THEORY AND PRACTICE OF LEADERSHIP | ROGER GILL

SAGE Publications
Los Angeles • London • New Delhi • Singapore

First published 2006
Reprinted 2007

SAGE Publications Ltd
1 Oliver's Yard
55 City Road
London EC1Y 1SP

SAGE Publications Inc.
2455 Teller Road
Thousand Oaks, California 91320

SAGE Publications India Pvt Ltd
B1/I1 Mohan Cooperative Industrial Area
Mathura Road, New Delhi 110 044
India

SAGE Publications Asia-Pacific Pte Ltd
33 Peking Street #02-01
Far East Square
Singapore 048763

British Library Cataloguing in Publication data

A catalogue record for this book is available from the British Library

ISBN 978-0-7619-7176-4
ISBN 978-0-7619-7177-1 (pbk)

Library of Congress Control Number: 2005928217

Typeset by C&M Digitals (P) Ltd, Chennai, India
Printed in Great Britain by The Cromwell Press Ltd, Trowbridge, Wiltshire
Printed on paper from sustainable resources

Contents

Tables

Figures

Cases

Preface

Writing this book was motivated by my dissatisfaction with the disparate range of theories and models that claim to explain 'leadership'. Each model or theory does so only in part: it is only one piece in a complex and confusing jigsaw puzzle. I believed that a more inclusive model of leadership is needed that has practical use as well as theoretical soundness. So six years ago I set out to explore what is common among the theories and models of leadership that could be presented in a way that both makes sense and is useful in practice. Defining the theory and practice of leadership was my mission, and this book is the result.

I discovered that several dimensions or forms of 'intelligence' underlie leadership: the intellectual or cognitive, the emotional, the spiritual and the behavioural. I also discovered that, to understand leadership more fully, we need to draw not just on psychology and sociology, traditionally its most popular base. During my journey of exploration I discovered that many other areas of human experience, ideas and knowledge also have something to tell us about leadership: ancient and modern philosophy, anthropology, political science, public administration, warfare, communication studies, history, theology, sport and the arts. In the arts I found specific contributions from literature, poetry, biography, journalism and reportage, and the performing arts, such as music and theatre, and even mythology and the visual arts. James MacGregor Burns' remark resonates with my own experience:

> **Many scholars based in traditional disciplines have found the study of leadership enormously expansive of their intellectual interests because of its creative intermingling of other disciplines. (Burns, 2005)**

I discovered five common themes that seem to capture the essence of leadership: vision and a sense of mission or purposefulness, creating a culture of positive shared values, developing and implementing strategies for the pursuit of vision and mission, empowering people to be *able* to do what needs to be done, and influencing, motivating and inspiring people to *want* to do what needs to be done. This is the model of leadership that this book presents.

Roger Gill
Ross-on-Wye and Kilmacolm

Acknowledgements

Many people have helped, influenced and inspired me in researching and writing this book over the past several years, and I would like to acknowledge who they are and how they did so.

Emeritus Professor Gerry Randell at the University of Bradford School of Management for his mentorship in my early years in academia and his intellectual stimulation ever since.

Distinguished Emeritus Professor Bernard M. Bass at the Global Center for Leadership Studies, the State University of New York at Binghamton, for stimulating my interest in the study of leadership.

Emeritus Professor Kees Van der Heijden, formerly at the University of Strathclyde Graduate School of Business and the University of Nijrenrode in the Netherlands, who first drew to my attention the limitations of current models of transformational leadership in respect of the importance of strategy and encouraged me to develop my new model.

Paul K. Winter, Chief Executive of The Leadership Trust Foundation, for giving me the time and space to write this book (though I remain responsible for its content, which does not necessarily reflect the views of the Trust), for permission to include Leadership Trust models, and for giving me the opportunity to put my ideas into practice in leadership development programmes for client organizations.

Professor John Adair for his wise insights and ideas on leadership.

Professor Jim O'Toole of the Marshall School of Business at the University of Southern California for his encouragement.

Patrick Wale, Ong Eng Kiat and Stephen Teo at Aviva Asia (formerly CGU Asia); BAT (British American Tobacco); British Sugar; Merck Pharmaceuticals; the University of Strathclyde; *Management Today* magazine; John Wiley & Sons, Inc.; Elsevier Ltd; The Manufacturing Foundations; Ian C. Buchanan of Booz Allen & Hamilton management consultants; and Richard Olivier: for their case material or permission to reproduce their copyrighted material.

Wilfred H. Gill, my father and honorary 'research assistant', for assiduously and tirelessly supplying me with a constant stream of corporate annual reports and newspaper and magazine articles on leadership.

Carol P. Kennedy for providing information and ideas on leadership in the media and the theatre and for comments on parts of the draft manuscript; Jonathan F. Kennedy for providing material on leadership in the world of theatre and the arts.

Dr Gareth Edwards, Senior Researcher in the Research Centre for Leadership Studies at The Leadership Trust Foundation, for providing an endless supply of articles on leadership and for helping me to find references; Dr Sharon Turnbull, my deputy at The Leadership Trust Foundation, for her useful comments on the first draft of the manuscript.

My doctoral and MBA students at the University of Strathclyde Graduate School of Business and at the School of Management and Economics at The Queen's University of Belfast for their ideas and frequently original insights into leadership; and participants in management and leadership seminars and workshops I have conducted and in conferences on leadership over the years for their useful ideas and material on leadership.

Former employers where I experienced good – and bad – leadership and who therefore enabled me to understand the very real importance of leadership.

Philip McDonnell, who incredibly painstakingly reviewed the first draft of my manuscript and provided very detailed and helpful comments and suggestions.

Kiren Shoman, Senior Editor, and Anne Summers, Assistant Editor, at SAGE Publications for their enthusiasm for this book and for their constant encouragement and remarkable patience while I was writing it. And Sharika Sharma, Production Editor, for her conscientious attention to detail throughout the production process.

If any attributions in this book are wrong, or if I have inadvertently failed to acknowledge any sources, I apologize.

1 Introduction: The Nature and Importance of Leadership

No man is a leader until his appointment is ratified in the minds and hearts of his men.

United States Infantry Journal, 1948

Overview

- Leadership has become a 'hot topic' with a burgeoning but fragmented literature in the past few years that draws on both the arts and the sciences. So far there is no agreed paradigm for the study and practice of leadership.
- Nevertheless the importance of leadership has long been recognized as crucial to both achievement and morale. Leadership is discussed in the contexts of politics, the public sector, business, the military and the arts.
- One fruitful approach to understanding leadership is to study followership: what followers expect of leaders and how leaders satisfy these expectations.
- Studies of the impact of leadership justify its vital importance. They include large-scale surveys, interviews and objective measures of leadership effectiveness.
- The concepts of management and leadership are defined, compared and contrasted. We manage things, but we lead people.
- The past emphasis on individual leadership is being superseded by an emphasis on shared and distributed leadership.
- There are similarities and differences in leadership across hierarchical levels in organizations. The collective leadership capacity and characteristics of an organization determine its 'leadership brand'.

We all experience leadership. From our early childhood in our families, through friendships, social, recreational and sports activities, school and higher education, to politics and government, and, of course, in our work, we all recognize leadership in other people and often in ourselves. Leadership has become a key issue in both the private and public sectors – a 'hot topic'. In government, global corporations and small businesses alike, the leadership role is becoming more demanding, more open to scrutiny and more difficult. David Collinson and Keith Grint (2005) point out that, while there is still 'little consensus on what counts as leadership, whether it can be taught, or even how effective it might be', the recent plethora of publications of all kinds on leadership '[extols] the need for excellence in management and leadership ... in part fuelled by a breakdown in confidence in leadership'.

Yet according to corporate chief and former US presidential candidate Ross Perot, 'The principles of leadership are timeless because, in a rapidly changing world, human nature remains a constant' (Perot, 2000). And Lt-Gen. Edward Flanagan of the US Army said:

> **Leadership is a timeless subject; it has been described, discussed, dissected and analyzed by management experts (who sometimes confuse management and leadership) for centuries. (Fitton, 1997)**

The burgeoning leadership literature ranges from highly cerebral academic research studies and scholarly treatises that few if any actual leaders read to idiosyncratic personal prescriptions of how to be an outstanding leader at the 'popular' end of the spectrum. Some of the contributions to the leadership literature are fictional and speculative:

> **[divining] the dubious leadership acumen of either long-dead military leaders [e.g. Attila the Hun] of questionable reputation or fictional characters [such as Winnie the Pooh and Captain Picard of *Star Trek*] in order to proffer it to the masses as pearls of wisdom. (Waclawski, 2001)**

This is not necessarily to eschew the contribution of fictional literature to our understanding of leadership. Indeed the arts have a distinct contribution to make, as we will see later. And in fact the study of leadership parallels the study of history. Bernard M. Bass, a foremost scholar of leadership at the State University of New York at Binghamton, says:

> **The study of leadership rivals in age the emergence of civilization, which shaped its leaders as much as it was shaped by them. From its infancy, the study of history has been the study of leaders – what they did and why they did it. (Bass, 1990a: 3)**

John Adair, the UK's first professor of leadership studies (at the University of Surrey), endorses the importance of history in leadership studies. 'The story begins,' he says, 'in ancient Athens, among the group that gathered around the philosopher of practical reason – Socrates' (Adair, 1989: 15). Socrates believed that effective leadership is situational (a contemporary theory which we will return to later) and that it depends on professional or technical competence. His pupil, Xenophon, extended the idea of technical competence to include several personal qualities and skills, such as the importance of giving direction, leading by example, sharing hardship and encouraging people.

The development of leadership theory also parallels the development of organizational theory (Gill et al., 1998). The bureaucratic form of organization is characterized by 'laissez-faire leadership' – whereby so-called leaders tend to avoid taking a stand, ignore problems, not follow up, and refrain from intervening – or transactional leadership, in which leaders practise management by exception, focusing only on deviations from what is required, and contingent reward, rewarding people (either materially or psychologically) for achieving what is required. The emergence of the post-bureaucratic form of organization in the late nineteenth century reflects the development of the concept of transformational leadership. These concepts of leadership are discussed further in Chapter 3.

Morgan McCall and Michael Lombardo (1978) at the Center for Creative Leadership in the United States suggested that students and scholars of leadership, and perhaps leaders themselves, would have discovered three things in their studies of leadership:

- The number of unintegrated models, theories, prescriptions and conceptual schemes of leadership is mind boggling
- Much of the leadership literature is fragmentary, trivial, unrealistic or dull
- Research results are often characterized by contradictions and by the Type III error – solving the wrong problems precisely

In the same year James MacGregor Burns, the political scientist and biographer of several US presidents, concurred: 'Leadership is one of the most observed and least understood phenomena on earth' (Burns, 1978: 2). But his seminal book on leadership that year changed the course of history, at least the history of leadership theory. Burns distinguished between transactional leadership and transforming leadership, and he stimulated a huge amount of future research, by Bernard M. Bass and many others, that would transform not only our understanding of leadership but also the way we recognize and develop effective leaders.

By the early 1980s, before the first major empirical study of leadership based on Burns' ideas was published (by Bass), the field was still confusingly fragmented. According to Robert Quinn (1984: 227):

> **Despite the immense investment in the enterprise [of the study of leadership], researchers have become increasingly disenchanted with the field. The seemingly endless display of unconnected empirical investigations is bewildering as well as frustrating.**

Henry Mintzberg in the early 1980s even said that leadership research was irrelevant to typical leadership practitioners (Mintzberg, 1982: 239–259). Warren Bennis and Bert Nanus (1985) suggested that each theory provides 'a sliver of insight but [remains] an incomplete and wholly inadequate exploration [of leadership]'. By 1993 leadership was still 'one of the most appealing and yet intractable subjects within management', according to Richard Whipp and Andrew Pettigrew (1993: 200). And Gary Yukl (1998: 493–494) described the field of leadership as having been:

> **in a state of ferment and confusion for decades... . The confused state of the field can be attributed in large to the sheer volume of publications, the disparity of approaches, the proliferation of confusing terms, [and] the narrow focus of most researchers... . As the old adage goes, it is difficult to see the forest for the trees.**

Stephen Zaccaro and Richard Klimoski (2001) saw the state of the art in 2001 as still incomplete and confusing:

> **The various parts of...[the empirical and conceptual leadership] literature still appear disconnected and directionless. In our opinion, a major cause of the state of the field is that many studies of leadership are context free; that is, low consideration is given**

to organizational variables that influence the nature and impact of leadership. Such research...tends to focus on interpersonal processes between individuals, nominally leaders and followers.

In Warren Bennis's view there is no agreed paradigm for leadership or framework for studying it:

Researchers have so far failed to come up with a widely accepted framework for thinking about leadership. There is no equivalent of *Competitive Strategy*, Michael Porter's 1980 classic, accorded near-biblical reverence by strategy experts... . I don't think [leadership] is yet a 'field' in the pure sense. There are something like 276 definitions of leadership. You can't say that there is a paradigm, any agreed-upon set of factors, that is generally accepted. (London, 2002)

Gary Yukl agrees:

Sometimes different terms have been used to refer to the same type of behaviour. At other times, the same term has been defined differently by various theorists. What is treated as a general behaviour category by one theorist is viewed as two or three distinct categories by another theorist. What is a key concept in one taxonomy is absent from another. Different taxonomies have emerged from different research disciplines, and it is difficult to translate from one set of concepts to another. (Yukl, 2002: 61)

Warren Bennis observes: 'Leadership is what the French call a portmanteau field – a field with many different variables' (London, 2002).

Different scholars have focused on different aspects of leadership according to their personal interests, rather than building on one another's work and creating general theories or models. And while studies have tried to develop generic models of leadership they fail to account for differences throughout organizational levels (Zaccaro and Klimoski, 2001: 4), which we return to later in this chapter.

Bob Hamlin points out the inadequacies of the dominant quantitative methods in studying leadership: they are too narrow and result in behavioural descriptions that are 'sterile' because of the need for generalization (Hamlin, 2004). Hamlin bemoans the lack of use of qualitative methods, particularly for confirming the results from quantitative methods such as survey questionnaires. Ken Parry (1998) and Mats Alvesson (2002) call for more studies of leadership based on social constructionism and grounded theory – a trend that is growing.

Nevertheless, Jerry Hunt points out that the field of leadership research is vibrant and fertile (Hunt, 1999). Two-factor theories (e.g. task versus relationships, transactional versus transformational), which have dominated the field, need to be de-emphasized, he says, as they may conceal important underlying ideas about leadership. However, there has been a renewed interest in the fundamental task/relationship dichotomy (Judge, Piccolo, and Ilies, 2004).

Researchers have approached the study of leadership from different perspectives, namely the 'meta', 'macro' and 'micro' perspectives (Covey, 1992: 295):

- Meta leadership concerns vision and stewardship of what is entrusted to the leader
- Macro leadership concerns strategy, organization and processes
- Micro leadership concerns relationships, legitimate power and followership

The 'micro skills' of leadership, for example, have been the specific focus of the 'Bradford approach' to leadership development pioneered by Gerry Randell and his colleagues at the University of Bradford School of Management (Randell, 1998). Studies from the macro perspective that focus on strategic leadership within the context of the organization's environment do not provide a complete picture. Zaccaro and Klimoski (2001: 3) say they 'ignore the cognitive, interpersonal, and social richness of [the phenomenon of leadership]' and they fail to provide 'strong conceptual frameworks [with] significant empirical support'.

Another way of looking at leadership is to classify the theories or models that have emerged. Keith Grint (2000: 2–3) identifies three popular approaches that differ in their emphasis on the individual and the context. The differences in emphasis reflect how knowable and critical the individual and the context are. He labels high emphasis as 'essentialist' and low emphasis as 'non-essentialist'. These three approaches focus on:

- Leadership traits that determine effective leadership universally
- Leadership situations that call for different leadership styles and behaviour
- Contingency – alignment between the situation and the person

Grint also describes a fourth, more recent approach – the constitutive approach. This approach questions any posited objectivity in defining the context and the leadership required and emphasizes the 'interpretive' nature of doing so:

> **We may never know...the true essence of an identity, a leader, or a situation...and must often base our actions and beliefs on the accounts of others from whom we can (re)constitute our version of events... . Leadership is an invention...[it] is primarily rooted in, and a product of, the imagination. (Grint, 2000: 10,13)**

This, Grint suggests, makes leadership more of an art than a science in four ways:

- A philosophical art – inventing an identity and constructing a community of followers
- A fine art – like painting, drawing or sculpting, for leaders paint, draw or sculpt the future when they construct a strategic vision
- A martial art – using an opponent's strength to defeat him or her or neutralizing his or her efforts
- A performing art – a theatrical performance of rhetoric and negotiation

The study of leadership, however, draws on both the arts and the sciences. But, according to Lord Snow in the late 1950s:

> **the intellectual life of the whole of western society is increasingly being split into two polar groups... . Literary intellectuals at one pole – at the other scientists... . Between the two is a gulf of mutual incomprehension. (Snow, 1959: 3)**

Leadership is a field in which there can be no 'gulf of mutual misunderstanding' between science and the arts if we are to have a truly full and useful understanding of this fascinating aspect of human behaviour. Charles Palus (1999) makes the point that both the arts and science are 'sensorily rich', personal (though replicable by others), based on enquiry, and experimental. Leadership is an art, he says, in terms of the imitative or imaginative skills needed to 'achieve form, function and meaning'. An example is the skills with which effective leaders create understanding and arouse positive emotions through language and speech, which we discuss in Chapter 8.

Leadership is also a science in terms of the systematic cognitive processes and formulated knowledge that effective leaders use in the 'forming and testing of ideas'. An example is the systematic scanning of the environment, analysis and interpretation of the findings in relation to existing knowledge, and decision making about the strategy to be employed (which we discuss in Chapter 6).

The contribution of the arts to leadership theory is expressed beautifully in the brochure for the Hart Leadership Program, *Leadership in the Arts*, in which Duke University undergraduate students spend a semester in New York City:

> **From the timeless power of a Shakespeare soliloquy to the timeliness of a dance work about the events of 9/11, the arts have the power to interpret and amplify the world around us. For ethics, plays and operas offer special advantages, illuminating dilemmas of individual responsibility, problems of public choice, conflicts about moral rules, and questions of character – loyalty and betrayal, integrity, honor and vainglory, courage and cowardice.**

The spirit of the Edinburgh International Festival in the UK is captured in its slogan: 'Engage the mind, touch the heart, feed the soul.'[1] This could well be our leadership slogan too. The Festival's brochure says: 'Challenging, moving, entertaining, profound – live performance can take you on a journey of discovery.' So too can the study and practice of leadership.

What is leadership?

There are many fewer examples of great leaders from the world of business than there are from the worlds of politics and the military. One reason for this, suggests Donald Krause (1997: xiv), may be that there is more disagreement about what effective leadership is in business organizations. Another reason, he says, may be that the media take much more notice of business leaders who are great 'showmen' – performing artists – rather than effective achievers.

If leadership is an art, it is at least a performing art. Metaphors for leadership come from the worlds of sport and the arts, especially from music. They include the leader as captain of the team striving to win the match, the sports coach, the conductor of an orchestra, and the leader's role rotating among members as in a conductorless orchestra or a jazz ensemble, where members improvise on a theme. Peter Cook (2000) says that the jazz band metaphor alludes to several features of the creative organization that have implications for leadership:

- The ability to learn and adapt to change through signposts which are understood by the whole organization
- Using both logic and intuition to guide the organization's direction
- Balancing structure and chaos according to stakeholders' needs
- Risk taking within a safe environment

- Personality differences overshadowed by 'a consuming mania with a shared purpose'
- Emergent strategy arising from the synthesis of collective capability

Such shared leadership can be a source of creativity and innovation, as Richard Hackman (2001) suggests:

> **Rather than relying on a charismatic, visionary leader who both calls the shots and engages members' motivation, might it be possible for all members to share responsibility for leadership and for differences and disagreements to be sources of creativity, rather than something that should be suppressed in the interest of uniformity and social harmony?**

Leadership, however, is not only a performing art. It is also the practical application of a science, an organized body of knowledge accumulated on the subject. This is what makes leadership so interesting: it straddles Snow's 'two cultures' – the arts and science (Snow, 1959). And this is what makes leadership such a fascinating intellectual, spiritual, emotional and behavioural phenomenon.

Leadership means different things to different people. 'Leadership is a popular concept rather than a scientific one,' says Victor Vroom; 'like many popular terms, it has been used in many different ways' (Sternberg and Vroom, 2002). And Alan Berkeley Thomas (2003: 164) says:

> **Even in everyday usage the term 'leadership' is ambiguous. It is used to refer to the holders of certain formally defined positions in an organisation, as when speaking of 'the party leadership' or 'the union leadership'. But it is also used to denote a particular type of behaviour; when someone is commended for displaying 'outstanding leadership' it is their actions that are being praised. Such a person may or may not occupy a position of leadership. On the other hand, a formally designated leader need not necessarily behave as a leader and in extreme cases may hardly be said to behave at all. So, for example, it has been claimed that Leonid Brezhnev (1906–1982), a former head of state of the now defunct Soviet Union, was barely alive in the later years of his premiership, let alone an active force capable of exerting decisive influence over events.**

According to a 1920s' definition of leadership, leadership is 'the ability to impress the will of the leader on those led and induce obedience, respect, loyalty, and cooperation' (Moore, 1927), a remarkably autocratic viewpoint by today's standards. At about the same time, Henry Ford was putting into practice his own view of organization and systems, with implications for leadership:

> **Industry is management, and management is leadership, and leadership is perfect when it so simplifies operations that orders are not necessary. (Nevins and Hill, 1954)**

Burns (1978) defines leadership as a mobilization process by individuals with certain motives, values and access to resources in a context of competition and conflict in the pursuit of goals. More recently, Nigel Nicholson speaks of leadership as either a position or a process (Bradshaw, 2002). If a process, he says, it is about influencing other people, and this requires knowing oneself, knowing those other people, and knowing how to influence them.

Seeking the answer to the question 'What is leadership?' is like searching for the Holy Grail: Gareth Edwards (2000) counted some 40 theories of leadership. For some this academic debate may be fascinating and now and again even illuminating. But it is an irrelevance to managers who are experiencing the realities of leading in today's demanding, turbulent and often chaotic environment. Joanne Ciulla (1999) says that 'the difference between the definitions rests on a normative question: "How should leaders treat followers?"' So what is *good* leadership? Barbara Kellerman (2004a) observes:

> **Scholars should remind us that leadership is not a moral concept. Leaders are like the rest of us: trustworthy and deceitful, cowardly and brave, greedy and generous. To assume that all leaders are good people is to be wilfully blind to the reality of the human condition, and it severely limits our scope for becoming more effective at leadership.**

Ciulla (1999) makes the point that 'good' has two senses that need to be related: 'good' in the moral sense and 'good' in the sense of being effective (even if 'bad'). Dave Ulrich and colleagues say:

> **Without...visible results, leadership never endures... . Conversely, leaders who achieve results but lack integrity, character, and values face a different challenge: winning the support necessary for long-term performance. (Ulrich et al., 2000)**

Kellerman addresses this issue exclusively in her book *Bad Leadership*, acknowledging the 'dark side' of human nature and how this affects leaders and followers alike (Kellerman, 2004b). She identifies seven major forms of bad leadership: incompetent, rigid, intemperate, callous, corrupt, insular and evil. Her argument is that, if bad leadership is to be avoided, it must be a shared responsibility.

In another insightful psychological analysis, Jean Lipman-Blumen explains how 'toxic' leaders first charm and then manipulate, mistreat, weaken and eventually devastate their followers (Lipman-Blumen, 2005). She explains how we human beings are psychologically susceptible to toxic leadership and how we can reduce our dependency on 'strong' leadership, identify 'reluctant leaders' and nurture leadership within ourselves. Michael Maccoby (2004) believes this dependency is the result of what Sigmund Freud called 'transference' – the tendency to relate to a leader as some important person from the past, such as a father or mother, a brother or sister, or even a nanny.

Leadership carries particular connotations for some eminent people. For example, Paul Keating, former Australian prime minister, said that 'Leadership is not about being nice. It's about being right and being strong.'[2] And in the UK Tony Blair, as the new Labour Party leader, before he became prime minister in 1997, said that 'the art of leadership is saying no, not yes. It is very easy to say yes.'[3]

Consulting the etymology of the word is a useful starting point for defining leadership. The word 'lead' comes from the Old English *lædan*, corresponding to the Old Saxon *ledian* and Old High German *leiten*, meaning 'take with one', to 'show the way' (Hoad, 1988). *Ledere* was the term for a person who shows other people the path to take and guides them safely along the journey (Kets de Vries and Florent-Treacy, 1999: 5). The Old Icelandic derivative *leidha* means 'the person in front', referring to the person who guided ships through the pack-ice in spring. The word 'leader' appeared in the English language in the thirteenth century, but 'leadership' appeared only in the early nineteenth century. Grint (2000: 420) sees leaders as 'in front', 'pulling' followers after them, and 'sharing the way' rather than showing the way.

Several contemporary statesmen such as former US secretary of state Henry Kissinger have suggested that a leader takes people to a place they have not been to before. Indeed we find in the Bible:

> I will bring the blind by a way that they knew not; I will lead them in paths that they have not known: I will make darkness light before them, and crooked things straight. These things I will do unto them, and not forsake them.[4]

Leadership has been variously defined in terms of traits, process, skill(s), competency, a relationship and a construct. Bass (1990a) identified over 1,500 different definitions of leadership. Underpinning the leadership development programmes at The Leadership Trust is the concept of leadership as 'using our personal power to win the hearts and minds of people to achieve a common purpose' (Edwards et al., 2002: 15). This concept of leadership implies that there must be a mission or common purpose and a clear strategy for pursuing it. Jim Collins and Jerry Porras (1996a) see the function of a leader as 'to catalyze a clear and shared vision of the organization and to secure commitment to it and vigorous pursuit of that vision'. The Leadership Trust's concept of leadership also brings out the issue of power and its use, which I discuss in Chapter 8. Moreover, this concept abrogates the use of position power (authority) in favour of gaining commitment through using personal power. Gary Hamel (2002) writes of a looming crisis in the use of authority:

> More than ever before, senior executives know they cannot command commitment, for the generation now entering the workforce is more authority-averse than any in history.

Leadership, according to Thomas Lenz (1993: 154–156):

> involves diagnosing situations, determining what needs to be done and marshalling collective effort sufficient to achieve a desired future or avert significant problems... . It entails the use of power and persuasion to define and determine the changing...problems and opportunities...of an organization, and...the solutions produced and actions taken by individuals and groups both inside and outside an organization to cope with such issues... . The purpose of exercising influence in organizational decision-making processes is to foster learning...and facilitate change.

Lenz's last point is key to our understanding of leadership. Warren Bennis and Bob Thomas (2002) suggest that most leadership failures in business are the result of failing to adapt to changing circumstances.

According to Howard Gardner (1995), leaders are those who, 'by word and/or personal example, markedly influence the behaviors, thoughts, and/or feelings of a significant number of their fellow human beings'. In discussing leadership in the public sector, Jo Brosnahan (1999) describes it as 'that special mix of gifts that include integrity, vision, the ability to inspire others, a deep awareness of self, courage to innovate, and instant and impeccable sense of judgment'.

Managers may be good at *managing* and nominally regarded as leaders, but the most effective managers exercise *effective leadership*. John Nicholls (1994) says:

> **When we say that an organisation lacks leadership we mean that its managers are neglecting their leadership responsibility. It is leadership that is missing, not leaders. If every manager understood and fulfilled his or her leadership responsibilities, there would be no shortage of leadership. It is attention to their managerial leadership responsibilities that converts competent administrators into effective managers.**

And Bass (1985: xiii) says:

> **Management is not only leadership, nor is leadership only management; however, those appointed to a position of responsibility as managers need to appreciate what leadership is expected of them.**

The importance of leadership is recognized in the well-known Excellence Model promoted by the European Foundation for Quality Management (EFQM) and the British Quality Foundation (BQF). The EFQM/BQF Excellence Model includes 'leadership' as an underpinning enabler in attaining key performance results. Leadership is defined as:

> **How leaders develop and facilitate the achievement of the mission and vision, develop values required for long term success and implement these via appropriate actions and behaviours, and are personally involved in ensuring that the organisation's management system is developed and implemented. (EFQM, 2000)**

Sub-criteria by which leadership is evaluated are:

- Leaders develop the mission, vision and values and are role models of a culture of excellence
- Leaders are personally involved in ensuring the organization's management system is developed, implemented and continuously improved
- Leaders are involved with customers, partners and representatives of society
- Leaders motivate, support and recognize the organization's people

Leadership also includes:

- Stimulating and encouraging empowerment, innovation and creativity
- Aligning organizational structure to support delivery of policy and strategy
- Supporting and engaging in activities that aim to improve the environment and the organization's contribution to society
- Personally communicating the organization's mission, vision, values, policy and strategy, plans, objectives and targets to people

Effective leadership results in a high degree of satisfaction that we are doing or achieving something worthwhile, to ourselves, to the organization we work for, and to the society we live in: in this way leadership has a spiritual dimension. Leadership is both extrinsic and intrinsic. Extrinsic leadership is leadership provided by another person, while intrinsic leadership comes from within ourselves – it is 'self-leadership'. People who have a vision, know what to do, are self-aware and are self-driven are displaying self-leadership. Leadership, whether extrinsic or intrinsic, creates a sense of direction, empowerment and the motivation we feel when we are doing or achieving something worthwhile.

Leadership and followership

The desire to follow is a basic human (indeed animal) instinct, Robert Ardrey (1970) suggests. While most theories of leadership focus on leaders, Stephen Covey (1992: 101) suggests that a 'more fruitful approach is to look at followers, rather than leaders, and to assess leadership by asking why followers follow'. This question can be addressed by looking at the needs and aspirations that people have and how leaders use power in helping people to satisfy them.

While sheep may naturally follow, human beings do not, for we make intelligent judgements for ourselves. When we follow, we do so either eagerly or reluctantly. As Stephen Fineman (2003: 76) says, we talk a lot about our leaders – our bosses and politicians – and we criticize them freely. But our desire to follow has deep emotional roots. And interestingly the Bible emphasizes followership more than leadership.

Many writers have identified a crisis in leadership, but there is perhaps also a crisis in followership. Robert Kelley (1992) reports a study indicating dissatisfaction among followers with their leaders: 40% questioned their ability to lead, a minority (14%) of leaders were regarded as role models, fewer than half were trusted, and 40% were regarded as having ego problems, were threatened by talented subordinates, needed to act in a 'superior' way, and did not share recognition. Burns (1978: 116) points out that:

> **One talent all leaders must possess [is] the capacity to perceive needs of followers in relationship to their own, to help followers move toward fuller self-realization and self-actualization along with the leaders themselves.**

This is about empowerment. Followership, according to one leadership development practitioner, results from being empowered – through delegation, creating team values, coaching and mentoring, and building a high-performance team (White, 2000a).

In the political world, leaders appear to have fewer and fewer followers. In democratic nations they are elected, but by whom? The 2001 general election in the UK was an example of a growing crisis in followership, where the lowest turnout for 80 years gave a large majority to the ruling Labour Party. Even so, only a small minority of the electorate actively supported the nation's political leadership, in effect were 'followers', as was the case again in the 2005 general election. And even within the Labour Party itself, there was dissension from the policies the government was following and in particular the prime minister's actions concerning Iraq. Nor was the Conservative Party immune from dissension, part of its downfall from government in 1997 and its several subsequent leadership crises. And what proportion of the US electorate 'follows' president George W. Bush? Fifty-one per cent, according to the 2004 election results.

The British government's 2001 report on *Strengthening Leadership* includes an interesting analysis of followership:

> **The most successful organisations appear to be those where the errors which the leaders inevitably make are compensated for by their followers: responsible followers prevent irresponsible leaders. But where followers are unable or unwilling to constrain their leaders the organisation itself may well suffer. This 'compensatory followership' operates right across the organisational and political spectrum such that, for example, the obsequient behaviour of most of Hitler's entourage (fortunately) failed to prevent him from making catastrophic strategic errors in the latter half of the Second World War. (PIU, 2001: D11)**

The report also gives a more contemporary example. In many hospitals, consultants are 'treated as "gods" and junior staff [are] afraid of "telling tales"'. Examples of tragic mistakes as a result of this culture appear all too frequently. Institutionalizing the role of devil's advocate is one way of preventing leaders from making mistakes (Kelley, 1992; Chaleff, 1995). Followers take turns to dissent from the group's decisions to focus the attention of the group and the leader on potential problems. According to the respondents in Kelley's study of followership, the best followers are those who think for themselves, give constructive criticism, are 'their own person', and are innovative and creative (Kelley, 1992). Kelley's review of follower characteristics revealed an additional dimension, namely active engagement in the task: the best followers take the initiative, participate actively, are self-starters, and do more than what is required.

The importance of leadership

Good leaders help people to make their dreams come true. Donald Krause (1997: 8) says 'the main goal of … leadership is to accomplish useful and desirable things that benefit the people being led'. The importance of leadership in determining what we achieve has been long recognized.

The rulers of ancient China studied leadership at great length. They were preoccupied with change and the associated chaos and uncertainty, as indeed we still are today. The writings on leadership of the general Sun Tzu in *The Art of War* and the philosopher Confucius in *The Analects* have endured over some two and a half millennia and are quoted far and wide today. One lesson from Sun Tzu is that even the most brilliant strategy requires effective leadership to be successful.[5] This is a lesson that receives scant attention from strategy theorists and eludes many business school texts on business strategy or at best is treated *en passant*. The importance of strategy to leadership is discussed in Chapter 6.

Leadership is the crucial issue, Rosabeth Moss Kanter (1993a,b) says, when a company is failing and survival is at stake. It matters most in respect of openness and honesty in dialogue, mutual respect, collaborative problem solving, and encouragement of initiative. She says that withholding information from employees and the public compounds a financial or strategic mess: the cover-up can be worse than the mistake.

Mutual respect is not gained by punishing those responsible for mistakes. It is gained through recognizing what people have to offer and involving them in problem solving and decision making, for example in strategy formulation. And problem solving and commitment to solutions in turnaround situations require collaboration across organizational boundaries. Kanter quotes as an example how Greg Dyke, on taking over as director-general of the BBC in 1999, used this approach in his 'One BBC: Making It Happen' strategy in rehabilitating a demoralized organization. Initiative can be encouraged by empowering employees to take action, again something that had been missing at the BBC and which Dyke introduced. Creating such a culture is the key for leaders in turnaround situations. In the words of Kanter: 'this is the true test of leadership: whether those being led out of the defeatism of decline gain the confidence that produces victories'.

The Industrial Revolution in the nineteenth century, starting in the UK, shifted the emphasis from political and military leadership to business and economic leadership – building industrial enterprises, opening up markets and innovation (METO, 2000: 27). Such leadership, however, was ascribed to the relatively few ('born' leaders?), who usually were autocrats. Said Douglas McGregor (1960) in his seminal book *The Human Side of Enterprise*:

> **Traditionally, leadership has tended to be equated with autocratic command and there are still many who see leadership mainly in terms of the issuing of orders which are eagerly obeyed by followers whose loyalty is largely determined by the charisma of the leader.**

Nearly half a century later, this is still true today.

Popular interest in leadership has grown rapidly in the past 20 years, though only more recently in the UK (Sadler, 1997: 11). Research by the Council for Excellence in Management and Leadership, set up by the British government in April 2000, revealed a need to 'increase the commitment of organisations of all sizes, in both the private and public sector, to develop better managers and leaders' (Cleaver, 2001). The Council acknowledges the 'direct link between leadership capability and sustained high performance' (CEML, 2001: 15). Its research findings included the following:

- There are still shortages in the quality and quantity of people with leadership skills. Yet the need for those with leadership skills is increasing all the time. There need to be some 400,000 new entrants to management and leadership positions each year.
- Larger organizations prefer customized leadership development programmes.
- Few professional associations require any management learning prior to membership and continuing professional development (CPD) requirements, despite recognition by professionals of the importance of leadership development.
- There is a lack of data on leadership development for benchmarking purposes.

The CEML research was the basis for proposals and an agenda for action on leadership development. These are described in the section on leadership development in Chapter 7.

Leadership in politics

In his discussion of political leadership Dennis Kavanagh (1990: 63–65) contrasts *reconcilers* with *mobilizers*. He cites, as British examples of mobilizers, Lloyd George,

Joseph Chamberlain and Tony Benn, who were primarily concerned with achieving policy goals rather than reconciling different interests, usually through radical change. Mobilizers therefore may be transformational leaders who emerge in conditions of dissatisfaction or crisis, like Lloyd George in 1916 and Winston Churchill in 1940. But in British politics, leaders who start out as mobilizers – as prime ministers Harold Wilson and Edward Heath did – usually do not last long as such and eventually become reconcilers as a result of the pressures of the consensus culture of political parties and government.

On the other hand, while the 'Iron Lady', prime minister Margaret Thatcher, transformed British society in the 1980s, she was eventually rejected because of her unwavering authoritarian leadership style. Her successor, John Major, lacked the 'essential attributes of a leader': the ability to define an agenda, mobilize support for that agenda, and then inspire followers with a vision of the destination, according to Anthony Seldon (1997). Similarly, Kevin Theakston (2003: 108–109) says of him:

> **No one would or could look to Major for visionary or innovative leadership. His skills were primarily those of a political manager – his approach was reactive, tactical and problem solving...a details man... . But he was not good on policy or on medium- and long-term strategy and objectives. He did not project a clear ideological position or a strong sense of policy direction.**

Following a good start as leader of the opposition and his party's election in 1997, prime minister Tony Blair began to appear in a shaky position from 2003 onwards, with declining ratings on 'trust' as a result of joining the dubious war in Iraq, increasing scepticism over his policies at home, and a much reduced Labour Party majority in the 2005 general election. He was perceived as committed to goals and values, and, Peter Riddell (2001: 35, 38) says, he preferred the 'big picture', strategy, values and images over policy detail. His 'Third Way', however, was unclear and pragmatic, and his 'modernization' mantra lacked direction and application. The Conservative Party elected and subsequently rejected two leaders in quick succession, William Hague and Iain Duncan Smith, who were succeeded in November 2003 by Michael Howard, a barrister and a consummate 'actor' (Sands, 2003) – one might say a 'performing artist'.

Political parties may from time to time lose their way, as evidenced by the disastrous performances of the British Labour Party in the 1982 general election and the Conservative Party in the 1997 and 2001 general elections. Such events have to do with leadership: failure is usually to do with vision, values and strategies that lack intellectual or emotional appeal. Robert Elgie (1995), in a discussion of political leadership, suggests that any differences in traits and styles of leaders are exercised through – and limited by – the institutional culture in which they operate. This is a point we will return to in our discussion of leadership, strategy and culture.

Former US president Richard Nixon is said to have used bargaining rather than display 'leadership', and he suffered a fatal credibility crisis over the Watergate affair (Cloud, 1996). The charismatic president Bill Clinton was castigated for lying about his sexual misconduct. His successor, George W. Bush, whose venture into Iraq to topple its president, Saddam Hussein, ostensibly on the grounds of his (illusory) possession of weapons of mass destruction, divided the American nation, won a second term in the 2004 presidential election with a 2% margin in the popular vote.

Doris Kearns Goodwin (1998), the Pulitzer Prize winner, historian and biographer, contrasts the leadership styles of three US presidents whose legacies have loomed large over several decades after they left office. Lyndon B. Johnson's great strength, she says, was his understanding of the legislative process, his brilliance both one-to-one and in small groups, his ability to create team spirit and his sense of timing. John F. Kennedy was the opposite in all of these respects. But he understood the power of language and the importance of symbolism, humour and image in mobilizing people towards a goal. Among modern US presidents, however, Franklin D. Roosevelt offers perhaps the best case study in leadership, Goodwin says. His greatest gift as a leader was his absolute confidence in himself and, even more important, in the American people. All three knew how to channel people's best impulses into positive outcomes. Their strengths lay in their extraordinary ability to reach out and move others, despite their weaknesses that were simply those of any human being. Their stories offer useful lessons for today's leaders in any kind of organization.

According to research by clinical psychologists Steven J. Rubenzer and Tom Faschingbauer (2004), however, US presidents who are rated most highly by historians tend not only to be intelligent (open to experience) but also to have ambitious goals and to be willing to 'bend' the truth. Rubenzer says that 'being a better liar than the others ... seems to increase their chances of putting their policies in place' (Dingfelder, 2004). But perhaps it is also one reason why electorates are so cynical about their political leaders.

The decline and eventual collapse of the Soviet Union and the introduction of perestroika and glasnost brought the heroic leadership of Michail Gorbachev into prominence. The French president, Jacques Chirac, was accused of financial corruption, though in 2003 he displayed strong leadership in standing firm against the US Iraq campaign. The German chancellor, Helmut Kohl, was accused of improper fund raising for his party. And the Spanish government was unexpectedly defeated in elections in 2004, partly owing to Spain's participation in a coalition with the United States and the UK in post-war Iraq but also as a result of a perceived dishonest misrepresentation, for political purposes, of the identity of the perpetrators of a terrorist bombing in Madrid. In Northern Ireland the Ulster Unionists led by Nobel Peace Prize co-winner David Trimble were overtaken by the more hard-line Democratic Unionist Party led by the Reverend Ian Paisley, putting the peace process in jeopardy. Indeed Trimble lost his parliamentary seat in the 2005 election.

Asia too has witnessed a series of political leadership crises. The Philippines president, Joseph Estrada, was accused of corruption and resigned. The Japanese prime minister Mori was criticized for his inability or unwillingness to define his vision for Japan as an IT leader and support it with tangible strategies, and he eventually resigned. Thailand's prime minister Thaksin Shinawatra promulgated 'new action, new thought' but took an antagonistic stance towards new civic reformist institutions and became regarded by some as an autocrat. Indonesia has had a succession of presidents since the fall of its dictator Suharto in 1998, as it gradually engages democracy. And new political systems in Afghanistan and Iraq after bloody wars have also been introducing democratic leadership.

Democracies, in which leaders are elected, are, however, beginning to meet with signs of disillusion, says Anthony Giddens (2000). Fewer people are voting, and more people are eschewing politics, believing the worst of politicians and political leaders.

Broadcaster and writer Jeremy Paxman (2002: 282–290) believes that this disillusionment with politics and political leaders is due to the remoteness of governments from the people and their increasing inability to make changes and get things done.

Ironically this may be due to government ministers behaving more like managers than leaders. Mark Goyder (2001) of the Centre for Tomorrow's Company points out that government ministers are drenched in statistics on progress, are questioned about specific cases in their functional domain, and are always expected to 'know':

> **New plans, new initiatives, new targets are thrown out to feed critics... . Ministers are drawn into managing when their job should be leadership. We want a minister for health, not a minister running the health service. Perhaps our political leaders could get back to being leaders, and let the people appointed to manage...[manage].**

Leadership in the public sector

The public sector in democratic nations is the instrument of elected politicians for pursuing their visions and missions. 'In public services,' Paul Joyce (2003) says, 'it is important to recognize the primacy of politicians in creating strategic visions.' Public sector managers are expected to articulate and sell the vision to employees at all levels.

In the report *Strengthening Leadership in the Public* Sector, the British government has identified leadership as key to meeting the challenges of the twenty-first century in the public services (PIU, 2001). The needs for modernization, meeting higher expectations from the public, partnerships and collaboration, and harnessing new technology all present leadership challenges. The government's report suggests that public services are failing to attract and retain the best leaders, recent leadership development initiatives are as yet unproven, with insufficient attention to leadership across organizational boundaries, and public service leaders' effectiveness is marred by a lack of freedom, support systems and challenges. Risk aversion and a blame culture are barriers to effectiveness. A lack of common understanding about what is required for effective leadership is also an issue.

The public sector is not comparable to the private sector. Politicians are responsible for regulating markets. And they – not public service leaders – establish values and remain ultimately accountable for public service delivery. Moreover, the public services are constrained by taxpayer funding, specifically three-year fixed funding in the UK, whereas private sector organizations can more often release funds where this increases revenue. Freedom to act is also constrained by legitimate public concern and clearly justified good practice. These constraints point to the differences between political and executive leadership. The government report says:

> **Many leaders...[see] their relationships with politicians as one-way: one [describes] it as a 'master-servant' relationship.Greater clarity in the respective roles of politicians and managers [is] recognised as one of the keys to better service delivery. (PIU, 2001: 4.14)**

This need also applies to the relationship between political leaders (elected councillors) and managerial leaders (chief executives and senior managers) in local government. One way forward in enhancing leadership relationships is joint training and development for political and executive leaders as adopted in local government, for example, in the UK, by Birmingham City Council (PIU, 2001: 4.19).

Comparative research in the British public sector (local government and the National Health Service) and the private sector shows two main differences in images of leadership: integrity and customer/stakeholder orientation (Alimo-Metcalfe and Alban-Metcalfe, 2002a). Integrity is valued more among public sector managers. And there is a more complex situation for them in addressing the needs of customers and other stakeholders, both internal and external. Gerald Gabris et al. (1998) describe leadership in the public sector as enigmatic. They say:

> **[Public sector leadership] involves the tension between the political and administrative spheres of responsibility. On the one hand, public administrators are expected to advocate innovative and creative solutions to complex problems. Yet, by acting as advocates, public administrators increase the risk that they will step on political toes or at some point appear overly brash. Administrators within the private sector do not often operate within such constraints. This often puts public administrators in the awkward position of being damned if they do and damned if they do not. The solution, for most of them, is to play it safe, adhering to the dictum that discretion is the better part of valor.**

Research by the Chartered Management Institute in the UK, covering local and central government, education, health and the armed services, found that public sector managers are looking for vision, integrity and sound judgement in their leaders (Charlesworth et al., 2003).[6] They also have a higher regard for their immediate bosses than for those more senior. The key leadership skills expected of leaders are communication, engaging employees with the vision, and creating an enabling culture.

Leadership in business

Business leaders too have not escaped criticism – usually over incompetence, corruption or 'fat cat' greed. Public confidence in business leaders has deteriorated in recent years, with disillusionment focusing largely on issues of ethics and values (Offermann et al., 2001).

In the business world, 'There's a greed in the air which is just mind-blowing … corporations have been captured by one insatiable group – the greediest of all – the shareholders', Henry Mintzberg says (Cunningham, 2001). The huge salaries and bonuses for CEOs that focus their attention on short-term share price rather than building the company are both dysfunctional and irresponsible. Roger Eglin (2001a) says:

> **Business has never been tougher. Stock markets demand constant improvements in performance, and chief executives' heads roll with unnerving frequency. Nothing can be taken for granted. The steady flow of mergers leaves victorious executives battling to justify the prices they have paid.**

Lord Taylor of Warwick (2000) expresses the pressure with a Caribbean proverb: 'The higher up the mountain you go, the more the wind blows.' And journalist Alison Eadie (2001a) says, 'The chief executives of our largest companies are sacked with increasing frequency.' Despite a 'publishing blizzard' on leadership and the array of available leadership development programmes, she says, we are still 'turning out duds'.

Warren Bennis and James O'Toole (2000) also point out that the job of the CEO in itself in the United States has become much more demanding in recent years, added to which are the pressures of recession, flatter organizations with more direct reports, increased travel due to globalization, the need for greater IT literacy and 'merger mania'. This has led to shorter and shorter tenures, known as 'CEO churning'. A report by *The Economist* (2003) suggests:

> **Swamped with e-mails (which some of them answer themselves), voicemails and demands for appearances on breakfast television and at grand dinners, many corporate leaders find it harder and harder to make time to think.**

According to Michael Goldstein (1992), 10% of all CEOs are removed from office for performing below expectations, with some 5% leaving within the first three years. He says of the remaining 90%, 'many that escape dismissal may still be plain vanilla or mediocre'. One may of course expect dismissals and resignations because of poor performance. A Korn/Ferry survey of 'Cause for removal of CEOs' for the Accenture Institute of Strategic Change in the United States revealed that 'ineffective leadership' accounted for 73% of the cases, exceeded only by financial or ethical malpractice and mental or physical incapacity (Bennis, 1998).

Management consultants Booz Allen & Hamilton calculated that, in 1995, the average tenure of those heading the world's 2,500 most valuable firms was 9.5 years; by 2001 it had dropped to 7.3 years (*The Economist*, 2002a). British figures are even more worrying. According to research at Cranfield School of Management, the average tenure for CEOs in the UK's top 100 companies in 1999 was four years (Coles, 1999). And the HayGroup reported that turnover of CEOs between 1999 and 2001 increased five-fold (HayGroup, 2001).

Institutional investors no longer tolerate poor shareholder value. John Kotter says, 'The pressure people are feeling at the top of organisations is unbelievable' (*The Economist*, 2003). He says that, if earnings growth drops by 3%, the share price may fall by 30%. An Ernst & Young study of institutional fund managers showed that there is a direct relationship between the effectiveness of the top team and valuation of the company (Mavrinac and Siesfeld, 1998). The top two non-financial criteria of effectiveness were 'execution of corporate strategy' and 'management credibility'.

CEOs now have less time in which to deliver results and, if they fail to do so, they are likely to be replaced by those who are tougher and more short-term focused and task oriented but leave a company in a financial mess. This short-term focus can be detrimental to the long-term sustainability of a company and thus poses a dilemma for CEOs. The short-term demands of shareholders may be the cause of this problem. On the other hand it may have to do with inappropriate leadership: obsession with growth and large personal rewards is another explanation for such failures.

Despite their CEOs' explanations of factors beyond their control – which occasionally are correct – companies usually fail because of leadership errors. Ram Charan and Jerry Useem (2002) say, 'What undoes them is the familiar stuff of human folly: denial, hubris, ego, wishful thinking, poor communication, lax oversight, greed [and] deceit.' Sometimes CEOs threaten to 'shoot the messenger': they do not welcome bad news. Then they make bad decisions without the necessary information, which is available but not communicated. Winston Churchill was aware of this risk during the Second World War. He set up a feedback process which bypassed his generals so that he would receive true information, however unwelcome. Lee Kuan Yew, as prime minister of Singapore, did likewise in the 1980s.

In his investigation of why CEOs fail, Sydney Finkelstein (2003a,b) discovered 'surprisingly few causes':

- They ignore the need for change
- They have the wrong vision: the logical and practical limitations of the 'one big idea' are not considered
- They 'get too close' to their companies: they treat their companies as extensions of themselves
- Arrogant attitudes
- Reverting to old formulae that once worked but no longer do so

John Baldoni (2004) suggests that many CEOs failed because they became 'intoxicated with their own image':

> **The pages of American business magazines were packed with laudatory profiles of men and women in charge, those who rule with power as well as impunity...corporate scandals were stoked in part by those at the top believing in their own invincibility as well as their own lack of accountability.**

CEOs in New Zealand appear to be much more optimistic than leaders at lower levels in their organizations, according to research by Ken Parry and Sarah Proctor-Thomson (2002). They found that CEOs see leadership in their organizations as much more transformational and much less transactional than the other leaders do. And hierarchical level appears to be related to such optimism, with supervisors (first-level managers) 'quite scornful of the leadership cultures of their organisations'. Their conclusion is that CEOs face a credibility gap that risks damaging the performance of their organizations. According to a public relations consultant, Lesley Gaines-Ross, CEOs' reputations used to be based on 'brand-name status, a track record and visibility'; now it is based on 'credibility' (*The Economist*, 2002a), a key requirement for effective leadership (Kouzes and Posner, 1993), to which we will return later.

Strategy is a key area of weakness. For example, Kmart, Tyco and AT&T followed the 'strategy *du jour*'; Tyco, WorldCom and AT&T were beset by 'acquisition lust'; and Cisco Systems failed in strategic thinking – the company omitted to test its basic assumption of growth and ignored indicative data (Charan and Useem, 2002). GEC, after its long-serving chairman Lord Weinstock's retirement in 1996, followed divestment and investment strategies that virtually destroyed the company (Aris, 2002).

Culture and corporate values are another key area of weakness. Charan and Useem (2002) quote 'dangerous' cultures that encourage profit taking without disclosure and conflicts of interest without safeguards: 'rotten cultures produce rotten deeds'.

Brian Baxter, senior partner at Kiddy and Partners, sees a shift from 'nurturing', people-oriented leadership to a 'tough, driving' style, which is 'not liked or admired but [is] widely respected' (Eglin, 2001a). The consequences of this shift, which can be explained by one major theory of leadership, unfortunately are the opposite of what is actually needed. These consequences are resentment, alienation and psychological withdrawal from work.

Bennis and O'Toole (2000) suggest that boards often do not understand what defines real leadership today. Finding it hard to 'measure' vision, inspiration and conviction, boards focus on 'hard' facts like shareholder value, market share, merger experience and technical skills as evidence of effective 'leadership'. Yet, Bennis and O'Toole say, when they do focus on their CEOs' visions:

> Boards are often seduced by articulate, glamorous – dare we say it – charismatic dreamers who send multiple frissons down their collective spines. William Agee seduced many boards with his 'chasing rainbows' number, creating rhapsodic scenarios for a vision-starved board and proceeding to 'fail upwards' because his glossy pitch always fell short of the directors' expectations.

Leaders have a 'shelf life' that expires through burnout, diminishing energy and inflexibility. James Champy and Nitin Nohria (2000) describe this, and the drive, persistence and optimism that leaders need to be effective, as the 'arc of ambition'. Of 're-engineering' fame, Champy believes that re-engineering must be combined with leadership, in particular ambition. For him, ambition includes an 'appetite for change'. The paradox is the need eventually to bow out gracefully and avoid the humiliation, rows, firings and sense of failure associated with the downward arc – difficult for ambitious leaders to do – for example as did Andrew Carnegie, the US steel baron, but Margaret Thatcher did not.

Changes in working methods associated with globalization and the digital economy – decentralization of operations and increased teamworking – are influencing the nature of leadership that is required: global virtual teams are becoming more widespread (Cascio and Shurygailo, 2003). Global virtual teams contain individuals who are culturally diverse, geographically or organizationally distributed worldwide, and interact in carrying out interdependent tasks guided by a common purpose and using computer-mediated communication technologies.

Leadership in the military

Military leaders like Hannibal, Rommel, Patton and Nelson are legends. The armed forces are often regarded as a paragon of virtue in respect of leadership. For example, journalist Godfrey Smith (2000) claims that, in the Battle of Britain in the Second World War:

> We won not because our pilots were better but because they were much better led. [Keith] Park [AOC, 11 Group, Fighter Command] has been compared to Wellington, but whereas Wellington had to concentrate for five hours at Waterloo, Park had to do it for five months.

Yet leadership in the British Army came under criticism in the 1970s in a seminal analysis by Norman Dixon (1976). He pinpointed, among generals, their fundamental conservatism and outmoded traditions; their tendencies to reject or dismiss information that challenged their preconceptions, to underestimate the enemy, to persist in pursuing an obviously doomed task, to prefer frontal assaults and brute force to proper reconnaissance and surprise, and to suppress or distort news from the front in the interest of morale; as well as their 'unnatural attachment' to mystical forces such as fate and luck.

The US Army's vision statement states: 'We are about leadership; it is our stock in trade, and it is what makes us different.'[7] When abuse of war prisoners occurs, as happened in Iraq after the 2003 war and during the subsequent occupation by coalition forces, it is worthwhile remembering the US Army mantra: 'The commander is responsible for everything the unit does or fails to do' (US Army, 1990: para. 2.6). In parallel with the rise in corporate scandals in the world of business, the military faces ethical criticism for its tactics and behaviour. Leonard Wong et al. (2003) say:

> For military leaders at the systems [strategic] level, new issues in ethics are...being confronted... . American military leaders are accustomed to waging war guided by moral obligations based on Western values, allegiance to the Constitution, and adherence to the laws of war. With the attacks of September 11th and the global war on terrorism, the U.S. military now finds itself in a situation of ethical asymmetry – fighting an enemy that does not follow the same moral guidelines [e.g. targeting civilians, using suicide bombers, etc.].

The military is not a monolithic organization but, they say, a 'diverse collection of organizations – army, navy and air force – roles, cultures and people'. Individual leaders, in a traditional hierarchy in which authority is distributed accordingly, therefore command relatively large numbers of subordinates and therefore have significant impact on people. The military's role has become much more varied since the end of the Cold War, with a lesser emphasis on conventional warfare and a greater involvement in anti-terrorist combat and peace-keeping operations in a wide variety of situations, many with considerable ambiguity and uncertainty, and often with extraordinarily far-reaching consequences. Leadership is required at strategic, operational and tactical levels, reflecting respectively national (or, in the case of UN forces, global) interests, policy and resource usage; major campaigns; and battles, engagement and close combat.

An underrated ability for strategic leadership is 'cognitive capacity' (which is discussed in Chapter 3). Wong et al. (2003) report research that stresses the importance of an independent perspective of the strategic environment and the use of abstract conceptual models in senior military leaders.

Leadership in the arts

The arts and cultural sector in the UK 'lacks good leaders', according to Sue Hoyle (2004), deputy director of the Clore Leadership Programme for the arts. She stresses the importance of personal qualities in leadership, especially passion for what one does. Howard Raynor (2004) comments, tongue in cheek:

> Christopher Columbus would have made the perfect arts administrator. After all, he set off with no clear idea where he was going; when he arrived he didn't know where he was; and when he returned he didn't know where he'd been – what's more, he did it all on someone else's money.

Lord Stevenson of Coddenham, chairman of the Pearson Group, believes that leadership in the arts in much more difficult than leadership in the business world (Stevenson, 2004). He says there is no bottom line by which to measure performance, no profit-and-loss account; leadership involves dealing with 'that very fragile thing called artistic judgement, artistic taste', and the arts world is generally 'exposed to much more scrutiny from far more audiences than a business is'. Leaders in the arts, he says, need 'a clear set of beliefs for what [they] are trying to achieve, and the confidence in [themselves] when [they] are in front of a shower of criticism'. Sir Peter Hall, a visionary, founder of the Royal Shakespeare Company, and one of the greatest drivers of British theatre, is an example. So is Tony Hall, the impresario at the Royal Opera House.[8]

Bruce Payne, director of the Hart Leadership Program in New York, *Leadership in the Arts*, believes that the people who succeed in the arts understand how to lead effectively: 'They know how to coach, they know how to encourage, they know how to praise, and they know how to love. Above all, they know how to express a vision that inspires rather than intimidates.'[9]

Studies of the impact of leadership

While there is considerable evidence for the positive effect of leadership on organizational effectiveness and employee satisfaction, the performance measures used in studies have usually been subjective evaluations (Koene et al., 2002). This has led to evidence for the importance of leadership that is less than compelling to sceptics.

A Conference Board study of some 400 *Fortune 1000* companies in the United States in the late 1990s found that 47% of executives and managers rated their companies' overall leadership capacity as poor or fair, while only 8% rated it as excellent (Csoka, 1998). And a survey by Development Dimensions International in 1999 found that only 36% of employees, including senior management, said they had confidence in their leaders (MacDonald, 1999). Employees identified weaknesses in 13 of 14 leadership skills, including strategic decision making, coaching and facilitating change. Only 49% of employees perceived empowering leadership in senior management, only 30% believed that their leaders had a vision, and 25% criticized strategic decision making.

Robert McHenry, chairman of OPP, suggests that:

- Managers do not think strategically or long-term
- People are expected to lead and manage without training
- Too many leaders are choosing entrepreneurship over strategic focus
- Managers often lack communication skills

(Eglin, 2002a)

A Chartered Management Institute (CMI) survey of leadership in the UK from the perspective of followers revealed that many leaders are failing to inspire the next generation and are struggling to meet today's business challenges, though organizations with leadership development programmes in place are doing significantly better

(Institute of Management, 2001; Hayhurst, 2002).[10] Similar to the Conference Board findings, more than one-third of all executives and nearly one-half of junior managers perceive the quality of leadership in their organizations as very poor. The chair of the project's advisory panel, Sir John Egan, commented:

> **Today's senior people have a new accountability to the people they lead. Good leadership is not elusive to describe nor to develop, but many companies have yet to rise to the challenge of creating programmes of leadership for all their managers.**

While 55% of managers identified inspiration as one of the three most important leadership characteristics, only 11% said their leaders provide it. They were more likely to see their leaders as knowledgeable (39%) and ambitious (38%) – characteristics perceived as important to their leaders' promotion but not as important to leadership per se. The other most important leadership attributes were the ability to provide a vision, look to the future and handle change, all of which were perceived as often lacking. The majority of executives favoured a role for leaders where they create a sense of purpose and a central vision or set of goals and then develop others around them to achieve the goals. Commenting on the survey results, Mary Chapman, director-general of the CMI, says there is a 'mismatch between what people want from their leaders and what they are experiencing': what they want is vision and inspiration, but what they get is ambition and technical knowledge (Simms, 2002).

The survey also revealed that leadership development is still a low priority. Almost half of respondents' organizations had no specific leadership development budget. However, where their organizations address leadership development, 57% of respondents rated quality of leadership highly in comparison with 21% of those in other organizations.

An interview survey of 1,000 employees in British companies with more than 500 staff by DDI in early 2004 revealed many as bored at work, lacking commitment, alienated and ready to quit (Eglin, 2004). The managing director of the firm conducting the survey, Steve Newhall, says:

> **Our research shows that organisations that fail to create a sense of meaning through their activities simply don't earn people's loyalty... . We all have hard jobs; we want to be sure they are worth the effort and help us grow.**

The 'inspiration gap' the CMI survey identified in the UK in no way applies to the top companies in the 2004 survey by *The Sunday Times* of the 100 best companies to work for and their 20,000 employees. Says Adèle Collins (2004: 8), 'The energy and inspirational qualities of a company's leader emerge this year as the major factors in making a company one of the best to work for.'

Another Conference Board leadership survey revealed a decline in the perceived strength of leadership in American companies. In 1997 about one-half of respondents rated their company's leadership strength as good or excellent; in 2001 only about one-third did so (Conference Board, 2002). And a survey by OPP (Eglin, 2002a) also revealed a significant dissatisfaction with leadership:

- Only 40% of respondents were satisfied with the leadership of their organizations
- The main cause of dissatisfaction was lack of trust

- 69% felt that the most important leadership quality is trustworthiness, but only 22% believed it was their boss's best attribute
- Almost 40% believed that the quality of leadership had declined in the past 10 years
- The greatest dissatisfaction was associated with taking risks or being entrepreneurial: 'People want leaders they can trust and with whom they feel confident about their future rather than those offering disruption' (Robert McHenry of OPP quoted by Eglin, 2002a)

In another survey – by the Manufacturing Foundation in 2003 of successful middle-market manufacturing firms in the UK – leadership style was ranked second, after strategic planning, in respect of its impact on company performance in more than half of the firms.

Annual surveys by *Fortune* magazine in the United States and *The Sunday Times* in the UK track 'the world's most admired companies' and the '1000 best companies to work for' respectively. They consistently identify leadership as a key factor contributing to high (and low) rankings. For example, Scott Spreier and Dawn Sherman (2003) of management consultants HayGroup, who conducted the 2002 *Fortune* survey, point out that the most admired companies are more focused on strategic issues, more successful at maintaining employee morale and commitment, and better led, with a greater emphasis on teams rather than individuals. Warren Bennis (1998) quotes a *Fortune* magazine comment:

> **The truth is that no one factor makes a company admirable, but if you were forced to pick the one that makes the most difference, you'd pick leadership...people are voting for the artist, not the painting.**

In *The Sunday Times* 2002 survey of the *100 Best Companies to Work for*, W.L. Gore & Associates, the GoreTex manufacturer, was ranked 16th overall, top for 'the most approachable management' and sixth for both 'the best work/life balance' and the 'most trusting managers'.[11] Mike Cox, technical director of the industrial products division, said:

> **Teamwork is everything. Gore is structured entirely differently from a classical organisation, to encourage everyone to contribute and to be inventive and creative. There is no positional power: you are only a leader if teams decide to respect and follow you, and we assess each other, which is rare but generates feedback and a sense of meritocracy.[12]**

By 2004, W.L. Gore was ranked as the best company to work for in the UK. Gore also gained the top score for putting into practice strong values and principles: between 80 and 90% of Gore's staff believed they could make a difference to the company, felt they made a valuable contribution to business success and felt the company was 'principled'.[13] And the majority of staff thought that Gore's corporate values did not reflect only one person's leadership. The 2004 survey supported the relationship between leadership and corporate values. Commenting on this, Collins (2004) says:

> **where staff perceive the values and principles within their company to be strong they are more likely to have a strong leadership and are more likely to view their company as a better place to work overall.**

And Alastair McCall (2004: 4) says:

> **Giving workers a sense of ownership is one of the key ingredients in creating the best companies to work for. Most often, the lead for achieving this comes from the top, making quality of leadership – and the ability of the boss to inspire the workforce – the single biggest influence on a company's ranking.**

The top ranking company for leadership in 2004 was Beaverbrooks, the jewellers. Beaverbrooks also ranked as the second best company to work for overall. McCall (2004) reports one employee as saying, 'The more senior people are a real inspiration. They have taught me so much about myself and continually support me. I feel a true sense of belonging here.' In *The Sunday Times* 2005 survey, W.L. Gore was the first company to rank first in two successive years, also leading the leadership category.[14]

Collins and Porras (1996a) claim that the research evidence shows that sustained success of companies is clearly associated with leadership. However, David Day and Robert Lord (1988) say that the effects of strategic (top-level) leadership cannot be assessed in less than two years. Lenz (1993: 171) explains:

> **Literature on corporate decline and failure indicates that such measures are 'lagging indicators'...[whereas] use of behavioral referents affords a means to evaluate leadership with 'leading indicators'...[which] may open the way for more rapid corrective action, if deficiencies are present.**

The best companies to work for in 2002 on average outperformed the rest of the FTSE-listed companies, with investment returns over the previous five years of 25.4% compared with –2%, 6.3% and 21.2% over the previous three years.[15] Apart from benefits to employees, being 'a good company to work for' makes a company an attractive investment. Numerous other studies show a relationship between leadership and financial performance, market share, organizational and workgroup climate, and employee job satisfaction, commitment and productivity.

A survey by the Accenture Institute of Strategic Change in the United States found that the stock prices of companies perceived to be 'well led' – creating cultures of adaptation – grew 900% over a 10-year period versus 74% for companies perceived to lack good leadership in this respect (Bennis, 1998). In research with Harvard Business School, executive search consultants Odgers, Ray & Berndtson (Gill, 2001a) found that the quality of leadership accounts for some 15–20% of the total variance in companies' performance, using a methodology that measures ROL ('Return On Leadership').

The importance of leadership has been recognized by the UK's Council for Excellence in Management and Leadership (CEML) in a radical recommendation of the voluntary reporting of leadership by public and private sector organizations in their annual reports, using evidence-based statements (CEML, 2002). Sue Law (2002) makes the point that the reporting of leadership is an 'inevitable next step' in the increasing emphasis on business accountability, including business ethics, the environment and social responsibility as a whole. The CEML has established several areas of leadership capability that might be included: morale (including employee job satisfaction), motivation (including surveys of employees' understanding of their companies' vision and strategy) and long-term development, including reviews of potential for leadership capability.

Leadership versus management

There is a continuing confusion between 'management' and 'leadership'. For example, Marcus Buckingham (2005), writing in *Harvard Business Review*, says:

> **[Great managers] discover what is unique about each person and then capitalize on it... . This is the exact opposite of what great leaders do. Great leaders discover what is universal and capitalize on it.**

This view is highly questionable: what Buckingham says is management is in fact a key aspect of effective leadership, posited specifically in one particular theory of transformational leadership that we discuss in the next chapter. Robert House and Ram Aditya (1997) suggest that:

> **Scholars of the traditional management and leadership literatures seldom take advantage of each other's contributions and, consequently, these two literatures are not adequately integrated.**

The term 'management' derives from *manus*, the Latin word for 'hand'. The term had to do with handling things, and it gained currency in its modern sense during the Industrial Revolution in the nineteenth century. The archaic French *ménager* meant 'use sparingly'.

In the oft-quoted words of Bennis and Nanus (1985: 21), 'Managers are people who do things right; leaders are people who do the right things.' For example, leaders ask the right questions about strategy and make sure the right answers are implemented (Bottger, 2000). Says David Wills, training manager for the Motherwell Bridge Group in Scotland:

> **Leadership is...about vision and having the courage to do the right thing – different from management, which is all about doing the thing right – even if there is a risk. (Abrahams, 2001)**

But this distinction is epistemologically unsound, according to Peter Gronn (2003):

> **It is an attempt to resurrect the traditional distinction between facts and values. Thus, 'things right' reduces to a competence or technical mastery, whereas 'the right thing' implies desirable ends, purposes or values.**

The Work Foundation (formerly The Industrial Society) in the UK defines the differences between management and leadership simply. Managers plan, allocate resources, administer and control, whereas leaders innovate, communicate and motivate.[16] Vision is one of the key differences between a manager and a leader, according to Stanley Deetz et al. (2000: 49). General Sir William Slim, the inspiring Second World War leader, saw the difference in the same way. In a speech in Adelaide as governor-general of Australia in 1957, he said:

> **We do not in the Army talk of 'management' but of 'leadership'. This is significant. There is a difference between leaders and management. [Leadership represents] one of the oldest, most natural and most effective of all human relationships. [Management is]**

> **a later product, with neither so romantic nor so inspiring a history. Leadership is of the spirit, compounded of personality and vision; its practice is an art. Management is of the mind, more a matter of accurate calculation of statistics, of methods, time tables, and routine; its practice is a science. Managers are necessary; leaders are essential. (Adair, 1989: 217–220)**

Bennis (1989: 45) suggests that the differences between leadership and management can be summed up as 'the differences between those who master the context and those who surrender to it'. These differences are detailed in Table 1.1.

Amin Rajan (2000a) contrasts management and leadership thus:

- Management is about path following; leadership is path finding
- Management is about doing things right; leadership is about doing the right things
- Management is about planning and budgeting; leadership is about establishing direction
- Management is about controlling and problem solving; leadership is about motivating and inspiring

John Kotter (1990a,b) says that management produces orderly results that keep something working efficiently, whereas leadership creates useful change; neither is necessarily better or a replacement for the other; both are needed if organizations and nations are to prosper.

Warner Burke (1986: 68) also agrees that both management and leadership are needed: 'For clarity of goals and direction, managers need leaders. For indispensable help in reaching goals, leaders need managers.' We 'manage from the left, lead from the right', Covey (1992: 248) says. In terms of brain dominance theory, the manager's role is mainly left-brain dominated, whereas the leader's role is right-brain based. The left hemisphere of the brain deals more with words, specific elements, logic, analysis, sequential thinking and time. The right hemisphere deals more with emotions, aesthetics, pictures, relationships among elements and the gestalt, synthesis and intuitive, simultaneous, holistic thinking, free of time constraints. An Eastern view is that leading involves the *yin* and managing involves the *yang*.

Table 1.1 *Differences between managers and leaders*

The manager	The leader
Administers	Innovates
Is a 'copy'	Is an 'original'
Maintains	Develops
Focuses on systems and structure	Focuses on people
Focuses on control	Inspires trust
Takes a short-range view	Has a long-range perspective
Asks how and when	Asks what and why
Imitates	Originates
Accepts the status quo	Challenges the status quo
Is a classic 'good soldier'	Is his or her own person
Does things right	Does the right thing

United Technologies, the aerospace and defence company, published an arresting notice in the *Wall Street Journal* and several other newspapers and magazines in 1984. Captioned 'Let's get rid of management', it read:

> **People don't want to be managed. They want to be led. Whoever heard of a 'world manager'? World leader, yes. Educational leader. Political leader. Religious leader. Scout leader. Community leader. Business leader. They lead. They don't manage. The carrot always wins over the stick. Ask your horse. You can lead your horse to water, but you can't manage him to drink. If you want to manage somebody, manage yourself. Do that well and you'll be ready to stop managing. And start leading. (Bennis and Nanus, 1985: 22)**

In 2002 United Technologies was ranked the world's most admired company in the aerospace and defence sector (Hjelt, 2003). The company's philosophy evidently has paid off, perhaps because we manage *things* but we *lead* people.

Individual, shared or distributed leadership?

Most texts on leadership assume that leadership is 'a solo act – a one-person undertaking – regardless of whether the organization being led is a nation, a global corporation or a scout troop' (O'Toole et al., 2002). The conventional view of leadership is that individual leaders make a significant and even crucial impact of the performance of their organizations. For example, Thomas argued, based on a study of large retail firms in the UK, that individual CEOs *do* make a difference (Thomas, 1988). Executive education and leadership development programmes even emphasize the individual leader:

> **The parsing of leadership styles has become de rigeur in American business schools. Professors teach students to adopt the right leadership style for themselves, using '360-degree feedback' to make them aware of how they are perceived by others – and how to manage those perceptions. A growth industry called executive coaching caters to the leadership-impaired. (Pasternack et al., 2001)**

Solo leadership is not necessary, not desirable, and probably impossible in today's organizations, according to James O'Toole (2001) and Bruce Pasternack et al. (2001). The latter claim there is little correlation between CEO leadership behaviour and organizational performance. And Richard Wellins and Patterson Weaver Jr (2003) quote a study of 83 leadership successions in 1997 and 1998 by Margaret Wiersma that showed little relationship between the loss of a CEO and the company's performance.

The new view of leadership is that the traditional role of a single leader who 'leads' by command and control no longer works because the challenges and problems facing organizations today are too complex and difficult for one person or even a small group of executives to handle alone (Drath, 2001a,b). 'Contextualists' argue that many situational factors constrain solo leaders (Thomas, 1988). What is needed, Wilfred H. Drath (2001a,b) says, is 'relational dialogue … people making sense and meaning of their work together … [creating] a world in which it makes sense to have shared goals or shared knowledge'.

The 'heroic' model of leadership, attributing greatness and infallibility to individual leaders, according to Grint, is 'both dangerous and dangerously naïve' (Eglin, 2003). Business leadership that depends on one all-powerful leader, Pasternack et al. (2001) say, is 'unstable in the long run'. Examples they give are the crumbling of the ITT Corporation after the CEO Harold Geneen's retirement and how General Motors after Alfred Sloan, Polaroid after Edwin Land and Coca-Cola after Roberto Goizueta seemed to lose their way. There are also many examples of once-lauded heroes falling out of favour: *The Economist* (2002b) quotes Bernie Ebbers of WorldCom, Diana Brooks of Sotheby's, Jean-Marie Messier of Vivendi Universal, Percy Barnevik of ABB, Kenneth Lay and Jeffrey Skilling of Enron, and even the iconic Jack Welch of General Electric. One problem is the celebrity status that is accorded solo leaders and feeds their egos. The result is that:

> **Nearly all CEOs think of themselves as the sort of all-knowing, tough, take-charge leader whose photo appears on the cover of *Forbes*, and they find irresistible the temptation to centralize authority in their offices, making all important...decisions themselves. (Pasternack et al., 2001)**

This phenomenon is not limited to 'heroes' in the business world of capitalism. It is apparent in communist culture too. For example, personality cults developed around communist leaders like Jiang Zemin and Zhu Ronji in the People's Republic of China. Said Susan V. Lawrence (2002) of the Beijing Bureau of the *Far Eastern Economic Review*, 'China's state media [are] increasingly given over to paeans to Jiang', and he has engaged in adorning public buildings with his calligraphic inscription 'with enthusiasm'.

Individual leadership nevertheless still has a place. It is necessary in small and start-up companies and in organizations where inspiration is needed to bring about transformational change (Pasternack et al., 2001). But Pasternack et al. also say:

> **CEOs of large companies should...see that it is more productive and satisfying to become a leader of leaders than to go it alone.**

Various references in the literature have been made to leadership that is shared, distributed, distributive, dispersed, collective or institutional. House and Aditya (1997) say:

> **The process of leadership cannot be described simply in terms of the behavior of an individual: rather, leadership involves collaborative relationships that lead to collective action grounded in the shared values of people who work together to effect positive change.**

To add to the terminology, they distinguish among delegated leadership, co-leadership and peer leadership. And co-leadership itself is interpreted in different ways. For example, David Heenan and Warren Bennis (1999) describe co-leadership in terms of one co-leader as 'playing second fiddle' to another, whereas Peter Troiano (1999) defines co-leadership as two leaders working side by side with equal managerial responsibility. Others use the term to mean the same as leadership shared among many individuals.

The survey by the Manufacturing Foundation in 2003 found that leadership in successful middle-market manufacturing firms in the UK tended not to reside in one person at the top but to be a shared role among the top management team. Shared leadership reflects shared ownership of problems, an emphasis on learning and development (empowerment) to enable sharing, understanding and contribution, and a culture of openness, mutual respect and trust. Michael Useem found that 'The best projects [by MBA students] come from the teams that learn to act together and exercise shared leadership' (Shinn, 2003). Shared leadership is characterized by:

- The quality of interactions among people rather than position in a hierarchy
- The effectiveness with which people work together in solving a problem rather than a solo performance by one leader
- Conversation rather than instructions
- Shared values and beliefs
- Honesty and a desire for the common good rather than self-interest, secrecy and spin

In 2001 Pasternack et al. (2001) in collaboration with the World Economic Forum and the University of Southern California surveyed over 4,000 people in leadership roles in 12 large organizations on three continents and interviewed 20 to 40 in each one. They found that many successful companies – such as Intel Corporation, Motorola and Hyundai Electronics Industries Company in South Korea – are developing an institutional leadership capacity rather than depending on a charismatic CEO: 'Rather than an aria, leadership can be a chorus of diverse voices singing in unison.' The measure they developed is known as the Leadership Quotient (LQ). Leadership, O'Toole (2001) says, is an 'organizational trait'. However, O'Toole et al. (2002) report the indifferent reception these findings had at the 2000 World Economic Forum in Davos, Switzerland, despite evidence of enough cases of shared leadership that attest to its success:

> **This resistance to the notion of shared leadership stems from thousands of years of cultural conditioning [starting perhaps with Plato's views]. We are dealing with a near-universal myth: in the popular mind, leadership is always singular.**

Marianne Döös and Lena Wilhelmson (2003) report a study showing that two-thirds of Swedish managers have a positive attitude towards shared leadership (or co-leadership). They studied four pairs of leaders in four Swedish organizations concerned with product development, management consulting, communications and soccer. Their common characteristics included shared values, mutual confidence, shared approaches to planning and visualizing, capitalizing on differences and receptivity to new ideas, and joint recognition of setbacks and successes.

Amana Corporation's CEO Paul Staman says:

> **[Shared leadership] allows more time for leaders to spend in the field; it creates an internal dynamic in which the leaders constantly challenge each other to higher levels of performance; it encourages a shared leadership mindset at all levels of the company; it prevents the trauma of transition that occurs in organizations when a strong CEO suddenly leaves. [What makes this work is] a shared set of guiding principles, and a team in which each member is able to set aside ego and 'what's in it for me' thinking.[17]**

The idea of institutional leadership was first described by Philip Selznick in 1957 (Selznick, 1957). The concept has gained currency only in recent years. Jeff Gold and Alma Harris (2003) describe a study of distributed leadership in two schools and how it occurs through 'mediation in the form of [dialogue] and representational symbols' with the aim of identifying actions for improvement and monitoring subsequent progress.

Gronn (2002), in his meta-analysis of empirical studies in 20 organizations with distributed leadership, observes that it often begins spontaneously but eventually becomes institutionalized. He identifies two features of distributed leadership: interdependence and coordination. Interdependence is characterized by overlapping of leaders' responsibilities and complementarity of responsibilities. Coordination and alignment among co-leaders are key to success, but not only at the top.

O'Toole (2001) has found that 'many of the key tasks and responsibilities of leadership [are] institutionalized in the systems, practices, and cultures of the organization'. Institutionalized leadership is characterized by empowerment to act like owners and entrepreneurs rather than 'hired hands', to take the initiative, accept accountability, and to create and adhere to agreed systems and procedures. O'Toole et al. (2002) suggest that the reason for the continued success of companies under the successive tenure of several CEOs – and for the failure of previously successful CEOs in new companies – is to do with organizational variables like systems, structures and policies, 'factors that are not included in research based on a solo leadership model'.

Flexible distributive leadership is required to cope with the increasing volatility, complexity and variety of organizations' external environments, according to Michael Brown and Dennis Goia (2002). Distributive leadership, Gronn (2002) says, has emerged as a result of the development of new organizational forms – such as flatter structures that are more organic and virtual organization – that require greater interdependence and coordination. The current interest in institutional leadership reflects a post-industrial division of labour characterized by distributed workplaces, such as 'hot-desking' and working from home. Such distributed working has been made possible by developments in IT.

Pasternack et al. (2001) suggest that whether and how the CEO builds institutional leadership, as did Jack Welch at General Electric and Yotaro 'Tony' Kobayashi at Fuji Xerox, make a difference to organizational performance. Pasternack says:

> **Too much is being written about the CEO as the great leader and not enough about organizations that demonstrate leadership capacity throughout the organization... . Really good leaders take their skill and abilities and build into their organizations the capacity for leadership all the way down the line. (O'Shea, 2000)**

Hierarchical level and leadership

If institutional leadership is important, then it would be useful to explore similarities and differences in leadership behaviour and effectiveness across the different levels of an organization's hierarchy. Most empirical research studies of leadership have focused on first-line or middle-level managers owing to the availability of access and large enough sample sizes (Sadler, 1997: 12). However, in line with the growing acceptance of qualitative research, we now see many more studies of CEOs based on interviews with them.

Organizational hierarchy is associated with 'command and control' leadership. Robert Fuller (2001) says that authority and hierarchy are associated with inflexibility, slow decision making and lack of responsiveness to customers. Frances Hesselbein says 'when people move into a circular system, enormous energy is released' (Shinn, 2003). But many organizations will probably always have hierarchies, and leadership in relation to organizational level is therefore worthwhile considering.

Likely hierarchical differences in leadership behaviour were pointed out long ago by Selznick (1957). According to Robert Lord and Karen Maher (1991: 97), 'the perceptual processes that operate with respect to leaders are very likely to involve quite different considerations at upper versus lower hierarchical levels'. Top-level leaders are responsible for the vision and mission of the organization – where it is heading, the development of appropriate strategies and strategic goals, and creating and promoting shared values throughout the organization. Lower-level leaders are responsible for formulating plans to implement strategies, accomplishing routine tasks and encouraging individual involvement and team working. Amitai Etzioni (1961) sees top management as concerned with ends rather than means, middle management with means rather than ends, and first-level management with daily operations. In common, however, are the need to empower people – to enable people to be *able* to do what needs to be done – and the need to influence, motivate and inspire them – to get them to *want* to do what needs to be done.

Bruce Avolio and Bernard Bass (1995) suggest that transformational leadership should be observed at all levels in an organization. Deanne Den Hartog et al. (1999) found that charismatic/transformational leadership behaviour is valued almost equally at top and lower levels of management. A study of commonalities and differences in leadership behaviour and effectiveness at different hierarchical levels in manufacturing organizations using a 360-degree leadership assessment instrument, Bass and Avolio's Multifactor Leadership Questionnaire (MLQ, see Chapter 2), revealed the following:

- Transformational leadership is displayed more at higher levels than at lower levels but its effectiveness is the same at all levels
- The use of both transactional leadership and laissez-faire leadership was found not to vary across the hierarchy
- The effectiveness of transactional leadership was found to decrease above middle-management level

(Edwards and Gill, 2003a,b)

These findings, for the use of transformational and transactional leadership, were replicated in another study. A separate study of leadership and organizational hierarchy, by Titus Oshagbemi and myself (Oshagbemi and Gill, 2004), also showed that, overall, transformational leadership is displayed more at higher levels than at lower levels while transactional leadership does not vary (except specifically for contingent reward, which differs between middle and first-level managers). The particular dimensions of transformational leadership that varied were intellectual stimulation and inspirational motivation. This study also showed that senior managers are less directive and more participative in their leadership style than first-level managers. There were also significant differences between senior, middle and first-level managers in their use of the delegative style, which was positively associated with hierarchical level: senior managers use this style most.

Hierarchical position therefore appears to be a moderator of the use of transformational leadership (a positive relationship) but not its effectiveness, which is constant throughout organizations. It is also a moderator of the effectiveness of transactional leadership (a negative relationship) but not its use, which in general is also constant across the hierarchy. Zaccaro and Klimoski (2001: 13) suggest that organizational context, of which hierarchical position is one feature, is often understated as a moderator: it is a boundary condition for theory building and model specification. More empirical research on the commonalities and differences in leadership across organizational hierarchies is needed.

The collective leadership capacity of an organization – institutional leadership – is the sum total of leadership behaviour at all hierarchical levels. When this is strong, we may say the organization has a strong leadership 'brand'. Barry Gibbons, former CEO of Burger King, says that 'leadership and ... branding have almost seamlessly merged into one' (Creelman, 2003a). Leadership brand is a characteristic of organizations rather than individuals. Cunningham (2002) says that 'a brand is a promise': the highest expression of who the organization is and a statement of its business philosophy and strategic intentions – it is about being distinct. Brands are a way to distinguish and market a product or service. For example, the Virgin brand, Gibbons says, is about fun, innovation and great value (Creelman, 2003a). Brands are a way to build customer commitment to the company, not just to its individual products. Leadership brand therefore is a way to build employee commitment to the company. Brand loyalty, in the case of leadership, is employee commitment and perhaps stakeholder commitment. Ulrich et al. (2000) say:

> **Leadership brand occurs when leaders at every level are clear about which results are most important, develop a consistent approach to delivering these results, and build attributes that support [their] achievement.**

Dave Ulrich and Norm Smallwood (2000) suggest that leadership brand is characterized by leadership attributes – the knowledge and skills that reflect how leaders behave – and results. Attributes such as innovating quickly are related to results such as being first in the market. Leadership becomes a brand because of the distinctive link between attributes and results in a given firm: leadership brand = leadership attributes × results (Ulrich et al., 2000).

Leadership brand is not merely the result of 'cascading' leadership, in which strong leaders empower other leaders throughout the organization. This is dependent, Pasternack et al. (2001) say, on the personality and support of whoever the top leader is at any particular time. Leaders throughout the organization behave more like owners and entrepreneurs, assuming responsibility and taking the initiative.

The nature of enquiry in this book

This book aims to shows how both individual and institutional leadership can be enhanced through a model that integrates the different approaches to studying and developing effective leadership. The approach to developing this integrative model is triangulation, whereby leadership is addressed from many different perspectives – psychology and sociology, traditionally its most common knowledge base, but also ancient and modern philosophy, anthropology, military and business strategy, political science, history, theology, sport and the arts – literature, poetry, biography, journalism and reportage, the performing arts (music, dance and theatre) and even mythology and the visual arts. The study of leadership is truly eclectic.

The rationale for this approach is that the basic axioms of quantitative and qualitative enquiry are arbitrary: it should be the fit of the methodology with the phenomenon to be studied that should decide which one to use (Guba and Lincoln, 1982; Salmon, 2003). Leadership draws on both science and the arts. Triangulation is arguably a good fit with leadership as a phenomenon because of its eclectic nature and the diverse range of methodologies that have been used to study it. Moreover, one might claim, as do David Rennie (2000) and Daniel Robinson (2000), that pushing back the frontiers of knowledge results not merely from deduction and induction but also from applying imagination, creativity and common sense.

Recognizing the adage that 'there is nothing more practical than a good theory', this book presents a new integrative and holistic model of leadership. The model aims to make a useful new contribution by integrating the several hitherto disparate strands of leadership thinking and research: the intellectual, spiritual, emotional and behavioural aspects of leadership. This model aims to be useful in practice to three groups of people: those who serve in – or aspire to – leadership roles in organizations, those who work as specialists and consultants in leadership development, and scholars and students who study or research leadership. As Donald Krause (1997: ix) says, 'Understanding the nature of leadership and developing strong leadership skills is probably the single most important task for society today.'

Further reading

John Adair (1989), *Great Leaders.* Guildford: The Talbot Adair Press.

W. Bennis, G.M. Spreitzer and T.G. Cummings (Editors), (2001) *The Future of Leadership.* San Francisco, CA: Jossey-Bass.

James C. Collins (2001a), *Good to Great: Why Some Companies Make the Leap – and Others Don't.* New York: HarperBusiness.

Stephen R. Covey (1992), *Principle-centered Leadership.* London: Simon and Schuster.

Gareth Edwards, Jan Bailey and Paul Winter (2002), *Leadership in Management.* Ross-on-Wye, Herefordshire: The Leadership Trust Foundation.

Keith Grint (2000), *The Arts of Leadership.* Oxford: Oxford University Press.

Barbara Kellerman (2004), *Bad Leadership: What It Is, How It Happens, Why It Matters.* Boston, MA: Harvard Business School Press.

Donald G. Krause (1997), *The Way of the Leader.* London: Nicholas Brealey.

Jean Lipman-Blumen (2005), *The Allure of Toxic Leaders.* New York: Oxford University Press.

James MacGregor Burns (1978), *Leadership.* New York: Harper and Row.

Gary Yukl (2005), *Leadership in Organizations, 6th Edition.* Upper Saddle River, NJ: Prentice Hall.

Stephen J. Zaccaro and Richard J. Klimoski (Editors) (2001), *The Nature of Organizational Leadership: Understanding the Performance Imperatives Confronting Today's Leaders.* San Francisco, CA: Jossey-Bass.

Discussion questions

1 Why is there no agreed paradigm for leadership?
2 How does the nature of leadership differ between business, politics, the public sector, the military and the third sector?
3 'Leaders are people who do the right thing; managers are people who do things right' (Warren Bennis). Discuss.
4 'And when we think we lead, we are most led' (Lord Byron). Discuss.
5 Is the day of the individual, 'heroic' leader giving way to the age of collective leadership?
6 How does the nature of leadership differ across hierarchical levels in organizations?

2 Current Thinking about Leadership: A Review and Critique

The Questioner, who sits so sly,
Shall never know how to Reply.
He who replies to words of Doubt
Doth put the Light of Knowledge out.

William Blake (1757–1827), *Auguries of Innocence*

Overview

- The major theories and models we find in textbooks have each helped us to understand leadership. Each one is a piece in the jigsaw puzzle of leadership. This chapter reviews the major theories of leadership, how they help us to understand it, but also how none of them alone provides a complete picture.
- Trait theories of leadership, also known as 'great man' theories, postulate common qualities or characteristics of effective leaders. These theories raise the question of whether such qualities are inherited or acquired.
- Theories of emergent leadership, including 'servant leadership', postulate that leaders may emerge who have the characteristics and skills to meet the needs of their group, organization or society at a given time.
- Leadership-style theories describe what leaders do and classify it into two categories: people focused and task focused. 'Action-centred leadership' is a development of leadership-style theory, focusing on task, team and individual.
- Psychodynamic theory, or leader–member exchange theory, explains the effectiveness of leaders as a function of the psychodynamic exchange that occurs between leaders and group members. Leaders provide direction and guidance through influence permitted to them by members.
- Contingency and situational leadership theories suggest that there is no one best style of leadership. Successful and enduring leaders use different styles according to the nature of the situation and the followers.
- The 'new leadership' comprises visionary, charismatic and transformational leadership theories. Transformational leadership occurs when leaders raise people's motivation to act and create a sense of higher purpose. It is distinguished from transactional leadership, which typically involves an exchange between leader and followers with an emphasis on correcting deviations from requirements and providing a material or psychological reward in return for compliance with the

leader's wishes. Other theories discussed include strategic leadership and pragmatic leadership.

- No theory or model of leadership so far has provided a satisfactory explanation of leadership. Indeed there are many definitions of leadership that vary widely.

Trait theories of leadership

Trait theories started with Hippocrates' description of personality types based on 'body humour'. Effective leaders were believed to show common characteristics that cause them to behave in certain ways. This was the era of so-called 'great man' theories (Van Sters and Field, 1990). For example, Luther Bernard (1926) attempted to explain leadership in terms of the 'internal' qualities that a person is born with.

Leadership trait studies are mostly psychological in approach. However, the sociological approach is to analyse the characteristics of leaders that result from their position in society: social class, education, gender and religious, ethnic and kinship networks (Whittington, 1993). The problem with the resulting social elite theory is that it deals with the generalities of social strata rather than with the analysis of the personalities and behaviour of leaders. As Burns (1978: 880) said, leadership involves not only the power of control but also the power to motivate: 'one must look for motives as well as the weapon'.

However, social structures can be seen as enabling rather than determining (Pettigrew, 1987). Richard Whittington (1993: 183) says: 'Society provides both the social resources, material and symbolic, that empower our actions, and the social rules of accepted behaviour that ... guides them.' Social structures provide people with the potential for leadership but it is the psychology of individuals, he says, that translates potential into actuality (Whittington, 1993: 184–185). 'Upper echelons' theory, favoured by macro-theorists and strategists (Waldman and Javidan, 2001), rejects the deterministic view taken by proponents of external control and focuses on the personal characteristics of top-level managers.

The idea that leadership is associated with superior intelligence originates in the teachings of Aristotle, Plato and Socrates and gained currency during the Age of Enlightenment. Intelligence is a particularly interesting trait, as it emerges in studies most often (Kotter, 1990b: 106):

> **People who provide effective leadership in big jobs appear to be always above average in some basic form of intelligence, although they rarely seem geniuses.**

Judge, Colbert and Ilies (2004), in their meta-analysis of studies of intelligence and leadership, found that intelligence and leadership are significantly associated. And Dean Simonton found that differences in intelligence account for about 10% of the variation in the 'greatness' of US presidents (Dingfelder, 2004).

Superior intelligence in the leader, however, can have disadvantages as well as advantages (Levicki, 1998: 98–99). For example, it has been shown that too high a level of intelligence may interfere with effective decision making (Gill, 1980, 1982). And there is evidence that leadership effectiveness is impaired when a leader's intelligence substantially exceeds that of the follower group (Bass, 1990a). Simonton suggests that 'The [US presidents] who are the most intellectually brilliant are often barely elected .... They have trouble speaking in sound bites and communicating with the public' (Dingfelder, 2004). The only US president rated as intelligent and with a PhD degree, Woodrow Wilson, was elected, Simonton notes, with only 20% of the popular vote.

Early studies of leadership and personality, in the 1930s and 1940s, assumed that effective leaders have special traits in common. Following a period during which the results of research aimed at identifying them generally have been inconclusive, more promising results have emerged more recently. Peter Northouse's analysis suggests that the main qualities appearing to be important for leadership, in addition to intelligence or cognitive ability, are integrity, self-confidence, dominance, sociability, and persistence or determination (Northouse, 1997: 17). In another study, employing the five-factor model of personality, Judge et al. (2002) also found significant relationships between several personality traits and leadership that were even higher than for intelligence and leadership, namely extraversion, agreeableness and conscientiousness, in addition to openness to experience (intelligence).

Another analysis, of successful CEOs, suggests the following characteristics:

- Integrity, maturity and energy
- Business acumen (a deep understanding of the business and a strong profit orientation)
- 'People' acumen (judging people, leading teams, coaching and growing people, and cutting losses (mismatches between people and jobs) where necessary)
- Organizational acumen (engendering trust, sharing information, listening expertly as well as diagnosing under-performance, delivering on commitments, change orientation, and being both decisive and incisive)
- Curiosity, intellectual capacity, and a global mindset (being externally oriented, eager for knowledge of the world, and adept at connecting developments and spotting patterns)
- Superior judgement
- An insatiable appetite for accomplishment and results
- A powerful motivation to grow and convert learning into practice

(Charan and Colvin, 1999)

Most of these characteristics are cognitive, emotional or interpersonal, and some are deeply embedded in individual values. Whether they are exhaustive or consistently displayed is highly questionable. And some tend to emphasize the individual in isolation rather than in relationships with others.

In a study of 17 CEOs, their top management teams (TMTs) and organizational performance, Randall Peterson et al. (2003) found the following significant associations between CEO personality and TMT dynamics and between TMT dynamics and organizational performance:

- CEO conscientiousness with TMT concern for legality and sense of control over the environment
- CEO emotional stability with team cohesion, intellectual flexibility and leader dominance

- CEO agreeableness with team cohesion and power decentralization
- CEO extraversion with leader strength (dominance)
- CEO openness with team risk taking and intellectual flexibility
- Income growth with TMT intellectual flexibility, optimism and cohesiveness

Joyce Bono and Timothy Judge (2004), in a meta-analysis of 26 studies of personality and the six dimensions of transactional and transformational leadership (which we discuss later in this chapter), identified by Bruce Avolio et al. (1999), found weak relationships between personality and leadership. With regard to transformational leadership in particular, the 'Big Five' personality traits (Digman, 1990) – neuroticism, extraversion, openness, agreeableness and conscientiousness – explained 12% of the variation in charisma (idealized influence and inspirational motivation combined) and only 5% of the variation in intellectual stimulation and 6% in individualized consideration. Extraversion was the strongest and most consistent correlate of transformational leadership. Correlations between personality traits and transactional and laissez-faire leadership were generally weak and of little practical significance.

A survey by management consultants Deloitte & Touche reported the most frequently identified characteristics of good corporate leadership (Table 2.1). The picture of personal qualities for leadership, however, is still not complete or even agreed. For example, recent research of databases of corporate results for companies that had been transformed into great companies going back to 1965 came up with only one finding: they all had leaders who displayed 'a paradoxical mixture of personal humility and professional will', an unusual mix of being 'timid and ferocious, shy and fearless' at the same time (Collins, 2001a).

Many traits undoubtedly develop in early life. Yet many people still believe that 'leaders are born, not made': leaders are born with the traits that mark them out as future leaders. Perhaps some traits are genetically determined or at least predisposed, which is a question we return to in Chapter 9. Meanwhile, suffice it to say that the search for the elusive 'leadership gene' continues.

It cannot be disputed that leaders who do not possess all the traits, whatever they are, are often effective. And leaders who possess many of them are often not effective. Mike Pedler et al. (2004) say:

> **There is no one correct definition of leadership, or any one set of personal qualities or competencies that characterise leaders.**

Even if trait theory stood up to scrutiny, it can still be argued convincingly that some strengths in excess can become weaknesses. For example, in the armed services, poor

Table 2.1 *Characteristics of good corporate leadership**

Characteristic	Frequency of mention (%)
Ability to make difficult decisions	92
Ability to lead a company during a crisis	89
Trustworthiness	85
Honesty	83
Intelligence and 'brains'	80

*Deloitte & Touche, *News 00Jan*, www.dttus.com.

decision making can result from 'cognitive dissonance' (Festinger, 1957), where decision makers reject new information after they have made their decision that suggests it was wrong (Dixon, 1976). Imbalance among traits can be dysfunctional: complementarity is needed.

Theories of emergent leadership

'Asking who should be the leader,' Henry Ford once said, 'is like asking who should sing tenor in the quartet' (Marshall, 1991: 19). The man with the tenor voice, of course!

Leaders may emerge who have the characteristics and skills to meet the needs of their group, organization or society at a given time. Such a leader is likely to be viewed as the most prototypical of the group (Hogg, 2001). The classic study of this was of a street corner gang in the United States (Whyte, 1943). Such leaders may emerge regardless of, or in the absence of, any formal leader appointed by others. Theories of emergent leadership emphasize the importance of followers (House and Mitchell, 1974). Leadership depends on an interaction between the goals of the followers and the leader. Vertical dyad linkage theory, or leader–member exchange (LMX) theory, has grown out of work in this area (Graen, 1976).

The emergence of 'natural' leaders is usual in politics, where leaders need to conform to followers' expectations. The nineteenth-century French politician Alexandre Ledru-Rollin (1807–1874) clearly recognized this: '*Eh bien! Je suis leur chef; il fallait bien les suivre*' ('Ah well! I am their leader; I really ought to follow them') (de Mirecourt, 1857).

Perhaps the most infamous example of an emergent leader is Adolf Hitler. However misguided, flawed and evil, Hitler's vision, values and oratory inspired a nation during a time of collective psychological depression. It was not only China's Mao Zedung who led people on a 'long march' in the wrong direction; in Hitler's case it was to total defeat and desolation.

The ability or desire to serve the needs of other people is usually the reason why leaders emerge. Great leaders serve others, according to the theory of 'servant leadership', associated with Robert Greenleaf (1977). Socrates and his pupil Xenophon saw leadership as serving others – as meeting their needs (Adair, 1989: 39). And St Paul said, 'I have made myself every man's servant, to win over as many as possible'.[18] Great leaders, then, display humility. But, as Major-General Tim Cross says, '[Jesus] served those who served the cause … but He certainly wasn't a doormat, rather a man of tremendous physical and moral courage' (Cross, 1998). It is no coincidence that the motto of the UK's Royal Military College at Sandhurst is *Serve to Lead* and that the Service prayer says, 'help us to be masters of ourselves that we may be servants of others, and teach us to serve to lead'.

What place does servant leadership have in the world of business? As CEO of the Toro Company, Ken Melrose believed that 'the great leader is a great servant': he said, 'I came to understand that you best lead by serving the needs of your people. You don't do their jobs for them; you enable them to learn and progress on the job' (Dess and Picken, 2000). And the founder of SouthWest Airlines, Herb Kelleher, says:

> **Leadership is being a faithful, devoted, hard-working servant of the people you lead and participating with them in the agonies as well as the ecstasies of life.[19]**

Retailer ASDA appears to be the only organization in the UK that uses the term 'servant leader', though many encourage the idea and put it into practice (Arkin, 2004). Service to other people is part and parcel of leadership in the trade union movement. As (Lord) Vic Feather once said to one company's management when general secretary of the UK's Trades Union Congress, 'They work for you, and I work for them' (Monks, 2000).

Many leaders have problems with the notion of servant leadership, especially if it is inconsistent with their self-image. Tom Marshall (1991: 67) has a different take:

> **After all, leaders lead, servants serve. If leaders are going to be the servants, what are the servants going to do, and who is going to do the leading?**

Greenleaf (1977) identifies two kinds of leaders: strong natural leaders, who take charge, make the decisions and give the orders, and strong natural servants, who assume the leadership role because they see it as a way in which they can serve. Strong natural leaders, he says, are assertive and driven by the need for acquisition or dominance, whereas strong natural servants are driven by the need to serve a cause. Greenleaf goes on to say that only natural servants ought to lead. The leadership issue here is natural servants who have the ability to lead but do not do so. Servant leadership is not a matter of leadership style, but of character and motivation – of traits?

Servant leadership entails strong values: servant leaders take on leadership roles because they want to serve others. And people follow servant leaders because they trust them. In Robert Greenleaf's words:

> **The servant-leader is servant first… . It begins with the natural feeling that one wants to serve, to serve first. Then conscious choice brings one to aspire to lead. He or she is sharply different from the person who is leader first, perhaps because of the need to assuage an unusual power drive or to acquire material possessions. (Bolden, 2004: 67)**

Greenleaf (1977: 23) suggests the test of servant leadership is whether those served 'become healthier, wiser, freer, more autonomous, more likely themselves to become [servant leaders]'. Servant leaders help followers develop their own values that support the organization in its mission.

The servant leader, Danah Zohar and Ian Marshall (2001: 33) say, 'serves the ultimate source of meaning and value'. They cite as examples Mahatma Gandhi, Mother Theresa, Nelson Mandela and the Dalai Lama. Less well known is Katsuhiko Yazaki, the Japanese owner of a global mail-order company, Felissimo (the Spanish and Italian word for 'happy'). Zohar and Marshall (2001: 261–263) describe how, after becoming wealthy through an inherited business, Yazaki emerged from a monastery with a new self-awareness and a vision of the 'proper' role of business as enhancing human happiness. He pursued his vision by helping his customers to imagine and achieve more fulfilling lifestyles and by investing his money in saving the environment and in educational projects.

A key issue for emergent leadership and servant leadership theories is that they ignore the wider organization or society that presents many demands in addition to those of a particular group of followers. Mandela in South Africa and Havel in the Czech Republic – and Yazaki – are examples of emergent leaders who did address such demands. But another issue is that these theories do not provide a sufficiently complete *explanation* of effective leadership.

Leadership-style theories

The lack of a consistent set of leadership traits – who effective leaders are – stimulated a new focus of attention – what effective leaders do. The 'scientific management' of Frederick W. Taylor at the start of the twentieth century promoted the importance of organizational goals and efficient methods and procedures and the associated task-focused leadership in a mechanistic bureaucracy. This found its highest expression in Henry Ford's factories. The 'human relations movement' emerging from Elton Mayo's work in the 1920s and 1930s at the Hawthorne Works of Western Electric refocused leadership on the importance of employees' feelings, attitudes and needs. This disjunction between task and human relationships, and later their conjunction, has characterized much of subsequent leadership theory.

The Michigan and Ohio State studies and their legacy

The first development was a set of influential theories that were popular from the 1950s to the 1960s. These theories of leadership style are articulated in various ways:

- 'Concern for task' (production orientation) and 'concern for people' (employee orientation) in the Michigan studies (Katz et al., 1950, 1951)
- 'Initiating structure' and 'consideration' in the Ohio State leadership studies or, for the former, the similar 'structuring' (Fleishman, 1953; Haplin and Winer, 1957; Fleishman and Harris, 1962)
- 'Task direction' (defining the goal, planning the solution, supplying the necessary knowledge) and 'social specialist' (maintaining the morale and motivation of the group) (Dixon, 1985a)

Rensis Likert (1961) categorized leadership styles as exploitative autocratic, benevolent autocratic, consultative and democratic. And Robert Tannenbaum and Warren Schmidt (1968) produced a similar continuum of leadership styles: autocratic, persuasive, consultative and democratic.

This model of leadership gave rise to assessment methods such as 'attitude toward men' (Likert, 1961) and the Managerial Grid (Blake and Mouton, 1964, 1978). The Managerial Grid describes leaders as '9,9' when they emphasize both task and people to a great extent, '9,1' when they emphasize task much more than people, '1,9' when they emphasize people much more than task, and '1,1' when they emphasize neither (Figure 2.1). Robert Blake and Jane Mouton later added a third dimension, 'flexibility'. This model gained, and still has, considerable popularity, particularly with leadership development specialists and consultants.

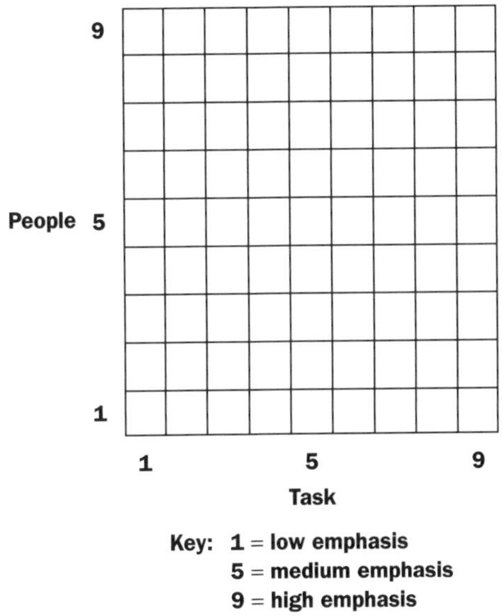

Figure 2.1 *Blake and Mouton's Managerial Grid*

Dorwin Cartwright and Alvin Zander (1968) define the two key roles – task and people orientation – as serving two objectives: goal achievement and group maintenance, the latter also termed 'socio-emotional' leadership (Bales, 1950). Bernard M. Bass and colleagues developed this simple model into one describing five styles, defined in Table 2.2 (Bass and Valenzi, 1974; Bass et al., 1975; Bass, 1976).

The descriptive model of leadership style was replaced later by a more prescriptive one that suggested that people-centred behaviour is more effective in getting results. However, preferences appear to vary: leaders' subordinates prefer their leaders to be people centred whereas leaders' bosses prefer them to be task centred (Alimo-Metcalfe, 1996).

Action-centred leadership

A popular British model of leadership that extends the ideas of task and people orientation is action-centred leadership (ACL), developed by Adair (1973, 1983, 1984). A key difference is that people orientation focuses separately on the individual and the team rather than 'people' as a whole. Effective leaders address needs at three levels: the task, the team and the individual (Figure 2.2).

According to this model, the more there is overlap, and the more balanced the needs of the task, team and individual, the more effective is leadership. The ACL model dismisses the idea that effective leaders possess a common set of traits but does propose that they possess the competence to handle a wide range of different situations. The problem with this model is not intrinsic but in how 'task' might be interpreted. If 'task' is taken literally to mean 'a piece of work to be carried out', then the scope of the model is limited. The model would gain more generality by extending 'task' to

Table 2.2 *Bass and colleagues' five styles of leadership*

Leadership style	Definition
Directive	You tell subordinates what to do and how to do it. You initiate action. You tell subordinates what is expected of them, specifying standards of performance and setting deadlines for completion of work. You exercise firm rule and you ensure that they follow prescribed ways of doing things. You also ensure they are working to capacity, reassigning tasks to balance the workload.
Consultative	You tell subordinates what to do, but only after discussing matters with them first and hearing their opinions, feelings, ideas and suggestions.
Participative	You discuss and analyse problems with your subordinates to reach consensus on what to do and how to do it. Decisions are made by the group as a whole and your subordinates have as much responsibility for decisions as you do. They participate as equals in decision making.
Negotiative	You employ political means and bargaining to gain desired ends, making political alliances, promising subordinates rewards for meeting expectations, releasing information to suit your interests, maintaining social distance, 'bending' the rules, encouraging subordinates to compete, and 'selling' decisions to them.
Delegative	You describe the problem or need and the conditions that have to be met, and you make suggestions, but you leave it to subordinates to decide what to do and how to do it.

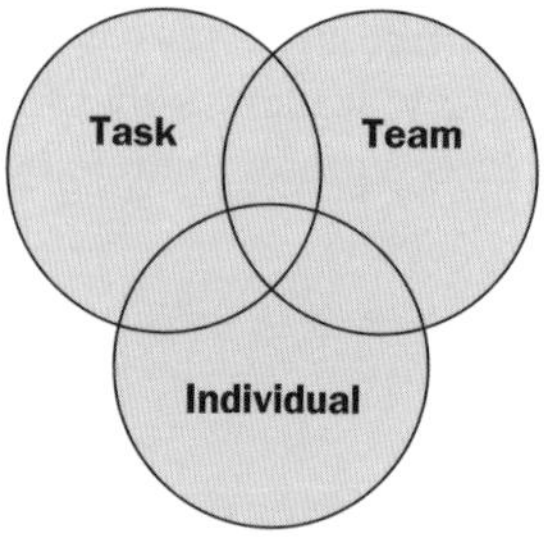

Figure 2.2 *Action-centred leadership*

encompass direction in terms of vision, mission and strategies. Adair (1989: 57, 61) suggests:

> The Biblical image of the shepherd well illustrates [the] three-fold responsibility [for meeting task, team and individuals' needs].... The shepherd [provides] direction, [maintains] the unity of the flock and [meets] the individual needs of the sheep.

This idea represents some key elements of the model described in this book.

Shortcomings of leadership-style theories

Leadership-style approaches have remained largely unfulfilled owing to their undue emphasis on the leader, followers and the task at the expense of the leadership situation (Whipp and Pettigrew, 1993: 205). Leadership-style theories fail to consider the contingencies in the leadership situation (Korman, 1966; Kerr et al., 1974; Schriesheim and Murphy, 1976; Katz, 1977; Schriesheim, 1980). These approaches also do not account for the behaviour of middle-level leaders who are expected to translate to subordinates the vision and strategies usually set by top-level leaders (Zaccaro and Klimoski, 2001: 16). And leadership-style theories focus on behaviour, but do not address values, except by implication: what values are relevant and effective in getting the job done and relating to subordinates and others, and what do these values mean to them? Moreover, Rob Goffee and Gareth Jones (2000) argue, contrary to Adair, that it is not leadership style that makes a great leader but the underlying personal qualities that make the style effective.

Research findings on the effectiveness of different leadership styles appear to be inconsistent (Korman, 1966; Larson et al., 1976; Nystrom, 1978). No one style consistently produces better results, though people or relationship orientation is more often associated with improvements. However, methodological shortcomings mean that it is difficult to identify the impact of leadership style because of extraneous factors in the situation. Most of the research findings have assumed rather than suggested that leadership style leads to performance and satisfaction, whereas in fact the reverse is sometimes the case (Greene, 1975). Studies have also mostly focused on the leader in relation to a group of followers, involving averaging their assessments of the leader, and thus failing to account for differences that reflect different behaviour by leaders towards different individuals (Schriesheim and Kerr, 1977: 9–45; Bryman, 1992: 8–9). This criticism, however, cannot be levelled at action-centred leadership, which introduces the idea of responding to and meeting individual needs.

Leadership-style research studies have also failed to take account of informal leadership, whereby leaders emerge regardless, or in the absence, of any formal structure, which was discussed earlier. Problems in leadership style research are that:

- The research instruments may not have been administered to the most appropriate persons
- Formal and informal leaders vary in their behaviour patterns
- These studies in any case also suffer from common problems of measurement associated with questionnaire instruments

(Bryman, 1992: 10–11)

Nevertheless, a recent study has rehabilitated the two components of leadership identified in the Ohio State studies: consideration and initiating structure. Judge, Piccolo and Ilies (2004) carried out a meta-analysis of the relationship of initiating structure and consideration with leadership. They found moderately strong correlations between both of them and leadership (0.48 for consideration and 0.29 for initiating structure), with consideration more strongly related to follower satisfaction, motivation and leader effectiveness, and initiating structure slightly more strongly related to leader job performance and group organizational performance.

Psychodynamic theory: leader–member exchange

This approach (LMX) defines the effectiveness of leaders as a function of the psychodynamic exchange that occurs between leaders and group members (followers or subordinates). Leaders provide direction and guidance through influence permitted to them by members. Exchange theories focus on the characteristics of the leader, their individual followers and their relationship. In contrast to leadership-style theories, LMX theories argue that leader–member relations are sufficiently variable to warrant focusing on each pair of leaders and members (each 'dyad') separately: members differ markedly in their descriptions of the same leader (Dansereau et al., 1975; Graen, 1976: 1201–1245; Graen et al., 1977). The essence of psychodynamic theory is the understanding of self and others and, as a result, the transactional nature of the leader–follower relationship (Stech, 2004).

This theory apparently was in use in ancient China. The 'Great Plan', dating from around 2200 to 1121 BC (the latter a date mentioned in the text) and drawing on astrology, morality, physics, politics and religion, prescribes how leaders should behave with their followers or subordinates – considering their attitudes towards social order and towards work:

> **The three virtues are rules, firmness, and gentleness. Spell out rules for peaceful people; deal firmly with violent and offensive people; deal gently with amenable and friendly people. Employ firm supervision with those who shirk or lack initiative, gentle supervision with those who are distinguished by their talents and good dispositions. (Karlgren, 1950)**

This prescription – some 1,700 years before Confucius – resembles Robert Liden and George Graen's Vertical Dyad Linkage model in which leaders reward subordinates who show commitment and work hard by showing consideration towards them and, towards others, acting impersonally and rigidly (Liden and Graen, 1980).

According to Douglas Brown and Robert Lord (2001: 181–202), leadership researchers have defined leadership mainly in terms of easily observable behaviours and their direct impact on outcomes or results rather than in terms of explanations of the underlying processes that lead to such outcomes. For example, they describe communicating a vision rather than *why* and *how* vision influences followers. This, they say, limits our ability as leaders to exercise influence over individuals, groups and organizations.

Attributional and social–cognitive theories of leadership focus on the perception of leaders' traits and behaviour by followers, such as charisma. We need therefore to emphasize the importance of feedback from followers and adjustment to them in effective leadership. The introduction of 360-degree feedback has helped in this.

Contingency theories of leadership

'Chaos is the midwife of dictatorship', according to the old adage. Disarray and crisis – bad social, political or economic situations – tend to spawn authoritarian leaders.

Contingency theories suggest that there is no one best style of leadership. Successful and enduring leaders use different styles according to the nature of the situation and the followers. They know how to adopt a different style for a new situation, regardless of how effective any one particular style has been in the past. The effectiveness of a particular style of leadership depends on the relationship between the characteristics of the leader, the followers and the situation. Bass et al. (1975) found that specific leadership styles are associated in different ways with organizational, task, personal and interpersonal characteristics. Philip Hodgson and Randall White (2001) say, 'Effective leadership is finding a good fit between behaviour, context, and need.'

Once again, contingency theory is nothing new. The ancient Chinese 'Great Plan' can be interpreted as advising leaders to behave differently according to two kind of contingency – the social context and the nature of the followers or subordinates (Karlgren, 1970).

Fiedler's contingency theory

Fred Fiedler was the pioneer of contingency theories in the late 1960s. His contingency theory suggests that the effectiveness of a leadership style – task oriented or people oriented – depends on the favourableness of a situation in terms of:

- How defined and structured work is
- How much position power (authority) the leader has
- The relationship between the leader and the followers

(Fiedler, 1969: 230–241)

A situation is highly favourable when work is clearly structured and the leader has great position power (authority) and good relationships with the group. An unfavourable situation is one that is characterized by unstructured work, little position power and poor relationships with the group. Fiedler's prescriptive model, however, is complicated. He suggests that it is more difficult for a leader to change his or her style to suit the situation than it is to change the leader according to the situation (Wright, 1996: 50, 88–89). The research underpinning Fiedler's model has been criticized for inconsistent results and confusion over the measurement instruments (Bryman, 1992: 20).

Path–goal theory

The path–goal theory of leadership employs the 'expectancy model' of work motivation (Evans, 1970; House, 1973; House and Mitchell, 1974). This proposes that a person's motivation (effort) depends on his or her assessment of whether the effort would lead to good performance, the probability of a reward – either material or psychological – as a result of the good performance, and the 'valence' (value of the reward to the person). The expectancy model of motivation is discussed in Chapter 8.

According to path–goal theory, the leader increases personal payoffs to subordinates for achieving work goals and paves the way to these payoffs by clarifying the path, removing or reducing roadblocks and pitfalls, and enhancing personal satisfaction along the way. Effective leaders adopt different styles – supportive, instrumental, participative or achievement oriented – in different situations. The situational factors that moderate subordinate performance and satisfaction are the personal characteristics of the subordinates and environmental and structural factors. Path–goal theory is primarily about transactional leadership: the leader offers rewards to others for successful achievement of the leader's goals.

Path–goal theory suffers from many of the same deficiencies as leadership-style theory, for example inconsistent findings, group averaging of ratings, lack of consideration of informal leadership, dubious causality, and measurement problems. These have been well documented elsewhere (e.g. Bryman, 1992: 13–20). But even if research findings were more consistent in predicting subordinate performance:

> **the plethora of leadership styles and situational factors that the theory and research have put forward do not provide leaders with clear guidance as to how they should behave. (Bryman, 1992: 20)**

Path–goal theory develops Fiedler's contingency theory and takes into account employee motivation in the choice of leadership style. However, the theory is questionable in situations in which goals are constantly changing and in which leaders cannot offer task direction owing to the highly specialized nature of work.

Situational leadership

Situational Leadership as a model of leadership behaviour developed by Paul Hersey and Kenneth Blanchard (1969, 1993) has gained even greater popularity than the Managerial Grid, with a range of available assessment instruments. It relates four leadership styles – 'telling' (directive), 'selling' (consultative), 'participating' and 'delegating' – to followers' or subordinates' readiness for them (maturity).

Readiness is defined as the ability and confidence to carry out a task. Followers or subordinates who lack a sense of responsibility or knowledge of a task need clear instructions from their leader, who accordingly adopts a directive or 'telling' style. As they grow in ability and confidence, so the leader should move to a more relationship-oriented and ultimately delegative (empowering) style. This model assumes flexibility of style in the leader – behavioural skills – as well as the ability to diagnose the situation and the style that is needed – a cognitive ability.

Reddin's 3-D theory of managerial effectiveness

Bill Reddin's 3–D model of leadership (Reddin, 1970a,b, 1987) goes one step further: it describes four styles that can be effective or ineffective, depending on their appropriateness to the situation (Figure 2.3). The four effective styles are the bureaucrat (similar to Blake and Mouton's 1,1 or Hersey and Blanchard's delegative style), the developer (1,9 or participative style), the executive (9,9 or consultative/selling style) and the benevolent autocrat (9,1 or directive style). Ineffective styles are the same four foregoing styles but used inappropriately: respectively termed the deserter, the missionary, the compromiser and the autocrat.

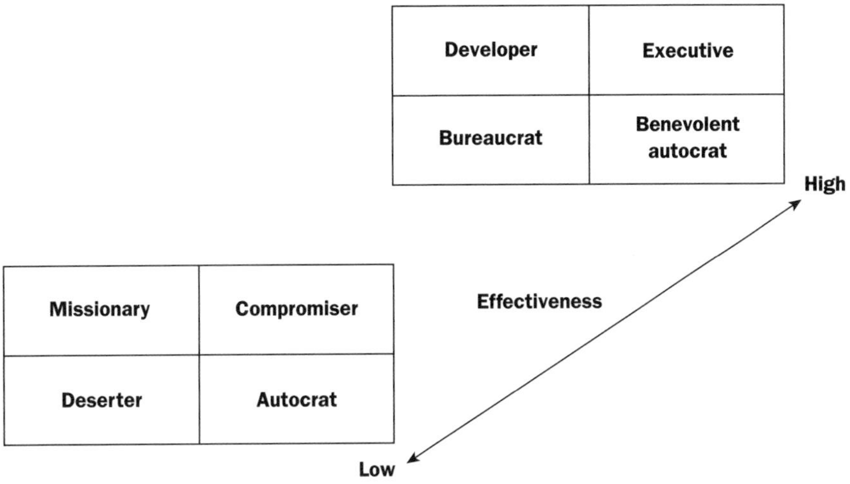

Figure 2.3 *Reddin's 3-D model of leadership*

Reddin uses the term 'situational sensitivity' to refer to the ability to 'read' a situation for what it contains and know what behaviour would most likely be effective. He uses the term 'style flexibility' to refer to the ability to change behaviour according to situational needs. And he proposes the idea of 'situational management' to describe changing the situation to increase managerial effectiveness, for example overcoming resistance to change.

Common features and shortcomings of contingency theories

The various contingency theories have contributed the idea that situational factors need to be considered in examining leadership behaviour. There is no doubt that one leadership style that works well in one situation will not necessarily work well in another.

These theories, however, do not explain *how* leadership styles vary according to organizational level or at (top) executive level (Zaccaro and Klimoski, 2001: 17). And they do not explain *how* leaders can change either their style or the situation (Nicholson, 2001). They also do not explain the leadership processes of acquiring and interpreting the meaning of information, social networking and strategic decision making (Fleishman et al., 1991). As Goffee and Jones (2000) say, 'given that there are endless contingencies in life, there are endless varieties of leadership ... the beleaguered executive looking for a model to help him is hopelessly lost'.

Situational and contingency theories do not refer explicitly to values, a key aspect of leadership, except perhaps by implication. Ciulla (1999) says:

> In some situations a person with particularly strong moral values must emerge as a leader...[for] example, Nelson Mandela and Václav Havel seemed to have been the right men at the right time...[they] both offered the powerful kind of moral leadership required for peaceful revolutions in South Africa and the Czech republic.

There is little conclusive research evidence to support situational and contingency models of leadership. Problems to do with methodology, analysis and ambiguity in its implications led to much disillusionment with the contingency approach – though never an outright rejection. It was, however, something else that stimulated the development of alternative approaches that collectively have been called the 'New Leadership' – the current phase (Bryman, 1992: 20–21).

The 'New Leadership': transformational, visionary, charismatic

Vision, charisma and transformation are the keywords for the New Leadership. The concept of transformational leadership arose from the study of rebel leadership and revolution in the early 1970s (Downton, 1973). However, it was a political historian and biographer, James MacGregor Burns, who in a seminal book in 1978 first described 'transforming leadership' and contrasted it with 'transactional leadership' (Burns, 1978).

Transforming or transformational leadership occurs when both leader and followers raise each other's motivation and sense of higher purpose. Transactional leadership on the other hand involves a transaction, or exchange, between leader and followers, such as providing a material or psychological reward in return for followers' compliance with the leader's wishes, with no sense of any higher purpose. Transforming leadership, according to Burns, addresses people's higher-order needs for achievement, self-esteem and self-actualization. It encourages people to look beyond self-interest for the common good. Transforming leadership raises both leaders and followers to 'higher levels of motivation and morality' (Burns, 1978: 20), whereas transactional leadership merely reflects what or how people *are*, appealing to their existing needs, desires and preferences.

Transformational leaders have strong values. Burns' theory distinguishes between the morality of ends and the morality of means. Transactional leadership, Ciulla (1999) suggests, concerns values implicit in the means of an act – 'modal' values like responsibility, fairness, honesty and keeping promises. Transformational leadership, on the other hand, is concerned with end-values like liberty, justice and equality. Rabindra Kanungo and Manuel Mendonca (1996) say that the moral aspects of transformational leadership are a prosocial orientation, a concomitant vision and values that reflect concern for others.

Micha Popper and Ofra Mayseless (2003) say, 'The impact of transformational leadership is reflected in motivation, empowerment, and morality [values].' In terms of Maslow's hierarchy of needs (see Chapter 8), they quote Burns as suggesting that transformational leaders motivate followers to pursue the highest level of need satisfaction, that is self-actualization. Transformational leaders, they say, empower followers to think independently, critically and creatively and by raising their levels of self-efficacy, self-worth, self-confidence, competence, autonomy and risk taking. And, again quoting Burns, they say (as do Kanungo and Mendonca) that transformational leaders emphasize prosocial values such as justice and equality rather than modal, instrumental values such as loyalty.

The Full-Range Leadership model

One of the most important recent models of leadership that includes and extends these ideas is Bernard Bass and Bruce Avolio's Full-Range Leadership model: laissez-faire, transactional leadership and transformational leadership (Bass, 1985, 1990a,b; Bass and Avolio, 1994). This model resulted from extensive empirical research by Bass in the early 1980s stimulated by Burns' ideas.

Laissez-faire

Laissez-faire leaders avoid taking a stand, ignore problems, do not follow up, and refrain from intervening. In terms of leadership-style theory (directive, consultative, participative and delegative styles), they use no particular style to any significant extent (Gill, 1999a).

Laissez-faire is non-transactional leadership, if indeed it is leadership at all. This behaviour may result in conflict and a lack of achievement. Examples that Bass and Avolio give are former US president Calvin Coolidge, who is reputed to have slept 16 hours each day; Louis XV of France, famous for his *'Après moi, le déluge!'*; and his successor, Louis XVI, who preferred to tinker with clocks rather than attend to matters of state.

Transactional leadership

Transactional leaders practise management-by-exception and contingent reward:

Management-by-exception. Management-by-exception is practised in two forms: passive and active (Bass, 1990a,b). Passive management-by-exception is displayed when a leader sets work objectives and performance standards but then waits for problems to arise, reacts to mistakes and intervenes reluctantly. The active form entails monitoring for deviations and errors and then correcting them, and enforcing rules and procedures.

Contingent reward. Contingent reward entails setting work objectives and performance standards, providing feedback, and providing financial or psychological rewards in exchange for performance that meets expectations. This may result in motivating people to achieve goals and to develop themselves, but not to the extent that transformational leadership behaviour does, as we shall see.

Transactional leaders appear to be strongly directive and they tend not to use the consultative, participative or delegative styles to any significant extent (Gill, 1999a). They set objectives and performance standards, but do so in a directive rather than participative manner. Transactional leaders, according to the Bradford micro-skills theory of leadership, are also more likely than transformational leaders to use closed and leading questions in their interactions with others (Wright and Taylor, 1994; Randell, 1998). These behaviours run the risk of gaining only compliance rather than commitment. Transactional leaders also tend to use rewards for performance on the basis of directives about objectives. And, while this can result in short-term achievement, it runs the risk of stifling human development, with consequential loss of competitive advantage.

Transformational leadership

Transformational leaders do more than 'transact' with subordinates or followers, and this is what makes a significant difference to people's motivation and development. They achieve 'performance beyond expectations' in their subordinates or followers (Bass, 1985). They stimulate followers to transcend their own immediate self-interest for the greater good of the group, organization or society. Transformational leadership makes a positive impact on empowerment, motivation and morality. According to the Bass and Avolio model, transformational leaders tend to use one or more of the four 'I's: individualized consideration, intellectual stimulation, inspirational motivation and idealized influence:

Individualized consideration. Transformational leaders display individualized consideration: they listen actively; they identify individuals' personal concerns, needs and abilities; they provide matching challenges and opportunities to learn in a supportive environment; they delegate to them as a way of developing them; they give developmental feedback; and they coach them. Transformational leaders practise MBWA – 'Management By Wandering Around'. This 'I' is similar to the dimension of consideration or socio-emotional orientation in leadership-style theories.

Intellectual stimulation. Transformational leaders use intellectual stimulation. They question the status quo. They present new ideas to followers and challenge them to think. They encourage imagination and creativity in rethinking assumptions and old ways of doing things. And they do not publicly criticize errors, mistakes or failure or ideas or approaches that differ from their own. Socrates, in his famous question-and-answer dialogues, is probably the greatest example of an intellectually stimulating leader (Avolio and Bass, 1990; Hazell, 1997: 8–12). Such leaders use and encourage intuition as well as logic. This is a recipe for personal growth. In the words of the American Supreme Court justice, Oliver Wendell Holmes, Jr (1841–1935): 'A mind once stretched by a new idea never regains its original dimension.'[20] With the increased emphasis today on knowledge work, intellectual stimulation is particularly important (Kelloway and Barling, 2000). Knowledge-based organizations require leaders who can create and maintain an environment where innovation thrives. Intellectual stimulation, together with individualized consideration, is the basis for an effective coaching and mentoring role.

Inspirational motivation. Transformational leaders display inspirational motivation. They communicate a clear vision of the possible future; they align organizational goals and personal goals so that people can achieve their personal goals by achieving organizational goals; and they treat threats and problems as opportunities to learn. They provide meaning and challenge to the work of their followers. And they speak (and write) in an appealing and exciting way. In Bass's words,

> **Quantum leaps in performance may be seen...when a group is roused out of its despair by a...leader who articulates revolutionary new ideas about what may be possible. (Bass, 1985: 4)**

As a result, followers want to meet expectations and they display commitment, not merely compliance, to the vision, goals and tasks. They are motivated and inspired.

Idealized influence. Transformational leaders also display idealized influence, something closely related to *charisma*. They express confidence in the vision; they take personal responsibility for actions; they display a sense of purpose, determination, persistence and trust in other people; and they emphasize accomplishments rather than failures. US football coach Paul 'Bear' Bryant captures this dimension of transformational leadership thus:

> **There's just three things I ever say. If anything goes bad, then I did it. If anything goes semi-good, then *we* did it. If anything goes really good, then *you* did it. That's all it takes.**[21]

Such leaders also gain the admiration, respect, trust and confidence of others by personally demonstrating extraordinary ability of one kind or another. They put the needs of other people before their own, and they display high standards of ethical and moral behaviour. Trust is perhaps the single most important factor in transformational leadership (Bass, 1997a). As a result of these behaviours, leaders become role models: people identify with them, and they want to follow and emulate them.

Transformational leaders tend to use the consultative, participative and delegative styles as well as the directive style to a significant extent (Gill, 1999a). The four 'I's are related to these four leadership styles in different ways. Transformational leaders are also more likely than transactional leaders to use open and probing questions and reflective responses. These findings are consistent both with what Tom Peters and Bob Waterman (1982) called 'loose–tight' leadership behaviour and with the findings of Abraham Sagie et al. (2002) in respect of the participative and directive styles. The latter researchers found that integrating these styles can be effective. The implication is that transformational leaders are more active and more flexible in their leadership behaviour.

Pseudo-transformational leadership

Transformational leadership may also take a dark form, what Bass and Avolio call 'pseudo-transformational leadership' (Bass, 1997a; Bass and Avolio, 1997: 93–94). Such leaders encourage an 'us-and-them' competitiveness and pursue their own self-interest rather than the common good. They use symbols of authority and hierarchical differentiation (Howell and House, 1993). Pseudo-transformational leaders may possess *dysfunctional* charisma. Their values are highly questionable, and they are likely to lead their followers to disaster and perdition.

Other models and concepts of transformational leadership

Noel Tichy and Mary Devanna's concept of transformational leadership proposes that transformational leaders are visionaries, see themselves as change agents, display courage in the face of resistance and risk, emphasize the need for motivation, empowerment and trust, are driven by strong values, see mistakes, errors and failures as learning opportunities, and cope with complexity, uncertainty and ambiguity (Tichy and Devanna, 1986b). This model, however, is based on observations of only 14 business leaders in action.

Alannah Rafferty and Mark Griffin (2004) propose another variation that they determined empirically, with the following five dimensions of transformational leadership:

- Vision – *expressing an idealized picture of the future based around organizational values*
- Inspirational communication – *expressing positive and encouraging messages about the organization, and making statements that build motivation and confidence*
- Intellectual stimulation – *enhancing employees' interest in and awareness of problems, and increasing their ability to think about problems in new ways*
- Supportive leadership – *expressing concern for followers and taking account of their individual needs*
- Personal recognition – *providing rewards such as praise and acknowledging effort for achievement of specified goals*

Visionary leadership

Marshall Sashkin's 'visionary leadership' concerns transforming an organizational culture in line with the leader's vision of the organization's future (Sashkin, 1988). Sashkin and Rosenbach also suggest that there are three personal characteristics that guide the leader's behavioural strategies: self-efficacy (self-confidence), power orientation (use of power in different ways) and cognitive capability (Sashkin, 1992; Sashkin and Rosenbach, 1998). Cognitive capability concerns understanding complex cause-and-effect chains to be able to take action at the right time to achieve desired outcomes (Streufert and Swezey, 1986).

Vision, as we will see in Chapter 4, is fundamental to leadership, and I discuss visionary leadership in more detail there. We also need to note, however, that there is more to leadership than vision, and I discuss this in Chapter 3.

Charismatic leadership

Outstanding leaders are often perceived as charismatic: they attract and inspire followers. Charismatic leadership is found at all levels in the organization, though most frequently at the top, Bass (1992) says, and it is associated with greater trust in leaders and achievement among followers. The charismatic leader 'weaves a spell' outside the organization too, attracting shareholders and investment in troubled times, according to research by Francis Flynn and Barry Staw (2004). David Waldman et al. (2001), however, in a study of senior managers in *Fortune 500* companies in the United States, found that charismatic leadership is associated with net profit margin, but only under conditions of environmental uncertainty. Charismatic leadership appears to be dysfunctional in predictable conditions, perhaps because it may generate unnecessary change.

Max Weber (1864–1920), the German sociologist, wrote the classic work on charisma (Roth and Wittich, 1968). He saw charisma as primarily a social relationship between leader and follower resulting from extraordinary personal qualities but which requires continual validation: followers' perception of the leader's 'devotion to … exceptional sanctity, heroism or exemplary character [and] the normative patterns of order revealed or ordained by him'. Weber saw charisma as a process of influence and commitment that arises in opposition to traditional bureaucracy.

Table 2.3 *Differences between distant and close leaders*

Distant leaders	Close/nearby leaders
Ideological orientation	Sociable and open
Strong sense of mission	Considerate of others
Courageous, rhetorical expression	Have a sense of humour
Little concern for personal criticism or sanction	High level of specific expertise
	Dynamic and active
	Impressive physical appearance
	Intelligent or wise
	Setting high performance standards
	Unconventional behaviour

A more contemporary view is that charisma is not something that is possessed by a leader but a consequence of the relationship between leader and followers (House, 1977: 189–207; Conger and Kanungo, 1987; Shamir et al., 1993). Followers appear to be attracted to different types of leaders, and followers' work values – favouring participation, security and extrinsic rewards – contribute to their leadership preferences (Ehrhart and Klein, 2001). Ciulla (1999) comments on charismatic leadership and values: 'The values of charismatic leaders shape the organization, but in some cases these values do not live on when the charismatic leader is gone.'

Distant and close leadership

Beverly Alimo-Metcalfe and Robert Alban-Metcalfe (2001) emphasize the importance of distinguishing between 'distant' leadership and 'close' or 'nearby' leadership. They contrast interview studies with top-level managers and studies at all levels of the *perceptions* of top-level managers ('distant' leadership) and immediate bosses ('close/nearby' leadership). Support for this contrast comes from the literature on leadership and social distance. For example, Boas Shamir's study of Israeli students (Shamir, 1995) produced the differences shown in Table 2.3.

Alimo-Metcalfe and Alban-Metcalfe (2001) suggest that most studies, including those using the MLQ, tend to describe distant leaders, and they do so in terms of charisma, vision and transformation, while perceptions of close leaders may be different. Their own research employed a grounded-theory approach but ensured content validity in their research questionnaire consistent with the transformational leadership literature. They identified the following nine scales with high reliabilities and convergent validities that formed the basis for a new instrument, the Transformational Leadership Questionnaire (TLQ):

- Genuine concern for others (similar to Bass's individualized consideration)
- Political sensitivity and skills
- Decisiveness, determination and self-confidence
- Integrity, trustworthiness, honesty and openness
- Empowering and developing of potential
- Inspirational networking and promoting
- Accessibility and approachability

- Clarifying of boundaries and involving of others in decisions
- Encouraging of critical and strategic thinking

Two second-order factors emerged: internal orientation and external orientation. Internal orientation concerns relationships within the department or organization; external orientation concerns relationships with the external world. The model requires confirmatory factor analysis and concurrent and predictive validation, and it is open to criticism of the use of same-source data that may produce 'halo' effects. However, the underlying model has benefited from using the 'richness' of grounded theory in addition to conventional empirical research, a higher than usual proportion of female subjects and subjects from four hierarchical levels.

In line with what might be expected in effective leadership at close quarters, 'Genuine concern for others' emerged as by far the most important factor whereas, in Bass's model and the MLQ, the closest factor, 'Individualized consideration', was the least transformational factor and is less 'rich' in its behavioural content:

> **The emphasis in the UK understanding of transformational leadership appears to be on what the leader *does* for the individual, such as empowering, valuing, supporting, and developing. In contrast, the US model is primarily about the leader acting as a role model and inspiring the 'follower'...with the leader envisioning a valued future, articulating how to reach it, and setting him/herself as an example with which followers can identify, and which they can emulate. (Alimo-Metcalfe and Alban-Metcalfe, 2001)**

This British model is close to Robert Greenleaf's 'servant leadership'. It emphasizes the social influence process in 'connectedness' between a leader and others. The differences between this model using the TLQ and Bass's using the MLQ have yet to be explored. Alimo-Metcalfe and Alban-Metcalfe (2002b: 3) suggest, as Bass does, that both transactional and transformational leadership are needed in organizations:

> **The real skill is in being transactional (i.e. setting objectives, planning, providing feedback, etc.) in a transformational way. But perhaps the greatest challenge is, how willing will those in the most senior positions – who may well have been appointed precisely because of their transactional strengths – be to adopt a transformational style?**

In reviewing Alimo-Metcalfe and Alban-Metcalfe's model of transformational leadership, Malcolm Higgs and Victor Dulewicz (2002: 113–117) note how it accounts for the organizational context and situational considerations. In particular the model identifies the following factors in leadership: vision, values and culture, strategy and a 'people' factor. The people factor implicitly addresses leadership behaviours to do with empowerment, motivation and inspiration.

Organic leadership

Gayle Avery (2004: 19) suggests that organizations of the future will require an 'organic' form of transformational leadership. She characterizes this as:

- Mutual sense-making within the group
- Emergence rather than appointment of leaders

- Buy-in to the group's shared values and processes
- Self-determination
- Emergence of vision from the group (rather than from a leader)
- Vision as a strong cultural element

The organic paradigm of leadership, she says:

> **involves letting go of conventional notions of control, order and hierarchy, replacing them with trust and an acceptance of continual change, chaos and respect for diverse members of the organization...the members are expected to be self-managing and self-leading. (Avery, 2004: 29–30)**

Critique of the 'New Leadership'

Bass and Avolio's Full-Range Leadership theory is supported by a meta-analysis of 87 relevant studies by Timothy Judge and Ronald Piccolo (2004), though contingent reward was found to be strongly associated with transformational leadership as a whole. Bass (1997b) claims universal applicability of his Full-Range Leadership model across national cultures, though he does say that specific behaviours that characterize the dimensions may vary. However, while the Full-Range Leadership model has enjoyed popularity, it is not beyond criticism.

Issues concern the validity of its factor structure (Den Hartog et al., 1997; Hinkin and Tracey, 1999) and the transformational leadership scales (Bycio et al., 1995; Carless, 1998). The results of various studies, including a confirmatory factor analysis by Bass and Avolio themselves, have led to the conclusion that a six-factor model is the best representation of his model, though there is low discriminant validity among the transformational and contingent reward (transactional) scales (Avolio et al., 1999).

Bass's model of transformational leadership incorporates communicating a vision as a source of 'inspirational motivation' and expressing confidence in it as 'idealized influence', but little more is said of vision, and nothing at all is said of mission or strategy. Vision is one of the key differences between a manager and a leader, according to Deetz et al. (2000: 49).

Generalizability of the Full-Range Leadership model across hierarchical levels in organizations has been questioned (Bryman, 1996: 276–292), though Bass (1997b) found transformational leadership at all levels. Other studies, however, have found it to be displayed significantly more at higher levels (Edwards and Gill, 2003a,b; Oshagbemi and Gill, 2004). Zaccaro and Klimoski (2001) point out that hierarchical level as a moderator in the use and effectiveness of leadership behaviour is a long-held theoretical assumption. And John Antonakis (2001) suggests that hierarchical level moderates Bass's 'full-range leadership' model. Kevin Lowe et al. (1996), however, had previously found that the effectiveness of transformational leadership does not differ across organizational levels. Indeed top-and middle-level managers appear to display transformational leadership more than lower-level managers do but it is effective at all levels (Edwards and Gill, 2003a).

Another criticism of the transactional/transformational leadership model is two-fold: transactional leadership appears to relate more to 'management' than to leadership; and the concept of transformation overemphasizes the role of the leader in the change process (Sadler, 1997: 45). In fact, Alan Bryman (1992: 97) says, transactional leadership can be equated with 'management' and the theories of 'leadership' style discussed earlier actually concern 'management' style rather than leadership. Transactional leadership reflects a control orientation, whereas transformational leadership is empowering and inspirational, resulting in changes in people's abilities, attitudes, values, beliefs and motivation. But Kets de Vries and Florent-Treacy (1999: 7–8) rightly argue that concentrating on transformational or charismatic leadership without considering the transactional role is too narrow: both roles are needed.

The various theories commonly categorized as the 'New Leadership' – charismatic leadership, visionary leadership and transformational leadership, with the exception of the organic paradigm – have been challenged as focusing on the individual rather than the organization as a whole. Critics say they fail to explain distributed leadership (Gronn, 1995a, 2002). Yukl (1999) and Gronn (1999) criticize contemporary leadership theories such as transformational and charismatic leadership for their assumption that one individual ('the leader') leads all of the other people in a group or organization towards its goals. Leadership has increasingly become regarded as shared among two or more people in a group or organization (which we discussed in Chapter 1).

Transformational leadership has rejuvenated leadership research since the mid 1980s (Hunt, 1999). It adds to the previously well-established dimensions of leadership, consideration and initiation of structure, the visionary aspect of leadership and the emotional involvement and development of followers or employees (Koene et al., 2002). What it does not do is to explain the nature of effective visioning and organizational mission or the place of values, culture and strategy in leadership.

Other theories: pragmatic and strategic leadership

Is effective leadership always concerned with organizational transformation? Clearly such transformation may be necessary when an organization or nation is performing poorly, there is new opportunity, or the business or economic environment changes adversely. But organizational transformation may not be necessary, and it may even be dysfunctional, when the organization or nation is performing well in conditions of relative stability. While radical organizational transformation may not be appropriate, transformational leadership is still desirable, entailing 'custody of the company's direction and its culture and values' (Leavy and Wilson, 1994: 161–162). Perhaps effective leadership, then, is about being 'right at the time', as Sir Peter Parker, as chairman of Mitsubishi Electric Europe BV, said:

> **The world of business is like a pendulum. So leadership Is about being right at the time. At present, the pendulum favours Branson rather than Hanson: modern, open, accessible, informal and egalitarian. (Rajan, 2000a)**

Pragmatic leadership

'Being right at the time' raises the question of pragmatic leadership. It has been argued that outstanding leaders like Benjamin Franklin, for example, may be neither transactional nor transformational, nor charismatic but pragmatic (Mumford and Van Dorn,

2001). In considering 10 cases of noteworthy leadership by Franklin, Michael Mumford and Judy Van Dorn suggest that outstanding leaders may simply take a functional, problem-solving approach based on their knowledge about, and sensitivity to, both social relationships and the problems people face.

A version of this is David Nice's 'warrior leadership' (Nice, 1998). Nice's model describes how political and military leaders behave in conflict and pre-settlement periods. They enter freely into conflict and strive to overcome the opposition, control information, emphasize results over methods, get to know those they seek to lead and defeat, and use intermediaries as buffers. Political leaders in Northern Ireland displayed such behaviour during the peace process. This brings us to the place of strategy in relation to leadership.

Strategic leadership

'Strategic leadership' rejoices in a plethora of definitions. Gerry Johnson and Kevan Scholes (2002: 38) define *strategic leadership* as encapsulating entrepreneurial processes and strategic vision. They also see strategic leadership as concerned with strategy development and change (2002: 65). In research by Philip Stiles (2001), one interviewee said, 'The mission is why we are in business. The vision is where we want to be. These are fundamentally the responsibility of the board.' A fundamental responsibility of the board is the vision and mission. Some writers argue that the sole role of the strategic leader is providing vision, mission and guiding principles (values and rules). Beverley Mobbs (2004), a quality management consultant, calls vision, mission and values 'critical success factors' in the pursuit of excellence.

Katherine Beatty and Laura Quinn (2002) give examples of strategic leadership: creating a shared vision of the future; linking the efforts of everyone in the organization to the organization's goals; not just accomplishing objectives but also steadily improving the organization. Essentially strategic leadership refers to the top management team, and strategic leadership theory has evolved from upper echelons theory (Hambrick and Mason, 1984). Another key role of top-level leaders is to decide and implement strategy (Johnson et al., 2001).

Using a model of strategic leadership developed by Michael Hitt et al. (1995), Abdalla Hagen et al. (2003) found that American CEOs ranked its six components in the following order of importance:

1 Determining strategic direction
2 Developing human capital
3 Exploiting and maintaining core competencies
4 Sustaining an effective corporate culture
5 Emphasizing ethical practices
6 Establishing strategic control

Beatty and Quinn (2002) describe the model of strategic leadership used by the Center for Creative Leadership in the United States:

> **Individuals and teams...exert strategic leadership when they think, act, and influence...in ways that enhance the organization's sustainable competitive advantage.**

Management consultant Bruce Nixon (2002), in his work on helping companies to deal with global forces, effectively uses a strategic leadership model that focuses on:

- Global forces – environmental trends, issues and opportunities
- Current state – how well the company is responding
- Purpose and values – both individual and corporate; the company's unique positioning
- Vision of a desirable future – for the world and for the company; the culture needed
- Strategy – key strategic actions, influence, networking, obstacles, implementation and support

Strategic leadership concerns developing the organization's vision, mission, strategies and culture and monitoring progress and changes in the business environment to ensure strategies are focused, relevant and valid. A key competency in strategic leadership is decision making about whether and when to act. Strategic leadership concerns monitoring how well organizational culture, including values, is supporting the organization's vision and mission. And it concerns monitoring human capital – employees' competencies, budgets and organizational structure and systems. However, little or no attention is paid in strategic leadership theories to the need for empowerment, motivation and inspiration. The place of strategy in effective leadership is discussed in Chapter 6.

Leadership theory: current status

No theory or model of leadership so far has provided a satisfactory explanation of leadership; indeed there is no consensus on the meaning of leadership in the first place. Many theories are partisan or partial, reflecting particular philosophical or ideological points of view. Many are based on limited, even biased, research: the answers one gets depend on the questions one asks. As a result the theories that emerge are often self-fulfilling prophecies and at best explain only some aspects of leadership. Yukl's wide-ranging review of the leadership literature in 1989 concluded:

> **Most of the theories are beset with conceptual weaknesses and lack strong empirical support. Several thousand empirical studies have been conducted but most of the results are contradictory and inconclusive.**

A related shortcoming of current leadership thinking is the separate tracks – cognitive, emotional, spiritual and behavioural – along which leadership research and theory have moved. For example, none of the theories and models reviewed, other than servant leadership, addresses the spiritual element of people's lives – the need for meaning (Kibby and Härtel, 2003). Some theories do attempt to combine the different tracks, but somewhat superficially. For example, research by the Industrial Society in 1996 identified 'observable leadership skills and behaviours, beliefs and trust' as the three key elements of 'liberating leadership'.[22] In terms of our model, these elements relate to the emotional and behavioural dimensions of leadership. But the 'Leader

Ship' model proposed by the Industrial Society (now The Work Foundation), in which the superstructure, hull and keel of a ship metaphorically represent these three elements respectively, omits any reference to vision and strategy. Current theories of leadership have failed to integrate the four tracks and put the pieces of the jigsaw puzzle together to produce a clear, coherent picture.

For example, strategy and leadership are topics that have been greatly researched and written about, but 'we still seem to be a long way from fully understanding these two concepts and how they are inter-related' (Leavy and Wilson, 1994: 1). None of the theories that have been reviewed deals much with strategy.

Understanding leadership as process centred on a relationship rather than on the individual has been receiving much attention recently. Leadership is exercised in all relationships, including upwards. Joseph Rost (1993) says that management takes place between managers and *subordinates*, whereas leadership takes place between leaders and *collaborators*: the essence of leadership is not the leader but the relationship. Leadership involves both leaders and collaborators in aiming to make real changes in an organization, where these changes reflect the common purpose of the leaders and collaborators, whereas management involves coordinating activities that reflect the organization's purpose.

Whipp and Pettigrew (1993: 207) point out that there has been insufficient attention to leadership as a process and to the interaction between leadership and context, in particular the difference that leadership can make to competitiveness. Alimo-Metcalfe and Alban-Metcalfe's model of close/nearby leadership contrasts with American models of distant leadership, also suggesting differences in leadership according to context (Alimo-Metcalfe and Alban-Metcalfe, 2001).

This chapter has reviewed the contribution and limitations of key leadership theories. Bruce Avolio likens the range of leadership theories to the periodic chart in chemistry: we are still discovering (or creating) new elements.[23] The variety of different theoretical frameworks constitutes a relatively fragmented and disparate body of knowledge, and this reduces their value (Wright, 1996). Such a variety of theories frequently serves to confuse those who wish to understand, practise or develop leadership in all its aspects and complexity. On the other hand, such fragmentation, Michael Katzko (2002) suggests, is a sign of the richness of a field of academic study. However, James MacGregor Burns says that there is a need for an integrative theory, a general theory of leadership, which draws on different disciplines.[24] There is a need for a theory or model that is at the same time conceptually inclusive, comprehensive, valid and useful in practice to those who perform in the role of a leader or are engaged in the development of leaders.

Keith Grint (1997a) analyses leadership theories in terms of tensions between a focus on the individual and a focus on the context and between subjective and objective assumptions about knowledge and data. He says the traits approach emphasizes the 'essence' of the leader but not the context, the situational approach emphasizes the context, and the contingency approach emphasizes both the individual and the context. The newest approach, he says, is the 'constitutive' approach. This emphasizes neither the individual nor the context. It postulates that there are many possible descriptions and interpretations of the individual leader and the situation. The emphasis is on *how* one constitutes one's version of events.

Current leadership theory appears to be a product of the economic and social context of the time. Gronn (1995a,b) suggests that 'theories of leadership wax and wane in keeping with wider cultural and economic shifts and developments'. They reflect the changing nature of work and authority in society as a whole. The mechanistic, bureaucratic organizations of the twentieth century spawned a traditional exchange or transactional kind of leadership. Avery (2004: 146–149) shows how the various approaches to leadership – theories from trait theory to visionary, charismatic and transformational theories – can be classified into four leadership paradigms: classical, transactional, visionary and organic. Organizations of the future, reflecting technological advances and societal change, and with organic forms and a greater proportion of knowledge workers, will require a form of transformational leadership *beyond* current models, such as Avery's organic leadership paradigm. Very few theories and models of leadership, Avery says, span all four paradigms.

The next chapter describes a model of leadership that attempts to integrate the range of current theories and provide a new view of leadership for the challenges ahead. It aims to provide another perspective within an organic paradigm.

Further reading

Gayle Avery (2004), *Understanding Leadership.* London: Sage Publications.

Bernard M. Bass (1985), *Leadership and Performance Beyond Expectations.* New York: Free Press.

Bernard M. Bass (1990), *Bass and Stogdill's Handbook of Leadership: Theory, Research and Managerial Applications, 3rd Edition.* New York: Free Press.

Bernard M. Bass and Bruce J. Avolio (Editors) (1994), *Improving Organizational Effectiveness through Transformational Leadership.* Thousand Oaks, CA: Sage Publications.

Robert Greenleaf (1977), *Servant Leadership.* New York: Paulist Press.

Keith Grint (Editor) (1997), *Leadership: Classical, Contemporary and Critical Approaches.* Oxford: Oxford University Press.

Tom Marshall (1991), *Understanding Leadership.* Tonbridge, Kent: Sovereign World.

P.G. Northouse (Editor) (2004), *Leadership: Theory and Practice, 3rd Edition.* London: Sage Publications.

Discussion questions

1. Which theory or theories of leadership come closest to providing an inclusive and useful picture of leadership?
2. What traits or personal characteristics do effective leaders have in common?
3. Do effective leaders always 'emerge'? Or can an effective leader have been 'appointed' by another individual or small group of people?
4. Do effective leaders always vary their style or behaviour according to the nature of the group of people they lead and the situation they are in?
5. Is having charisma essential to being an effective leader?
6. What contribution has Bass's 'Full-Range Leadership' model made, and what are its limitations in helping us to understand leadership fully?

3 Redefining Leadership: A New Model

It could be said of me that in this book I have only made up a bunch of other men's flowers, providing of my own the string that ties them together.[25]

Montaigne (1533–1592), *Essais*

Overview

- There is a widespread view, but so far not a unanimous one, that a new, more integrated conceptual framework for leadership is both possible and necessary.
- The different tracks of research and thinking followed in the past appear to reflect four dimensions or forms of 'intelligence' underlying leadership: the intellectual or cognitive, the emotional, the spiritual and the behavioural.
- The intellectual or cognitive dimension of leadership comprises abilities to perceive and understand information, reason with it, imagine possibilities, use intuition, make judgements, solve problems and make decisions.
- The emotional dimension of leadership – emotional intelligence – comprises understanding oneself and others, practising self-control and responding to other people in appropriate ways.
- The spiritual dimension of leadership – spiritual intelligence – concerns understanding that human beings have an animating need for meaning, value and a sense of worth in what they seek and do, and responding to that need.
- The behavioural dimension of leadership comprises the skills of both using and responding to emotion, for example through body language, communicating in other ways (through writing, speaking and active listening), using personal power, and physical activity.
- Cognitive processes, emotions and volitional action (behavioural skills) interact, and we need to understand how.
- Five common themes have emerged that capture the essence of leadership: visioning, creating a culture of shared values, strategy forming and implementation, empowerment of people, and influence, motivation and inspiration. Evidence supporting this inclusive and practical model is provided.

There is a widespread view, but so far not a unanimous one, that a new, more integrated conceptual framework for leadership is both possible and necessary. Roseanne Foti and John B. Miner (2003), for example, say: 'It is entirely possible that a single overarching theory of leadership is beginning to emerge from [the] conglomeration' of overlapping current theories of leadership. What is required is the 'string that ties them together'.

In November 2001 James MacGregor Burns convened an interdisciplinary group of leadership academics. He outlined his vision for a 'general theory of leadership' – a set of principles that are universal and can be adapted to different situations (Mangan, 2002).

I believe that leadership can be redefined to integrate the different tracks of research and thinking. After all, Edwin Locke (1997: 375–412) has made an attempt to create an integrated model of work motivation, a field blessed (or cursed) with as much fragmentation and richness as leadership. Frank Schmidt (1992) has recommended using 'mega-analysis' to build integrated theories or models. Mega-analysis combines all known meta-analyses of empirical studies that are relevant to each path or connection in a theory or model. Schmidt et al. (1986) have already done this on a small scale in the field of human resource management. Creating an integrated theory or model of leadership that is based on just such mega-analysis is the next step and an exciting and worthwhile challenge.

The different tracks of research and thinking reflect four dimensions to leadership:

- The intellectual or cognitive
- The emotional
- The spiritual
- The behavioural

These dimensions are forms of intelligence. They underlie the integrative, holistic model of effective leadership that I propose in this book, that effective leadership requires vision and a sense of mission, shared values, strategy, empowerment, and influence, motivation and inspiration. Let us first briefly consider some of the evidence for these dimensions.

The dimensions of leadership

In his analysis of attitudes, Tom Marshall (1991: 75) identifies three basic components:

- A cognitive element: intellectual beliefs or convictions
- An emotional element: feelings we have about these beliefs
- A volitional element: behavioural responses we make because of our beliefs

In reviewing what CEOs need to address if their organizations are to be successful, Zaccaro and Klimoski (2001: 5) conclude that these needs are to meet cognitive, social and personal demands and requirements. More specifically, Zaccaro et al. (2001) describe leader–team dynamics in terms of cognitive, motivational, affective and coordination processes.

Manfred Kets de Vries and Elizabeth Florent-Treacy (1999: 8) describe effective leadership in terms of cognitive and emotional 'competencies' and behavioural characteristics that contribute to them. Marshall Sashkin and Molly Sashkin (2003) describe the elements of transformational leadership as 'ABC':

- Affect – emotion and feelings
- Behavioural intent – confidence to act
- Cognition – the basis for vision

Research in AT&T identified cognitive skills, the need for power and interpersonal skills as associated with the career advancement of managers (Bray et al., 1974; Bray, 1982; Howard and Bray, 1988). The ability to motivate and inspire followers is a form of power as well as a set of interpersonal skills. And Gilbert Fairholm (1996) describes a spiritual dimension to leadership associated with integrity, independence and justice, one that is concerned with meeting people's needs for meaning and value in what they do.

Studies of how and why leaders succeed, Ulrich et al. (2000) suggest, focus separately on three clusters of leadership factors:

- What to *know*. The knowledge cluster, which includes knowing *how*, concerns setting direction (understanding the business environment and developing a vision), mobilizing individual commitment, and creating organizational capability.
- How to *be*. The second cluster, about *being*, concerns personal values and motives such as integrity, ambition, concern for others, loyalty and self-awareness.
- What to *do*. The *doing* cluster refers to the behaviour and actions of leaders, such as where, how and with whom leaders spend their time.

Russ Moxley (2000) has called for a more holistic kind of leadership that integrates four arenas of the human condition: the mind (rational thought), the heart (emotions or feelings), the spirit and the body.

These analyses support the basis for the integrative, holistic model of leadership described in this book: the intellectual or cognitive dimension of leadership – the *mind*; the emotional dimension – the *heart*; the spiritual dimension – the *spirit*; and the behavioural dimension – the *body*. Let us now consider each of these dimensions of leadership in turn and how they interact.

The intellectual or cognitive dimension of leadership

'Few characteristics are more valued, or valuable, in modern Western society than intelligence', say Judge, Colbert and Ilies (2004). Intelligence was found in a study by Robert Lord et al. (1984) to be the only attribute that is seen as critical to a leader. Fiedler (2002: 91), however, believes that 'Intellectual abilities ... do not predict leadership performance to any appreciable degree.' Most scholars and commentators nevertheless would agree that effective leadership requires the abilities to perceive and understand information, reason with it, imagine possibilities, use intuition, make judgements, solve problems and make decisions. Indeed Judge, Colbert and Ilies (2004) found a significant but moderate association between intelligence and leadership.

These abilities are necessary for creating vision, mission, shared values and strategies for pursuing the vision and mission that 'win' people's minds.

According to Sun Tzu (*The Art of War*) and Confucius (*Analects*), effective leadership entails following three principles: being proactive, reducing complexity and concentrating effort on the essential tasks, and seeking improvement (Krause, 1997: 8–9). And the early nineteenth-century military historian Karl von Clausewitz added that:

> A leader must know the character, the feelings, the habits, the peculiar faults and inclinations of those whom he is to command...These are matters only to be gained by the exercise of an accurate judgement in the observation of things and men. (Howard and Paret, 1984)

The ability to think and decide is a key requirement to be able to lead a group, organization or nation (Adair, 1989: 73). This ability reflects Aristotle's element of rhetoric, *logos*. Emmett Murphy (1996) refers to 'leadership intelligence', quoting *Webster's Dictionary*:

> the degree to which a leader is able to use the faculty of reason – the ability to learn from experience, to otherwise acquire and retain knowledge and to respond successfully to new situations.

The cognitive skills of leadership

Peters and Waterman (1982: 287) argue that:

> An effective leader must be the master of two ends of the spectrum: ideas at the highest level of abstraction and actions at the most mundane level of detail.

This is commonly known as 'helicopter view': the ability both to see a problem or issue in context (from a high vantage point) and to focus on the detail and to move easily between each activity – to be able to see both the 'forest' and the 'trees'. Helicopter view is an example of 'complementarity': the ability to do one thing without prejudice to being able to do the opposite. For example, Johnson and Scholes (2002: 550) describe strategy creation and implementation as involving both detailed analysis *and* visioning about the future, both having insight about the future *and* making things happen, and both maintaining credibility and carrying people with change *and* questioning current ways of doing things.

The cognitive skills that make up what Robert Sternberg calls 'successful intelligence' are memory, analytical abilities and creativity, and he believes that these are important for effective leadership (Sternberg and Vroom, 20002). But they are not sufficient, for Sternberg in his correspondence with Vroom argues that 'wisdom' is also necessary. He defines wisdom as:

> the extent to which [a leader] uses successful intelligence as moderated by values to...seek to reach a common good...by balancing intrapersonal (one's own), interpersonal (others'), and extrapersonal (organizational/institutional/spiritual) interests... over the short and long term, to...adapt to, shape, and select environments.

Underlying the intellectual/cognitive dimension of leadership are several further forms of intelligence (Gardner, 1993): the ability to think in words and use language to express and understand complex meaning (linguistic intelligence); to understand cause-and-effect connections and relationships among actions, objects, events or ideas (logical–mathematical intelligence); and to think in pictures, use imagination and perceive the visual world accurately in three dimensions (visual–spatial intelligence).

Leopold Vansina (1988) studied successful general managers in a multinational company. He found they think holistically, backed up by subsequent analysis, in attempting to understand a situation, which in turn leads to a vision of what the company should be in the future. Future orientation is a necessary requirement for effective leadership. While all of us need goals – we all need to be heading for somewhere – leaders, Marshall says, must be able to deal with the future: they need foresight (Marshall, 1991: 10–11). Foresight in turn, he says, requires vision – seeing possible futures, identifying opportunities and possibilities, and knowing how to respond – and intuition – a sense for the unknown.

Both visioning and strategy development require well-developed cognitive ability. High-level leaders in particular have to produce a fit between the organization and its anticipated environment at some future time (Jacobs and Jaques, 1987; Sashkin, 1988; Lewis and Jacobs, 1992). They have to process ambiguous and complex information and produce a logical framework, understand how their organizations may evolve in the context of the vision, and develop the appropriate strategies and tactics (Zaccaro and Banks, 2001: 202). This requires both logical intelligence and creativity. John Kotter (1988: 29) says:

> **Great vision emerges when a powerful mind, working long and hard on massive amounts of information, is able to see (or recognize in suggestions from others) interesting patterns and new possibilities.**

Turning vision into goals or objectives requires conceptual skills. Conceptual ability takes disjointed, inconsistent and 'sometimes apparently contradictory ideas, phenomena and opinions and builds them into a mental image in which each element has a logical and integral relationship with the whole' (Marshall, 1991: 20–21). Based on a study of the research literature, Stephen Zaccaro and Deanna Banks (2001) suggest that high-level leaders need 'meta-cognitive' skills – inductive reasoning, deductive reasoning, divergent thinking, information processing skills and verbal reasoning. Such skills – for example, the selective encoding, combination and comparison of information – are particularly important for unstructured problems requiring insight and creativity (Davidson et al., 1994).

Another cognitive ability in effective leadership is the ability to take the adversary's perspective on one's own frame of reference – one's mental model – for strategy development (Dahl, 1998). Research reported by Owen Jacobs and Michael McGee (2001: 74) suggests that cognitive ability is associated with reflection on experience, openness to new ideas, and the capacity to form and integrate multiple perspectives on one's environment and experience. Gary Hamel and Liisa Välikangas (2003) say that, for an organization to become resilient in the turbulent modern business environment, the cognitive challenge is for it to 'be entirely free of denial, nostalgia, and arrogance ... [and] deeply conscious of what's changing and perpetually willing to consider how those changes are likely to affect its current success'.

Strategists implicitly use mental models in scanning, analysing and making sense of the competitive environment. A mental map is known as a paradigm: 'the set of assumptions and beliefs that resides deep within [the organization's] culture and influences the thinking, decisions and actions of it members' (Moncrieff, 1998). 'Cognitive mapping' has been used to describe individuals' mental models and to understand how leaders formulate visions, interpret the competitive environment and develop strategies (Huff, 1990). This is discussed further in Chapter 6.

When managers fail to use (or to have) effective cognitive processes and models of their organizations, they tend to resort to simplistic management 'fads' (Shapiro, 1996; Grint, 1997b). Naomi Brookes and Michel Leseure (2003), investigating the relationship between managers' cognitive processes and organizational performance, found three themes emerging: managers use extremely simple models; cognitive processes are characterized by a small series of steps in chronological order; and their cognitive models are highly pictorial in nature.

Hodgson and White (2001) suggest four perspectives of leadership that characterize the intellectual dimension:

- *The economic and strategic perspective*. This focuses on what the organization should be trying to do – its 'strategic intent' (Porter, 1985; Hamel and Prahalad, 1994). It seeks a good fit between what the organization needs to become and the constraints and opportunities in its business environment.
- *Internal culture*: developing the organization's culture to enable it to do what needs to be done. This means first establishing a clear vision and set of corporate values. Leaders then take one or more of three stances: command and control, empowerment or 'difficult learning'. Command and control might work in an organization where expertise (assumed to be vested in a few) is highly valued and senior executives are expected to make the right decisions. Empowerment assumes – and ensures – that people can produce the necessary solutions to problems (which we discuss in Chapter 7). In 'difficult learning', the leader responds to uncertainty through 'an evolving, continuous process of discovery and reinvention', which can lead to achieving competitive advantage.
- *The overall aims of the leader*, for example maintenance of the status quo or revolution.
- *The leader's own knowledge and skills*, such as (a) strategic knowledge concerning the needs and goals of stakeholders and competitors and planning techniques; (b) tactical knowledge of how to identify emerging threats and opportunities and respond to them quickly and appropriately, within the strategic framework, through innovation and improvisation (Krause, 1997: 6); and (c) handling uncertainty during change.

Another track of research that has contributed to our understanding of the cognitive processes in leadership is the organizational systems approach. This approach, exemplified by the work of Daniel Katz and Robert Kahn (1978), emphasizes the role of leaders in spanning organizational boundaries and coordinating activity across them. Such boundaries comprise interfaces with the external environment or between organizational levels.

In Ruth Tait's interviews of business leaders, she found some ambivalence among them on the importance of intellect or cognitive skills (Tait, 1996). On the one hand, Sir Christopher Hogg, chairman of Courtaulds and Reuters, says:

> **Whatever else it is, business is an intellectual exercise...it [is] fantastically demanding on intellectual resources. You are dealing with an enormous range of variables. You are always trying to make decisions on inadequate information and against time. It means a constant process of selection of priorities.**

But on the other hand, Gerry Robinson, chief executive of Granada, says:

> **The danger of a high intellect is that it can veer into over-intellectualizing a business problem that is essentially very simple. People with lots of nous but average intelligence can be enormously successful in running large companies.**

The American writing-style guru Albert Joseph (1972) says, 'Thinking is the process of simplifying the relationships between ideas. Therefore simplicity is not only desirable – it is the mark of the thinking person.' It requires considerable cognitive intelligence to be able to summarize information and communicate it accurately and clearly.

The danger of over-intellectualizing about problems carries some credence. In a study that explored management potential as a concept of 'trainability', it was found that the most intelligent individuals (as measured by an intelligence test) did not improve their ability to prioritize items in their in-basket or to make effective decisions as a result of coaching as much as those of above-average (but not very high) intelligence did (Gill, 1980, 1982). Intelligence was related to prioritizing and decision making in a curvilinear manner. The most intelligent individuals tended to analyse problems at the expense of making decisions about what to do.

Intuition

In addition to analytical and reasoning skills, intuition and imagination are generally regarded as important characteristics of effective leadership. Intuition is often called the 'sixth sense' or 'gut feeling'. The gut feeling that occurs, Baroness Susan Greenfield (2003) says, is due to the release of peptides in the abdomen that act as chemical messengers to the brain.

'Intuition' and 'instinct' are often casually used interchangeably. However, a distinction is necessary. The *Concise Oxford English Dictionary* defines intuition as 'the ability to understand something immediately, without the need for conscious reasoning', and instinct as 'an innate pattern of behaviour in animals in response to certain stimuli ... a natural ... way of acting or thinking ... a natural propensity or skill'.[26] Instinctive behaviour is unlearned and largely genetically programmed. Simply expressed, instinct is innate behaviour; intuition is insight. Lord Robert Winston (2003) suggests that both instinct and intuition play a part in leadership, for example in relation to social behaviour.

We have always placed a great emphasis on developing the intellect in our schools, universities and, indeed, MBA and other management development programmes. Admission to graduate business schools often requires high scores in the GMAT (Graduate Management Admissions Test), which measures verbal and quantitative reasoning skills. 'This exclusive trust in the intellect', Allen Dorcas (2000) says, 'has led to a mistrust of other modes of apprehending reality, namely more intuitive modes.' While some people are reticent about arguing for their intuitive judgements because they feel that doing so is not 'intellectually respectable', many others – Einstein, for example – regard intuition as a gift possessed by great people (Adair, 1989: 89). Lord

Simon of BP and an architect of the British government's competitiveness initiative says: 'You don't have to discuss things. You can sense it. The tingle is as important as the intellect' (Dearlove, 1997a).

Intuition is the perception of a truth that occurs without any conscious cognitive process. Psychologists take it to be a subconscious process of reasoning based on implicit knowledge gained through experience. Ignoring intuition, whether for rational or emotional reasons, presages error and failure, as many of us – and many leaders – have discovered: 'Dawn does not come twice to awaken a man' says an Arab proverb (Adair, 1989: 90).

People tend to differ in their cognitive style – their 'preferred ways of organizing and processing information and experience' (Messick, 1976: 5). Cognitive style reflects other traits in addition to cognitive ability. People tend to be either analytical or intuitive. These modes of thinking are often associated, perhaps over-simplistically (Rao et al., 1992), with the left brain and right brain respectively (Sperry, 1973). An analytical person tends to be compliant, structured and systematic, whereas an intuitive person tends to be unconventional, quick, random and holistic in problem solving and decision making. Intuitive leaders may be less dominating with their subordinates than analytical leaders are, and they are more liked and respected by analytical subordinates than analytical leaders are liked by intuitive subordinates (Allinson et al., 2001).

Jill Hough and dt Ogilvie (2005) say that cognitive styles 'help explain why managers with the same skill set and level of ability make different decisions … . [They reflect] "how", rather than "how well", we perceive and judge information.' Using the MBTI (Myers–Briggs Type Indicator) to study executives' strategic decision making, Hough and Ogilvie found that 'intuiting' and 'thinking' (logical) managers used their intuition to make better decisions than 'sensing' and 'feeling' managers did.

Intuitive capacity is important to strategic vision. Johnson and Scholes (2002: 66) point out that there are leaders who see what other executives do not see and who champion new ways of working. There are many anecdotes of defining moments of intuition. Sir Richard Branson's decision in 1984 to go into the airline industry, against all the advice of colleagues and friends based on rationality, was intuitive (Dearlove, 1997a). He created a successful airline with a unique brand. Another such moment defined the survival of Chrysler in the 1990s (Hayashi, 2001). One weekend in 1988, the then-president of Chrysler, Don Lutz, was driving his Cobra. Relaxed and ruminating on criticisms about the company, he formed a vision of a car that would be a 'muscular, outrageous sports car that would turn heads and stop traffic'. He put his intuitive decision into action on the Monday. The Dodge Viper was to become a 'smashing success', the right car at the right time. His intuition, he says, was 'this subconscious, visceral feeling … [that] just felt right'.

According to Ralph S. Larsen, chairman and CEO of Johnson & Johnson, intuition appears to be more important and more valued at more senior levels of management, where problems become more complex and ambiguous and less amenable to quantitative decision making (Hayashi, 2001). However, Randall White et al. (1996) say:

> **Most executives can't and won't talk about it. Shareholders and institutional investors are particularly unimpressed by intuitive decisions and judgements. As a result, annual reports and the like have become works of incredible fiction. If a chief executive hits on a brilliant idea while in the bath, it is not something that he will proclaim at the AGM.**

Yet ignoring intuition is dangerous. Chet Miller and Duane Ireland (2005) point out that, while there are risks and problems with intuition, when treated as 'holistic hunch' in exploration, for example in exploring new strategies and technologies, it can be beneficial. Intuition is an emotional process that occurs faster than rational thought. Intuition may be accompanied by physical reactions: 'first the feeling, then the thought'. Intuitive feelings guide decision making so that the mind can make good choices.

Imagination

Imagination, says Ralph Rolls (1976: 14), is the human being's 'most powerful weapon for attack, defence, survival – but above all for invention and creativity'. In the words of poet William Wordsworth, imagination is 'that inward eye which is the bliss of solitude',[27] with which 'man can see beyond himself, beyond his immediate environment and circumstances' (Rolls, 1976: 14). Imagination is 'the vanguard or advance scouting party of thinking' (Adair, 1989: 93). It leads to exploration of uncharted waters, experimentation, creativity, invention and innovation. While imagination may be fanciful, silly or cranky, it characterizes the pathfinder.

Richard Olivier (2001: 5) points out that the word 'imagination' shares the same root as 'image', 'magic' and 'magi'. Images, he says, stimulate our own magic and wisdom and are the source of creative inspiration. He quotes Einstein as saying:

> Imagination is more important than knowledge – for while knowledge points to all that is, imagination points to all there will be. (Olivier, 2001: 6)

Greenfield (2003) describes how even learning skills may occur through imagination: imagination helps to establish neural connections in the brain. She quotes the example of learning to play the piano, which can be aided by imagining one is playing it as well as by actually doing so.

The emotional dimension of leadership

Emotion at work

We all experience emotion in our lives, not least at work. While psychologists have studied emotion for many decades, it has not figured much in the study of work in general and leadership in particular until recently. Moreover, 'the emotional impact of a leader is almost never discussed in the workplace, let alone in the literature on leadership and performance', say Daniel Goleman et al. (2001). Why? Steve Fineman (1996) suggests a reason:

> Deeply rooted in Western (especially male) cultural beliefs about the expression of emotion is the belief that organizational order and manager/worker efficiency are matters of the rational, that is non-emotional, activity. Cool strategic thinking is not to be sullied by messy feelings. Efficient thought and behaviour tame emotion. Accordingly good organizations are places where feelings are managed, designed out, or removed.

Guy Lubitsh and John Higgins (2001) describe how ignoring emotions can result in tragic consequences – for example, in the *Challenger* disaster. Engineers did not feel they could let management know of a crucial fault in the Space Shuttle because of management's perceived unwillingness to listen to opposing or unpopular views and their alleged bullying attitude – a leadership failure. Peter Frost (2003: 13) describes how emotionally insensitive attitudes and the behaviour of managers in organizations may create 'emotional pain' that becomes toxic and debilitates the organization. Listening to employees, he says, is a way of 'cleansing' emotional toxins. We need feeling as well as thinking people, says Kjell Nordstrom (2000):

> In an excess economy success comes from attracting the emotional consumer or colleague, not the rational one... . We need not only agile thinkers, but acting, feeling and communicating human beings as well.

The expression of positive emotions may have very positive outcomes. For example, excitement is contagious: it can stimulate others into action (Hatfield et al., 1992). Jonathan Haidt's research into morality found likewise:

> When people witness acts of moral beauty – a young person helping an elderly woman shovel her driveway, Mother Teresa ministering to the poor – they experience a distinct emotion [called] elevation – an emotion that involves a physical feeling, typically in the chest, and motivates people to want to help others. (Carpenter, 2001)

And Goleman et al. (2001) say:

> When the leader is in a happy mood, the people around him view everything in a more positive light. That, in turn, makes them optimistic about achieving their goals, enhances their creativity and the efficiency of their decision making, and predisposes them to be helpful.

Emotional reactions may have adverse effects on one's own judgement, task performance and well-being as well as on one's relationships with others (Ostell, 1996). Kevin Daniels (1999) suggests that negative emotions, for example, may affect the way managers make major strategic decisions about their organizations. Time and again we see calmness under pressure – self-control – as a characteristic of effective leaders. It is often emotions that explain why irrational decisions are made. The heart may 'rule' the head with adverse consequences even at the top level in an organization. The damaging effects of strong negative emotions at work are well documented. Lubitsh and Higgins (2001) say:

> It is not unusual to find a senior executive bullying his senior team, accusing it of laziness, an accusation which has nothing to do with the diligence of the team – or the need for performance – and everything to do with the senior executive's emotional need to disown and reject some of his own 'bad' emotions or past experience of being in an organisational setting where the senior management team did become lazy and indulgent, and the organisational costs were great.

First the feeling, then the thought. The emotional mind is far quicker than the rational mind, springing into action without pausing even a moment to consider what it is doing. This suggests that emotion has a more immediate and perhaps even greater impact on our behaviour than rational thought. However, it is difficult in practice, and perhaps even unrealistic, to separate feeling from thinking. For the 'emotional brain', housed in the structure in the limbic system called the amygdala, works very closely and speedily with the 'thinking brain' in the prefrontal cortex. This relationship provides us with what we call 'emotional intelligence' (Goleman, 1998a). It is well known that effective learning, for example, depends on the interaction between cognitive and emotional processes. In contrast to learned behaviour, instinctive behaviour such as fear and competitiveness in human beings, according to Winston (2003), also arises in the amygdala.

We now understand a great deal about emotion and its relationship to our behaviour. And we have come to accept the need to 'manage' both our own and other people's emotions. Sharon Turnbull (2003) makes the point that 'charismatic and transformational leadership has at its heart the assumption that the control of emotion is the most effective way to lead'. But this is not about encouraging the exploitation of other people's feelings. It is instead about enabling both ourselves and people we interact with to function effectively, achieve results and enjoy job satisfaction. It is about emotional intelligence.

Emotional intelligence

The concept of emotional intelligence was developed rapidly during the 1990s. Its roots go back to the 1920s with Edward Lee Thorndike's concept of 'social intelligence' (Thorndike, 1920), defined by Kimberly Boal and Robert Hooijberg (2000) as the understanding of one's social environment. One of the earliest definitions of emotional intelligence comes from Howard Gardner (1985: 239): the ability 'to notice and make distinctions among other individuals ... in particular, among their moods, temperaments, motivations, and intentions'. Peter Salovey and John Mayer (1990) reconceptualized it as: 'the ability to monitor one's own and others' feelings and emotions, to discriminate among them and to use this information to guide one's thinking and actions'. And John Mayer et al. (1999) later defined emotional intelligence as:

> **an ability to recognize the meanings of emotions and their relationships, and to reason and problem-solve on the basis of them. Emotional intelligence is involved in the capacity to perceive emotions, assimilate emotion-related feelings, understand the information of those emotions, and manage them.**

Two forms of intelligence identified by Gardner (1993) underlie the emotional dimension of leadership: the ability to understand and manage oneself, one's thoughts and feelings, strengths and weaknesses, and to plan effectively to achieve personal goals (intrapersonal intelligence); and the ability to understand other people, display empathy, recognize individual differences and interact effectively (interpersonal intelligence). Together, these abilities constitute emotional intelligence.

Notable models of emotional intelligence have been developed by Robert Cooper and Ayman Sawaf (1997), Daniel Goleman and Richard Boyatzis (Goleman, 1995, 1998a,b) and Victor Dulewicz and Malcolm Higgs (Higgs and Dulewicz, 1999; Dulewicz and Higgs, 2000). A comparison of the characteristics of emotional intelligence that these authorities agree on is provided in Table 3.1. Comparable terms are grouped together.

Cooper (1997) defines emotional intelligence as 'the ability to sense, understand and effectively apply the power ... of emotions'. Cooper and Sawaf (1997) suggest that

Table 3.1 *Characteristics of emotional intelligence*

	Cooper and Sawaf	Goleman and Boyatzis	Dulewicz and Higgs
Self-awareness	✓	✓	✓
Awareness of others Organizational awareness Interpersonal sensitivity	✓	✓	✓
Resilience	✓		✓
Interpersonal connections Building bonds	✓	✓	
Compassion Empathy	✓	✓	
Personal power Influence Persuasion	✓	✓	✓
Integrity Trustworthiness	✓	✓	✓
Conscientiousness		✓	✓
Achievement orientation Motivation		✓	✓

there are three broad aspects of emotional intelligence – emotional literacy, emotional competencies, and values and beliefs – with 14 factors within them. Unique to their model are emotional expression, intentionality, creativity, constructive discontent, outlook, intuition, and trust radius.

According to Goleman (1995), 'emotional intelligence refers to a different way of being smart. It's not your IQ. It's how well you handle yourself and handle your relationships, how well you work on a team, your ability to lead.' And it is 'the capacity for recognizing our own feelings and those of others, for motivating ourselves, and for managing emotions well in ourselves and in our relationships' (Goleman, 1998b). Research by Goleman and Boyatzis produced four dimensions of emotional intelligence – self-awareness, self-management, social awareness and social skills – and 20 factors within them.[28] Unique to Goleman's model are accurate self-assessment, self-confidence, self-control, adaptability, initiative, service orientation, developing others, leadership (in its own right), communication, change catalysis, conflict management, and teamwork and collaboration.

Research by Dulewicz and Higgs (2000) suggests there are seven dimensions of emotional intelligence.[29] Unique to their model is decisiveness.

Is 'emotional intelligence' merely a recycling of what we used to call the 'soft' skills of management and leadership? Is it not just another case of 'old wine in new bottles'? I do not believe this is so. So-called soft skills generally concern *interpersonal intelligence* – relating to others – whereas emotional intelligence also involves *intrapersonal* intelligence – knowing oneself, which, Tim Sparrow says, is necessary before one can understand others (Pickles, 2000). The former leader of an executive team at Ford Motor Company, Nick Zenuik, says, 'Emotional intelligence is the hidden competitive advantage. If you take care of the soft stuff, the hard stuff takes care of itself' (Cooper, 1997).

Recent work on emotional intelligence has refocused what we know about the place of emotion in human behaviour. And because human behaviour is the focus and outcome of leadership, we have now come to understand leadership not only as an intellectual, cognitive process but also as a social, behavioural, spiritual and emotional process. The key feature in our understanding of this is the new importance in our leadership role that we now give to self-awareness.

Emotional intelligence and self-awareness

'We lie loudest when we lie to ourselves,' says Eric Hoffer, the American sociologist (Cooper and Sawaf, 1997: 10). How can we recognize and respond to other people's feelings if we fail to recognize and respond to our own feelings?

Self-awareness includes knowing how others see us. In the immortal words of the Scottish poet, Robert Burns:

> **O wad some Pow'r the giftie gie us**
> **To see oursels as others see us!**
> **It wad frae mony a blunder free us,**
> **And foolish notion.**[30]

Awareness of the importance of self-awareness is nothing new: sociologist Charles Cooley coined the term 'the looking glass self' in 1902. Yet there are some commentators, such as journalist Lucy Kellaway (2003), who dismiss self-awareness as 'tosh'. Referring to the UK Home Office selection criteria for recruiting bankers, she asks: 'Have you ever met anyone who was "fully aware of their own strengths, weaknesses and motivations"?' She suggests that what people say about themselves, for example about how they learned from failure, may have nothing to do with their actual ability to lead effectively.

Nevertheless, as leaders we need to know and control ourselves first before we can lead and enable others. This is not a new principle: Philip Massinger in 1624 said: 'He that would govern others, first should be the master of himself.'[31] Understanding ourselves helps us to understand better other people. Allan Church (Church, 1997; Church and Waclawski, 1999) has shown that high-performing managers are significantly more self-aware than average performers.

Lack of self-awareness may result in reading other people's responses wrongly, incorrect assumptions about people and situations, and inappropriate behaviour (Bass and Yammarino, 1991). Self-awareness gives individuals greater perceived control over interpersonal events (Sosik and Magerian, 1999). And transformational leaders who are self-aware display high levels of self-confidence (Sosik and Margerian, 1999). Rob Goffee sums up the importance of self-awareness: 'At the heart of good leadership is self-knowledge: knowing your strengths and weaknesses and using them to your advantage' (Crainer, 1999). Self-awareness, then, is the starting point for self-development, and this is a prerequisite to become a good leader. So what characterizes self-awareness?

Personal insight Personal insight is our awareness of how we are feeling and why we are feeling that way. It is also our awareness of our behaviour that is being driven by our feelings and values. More importantly, it is our awareness of the impact of our behaviour on others. Thirdly, it is our awareness of our strengths and how we best perform. Peter Drucker (1999a) makes the point that performance can only be built on strengths and that it is therefore important to know our strengths. To achieve personal insight requires honesty about ourselves.

Accurate self-assessment Accurate self-assessment adds to personal insight and entails understanding our strengths and limitations as well as our emotional needs. To achieve such understanding we need constant feedback on our leadership style and its impact on others. Effective leaders create a culture of openness and feedback, whether informally or formally, through 360-degree processes. David Dunning says, 'People overestimate themselves [in relation to their abilities] … [and] they really seem to believe it' (DeAngelis, 2003). He found that the least competent performers (among students) inflate their abilities the most. The reason for this appears to be ignorance – inaccurate self-belief – rather than arrogance. One reason for this ignorance is lack of accurate negative feedback that would help to improve performance.

Humility Some managers find it difficult to offer an apology for making a mistake, believing that they will expose themselves to criticism or loss of face. In fact the converse may often be the case. Managers may gain credibility and respect for having 'owned up' to a subordinate, who then feels that justice has been done and as a result is willing to focus on resolving the problem (Ostell et al., 1999). John Hunt (1998) says that, by exposing a flaw or weakness, leaders reduce their 'psychological distance' from followers and thereby attract help and support.

Leaders who are self-aware take responsibility for their actions. In this sense they display humility. The ability to say 'I was wrong', 'I don't know', or 'You are right, and I think I need to change the way I see this' is not an admission of weakness but arguably a strength (except in some traditional cultures). Humility, then, is the basis for developing self-confidence. The poet John Ruskin recognized this: 'The first test of a truly great man is his humility' (Holden, 2000).

Self-confidence Self-confidence is undoubtedly a characteristic of effective leaders (House, 1977; Bass, 1985; Boal and Bryson, 1988; Atwater et al., 1991; House and Howell, 1992). According to Paxman (2002: 8–9, 43) it is a *sine qua non* for political leaders. And Zaccaro and Banks (2001: 203) say:

> [Self-confidence] contributes to the envisioning process in several ways. First, high self-confidence helps leaders develop an innovative vision that breaks with the status quo. Second, it helps them confront the difficult challenges associated with implementing such a vision. Finally, when leaders display a strong sense of confidence, they convey a positive message to their followers about the feasibility...of their vision; accordingly, they facilitate the trust necessary for successful vision implementation... . Low self-confidence leads to more reward-based or coercive modes of leader influence.

James Minchin (1986: 325–326) writes of Singapore's 'founding father' and former prime minister, Lee Kuan Yew:

> **Anyone who examines [Lee Kuan Yew's] leadership will discover that one rock-solid feature of the psychological landscape is always in evidence. It is that Lee does not, perhaps cannot, criticise or doubt himself.**

Personal vision A key part of self-awareness is understanding who we are and what we want from life: our personal vision. When we ask who we are, we are asking what our values are, what we stand for. If we do not know this, how can we have anything against which to judge ourselves? One way of capturing our personal vision is to ask what legacy we want to leave as a leader.

Emotional intelligence and self-control

Self-awareness is the foundation for emotional intelligence, but by itself it is not enough. The emotionally intelligent leader exercises self-control. David Gilbert-Smith (2003: 10), the first chief executive of The Leadership Trust, says:

> **All leadership starts with oneself, with learning to know and control oneself first, so that then and only then can one control and lead others.**

The importance of self-control is highlighted in a case study of Gravitas Public Relations in Cheltenham (Pickles, 2000). While staff had high levels of 'happiness' as a team, their impulse control was weak. Understanding that and emphasizing self-control when the company recruited a new person proved more effective.

We can develop considerable self-awareness by attending courses and through feedback. But we will never develop and grow unless we have the desire and courage to change our behaviour. This means sometimes pushing ourselves out of our 'comfort zone'. It means developing what Konosuke Matsushita called *torawarenai sunao-na kokoro* ('a mind that doesn't stick') – an agile and innovative mind (Nordstrom, 2000: 177). John Kotter (1997a: 206) describes one of Matsushita's guiding principles: 'Solving difficult problems requires, above all, an open mind and the willingness to learn.' In his book, Matsushita (1978: 63) says:

> ***Sunao*** **is a Japanese word that usually denotes weakness or tractability in a person, an openhearted innocence and a willingness to be sincere. One could say that a sunao mind is an untrapped mind, free to adapt itself effectively to new circumstances.**

Daniel Goleman refers to the ability to manage our emotions. Robert Cooper refers to 'effectively applying' our emotions. Our ability to effect personal change, and indeed to influence others, depends on how we manage our emotions and whether we can maintain a self-empowering mindset. Consider the model in Figure 3.1 and think about your attitude towards organizational change.

It is a fact that change is going to happen. With it there will be uncertainty or even chaos. The way we lead other people through change will depend on how we lead ourselves through it. If we find it difficult to accept the fact of change, then our mindset may be resentment. We start to talk in a resentful way: 'They shouldn't be doing this to me' (whoever 'they' are); 'I could do some really cool things around here if only my

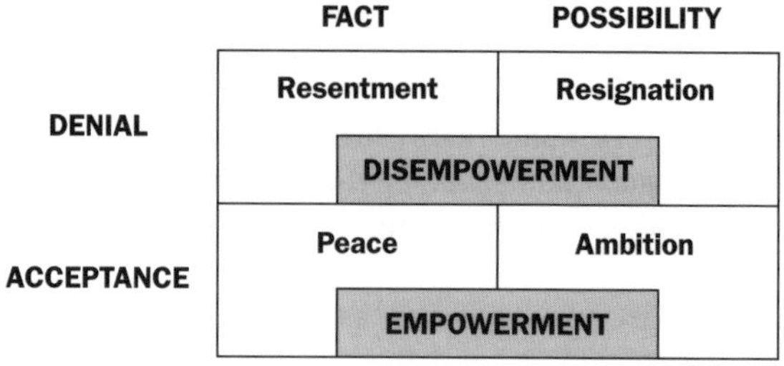

Figure 3.1 *Self-empowerment model*

boss would let me'. From here it is only a small step to personal resignation: 'There's nothing I can do. What's the use of trying? They never listen anyway.' At best, all you are going to do is to achieve the status quo. But you are effectively disempowering yourself by saying that you cannot do anything to change or influence the situation.

In contrast, accepting the situation immediately brings an inner peace. Only from this launch pad can you create an ambition to take control of your situation and how it affects you. You are then empowering yourself. As Nordstrom (2000) says, 'It is what it is.' Only when we accept this axiom can we do something about it.

A good clue as to where you are 'internally' is to look at the external, visible signs. Listen to the language you use and the conversations you have with others. Ask a colleague to give you feedback. If you are in the top two boxes of the model above, ask yourself what effect it is having on those whom you're leading.

Self-control first requires self-awareness – recognizing one's own emotions. Then it requires controlling one's own emotional behaviour. For example, in exercising such self-control, it is important to deal with a person's emotional reaction before attempting to resolve the problem (Ostell et al., 1999). What may get in the way of this is 'unconstructive mood matching', which is what happens when we display an emotional state that is similar to that of another person, with adverse consequences: for example, displaying anger with somebody because the latter is angry with you (Ostell, 1996). Self-control means avoiding the use of emotive verbal expressions and negative body language that would exacerbate another person's negative emotion. Self-control involves self-awareness, displaying integrity, self-empowerment and being agile in our behaviour.

Emotional intelligence and awareness of others

Self-awareness and self-control are critical prerequisites if we are to excel in the third major competency of emotional intelligence – awareness of others. Interpersonal insight is characterized by understanding others' motivation, aspirations, needs, interests, preferences, likes and dislikes, and feelings. The key to awareness of others is empathy. Says Peter Drucker, 'The number one practical competency for leaders is empathy. Today, perceptiveness is more important than analysis' (Cooper, 1998). A study of the US presidential election in 2000 revealed that voter perceptions of the emotional empathy of candidates Al Gore and George W. Bush were associated with ratings of their transformational leadership and attributed charisma, which in turn had a strong relationship with voting behaviour (Pillai et al., 2003).

The essence of empathy is sensing what others feel without their saying so. We sense other people's feelings not through the words they use but through their body language – their eye contact, tone of voice, facial expression, gestures and posture. For Nelson Mandela, 'To see the world through another man's eyes, you have to walk a mile in his shoes' (Mandela, 1994).

Empathy is the foundation for social competencies – understanding other people's feelings and needs, whether colleagues, subordinates, customers or bosses. Empathy is not necessarily agreeing with people; it is showing understanding of their feelings and needs. And when people believe their feelings and needs are perceived and understood, they are more trusting and therefore open. The film *Dead Poets' Society* provides a vivid example. Teacher John Keating (Robin Williams) displays impressive empathy with student Anderson over his fear of creating and reciting a poem in class. He uses humour. Humour diffuses anxiety and tension. Leaders like Hannibal and Churchill knew this and used it liberally to good effect.

How do we achieve empathy? Emotionally intelligent leaders who do so use well-developed questioning skills – open and probing rather than closed and leading questions. They use active listening skills – paraphrasing the meaning or content of what the other person has just said and reflecting the feeling displayed through that person's body language. Active listening confirms to another person your understanding of his or her meaning and feelings. Understanding builds trust. And trust breeds powerful relationships. As such, trust is a common corporate value, which we discuss in Chapter 5.

Emotional intelligence and leadership

According to Daniel Goleman, emotional intelligence is twice as important as cognitive or technical skills for high job performance, and at the top level almost all-important, according to findings from profiles of top executives in 15 global companies including IBM, PepsiCo and Volvo (Pickles, 2000). And Robert Sternberg says that IQ accounts for as little as 4% of exceptional leadership, job performance and achievement; emotional intelligence (EQ) may account for over 90% (Sternberg, 1996). A study of 100 management and business leaders in the UK over seven years by Higgs and Dulewicz (1999) revealed that 'emotional intelligence was more highly related to success than IQ alone'. And taken together, EQ and IQ predict managerial success even better (Dulewicz and Higgs, 2000). According to Goleman (1997):

> **High IQ makes you a good English professor; adding high EQ makes you chairman of the English Department... . High IQ makes you a brilliant fiscal analyst; adding high EQ makes you CEO.**

But the case for emotional intelligence is put perhaps most powerfully by Bennis (1994), one of the world's foremost thinkers and writers in the field of leadership:

> **Emotional intelligence is much more powerful than IQ in determining who emerges as a leader. IQ is a threshold competence. You need it, but it doesn't make you a star. Emotional intelligence can.**

Intellect – verbal, numerical and thinking skills – is necessary for effective leadership. However, it is not sufficient: emotional intelligence is an essential requirement for success.

The emotional and interpersonal dimension of leadership concerns values, strategy, empowerment, and inspiration and motivation. The leader's self-concept and emotional intelligence are the key. Feelings are the manifestation of both motivation and the frustration and satisfaction of needs. Emotion is a powerful moderator of intellectual understanding and reasoning and behaviour, in both leader and follower. Inspiration is the ultimate 'level' of motivation. *Communicating* the vision, values and strategy, empowering people, and inspiring and motivating them are both emotional and behavioural processes and require considerable interpersonal skills.

Openness and curiosity in leaders stimulate exploration and learning and the creative problem solving necessary in visioning and strategy development (Keller, 1986; McCrae and Costa, 1987; Barrick and Mount, 1991; Mumford et al., 1993a,b). Risk propensity is also important: visionary leaders are intellectually and emotionally courageous (Tichy and Devanna, 1986a,b). They know when to confront painful situations and they can resist conforming. Effective leaders also display skills in complex interactions with others, behavioural flexibility, conflict management, social awareness and reasoning, persuasion and empathy (Zaccaro et al., 1991; Zaccaro, 1999). Understanding the moods and emotions of stakeholders is important to leaders, for example in deciding how to communicate strategies (Boal and Hooijberg, 2000). Chief executives need to understand and manage the dynamics of the top team, which calls for emotional intelligence, in ensuring clear goals and cooperation. Studies by HayGroup clearly reinforce the need for emotional intelligence:

> **The most successful teams are distinguished by empathy and integrity, rather than brainpower...[they] excel at working with others and are adaptable, capable of self-control and able to manage 'productive conflict'...over ideas rather than personalities. (Maitland, 2001a)**

A study of 12 skippers in the 2000/2001 BT Global Challenge Round-the-World Yacht Race found (using Dulewicz and Higgs' model) that the more successful ones displayed greater emotional intelligence, in particular interpersonal sensitivity, and that their intuitiveness increased during the race (Dulewicz and Higgs, 2002). Interviews reported by Jane Cranwell-Ward indicated the importance for success of self-confidence, self-belief, a strong set of values and an ability to cope with emotions (Dulewicz et al., 2002). She also found that skippers who were 'performance drivers' motivate teams to achieve when projects are short term and need to be completed quickly, whereas 'performance enablers' inspire teams to maintain commitment and loyalty over a longer period, which is critical during times of uncertainty.

Neal Ashkanasy and Catherine Daus (2002) suggest, however, that 'there is much more to emotions than just emotional intelligence'. They show how affective events theory can explain positive or negative emotions that influence both work attitudes, such as job satisfaction, commitment and loyalty, and affect-driven behaviours, such as impulsive acts, spontaneous helping and transient effort (Weiss and Cropanzano, 1996). In turn, work attitudes influence judgement-driven behaviour, such as quitting, antisocial or prosocial behaviour and productive work. Positive and negative emotions, according to the theory, are a consequence of daily work events, such as hassles and uplifts, and personal disposition in terms of 'trait affect' (a general tendency to be in a positive or negative mood) and emotional intelligence. In addition to having emotional intelligence, managers need to investigate the events that cause emotions in organizational settings.

Goleman et al. (2001) say, 'Emotional leadership is the spark that ignites a company's performance, creating a bonfire of success or a landscape of ashes.' Higgs and Dulewicz (2002: 113–117) report several studies that indicate a link between emotional intelligence and leadership. They speculate that leadership effectiveness (LQ) is a sum of emotional intelligence (EQ), intellectual intelligence (IQ) and managerial competence (MQ):

$$LQ = EQ + IQ + MQ$$

In a study of innovation and enterprise course participants at the Swinburne University of Technology in Australia, Benjamin Palmer et al. (2001) found that emotional intelligence correlated with the transformational leadership behaviours of individualized consideration and inspirational motivation and (as Julian Barling and colleagues also found) with the contingent reward element of transactional leadership. In a further study, Lisa Gardner and Con Stough (2002), studying 110 senior managers, found that emotional intelligence correlated highly with all aspects of transformational leadership (individualized consideration, intellectual stimulation, inspirational motivation, and idealized attributes and behaviour (derived from idealized influence)). Understanding others' emotions and emotional management were the best predictors of transformational leadership, and there was a negative relationship with laissez-faire behaviour.

Despite all the research studies of emotional intelligence, there is still a 'macho' mentality (emotionality?) among some journalists and executives about what it takes to be an effective leader. Stefan Stern (2003) quotes research by Graham Jones at the University of Wales that 'will cause Dr Goleman and his followers to rethink their theories on touchy-feely management'. This research focuses on 'mental toughness' – the ability to persist and sustain high levels of performance even under extreme pressure. Mental toughness is characterized by 10 features, according to Stern's report:

- self-belief
- resilience – the ability to recover from setbacks
- focus in the face of distractions
- drive to succeed
- control – the ability to regain control after unexpected events
- resolve – pushing back the boundaries of pain while maintaining discipline and effort under distress
- 'nerves of steel' – accepting anxiety or pressure as inevitable and knowing one can cope with it
- independence
- competitiveness
- 'chillability' – the ability to 'switch the focus' on and off as required

Stern (2003) says, 'The mentally tough don't let the latest quirk of fate shake them', quoting Nietzsche: 'That which does not kill me makes me stronger.' What is of concern here is how these findings for 'true grit' can be reconciled with those for the characteristics and positive consequences of emotional intelligence. I would argue that they *add* to emotional intelligence.

Effective leadership, then, requires well-developed emotional intelligence – the ability to understand oneself and others, to practise self-control, and to use interpersonal skills to respond to other people in appropriate ways. Effective leaders 'win people's hearts'. They use personal power of emotional intelligence rather than position power (authority). Emotional intelligence, in addition to cognitive skills, is key to identifying and promoting shared values that support the pursuit of vision, mission and strategies and to empowering and inspiring people. Visioning, strategic thinking and goal setting without effective emotional leadership are impotent. But the converse is dangerous. And without spiritual leadership, both intellectual and emotional leadership are barren.

The spiritual dimension of leadership

Effective leadership concerns both cognitive and emotional intelligence, but it concerns something else too. Nietzsche said, 'He who has a *why* to live can bear with almost any *how*' (Allport, 1983: 12). Effective leadership requires spiritual intelligence: providing *meaning* and *value* in what we seek and what we do. 'Spirit', according to *Webster's Dictionary* and the *Oxford English Dictionary*, is a person's animating principle. And, in the words of Frances Hesselbein, 'people are hungry for meaning and significance' (Shinn, 2003). Spiritual intelligence (SQ) concerns understanding that human beings have an animating need for meaning, value and a sense of worth in what they seek and do. Spiritual leadership is about satisfying that need. Underlying the spiritual dimension of leadership in part is what Gardner (1993) calls linguistic intelligence: the ability to think in words and use language to express and understand complex meaning.

Louis Fry (2003) defines spiritual leadership as:

> creating a vision wherein organization members experience a sense of calling in that their life has meaning and makes a difference [and] establishing a social/organizational culture based on altruistic love whereby leaders and followers have genuine care, concern, and appreciation for both self and others, thereby producing a sense of membership and feel understood and appreciated.

Leadership as involving 'sense-making' or 'meaning-making' is a fairly recent view (Weick, 1995). Interpreting the environmental complexities – the threats and opportunities of the organization's external environment and the strengths and weaknesses of its internal environment – requires the cognitive skills discussed earlier in this chapter. Leadership from the social constructivist or constitutive viewpoint concerns providing meaning and value to followers by displaying behaviour and articulating messages that reflect the needs and wishes of others who have it in their gift to confer the status of leadership.

Danah Zohar and Ian Marshall (2000: 5) contrast SQ with EQ:

> My emotional intelligence allows me to judge what situation I am in and then to behave appropriately within it… . But my spiritual intelligence allows me to ask if I want to be in this particular situation in the first place. Would I rather change the situation, creating a better one?

On this Adam Blatner (2000) says:

> **One of the components of feeling a sense of meaning in life is the ability to become aware of feelings and to think about relationships... . Emotional intelligence and personal meaning are complementary, the former offering methods for the energizing of the latter.**

The quest for meaning in liberal Western society is vividly captured by Michael Novak (1982):

> **Many regard the emptiness at the heart of pluralism as a flaw. Its consequences among individuals are looked upon as illnesses: anomie, alienation, loneliness, despair...at the spiritual core there is an empty shrine.**

Zohar and Marshall (2000) believe that managers not only have avoided recognizing emotions; they have also lost their sense of purpose and their 'spirituality'. We human beings, Charles Handy (1997: 108), the British writer and management philosopher, says, need a purpose in life that gives us 'energy for the journey'. Meaning and value are what comprise 'spirituality'. He quotes a definition of spirituality from an unlikely source, the British government's Department of Education: 'The valuing of the non-material aspects of life, and intimations of an enduring reality' (Handy, 1997: 108). We can influence this 'enduring reality', Handy says, by leaving 'a bit of ourselves behind'.

The 'deregulation of employment' (Cappelli, 1995) – the disappearance of security and tranquillity in the workplace – has created a 'spiritual vacuum' for a growing number of people. And this spiritual vacuum has extended beyond work to human life in general. It has created a growing need for 'spiritual leadership', or what Leigh Kibby and Charmine Härtel (2003) call 'noetic' leadership after the Greek word *noös*, 'spirit'.

Historian Theodore Zeldin (2004), from his conversations with them, believes that the majority of business leaders and MBAs 'are not primarily interested in making money':

> **They need money of course, but there is a deep desire to do something more useful with their lives. Our business leaders are prisoners of the system that they have inherited, entangled in bureaucratic cobwebs from which they cannot escape. Corporations were invented 100 years ago: they are no longer suitable for our aspirations today. We have to rethink how we want to organise business and what we want to replace corporations with.**

These ideas about meaning and value are supported by research findings by Laura Nash and Howard Stevenson (2004). From their studies of successful professionals, top executives attending Harvard Business School programmes, HBS alumni, and members of the Young Presidents' Organization, they concluded that there are four 'irreducible components of enduring success' that people pursue and enjoy:

- Achievement – accomplishments that compare favourably against similar goals that others have striven for
- Significance – the feeling of having made a positive impact on people cared about

- Legacy – establishing one's values or accomplishments in a way that helps others to find future success
- Happiness – feelings of pleasure or contentment about life

Mihaly Csikszentmihalyi (1999) points out that material wealth does not correlate with happiness. Martin Seligman, leading researcher into happiness and former president of the American Psychological Association, regards the sensual pleasures (often associated with material wealth) – 'the pleasant life' – as the lowest level of happiness, bettered by 'the good life' – enjoying doing something we are good at – and the highest level, the most lasting form of happiness, 'the meaningful life' – that comes from doing something one believes in, that has meaning and value (Seligman, 2002; Elliott, 2003). And the Chief Rabbi in the UK, Sir Jonathan Sacks, says:

> **Living for yourself may be pleasurable, but pleasure is not happiness. Happiness comes from a life lived with and for others within a framework of mutual responsibility. (Appleyard, 2004)**

Catherine Fletcher (1976: 4) says, 'The search for meaning ... brings purpose and enrichment into our lives.' What is 'meaningfulness'? Baumeister (1991) suggests that people experience a meaningful life when they have a sense of purpose or direction, a sense of self-efficacy or control, a set of values that inform their actions and behaviour, and self-worth. Richard Sennet, the sociologist, suggests that certain features of modern capitalism are a cause of the lack of meaning in people's work:

> **The uncertainties of flexibility, the absence of deeply-rooted trust and commitment, the superficiality of teamwork; most of all the spectre of failing to make something of oneself in the world, to 'get a life' through one's work. All these conditions impel people to look for some other scene of attachment and depth. (Overell, 2002)**

Mike Emmott, adviser to the UK's Chartered Institute of Personnel and Development, says that the search for meaning at work includes job satisfaction and commitment but also extends to 'a sense of the wider purpose in doing the work' (Overell, 2002). The 2004 Roffey Park survey found that managers are seeking different kinds of meaning in their work: associated for some with personal values and ideals, for others with spiritual beliefs or personal fulfilment (Hoar, 2004). Mike Martin suggests that meaning lies at the core of professional ethics: meaningful work is about 'self-fulfilment and self-betrayal, and the interplay of private and professional life' (Martin, 2000; Overell, 2002). Norman Bowie writes:

> **Meaningful work is work that is freely entered into, that allows the worker to exercise their autonomy and independence; that enables the worker to develop their rational capacities; that provides a wage sufficient for physical welfare; that supports the moral development of employees and that is not paternalistic in the sense of interfering with the worker's conception of how they wish to obtain happiness. (Overell, 2002; see also Bowie, 1998)**

Neal Chalofsky (2003) suggests that meaningful work – work that expresses our inner being – depends on several factors, among them:

- Knowing one's purpose in life and how work fits into that purpose
- Having a positive belief about one's ability to achieve that purpose and pursuing the opportunity to do so through work
- Empowerment – autonomy and control over one's environment
- Recognizing and developing one's potential through learning
- The nature of work itself

Spiritual leadership takes followers beyond self-interest. It is associated with integrity, independence and justice, says Gilbert Fairholm (1996). He suggests that the foundation for spiritual leadership is morality, stewardship and community. Spiritual leadership is about identifying and affirming shared core values, beliefs and ethics, a shared vision and a shared purpose that have meaning for everybody, meaningful work, empowering people, and stewardship – holding the community's, and indeed the world's, resources in trust. Spiritual leadership is about creating Aristotle's *ethos*.

Fry's model of spiritual leadership (Fry, 2003) comprises vision, 'altruistic love' (values) and 'hope and faith' (effort or motivation). Vision, he says, provides a broad appeal to key stakeholders, defines the destination and the journey (the strategy), reflects high ideals, encourages hope and faith, and establishes a standard of excellence. Altruistic love concerns the values of forgiveness, kindness, integrity, empathy and compassion, honesty, patience, courage, trust and loyalty, and humility. Hope and faith provide endurance, perseverance, stretch goals, the desire to do what it takes, and the expectation of reward or victory.

The concept of spiritual leadership tends to be focused more on the characteristics and behaviour of the individual leader than on the relationship between leader and followers, their situation or the leadership process, according to some writers. Douglas Hicks (2002) suggests that 'the concept of spirituality is more disparate and contested than the current leadership literature acknowledges'. Ron Cacciope (2000) says:

> The meaning of the term spirituality is often misunderstood and can have negative connotations for many people. Spirituality is often seen in the same context as organized religion, with particular beliefs, moral rules and traditions. Spirituality, however, is not formal, structured, or organized. Organized religion has more of an external focus where spirituality involves a person looking inward and therefore is accessible to everyone whether religious or not. Religion often has salvation as its major aim. Spirituality is above and beyond any specific religious denomination and seeks to find and experience the common principles and truths that each religion offers.

Ian Mitroff and Elizabeth Denton (1999a,b) report that most managers they surveyed or interviewed in the United States are positive towards spirituality but negative towards religion. Hicks (2002) believes that 'The opposition between spirituality and religion creates a problem for leadership scholars who acknowledge that the "whole person" comes to work.' Hicks believes the distinction between spirituality and religion is not tenable. He argues that effective leadership is not about promoting 'a single spiritual framework but … [about creating a] culture in which leaders and followers can respectfully negotiate religious and spiritual diversity' – a culture of 'respectful pluralism' (an example of individualized consideration). The Dalai Lama for one, however, is very clear about the difference between spirituality and religion:

> **Religion I take to be concerned with faith in the claims of one faith tradition or another, an aspect of which is the acceptance of some form of heaven or nirvana. Connected with this are religious teachings or dogma, ritual prayer, and so on. Spirituality I take to be concerned with those qualities of the human spirit – such as love and compassion, patience, tolerance, forgiveness, contentment, a sense of responsibility, a sense of harmony – which bring happiness to both self and others. (Dalai Lama XIV, 1999: 22)**

Zohar and Marshall (2000: 285) say that 'Self-awareness is one of the highest criteria of high spiritual intelligence but one of the lowest priorities of our … culture.' Danah Zohar and Jacquie Drake say that leaders with high SQ behave in characteristic ways that are not 'God-given' but can be developed (Zohar and Drake, 2000; Zohar and Marshall, 2000: 15). They say that such leaders are:

- Flexible – receptive to suggestions, surprises and change, and able to cope with ambiguity
- Self-aware – reflective and critical of themselves
- Led by their personal vision, sense of purpose and values
- Able to cope with and learn from failure and suffering and turn the lessons learned into wisdom
- Holistic – focused on the whole person and the whole situation
- Welcoming of diversity
- Independent and willing to take a stand on issues
- Questioning, particularly in respect of reasons for actions, decisions and events
- Able to reframe situations using new perspectives and creating new options
- Spontaneous – in tune with the moment and unafraid of responding or initiating action

Spiritual leadership is about creating meaning and value for people, in work life, family life or community life. Zohar and Marshall (2000: 16) suggest that a high-SQ leader is likely to be a servant leader: 'bringing higher vision and value to others and showing them how to use it … a person who inspires others'. Spiritual intelligence does not merely reflect existing values: it leads to new values.

Zohar and Marshall (2000: 7) point out that spiritual intelligence is the result of the integration and unification of activity in the cognitive and emotional domains of the brain – 'a dialogue between reason and emotion, between mind and body' – that gives meaning to our existence. While science, including psychology, has not explicitly addressed spiritual intelligence, Zohar and Marshall (2000: 11–13) point out that much evidence for it has resulted from neurological, psychological and anthropological studies. As in the field of leadership, there are several streams of research that have scarcely yet converged:

1. The existence of a 'God spot' in the brain – a spiritual centre in the temporal lobes which, in scans using positron emission topography, lights up whenever subjects are exposed to spiritual or religious topics (Persinger, 1996; Ramachandran and Blakeslee, 1998).
2. The existence of a neural process in the brain that is devoted to unifying and giving meaning to our experience (Llinas and Ribary, 1993; Singer and Gray, 1995; Singer, 1999). Serial neural connections are the basis of IQ; haphazard interconnections

among huge neuron bundles are the basis for emotional intelligence; and synchronous neural oscillations suggest the basis of spiritual intelligence.

3 Language as a uniquely human, symbolic activity that evolved in parallel with the development of the brain's frontal lobes and that enables meaning and symbolic imagination (Deacon, 1997).

Viktor Frankl (1984) suggests that our search for meaning is our primary source of motivation. Zohar and Marshall (2000: 19–32) give many examples that support this notion. The spiritually intelligent leader provides 'a consistent focus on mission … a clear sense of direction and the opportunity to find meaning in … work' (Hesselbein, 2002). Bennis and Thomas (2002) share this view: they argue that effective leaders create shared meaning. Meaning, whether to do with work or life in general, is captured in the goal – the vision – and the values that have meaning for people and thereby motivate and inspire them. Meaning has 'meta-value'; Kets de Vries and Florent-Treacy (1999) say:

> **When people see their jobs as transcending their own personal needs (by improving the quality of life for others, for example, or by contributing to society)...the impact can be extremely powerful.**

They cite as an example the pharmaceutical industry, in which the preservation and improvement of human life through the development of new medicines provides this meta-value and is a source of motivation and inspiration. They argue that effective leadership entails meeting human motivational needs: effective leaders 'pay attention to individuals' desire for *identity*; their sense of usefulness or *meaning* in life; and their feeling of *attachment* or human connectedness'. It is when there is alignment between employees' motivation and organizational values, they say, that people's subjective experiences and actions become meaningful.

The Roffey Park report says that it is employees rather than employers who are leading the trend towards greater spirituality, perhaps because employers find the subject too vague and perhaps, according to consultant Geraldine Brown, because of its association with weird cultism (Watkins, 2003). Jon Watkins quotes Richard Cree of the Institute of Directors as saying that:

> **The issue of spirituality is not the kind of thing companies should be getting involved in... . It has to come from the employees...there are still...a lot of people that are not convinced by it. (Watkins, 2003)**

Paul Gibbons, a management consultant with PricewaterhouseCoopers, is quoted by Watkins (2003) as saying that spirituality is merely another management fad. On the other hand, Watkins also quotes a training manager, Simon Burton of pub chain Greene King, as saying that spirituality is linked closely to inspirational leadership and empowerment – giving employees autonomy, giving them the room to be creative and make mistakes, and the building of trust between employees and the employer. Burton says that inspirational leadership models use 'all the words … associated with spirituality'. The increasing popular interest in spirituality in the workplace is captured by Fleur Britten (2005) in *The Sunday Times' Style* magazine, describing spiritual development activities and programmes at several organizations, including Apple,

McKinsey, the World Bank, Orange and Kwik-Fit, and residential programmes run by specialized providers such as Golcar Farm in West Yorkshire in the UK, The Big Stretch in Spain and Shreyas in India.

Reviewing studies that demonstrate the value of spirituality in work organizations, Len Tischler et al. (2002) say, 'evidence exists that suggests a link between workplace spirituality and enhanced individual creativity, increased honesty and trust within the organization, enhanced sense of personal fulfilment ... and increased commitment to organizational goals'. The concept of spirituality, to do with meaning, purpose and value in what we do, is key to intrinsic motivation and to leadership. Inspiration comes from leadership that provides meaning, purpose and value, and, Jill Graham (1991) says, this is more powerful than charisma alone, which may lack a basis in values and therefore may not protect followers from immoral action. And Zohar and Marshall (2004) argue for a new form of capitalism – 'spiritual capital' – that is based on spiritual intelligence and the higher motivations we associate with transformational leadership.

Related to the concepts of emotional intelligence and spiritual intelligence is what Doug Lennick and Fred Kiel (2005) call 'moral intelligence'. They define this as 'the ability to differentiate right from wrong as defined by universal principles'. Moral intelligence, they say, concerns the key elements of integrity, responsibility, compassion and forgiveness. These elements overlap with Fry's (2003) concept of spiritual intelligence.

The behavioural dimension of leadership

The behavioural skills that are necessary in leadership include both using and responding to emotion, for example through body language. But they also comprise communicating in other ways through writing, talking and listening – using personal power – and physical activity. While little research has been carried out on political behaviour, political skill has been argued as an important behavioural competency in leadership (Mintzberg, 1983, 1985; Perrewé et al., 2004; Treadway et al., 2004).

Underlying the behavioural dimension of leadership again are several forms of intelligence (Gardner, 1993): the ability to use language to express and understand complex meaning (linguistic intelligence), to manage oneself, one's thoughts and feelings (intrapersonal intelligence), to interact effectively (interpersonal intelligence), and to use the body in skilful and complicated ways, involving a sense of timing, coordination of movement and the use of the hands (kinaesthetic intelligence).

Emotional and spiritual intelligence models generally include interpersonal skills, but such skills can also be categorized as belonging to the behavioural dimension of leadership. Such skills are learned behaviours. Following Marshall's model of attitudes, the behavioural dimension – Marshall's volitional element (1991: 75) – comprises the behavioural responses we make as a result of our knowledge, beliefs, values and feelings. The behavioural dimension of leadership contains more behaviours than those associated primarily with emotion.

The behaviours associated with emotional intelligence include communicating with other people, active listening, building relationships, managing conflict, teambuilding, collaborating with other people, developing and empowering them, influencing them, and inspiring and motivating them. However, in addition to these behaviours there are those that result mainly from *thinking*. Examples of such behaviour are speaking (other than inspirational oratory) and writing (including computer keyboard activity). As Albert Joseph says, 'You cannot write clearly unless you have thought it out clearly' (Joseph, 1986: 34). The same applies to speaking.

The Bradford model of leadership focuses on the interpersonal 'micro skills' of effective leadership behaviour (Wright and Taylor, 1994; Randell, 1998; Wright and Taylor, 2000). These are ways in which effective leaders structure their interactions with followers and others and manage emotion. They comprise the perception of others' thoughts and feelings through their behaviour, appropriate questioning, making judgements from the answers, and responding appropriately both verbally (using active listening by paraphrasing meaning) and non-verbally through body language (reflecting implied feelings).

Political skill has been defined by Gerald Ferris et al. (2002) as:

> **an interpersonal style construct that combines social perceptiveness or astuteness with the capacity to adjust one's behavior to different and changing situational demands in a manner that inspires trust, confidence, and genuineness, and effectively influences and controls the responses of others.**

Political skill enables leaders to network, influence and control people and situations effectively.

Leaders' behavioural repertoires influence their effectiveness and consequently that of their organizations (Bullis, 1992; Hart and Quinn, 1993). Behavioural skills, together with cognitive skills, include the ability to choose and use the appropriate leadership role for the situation (Boal and Hooijberg, 2000) and influencing behaviour upward, downward and laterally (Yukl and Falbe, 1990; Yukl and Tracey, 1992). Subordinates or followers, peers and bosses alike frequently see managers who perform a broad range of leadership roles (styles) as more effective (Hooijberg, 1996). Typical leadership styles, which we discussed in Chapter 2, are the directive, consultative, participative and delegative styles. Situational sensitivity and behavioural flexibility in leadership style are inherent in effective leadership.

Leaders may be able to discern and understand the need for particular behaviour, but they may not necessarily be able to act in that way. An example is effective time management. This requires not only cognitive skills but also emotional skills such as self-discipline and self-control. The interaction between thinking and *behaving* (Johnson et al., 2001) and the emotional or *affective* aspect of this interaction (Walsh, 1995) therefore must be considered.

The relationship between the cognitive, emotional, spiritual and behavioural dimensions of leadership

Concentrating on the separate dimensions of leadership in a mutually exclusive way inevitably entails failure to understand the interaction among the cognitive processes, emotions and volitional action (behavioural skills) in leadership. Emotions and moods interact with cognition (Parkinson, 1995). For example, anxiety and sadness adversely affect attention to stimuli and information recall (Dalgleish and Watts, 1990; MacCleod,

1991; Mathew, 1993; Williams et al., 1996). And the affective and cognitive components of attitudes also interact. Affective–cognitive consistency is a significant moderator of the relationship between job satisfaction and job performance: the greater the consistency, the stronger the relationship between job performance and job satisfaction (Schleicher et al., 2004).

Martha Nussbaum (2001) suggests that emotions are ways in which human beings direct their attention to objects and cannot be separated from perception or cognition. Mary Warnock (2002a) argues likewise:

> **[Jean-Paul] Sartre...was convinced...that one cannot separate the emotions from the intellect, that the emotions have objects (they are intentional) and that loving or hating or feeling disgust for an object is a way of perceiving that is bound up in all our understanding and knowledge of the world, giving intelligibility to that world.**

Nussbaum (2001) in particular argues that compassion is socially useful provided it is informed by reason. Emotional intelligence may *enable* the intellect: once the contagion of negative emotion is dissipated or controlled, the rational, analytical mind can function more effectively. On the other hand the intellect benefits from positive emotion; indeed the synergy of reason and emotion is the fount of human achievement. Charles Rennie Mackintosh (1868–1928), the iconic Scottish architect, designer and artist, in contrast to Nussbaum, with a converse message, put it this way:

> **Reason informed by emotion...expressed in beauty...elevated by earnestness...lightened by humour...[that is] the ideal that should guide all artists. (McKean and Baxter, 2000: 139)**

Higgs and Dulewicz (2002: 141–143) suggest the need for balance between the rational (cognitive) and emotional in achieving results. The cognitive aspects of leadership, they say, comprise corporate business plans which are cascaded down into individual goals or objectives; the emotional aspects comprise vision, values and the resulting behaviours.

The interaction between thinking, feeling and behaviour is complicated. Using functional magnetic resonance imaging, Jeremy Gray and colleagues found that activity in the lateral prefrontal cortex of subjects' brains as they were carrying out verbal and non-verbal tasks under conditions of emotional arousal and non-arousal was influenced by the combination of emotion and cognitive activity but not by either one alone (*Monitor on Psychology*, 2002). They also found that pleasant emotions heralded better performance on verbal tasks but worse performance on non-verbal (visual) tasks. And the reverse was true for negative or anxious moods: anxious subjects did better on visual tasks and worse on verbal tasks.

Cognitive resource theory suggests that there are several moderators of the association between intelligence and leadership that concern emotion, for example the supportiveness of followers, leader stress and leadership style (Fiedler and Garcia, 1987). The theory suggests that stress experienced by a leader moderates the relationship between intelligence and leadership effectiveness because of negative emotions associated with fear of failure, doubts of self-efficacy and anxiety about evaluation (Fiedler, 1986). Judge, Colbert and Ilies (2004), in their meta-analysis of studies of intelligence and leadership, indeed found that intelligence and leadership are more strongly related when leader stress is lower. Cognitive resource theory also predicts that leaders need to be directive in their leadership style if followers or subordinates are to benefit from their superior intelligence, which shows itself in better strategies and decisions. Again, Judge et al. found support for the moderating effect of directive behaviour in the relationship between intelligence and leadership.

According to Catherine Cassell and Kevin Daniels (1998), 'The process of strategic management is essentially a rich social and cognitive process.' Strategic analysis, they say, entails the analysis and selection of strategic options by management teams 'on the basis of incomplete and ambiguous data', often through 'intense debate and negotiations over ... months or even years', influenced by 'the vested interests of stakeholder groups'. Cognitive processes are involved in the associated judgement and decision processes. And cognitive, emotional and social processes are involved in handling the consequences of strategic decisions, e.g. downsizing as a result of restructuring.

The relationship between thinking, emotion and behaviour is captured in the Leaderplex model of Robert Hooijberg et al. (1997). This model proposes that behavioural complexity is informed by the cognitive and social (emotional?) complexity of the leader. And cognitive complexity, social or emotional intelligence and behavioural complexity are suggested by Boal and Hooijberg (2000) to have a positive association with absorptive capacity, capacity to change and 'managerial wisdom', although, interestingly, there appears to be no significant direct relationship between social or emotional intelligence and cognitive intelligence – IQ (Sternberg, 1985; Rosnow et al., 1994; Sternberg et al., 1995). Moreover, Boal and Hooijberg (2000) say that having a clear vision and charisma are moderators in this relationship: they strengthen it.

Boal and Hooijberg (2000) argue that cognitive intelligence and social (emotional) intelligence are particularly important at the highest levels in organizations. Top-level leaders who display higher levels of cognitive and social or emotional intelligence and behavioural complexity anticipate environmental changes, e.g. deregulation, see trends more quickly, and start to reformulate their organizations' strategies ahead of the competition. Visioning and strategy development usually take place in a group environment, except perhaps in some owner-managed small enterprises (Johnson, 1998). The dynamics need to be understood. For example, individuals may behave in a way that is cognitively dissonant to maintain membership of the group.

An integrative, holistic model of leadership

From the previous sections, we can see therefore that effective leadership entails the following defining functions:

Vision and mission. Effective leaders define and communicate a meaningful and attractive vision of the future and a mission or purpose through which the organization will pursue it.

Shared values. Effective leaders identify, display and reinforce values that support the vision and mission and that followers share.

Strategy. Effective leaders develop, get commitment to, and ensure the implementation of rational strategies that enable people to pursue the vision and mission and that reflect the values they share.

Empowerment. Effective leaders empower people to be *able to do* what needs to be done.
Influence, motivation and inspiration. Effective leaders influence, motivate and inspire people to *want to do* what needs to be done.

The new model of leadership is an attempt to bring together scholarly research findings, the findings of leadership surveys, what organizations have found to describe best practice, lessons from the arts, and theoretical speculation. Each of the elements and processes in the model is discussed in detail in the chapters that follow. But first I consider further evidence, not quoted so far, that supports the model.

Robert Kreitner and Angelo Kinicki (1998) identify vision, values and empowerment as the new leadership paradigm:

> **Traditional organizations and the associated organizational behaviors they created have outlived their usefulness. Management must seriously question and challenge the ways of thinking that worked in the past if they want to create a learning organization. For example, the old management paradigm of planning, organizing and control might be replaced with one of vision, values, and empowerment.**

In their studies, Arthur Yeung and Douglas Ready (1995) found that expressing 'tangible vision, values and strategy' ranks in the top three globally valued leadership capabilities. And according to a survey by The Manufacturing Foundation (2003), successful middle-market manufacturing firms in the UK[32] are characterized by visionary and inspirational leadership, a clear strategic direction, a supportive corporate culture, and employees who are empowered to make decisions and act. Moreover, the '100 Best Companies to Work for in America' (Levering and Moskowitz, 1993) have three common characteristics: an explicit mission or purpose, a strategy for achieving that purpose, and cultural elements that support the mission and strategy (Lipton, 1996). And one highly successful company chairman and CEO who supports vision, values and strategy as key to shareholder value is William W. George of Medtronic, Inc., one of the world's leading medical technology companies, based in Minneapolis. He says:

> **The best path to long-term growth in shareholder value comes from having a well-articulated mission that employees are willing to commit to, a consistently practiced set of values, and a clear business strategy that is adaptable to changing business conditions. (George, 2001)**

Probably the models closest to mine are Kotter's and Kouzes and Posner's. Kotter (1990a) says that leadership concerns the following:

- Setting a direction
- Developing a vision of the future and expressing it in terms of the values of the followers
- Developing strategies for achieving the vision in a participative way
- Aligning people (obtaining their commitment to the pursuit of the vision)
- Motivating and inspiring people

In later writing, Kotter says that leadership is about empowering other people, and that there may be unusually capable people at the top but that their effectiveness is based on communicating 'their visions and strategies broadly … [obtaining] understanding and commitment … [motivating] large numbers of their middle managers … [and building] coalitions' (Kotter and Heskett, 1992).

James Kouzes and Barry Posner (1995) see leadership as:

- Inspiring a shared vision
- Enabling others to act
- Modelling the way
- Encouraging the 'heart'

The Burke–Litwin model proposes that individual and organizational performance are a function in part of mission, strategy, culture, individual knowledge and skills (an element of empowerment), and motivation – the key idea in Burke and Litwin's concept of leadership (Burke and Litwin, 1989; 1992). They define individual and organizational performance in terms of productivity, customer satisfaction, self-satisfaction, profit and quality. Fred Cannon's modified model, resulting from an empirical study of 462 managers at all levels in one financial services organization, proposes that leadership is a function of personal and professional qualities, the creation of vision, building and sustaining commitment, and ensuring execution, with strategy and culture as two situational or contextual factors (Cannon, 2004).

Zaccaro and Banks (2001: 181) suggest that most models of leader effectiveness specify setting the direction – defining the organizational purpose and a vision of the future as 'a direction for collective action' – as a central role of organizational leaders. It also entails 'facilitating or enabling' people to achieve it, according to Zaccaro and Klimoski (2001: 6–7), and this is done 'through mission, vision, strategy, goals, plans, and tasks'. They suggest that, in addition to the 'social or interpersonal influence processes … cognitive processes [are] equally critical to leader effectiveness', for example interpreting environmental demands and strategic thinking. The role of top-level organizational leaders is to align the organization and its environment (Lawrence and Lorsch, 1967; Thompson, 1967; Wortman, 1982; Bourgeois, 1985). This entails making sure that strategic choices and their implementation are effective.

Support for the model of leadership described in this book comes not only from the academic literature but also from real-life case examples, such as British Sugar and BAT.

CASE EXAMPLE

British Sugar's Leadership Competency Model[33]

British Sugar's 'leadership competencies' were developed through interviews with managers and board members and testing the conclusions with wider audiences. Behavioural statements were generated, together with specific descriptors. The focus was business challenges and opportunities in the future and associated leadership behaviours. British Sugar's leadership competency model proposes three competency dimensions that reflect vision, values, strategy, empowerment and motivation:

- *Understanding people:* winning their 'hearts' by winning their trust, respect and confidence in us as a leader, by making them feel wanted, valued, listened to and involved, and by giving them pride in their job, in [the company] and most importantly in themselves. Key elements in understanding people are building relationships, flexibility of style, integrity, motivating others, developing others, tenacity, providing direction, interpersonal sensitivity, empowering people, and teamwork.
- *Business thinking:* winning people's 'minds' by understanding and clarifying the business challenges that face them and [the company], and by enabling them and ourselves to improve our business knowledge and skills to perform to the highest level of our ability in handling these changes. Key elements are strategic thinking, cross-functional awareness, technical skills, information gathering, judgement, problem solving, and innovation.
- *Understanding yourself:* first learning to lead ourselves, before we earn the right to lead others, by knowing and controlling ourselves first and increasing our knowledge of how others see us, against what is expected from us as a business leader. Key elements in understanding oneself are self-awareness, self-motivation, drive and energy, communication skills, decisiveness, impact, and self-confidence.

CASE EXAMPLE

British American Tobacco's Leadership Model [34]

BAT (British-American Tobacco) defines effective leaders as having a clear vision for the business, aligning, energizing and enabling those around them, fostering innovation, and contributing to building a global enterprise. Effective leaders foster an open, confident culture that encourages change and innovation and is shaped by the Guiding Principles ('Enterprising Spirit, Open Minded, Freedom through Responsibility and Strength from Diversity') and they inspire people to perform and enjoy. They develop a learning culture by building the capabilities of the organization and people, with a focus on coaching.

Having followed Montaigne's approach in providing the string that holds the flowers together, let us now consider the flower arrangement. The next chapter considers the first (and fundamental) characteristic of leadership: having and communicating a vision and mission.

Further reading

Robert Cooper and Ayman Sawaf (1997), *Executive EQ*. London: Orion Business.

Viktor E. Frankl (1984), *Man's Search for Meaning, 3rd Edition.* New York: Simon & Schuster.

Howard Gardner (1993), *Frames of Mind: The Theory of Multiple Intelligences.* New York: Basic Books.

Daniel Goleman (1995), *Emotional Intelligence.* New York: Bantam Books.

Daniel Goleman (1998), *Working with Emotional Intelligence.* London: Bloomsbury.

Charles Handy (1997), *The Hungry Spirit: Beyond Capitalism – A Quest for Purpose in the Modern World.* London: Hutchinson.

Malcolm Higgs and Victor Dulewicz (2002), *Making Sense of Emotional Intelligence, 2nd Edition.* London: ASE.

James Kouzes and Barry Z. Posner (2002), *The Leadership Challenge, 3rd Edition.* San Francisco, CA: Jossey-Bass.

R.S. Moxley (2000), *Leadership and Spirit.* San Francisco, CA: Jossey-Bass.

Martha C. Nussbaum (2001), *Upheavals of Thought: The Intelligence of Emotions.* Cambridge: Cambridge University Press.

R.E. Riggio, S.E. Murphy and F.J. Pirozzolo (Editors) (2002) (*Multiple Intelligences and Leadership*. Mahwah, NJ: Erlbaum.

Robert J. Sternberg (1996), *Successful Intelligence.* New York: Simon and Schuster.

Danah Zohar and Ian Marshall (2000), *Spiritual Intelligence: The Ultimate Intelligence.* London: Bloomsbury.

Danah Zohar and Ian Marshall (2004), *Spiritual Capital: Wealth We Can Live By.* San Francisco, CA: Berrett-Koehler.

Discussion questions

1 Do you think it is possible to create a single inclusive and holistic model of leadership?
2 How important is the intellectual or cognitive dimension of leadership in relation to the other dimensions?
3 What is the relationship between the emotional and spiritual dimensions of leadership?
4 How does the use of personal power show itself in the behaviour of effective leaders?

4 Leadership, Vision and Mission

Without vision, a people perish.

Proverbs, 29:18

Overview

- The proposition of this chapter is that effective leaders define and communicate a meaningful and attractive vision of the future and a mission or purpose through which the group or organization will pursue it.
- A vision is a statement of what or where you want to be. It represents 'true north', and a vision statement is your compass. Vision is the basis for effective leadership and the driving force for organizational change.
- Having a vision that is brief, clear, valid and desirable, contains relevant imagery, and is communicated and implemented in everyday actions and behaviour makes a vital difference to organizational performance.
- While entrepreneurs usually have a vision already, creating a vision should be a participative process, concluding with a vision that all stakeholders share.
- Effective leaders ensure that people understand and are committed to the vision throughout the organization.
- Clear vision without effective emotional, spiritual and behavioural leadership is impotent. Effective leadership ensures the vision is translated into reality.
- The organization's mission flows from the vision (though sometimes a vision comes afterwards) and provides its identity. It describes its purpose, distinctiveness, intended products or services and markets, and usually its core values.
- Mission statements need to be short enough to be memorized and generic enough to encompass likely developments in the organization's business environment.

So does an organization. Without a common vision, an organization flounders, 'rudderless in a sea of conflicting demands, contradictory data, and environmental uncertainty' (Sashkin, 1986).

Vision and mission statements are used by 70% of respondents' organizations, according to a 2001 survey of 451 senior executives by management consultants Bain &

Company (Rigby, 2001). Their main benefit is that they help to integrate effort throughout an organization. And a survey of 250 senior and middle-level managers in the UK revealed a similar usage: 73% of their companies have a vision, while 14% were unsure (The Leadership Trust, 2002). In those companies with a vision, however, while over 90% of managers said it was coherent, consistent and well understood, only 42% saw their companies as fully on track in pursuing the vision.

Less than one-third of employees say that management provides clear goals and direction, according to a Harris study; yet most CEOs in a survey of 164 large companies in the UK said they could not afford the time to communicate with their employees (Quirke, 2002). Bill Quirke, a communications consultant, emphasizes the need for employees to understand the company mission for strategies to succeed, and they need to know not only *what* but also *why*. While most companies have vision, mission or strategy statements, however, in less than 10% are they understood even by middle management and employees, according to another survey (Creelman, 1996).

A study of top teams in telecommunications, airlines, computer software and manufacturing in the United States by HayGroup found that they frequently do not have a common vision of what they are trying to achieve (Maitland, 2001a). For example, when asked to write down the team's number one priority, the 10 members of the top team in an oil refining business listed several different ones, relating to safety, cost cutting, environmental compliance and new markets. The chief executive's priority was to reduce refining costs. The risk in a lack of common vision is 'a potentially dangerous situation where each member promotes his or her own agenda'. It is generally recognized that people in successful organizations have a shared view of the future that stretches the organization beyond its current capabilities (Middleton and Gorzynski, 2002: 105). A shared vision creates alignment. Peter Senge (1990) puts it this way:

> In a corporation, a shared vision changes people's relationship with the company. It is no longer 'their company'; it becomes 'our company'. A shared vision is the first step in allowing people who mistrusted each other to begin to work together. It creates a common identity.

The British government identified leadership as key to meeting the challenges of change in the public services (PIU, 2001). But change in the public sector must start with a political vision:

> The Government has to present a clear picture...of the kind of society it [wants] from its reforms and stop being seen as a 'value-free zone', says [former] health secretary Alan Milburn... . Prime minister Tony Blair responds: '[New Labour] needs to rediscover its political vision...building a Britain of opportunity for all'. (Waugh and Morris, 2002)

The Chartered Management Institute survey of 1,900 managers in the UK's public sector found that vision is the most sought-after feature of leadership and engaging employees with the vision is one of the top three skills expected of leaders (CMI, 2003).[35] The CMI report includes a telling quotation from one borough council (local government) manager:

> We are suffering the syndrome of jumping on every latest bandwagon, often with no clear sense of direction as to where the next journey will take us.

What is vision?

Vision, according to the *Concise Oxford English Dictionary*, is 'a mental image of what the future will or could be like'; it involves 'the ability to think about or plan the future with imagination or wisdom'.[36] Vision defines what or where the organization wants or needs to be. For example, First Quench Retailing, a drinks retailer that is one of the UK's '100 Visionary Companies': to be 'an enjoyment and celebration company' (Management Today, 2001). And in 1990, General Electric's then CEO, Jack Welch, promoted the following vision:

> **Our dream for the 1990s is a boundaryless company...where we knock down the walls that separate us from each other on the inside and from our key constituents on the outside. (Crainer, 1996)**

In the UK's higher education sector, the University of Strathclyde's vision is still, more than 200 years since the University's founding by John Anderson, driven by his vision of the University as 'a place of useful learning', recently amended to '*The* place of useful learning':

> **The University of Strathclyde aspires to be a dynamic top-ranking European university dedicated to excellence through its core mission of promoting useful learning.[37]**

Zaccaro and Banks (2001: 184–185) give two pages of definitions of what visions are. They identify what is common among the many definitions:

- 'Visions provide an idealized representation of what the organization should become.' For example, McDonald's wants to be 'the world's best quick service restaurant experience' – 'consistently satisfying customers better than anyone else through outstanding quality, service, cleanliness, and value'.[38]
- Visions relate to a longer time span than strategies do. Visions may have a time span of three to twenty years, while strategies typically last for one to five years (Kotter, 1990b).
- Visions reflect values – preferences – and in that respect do not change (Conger and Kanungo, 1987). In this sense visions may be ideological and expressed in moral terms (Shamir et al., 1993; Kirkpatrick and Locke, 1996). However, environmental factors dictate how they are translated into strategies.
- Visions are symbols of change for harnessing the collective effort of organizational members. They are means of giving meaning to work and inspiring people (Shamir et al., 1993).

Both findings from academic research and the practical experience of business leaders suggest that a clear vision is essential to the survival and success of an organization (Harvey-Jones, 1988: 18–19; Kotter, 1995a; Kakabadse, 2001). Covey (1992: 96) says that vision provides a 'compass' for everybody in the organization. And Kouzes and Posner (1991: 135) say, 'Vision [is] the magnetic north.'

A vision has to be aligned to the needs and expectations of the organization's stakeholders. Where strongly held personal visions are not aligned, individuals will resort to political means to pursue their own. This will leave the organization without a sense of direction and less capable of responding to the need for change (Van der Heijden, 1993: 142). Positioning the organization for change is key to the leadership role (Flanagan, 2000).

The effective articulation of a viable vision is related to organizational performance (Kirkpatrick and Locke, 1996; Lowe et al., 1996), implicit conceptions of leadership (Den Hartog et al., 1999) and effective group interaction (Sosik et al., 1999; Parry and Proctor-Thompson, 2001). Jill Strange and Michael Mumford (2002), in reviewing vision studies, concluded that vision serves five purposes:

- Specifying direction, purpose and uniqueness of a venture
- Providing a motivational force by organizing action around an evocative future goal
- Providing a sense of identity and meaning for work
- Enabling coordination and integration of activities by providing a framework for action
- Providing a basis for developing organizational norms and structures as a result of the prescriptive beliefs embedded in it

John Kotter (1997b) makes the point that, for organizational change, only an approach based on vision works in the long term. He says a shared vision:

- Clarifies the direction of change and ensures that everything that is done – new product development, acquisitions, recruitment campaigns – is in line with it
- Motivates people to take action in the right direction, even though the initial steps in the change process may be painful to some individuals
- Helps to align individuals and coordinate their actions efficiently

Vision is not the preserve of top management only, but a feature of effective leadership at any level, in any function, in an organization. The specific nature and content of visions will vary at different levels in any organization. The top-level leader defines a broad, long-term (and often ambiguous) vision and translates it into specific organizational strategies. The middle-level leader translates the organizational vision into a departmental vision or goals and more short-term strategies. And the lower-level leader in turn translates these goals and strategies into more short-term goals and operational plans and tasks (Kotter, 1990b; Kelly, 1993). As we move down the organization, vision and goals change from the abstract to the concrete, from the long term – from years, even decades – to the short term – monthly, weekly and daily (Jacobs and Jaques, 1990, 1991; Zaccaro, 1996). In this respect top-level leaders set the stage; lower-level leaders are the actors. Crucially, however, the multiplicity of visions throughout the organization must support the overall view of the future.

Vision without mission, however, is moribund. To be effective, vision has to be translated into a mission – a purpose – for the organization and then into specific goals or objectives and action plans. We consider the relationship between vision and mission later in this chapter. Deetz et al. (2000: 73) say:

> **Visioning is essential to creating the norms, mission, and rules of an organization, components that make up the organization's formally espoused goals... . Vision [is] an organizational *ideal*.**

So if vision is an ideal, what is a useful vision?

What is a useful vision?

A vision is a statement of the aspirations or desired future of a group, organization or nation. Good leaders communicate an appealing vision of the future. Several examples come from the world of politics and government:

- General Charles de Gaulle's vision of France as a front-rank nation in the vanguard of progress
- Russian president Vladimir Putin's vision of Russia as 'a full-fledged part of Europe, taking its rightful place alongside Germany, France, and Britain' (Starobin, 2002)
- Former prime minister Lee Kuan Yew's 1984 vision of Singapore as 'the Switzerland of the East by 1999'
- Former prime minister Mohamed Mahathir's 'Vision 2020' for Malaysia: that Malaysia would be a fully developed nation according to OECD criteria by 2020

Leadership research shows that having a vision that is brief, clear, valid and desirable, contains relevant imagery, and is communicated and implemented in everyday actions and behaviour makes a vital difference to organizational performance and often, indeed, society. An example is Henry Ford's vision of 'a car for the great multitude [the Model T Ford introduced in 1908] ... so low in price that no man will be unable to afford one'. Ford's vision led to a mass market for cars and the invention of the dealer franchise system for selling and servicing them (Friedman, 2001).

The research literature suggests as important several particular attributes of vision, the imagery of the vision content and the way the vision is communicated. Ruth Tait's series of interviews with 18 business leaders found that vision, the foundation of effective leadership, should preferably be conceptualized and expressed in simple terms (Tait, 1996). She quotes one of the participants in the study, Gerry Robinson, then chief executive of Granada, as saying:

> **There is a tendency to think of vision as something rather sophisticated and complex but actually most visions are terribly simple... . You do have a vision as to what it is you are trying to do, at both a personal level and at a corporate level. It is very important to be very clear, very repetitive, very simple about that. It is essential that people know what success is.**

Tom Peters (1987) says a good vision is challenging, effective and inspiring, quoting Steve Jobs, who wanted to revolutionize the way people process information, think and deal with the world. In probably the only such study, Robert Baum et al. (1998) investigated entrepreneurial firms and their growth (sales, employment and profit) over two years in relation to the attributes and content of their visions and the way their visions were communicated. The criteria they used were brevity, clarity, abstractness, challenge, future orientation, stability and desirability or ability to inspire. The visions they found were various mixtures of mission, strategy, values and goals: the particular mixture seems to be the way that a particular leader creates a guide to future action. They discovered several relationships between vision and growth:

- Those firms with a vision grew significantly more than those without one.
- The brevity, clarity and desirability of the vision are particularly important.
- Imagery of growth in the vision statement is related to actual growth. For example, in one firm, wanting to be 'known nationally as the manufacturer of leading-edge, highly technical and deeply designed artistic architectural woodwork' was related to actual growth in the firm.
- Communicating the vision effectively entails oral, written and non-verbal means – dramatic gestures, role modelling, and the way the firm selects, trains and rewards employees. Simply having and communicating a vision is not enough: leaders must show that they are pursuing the vision in their actions and behaviour.

Organization growth is clearly associated with the characteristics of the vision, its content and the extent to which it was communicated to employees. In other studies visionary leadership behaviour is associated with enhanced individual performance, trust and satisfaction among subordinates and with business unit performance (Hater and Bass, 1988; Podsakoff et al., 1990; Howell and Avolio, 1993; Yammarino et al., 1993).

Having a vision, however, even an emotionally appealing one, is not enough. The vision must make sense – it must be intelligent. And it must be based on imagination or wisdom. Visions likely to enhance organizational performance, according to Paul Nutt and Robert Backoff (1997), have several features:

1 They offer new possibilities: they are 'innovative ... unique, vibrant ... inspirational, and ... offer a new order'
2 They are desirable, '[drawing] upon the organization's values and culture, and [connecting] the possibilities to these values'
3 They are actionable, '[pointing] to activities that people can undertake to move towards a desirable future'
4 They can be articulated using powerful imagery representing what people want

Gary Hamel and C.K. Prahalad (1994) argue that a compelling and engaging vision necessarily includes a focus on the 'top as well as the bottom line'. They argue that innovation for revenue growth is the critical success factor. This is significant in the light of the growing attention since the 1980s to cost reduction as a strategy for achieving greater performance and competitiveness.

Visions are not merely goals, according to Bert Nanus (1992): visions must have an explicit ethical or moral component to them. Lindsay Levin, CEO of the Whites Group, says they must at least be in line with values (Levin, 2000). Such visions, for example, often concern improving the quality of life. Vision may even be expressed in terms of values. Kees Van der Heijden (1993: 137–150) quotes the example of Levi Strauss: 'To be a company that our people are proud of'. Zaccaro and Banks (2001: 188) suggest that the ethical and moral aspects are perhaps the most important features of a vision. Shamir (1995) shows how a vision is most effective when it is congruent with followers' personal values. Subordinates or followers judge vision in terms of what is 'good' and 'right'. And values, because they create passion and conviction about the vision, are central to it (Senge, 1990). Effective visions reflect values that are associated with an aspiration for growth and change.

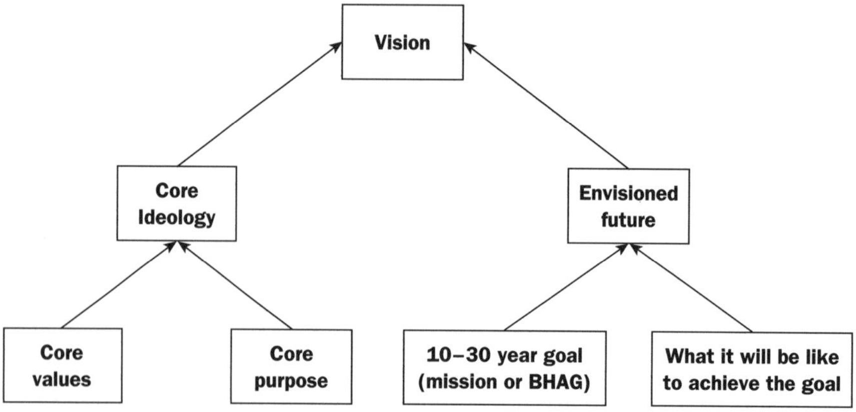

Figure 4.1 *Collins and Porras's components of vision*

A six-year study at Stanford Graduate School of Business by Collins and Porras (1996a) compared 18 successful and long-lived companies that had all outperformed the stock market between 1925 and 1975 by 12 times. These companies included Hewlett-Packard, 3M, Johnson & Johnson, Procter & Gamble, Merck, Sony, Motorola and Nordstrom, and they were compared with 18 of their major competitors. Collins and Porras found that successful companies have a core ideology – core values and a core purpose – and a vivid vision of the future 10 to 30 years ahead – a 'BHAG' (a 'Big, Hairy, Audacious Goal'). Figure 4.1 shows Collins and Porras's components of vision.

Collins and Porras (1996b) define core ideology as:

> **what we stand for and why we exist...the enduring character of an organization...a consistent identity that transcends product or market life cycles, technological breakthroughs, management fads, and individual leaders.**

Their 'envisioned future' is 'what we aspire to become, to achieve, to create'. Core values are a system of 'timeless' guiding principles and tenets. And core purpose (mission) is 'the organization's most fundamental reason for existence'.

Work Systems Associates (1996: 30), a management consulting firm, defines a meaningful vision as one that has direction, clarity and emotional appeal. I.M. Levin (2000) says it should be future oriented, compelling, bold, aspiring and inspiring, yet believable and achievable. According to Kotter (1997b), a good vision has six characteristics. It is:

- Imaginable – conveying a picture of what the future will look like
- Desirable – appealing to the long-term interests of all stakeholders
- Feasible – realistic and attainable
- Focused – clear enough to provide guidance in making decisions
- Flexible – allowing individual initiative and differing responses in the light of changing conditions
- Communicable – easy to communicate (and able to be explained within five minutes)

Kotter (1988) says that vision must also meet the needs of the organization's stakeholders – shareholders, employees and customers – and it must be easily translated into strategies that improve its competitiveness in its industry. One reason for the failure of so many dotcom companies, Internet guru Patricia Seybold says, is their lack of vision in how they can competitively deliver market needs (Maruca, 2000). Deetz et al. (2000: 53) say that 'A strong long-term vision gives cohesion to the work of an organization.' Without it, initiatives like TQM, BPR, quality circles, benchmarking and the like become ineffectual fads.

How specific should visions be? According to Gregory Dess and Joseph Picken (2000):

> **The most powerful visions are clear about the direction and objectives and proactive in approach, but deliberately vague about the means – leaving room for flexibility in developing viable strategic options and solving complex problems.**

David Butcher and Mike Meldrum (2001) point out that visions sometimes can be 'short-lived, misguided and even embarrassing once the world has moved on', as with British Airways' self-image as 'the world's favourite airline' – at the time 'a label at odds with its poor results and sustained adverse publicity'.

Visions must be communicated not only to employees but also to other stakeholders, and they frequently refer to them. Sally Lansdell (2002: 43) says they must also be backed up by action that is consistent if they are not to invoke distrust. She describes how in February 2000 CEO Matthew Barrett of UK-based Barclays Bank described his vision of 'superiority in the range of products, services, and value propositions available to customers'. This was badly received by customers of small village branches, 171 of which were to be closed within two months, causing hardship to them. And the City does not like false promises contained within vision or mission statements, as a sliding share price reflecting Rentokil's unfulfilled goal of a 20% annual increase in profits illustrated (*Guardian*, 2000).

Creating the vision

Eleanor Roosevelt is reputed to have said, 'The future belongs to those who believe in the beauty of their dreams.' And a Nepalese Buddhist mantra says 'Never laugh at anybody's dreams. People who don't have dreams don't have much.' A vision starts with a dream. Greenleaf (1991) says:

> **Not much happens without a dream. And for something great to happen, there must be a big dream. Behind every great achievement is a dreamer of great dreams. Much more than a dreamer is required to bring it to reality; but the dream must be there first.**

Sal Marino (1999), a columnist with *Industry Week*, takes up this theme:

> **Dreaming things that never were is not a science. It's an art practiced by visionaries who manage by faith instead of by formula. They are driven by an unquestioning belief that the lessons of the past will inevitably invent the successes of the future. They see visions where others see vacuums. They say 'We can' when others say 'We can't'.**

John Middleton and Bob Gorzynski (2002: 106) say:

> **Vision is deeply paradoxical. It is partly mystical, partly common sense. It is sometimes a picture of the future, sometimes a feeling. It is sometimes fully-formed, often not. But it is almost always the ability to see things differently or to integrate disparate and seemingly unrelated information in new ways. Sometimes it is merely asking questions that others cannot or will not ask. As John F. Kennedy put it: 'Some people see things and ask "Why?" I see things and ask "Why not?"'**

The most effective leaders spend some 20% of their time in creating a vision for the future, according to a survey of 7,500 chairmen, CEOs and directors of large and medium-sized companies by Andrew Kakabadse and Nana Kakabadse (1996). They quote Bernard Le Bargy, human resources director at Vickers, as saying that such work by the top team was necessary for the radical refocusing of the company. And Margaret Coles (1998) quotes Chris Rodriguez, CEO of Bradford & Bingley Building Society, as saying:

> **the process of creating a vision is a combination of listening a lot, getting creative input from a wide variety of people and then thinking hard.**

Colin Sharman, global partner of KPMG management consultants, goes farther: he suggests that 40% of the time should be spent on vision (Coles, 1998).

The poet David Whyte (1997) says, 'If you can see more than one step ahead of you, it is not your path.' The path well trod is not one's unique way. 'Effective leaders go against the grain,' says Jo Owen (2002). What makes the difference, she says, is being 'unreasonable' – having a vision and goals that are not based on reason and logic alone, that are based on translating dreams into reality, that involve taking risks, that stretch the organization and that make a huge difference, and whose promulgators are remembered for it. Examples she gives are Sir Richard Branson's taking on British Airways, US president Kennedy's vision of putting a man on the moon by the end of the decade, CNN's creation of 24-hour news, and Dell's displacement of Apple and Compaq. She reminds us of Henry Kissinger's definition of leadership as 'the art of taking people where they would not have gone by themselves'.

The two main roles of the founder of a company, according to Edgar Schein (1991), are creating a vision – the critical step – that leads to strategies and creating an organizational culture that reflects the founder's philosophy. The individual entrepreneur personally decides the vision and takes the risk of failure, though in large, mature organizations the management team shares decision making and creates a shared vision through 'strategic conversation' (Van der Heijden, 1993: 137–139).

A vision is the driving force for strategy formation. For the individual entrepreneur this is personal, Van der Heijden (1993: 137–150) says, but in a management team the driving force is a shared vision. He says, '[The] shared vision [is] arrived at through communicating and modifying personal views in the team through a conversational process.' 'Visions,' he says, 'tend to be tacit, taken for granted … seldom made explicit … [operating] in the background.' Andrew Kakabadse (2001) says that:

> **Effective visioning requires a willingness to consider all the options and to share information that is needed to develop them. It also demands that staff commit to a plan**

of action that is in the best interests of the organisation...[it] is not a managerial fad...but a fundamental element of best practice for senior executive teams. It provides an effective organisational force, a binding cohesion, initially at senior management levels, but then throughout the organisation, guiding and motivating people's actions.

A useful vision contains an entrepreneurial idea, and strategic vision is a view of an organization's future 'in terms of a business idea, size, scope or success formula ... that will indicate direction for action' (Van der Heijden, 1993: 140).

Some outstanding leaders do sense opportunity, create a new vision, communicate it in an inspiring way, build trust in it, and achieve the vision through empowering people. As a result they are often perceived as charismatic (Conger, 1989). The vision challenges the status quo, addresses followers' personal aspirations and often involves the leader in taking a risk. It can be argued, therefore, that entrepreneurs, to be successful, *must* be effective leaders.

Vision must have intellectual acceptance among followers: it must make sense in being challenging but also achievable (Handy, 1992a). The term 'followers' implies not only subordinates or employees, but all stakeholders – investors, suppliers and customers too. In fact one can argue that, in one sense, they are also part of the organization.

Most people in a company expect the CEO to have a personal vision of where it should be going, but John Harvey-Jones (1988: 26) believes this vision needs much discussion and consideration of the processes required to get there. This is essential to getting commitment to the vision. He says:

I do not believe in the myth of the great leader who can suddenly engender in his people a vision and lead them to an entirely new world. I believe that the reality is more traumatic and more demanding. (Harvey-Jones, 1988: 97)

Van der Heijden (1993: 146) says, 'The vision needs to have the power to convince people that the proposed future is not a "pipe-dream", that a feasible process can be envisaged which will cause its realisation.' Arriving at such a vision entails discussing the following:

- The business environment, particularly developments in society and new ideas
- Definition of the business and areas for exploitation
- The distinctive competencies and resources that now exist in the organization or can be developed
- The constraints to imitation by other organizations and making the organization's distinctive competencies and resources sustainable
- The feasible path from the present to the future situation by which new distinctiveness can be developed from existing distinctiveness – the 'formula for success' (Van der Heijden, 1993: 149)

Keith Denton (2001) describes how senior and middle-level managers in a medical centre in the United States had many and varied visions of its future. They had common threads, but there was no common vision. There will usually be several competing entrepreneurial visions in an organization. The foregoing considerations provide a process – and objective and rational criteria – for convergence towards a common understanding and, thereby, organizational learning and progress.

Visions emerge from two sources, according to Zaccaro and Banks (2001: 190– 191): from 'sense-making and consensus-seeking and [consensus]–making processes' and from the values of the top-level executive. Visions may result from interpreting the misalignment between the organization and its environment and the need for organizational change and negotiation among the top-level team (Robbins and Duncan, 1988: 229). Zaccaro and Banks (2001: 192) suggest that the influence of visionary leaders:

> **resides not in their environmental analysis or negotiation skill but rather in the values they seek to propagate through organizational change.**

Andrew Dubrin (2001) suggests several sources as a basis for creating a vision: annual reports, management books and magazines, group discussions (with both work colleagues and friends), the work of futurists, and not least one's own intuition. Creating a vision can be viewed as an entrepreneurial activity involving imagination, perception, analysis, interpretation and synthesis. Vision may be formulated rationally (Bennis and Nanus, 1985) and intuitively (Kouzes and Posner, 1987). It requires both reflection and intuition, both insight and foresight. It is an intellectual activity, and its outcome requires validity in the minds of followers.

In forming a vision, Richard Allen (1995) suggests several key questions should be considered:

1 What is our purpose?
2 What is our driving force?
3 What are our core values?
4 What do we do best?
5 What do we want to accomplish?
6 What do we want to change?

Thomas Bateman et al. (2002) provide a useful taxonomy of goal content and goal hierarchy for top-level leaders in business organizations that could be used in the visioning process. And Monica McCaffrey and Larry Reynolds (2003) describe a useful workshop approach to creating a vision using a facilitator, described in the following case example.

CASE EXAMPLE

McCaffrey and Reynolds' Approach to Creating a Vision

This approach consists of several phases: setting the scene, taking stock, scenario planning, agreeing the vision and taking action.

1 Setting the scene.
   (a) Clarify the purpose of the process.
   (b) Ask participants what they find both enjoyable and frustrating about their jobs, which may imply the kind of vision that would be exciting.

2 Taking stock produces a picture of where the organization is at present.
   (a) Participants in small groups identify and report positive and negative features of the organization under several headings, for example customers, competitors (or, in the absence of competitors, regulatory or political matters), people (employees) and processes (organization and systems).
   (b) Based on the feedback, participants then are asked to say where they would like to see the organization going.
3 Scenario planning, whereby a range of possible futures is identified, with implications for action now (explained in Chapter 6).
   (a) Small groups use a PESTLE framework (see Chapter 6), including customers, competitors and demographics, to identify political, economic, social, technological, legal and ecological forces that could lead to change for the organization. Different groups focus on optimistic, pessimistic, status quo and 'wild card' scenarios (whereby a group imagines an unpredictable event that would have huge consequences for the organization).
   (b) Based on the groups' reports, implications for action are discussed for each scenario.
4 Agreeing the vision.
   (a) Each small group creates a vision in words or pictures and then presents it to all participants.
   (b) The whole group discusses each vision's merits and demerits and identifies the common themes of all the visions.
   (c) A single vision statement is created through rewriting until it meets with a consensus.
5 Taking action. This involves discussing:
   (a) How and when the vision will be communicated.
   (b) What needs to be done to create strategies to pursue the vision and turn it into reality.

Writers on leadership usually attribute *creating* a vision to leadership (Bennis and Nanus, 1985; Kotter, 1990b; Tichy and Devanna, 1990; Kirkpatrick and Locke, 1991; Kotter, 1996). Effective leaders invariably communicate vision in an inspiring way, whether they create it or not. But many business and political leaders do not create the vision they communicate. For example, it was Karl Marx's vision that underpinned the leadership of Lenin and Stalin in the former Soviet Union (Edwards, 2000). Jan Carlzon's vision, to turn Scandinavian Airlines into the best airline in the world for the business traveller, was not original in the sense that it was based on common knowledge in the airline industry (Kotter, 1988).

Typically a board of directors works together to produce a vision, and the chief executive communicates it to the rest of the organization. But visionary thinking is not the exclusive province of the CEO or even the board. Dess and Picken (2000) say:

> **Broad participation in the formulation of a strategic vision offers multiple perspectives and encourages commitment.**

They quote the case of Sears' dramatic transformation after 1994 when 120 of the firm's senior executives formed task forces and came up with the vision for Sears: to be 'a compelling place to shop, work, and invest'. And Jim Renier, former CEO of Honeywell, says that, while the vision may be a single-minded CEO's, it often evolves through dialogue with others on possible desired future states:

> **What you've got to do is constantly engage in iterating what you say [about the vision] and what they say is possible. And over a couple of years the different visions come together. (Tichy and Devanna, 1986b)**

Robert House (1995) says leaders at any organizational level may formulate visions. Indeed every department or business unit should have its own vision. But such visions need to be framed within the context of the organizational vision. Involving people in the visioning process gathers people around a shared, common vision and achieves maximum commitment to it. Individual leaders who already have a vision have a more difficult task. Olivier (2001: 34) says that, if a group rejects a leader's vision, it is difficult to revisit it. The leader has to explain the reasoning behind the vision and the values that inform it. Values are the subject of the next chapter, and we will see how important it is for vision and leadership to reflect shared values in a group or organization.

Olivier uses the following exercise in helping individuals to create a vision:

1 Think about your experience and your core values. What do you really care about in your life? What kind of things, habits, people, behaviours, activities and situations do you tend to gravitate towards? And avoid or move away from? Answering these questions may yield some common themes not previously apparent.
2 Now think about times when you felt closest to inspiration and vision, and the times you felt farthest away from them. What was happening at those times, who was involved, what were you doing, and how did you feel? This process likewise should produce some signposts.

Olivier (2001: 40) suggests that, in creating a vision, 'It is politically intelligent to listen to those who have moved in the corridors of power longer than you.' In the case study on leadership and inspiration in Chapter 8, Shakespeare's *Henry V* is contemplating his vision of reuniting England and France. He speaks to his senior nobles and advisers, usually in private, asking: 'If I was to suggest going to France what would you think? Is it the kind of project you could support? If not, why not?' (Olivier, 2001: 41). Olivier says that it was only when Henry knew he had enough support for his vision that he went public. That was the start of shared ownership of the vision.

Lansdell (2002: 45–47) describes other ways of developing visions:

Pictorial vision statements. An abstract verbal statement is translated into a colourful image that communicates both the cognitive and emotional aspects of the vision. Small groups of three to six members, each representing a business function, meet for one hour with the CEO's liaison and an artist–facilitator. The artist–facilitator draws how group members see the business today and tomorrow and their role in it. The artist–facilitator later produces illustrations representing the patterns and issues arising in each group. These are used by the CEO and group of senior managers to create a single picture for the vision of the organization as a whole.

Storytelling. 'Storytelling is how we make sense', say Michael Lissack and Johan Roos (2000: 143–153): 'The power of a story is that it allows the listener to recreate an experience in their mind . . . . The power of storytelling helps us consolidate our experiences to make them available in the future, whether to ourselves or to others.' Steve Hoffmann of Agilent Technologies uses stories, such as the old Chinese proverb that parents can give their children two things: roots and wings (O'Brien, 2001). He tells his employees that, if they are working in the 'roots' area of the business, they can get ahead in their career because it is critical to the business; and that, if they are in the 'wings' area, they can do something new. He says he finds stories useful because they help to frame and simplify messages such as the organization's vision and its importance, and they are more memorable than slide presentations or speeches.

Peter Senge et al. (1994) say:

> **Visions which tap into an organization's deeper sense of purpose, and articulate specific goals that represent making that purpose real, have unique power to engender aspiration and commitment... . The content of a true shared vision cannot be dictated: it can only emerge from a coherent process of reflection and conversation.**

Communicating the vision

Effective leaders ensure that people understand and are committed to vision throughout the organization. Zaccaro and Banks (2001: 192–193) explain how communicating and implementing a vision for growth can make a crucial difference. Visions provide a frame of reference for both leaders and followers for the strategic direction of the organization. They provide 'a source of impassioned empowerment that motivates followers'. This comes from the values and ideology implicit in the vision. For example, according to Burns (1978: 97), effective leaders 'emphasize fundamental values such as beauty, order, honesty, dignity, and human rights'. The way that leaders articulate and communicate the vision may galvanize commitment to it.

Communicating a vision in a confident and attractive way and taking overt action to implement and pursue the vision are two core components that are common across current leadership theories. In fact vision is far more powerful than charisma or personality in its effects on the performance and attitudes of followers (Baum et al., 1998). The key is the link between the values expressed in the vision and the self-concepts of the followers (House and Shamir, 1993). The way vision is communicated determines whether and how much followers identify with it, their loyalty to it, and their motivation and efficacy to pursue it through strategic and tactical goals (House, 1977; Eden, 1984; Eden, 1990).

Failing to communicate a vision effectively is one of the main reasons for the failure of strategies to implement it – 'by a factor of 10 (or 100 or even 1,000)', says Kotter (1996). Top-level leaders are responsible for communicating the organizational vision and making sure all members of the organization understand it, are committed to it and implement it. Kouzes and Posner (1991: 124) say that communicating a vision:

> **isn't a one-way process; on the contrary, it's a process of engaging constituents in conversations about their lives, about their hopes and dreams… . Leadership isn't about imposing the leader's solo dream; it's about developing a *shared* sense of destiny… . A vision is *inclusive* of the constituents' aspirations; it's an ideal and unique image of the future for the *common* good.**

Lansdell (2002: 40) says it is not necessary to have a written vision. More important is the ability of a leader to explain the organization's vision 'in a compelling way in five minutes or less'. Otherwise it will be ineffective.

Having a vision, and even translating it into goals and strategies, is not enough. Effective leadership entails communicating it in a way that attracts followers. Marshall (1991: 35) suggests, perhaps controversially, that people do not follow visions: they follow leaders. Such leaders, he says, not only have the 'right' visions and goals that reflect the aspirations of people. They also effectively use persuasion and build relationships with their followers.

The vision must point the way forward. It must be sustainable. It must be exciting and fire the imagination. It must challenge people to participate in pursuing it. Timing in communicating a vision is of the essence in leadership. A premature vision may be rejected because it leaves too many questions unanswered. The leader's task is never accomplished until people own the vision for themselves. And communicating the vision does not stop there. Organizations go through good times and bad, and initiatives, promoted – and received – with enthusiasm, can fade away. The leader's role, therefore, as Marshall (1991: 40) says, 'is to continually reiterate, reinforce, clarify and redefine goals along the way'. As Deetz et al. (2000: 49) say, 'people respond to the vision they hear, not the one that was meant':

> **To be effective…a vision statement must be collaboratively constructed and 'owned' by members across organizational levels. Unless the vision is clearly communicated and integrated unto organizational practices, it is likely to have little effect…some of the world's premier organizations have turned a commitment to a strong vision into unparalleled success.**

Ways in which commitment to vision may be achieved, they say, include:

- Involving all stakeholders in creating it
- Linking vision explicitly to shared values or guiding principles, the work objectives of all groups and individuals to create alignment, criteria for performance appraisal and improvement, and reinforcing individuals' behaviour that relates to it

- Using inspirational language to communicate it and constant repetition in team briefings and workshops, supported by brochures or booklets, Internet dissemination, 'road shows', videos with the CEO talking about the vision, and a vision jingle or song
- Surveys on employees' understanding of the vision and their attitudes to it, with remedial action where necessary

The importance of communicating the vision passionately is clear:

> **You have got to know where you are going, to be able to state it clearly and concisely – and you have to care about it passionately. That all adds up to vision, the concise statement/picture of where the company and its people are heading, and why they should be proud of it...The issue here...is not...the substance of the vision, but the importance of having one, *per se*, and the importance of communicating it consistently and with fervor. (Peters and Austin, 1985: 284)**

It is one thing to formulate a vision but quite another to communicate it in a way that gains people's commitment to it and their everyday action on it (Deetz et al., 2000: 73). This requires *framing* the vision. Framing entails aligning people's understanding with what is meant through the use of language, for example metaphors. We return to this theme – communicating in an inspiring way – in Chapter 8.

Gail Fairhurst and Robert Sarr (1996) describe how one company framed the mission using metaphor. The public affairs team came up with a three-fold mission statement for their department: to disseminate corporate information; to communicate responsibly with the public; and to engage in more dialogue with the public through membership of stakeholder organizations. Each of these elements was regarded as equal in importance and interdependent in carrying out the overall mission of winning public trust. Thus was born the metaphor of a three-legged stool for their mission.

Storytelling is also a way of communicating the vision, Beverly Kaye and Betsy Jacobson (1999) say, essentially comprises the following parts: telling the story, understanding of the implicit metaphor by the listeners, and the creation of shared meaning. Stories tap into both the intellect and the emotions and help people to understand in relevant and meaningful ways when stories are vivid and memorable. And they help in the sharing of meaning, because storytelling is a collective act.

Communicating the vision in an inspiring way has both content and stylistic aspects. Inspiring content is characterized by emphasizing the importance of the vision, expressing confidence in people's self-efficacy and ability to achieve it, reference to values and moral justification, emphasizing the common goal and collective identity, and reference to hope and faith (Howell and Frost, 1989; Shamir et al., 1994; Den Hartog and Verburg, 1997). Inspiring communication of vision is characterized by a captivating tone of voice, pacing and sitting, leaning forward, direct eye contact and animated facial expressions (Howell and Frost, 1989; Holladay and Coombs, 1994; Awamleh and Gardner, 1999). Michael Frese et al. (2003), using a novel research design without the conventional control group, found that the inspirational communication of vision can be trained.

Communicating a vision is difficult – so much so that some companies have resorted to specialist agencies to help them do it, says Eglin (2001b). He reports the managing director of one such agency as saying:

> **Many companies are still using old-fashioned methods. You get a typical situation where a large company has been through a merger and the chairman wants to communicate a new vision. He appears on stage backed by expensive audiovisuals and tries to sell the vision in an Orwellian sort of way. It is generally appalling and doesn't work.**

For many companies, such as DHL, Axa Sun Life and Abbey National, the approach has been to get staff together to discuss and agree on how to get the message across, resulting in enhanced commitment to the vision – an example of participative leadership.

Creative ways of communicating the vision in global companies go beyond company newsletters and e-mail. Federal Express uses an internal private business television network, called FXTV, operated via satellite, with a daily five-minute broadcast to employees around the world focused on how the individual efforts of employees contribute to the company's vision (Grensing-Pophal, 2000). Immediately after its annual meeting of its top 500 executives, General Electric circulates a video of the CEO's speech on the company's direction with instructions to attendees on how to use it with their teams (Byrne, 1998). Within a week 750 videos in eight languages are distributed worldwide.

Lansdell (2002: 52–68) provides several case studies of how companies communicated and implemented their visions and the impact on their businesses as a result. One example is Boehringer Ingelheim GmbH, a multinational German pharmaceutical company, whose vision statement is '*Werte schaffen durch Innovation*' ('Value through Innovation') (see case example below).

CASE EXAMPLE

Boehringer Ingelheim's Approach to Communicating and Implementing a Vision

The process followed these steps:

1 Analysis of the company environment and competitors' corporate philosophies
2 Research into how the company would grow and rank among the best
3 Testing of the resulting vision in terms of likely consequences
4 Communicating the vision in novel ways at the group's annual top management conference
5 Workshops on the vision for all employees
6 Reinforcement of the vision in action by using rewards for new ideas
7 Introduction of a new company magazine called *Vision*
8 Development of a set of associated leadership principles accompanied by workshops
9 An annual 'Value through Innovation' event to maintain the momentum

Since the process was introduced, collaboration internally and externally has improved, recruitment has become easier, morale has increased, processes have been speeded up, purchasing waste has dropped, and sales tripled over seven years.

Vision as a driving force

Vision is the driving force for motivation and achievement. To be a driving force, a vision must be positive, not negative (Senge, 1990: 225). Energy is better directed towards making something happen rather than preventing it from happening. For example, following the merger in the UK of UMIST and the Victoria University of Manchester in October 2004, the vision for the new University of Manchester is 'a 21st century university that will become an international research powerhouse and a favoured destination for the best students, teachers, researchers and scholars in the world'. Positive visions connote a sense of power rather than the powerlessness associated with negative visions. And positive visions persist, whereas negative visions last only as long as the threat exists.

Vision reflects ambition. And as Champy and Nohria (2000) say in their book, *The Arc of Ambition*, 'ambition is the root of all achievement'. Their thesis is that 'the careers of ambitious people typically follow a predictable path – the *arc of ambition*' (2000: 3). The curve is different for everybody. It rises slowly for some, such as Sam Walton of Wal-Mart, with long-harboured secret dreams, and quickly for others, like Michael Dell of Dell Computer Corporation. But at some point it provides for all a springboard for action and achievement through perseverance and courage. It then tails off with the decline of ambition, with which all leaders must come to terms. Champy and Nohria's book describes how ambition transforms dreams into reality, drawing on dozens of contemporary and historical figures from the worlds of business, politics, science and the arts.

Olivier (2001: 12–13), in drawing from Shakespeare, supports this view but cautions against excessive or misdirected ambition. He cites examples from *Macbeth*, *Richard III* and *Coriolanus*, where over-ambitious leaders turn into tyrants. He points out that the word 'ambition' comes from 'ambit', the Greek root of which also means 'wingspan'. 'Ambition' therefore is associated with how far we can stretch our wings. Too little, and we will never fly; too much, and we may crash to the ground.

Translating vision into reality

'Action without a vision is stumbling in the dark, and vision without action is poverty-stricken poetry,' says Bennis (1989). Put another way, effective emotional, spiritual and behavioural leadership without clear vision and strategic thinking is dangerous; the converse is impotent.

'A vision is always just out of reach', say Deetz et al. (2000: 52). It is a state of affairs to strive for, something that exists only in the imagination and that 'may never

Figure 4.2 *Translating vision into reality*

become a reality … [requiring] an act of faith' (Nanus, 1992: 25–26). This idea of a vision is commonplace among many commentators. Domino Pizza's chairman says, for example, that the company's vision is a 'finishing line' – 'if there ever is one' – in a 'marathon rather than a sprint'.[39]

Translating vision into reality is a leadership responsibility throughout the organization. Mobbs (2004) says there is often a 'lack of linkage between vision, strategy and day-to-day activities' but that linkage may be achieved by using the 'Balanced Scorecard' (see Chapter 6). Figure 4.2 shows a simple model for translating vision into reality.

The impact of vision

In 1990 and 1991 Robert Stempel and his top management team at General Motors were blamed for losing $12 billion dollars. One reason, David Day (2001: 385) says, was Stempel's lack of a new vision for GM. The right vision can have several benefits for an organization, according to Nanus (1992):

- It stimulates commitment to the organization and energizes people
- It provides meaning to people's lives
- It provides a standard of excellence to aim for and encourages improvement
- It focuses the organization on a desired future state

Danny Miller and John O'Whitney (1999) say a vision gives a company 'character and direction, harmonizes strategy and processes, and motivates people to work towards a common objective'. Mark Lipton (1996) identified five benefits of managing with a vision, based on an analysis of over 30 international studies:

1 Performance improvement on measures such as profit, return on shareholder equity, employee turnover and rate of new product development
2 Promotion of change by serving as a guide during organizational transformation
3 Provision of the foundation for a strategic plan
4 Motivation of employees and attraction of talented people
5 Keeping decision making on track, providing focus and direction

One obvious problem with visions and vision statements is that they may be bland and uninspiring: they do not actually provide direction, set a common goal or motivate. They may be an ego exercise by the CEO: 'some corporate leaders [can't] distinguish between vanity and vision ... implementation and basic blocking and tackling are increasingly regarded as more important than vision'.[40] Questions start to be asked about this 'vision thing'.

But clear visions, according to Kouzes and Posner (1991: 124), are associated with high levels of job satisfaction, motivation, commitment, loyalty, *esprit de corps*, clarity about the organization's values, pride in the organization and organizational productivity. Boyett and Boyett (1996) say, 'It is next to impossible to have an energetic, creative, innovative, flexible, competency-driven company without a vision.'

It is important for the leader to model the attitudes, values and beliefs implicit in the vision. This fosters trust, sets high performance expectations and shows confidence in the ability of people to meet these expectations. Leaders exert charismatic influence when their visions encompass current organizational problems or crises, their visions are perceived to represent a solution to them, and their visions are perceived as rational, cogent and persuasive in doing so (Kanungo and Conger, 1992).

Bass goes further, describing how vision transforms the expectations people have (Bass, 1985; Bass, 1990a; Bass and Avolio, 1993; Bass, 1996). Transformational leaders also encourage their followers to examine problems from new perspectives – intellectually stimulating them – and provide individual attention to them (individualized consideration). This avoids the undesirable blind obedience that purely charismatic leaders often engender (Bass, 1990a: 216). Sashkin adds the need for discussion of the vision with followers, demonstration by leaders of consistency, respect for followers, risk taking and trustworthiness to reflect sincerity, commitment and values implicit in the vision (Sashkin, 1988; Sashkin and Fulmer, 1988).

Zaccaro and Banks (2001: 196–197) present a model that shows how visions influence organizational effectiveness (Figure 4.3). In the model, 'inclusive language' refers to language that unifies rather than divides – using words like 'we' and 'our' rather than 'them' and 'they' (Fiol et al., 1999). This is an aspect of framing our speech, which we discuss in Chapter 8.

CASE EXAMPLE

Visionary Leadership at the Generics Group[41]

Visionary leaders bring change by designing a new future for their organizations rather than settling for incremental improvement. The Generics Group is a technology incubator organisation whose vision is to turn intangibles into tangibles. The Generics Group have a design approach and a vision that have been created and implemented by someone who demonstrates clarity, judgement and a total commitment to success – a person who stands apart from the rest.

Professor Gordon Edge founded the Generics Group with the clearly expressed vision of creating wealth through technology. Today [2001], his Cambridge-based ideas factory has a global reputation, not only for technological consulting but also for turning brainwaves into businesses.

Since 1986, the Generics Group has established or invested in more than 40 companies in areas such as telecommunications, biotechnology and materials engineering. With 250 employees, research laboratories in Cambridge, Stockholm and Baltimore, and offices in Boston, Stockholm, Zurich and Tokyo, Generics was valued at more than £220 million when floated in December 2000.

Edge's visionary approach to turning technology ideas into revenues was honed during a training that began in the 1970s at Cambridge Consultants. Later he started PA Technology as an offshoot of the PA Consulting Group, before leaving to establish Generics in 1986. Edge's vision for Generics was to create a radically new environment in which to foster technology entrepreneurship.

'You can't organise people into being more creative, but you can create an environment in which creativity is part of the culture,' he says.

At Generics' headquarters, employees from fields as diverse as biotechnology and engineering work together. 'It's an interdisciplinary culture,' Edge stresses. Employees are encouraged to invest personally in spin-off companies and the entrepreneurial are encouraged to develop their own ideas.

A novel feature of Generics' innovation process is its Innovation Exploitation Board (IEB). The IEB is a large committee of employees drawn from across the company that discusses all the technology and business opportunities that Generics receives. 'It's a peer-group review process that is effective in providing a rigorous challenge to an emerging opportunity,' argues Edge. The IEB can also draw on a £1 million fund to test ideas further if required.

Creativity is so important to Generics that it is measured using a mixture of objective and subjective metrics. 'Objectively, we can point to numbers such as how many patents a person has produced,' says Edge. 'But we also use the mechanism of peer-group review, as no-one is better than your colleagues at assessing your performance as a creative worker.'

Edge's vision for his company is so strong that the strategy, culture and organisation remain unchanged after 14 years – only the size is different. The secret of his leadership success, he believes, is always to recruit people whom you genuinely believe to be better than yourself.

Case discussion questions

1 What is Generics Group's vision?
2 How well does it meet the criteria for good visions?
3 What part has vision played in the company's success?

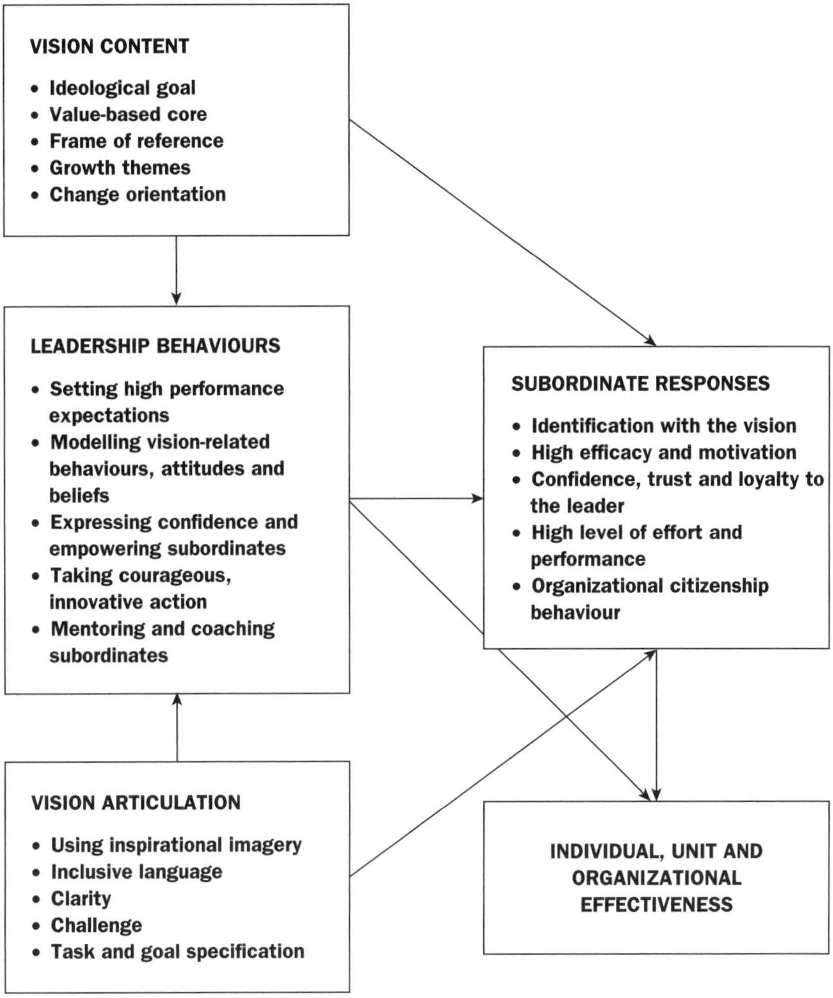

Figure 4.3 *Model of leadership vision and organizational effectiveness (adapted from Zaccaro and Banks, 2001: 197)*

Source: Adapted from Stephen J. Zaccaro and Deanna J. Banks, Figure 7.1, Model of Leadership, Vision, and Organizational Effectiveness, in Chapter 7, 'Leadership, Vision, and Organizational Effectiveness', page 197, in Stephen J. Zaccaro and Richard J. Klimoski (Editors) (2001), *The Nature of Organizational Leadership: Understanding the Performance Imperatives Confronting Today's Leaders.* San Francisco, CA: Jossey-Bass. Copyright © 2001, Jossey-Bass Inc. Reprinted with permission of John Wiley & Sons, Inc.

Organizational mission

Mission in the organizational context, according to the *Concise Oxford Dictionary*, is 'a strongly felt aim or calling'.[42] So mission is not about where or what the organization wants to be, which is vision, but how it sees its purpose or task. Purpose or task depends on the vision. On this argument, first comes vision, from which the mission follows, though the converse may also hold true sometimes.

Both a vision and a mission provide a context for people in an organization to make sense of the tasks they are performing. Both vision and mission can be inspiring and motivating in themselves. As Sanjay Menon (2001) says, 'The energising power of a mission or valued cause has often been noted in the context of religious or missionary work and sovereignty movements.' Faced with 'compassion fatigue' among the general public, charities, Owen Hughes (2003) says, 'need to make people understand not only what they do but also what they are like as an organisation'. He says images help to do this where they reflect the core idea of what the organization stands for, illustrate benefits rather than problems, and connect and inspire rather than shock.

When all employees share a belief in the mission, they are enthusiastic, say Milton Moskowitz and Robert Levering (2003), who have carried out an annual survey of the best US workplaces for *Fortune* magazine. C. William Pollard (2000), CEO of ServiceMaster, one of the world's most respected companies, ranked the top service company among the *Fortune 500*, believes that:

> People want to contribute to a cause... . When we create alignment between the mission of the firm and the cause of its people, we unleash a creative power that results in quality service to the customer and the growth and development of the people who do the serving. People find meaning in their work.

However, Stephen Covey says, 'Go and ask people what the purpose of the company is and you'll get 10 different answers ... . They don't know the purpose of the company' (Skapinker, 2002). Richard Scase (2004) agrees, adding that:

> mission statements are rarely taken seriously and are usually seen as irrelevant. Too often, they are simply the manufactured product of some PR consultancy. Companies have them because they are supposed to.

In two pieces of action research on leadership in strategic business units, Vansina (1988, 1999) found that successful general managers engaged in large-scale organizational change 'direct their efforts towards the "embodiment of purpose" within the whole company', shaping or strengthening corporate identity. The purpose – or mission – is regarded as realistic and achievable but challenging, appealing to competitive spirit and 'igniting' the energy of everybody. This view is agreed by Scase (2004) as true when mission statements are taken seriously by top management, quoting, for example, the appeal to young people of BP's commitment in its mission statement to environmental sustainability and 3M's emphasis on innovation.

Olivier (2001: 20) says that an organization's mission is the sum of vision plus action: 'Vision + Action = Mission'. He says:

> If the vision has no mission, it will remain in the air, a good idea without application. A vision is more internally driven, a mission more externally. If the vision is being achieved you feel it, if the mission is being achieved you can measure it.

Vision and mission as distinct

Alex Miller and Gregory Dess (1996: 9–10) usefully contrast vision and mission: vision is a group's or an organization's aspirations for the future that appeal to the emotions and beliefs of its members; mission is a matter of group or organizational identity and comprises its purpose, distinctiveness, intended products or services and markets, and its core values. Deetz et al. (2000: 51) say:

> **Most organizations have a mission statement that articulates the overall purpose that the organization was founded to accomplish... . A mission tells you where the organization wants to go... . A vision, however, helps you see the importance of getting where you want to go and understand why some paths there are better suited.**

Denton (2001) quotes Disney as an example: the company's mission is 'to make people happy', and its vision is 'to become the leading entertainment company in the world'.

Vision and mission are often confused or ill-defined. Michael Raynor (1998) believes that many executives are frustrated in their attempts to realize their full value. An example of this confusion is the British Civil Service Management Board's Vision for the Civil Service: 'To make a difference to the success of the country; to serve with integrity, drive and creativity' (PIU, 2001: 5.26). This is a mission statement.

FirstGroup plc similarly confuses its vision with its mission. It states its vision as 'to transform travel, providing public transport services that are safe, reliable, high quality, personal and accessible'.[43] This is a statement of mission or purpose. However, its vision is expressed as a stated 'aim': 'to be the number one public transport provider'. The chairman's report unfortunately does not make reference to the company's vision or mission, focusing only on financial performance and strategy.

Conversely, an early mission statement of Cadbury-Schweppes Beverages, later changed, stated the company's mission as 'To be the biggest non-cola company in the world' (Rigby,1998). This is actually a vision statement: it states what the organization wants to be, not what it does. And it lacks appeal: as Rhymer Rigby (1998) says, it is better 'to define yourselves in terms of what you are, not what you aren't'.

Another example of the confusion between vision and mission is the 'vision' of Perot Systems in the United States: 'to deliver innovative services and solutions that serve the particular needs of our clients and their customers' – really a mission or purpose – though later in its annual report for 2001, director Ross Perot Jr, says:

> **Our vision for Perot Systems is to become the most admired information services company in the world. Admired for the service we provide, the commitment and expertise of our employees, and the results and value we bring to our customers.[44]**

Different writers posit different, and sometimes conflicting, characteristics of useful mission statements (e.g. Pearce, 1982; David, 1989). And mission statements often appear to be 'either banal [or] situation specific' (Raynor, 1998), or 'a muddled stew of values, goals, purposes, philosophies, beliefs and descriptions' (Collins and Porras, 1991). Several writers confuse the issue:

> The mission statement, or purpose, of your organization is the broad description of its reason for existence. It is the single statement that differentiates your organization from other organizations in the community. It is the source from which all of your organizational plans and dreams, strategies, objectives, policies and outcomes flow. (Vogt, 1994)

> An effective mission statement describes the firm's fundamental, unique purpose...[it] indicates what the organization intends to accomplish, identifies the markets in which the firm intends to operate, and reflects the philosophical premises that are to guide actions. (Ireland and Hitt, 1992)

> ...mission [is] the intent, spirit, or rallying cry which constitutes the organization's and its members' primary duty or way of behaving, the foundation and force which throws, sends or casts itself into the future towards its goals and targets. (Cummings and Davies, 1994)

This selection of examples is a pot-pourri of references to 'reason for existence', 'a rallying cry', identifying markets, and indicating 'what the firm intends to accomplish' (Raynor, 1998). And yet the mission statement, says Stephen Covey (1989a), should be 12 words or less, easily memorized and inspirational. These multiple demands only give weight to the argument for well-developed cognitive skills in defining mission. But, Raynor (1998) says, 'Like the panoply of Greek gods, it is just possible that these concepts [vision and mission and many other, related ones] are so tied together that to speak of one is to invoke them all.' One response to this confusion has been to create several statements:

- A vision statement – describing what or where the organization wants to be
- The mission statement – describing the nature and purpose of the organization's business and its competitive positioning
- An ethics statement – providing guiding principles for handling conflicts of interest
- A statement of operating philosophy or core values – providing guiding principles for employee behaviour

Olivier (2001: 46–47) describes how activities (with their own laudable purpose) may get out of line with the organization's overall mission ('core purpose') quoting the case of a group of British police officers:

> [The] constabulary had done their best to take on board the recommendations of the Stephen Lawrence Report and combat 'institutional racism'. One of their new missions was to build a community centre where they could meet local youths, play football, table tennis, etc, and generally come into contact in a non-confrontational way. Sounds great. The trouble was that the crime rate was going up and the local community now felt less safe than they had before the project started. The mission had so involved and stimulated everyone around it that the core purpose of 'Making Britain safer' was no longer being served. The mission, however noble, had got out of line...and the core purpose was suffering. Those concerned had to rein in the runaway mission and refocus in order to serve the core purpose.

What is a useful mission statement?

Mission statements need to be short enough to be memorized and generic enough to encompass likely developments in the organization's business environment, which may be extremely rapid, as in the IT industry. Examples are Tesco's 'core purpose': 'Creating value for customers, to earn their lifetime loyalty',[45] and Marks & Spencer's mission: 'Making aspirational quality accessible to all'.[46]

The organizational mission determines the organization's goals, context and coherence (Covey, 1992: 296). The lowest common denominator for a mission statement, Covey suggests, might read like this: to improve the economic well-being and quality of life of all stakeholders. Covey argues cogently for these elements in a mission statement. Organizations largely serve economic purposes by providing goods and services, and employment provides livelihoods. Quality of life, and quality of work life in particular, is of increasing moral, psychological and social importance.

An organization's mission defines why the organization exists and what it does. It defines *how* the vision will be attained. A mission is a practical way of putting the vision into action. A mission statement therefore includes some or all of the following:

- Who are we? A definition of the business we are in.
- What do we do? The markets we serve.
- Why do we exist? Our corporate values, beliefs and guiding principles.

The kind of mission that makes people proud to be associated with a company comes from Percy Barnevik as CEO of the Swedish–Swiss company that owns Asea-Brown Boveri. He says:

> **I would like to create and develop an image of us as helping to improve the world environment. For example, transferring sustainable technology to China or India, where they have a tremendous need to clean up their coal-fired power plants. Our employees can...see that we contribute something beyond shareholder value. (Dess and Picken, 2000)**

Yukl (1994: 362) says that the organization's mission statement is the core of a vision. He says that the mission statement is an overall picture, reflecting the important themes and values of the organization, rather than a detailed blueprint. 'A good mission statement should be distinctive, relevant and memorable,' says Hilary Scarlett, at communications consultants Smythe Dorland Lambert (Rigby, 1998).

Both vision and mission statements sometimes attract scepticism and criticism. They are too often 'a collection of business buzzwords,' says Lansdell (2002: 3). Scott Adams in *The Dilbert Principle* describes a mission statement as 'a long awkward sentence that demonstrates management's inability to think clearly' (Adams, 1997: 36). Lansdell (2002) relates a story from the *Dallas Morning News* in the United States of how Adams duped Logitech's senior executives (with the connivance of the company's co-founder and vice-chairman):

> **[Scott Adams] was asked...to pose as...a management consultant who was going to help executives draft a new mission statement for the company's New Ventures group. Adams disguised himself with a wig and a false moustache, before deriding the existing**

> **statement – 'to provide Logitech with profitable growth and related new business areas' – and leading an exercise in which managers brainstormed words and ideas for a new one. The result? 'The New Ventures Group is to scout profitable growth opportunities in relationships, both internally and externally, in emerging, mission inclusive markets, and explore new paradigms and then filter and communicate and evangelize the findings'. Drawing a last diagram, a picture of Dilbert, Adams took off his wig and the Logitech managers realized they'd been duped, although they apparently enjoyed the joke.**

In the past, a mission statement has served three purposes, according to Christopher Bart and John Tabone (1998):

- To provide a focused basis for allocating resources
- To motivate and inspire people throughout the organization (or group or nation) to achieve a common goal or purpose
- To create a balance among the competing interests of the various stakeholders in the organization

Paul Joyce and Adrian Woods (2001: 69–71) add some more contemporary reasons:

- To refocus the organization during a crisis
- To create standards of behaviour
- To provide a common purpose or direction
- To define the scope of the business
- To allow the CEO to assert control over the organization
- To develop shared values or culture in the organization
- It is expected

Why do organizations exist and what do they do? A frequently stated purpose is to maximize shareholder value, for example Lloyds TSB Group's 'governing' objective.[47] 'Leaders are not measured by vision, mission statements or codes of ethics,' Iain Mangham (2004: 53) says, 'but like the wrapping on Christmas presents these serve as appropriate decoration. They are measured by the growth in shareholder value … . Not surprisingly, leaders give their full attention to that.' Collins and Porras (1996b) say: 'A primary role of core purpose is to guide and inspire. Maximizing shareholder wealth does not inspire people at all levels of an organization, and it provides precious little guidance.'

Another frequently stated purpose is to meet market demands and needs and satisfy customers or clients. Peter Drucker always argued that companies should exist not to make profits but to create and satisfy customers. He says:

> **Aristotle said there can only be one end, but there can be many means. Profit is a means, very much like oxygen to the human body. It is absolutely necessary, but you don't exist for its sake. (Jackson, 1999)**

Peter Doyle (1996) says that a vision (or mission) focused on short-term profits and return on capital makes it very difficult to maintain market share in competitive markets. Companies like BMW, Siemens and Hewlett-Packard, he says, with returns on capital of much less than the average, are the first choice of customers. Focusing on providing customer value, not shareholder value, paradoxically produces greater shareholder value. This is argued compellingly, with several examples, by William W. George, chairman and CEO of Medtronic, Inc. – one of the world's leading medical technology companies based in Minneapolis – and the Academy of Management's 2001 'Executive of the Year' (George, 2001).

George also argues that people today in their work seek meaning and purpose – the spiritual dimension we discussed in Chapter 3. When they find it, '[they] will buy into the company's mission and make the commitment to fulfilling it' (George, 2001). Dess and Picken (2000) quote Xerox PARC guru John Seely Brown as saying: 'The job of leadership today is not just to make money: it's to make meaning.'

Richard Ellsworth (2002) emphasizes the importance of corporate purpose or mission, and he denigrates the preoccupation with shareholder value on both economic and humanistic grounds. Instead, he says, only 'a customer-focused corporate purpose provides the key to outstanding performance and to enhancing the lives of those the company serves and of those who serve it' (Ellsworth, 2002: xi). In his commentary on Ellsworth's thesis, Scott Snook (2003) says:

> **Everything flows from a customer-focused purpose. A singular focus on serving customers defines the ultimate end for corporate visions, missions, and strategies. Ultimately, all strategic direction flows from this clearly understood answer as to why the corporation exists.**

Another view is that organizations exist to serve the interests of *all* their stakeholders. In 1995, the Royal Society for the encouragement of Arts, Manufactures and Commerce (RSA) published a report on its inquiry into 'Tomorrow's Company: the role of business in a changing world'. The report argues:

> **The companies which will sustain competitive success in the future are those which focus less exclusively on shareholders and on financial measures of success - and instead include all their stakeholder relationships, and a broader range of measurements, in the way they think and talk about their purpose and performance. In short it is this inclusive approach which differentiates Tomorrow's Company from yesterday's companies. (RSA, 1995)**

Every organization has a range of stakeholders – customers, owners and investors (shareholders), suppliers, distributors, the government, the community in which it operates, society at large and not least its employees. Each stakeholder will ask how the organization serves its interests. Stakeholder interests therefore have to be taken into account in the round in deciding the organizational mission – why the organization exists and what it does. An example of a mission that does so is Barclays', focusing on customers, employees and communities as key stakeholders: 'to be an innovative, customer focused Group that delivers superb products and services, ensures excellent careers for our people and contributes positively to the communities in which we live and work'.[48]

Creating a mission statement

A key challenge to leadership is to create a mission shared by all stakeholders based on a shared vision for the organization's future. Raynor (1998) points out that there is lack of agreement on how to create both a vision and a mission: what is needed is clarity about the meaning of these concepts. He suggests that the organization's mission should emerge from an understanding of its core competencies and be informed by its core values. Clarifying and agreeing a mission statement can take months, even years, to do. For example, it took two years for AT&T to produce a 250-word mission statement (Jones and Kahaner, 1995).

Kim Kanaga and Sonya Prestridge (2002) provide a useful procedure for creating a mission statement. The key questions to be considered are as follows:

- What purpose does the organization serve?
- Who are the organization's customers?
- What do the organization's customers have to gain from it?
- What are the organization's distinctive competencies?
- What does the organization want to change (represented in its vision)?
- What energizes the organization?
- What are the organization's core values, and how do they inform its vision and mission?
- What legacy should the organization aim to leave (hypothetically)?

These questions are subjected to a brainstorming process:

1 One sheet on a flip chart is devoted to each question. Members of the group call out ideas, either randomly or in turn, that relate to each question, considered one at a time. All suggestions are recorded, regardless of quality or repetition, and this process is continued until ideas dry up.
2 The sheets are posted around the room. All members study them and then identify and report patterns and themes, looking for common words and repetition.
3 The themes and patterns are then discussed to identify the key ideas for a mission statement.
4 All members individually write a mission statement.
5 Members form groups of three or four and share their statements and create a common one.
6 The whole group reconvenes, shares the small groups' mission statements, and creates a single, agreed statement. A sub-group may be assigned to add the finishing touches for approval by the whole group if desired.

Vision is about the future of the organization – its future positioning, what or where the organization wants or needs to be. Raynor (1998), contrary to my thesis, sees vision as determined by the organization's mission and by the recognition of the market forces that will impact on its future. However, one may argue conversely that an organization's mission is a consequence, not a precursor, of vision. While some scholars debate this, practitioners generally regard vision as the first step – the foundation – for developing the organization's mission (O'Brien and Meadows, 2000). And the various theories of transformational leadership share a common core idea: outstanding leadership depends on effectively articulating and communicating a viable and valid vision (Mumford and Van Doorn, 2001).

The organization's mission, based on a clear, appealing vision of the desired and possible future, provides a simple but powerful mantra for the organization. To deliver the best results, Collins says, the opportunities we pursue must meet three basic tests:

1 Do they square with our mission?
2 Do we have the capability to deliver against them better than any other organization?
3 Do the opportunities 'make sense within the context of the economic engine and resources of the institution'?

These questions are questions of strategy, which is the subject of Chapter 6. But it remains the case that the fundamental driving force of the organization is one thing and one thing only – a mission based on a vision of its future. It is, Scase (2004) says, 'the glue holding the whole business together'.

Visionary leadership in action

While there is more to leadership than vision, as I argued in Chapter 3, vision is of fundamental importance. Visionary leadership is a theory of leadership in its own right, as I briefly mentioned in Chapter 2. In this section we consider in more detail visionary leadership in both theory and practice.

A 1989 global survey of 1,500 CEOs representing companies producing 10% of the gross world product identified the overwhelming importance of visionary leadership in anticipating the company's future and its place in global business, setting ambitious corporate goals and inspiring managers to achieve them (Korn/Ferry, 1989). The need for vision is culture-free.

J.W. Thompson says, 'Visionary leadership is no longer just desirable; it is ... the cornerstone of corporate survival' (Thompson, 1992). Yet in fewer than half (42%) of UK PLCs is the board of directors exclusively responsible for creating the vision and mission, according to research by Stiles (2001), and in over 17% it is exclusively or mostly management's responsibility.

'The best way to predict the future is to create it,' says Drucker (1966). According to Joseph Jaworski (1996), true leaders 'create the future' through their commitment to others, through 'synchronicity'. Larry Reynolds (2000) calls this 'transcendental' leadership. It is leaders that make companies appear 'visionary', according to a study of 18 companies (Collins and Porras, 1994). Their leaders consistently promoted an organizational identity and a set of organizational values not just through 'framing' them but also through programmes for their implementation, socialization and recognition.

Visionary leadership, according to Glenn Rowe (2001):

> **is future-oriented, concerned with risk-taking, and visionary leaders are not dependent on their organizations for their sense of who they are. Under visionary leaders, organizational control is maintained through socialization and the sharing of, and compliance with, a commonly held set of norms, values, and shared beliefs.**

A characteristic shared by charismatic leaders, Jay Conger says, is the ability to craft a compelling vision, a story of where the organization is going (Rush and Wilcox, 2001).

But he says that having a vision statement or mission statement is not the same as being visionary. Based on in-depth interviews and biographical research, Conger found that there are different ways of being a visionary leader:

- Those who have an idea about the way the world is heading and focus the organization in that direction, for example Fred Smith, FedEx head
- Those who are opportunists who see a gap in the market place and take advantage of it, for example Yvon Chouinard, founder of recreational clothing company Patagonia
- Those who are not visionaries in the usual sense, such as those who have visions in more than one form, for example Ray Kroc, who took two McDonald brothers' idea and set up a new form of franchise and real estate leasing

Visionary leaders all have help in shaping and implementing the vision. For example, at FedEx Vince Fagan helped Fred Smith see the possibility of a market in law and accounting firms. This may take time, great effort and finetuning in the light of market and resource constraints. And visioning is not a linear process: it is beset by crises, accidents, experiments and customer feedback.

Visionary leaders, Champy and Nohria (2000: 31) say, 'see the world [or their company] differently and dare to make [the] dream come true', quoting the Wright brothers and their vision of powered flight. Visionary leadership concerns creating and communicating the mission of the organization – what it stands for – and a vision of its future. The everyday concept of vision has to do with a broad world-view, deep understanding or insight, and future orientation (Van der Heijden, 1993). Bryman (1992: 168) says:

> it is often not easy to see what is visionary about...visions...there is little to distinguish leaders' visions from...strategy. In the case of [Steve] Jobs, the term seems warranted because he was concerned at Apple to transform people's lives through computers... . It is not surprising that it tends to be those leaders whose 'visions' are either innovative or deal with ultimate values...[who] are regarded as charismatic. Leaders who adopt visions that are barely distinguishable from strategic intent or from broad aims and which lack innovativeness (for example, stereotyped proclamations about competitiveness, emphasis on quality or the customer) are creating visions in name only.

Philip Williams (1982), in his discussion of political leadership, calls visionary leaders who move the party's policies in a new direction 'pathfinders'. He contrasts them with 'stabilizers', who play a unifying role. Pathfinders in British political parties include Hugh Gaitskell, Neil Kinnock, Margaret Thatcher and Tony Blair. Stabilizers include Clement Attlee, Harold Wilson, James Callaghan, Michael Foot, John Major and Michael Howard. Another example of a visionary leader and pathfinder is Singapore's founding father and former prime minister, Lee Kuan Yew, who says:

> Because of our unusual circumstances – no natural resources, nothing except people on a small island – [the next generation of political leaders] must have the imagination and vision to use the technologies that come along and carve out a future for ourselves. (Thornhill et al., 2001)

Table 4.1 *Ideological and charismatic leaders*

	Ideological	Charismatic
Socialized	Charles de Gaulle Margaret Thatcher Eleanor Roosevelt Mohandas Gandhi Ronald Reagan Woodrow Wilson	Franklin D. Roosevelt Henry Ford John F. Kennedy Jomo Kenyatta Winston Churchill J.P. Morgan
Personalized	Che Guevera Deng Xiaping J.D. Rockefeller Vladimir Lenin Mao Zedong Joseph Stalin Joseph McCarthy	Benito Mussolini Idi Amin J. Edgar Hoover François Duvalier (Papa Doc) Neville Chamberlain Nicolae Ceausescu Huey Long

Robert House and Jane Howell (1992) distinguish between vision focused on the enhancement of a social institution (that of a 'socialized' leader) and one focused on enhancing a leader's personal power (that of a 'personalized' leader). They contrast Franklin Delano Roosevelt and Hitler respectively. Unsurprisingly, socialized charismatic leaders are more likely than personalized charismatic leaders to articulate visions that result in positive outcomes for society (O'Connor et al., 1995).

Strange and Mumford (2002) analysed the biographies of 60 notable historical leaders of both kinds and found that, in constructing their visions, ideological leaders emphasize personal values and standards and charismatic leaders emphasize social needs and change. They suggest that leaders form mental models based on their experience that they use to do this (Mumford and Strange, 2002). Examples of well-known leaders they give using this classification are shown in Table 4.1.

Colin Wilson (1963: 222) says that the visionary 'starts from a point that everybody can understand, and very soon soars beyond the general understanding'. And visionary leaders, Rowe (2001) says, tend to take risks, create disorder and excitement, and change 'the way people think about what is possible, desirable and necessary .... They work in, but do not belong to, organizations.' They are often driven by strong personal values (Hosmer, 1982; Zaleznik, 1990; Sooklal, 1991; Evans, 1997).

The visionary leader is an outsider. The outsider is a person who perceives the unstable foundations on which human life is built and feels that chaos and anarchy lie deeper than the order that most others believe in – a person not at home in the world and who cannot accept its values. H.G. Wells' hero in *The History of Mr Polly* typifies the visionary as an outsider: 'If you don't like your life you can change it.' The visionary wants to 'go out and *do* something' (Wilson, 1963: 225).

The self-confidence of the visionary may result from a long period of self-doubt, leading to discovery of what he or she may be capable of (Wilson, 1963: 227). We all possess a 'visionary faculty' (Wilson, 1963: 254). But living from moment to moment clouds vision: for example, the need for short-term profit and the trouble-shooting and fire-fighting that preoccupy the lives of many managers at work. Our visionary faculty is impaired by excessive stress in our everyday lives. Too often we see only what is the case, not what may be possible. Visionaries are lateral thinkers. Wilson (1963: 260) says, 'imagination is the instrument of self-knowledge'. And imagination comes into play when we are relaxed and we daydream. Managers need to release themselves from the prison they live in, to develop their visionary faculty. We need to daydream.

One difference between visionaries who are leaders and those who are not is the time frame in which they operate. Marshall (1991: 30) says:

> **The visionary or the dreamer lives almost entirely in the future, he dreams his dreams or she paints her visions of what could be, but neither of them have to do anything to actualise their pictures. The leader on the other hand has to operate on the boundary line between the future and the present...he or she has to take the critical decisions that will draw the future into the present, that will attempt to actualise the vision and will commit resources and manpower to the task of concretising the dream.**

A visionary does not necessarily make things happen. Robert Craven (1998), considering the Beatles' Paul McCartney as the group's creative leader who masterminded the group's success, quotes Yoko Ono, widow of John Lennon, as saying:

> **John did not make the phone calls, he was not on that level as a leader – he was on the level of a spiritual leader. He was the visionary and that is why the Beatles happened.**

For Glenn Rowe, visionary leaders will probably create more wealth than 'managerial leaders', but with a high degree of risk, particularly in the short term. An organization needs managerial leaders too. What is also needed, however, is a strategic element in leadership, which we discuss in Chapter 6.

The UK's 100 most visionary companies were identified in a competition organized by BT and Cranfield School of Management. Companies were judged in six categories:

- Relationships with clients, customers, suppliers and citizens
- Supply-chain management
- Knowledge management
- Visionary leadership
- Organizational transformation
- Unexpected outcomes of vision

Judging was based on several criteria. These included clarity of vision, the existence of new and better competencies resulting from the vision, and evidence of measurable and beneficial results. The judges looked for evidence of 'thinking outside the box' and proof that companies had anticipated a desired future and were aligned to their vision.

Visionary companies share several features, according to Collins and Porras (1994):

- A fundamental belief in, and passion for, the business they are in
- Remaining true to an enduring set of values while adapting strategies and other aspects of culture according to environmental demands
- An enduring core ideology, reflected in their values, that transcends customer demands and market conditions, guides and inspires people, and creates alignment and *esprit de corps*
- BHAGs ('Big, Hairy, Audacious Goals') that motivate people to achieve greatness in the long term – for example, NASA's goal in the early 1960s to put a man on the moon by the end of the decade

Organizations can become visionary through 'strategic innovation' and through individual entrepreneurs who are not blamed for failures (rates will always be high) but who learn from them and try again – and again. Also important is developing a culture that values innovation. Visionary companies all have a deep dedication to the customer. Becoming more visionary comes from understanding the customer, trends in the industry, connections with things beyond the business that are changing, and front-line staff who know how the world is changing every day. It also comes from brainstorming not why or how things will not work but how to create something that will work.

A visionary leader puts into words a compelling vision for a nation, organization or other group of people, persuades or even inspires people to commit to it, and empowers people to achieve it. But Jim Collins (1996) says:

> **[The] difference between being an organization with a vision statement and becoming a truly visionary organization...lies in creating alignment – alignment to preserve an organization's core values, to reinforce its purpose, and to stimulate continued progress towards its aspirations.**

Collins and Porras (1995) add a suitable concluding note for this chapter: 'Visionary leaders die. Visionary products become obsolete. Visionary companies go on forever.' So the best kind of leadership, one might argue, creates a visionary culture. We now turn to this in the next chapter.

Further reading

James C. Collins and Jerry I. Porras (1996), *Built to Last: Successful Habits of Visionary Companies*. London: HarperBusiness.

Stanley A. Deetz, Sarah J. Tracy and Jennifer Lyn Simpson (2000), *Leading Organizations through Transition*. Thousand Oaks, CA: Sage Publications.

Richard R. Ellsworth (2002), *Leading with Purpose: The New Corporate Realities*. Stanford, CA: Stanford Business Books.

Sally Lansdell (2002), *The Vision Thing*. Oxford: Capstone Publishing.

B. Nanus (1992), *Visionary Leadership*. San Francisco, CA: Jossey-Bass.

Stephen J. Zaccaro and Richard J. Klimoski (Editors) (2001), *The Nature of Organizational Leadership: Understanding the Performance Imperatives Confronting Today's Leaders*. San Francisco, CA: Jossey-Bass.

Discussion questions

1 Which should come first: vision or mission?
2 How can you create a vision that all stakeholders share?
3 How can you ensure that people throughout the organization understand and are committed to the vision?
4 Should a vision be attainable or not quite?

5 Leadership, Values and Culture

Open your arms to change, but don't let go of your values.

Nepalese Buddhist mantra

Overview

- The proposition of this chapter is that effective leaders identify, display and reinforce values that support the vision and mission and that followers share, and they create a strong, positive organizational culture.
- Values are beliefs and principles that are held dear in people's hearts. 'Moral' values are values that are regarded as good as opposed to bad, right as opposed to wrong. A useful distinction is that values are personal and subjective, whereas 'corporate values' or guiding principles are impersonal and objective. Moral values may be institutionalized as 'corporate values' or guiding principles for behaviour for everybody in a group or organization. Such values that are translated into rules of conduct in a business context are known as business ethics.
- Culture is often simply defined as 'the way we do things around here'. It is characterized by overt and covert rules, values, guiding principles, habits and psychological climate.
- A strong culture is characterized by values that are shared throughout the organization. And a strong culture with the right values – those that support the organization's vision, mission and strategies – characterizes an effective organization.
- Shared values make a significant impact on both the job satisfaction and morale of people in an organization and their job performance and contribution.
- The best companies to work for have cultures with clear, shared values such as mutual respect and trust, work–life balance, opportunity to advance in the job and learn new skills, and pride in the company's role in the community or the way it serves its customers. Trust and trustworthiness are perhaps generally the most important value. Trust is the basis for credibility, cooperation and collaboration.
- The actions and decisions of effective leaders reflect both the organization's guiding principles or corporate values and their personal values: this is 'behavioural integrity'. A mismatch displays hypocrisy.

- National cultural differences pose a special challenge for leaders in global and multinational organizations, and there are many examples of their failure to recognize and appropriately respond to them.
- We discuss the alleged decline in ethical standards in business over the past few decades and the implications for leadership.
- The argument continues to run that there is one and only one social responsibility of business: to maximize profits and shareholder value. However, corporate social responsibility (CSR) can be justified on the arguments that it does maximise long-term profitability and that it reflects shared values and beliefs. The chapter concludes by describing company CSR practices and identifying the implications of CSR for leadership.

Aristotle recognized the characteristic spirit and beliefs of a community. We call this the *ethos* of an organization. A strong culture is characterized by values that are shared throughout the organization. Where this is the case, leaders are more likely to get commitment to a vision of the organization's future and to strategies for its pursuit. The most effective organizations are communities that share ethical values (Tichy and Sherman, 1994; Fukuyama, 1995). But what values? And how can leaders ensure the 'right' values are shared and inform everybody's behaviour?

Since the landmark book *In Search of Excellence* was published in 1982 (Peters and Waterman, 1982), *Fortune* magazine has listed the most admired American companies. Manfred Kets de Vries (2000) suggests they are distinguished by a common set of values: trust, teamwork, customer focus, change orientation and a learning environment. American corporate culture, however, has been criticized by German Chancellor Gerhard Schroeder, who suggested that it values shareholder value far more than the individual and that 'Egoism at the top does not suffice to have lasting economic success.'[49] Indeed, the UK's 100 best companies to work for, according to the 2001 *Sunday Times* survey, were characterized most of all by how much they value the contribution of every individual.[50] For example, Charles Krulak, chairman and CEO of MBNA International Bank, says:

> **we realise that our greatest asset is the people who work here. Each one is absolutely fundamental to the company's continued success in providing superior customer service, day in, day out. (Fray, 2001)**

The *Sunday Times* 2002 survey revealed that the best companies to work for have stimulating workplaces and that their employees feel motivated and valued – a deliberate policy of top management.[51] It is not just pay that creates this positive culture. ASDA, ranked top, has flexible employment policies and practices, employee share options, employee participation and recognition schemes, health insurance schemes that are responsive to employees' needs, and social and recreation schemes. The company's 'people director', David Smith, says, 'I am humbled when new starters tell me that our values really are not just a plaque on the wall.'

The *Best Workplaces 2003* survey reported by the *Financial Times* found that what employees value most at work are consideration for personal circumstances, knowing what is going on and, above all, trust.[52] The survey found close similarities between European

Union countries and the United States. Michael Skapinker (2004), analysing the 2004 findings,[53] identified four broad themes that make a company a good place to work:

- Respect and trust
- Work–life balance
- Opportunity to advance in the job and learn new skills
- Pride in the company's role in the community or the way it serves its customers

A survey of employers in Singapore in 2002 by JobStreet, with 1,537 respondents, showed Singapore Airlines as the best local employer, beaten only by Hewlett-Packard and ahead of IBM, Citibank and Agilent Technologies (Divyanathan, 2002). Singapore Airlines was cited for its effective leadership and fairness during difficult economic conditions and HP for its genuine 'people-oriented' culture of empowerment and mutual trust and respect. Corporate values like these are a major feature of a strong, positive culture. Eadie (1999) reports research findings by communications consultancy Smythe Dorward Lambert that certain corporate values appear to be universal: chief executives generally say they believe in integrity, trust, empowerment, flexibility and openness (as do employees).

Values, and behaviour that reflects them, are the basis for effective relationships in business organizations, and they shape the business persona on which its brand and reputation depend, says Mark Goyder (1999). Thomas J. Watson Jr, son of the founder of IBM, argued that beliefs (values) – IBM's were respect for the individual and liberating the talents and energies of its people – must inform vision, mission and culture:

> **Any organization, in order to survive and achieve success, must have a sound set of beliefs [values] on which it premises all its policies and actions. Beliefs [values] must always come before policies, practices and goals. The latter must always be altered if they are seen to violate fundamental beliefs [values]. (Wickens, 1999b)**

Values in business organizations appear to be a field which academics shy away from. Sally Stewart and Gabriel Donleavy (1995) suggest several reasons for this. First, academics believe they risk charges of ethnocentricity and of promoting a particular set of values. Second, they tend to be unwilling to counter the argument that business needs only to obey the law. Third, the theoretical problems of dealing with such an abstract subject are formidable. Business school faculty tend to leave it to their philosophy colleagues, who treat the subject 'academically'. The result, according to Simon Webley (1999), is neglect of business ethics and values as a subject.

Professional bodies, such as the Chartered Management Institute and the Institute of Directors in the UK, promote professional codes of practice.[54] But there are also cross-cultural organizations that promote values-based leadership. For example, Webley (1999) quotes the International Chamber of Commerce based in Paris, the Caux Principles, which were published in 1996 reflecting a stakeholder model and promoting the shared values of the common good (*kyosei*) and human dignity,[55] and the Interfaith Declaration on International Business Ethics published in 1994 under the auspices of the Duke of Edinburgh, Crown Prince Hassan of Jordan and Sir Evelyn de Rothschild.[56] The Interfaith Declaration, based on a common religious heritage, promotes four key values: justice, mutual respect, stewardship and honesty.

Table 5.1 *Frequency of mention of values in 15 corporate codes*

Value	No. of mentions
Integrity	11
Highest ethical standard	9
Responsibility	8
Reputation	7
Honesty	6
Openness	4
Fairness	3
Competitiveness	3
Trustworthiness	2
Profitability	2
Truthfulness	2

Some British corporations appear to be reticent about using value-based terms and they confuse values with performance criteria, according to Webley (1992). Attempts have been made to define generally accepted societal values (e.g. Lodges and Kidder, 1997). A review of codes of business ethics of 15 large British corporations (Webley, 1992) revealed the espoused values shown in Table 5.1.

James Sarros and Joseph Santora (2001), in a study of leadership behaviour and value orientations of Australian executives, found a close association of transformational leadership behaviours and the use of contingent reward (one aspect of transactional leadership) with the values of achievement, benevolence, self-direction (intellectual autonomy) and stimulation (intellectual challenge). Unsurprisingly they found little association of these values with management-by-exception (another aspect of transactional leadership) and laissez-faire leadership behaviour.

A study of middle-level managers in the UK and Canada suggests that a high level of moral reasoning tends to be associated with transformational leadership (Turner et al., 2002). O'Toole (1995: 9) says, 'Moral and effective leaders listen to their followers because they honestly believe that the welfare of followers is the "end" of leadership (and not that followers are merely the means to achieving the leader's goals).'

'Moral intelligence' is a recent label for intelligence based on values, namely the ability to distinguish between right and wrong according to universal principles (Lennick and Kiel, 2005). Moral intelligence, according to Lennick and Kiel, comprises several key elements:

- Integrity – acting consistently with principles, values and beliefs
- Responsibility – willingness to accept accountability for the consequences of actions and choices and admit mistakes and failures
- Compassion – actively supporting the choices and goals of one's staff (other than bad behaviour)
- Forgiveness

Transformational leaders display a strong morality both in their prosocial orientation – a desire to benefit others in the organization or in society at large – and in their behaviour that reflects values of empathy, care, concern and respect for others: they take an altruistic rather than egotistical stance (Kanungo and Mendonca, 1996: 46). Transformational leaders model prosocial and altruistic behaviours: Popper and Mayseless (2003) see transformational leaders as 'good parents'.

What are values?

Values are beliefs and principles that are held dear in people's hearts. A more technical definition is that values are latent constructs involved in evaluating activities or outcomes (Roe and Ester, 1999). 'Moral' values are values that are regarded as good as opposed to bad, right as opposed to wrong. They serve as a 'normative regulatory guide for individual workers' (Meglino and Ravlin, 1998). For example, Lord (Hartley) Shawcross, in presenting the case at the Nuremberg trials in 1945 against Germans accused of aggressive war and crimes against humanity, stated the now-famous dictum: 'There comes a point when a man must refuse to answer to his leader if he is also to answer to his own conscience.'[57]

Geert Hofstede (1991: 8) defines values as 'broad tendencies to prefer certain states of affairs over others'. Schwartz (1992: 2) provides a particularly useful definition: values are 'desirable states, objects, goals, or behaviors transcending specific situations and applied as normative standards to judge and to choose among alternative modes of behavior'. Values thus provide a sense of purpose to behaviour.

Covey (1992: 19) makes a useful distinction between values and guiding principles. Values, he says, are personal, subjective and internal to the individual, whereas guiding principles are impersonal, objective and external. Humphrey Walters (2002), member of a successful round-the-world yachting team, agrees: he says values are personal but guiding business principles are corporate. And they are enduring. Covey (1992: 19) says:

> **Principles apply at all times in all places. They surface in the form of values, ideas, norms, and teachings that uplift, ennoble, fulfil, empower, and inspire people.**

And Warren W. Wiersbe (Clinton, 1988), a Christian evangelist, says:

> **Methods are many;**
> **Principles are few.**
> **Methods may change;**
> **Principles never do.**

The late Pope John Paul II is an example of a leader who insisted on the observance of traditional values (guiding principles) in the Roman Catholic Church despite secular changes. In this he was authoritarian. His successor, Pope Benedict XVI, the former Cardinal Josef Ratzinger, is similarly conservative. Guiding principles never change.

The 'corporate values' defined by many companies are really guiding principles for people's behaviour in the organization. Nevertheless, the corporate values officially espoused and promoted by an organization do – and ought to – reflect values. They are beliefs about what is good for its business and accordingly how people in the organization are expected to behave. Interestingly, in a study of a culture change programme in a large engineering company in the UK, Turnbull (2001) discovered that the content of the company's new corporate values was less important than the fact that corporate values now existed: employees apparently wanted to identify with *something*.

Values-based guiding principles govern behaviour rather than motives (Bartels, 1963: 116). Motives in fact reflect personal values. The more values and guiding principles are aligned – the more the 'maps of the territory reflect the reality of the territory' – the more effective they will be in building a strong, favourable culture, says Covey (1992). Effective leadership therefore entails creating shared values in the organization.

If Covey is correct about the individuality of values and beliefs as distinct from organizational guiding principles, can one create an organization-wide value system? Perhaps the 'organizational' values on which its guiding principles are based can only be aspirations towards which it continuously strives. An example of an effective guiding principle was UK-based insurance company Commercial Union's promise to customers that 'We won't make a drama out of a crisis.' Following this principle became a source of pride for employees and succeeded in retaining customers even when premiums rose. Miranda Kennett (2004) says, '"values" are valueless if they are not relevant to those who buy or use your products or services'.

Ralph Larsen, as CEO of Johnson & Johnson, emphasized the importance of core values regardless of their commercial pros and cons:

> **The core values embodied in our credo might be a competitive advantage but that is not why we have them. We have them because they define for us what we stand for, and we would hold them even if they became a competitive disadvantage in certain situations. (Yearout et al., 2001)**

Former British prime minister Margaret Thatcher (2002) presents another issue: 'In this age of spin doctors and sound bites, the ever-present danger is that leaders will follow fashion and not their … beliefs.'

Former president of Scandinavian Airline System Jan Carlzon (1987) described his personal beliefs and values as follows:

- Everyone needs to know and feel that they are needed
- Everyone wants to be treated as an individual
- Giving someone the freedom to take responsibility releases resources that would otherwise remain concealed
- An individual without information cannot take responsibility; an individual who is given information cannot help but take responsibility

And an example of a corporate leader's values that go beyond the company's immediate interests is those of William Clay Ford Jr, chairman of the Ford Motor Company. He says:

> **We see no conflict between business goals and social and environmental needs. I believe the distinction between a good company and a great one is this: a good company delivers excellent products and services; a great one delivers excellent products and services and strives to make the world a better place.[58]**

Drucker (1999b: 177), the father of modern management, gives a practical example of differences in values that many companies will identify with:

> **In any conflict between short-term results and long-term growth, one company decides in favor of long-term growth; another company decides...in favor of short-term results...this is not primarily a disagreement on economics. It is fundamentally a value conflict regarding the function of a business and the responsibility of management.**

Domino's Pizza takes a clear stand in this respect, seeing operating and developing its business as 'running a marathon':

> **For us, the race is always a long-range one, never a sprint. So our decisions are always made with long-term goals in mind. We have always resisted focusing on short-term goals, which can only cloud the road ahead.**[59]

Corporate identity is a concept that came into popular use in the mid twentieth century. But one of the earliest recorded examples is Pericles' funeral oration in 431 BC in his effort to inspire unity among Athenians in their war with Sparta. In effect he made it clear, in an inspiring way, what was different about them (Clemens, 1986). However, with superficial catchy names, logos and advertising taglines, corporate identity – 'that rich and varied set of characteristics that fuels differentiation and fires contribution' – has not been fully appreciated as 'a powerful force ... in shaping the fortunes of organizations', according to Laurence Ackerman (2000).

Organizational leaders commonly articulate and claim what is unique, central and enduring about their organization (Pfeffer, 1981; Albert and Whetten, 1985). Corporate identity, though, is what members perceive it to be (Albert and Whetten, 1985). For example, one may perceive corporate identity as social responsibility, technical expertise and democracy in one case and as being conservative, providing superior service and bureaucracy in another (Dutton and Penner, 1993). Corporate identity reflects an organization's vision, mission, strategies and values: what it wants to be, what it does, how it does it and what it stands for. Above all, it reflects what the organization wishes to become.

A sense of history of an organization or nation can help us to understand its core values. Christopher McKenna (Eglin, 2002b) says:

> **History captures all the values and legacy of a company. It holds the fabric of the company together in difficult times and it makes the brand.... You ignore history at your peril.**

Companies' statements of values are often criticized for being no more than a belief in 'motherhood and apple pie'. Many companies' value statements are meaningless and even harmful, says Patrick Lencioni (2002). He cites common ones – communication, respect, integrity, excellence. But, according to the company's 2000 annual report, these were Enron's – hardly a model of meaningfulness. Lencioni says:

> **Most values statements are bland, toothless, or just plain dishonest.... Empty values statements create cynical and dispirited employees, alienate customers, and undermine managerial credibility.**

The 2004 Roffey Park survey in the UK found that 52% of the 735 managers surveyed were sceptical about their companies' value statements (Hoar, 2004). Ever since

Collins and Porras in 1994 published *Built To Last*, which argues that the best companies adhere to an explicit set of core values, many companies have created their own statements of core values, Lencioni says, because they felt they had to do so:

> **Today, 80% of the *Fortune 100* [companies] tout their values publicly – values that too often stand for nothing but a desire to be au courant or, worse still, politically correct. (Lencioni, 2002)**

Such actions, Lencioni says, debase values statements, create cynicism – the very opposite of what is intended – and waste the opportunity to define what distinguishes a company from its competition by 'clarifying its identity and serving as a rallying point for employees'. True core values, he says, 'inflict pain':

- They make some employees feel like outcasts
- They limit the organization's freedom, strategically and operationally, and constrain, as well as guide, its people's behaviour
- They require leaders in the organization to be role models and paragons of virtue

Lencioni suggests that there is much confusion about values which hinders clear debate. He defines several types:

Core values. Inherent, sacrosanct values that distinguish a company and serve as guiding principles for everybody's behaviour. They are often the values of the founders, as with Hewlett-Packard's 'The HP Way'.

Aspirational values. Values that an organization needs to be successful in the future but currently lacks. Lencioni quotes an example of a *Fortune 500* company which cited 'a sense of urgency' as a core value because employees were complacent: this is not a core value but an aspirational value.

Permission-to-play values. Like core values but they merely reflect the minimum behavioural standard required of all employees. It is these – such as integrity, teamwork, quality, customer satisfaction, innovation – that we see as common to many companies, but they do not create distinctive identity.

Accidental values. Arise spontaneously, reflecting the common interests or values of employees, such as dress code, thus creating a sense of inclusivity. But they may limit a company's opportunities and development by being too exclusive. They are false core values.

Values and behaviour

'Leaders walk their talk; in true leaders, there is no gap between the theories they espouse and their practice,' say Warren Bennis and Joan Goldsmith (1997: 145). For 'theories' read 'values'. The importance in leadership of setting an example as a model for the behaviour of followers is nothing new: it was recognized in ancient writings of Sun Tzu and Confucius.[60] Tony Simons (1999) calls the perceived fit between espoused and enacted values 'behavioural integrity'. He points to a pattern of increasing divergence between managers' words and deeds, driven, he says, by managerial fads and organizational change efforts. He goes on to say:

> the divergence between words and deeds has profound costs as it renders managers untrustworthy and undermines their credibility...[and sacrifices] the trust and commitment of their subordinates.

Covey (1992: 168) says:

> Many executives say they value capitalism, but they reward feudalism. They say they value democracy, but they reward autocracy. They say they value openness and *glasnost*, but they behave in ways that value closeness, hidden agendas, and politicking.

A telling example of the mismatch between values and behaviour comes from the Revlon Corporation:

> At the Revlon Corporation the story is told about Charles Revlon, the head of the group, who insisted that employees arrived for work on time, but seldom arrived himself much before noon. One day Charles wandered in and began to look at the sign-in sheet, only to be interrupted by the receptionist who had strict orders that the list should not be removed. Both insisted that they were in the right until finally Charles said 'Do you know who I am?' And she said 'No sir, I don't'. 'Well, when you pick up your final pay check this afternoon, ask 'em to tell ya'. (Brown, 1995: 15)

True leaders practise what they preach. Unfortunately this is not very widespread (Hooper and Potter, 2001: 7). When espoused values do not match behaviour, this is hypocrisy. But perhaps even behaviour is less important than motive (reflecting values). In the words of the poet W.B. Yeats:

> The Light of Lights
> Looks always on the motive, not the deed,
> The Shadow of Shadows on the deed alone.[61]

William W. George (2001) points out that companies vary little in their stated values – customer orientation, quality, integrity in business dealings, respect for employees, and good citizenship – and that it is difficult to create a unique set of values. He says that what makes the difference is the reinforcement and *practice* of these values, particularly by top management. Without this, trust evaporates. And so does belief in the organization's mission. He argues that:

> Integrity is everything. It takes many years to establish the reputation for integrity, yet it can be lost in a single act. Witness the *Exxon Valdez* and Union Carbide Bhopal, or the Lockheed payoffs of the 1980s. Or, more recently, Firestone and Ford.

Joseph Badaracco and Richard Ellsworth (1989) propose a model that regards integrity – in the sense of wholeness, coherence and moral soundness – as at the heart of leadership. High achievement, they say, results from consistency among personal values, aspirations for the organization, and actions. Personal values comprise strong personal ethics, trust in others and a compelling vision for the organization. Aspirations for the organization relate to having competent people, sharing in the vision and values, openness in communication and expression of feelings, and empowerment. Effective action is consistency with values.

Leaders sometimes lack the ability, moral courage, time or energy to act in accordance with their values. Moral courage is standing up for a set of beliefs and values when the sand shifts beneath one's feet. Yet, Adrian Furnham (2001a) says, few companies have courage as a core value.

Honesty is a core value proclaimed by many organizations. But leaders often face a dilemma here. Olivier (2001: 138) recounts the experience of a human resources director who learned about one scenario which the company was planning for entailed redundancies and relocation for many employees. When frequently asked what was happening, he was not free to reveal what he knew. He faced a dilemma: tell the truth and breach the confidence entrusted to him, pre-empt the management's decisions and action and worsen morale, or lie. Instead, he decided to be truthful about the extent to which he could be honest. He said, 'I do know what is being planned and at the moment there are good reasons why I can't tell you all about it. Here's what I can tell you ... and this is when I will be able to tell you more ... .' He was able this way to retain the trust and respect of the employees despite not giving them what they wanted to know.

One of the reasons why companies are felt by employees to be good to work for is the level of trust they enjoy. Drucker (1999b: 187) says:

> **Organizations are...increasingly built on trust. Trust does not mean that people like one another. It means that people can trust one another. And this presupposes that people understand one another.**

The top three companies in the UK in 2002 in terms of 'the most trusting managers' were Timpson, the shoe repair and key cutting firm, Hewlett-Packard and Microsoft, according to *The Sunday Times* survey of the best 100 companies in the UK to work for.[62]

Trust in a leader has a considerable impact on team and organizational performance: it affects the team's willingness to accept the leader's activities, goals and decisions and to work hard to achieve the goals (Dirks, 2000). Trust is both a cause and a consequence of effective team performance (Dirks, 2000). It is probably the single most important variable that moderates the effects of transformational leadership on the attitudes, performance and satisfaction of followers (Podsakoff et al., 1990). And trust, Marshall (1991: 146) says, is probably the most important aspect of relationships between leaders and followers. Peters (1992: 463) says that trust must be 'unilateral on the part of management'. Showing trust engenders trust.

Francis Fukuyama (1995) relates leadership behaviour to levels of trust in different cultures. High levels of power distance and strong hierarchy, with authoritarian, compliance-oriented leadership, he says, characterize societies or organizations in which there is a low level of trust. Conversely, high levels of communal solidarity and purpose characterize those in which there is a high level of trust, and effective leadership behaviour is likely to be facilitative and empowering, with open communication and internalized controls.

Trust is key to innovation, delegation, self-esteem and effectiveness in virtual teams, where their members are dispersed geographically. Roy Howells says:

> **Learning about emotions and their impact is crucial for anyone who wants to get the best for themselves and their team. It is about learning the value of trust between**

managers and their staff – something that will be a way to deliver high standards of service. (White, 2000b)

Lynda Gratton (2003) describes how she was impressed by the efficiency, mutual trust and happiness of the crews of ferries on Lake Como in Italy. Reflecting on her experience, she muses how there is increasing monitoring and (financial) rewarding of performance today that may be 'eroding the basis of trust'. She says:

> **The balance to be struck is between accountabilities, obligations and trust...to trust without accountabilities and obligations is likely to become one-sided; that is, it will slide into dependence. At the same time, accountability without trust would lead to the continual scrutiny of the motives and actions of others. [To encourage growth and performance] requires us to credit others to be trustworthy without the need to audit their behaviour continually.**

Lack of trust, and lack of truthfulness that is associated with it, is associated with a control-based work environment, says Rob Lebow (Creelman, 2003b). He describes how managers are often not expected to disclose secret information to subordinates, how subordinates are often unwilling to disclose 'the truth' to their managers for fear of damaging their career prospects, and how managers in highly competitive business environments, with control-based mindsets, assume that people are not trustworthy. He says:

> **How often have you called up a company and heard, 'We may be recording this [telephone call] for quality [or training] purposes'. Are we kidding each other? It's not about quality [or training] – *it's about control.***

'If there is no sense of trust in the organisation, if people are preoccupied with protecting their own backs, creativity will be one of the first casualties,' says Manfred Kets de Vries (Cooper, 1997). And John Whitney of the Deming Center for Quality Management says that up to half of all daily business activities may be wasted or compromised due to mistrust (Cooper, 1998).

Trust also has a direct impact on an organization's financial performance and profitability, according to Michael West.[63] In an empirical study of employee trust in their general managers in a catering company consisting of nine restaurants, level of trust – based on perceptions of their ability, benevolence and integrity – was found to be significantly related to sales, profits and employee turnover (Davis et al., 2000). Rob Lebow has also established a relationship between trust and profitability (Creelman, 2003b). And studies in a division of Hewlett-Packard have corroborated this relationship between trust and organizational performance (Gratton, 1997).

Bennis and Nanus say that 'trust is the "emotional glue" that binds leaders and followers together' (1985: 153), a view echoed by Peters (1997: 142). Trust is one's readiness to give someone or something you hold valuable to someone else and believing that it will be safe. Examples of what we hold valuable are money, knowledge, freedom, information and secrets. A study of the 2000 US presidential election showed that trust in the candidate mediated the relationship between perceptions of leadership and voting behaviour (Pillai et al., 2003). Roger Mayer et al. (1995) give the most widely cited definition of trust: a willingness to be vulnerable based on the expectation that the person trusted will do something important to the person trusting the other, regardless of the latter's ability to control the person trusted. Saj-nicole Joni (2004) distinguishes between personal trust based on affinities and personal relationships, 'expertise trust' reflecting reliance on a person's ability in a specific field, and 'structural trust' based on roles and responsibilities – professional relationships that provide informed, disinterested, objective advice.

Covey (1992) says that leadership is as much about *who you are* as about what you do – it is about personal integrity, credibility and trust. He also says:

> **Integrity includes but goes beyond honesty. Honesty is telling the truth – in other words, conforming our words to reality. Integrity is conforming reality to our words – in other words, keeping promises. (Covey, 1989b: 195)**

James Scarnati (1997) says that trust cannot develop without honesty and integrity, and trust leads to credibility, cooperation and collaboration. Jeffrey Garten (2001: 125–126) says that:

> **Trust...requires integrity. CEOs who say one thing and do another...who blame others for their own faulty decisions...who ask the troops to tighten their belts while they purchase more elaborate corporate jets obviously arouse suspicion among employees. [Conversely] an executive's integrity [and hence trustworthiness] is enhanced when he or she takes responsibility for a mistake or a strong position on ethical issues.**

The foundation of trust is trustworthiness, which in turn results from character and competence (Covey, 1992: 31). Not living the values that are espoused, however, seriously damages a leader's trustworthiness and credibility. Collins and Porras (1997: 47–49, 56–58) cite the trustworthiness and credibility of great CEOs like David Packard and George Merck II. David Packard emphasized Hewlett-Packard's values in its mission 'to design, develop and manufacture the finest electronic [equipment] for the advancement of science and the welfare of humanity'. Profit is a means to pursue your mission, not vice versa. Merck insisted that 'medicine is for the patient ... not for the profits ... [the] profits follow'.

To err is human. Unfortunately, in 2002 Merck Pharmaceuticals was accused of inflating revenues to enhance profitability. And HP's image suffered as a result of shareholder battles over its merger with Compaq involving the company's president and Hewlett's son. These events, together with a rash of scandals in 2001 and 2002 such as those involving auditors Arthur Andersen, Enron, WorldCom and Qwest, severely damaged the US stock market and confidence and trust in corporate leaders. This was so severe that even the US president George W. Bush had to intervene and call for a new ethical culture in American business.

Trust has to be earned, and building a climate of trust in an organization can take place only gradually. Covey (1992: 31) depicts trust as an emotional 'bank account', in which people make deposits and withdrawals with one another. Trust, once broken, however, is seldom restored. In the words of novelist Ken Follett (2000: 230) in *Code to Zero*:

> **Trusting someone [is] like holding a cup of water in your cupped hands - it [is] so easy to spill the water, and you [can] never get it back.**

Goodwin (1998), in her analysis of US presidential leadership, says trust is the most fragile yet most important attribute of leadership. Two recent US presidents have discovered this principle – to their cost. Likewise Thatcher (2002: 467) says that the highest form of trust is that held by one who leads a nation, an issue that the British prime minister Tony Blair faced after going to war with Iraq in the belief that it possessed weapons of mass destruction. Matthew Symonds (2003), political editor of *The Economist*, describes how trust in Tony Blair was 'collapsing' in late 2003 as a result both of his blindness to evidence or arguments against joining the Iraq War, having made up his mind that it was the right thing to do, and of increasing scepticism over his policies at home in respect of health, education, public sector reform and joining the euro. The electorate made its judgement in the May 2005 general election, returning the Labour government with a much reduced majority and calls for Blair's resignation.

Skapinker (2003) says that 'the destruction of trust can be seen everywhere'. Particular areas he quotes are organizational downsizing and the closure of final-salary pension schemes to current members. But trust also breaks down when a manager responds with frustration to poor performance by an employee and this remains unresolved, and when bullying occurs (Martin and Fahy, 2003). Such breaches of trust may reach the law courts, which take a dim view of such behaviour.[64]

In contrast, Onora O'Neill in her Reith Lectures (2002) questions whether there really is a 'crisis of trust'. She points out that we place our trust in others perforce, citing doctors, politicians, lawyers, estate agents, and so on. However, in her review of O'Neill's lectures, Warnock (2002b) suggests that:

> To be forced to take as truth what is offered as truth by the media, or by our political masters, when we have no way of knowing whether we are being deceived, is to turn us into a society of cynics, who in the end may be ungovernable. Good behaviour, whether in the City or on the streets, depends on non-cynical trust.

O'Neill considers, with suspicion, the ways in which attempts are being made to restore our trust: human rights movements, a new insistence on 'accountability', 'transparency' and a 'public culture' of communication. She sees these developments as illusions. For example, accountability – the 'unending stream of new legislation and regulation, memoranda and instructions, guidance and advice' that overwhelms public institutions with bureaucracy – does nothing to restore trust. And transparency – 'The very technologies that spread information so easily and efficiently are every bit as good at spreading misinformation and disinformation' – is no better. 'Some sorts of openness ... may be bad for trust,' she says. O'Neill points out the inverse relationship in recent times between openness and public mistrust. A free press is 'good' only in so far as it truthfully informs and makes debate possible, but we have no way of knowing 'whose truth'. O'Neill concludes that society's efforts, and government's in particular, to increase trustworthiness and thereby trust are failing. In commenting, Warnock (2002b) says:

> The intrusiveness and constant checking and double-checking on performance and adherence to codes of conduct, the insistence on calling everyone to more and more detailed account may in fact make people behave worse, and therefore be less worthy of trust.

This is transactional leadership. Transformational leadership, on the other hand, is about creating a culture in which people take seriously not their rights (that others act when we feel we have been deprived of what we deserve) but their responsibilities: in Mary Warnock's words, '[to refuse] to succumb to political pressure ... to use the language of deception ... [to reject] the politically correct ... [to refuse] to endorse slogans and half-truths'. O'Neill argues against the idea that having rights entails having obligations: she says this is not the relation that exists between rights and obligations. If I claim a right, she says, then someone else must have an obligation to secure that right for me or not to prevent my exercising it – an argument that is, in Warnock's view, 'masterly'. Leadership, therefore, must be grounded in legitimacy.

Values, and in particular trust and respect, are inherent in transformational leadership (idealized influence). A key feature of the leadership role is to foster a working environment where people cherish and value one another (Flanagan, 2000). Noel Tichy and Eli Cohen (1997: 106) implicitly relate trust to shared values and empowerment:

> **When you can't control, dictate or monitor, the only thing you can do is trust. And that means leaders have to be sure that the people they are trusting have values that are going to elicit the decisions and actions that they want.**

Trust is about the use of power. Leaders depend on power, but, in BP's Group CEO Lord Browne's words:

> **If you inadvertently punch with the strength of a heavy weight, you may knock someone out you don't want to knock out...all power must be proscribed...we will not use it in one-off transactions with people to take advantage of them, recognizing that we can't come back and do business again – in other words, create a relationship which isn't...mutual. (Garten, 2001: 130)**

Trust results from demonstrated concern for the interests and needs of both the organization and the individual, as both Michael Armstrong, chairman and CEO of AT&T, and Dr Rolf-E. Breuer of Deutsche Bank's board of managing directors emphasize (Garten, 2001: 123–124). Achieving results and contributing to stakeholders' well-being also lead to trust:

> **A leader gains trust by getting results: by setting corporate targets and achieving them, by creating value for shareholders, by running a company profitable enough to create good jobs at good wages, and by having the resources and willingness to contribute to the communities in which the company operates...[by making] decisions openly and fairly...[by having strategies that are] seen as deliberate and thoughtful, with promotions and compensation based on objective criteria that everyone understands. (Garten, 2001: 116–117)**

Employees appear to be trusting their bosses less and less. Why? Garten (2001: 126–127) suggests three reasons:

- Loss of jobs and anxiety among employees remaining due to corporate restructuring, in turn due to financial pressures
- Loss of job security due to globalization and the transfer of functions, especially manufacturing, to developing countries

- Ever shorter tenures and larger severance packages of failing CEOs – $50 million for Jill Barrad at Mattel, $25.5 million for Doug Ivester at Coca-Cola and almost $10 million for Durk Jaeger at Proctor & Gamble – reflecting stock market volatility and the lure of stock options in an increasingly active job market

Loss of trust in leaders in both the private and public sectors has much to do with their lack of credibility or unethical behaviour, issues that reached crisis proportions at the beginning of the twenty-first century. Some 2,500 years ago Confucius told his disciple Tsze-kung:

> **Three things are needed for government - weapons, food and trust. If a ruler can't hold on to all three he should give up the weapons first and the food next. Trust should be guarded to the end. Without trust we cannot stand. (Giles, 1976)**

Valuing loyalty has fallen out of favour in recent years. Employees are said to focus more on their careers and their 'self-actualization' than on serving the interests of their employers. And employers are said to focus more on creating shareholder value than on serving the wider interests of all stakeholders, including employees. Yet many organizations still profess mutual loyalty as a core value, perhaps often more as a social expectation – as 'window dressing' – than as a deep and honest belief. Is loyalty, then, an important value in leadership?

Frederick Reichheld (2001) believes it is. He speaks of 'loyalty leaders'. Among a diverse range of companies – Northwestern Mutual, Vanguard, Chick-fil-A, Enterprise Rent-A-Car, Harley-Davidson and Intuit – he sees 'relationship strategies that are strikingly similar' that are related to profitability:

- Practising what you preach – for example, honesty and openness
- Playing to 'win–win' – all stakeholders benefit in the drive to create customer and – consequentially – shareholder value
- Being selective about employees with compatible values
- Simplifying the rules for decision making for speed and flexibility – for example, 'do whatever is in the customer's best interest' (in the words of Jim Ericson, CEO of Northwestern Mutual), and avoiding excessive bureaucracy
- Rewarding the right results
- Listening carefully and talking frankly – to promote trust, which in turn promotes loyalty

Quoting a survey report published by Bain & Company, management consultants,[65] Reichheld (2001) identifies the personal integrity of the senior leadership team as implicit in promoting loyalty: 'Through loyalty to ideals, leaders become worthy of loyalty from their partners.'

In Shakespeare's *Hamlet,* Polonius advises Laertes, 'This above all, to thine own self be true.'[66] Charles Handy (1992b) puts it in a more contemporary way: 'One's personal principles and values cannot be left on the coat-stand when you walk through the office door.' Bennis and Nanus (1985: 46) endorse this counsel of authenticity in leadership:

> **[Leaders] acquire and wear their visions like clothes. Accordingly, they seem to enroll themselves (and then others) in the belief of their ideals as attainable, and their behaviour exemplifies the ideas in action.**

Values statements are sometimes not considered carefully enough. The case of Borg-Warner is an example (Goodpaster, 1983). CEO Jim Beré developed an exemplary code of ethics that included statements such as 'We believe in the dignity of the individual', 'We believe in the commonwealth of Borg-Warner and its people', 'We must heed the voice of our natural concern for others', and 'grant others the same respect, cooperation, and decency we seek for ourselves' (Murphy, 1998: 27). Following a turnaround in one division resulting from union–management cooperation and the introduction of effective quality circles after years of losses and labour disputes, without warning some operations were transferred overseas to save on labour costs. Three hundred jobs were lost. The way the decision was carried out showed no respect for those who had worked so hard to achieve success. The efforts, goodwill and commitment of employees were ignored; so were the 'exemplary' values.

A happier story comes from Merck Pharmaceuticals (Useem, 1998: 29). George C. Merck, son of the founder, reinforced the company's belief that medicine was for people, not profits, but that, if medicine was for people, profits would follow. The company had developed a drug that was effective in treating river blindness, a disease that threatened some 85 million people in 35 developing countries. However, the drug was unaffordable for them. CEO P. Roy Vagelos and his directors announced in 1987 that they would give away the drug free, for ever. By 1996 the drug had reached some 19 million people, and by 1997 the gesture had cost the company $200 million. The values of the company, and the founder, had guided the actions of its leaders in pursuing the company's mission:

> **to provide society with superior products and services... . We are in the business of preserving and improving human life...All our actions must be measured by our success at achieving this goal... . We expect profits from work that satisfies customer needs and that benefits humanity.**

This was not the first time the company had acted this way. After the Second World War, tuberculosis spread in Japan, and most Japanese could not afford Merck's powerful drug, Streptomycin. So Merck donated a large supply free. Many years later, remembering Merck's gesture, the Japanese permitted the company to purchase a controlling share in a Japanese pharmaceutical firm to become the largest American firm in that industry. Other pharmaceutical firms – GlaxoSmithKline and DuPont – have since acted likewise. Merck had set the benchmark for moral behaviour. And its leaders had set a moral benchmark for the industry.

The importance of shared values

The challenge of change has stimulated the emergence of values-based leadership. Lee Bolman says, 'you can't talk sensibly about leadership without talking about how leadership is based on … purpose and values' (Shinn, 2003). O'Toole (1995: xiii) says that there is a widespread belief among corporate executives in the need to create strong, shared values to unite people in a fragmented world. The fear, though, is the danger of 'groupthink'. Yet, if there is one organizational characteristic that provides the 'glue' in uniting people, it is trust. And trust, O'Toole suggests, 'emanates from leadership based on shared purpose, shared vision, and especially, shared values' (O'Toole, 1995: xiii).

Peters and Waterman (1982: 76) say that 'People way down the line know what they are supposed to do in most situations because the handful of guiding values is crystal clear.' They say that a strong organizational culture is one in which values are shared, intensely held, and clearly known by employees. Robert Haas quotes Levi Strauss, where shared values contribute to competitive success: 'values drive the business' and provide a common language that unites employees and leaders (Howard, 1990). And Tony Morden (1997) concluded that General Electric's success depended significantly on shared values, which former chairman and CEO Jack Welch promulgated.

Shared values make a significant impact on both the job satisfaction and morale of people in an organization and their job performance and contribution. For example, congruence between employee values and organizational culture is positively related to employee commitment, according to Chatman (1991). And Karen Jehn et al. (1997) found that value congruence among group members decreased conflict associated with both relationships and tasks and increased group members' performance and satisfaction. Mark Tannenbaum (2003) concluded from his study of seven public and private organizations that:

> An analysis of these successful companies and their competitors demonstrated that focusing first on alignment of values and strong cultural norms were distinguishing factors with measurable bottom-line revenue and profitability results.

A study of 11 US insurance companies showed that those whose managers did not share the same perception of corporate values performed less well than those with shared values (Gordon and DiTomaso, 1992). Ann Nicotera and Donald Cushman (1992) say:

> If the value systems of individuals do not complement the value system of their organization, those individuals will eventually be faced with insoluble ethical dilemmas.

Drucker (1999a) agrees:

> To work in an organization the value system of which is unacceptable to a person, or incompatible with it, condemns the person both to frustration and to non-performance.... Organizations, like people, have values. To be effective in an organization, a person's values must be compatible with the organization's values. They do not need to be the same. But they must be close enough to coexist.

And so does Joseph D. Williams, CEO of Warner-Lambert:

> Unless company objectives are in harmony with your [employee] objectives, unless our corporate way of life is compatible with the way you want to work and what you want to achieve, there is no way we can succeed, no chance to excel. (Deetz et al., 2000: 51)

William O'Brien, CEO of Hanover Insurance, believes that people must share values and a vision of the future before there can be meaningful participation: 'people have a real need to feel that they're part of an ennobling mission' (Dess and Picken, 2000). And Lord Browne of BP says:

> **The people who make up our company...have hopes and fears for themselves and for their families. Companies that want to keep operating successfully have to uphold their employees' values, just like customers' values. We cannot isolate ourselves. (Garten, 2001: 4)**

Brand values that are shared characterize EasyJet and the stable of Easy companies founded by Stelios Haji-Iaonnou:

> **Over the last five years [since 1995], we've acquired brand values. Value for money, easy for the consumer, fighting the big boys, orange, innovative – these are what Easy means. Not because I decided, but because that's what people think of it. (Hall, 2000)**

Value congruence mediates the relationship between leadership style and performance outcomes (Jung and Avolio, 2000). When the values of the leader and the followers coincide, the leader gains legitimate power through credibility. Legitimate power is the ability to motivate people because of their belief in the leader and in what the leader is trying to accomplish (Covey, 1992: 102). Margaret Thatcher's demise as British prime minister in 1990 – after a successful start in this respect – was largely due to her failure to maintain or reflect shared values among her followers in her leadership behaviour (Horn, 2001). The very essence of transformational leadership is the achievement of 'value congruence within the group, organization, or society [that] gives rise to behaviour that is itself congruent with these values' (Price, 2003). Transformational leaders create and promote a culture of shared values and beliefs that support and facilitate the pursuit of the vision, mission and strategies of the group, organization or society.

A culture that is strong – where values are widely shared and deeply held – tends to endure, and the founder's vision and strategies are likely to become a legacy – or a hangover – depending on their flexibility and environmental conditions (Ogbonna and Harris, 2001). But John Gardner (1990: 191) says:

> **One of the tasks of leadership – at all levels – is to revitalize...shared beliefs and values, and to draw on them as sources of motivation for the exertions required of the group.**

A survey of senior and top-level managers by Ashridge Management College revealed significant tensions between their personal values and corporate ethics (Faruk, 2002a,b). One respondent reported: 'My organisation has one mission – maximise shareholder value – everything else they do is secondary ... environmental destruction is the result.' Some 44% said they had supported social or environmental campaigns in their private lives and one-quarter of these believed their actions to be inconsistent with what they are expected to do at work. These findings call into question the extent to which corporate values are genuinely shared.

The leadership challenge is to create 'transcendent' values that accommodate different aspirations, to appeal to common, higher-order values that transcend narrow self-interest. (This is transformational leadership – that raises us to go beyond our self-interest and pursue the common good.) An example that O'Toole (1995: 258–261) quotes is Vaclav Havel, former president of the Czech Republic. Havel always made

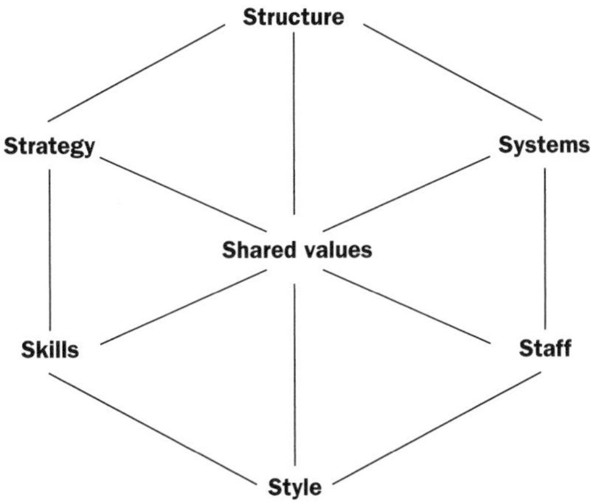

Figure 5.1 *The McKinsey 7S model*

decisions on the basis of his principle of 'civility' – the collective practice of respect for people. He did just this in reluctantly allowing the dissolution of Czechoslovakia into the Czech Republic and Slovakia.

Ian Davis (2003) suggests that people will increasingly be seeking employment with companies that uphold their personal values:

> **The best companies will create jobs and roles where employees feel they have some control over what they do, where professional relationships are valued, where more than lip-service is paid to work-life balance and where there is real belief in the social and ethical responsibility of the employer.**

Shared values are part of the well-known McKinsey '7S' framework (see Figure 5.1), which is useful for understanding the culture of an organization and its strengths and weaknesses and for considering the factors affecting strategy implementation (Sharplin, 1985: 69).

Employing elements of the 7S model, Brother Uttal (1983) defines corporate culture as:

> **A system of shared values (what is important) and beliefs (how things work) that interact with a company's people, organizational structures, and control systems to produce behavioral norms (the way we do things around here).**

Certain values or beliefs, according to Roy Eidelson and Judy Eidelson (2003), are more likely to lead to individual or intergroup conflict. These are a sense of superiority, perceived injustice to oneself or one's group, a sense of vulnerability, distrust and a sense of helplessness. An example of superiority as a dangerous core belief is Hitler's ideology of Aryans as a master race with the right and destiny of ruling over other people (Gonen, 2000). Political leaders may express such core beliefs in inspirational speech, with potentially dangerous consequences (see Chapter 8).

The clash of values underlying the terrorist attacks on the World Trade Center and the Pentagon on 11 September 2001 – the perception of corrupt American power and materialism – 'more than any other single issue, will define the shape and soul of this new century', says former US president Bill Clinton (2001). He says:

> **Most of us believe that our differences [in political and religious beliefs] are important and make our lives interesting but that our common humanity matters more.**

Clinton is talking here about shared values at the global level, and values that need to be reflected and displayed in the global vision and strategies that our leaders pursue.

Management consultant Rob Lebow points out that shared values '[create] a context in which people [can] work ... of how we [can] treat each other and our customers' (Creelman, 2003b). Productive customer relationships, he says, require those who deal with customers to have freedom rather than control, but in a culture of shared values:

> **A freedom-based workplace expects that every front-line worker is both responsible and accountable for delivering [productive customer relationships]; and shared values allow people to relate to each other as thinking and responsible adults.**

Shared values alone, Lebow says, is not sufficient: a freedom-based, not a control-based, environment in which people are trusted to do the right thing is necessary. But 'it is the sharing of our values that is the oil that lubricates the [organizational] machine'.

Peter Wickens (1999a) suggests that, if an organization wants to have genuinely shared values, it is necessary first to discover the existing values and then determine what values are desired. This discovery process, he says, should be led, but not dictated by, the enterprise's leadership. In the Barnsley Alcohol and Drug Advisory Service in the UK, he applied this process, following 10 steps:

1. Introduce the concept of values
2. Identify possible relevant values, both positive and negative
3. Ask everybody individually to select six that best describe their perception of the current values of the organization as demonstrated by the behaviour of themselves, the top management and others
4. Have small groups of people (of about the same organizational level) reach consensus on six to eight of the perceived current values
5. Report the conclusions to a plenary session (in the Barnsley Alcohol and Drug Advisory Service only 'humour' emerged as common, and many values were negative) and get plenary session consensus.
6. Returning to the original list, ask everybody individually to select values that are desired, have small groups, this time multi-functional and multi-level, reach consensus on about six
7. Following reports once again to the plenary session distil desired values into a final list
8. After the workshop, ask participants to discuss the results with their colleagues, aiming to involve as many people as possible as 'insiders'
9. Reconvene to report and discuss the consultation process and refine the values
10. Translate the values into behaviour, goals and measures, including working on the negative current values that were identified earlier to eliminate them

Wickens (1999b)

CASE EXAMPLE

Introducing New Values at Claridge's

Claridge's, one of London's most luxurious hotels, is a case study in rehabilitation through the way in which a new vision and set of values was introduced. Catherine Edwards (2004) reports how in 1998 a new human resources director, Sara Edwards, had to confront lowered occupancy rates, high staff turnover (73%), guest complaints and poor staff morale. Underlying her approach was the principle: 'If you don't get it right with the employees, you won't get it right with the guests.' The executive team formulated a new vision – to be 'the first choice for any guest coming to London looking for style and quality service, and the first-choice employer' – and a set of seven values concerning communication, passion, team spirit, interpersonal relations, service perfection, maximizing resources and responsibility for actions, shown pictorially as a rainbow.

At an away-day with the executive team, managers were asked to stage a five-minute sketch, song or dance to illustrate one of the values. Edwards says the impact was remarkable, and, with all executives and managers putting the values into action, appraisal linked entirely to values (not skills), staff winning a range of attractive prizes for exceptional demonstration of a value, and other HR initiatives, by 2002 staff turnover had fallen to 27% and morale had increased dramatically.

Ownership of the values is a key issue. Lencioni (2002) does not believe that this should be achieved by seeking consensus. He says this risks including suggestions from employees 'who don't belong in the company in the first place' and '[creating] the false impression that all input is equally valuable'. The best values initiatives, he says, are 'driven by small teams that include the CEO, any founders who are still with the company, and a handful of key employees'. Values initiatives, he says, are 'about imposing a set of fundamental, strategically sound beliefs on a broad group of people'.

Rob Lebow carried out a meta-analysis of several million surveys of job satisfaction and performance up to 1972. He identified several universally shared values:

- Treating one another with uncompromising truth
- Trust
- Mentoring unselfishly
- Being receptive to new ideas regardless of their origin
- Taking risks for the organization
- Giving credit to others
- Honesty
- Putting the interests of others first

(Creelman, 2003b)

Effective leaders provide ways to recognize, encourage and develop shared values among followers. Deetz et al. (2000: 76) say, 'If leaders want to ensure that their values are inculcated into organizational members, then they must also provide organizational systems that correlate with their espoused goals.' For example:

> **if innovation is a top priority in an organization, then leaders must build mechanisms in the culture to ensure that such innovation is stimulated among colleagues who may or may not have direct contact with the leader on a daily basis. (Avolio and Bass, 1994: 206–207)**

Creating a sense of shared core values that support the organization's vision, mission and strategies requires their integration into every policy, procedure and process concerning employees: recruitment and selection, performance management and appraisal, training and development, promotion and rewards. Successful companies reflect their shared values in their recruitment processes to attract the 'right' people and in their culture by introducing them into their corporate literature, communication policies and practices, competency models, training and development programmes, promotion practices and performance appraisal processes. In its recruitment and selection strategy, the RAF uses a procedure that assesses first an individual's values and then skills for a role. This reduces the risk of incompatibility with the organization's culture.

Another strategy that organizations use to create a strong corporate culture is performance appraisal and linked rewards and promotion. Here, those whose actions and behaviour reflect or promote organizational values or guiding principles enjoy rewards and promotion. This is Bass's contingent reward (transactional leadership) in action (see Chapter 2). Employees may feel that the organizational values are being 'forced' upon them and that their own values are less important. This may result in disaffection and alienation. However, transformational leadership, in particular individualized consideration and the three other 'I's, has an advantage over transactional leadership in creating trust, respect and confidence in management.

In the context of culture change, some organizations go further, using indoctrination, or what Edgar Schein calls coercive persuasion (Schein and Coutu, 2002). He says this is more typical of companies in some East Asian countries, and is known as *xinao*, or 'cleansing of the mind'. For example, Schein quotes GE's Jack Welch's non-negotiable requirement: 'if you wanted to stay at the company, you had to learn what he wanted you to learn. Heavy socialization is back in style in American corporations.' Schein also says that culture change is more difficult than is perhaps appreciated and takes a long time – for example 25 years in the case of Procter & Gamble. He argues that coercive persuasion is the only viable alternative to starting with a completely new set of employees who already possess the desired values.

CASE EXAMPLES

Corporate Values

STONYFIELD FARM

Gary Hirshberg (2002), president and CEO of Stonyfield Farm, a fast-growing American yoghurt company, describes his company as values driven. He says, 'our values and social mission are central to everything that we do ... we are in business to do far more than simply attain a positive financial goal'. Chapter 4 describes the company's mission.

DARDEN RESTAURANTS

Joe Lee, chairman and CEO of Darden Restaurants, Inc., a successful casual-dining restaurant company in the United States and the largest in the world, sees the values of integrity, fairness, and respect and caring for people as critical to the success of the company (Ford, 2002). The corporate culture depends, he says, on recruiting employees who share those values.

TESCO

Tesco is one of the few companies to state its values in its annual review: 'In the UK and internationally, the way we do things ... is defined by our values. They are fundamental to our business and support the core purpose.'[67]

• No one tries harder for customers	Understand customers better than anyone Be energetic, innovative and first for customers Use our strengths to deliver unbeatable value to our customers Look after our people so they can look after our customers
• Treat people how we like to be treated	All retailers, there's one team ... the Tesco Team Trust and respect each other Strive to do our very best Give support to each other and praise more than criticize Ask more than tell and share knowledge so that it can be used
• Enjoy work, celebrate success and learn from experience	

VODAFONE

Sir Chris Gent, former chief executive of Vodafone, one of the world's leading mobile telecommunications companies, says:

> Increasingly, we are bound together by core values which run throughout the Group – professionalism, excellence in service, customer focus and a determination to deliver the benefits which corporate social responsibility can bring for us all. We are passionate about our customers, passionate about our people, passionate about achieving results and passionate about the role we play in the community at large. We hope and expect that this will be manifest in everything we do.[68]

Vodafone states its corporate social responsibilities in two pages in its annual review and in a separate report,[69] indicating its focus on 'core values and principles that have always been part of the Vodafone philosophy' and setting out its determination to address issues in its social, environmental and economic impact.

Culture and values

The case for the importance of corporate culture in business organizations has been strongly argued. For example, Gideon Kunda and Stephen Barley (1988) say:

> **Culture enhances social integration; social integration eliminates the need for bureaucracy, and increases levels of investment which, in turn, enhance performance and productivity. Thus, by manipulating culture, substantial increments in profitability should accrue.**

However, Jennifer Chatman and Sandra Eunyoung Cha (2003) take a more measured view:

> **We [do] not claim that by simply managing culture, leaders will be assured of organizational success, or by neglecting culture they will be doomed to failure. Leveraging culture is but one of a number of key leadership tools. We [do] claim, however, that by actively managing culture, an organization will be more likely to deliver on its strategic objectives in the long run.**

What is culture?

'Culture is to people what software is to computers – the programming of people's thinking and behaving', say Henry Lane et al. (2000). Shared values and beliefs are 'the templates through which groups and group members interpret their shared experience ... [and] ... are an essential component of group culture' (Eidelson and Eidelson, 2003). Harry Triandis (1996) says that culture is reflected in 'shared cognitions, standard operating procedures, and unexamined assumptions'.

Culture has been described in many ways, and it is difficult to find a consensus. In any case, culture describes what an organization *is* (Smircich and Calás, 1987: 228–263). Andrew Leigh and Michael Maynard (2000) see culture as 'a heady mixture of vision, values, tradition, ethos and self-image'. And Work Systems Associates (1996: 22) describe culture as:

> **the lifestyle of [the] organization: the core values; hidden assumptions or beliefs; [the] systems, policies, and procedures; the way [it does] business every day.**

Understanding the corporate culture – and, by implication, the national culture in the case of expatriate managers – is part and parcel of leadership.

> [The] ability to perceive the limitations of one's own culture and to develop the culture adaptively is the essence and ultimate challenge of leadership. The most important message for leaders at this point is 'Try to understand culture, give it its due, and ask yourself how well you can begin to understand the culture in which you are embedded. (Schein, 1992: 2)

Understanding of culture was advanced in the early 1980s by three complementary, hugely popular books, focusing our attention on vision, values and leadership: William Ouchi's *Theory Z;* Terrence Deal and Allan Kennedy's *Corporate Cultures: The Rites and Rituals of Corporate Life;* and Tom Peters and Robert Waterman's *In Search of Excellence* (Deetz et al., 2000: 7). Ouchi's *Theory Z* argued for the need to integrate the typically Western values of individual achievement and advancement with the Japanese sense of community (Ouchi, 1981). This sense of community, however, has its downside. Michiyo Nakamoto (2001) argues that Japan's culture of group solidarity may have to give way to the entrepreneurial spirit of the individual. He quotes Martin Reeves at Boston Consulting Group as saying that such group solidarity has often counted for more than results, and Ichiro Hatanaka of Accenture as saying:

> The skill that has been most valued at Japanese companies has been the ability to coordinate the various elements of the group so as to maintain the harmony of the whole. And that is why Japan's business leaders break down in tears as they announce a drastic restructuring or a corporate failure: they have failed the group.

Leadership and corporate culture

Terrence Deal and Allan Kennedy (1982) identified five components of a strong corporate culture: the organization's external environment, corporate values, organizational heroes, rites and rituals, and the cultural network. And Peters and Waterman (1982) discovered eight cultural features that characterize 'excellent' companies: a bias for action, closeness to the customer, autonomy and entrepreneurship, productivity through people, being hands-on and value driven, sticking to the knitting, having a simple form and lean staffing, and having simultaneously loose–tight properties.

Emmanuel Ogbonna and Lloyd Harris (1998) caution that 'the complexities and intricacies of the concept of organizational culture have done more to confound executives and researchers than to enlighten them'. They explain that organizational culture is not the same as organizational climate or power and politics, and it not a unitary concept. Susan Schneider and J. Rentsch (1988: 27) distinguish between culture and climate thus:

> Climate refers to the ways organizations operationalize the themes that pervade everyday behaviour...'what happens around here' [while] culture refers to the history and norms and values that members believe underlie climate...'why...things happen the way they do'.

Warner Burke and George Litwin (1989: 16) define culture similarly as 'the way we do things around here' and the collection of overt and covert rules, values and principles that guide organizational behaviour, and climate as:

> **The collective current impressions, expectations, and feelings that members of local work units have that, in turn, affect their relations with their boss, with one another, and with other units.**

Organizational culture comprises multiple sub-cultures, typically of a departmental, occupational and professional, and geographical kind. Ogbonna and Harris (1998) carried out an in-depth case study of three British retailing companies and found that the cultural perspectives of their employees were directly linked to their hierarchical positions in their organizations. Head office managers tended to perceive organizational culture in an integrative way, emphasizing consistencies (possibly neglecting sub-culture differences). Store managers perceived it in a differentiated way, recognizing the existence of sub-cultures (e.g. head office) and balancing their demands. Shop floor staff perceived organizational culture as fragmented, as in a constant state of flux, and indicated confusion about the company's values.

Ogbonna and Harris conclude that 'any change initiative which is based solely on head office values and perceptions is likely to be ineffective'. They suggest that:

> **There is an inherent difficulty in achieving an organization-wide consensus in values... [and that] it may be advisable to...recognize the existence of subcultural differences... and look for ways of reconciling only the key differences which directly impact upon the performance of the organization.**

A study of a large Danish insurance company by Geert Hofstede (1998) also revealed not one corporate culture but three distinct sub-cultures – a professional sub-culture, an administrative sub-culture and a customer-interface sub-culture. Failure to understand this led to values-based rifts and adverse consequences in the form of losses and a change in ownership and top management.

Corporate culture is socially constructed by employees. The most common conceptions of culture are:

- The behavioural regularities observed when people interact – such as language, traditions and rituals
- Group norms, standards and values
- Espoused or articulated values
- Formal philosophy
- Rules of the 'game'
- Learning the organizational 'ropes'
- Corporate climate – the feeling portrayed through the organization's physical layout and the way people relate to one another
- Embedded skills or the special abilities of the organization
- Habits of thinking, mental models, and other linguistic paradigms
- Shared meanings
- 'Root metaphors', or integrating symbols

(Schein, 1992: 9)

Corporate values are perceived in the artefacts of corporate culture. These include organizational structure, office layout, dress codes, stories and legends, distribution and sharing of power, reward systems, communication style and methods, behavioural norms and expectations, unwritten rules, and the taken-for-granted beliefs and assumptions at the heart of corporate culture.

Values affect behaviour, and behaviour affects values. Karen Legge says:

> [Culture] is both produced and reproduced through the negotiation and sharing of symbols and meanings - it is both the shaper of human action and the outcome of the process of social creation and reproduction. (Buchanan and Huczynski, 1997)

However, in building a corporate culture:

> Leaders have more direct control in shaping communication patterns and overt behaviors than they do in changing deep-rooted value systems. Therefore...leaders [need to] create and change a culture through the way they communicate...[affecting] the espoused values, norms, and rules of their organization through visioning...[shaping] employees' identification with the organization...[and framing] organizational stories, myths, and everyday communication...in line with the values that are best for the organization. (Deetz et al., 2000: 11)

The need for leaders to create and manage organization culture is consistent with the increasingly accepted importance of organization-wide leadership – shared or distributed leadership (Ashkanasy et al., 2000).

Culture operates at the emotional level and therefore is a powerful force. J.M. Beyer and David Nino (2001: 173–197) suggest five ways in which culture shapes emotions:

- Managing the anxieties arising from uncertainties. Organizational culture, Schein (1990) argues, provides meaning, stability and comfort for members.
- Providing ways to express emotions, for example rites and rituals. Rites and rituals are held on to long after they have ceased to be useful because they have emotional meaning. Fineman (2001: 214–239) says it is our self-control, not managerial control, that manages the tension between private feelings and public display and enables social control.
- Encouraging and discouraging emotional experience. Culture may shape emotions in a subtle way, sometimes insidiously, whereby people, assured they are empowered and free, may 'roam [but] at the end of a leash, constrained ... by the governing cultural assumptions of the organization' (Tourish and Pinnington, 2002).
- Engendering identification and commitment to the organization. Cultures provide a social identity and thereby an emotional bond or attachment among organizational members and with the organization itself.
- Producing ethnocentrism. A 'strong' culture is characterized by 'like-minded, like-feeling, like-behaving employees' that may yield competitive advantage (Tourish and Pinnington, 2002) but may create an unhealthy organization, for example in the case of lack of diversity and a lack of openness to diversity (Härtel and Fujimoto, 2000). The dangers of 'groupthink' (Janis, 1982) and unquestioning compliance or obedience in respect of orders from superiors (Milgram, 1963) are well known.

Lane et al. (2000) provide a Cultural Orientations Framework that identifies six areas that need to be addressed in considering culture:

- Relationship of people to the environment: harmony, mastery or subjugation
- Relations among people: collective, individualistic or hierarchical
- Mode of activity: being, doing or thinking
- Human nature: 'blank slate', predisposition to 'goodness' or predisposition to 'badness'
- Time: monochronic (linear time, requiring its measurement and management), polychronic (time viewed as flexible), and past, present or future orientation
- Space: sense of shared or personal ownership (public or private)

A distinctive and strong corporate culture can give one business a competitive advantage over another in the same industry, according to Deetz et al. (2000: 31). This view is endorsed by Adam Zuckerman (2002), who says that companies that outperform their competitors and enjoy better returns on investment, higher net income growth and bigger increases in share value tend to have stronger corporate cultures, where values and behavioural norms are widely shared and strongly held. For example, in their analysis of the Silicon Valley cluster of interconnected companies, John Micklethwait and Adrian Wooldridge (2000) identify what they call 'the ten habits of highly successful clusters':

- A strong belief in meritocracy
- A very high tolerance of failure
- Tolerance of 'treachery' – talent-intensive businesses inevitably lose both secrets and employees
- Collaboration – short-term alliances between companies and individuals
- Risk orientation – one winning idea pays for scores of failures
- Reinvestment – money that is made is ploughed back into the company
- Change orientation – getting stuck in a rut risks demise
- Obsession with a winning product
- Opportunity and achievement orientation – success is admired and aspired to rather than begrudged
- Sharing of wealth – founders share proceeds with employees when firms are sold

Ogbonna and Harris (2000) carried out a multi-industry study in the UK, investigating the relationship between leadership style, organizational performance and organizational culture. They identified four distinct types of culture – innovative, competitive, bureaucratic and communitarian – and three leadership styles – participative, supportive and instrumental (akin to directive or transactional leadership). Performance was measured by a composite of customer satisfaction, sales growth, sales volume, market share and competitive advantage.

They found that competitive and innovative cultures are associated with organizational performance. They also found that strongly held shared values are associated with organizational performance, but only if organizational culture is oriented towards the external environment. With regard to leadership style, they found 'significant, indirect pervasive effects on organizational performance' and strong causal associations with competitive and innovative cultures (and hence on organizational performance). Supportive and participative leadership styles were positively related to organizational performance, and instrumental leadership was negatively related. Ogbonna and Harris's overall conclusion was that organizational culture mediates the relationship between leadership style and organizational performance.

Jesper B. Sorensen (2002) found that firms with stronger cultures also perform more consistently, except when industry volatility increases. The reason may be that a strong culture may impede adaptability:

> **The findings of a good deal of case study work in industry, and particularly that with an ethnographic or an anthropological focus, have suggested that work cultures are highly distinctive, resilient and resistant to change. (Ackroyd and Crowdy, 1990)**

Employees are often more satisfied when they work in a 'strong culture' in which values are widely shared (Deetz et al., 2000: 33). But too strong a commitment to the values and 'desired' behaviours might decrease flexibility and inhibit creative problem solving (Cooper and Hartley, 1991). Deetz et al. (2000: 32) say:

> **A strong culture can become a limitation when important shared beliefs and values interfere with the goals of the organization or members and the direction it needs to go to stay competitive...[it] can actually hurt an organization or even lead to unethical behavior. Therefore, a strong culture may best be thought of as a balance between extremes.**

Empirical studies of the relationship between corporate culture and performance, however, do not always show clear-cut results. One study, by John Kotter and James Heskett (1992), for example, showed a positive but weak correlation between the strength of the corporate culture and economic success. However, they also found that high-performing companies – producing shareholder value four times greater over 10 years compared with low performers and a return on capital of 11.3% compared with 7.7% – were characterized by the greater value they placed on leadership, customers, employees and shareholders. And 'visionary companies', in which vision was not merely the preserve of the CEO but embedded in the organization, were differentiated from 'also rans' by displaying historical continuity of values, actions consistent with values, investment in people, objectives beyond profit, and investment for the long term (Collins and Porras, 1995: 83). Their average return on investment over 50 years was 15 times the stock market average.

David Buchanan and Andrzej Huczynski (1997: 530) say, 'the popular view that a strong corporate culture [leads] to economic success [is] just plain wrong'. Perhaps the truth of the matter is that the corporate culture should not just be *strong* but should be *positive* in terms of the values supporting and informing the organization's vision, mission and strategies. So a question for a leader is to decide whether the organization's 'strong' culture is the appropriate culture in relation to its vision, mission and strategies. The existing culture may be at odds with these – a huge challenge for leadership. This question must be addressed through input from all stakeholders, particularly employees. For this to happen, employees need to be empowered to provide such input, which we consider in Chapter 7.

Ross Perot, chairman of Perot Systems Corporation, emphasizes the importance of corporate culture in stating in the company's annual report the intention to 'Create an environment where the hopes and dreams of every person can materialize if the company is successful.'[70] The company believes that its 'unique culture' – reflecting the values of initiative, flexibility, accountability and integrity – 'produces energy and results'. Its annual report is itself unique in providing examples of how its values are translated into real-life behaviour.

Founders of companies create organizational cultures that often endure long after their passing (Deetz et al., 2000: 162–163). They often create a company to put their deeply held values into practice. Their values appear in their companies' mission statements and in their visions of a desired future as well as in 'the way we do things around here'. Why do such organizational cultures endure?

One explanation comes from the study of memes, a term coined by Richard Dawkins (1998). Memes are items of information through which culture is inherited. They lead to 'copycat' behaviour and enduring cultural characteristics such as 'dress, diet, ceremonies, customs and technologies' (Blakemore, 1999: 6). For example, memes characterize the way proponents of 'manoeuvre warfare' talk about the Wehrmacht's *Sturm und Drang, Schwerpunkt* and *Auftragstaktik* rather than 'main effort' and 'mission tactics' (Hooker, 1993: 27–28). In talking this way the speakers are promoting an authoritative and warlike image characteristic of the German Second World War military machine. Modern examples of memes are the use of the terms like 'boat people' and 'asylum seekers' and George W. Bush's 'axis of evil'. 'Mimetic engineering' is the term used for embedding desirable (shared?) values into the collective minds of people in an organization through the use of memes.

Successful leaders create strong, positive cultures: the culture supports the vision and mission of the organization or group and facilitates their pursuit. Deetz et al. (2000: 21) say:

> If company values are consistent with national and community values and with different levels in the organization and across the industry, the strength of the culture is increased. If the various systems are contradictory, the strength is reduced... . Cultural strength is increased when company values are carefully integrated with deeply held values of employees...[and when] pay systems, employee relations, and espoused values are consistent.

Research in the early 1990s reported by Rajan (2000b) showed that a large majority of companies still had 'strong elements of paternalism and bureaucracy in their culture'. This research also noted that 'their change programmes sought to replace them by elements of democratic culture of high performance and employee empowerment' and that some 'also tried to embrace elements of the anarchic culture of excellence and continuous improvement', on which the 'jury' was still out seven years later. One problem, according to a chief executive whom Rajan quotes, was the 'leadership gap':

> It is one thing to talk about creating a new organisation for the new age. But not creating the requisite leadership qualities at the outset is like putting the cart before the horse.

Leadership and national culture

Can there be 'leadership *sans frontières*' (Gill, 2001b)? Those who work in multinational or global organizations may have a particular interest in the similarities and differences in the behaviour of effective leaders in different cultures. In the UK, Tom Cannon (2000) says, the nature of effective leadership is changing because we have moved from a monoculture to a multiculture.

Examples of areas in business in which understanding cross-cultural aspects of leadership styles and behaviour can help are dealing with global competition, international mergers and acquisitions, assessing new market opportunities, international transfer of executives, localization of management, and international management and leadership development programmes. Managers, in working in multinational organizations, can as a result better predict the problems arising in adopting parent-company organizational policies and leadership practices. Cross-cultural studies suggest the need to avoid global generalizations and to focus on local cultures (Kabasakal and Dastmalchian, 2001).

Values define both corporate and national cultural differences. So if effective leaders create a strong culture of shared values, is leadership universal or culture specific? Cultural differences pose a special challenge for leaders in global and multinational organizations. For example:

> **Exporting participative leadership to countries with authoritarian cultures is like preaching Jeffersonian democracy to [those] who believe in the divine right of kings. (Haire et al., 1966)**

Research evidence tends to support 'travellers' tales' about differences in the behaviour of leaders in different cultures (Bass, 1997b). But popular views or stereotypes of cultural characteristics do not always stand up. For example:

> **The idea of consensus has a powerful appeal for Japanese, who seem convinced, despite abundant evidence to the contrary, that their society and culture are built on a foundation of *wa*, harmony. (*The Economist*, 2001a)**

The way of Lao Tzu, however, is still reflected today in Japanese culture. Adair (1989: 55) writes:

> **The Japanese practise a more self-effacing style of leadership than is customary in the West. In Japan the group is still valued more highly than the individual.**

Yet 'leadership' is a universal phenomenon: there are leaders everywhere. Universally, in democracies, effective leaders gain the voluntary commitment of people – not merely their compliance – to strive towards goals: they get people to *want* to do the things that help the organization (or nation) succeed. And they empower them to do so. According to a survey by PA Consulting Group (1996), universal aspects of leadership across cultures are vision, inspiring people and creating a learning organization. British Telecom focuses on five key skills and characteristics in its cross-cultural leaders: emotional resilience, flexibility and openness, perceptual acuity and sensitivity, personal autonomy and humility (Griffiths, 1999).

In a comparative study of Southeast Asian and British managers, Southeast Asian emerged as significantly more directive and less delegative than British managers (Gill, 1999b). Both groups were about the same in their use of the consultative and participative styles. Southeast Asian managers, however, varied more in their use of the latter two styles.

The greater directiveness and lesser delegativeness of Southeast Asian managers are not surprising. The cultures they work in are generally more authoritarian than British culture. In some traditional Asian cultures, people expect to be told what to do and how to do it. They regard initiative and decision making on direction and methods as the manager's responsibility. Moreover, they do not necessarily even want to be consulted. Being consulted about what to do or how to do it may be seen as a weakness in the manager (he or she does not know) rather than a strength – helping the individual to develop and grow or gaining his or her commitment through ownership of ideas. This means that participative (Western) management practices such as management-by-objectives may not work as well as they do in the West. Southeast Asian managers may well find their subordinates more dependent on them. They may also find themselves more overloaded as a result of lack of delegation. The greater variation in Southeast Asian managers' use of consultation and participation might reflect a more heterogeneous management culture than in the UK, with its mix of Western-educated managers and traditional Asian managers.

Consultative and participative styles of leadership in the Near East and Middle East cannot be equated to those in the West (Kabasakal and Dastmalchian, 2001). The consultative style, they say, is used to 'pander to egos' rather than to improve the quality of decision making, and the participative style is used to induce feelings of belonging to the group rather than to achieve consensus on decisions. Mansour Javidan and Ali Dastmalchian (2003), in respect of Iranian managers, much like Southeast Asian managers, say they 'have become accustomed to autocratic leaders who make decisions without much participation from their employees .... They expect the leader to develop a vision and communicate it to them.'

Southeast Asian managers also emerge as more laissez-faire than British managers (Gill, 1999b). Perhaps Southeast Asian culture conditions them to avoid conflict, and therefore to avoid confronting people, and to be more 'psychologically distant' from their subordinates. The greater use of management-by-exception that also emerged might reflect their greater workload as a result of a disinclination to delegate. And, with respect to their greater use of contingent reward, other findings suggest that extrinsic rewards like money are more effective for Southeast Asian managers in motivating employees than for British managers. Performance-related pay has become increasingly controversial in the UK in recent years. Greater psychological distance between Southeast Asian managers and their subordinates may also explain another finding: their lesser individualized consideration. In general, the differences in leadership styles and in transactional and transformation leadership between Southeast Asian countries and the UK are consistent with Geert Hofstede's model. This is probably the best-known model of national cultural differences. According to this model, national cultures vary in terms of power distance, uncertainty avoidance, independence and 'masculinity/femininity' (Hofstede, 1984, 1991, 1994).

A study of national cultural differences in a large international chemical company across several European countries and including the United States revealed differences in people-oriented leadership but not in task-oriented leadership (van Beek, 2000). For example, managers in the Czech Republic tend to rely more on their own experience when making decisions than British managers do (Smith, 1999). This has implications for empowerment, participation and consequently the commitment of those who have to implement management decisions. The Latin European countries value people-oriented leadership more.

Cultural values appear to affect organizational commitment. Arzu Wasti (2003), in a study in Turkey, found that, for employees who endorse individualist values, satisfaction with work is a key determinant of emotional attachment to the organization and a feeling of obligation to remain with it. On the other hand, for those with collectivist values, satisfaction with the supervisor is more important.

That values differ between the West and the East is scarcely contested. Lee Kuan Yew, former prime minister of Singapore, has frequently argued this. But Malaysia's former prime minister, Dr Mahathir Mohamad, said, 'Asian values are actually universal values and Western people used to practise the same values'.[71]

Fons Trompenaars (2000) proposes that the solution to the problem of cultural differences is not ethnocentric domination or even compromise, but the reconciling of opposing values. The challenge to organizational leadership is to develop a corporate culture that recognizes the diversity of values across national cultures and reconciles them within a corporate culture that supports the organization's vision and strategies. Lansdell (2002: 33) quotes, for example, global management consultants McKinsey & Co. as achieving just such a balance. By 1999, she says, only 40% of its 4,800 consultants were from the United States, the rest representing some 80 nationalities. All consultants are expected to adhere to a set of corporate values and aspirations, for example an obligation to see things from others' points of view. But within this framework there is freedom to act in line with what is best for the company.

CASE STUDY

The GLOBE Project

A major contribution to understanding the relationship between national (societal) culture and leadership has been made by the long-term GLOBE project, started in 1993 (House et al., 1999: 171–233; House et al., 2001). This project aimed to identify the 'etic' (the universal characteristics) and the 'emic' (the culture-specific characteristics) of effective leadership. It also aimed to develop an empirically based theory to answer, among others, the following questions:

1 Are there leadership behaviours and attributes that are universally effective across cultures?
2 Are there some that are effective only in some cultures?
3 How do societal and organizational cultures affect leadership behaviour that is effective?
4 What is the effect of violating cultural norms relevant to leadership behaviour?

The GLOBE project gathered data from 17,000 middle managers in some 825 organizations in 61 countries. The project studied nine cultural dimensions drawing on previous work on culture, including Hofstede's. These are uncertainty avoidance, power distance, societal collectivism, group collectivism, gender egalitarianism, assertiveness, future orientation, performance orientation and humane orientation.

A sub-study of over 6,000 managers in European countries revealed that leadership concepts vary by culture within Europe (Brodbeck et al., 2000). Countries that share cultural values also share leadership concepts. However, Den Hartog et al. (1999) found that certain aspects of charismatic/transformational leadership are strongly and universally endorsed across cultures.

An analysis of the GLOBE data for future orientation – planning and forecasting, investing in the future and delaying gratification – revealed that Iran, Kuwait, Turkey and Qatar are similar to one another but below the world average (Kabasakal and Dastmalchian, 2001). The concept of 'fate' or destiny in Islam (Ilmihal, 1999) – that all past and future deeds are pre-ordained – influences future orientation negatively. However, this appears to be true only at the overall societal level and not in organizations, where leaders are expected to be future oriented and 'visionary' (Kabasakal and Bodur, 1998; Abdalla and Al-Homoud, 2001; Dastmalcian et al., 2001; Pasa et al., 2001).

As part of the GLOBE project, Felix Brodbeck et al. (2002) found that middle-level managers in the telecommunications, food processing and finance industries in Germany share a strong performance orientation and a lack of compassion and interpersonal consideration. The authors believe that sensitivity to the feelings of people is an important development need among business leaders in Germany to cope successfully in the future with the challenges of globalization and multicultural teams.

Leadership and business ethics

Ethics are a set of moral values translated into rules of conduct that reflect a distinction between what is good and bad or right and wrong. Ethics are supposed to govern actions and behaviour. Ethics, philosopher Anthony Grayling (2004) says, 'is about one's "ethos", one's whole way of life ... what sort of person one is'. The place of ethics in business leadership has long been recognized. In 1938 Chester Barnard wrote about the need for balance between an organization's financial performance and moral values and ethical standards in employees:

> **To suppose that leadership, that the moral elements, are the only important or significant general factor in organization is as erroneous as to suppose that structure and process of cooperation without leadership are sufficient. (Barnard, 1938)**

A survey by a Jesuit priest in 1961 reported in the *Harvard Business Review* found that conflict between personal values and business pressures had arisen for only three out of every ten people (Baumhart, 1961). The main areas of conflict were dismissals, lay-offs and dishonesty in advertising, contracts and promises. Business executives tended to believe that 'good ethics is good business' because it leads to repeat sales, lower labour turnover, a good reputation, and public and customer acceptance. The survey also found that unethical practices increased with both too little as well as too much competition.

The decline in ethical standards in business

A decline in ethical standards in business has been perceived over the last decades of the twentieth century, inversely matched by an increasing emphasis on organizational productivity and financial performance (Cohen, 1995). There is evidence that leadership is a key influence: leaders may either encourage or discourage followers to behave in an ethical or unethical way (Brief et al., 2000). Leadership behaviour can influence ethical conformity, according to other research findings (Schminke et al., 2002). Organizational culture, including ethical values, is established by the founders of organizations (Dickson et al., 2001). It is maintained or modified subsequently by successive leaders according to how they perceive and interpret it.

The plethora of cases of corrupt business practices in the United States from late 2001 and into 2002 created alarm in stock markets around the world. Enron, the energy-trading company, was accused of using complex deals to hide losses and exaggerate profits. WorldCom, America's second largest long-distance telephone company, was accused of the world's largest fraud in reclassifying expenses of $3.9 billion to bolster profits and declared itself insolvent. Conglomerate Tyco was accused of 'aggressive' accounting and its former CEO of tax evasion. Qwest, the telecommunications company, was investigated for dubious accounting practices and swap deals to exaggerate revenues.

AOL Time Warner, Halliburton and several other companies were being investigated for questionable accounting practices. John Rigas, the former head of bankrupt Adelphia, one of America's largest cable-television companies, was accused, together with two sons, of misusing the company's funds for personal benefit. And Arthur Andersen, the audit and accounting firm, the 'auditor of choice for the bad guys' – Enron, WorldCom, Qwest and others – was convicted of destroying evidence in the Enron case (Rushe and Durman, 2002). The rot is not only in the United States. The fast-growing German life insurance company, MLP, was raided and accused of inflating its profits through questionable reinsurance deals (Rushe and Durman, 2002). And in the UK there has been the mis-selling of life assurance.

Many organizations, of course, take business ethics seriously. The US Army has a long track record – with some notable failures – in emphasizing and training for ethical decision making and instilling ethical core values (Dickson et al., 2001). And following Lockheed's conviction for conspiracy in 1995 to commit bribery and falsification of records – and a fine of almost $25 million – the company introduced a corporate ethics programme, continuing after its merger with Martin Marietta to form Lockheed Martin, focusing on building trust.[72] Many other organizations are doing likewise. Some, however, have not had a second chance.

In response to the spate of corporate scandals over greed and corporate wrongdoing, many university business schools such as Strathclyde and Harvard have introduced business ethics and social responsibility courses into their MBA programmes (Bradshaw, 2003). However, the scepticism that exists towards the practice of business ethics and corporate social responsibility is evident in the words of Philippe de Woot, chairman of the University of Louvain:

> **The protagonists of the recent financial scandals in the United States were successful students of business ethics in prestigious international business schools. Some even taught business ethics[!] (Oliva, 2004)**

Business ethics, culture and value systems

Ethical standards of behaviour in organizations, George Steiner (1975: 213, 217–220) suggests, arise from several value systems. Religious values of right and wrong emphasize human dignity and worth and the need to recognize the rights and obligations of other people – employees, customers, shareholders and the general public. Philosophical ideas, through reasoning, produce ethical norms, such as the Aristotelian Golden Rule that we should behave to others as we would wish them to behave towards us, or the first-century Jewish sage Hillel's principle that 'What is hateful to you, don't do to your fellows.' Culture – group, organizational or national – is associated with values that maintain or advance people's interests and well-being.

The legal system codifies customs, ideas, beliefs and behavioural standards which society wishes to preserve and enforce, such as employment protection, rights to negotiate pay and conditions of employment, and health and safety at work. And professional and business codes of practice promote ethical corporate behaviour, for example in recruitment, career development and consultation procedures.

The Right Reverend Hugh Montefiore (1976) suggested that excessive regulation may restrict personal initiative (which is intrinsically good) but may also restrict exploitation (which is intrinsically bad), while freedom may encourage personal acquisitiveness (which is bad) but may obviate dependency (which is good). Montefiore argued that a balance was needed. More recently, Sir William Barlow (2002), former president of the Royal Academy of Engineering and former chairman of the Post Office, argued that privatization of the utilities and associated government regulation have harmed their performance. Such regulation, he says, has limited infrastructure investment and technological innovation and emphasized competition over and above efficiency and quality of service or product delivery.

Leadership and business ethics: implications for leadership

As with vision, values have ethical and moral aspects. Subordinates or followers judge values in terms of what is 'good' and 'right'. But what are 'good' and 'right' values? The theory of transformational leadership assumes that transformational leaders know the answer to this question (Rost, 1991). However, Terry Price (2003) suggests that this is not necessarily the key issue; nor is it where transformational leaders act in their self-interest rather than 'morally' correctly. He argues instead that leaders may act according to other values they are committed to that they think override general moral requirements. Transformational leadership, he says, is about more than being authentic – being true to oneself. It is also about sacrificing some values when generally applicable moral requirements legitimately compete with them. Hitler, for example, while in some respects an effective leader, infamously failed this crucial test. So have several CEOs in business organizations more recently.

The ethical leadership challenge is to create, promote and reinforce, in every way possible, corporate values and ethical standards of behaviour that both reflect the shared personal values of all individuals in the organization (and its other stakeholders) *and* serve its vision, mission and strategies. This is the basis for corporate social responsibility.

Leadership and corporate social responsibility

If the corporation were personified, what kind of a person would it be? This is a question asked in a film released in the UK in 2004, *The Corporation*,[73] and based on a book by Joel Bakan (2004). The answer it gives is – a psychopath. *The Economist* explains:

> Like all psychopaths, the firm is singularly self-interested: its purpose is to create wealth for its shareholders. And, like all psychopaths, the firm is irresponsible, because it puts others at risk to satisfy its profit-maximising goal, harming employees and customers, and damaging the environment. The corporation manipulates everything. It is grandiose, always insisting that it is the best, or number one. It has no empathy, refuses to accept responsibility for its actions and feels no remorse. It relates to others only superficially, via make-believe versions of itself manufactured by public-relations consultants and marketing men. In short...the corporation is clinically insane. (The Economist, 2004)

The film makes the point, *The Economist* says, that, 'through their psychopathic pursuit of profit, firms make good people do bad things', such as exploiting the relationship between children and their parents, acting deceitfully as an impostor to extract business intelligence, and selling tobacco and thereby 'spreading cancer'. 'Human values and morality survive the onslaught of corporate pathology,' *The Economist* says, 'only via a carefully cultivated schizophrenia.'

More than 40 years before, Nobel Prize winning economist Milton Friedman (1962: 133) famously argued that:

> There is one and only one social responsibility of business – to use its resources and engage in activities designed to increase its profits so long as it stays within the rules of the game... . Few trends could so thoroughly undermine the very foundations of our free society as the acceptance by corporate officials of a social responsibility other than to make as much money for their stockholders as possible. This is a fundamentally subversive doctrine.

The debate still rages today, but on different arguments.

Corporate social responsibility – concern for the environment, concern for the working conditions of suppliers' employees, and supporting human rights around the world – is justified, Geoffrey Colvin (2001) says, on grounds of corporate self-interest – to maximize long-term profitability. Colvin says it is also justified on grounds of consumer demand: increasing capitalism and prosperity around the world, he says, has 'made room for those issues on the mainstream agenda'. However, Simon Zadek (2001) disagrees with Colvin's first point. He believes that economics and ethics do not always walk hand in hand – that there is a trade-off between socially responsible corporate behaviour and the profitability of the firm:

> **Doing good clearly does not guarantee financial success...just as being less than ethical does not guarantee financial disaster.**

On Colvin's second point, Zadek agrees, and he suggests that the market system can ensure social responsibility is afforded an economic value through a model of 'civil regulation'. This model shows how the profitability of a firm in certain circumstances can be positively correlated with its reputation in terms of perceived ethical behaviour. The existence of the FTSE4Good index in the UK recognizes the importance of social responsibility to investors.

Steven Carden and Olive Darragh (2004) of management consultants McKinsey & Co. report a study of an investment portfolio defined as 'socially responsible' over 10 years. It generated returns of 8 to 14%, lower than the rate typically earned from direct equity investments in entrepreneurial ventures but comparable to S&P 500 capital-market returns and acceptable to the majority of the investors.

Andrew Wilson (2001) suggests there may be 'elasticity' of demand for corporate social responsibility: different groups in society may be prepared to pay more for goods and services from more socially responsible organizations. And Zadek (2001) argues convincingly that corporate social responsibility encourages innovation and creativity.

Research at Ashridge in the UK revealed that 77% of its alumni, mostly senior and top-level managers, rated responsible business practice as 'very important' to the long-term success of a company (Faruk, 2002a,b). Some 75% rejected the proposition that companies should be run for the benefit of shareholders with all other considerations secondary. The survey also found tensions between managers' personal values and corporate ethics. The 2004 Roffey Park survey found that 80% of the 735 managers surveyed in the UK stated it was important to them personally that their companies are environmentally and socially responsible (Hoar, 2004).

A survey of top corporate executives in 200 major companies in Europe by Business in the Community, a corporate social responsibility organization based in London, reported by Peggy Anne Salz (2003), suggests that integrating responsible business practices makes a company more competitive and that 73% believed that this can significantly improve profitability. She quotes how British pharmaceutical company GlaxoSmithKline's share price rose by over $1 in the week following the announcement of its decision to reduce further the not-for-profit price of its HIV/AIDS medicines for the world's poorest countries by up to 47%. She describes how investors and employees alike want organizations to attend to social issues. And she quotes James Despain of Caterpillar as providing first-hand evidence that values-based leadership can create outstanding financial and social results:

> **To restore employee – and ultimately customer and stakeholder – satisfaction, management must lead by example and build an organization around vision and values employees are proud to share... . [The increased focus on corporate social responsibility forces companies to] make sure it's not just the business that is being run ethically... .**

> **The objective must also be to give employees a workplace where they can express themselves without fear or intimidation of threat, and leave each day with a sense of worth and self-dignity.**

Social responsibility as business policy has its roots with Robert Owen, the cooperative movement and the Quakers in the UK, and with the Amish and the Shakers in the United States. Leaders in global organizations, says the founder of The Body Shop, Anita Roddick (2000), have a global social responsibility: their decisions impact not just on economies but on human poverty, the environment and security. The key to developing social responsibility, she says, is the empowerment of employees:

> **There aren't many motivating forces more potent than giving your staff an opportunity to exercise and express their idealism to influence change: locally, nationally and globally.**

The social responsibility of leaders and their companies must extend explicitly to recognizing and upholding employees' values, says Lord Browne of BP Amoco:

> **Companies are an integral part of the societies in which they work. We don't make our profits and then go and live somewhere else. This is our society, too. The people who make up our company are also citizens. They have hopes and fears for themselves and for their families. Companies that want to keep operating successfully have to uphold their employees' values, just like customers' values. We cannot isolate ourselves. (Garten, 2001: 4)**

And former chairman of ICI, Sir John Harvey-Jones (1988: 249), says:

> **Enduring values in companies, which spread the whole way down the line, are reinforced by business success, and become almost articles of faith.**

The growing interest in the importance of corporate social responsibility has been reflected in the establishment of the European Academy of Business in Society, sponsored by several business schools and companies. One of the fundamental and growing criticisms of business is the prevalent focus on creating value for shareholders rather than for society as a whole. Henry Mintzberg states the issue this way: the system 'allows companies to damage society within the law and executives to amass untold riches, despite destroying value' (Cowe, 2002). The role of leadership in emphasizing corporate social responsibility is to be one of the Academy's research thrusts.

Corporate social responsibility: what companies do

Europe's business leaders believe responsible business practices lead to greater innovation, competitiveness and profitability, according to a survey reported in the *Financial Times* (Maitland, 2002). Yet few regard it as the concern of every department – and by implication every leader – in the company. The survey also shows that, while 43% of British directors believe that all departments should be actively involved in corporate social responsibility (CSR), only 10% of directors in the rest of Europe do. And less than one-third of the 200 chairmen, CEOs and directors surveyed have credos or codes of conduct that deal with environmental, ethical and social issues.

Some industries are particularly at risk of criticism about how they perceive and discharge their social responsibilities. The utilities sector is an example. ScottishPower stated in 2001 that it saw 'Balancing economic goals with the needs of society and the natural resources on which we depend … [as] at the heart of sustainable development.'[74] Specific actions the company has taken include CO_2 reduction, customer education in efficient energy use, moving towards more sustainable energy supplies to reduce adverse long-term environmental damage (as part of its vision of being a leading renewables operator), and implementation of strategies to enhance the safety of employees, customers and the general public.[75] Ranked top in the 2000/2001 *Financial Times*/BiE Survey of Corporate Environment Engagement, the company has also received a Queen's Award for Enterprise in Sustainable Development.

Vodafone also recognizes its social responsibilities. In 2000 it set up a Group Corporate Responsibility team, aiming to 'help manage the environmental and social impacts of the Group'.[76] BT regards the way employees are treated, equal opportunities, health and safety, and business ethics as crucial CSR issues (Persaud, 2003). According to its head of sustainable development and corporate accountability, Chris Tuppen, CSR activities impact directly on customer satisfaction. The company, he says, found that, 'For every 1 per cent increase in our socially responsible activities, we get a 0.1 per cent increase in customer loyalty.'

Anita Roddick, founder of The Body Shop, stresses CSR as a priority for the company – and indeed any company. She says, 'It is a basic responsibility of business to be open and honest about its environmental and social impacts' (Persaud, 2003). Roddick says that The Body Shop's approach is 'putting our money where our heart is'. It monitors its performance through regular social and ethical audits, and has achieved rankings for CSR of 1 in the UK, 10th in the United States and 14th worldwide (Lansdell, 2002: 32).

In the annual report for 2002, Cadbury Schweppes' CEO, John Sunderland, states that the company's success 'has been built on … a strong commitment to build on long-established values', incorporating them into its statement of purpose and values, and recognizing that 'enduring corporate success requires a clear sense of purpose and values to which all our colleagues are committed'.[77] The company, Sunderland says, also places 'great importance on corporate and social responsibility' to all stakeholders, with a Corporate and Social Responsibility Committee chaired by Baroness Wilcox. A 'particularly challenging issue' in 2001, he continues, was 'the reported use of the worst forms of enforced child labour in cocoa production in the Cote d'Ivoire'. The company is included in the FTSE4Good and Dow Jones Sustainability indices, and in 2002 started publishing a CSR report. The four 'defining characteristics' of its CSR policy are shown in Table 5.2.

Table 5.2 *Cadbury Schweppes' CSR policy: defining characteristics*

- We take an **inclusive approach**. CSR touches many aspects of our business and is integral to our relationship with **all our stakeholders**.
- Our formal statement of *Business Principles* sets out **our beliefs** and establishes **a framework for behaviour** right across the Group.
- CSR is a **Board-level responsibility**. The Board's Corporate and Social Responsibility … oversees the integration of CSR. The Board's Audit Committee considers it as part of our risk management processes.
- We work with **partners, suppliers and customers**, with whom we share a responsibility for ensuring high standards throughout the value chain.

Source: Annual Report and Form 20F 2001, Cadbury Schweppes plc, pp. 26–7.

The company also has a human rights and ethical trading policy, which covers core labour rights, health and safety, and respect for diversity. In practice this includes a *global supplier code*, pilot studies 'to examine areas of particular importance in the supplier chain', collaborative action on the 'reported use of child labour on cocoa farms in West Africa', and participation in the Global Industry Protocol.

Cadbury Schweppes' CSR policy also includes an undertaking to:

> **meet the learning and development needs of all employees...policies and procedures to promote equal opportunities in diverse cultures...high standards of health and safety...investment in [and encouragement of employee participation in]...community programmes [around the world]...aligned to the Group strategy of creating value in the community...and sound and responsible environmental management...measured against detailed performance targets in all parts of our operations.**

Stefan Stern (2004) points out that 'When companies sign up publicly to something called "CSR" they open a can of worms. Every business decision, every investment or closure, can immediately be subjected to the CRS test,' quoting the example of banking group HSBC. He quotes how HSBC's website proclaims employees to be the biggest beneficiaries of the business – ahead of shareholders – and yet HSBC transferred its call-centre operations from the UK to Asia, retrenching some 4,000 employees. He also quotes the example of the leading supermarket firm Tesco, which aids regeneration in deprived inner-city areas, creating employment (and new customers?), and provides computers for schools – 'marketing in disguise' in the classroom – yet squeezes suppliers to generate maximum profits.

Boots was nominated for a *Business in the Community* award in 2003. The company also takes CSR seriously, being 'among the first to champion family-friendly policies for employees ... [and] ... the first organisation to offer staff formal accreditation for their work in the community' (Persaud, 2003). The company's reputation was dented in January 2004, however, when it announced substantial job losses.

A tool for evaluating the competing demands of shareholders, government and society at large is Roger Martin's 'virtual matrix' (Martin, 2002). This provides a conceptual framework for addressing questions of social responsibility, depicting the forces that create it:

- The norms, customs and laws that govern corporate practices and engagement in these practices either by choice or by statutory compliance
- The organization's structural or strategic innovations in socially responsible behaviour

In the 1960s, the late Martin Luther King Jr was fond of quoting a black Southern minister:

> **Lord, we ain't what we ought to be.**
> **We ain't what we want to be.**
> **We ain't what we're going to be.**
> **But, thank the Lord, we ain't what we was. (Steiner, 1975: 173)**

The sentiment in respect of CSR arguably is still true today. But this discussion of social responsibility cannot end without a comment on social responsibility and the state. *The Economist* argues that the modern state is potentially 'a more dangerous psychopath than any corporation can ever hope to become', citing the examples of the 'environmental destruction wreaked by Japan's construction industry' and North Korea (*The Economist*, 2004).

CSR: implications for leadership

The key leadership tasks in resolving the issues of CSR are:

- Providing a clear mission and vision for the company: 'What are we here for?' and 'What do we want to be?'
- Recognizing employees' values and beliefs in the company's core values and guiding principles in respect of CSR
- Empowering employees to voice their opinions and influence change
- Displaying 'spiritual intelligence' and leadership by providing meaning and value in work

Values and guiding principles inform not only vision and mission in effective leadership but also the strategies for pursuing them. We therefore now turn to strategy, the third essential element in our model of leadership.

Further reading

N.M. Ashkanasy, C. Wilderom and M.F. Peterson (Editors) (2000), *Handbook of Organizational Culture and Climate.* Thousand Oaks, CA: Sage Publications.

Joel Bakan (2004), *The Corporation: The Pathological Pursuit of Profit and Power.* New York: Free Press.

A. Brown (1995), *Organisational Culture.* London: Pitman.

James C. Collins and Jerry I. Porras (1997), *Built To Last: Successful Habits of Visionary Companies, 2nd Edition.* London: Century/Random House Business Books.

Stanley A. Deetz, Sarah J. Tracy and Jennifer Lyn Simpson (2000), *Leading Organizations through Transition.* Thousand Oaks, CA: Sage Publications.

F. Fukuyama (1995), *Trust: The Social Values and the Creation of Prosperity.* London: Hamish Hamilton.

Geert Hofstede (1994), *Cultures and Organizations: Software of the Mind, Paperback Edition.* London: HarperCollins.

R.N. Kanungo and M. Mendonca (1996), *Ethical Dimensions in Leadership.* Beverly Hills, CA: Sage Publications.

J. Kotter and J.L. Heskett (1992), *Corporate Culture and Performance.* New York: Free Press.

Edwin Schein (1992), *Organizational Culture and Leadership, 2nd Edition.* San Francisco, CA: Jossey-Bass.

Discussion questions

1 What values would you wish to promote in an organization, and why?
2 How can we create a culture of 'shared values'?
3 Who decides what the guiding principles should be? And how can they be communicated and effectively applied?
4 How can we know that an organization's culture is the 'right' culture for it?
5 Why are some managers hypocrites?
6 Why have business ethics declined?
7 Why do corporations practise corporate social responsibility (when they do)?

6 Leadership and Strategy

Without strategies, vision is a dream.

Overview

- The proposition of this chapter is that effective leaders develop, get commitment to, and ensure the implementation of rational and intelligent strategies that both enable people to pursue the vision and mission and reflect the values they share.
- Expressed in the simplest possible way, strategy is about how to get from where we are now to where we want to be. It is a journey plan and a route map for travelling to the destination (vision). Strategy also serves an organization's or nation's core values. Strategies are ways of pursuing the vision, identifying and exploiting opportunities, anticipating and responding to threats, and not only responding positively to the need for change but also creating change.
- Studies show that the lack of strategic thinking and strategies is a common management weakness, except in the most admired companies and those that are most successful. We discuss briefly the place of shareholder value as the sole strategic focus in commercial organizations in relation to corporate mission and values, particularly with respect to customers and employees.
- Strategic thinking can be classified into various approaches: the classical, evolutionary, systemic and processual. And strategies are developed at several levels: corporate, business and functional.
- This chapter discusses the concept of core competencies and distinctive capability in strategic thinking and the Balanced Scorecard as a useful basis for developing strategy. Several examples of corporate strategies are provided. The case study of CGU Asia illustrates an analytical approach to business strategy that underscores the importance of the intellectual dimension of leadership.
- Developing strategy entails 'strategic conversation' in the organization – a participative approach – and alignment of people's tasks and actions. We discuss the way this can be done through 'sense-making' and the cognitive skills and social and

emotional processes involved. We also discuss the effects of emotion and mood in the strategy process.

- We discuss methods of strategic analysis, in particular environmental scanning, PESTLE analysis, industry and competitor analysis, SWOT analysis, benchmarking and scenario planning.
- Deciding on a strategy may entail reconciling a variety of individual interpretations and choices to achieve consensus. Decisions reflect decision makers' mental maps and political processes (including their use of power), which in turn reflect the organizational culture. Strategies on the other hand may emerge: they may *form* rather than be *formulated*. Influences on this process are history and context.
- Leadership is also about ensuring that strategy is implemented effectively. This entails enabling and ensuring commitment to it through ownership of it as well as the control mechanisms that are part and parcel of 'management'. Leaders who focus on strategy in pursuing a vision or set of long-term goals can be called strategic leaders.

Leadership starts with a dream – a vision of where or what we want to be. If leadership is about showing or even 'sharing' the way, then what is 'the way'? The way is the strategy. So leadership necessarily entails deciding the strategy. And strategy concerns choices that determine whether an organization survives, prospers or dies.

The difference between 'what we are' and 'what we want to be' creates what Vansina (1999) calls 'psychic tension'. This tension lies in the feasibility of moving from what we are to what we want to be. This requires both will and coordinated action. The key to realizing a vision or fulfilling a mission is strategy. Vansina presents two positions: 'A mission becomes feasible through … strategy.' And 'a mission is feasible when we believe in our capacity to design an appropriate strategy to reach it.' It requires greater self-confidence to decide the latter.

John Kotter says, 'Strategy without vision can only go so far and vision without strategy translates into hope without a practical reality' (Finnie and Norris, 1997). In the words of an old Chinese proverb: 'It is not the call of the duck, but its flight, that makes the flock to follow.' It is perhaps not the leader per se who creates followers, but the leader's vision and strategies. As with vision, strategies require intellectual validity, spiritual meaning and emotional appeal in the minds and hearts of followers. Winston Churchill as a leader in wartime achieved all with his proactive strategies:

> **To [Parliament] he gave the realisation of his unrivalled grasp of the grand design that must unfold through the years ahead. (Ferrier, 1965: 6)**

'Asking a management theorist to define strategy,' *The Economist* (1997) says, 'is rather like asking a philosopher to define truth.' Good strategies, however, result from the organization's vision and mission statement, and good strategic planning reflects the values of the organization and its environmental realities (Covey, 1992: 166–167). A strategy outlines how the organization intends to pursue its mission and realize its vision for the future.

In a celebrated lecture at the Harvard Business School in 1931, Alfred North Whitehead, the eminent philosopher, identified strategic foresight as 'the crucial feature of the competent business mind' (Fiol and O'Connor, 2002). By this he meant the ability to anticipate future developments – to reflect on change and novelty, see through confusion, foresee trends, see emerging patterns, and understand social currents that are likely to shape future events. Some 500 years ago, the Japanese military leader Miyamoto Musashi said: 'In strategy it is important to see distant things as if they were close and to take a distanced view of close things' (Beatty and Quinn, 2002).

Today's leaders, contemplating mergers and globalization, Champy and Nohria (2000: 12) say, frequently have great visions, but 'getting from A to B is often as dangerous and mysterious as sailing off into unknown waters was in the age of exploration'. Markets and competition are increasingly complex and dynamic. Global integration and coordination of operations, demand for local country and market responsiveness, and the need for innovation and new business development pose ongoing challenges to be met.

Strategic leadership models emphasize the thought processes of leaders. They propose that strategic decisions reflect a careful analysis of the environment and organizational strengths and weaknesses, opportunities and threats, using defined criteria (Pearce, 1981; Bourgeois, 1984, 1985; Hitt and Tyler, 1991). Senior executives may consistently misinterpret environmental threats and opportunities (Dutton et al., 1983; Dutton and Jackson, 1987; Dutton et al., 1989). How this can happen is well understood in the concepts of cognitive dissonance (Festinger, 1957) and the perseverance effect (Fiske and Taylor, 1991). This can lead to strategic drift (Johnson, 1987) and serious consequences. Johnson and Scholes (2002: 550) identify several cognitive characteristics of strategic leaders: visionary capacity, mental ability and the ability to cope with complexity, and expressing ideas simply.

Strategic thinking is a crucial cognitive competency of leaders. Yet, according to John Adair, sadly British business culture is short term and pragmatic: 'We don't even believe in strategy, let alone strategic leadership' (Simms, 2002). Only 44% of companies' annual reports mention corporate strategies, with only 36% stating clear objectives for the company and few stating its direction, according to a study in the UK Europe and United States (Parker, 2003). The best reports were from GlaxoSmithKline, BT, Vodafone, AstraZeneca and Aviva; the worst were from UBS, Tesco, Berkshire Hathaway, Deutsche Telekom and Kingfisher. The world's most admired companies (headed by GE, Wal-Mart and Microsoft), according to the 2002 survey conducted for *Fortune* magazine, however, do have clear and focused strategies (Chen, 2002).

A survey of small and medium-sized enterprises in one region of the UK revealed that 64% had a formal strategic planning process (Nadin et al., 1998). And according to a 2001 survey of 451 senior executives by management consultants Bain & Company, strategic planning is used by 76% of respondents' organizations (Rigby, 2001). The main benefits of strategic planning were reported as strengthening integration effort across the organization and improving competitive positioning, performance capabilities and financial results. For example, a study by management consultants PricewaterhouseCoopers found that companies with documented HR strategies typically show 35% higher revenue per employee than the 42% of companies without one (Willmott, 2003).

Bureaucratic organizations are often regarded as poor in strategic behaviour. Universities, for example, are weak in competing with one another and slow in responding to a fast-changing environment, according to Michael Diamond (2002). Kasturi Rangan (2004) reports that many not-for-profit organizations do not have any strategy and most make programme decisions based on their mission rather than a strategy. However laudable their actions, acting this way, Rangan says, 'can stretch an agency's core capabilities and push it in unintended directions'. He analyses a children's aid agency, SOS Kinderhof, based in Austria, as an example. This is not to denigrate loyalty to the mission, for this is the source of inspiration for the organization and its funding sources. On the other hand, organizational missions must keep pace with the times.

Competitive advantage plays a central role in defining strategy (Kim and Mauborgne, 2003). Michael Porter (1980) is well known for his theory of strategy development and implementation based on an understanding of competitiveness and the environment and for his 'five forces' model:

- The threat of new entrants and the appearance of new competitors
- The degree of rivalry among existing competitors in the market
- The bargaining power of buyers
- The bargaining power of suppliers
- The threat of substitute products or services that could shrink the market

However, Chan Kim and Renée Mauborgne's research suggests that this approach may be dysfunctional: it discourages creativity, with old, young and new industries alike, and it focuses on the competition – a 'vicious cycle of competitive benchmarking, imitation and pursuit ... [that achieves] mere incremental advantage over market rivals' – instead of value and innovation for the customer. The customer, not the competition, should be the focus of strategy. Kim and Mauborgne quote Pret A Manger, Borders Book Stores, Starbucks, Bloomberg and IKEA as examples of success in this respect. Hamel and Prahalad (1994) concur. They argue that businesses need to focus on aligning their own strengths – their core competencies – with customer needs rather than focusing on the competition. And they need to focus on innovation, aimed at exceeding customer demands – thereby staying ahead of the competition (Hamel, 2001).

In a very different context Sir Ernest Shackleton, the Antarctic explorer, who was particularly interested in the 'mental' side of leadership, thought out brilliant strategies for survival in terrible conditions. He made contingency plans in great detail while still remaining flexible. Today we call this scenario planning. In all ways, from planning his missions – including fund raising – to responding to threats and opportunities during his voyages, Shackleton set the standard for 'best practice' in strategy formation and implementation. He taught us lessons that are particularly relevant to today's high-risk, turbulent and entrepreneurial business environment.

What is strategy?

The word 'strategy' comes from the Greek, *strategos,* which originally referred to a general in command of an army. Its meaning evolved over several centuries BC to mean successively the art of the general, managerial skills as well as oratory and power, and ultimately 'the ability to employ forces to defeat opposing forces and to develop a unified system of global governance' (Evered, 1980; Quinn, 1980; Mintzberg and Quinn, 1996). Moshe Farjoun (2002) defines strategy as:

> **the planned or actual coordination of the firm's major goals and actions, in time and space, that continuously co-align the firm with its environment.**

Goals 'state what is to be achieved and when results are to be accomplished, but do not state how the results are to be achieved' (Quinn, 1980). Actions are 'resource deployments, initiatives, responses, moves, deals, investments, and developments' (Farjoun, 2002). Coordination refers to goals and means for achieving them, resources and administrative infrastructure. Strategy reflects vision and purpose (mission) and core values. Co-alignment refers to adapting to, and at times adapting, the environment (Pfeffer and Salancik, 1978; Bourgeois, 1984; Itami and Roehl, 1987; Porter, 1991). Strategy thus is a matter of content (goals and action), coordination and context, and it is interactive, adaptive and integrative (Farjoun, 2002).

Expressed in the simplest possible way, strategy is about how to get from where we are now to where we want to be. It is a 'journey plan' (Grayson and Hodges, 2004: 157). Strategy is generally viewed as 'a posture and a plan', where posture is 'a fit or alignment ... between [for example] activities and organizational structure, and environmental elements, such as a customer group' (Farjoun, 2002). Christopher Bartlett and Sumantra Ghoshal (1989) pointed out in the late 1980s the need for multinational and global organizations to meet demands for both global efficiency and local responsiveness at the same time. This, they argued, entails replacing centralized, hierarchical structures with networks of far-flung teams and resources.

Strategies are route maps. Strategies are ways of pursuing the vision or mission of the organization, identifying and exploiting opportunities, and anticipating and responding to threats. According to Porter, strategy is about optimum competitive positioning in the market. However, the turbulence of today's business environment requires a redefinition: strategy is not about position but about process – about developing processes to enable exploitation of advantages (Gary, 2001). In the words of Orit Gadiesh, chairman of Bain & Company, this entails having a 'strategic principle', grounded in economic reality, about company direction (Gary, 2001).

Modern thinking about strategy and its application to business start with Alfred Chandler in the 1950s and 1960s. He defined strategy as:

> **the determination of the long-term goals and objectives of an enterprise, and the adoption of courses of action and the allocation of resources necessary for carrying out these goals. (Chandler, 1962)**

Chandler's approach was based on an assumption that organizations act in a rational and sequential way. His famous dictum that 'structure follows strategy' was challenged only in the 1980s, by writers like Tom Peters and Richard Pascale. Igor Ansoff (1962) developed Chandler's ideas by providing a prescriptive approach to strategy, using analytical tools. Such thinking constituted the first of several approaches to strategic thinking:

The classical school. Ansoff and Chandler, together with Porter, are advocates of the 'classical school' of thinking about strategy. This view assumes that there is one best answer to the strategy question and that rational thinking will lead to it. Profitability is the supreme goal. Rational planning is the means to achieve it. From the point of view of leadership, the challenge in implementing strategy is to get people to see the underlying logic and to motivate them to act accordingly. Porter's model provides generic strategies for managing the future that capture the maximum value embodied in the firm's products and services (Porter, 1980). Middleton and Gorzynski (2002: 17) say that Porter's approach is flawed in a further way:

> **It is based on a static view of the world, in which the size of the economic pie is given and finite...all that is left to be decided is how the pie is to be divided up, and corporate profits must...come at a cost to society.**

The evolutionary school. Another school of thought is the evolutionary school, which argues that markets, not managers, determine success. Success is achieved through 'survival of the fittest', which entails adaptability rather than deliberate strategic choice. So the best strategy is flexibility.

The systemic school. The systemic school of thought argues that social context is all-important. The social and economic contexts in which firms are embedded vary. Competitors' strategies need to be analysed in terms of their social and economic contexts. Therefore there can be no universal model of strategy.

The processual school. The 'processual' school of thought rejects the notion of 'rational economic man'. This view asserts there are cognitive limits to rational action, varying personal objectives and agenda, and cognitive biases. Emotion plays a part. Strategy is about 'satisficing': achieving solutions that are not perfect or ideal but are good enough and workable (Simon, 1957). Satisficing – sufficing and being satisfactory – is an emotional acceptance that there are too many uncertainties and conflicts in values for there to be any hope of obtaining the ideal solution.

Strategy is determined at several levels:

- Corporate strategy – focusing on business portfolio and scope, the business concept, resource allocation, and investments and divestments. This sets the context for two other levels of strategy.
- Business strategy – focusing on markets, customers and efficiency.
- Functional strategies – for example, marketing, operations or production, finance, research and development, and human resources.

Thinking about strategy during the 1990s moved away from 'long-term planning' to concern aligning the organization to the demands of a rapidly changing world – a leadership dimension to the strategy process. Perhaps the most prominent thinkers here are Bartlett and Ghoshal (1994, 1995a, b, 1998), who argued that:

- Leaders need to change their focus from devising formal systems to developing organizational purpose
- They should replace top-down vision and direction by bottom-up initiatives from those people who are closest to the customer
- Top-level leaders should replace directing and controlling middle and frontline managers by creating an environment whereby they can manage themselves

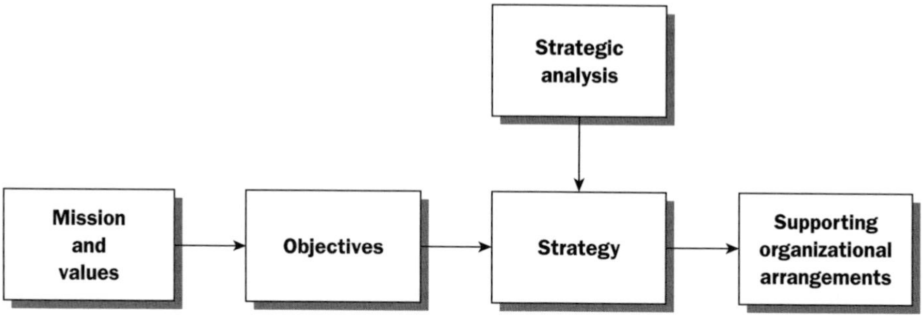

Figure 6.1 *The place of strategy*

In other words, strategy is about defining the vision and mission (purpose) of the organization and empowering people to pursue them. These are key themes in our model of leadership. Donald Hambrick and James Fredrickson (2001) depict the place of strategy as shown in Figure 6.1. This shows strategy as driven by strategic analysis and strategic objectives that reflect the organization's mission and values. Organizational arrangements relating to structure, processes, policies, people and rewards support strategy.

Robert Kaplan and David Norton (2001a) identify five characteristics of strategy-focused organizations:

- Strategy is a continual process, through linking it to budgets, strategic learning and information systems
- Strategy is everyone's job, using strategic assessments and personal 'scorecards'
- The organization is aligned to its strategy through business and support unit synergies
- Strategy is translated into operational plans, using strategy maps and the 'Balanced Scorecard' (see below)
- Change is mobilized through executive leadership

Strategies are ways of pursuing the vision, identifying and exploiting opportunities, anticipating and responding to threats, and not only responding positively to the need for change but also creating it. If opportunities are not identified, they will become threats, BT's CEO Bill Cockburn (2000) said. Porter (1997: 54) adds:

> **Today, the only way to have an advantage is through innovation and upgrading... . There has to be a strategic vision within which you are innovating.**

C.K. Prahalad (1999) says, 'Strategy is not about positioning the company in a given industry space but increasingly one of influencing, shaping and creating it.' It is about pursuing an imaginative vision of the desired future. There is general consensus that the strategy process comprises scanning and analysis of the organization's business environment, formation of strategy and its implementation (Milliken and Volrath, 1991). Prahalad (1999) sees the differences between the traditional and emerging views of strategy as given in Table 6.1.

How the strategy process is incremental and informed by shared beliefs and values is depicted in the model shown in Figure 6.2. This view has been taken further by David

Table 6.1 *The new view of strategy*

Traditional view	Emerging view
Strategy as *fit* with resources	Strategy as *stretch and leverage*
Strategy as *positioning in existing* industry space	Strategy as *creating new industry* space
Strategy as *top management* activity	Strategy as *total organizational* process
Strategy as an *analytical* exercise	Strategy as an *analytical and organizational* exercise
Strategy as *extrapolating* the past	Strategy as *creating the future*

Grayson and Adrian Hodges. They point out that corporate social responsibility (CSR) is widely perceived to add costs and extra regulatory burden, yet it has simultaneously created untapped opportunities for product innovation, market development and non-traditional business models (Grayson and Hodges, 2004). They argue that 'corporate social opportunity' – exploiting the opportunities arising from stringent social, ethical and environmental standards – 'lies in building CSR *into* business strategy, not adding it *on* to business operations'.

A sound business strategy that is adaptable to changing business conditions is one of three conditions necessary for sustainable growth in shareholder value, according to George (2001). Examples of strategic inflexibility that he gives are DEC in the 1980s and Apple Computers in the early 1990s, contrasted with Microsoft's responsiveness to the Internet in the late 1990s. George argues that 'Employees can adapt to major strategic shifts as long as the company's mission and values remain constant', which is an important factor in maintaining their trust in top management. Medtronic is 'completely reinvented' every five years in terms of its business strategies. For example, between 1989 and 1994, the company was transformed from a pacemaker company into a broader cardiovascular business, with revolutionary new therapies during the following five years, and with further innovations expected, reflecting its 'Vision

Figure 6.2 *The process of strategy*

2010'. Meanwhile, mission and values (see Chapters 4 and 5 respectively) have remained constant and, George says, will continue to do so.

Core competencies and distinctive capability

Firms in the same industry vary in their performance and competitive advantage. Why? One explanation in strategy theory, the resource-based view, is that market position derives from a firm's 'unique bundle of resources and capability' (Hoopes et al., 2003). To be a source of competitive advantage, to maintain a unique and sustainable position in the market, such resources and capability according to this view must be valuable, rare (available in short supply relative to demand), and not easily transferred, imitated or replicated. The resource-based theory of strategy was developed by Bo Wernerfelt from ideas first set out 20 years earlier by Edith Penrose (Kay, 1996). From the standpoint of leadership, the resource-based view implies the need to develop a strong culture and set of shared values that support the firm's vision, mission and strategies as well as distinctive competencies among its employees. An even broader implication of the resource-based view is the need to develop the firm's collective leadership capacity – 'institutional leadership' – and its leadership 'brand' (which was discussed in Chapter 1).

Central to the resource-based theory of strategy is the idea of core competencies. 'Core competencies [attributed to C.K. Prahalad and Gary Hamel] is one of the most used and abused phrases in business strategy', says the economist John Kay (1996). The term is used variously, he says, to describe the resources an organization has (such as economic and business knowledge), what it does (such as solving problems and project management), and characteristics it needs but may not have (such as innovation and customer focus). The main strategic question for any organization, Kay says, is how well what it is matches what it does. He makes the distinction between distinctive capability and skills. Distinctive capability is idiosyncratic to an organization; skills can be readily bought in the marketplace – or trained.

An example of distinctive capability that Kay gives is from his own company, London Economics: its exceptional economic expertise and an established position in the market that other organizations – competitors – would find it difficult to replicate. Another example is from the Säid School of Business at the University of Oxford: the Oxford brand, which, he says, 'immediately implies an intellectual, relatively academic, positioning'.

In defining a strategy, a company needs first to identify the markets where its distinctive capability is relevant and then acquire and deploy the skills required to capture and serve these markets. As Andrew Pettigrew and Richard Whipp (1993: 201) say, competing successfully depends on two abilities: 'to comprehend the competitive forces in play and how they change over time ... [and] the linked ability ... to mobilise and manage the resources necessary for the chosen competitive response through time'. Competitive advantage, Kay says, is associated with distinctive capability, not with pursuing new lines of business just because they provide easy pickings in markets that are growing or profitable. A leadership responsibility, he says, is 'to put together the resources which complement the organization's distinctive capability in achieving [its] market position'. It follows, he says, that 'any effective strategy is specific to the business that deploys it'. One size does not fit all.

The Balanced Scorecard and strategy maps

As a framework for creating strategy, Kaplan and Norton (1992) introduced the 'Balanced Scorecard' in the early 1990s. The Balanced Scorecard, they say, is the basis for 'a strategic management system that institutionalizes the new cultural values and processes into a new system for managing' (Kaplan and Norton, 2001b).

The basis for the Balanced Scorecard is a 'strategy map' that defines the 'architecture' of strategy:

- Financial – the strategy for growth, profitability and risk, viewed from the shareholder's perspective
- Customer – the strategy for creating value and differentiation from the customer's perspective
- Internal business processes – the strategic priorities for various business processes that create customer and shareholder satisfaction
- Learning and growth – the priorities to create a climate that supports organizational change, innovation and growth

Kaplan and Norton say that 'organizations build their strategy maps from the top down, starting with the destination and then charting the routes that lead there'. This first requires senior executives to review their mission statement (why the company exists) and core values (what the company believes in). On this basis, a strategic vision is developed – what the company wants to become. The strategy map defines the core competencies, technologies and corporate culture needed. Strategies identify the paths for reaching that destination.

Kaplan and Norton (2000) suggest 'strategy maps' as useful ways of communicating strategy. Strategy maps give a visual representation of how a company plans to convert its range of assets into desired outcomes. For example, they cover the company's key objectives, targeted markets, value propositions for customers, the role of innovation and product, service and process quality, and investment. They show the causal relationships among improvements and desired outcomes. Kaplan and Norton say, 'Strategy maps will help organizations view their strategies in a cohesive, integrated, and systematic way', thereby '[increasing] the likelihood of [their] successful implementation'. They describe how Mobil North American Marketing and Refining used strategy maps to transform itself from a centralized manufacturer of commodity products to a decentralized, customer-driven organization, thereby increasing its operating cash flow by over $1 billion per year.

One benefit of the Balanced Scorecard, Tom Lester (2004) says, is that it 'helps to clarify objectives and the resources available and communicate them effectively'. Objectives and measures agreed under each of the four headings help the organization to pursue and fulfil its vision and mission. Lester quotes the Ministry of Defence in the UK as a leading user of the Balanced Scorecard in a public sector context focusing on: output and deliverables (what the government requires), process involvement (the 'how'), learning and development, and resource management.

The real benefit of the Balanced Scorecard, however, whether in the public or private sector, according to Jonathan Chocqueel-Mangan, is gained only if it helps to clarify and rationalize strategic purpose or mission (Lester, 2004). Objectives, targets and measures 'must all tell the same story', he says, and this story must be about the vision and mission of the organization. Julian Taylor describes how Scottish Enterprise, Scotland's economic development agency, junked its formulaic use of the Balanced Scorecard:

> **We decided to forget about targets and think carefully what 'a smart successful Scotland' really meant, and so determine what to do more of, what less of. We could then decide how to measure it. (Lester, 2004)**

Examples of corporate strategies

Polaris Industries Tom Tiller, immediately after his appointment as president and Chief Operating Officer of Polaris Industries, focused everybody's attention on two questions: 'what are we going to try to accomplish, and how are we going to get there?' (Barnett and Tichy, 2000). His strategy statement occupies one page – providing the business theory and a simple 'roadmap' for everyone to follow (see the case example below). It became known as 'the one-pager' or 'the chart'.

CASE EXAMPLE

Polaris Industries' Strategy Statement*

The Goals ...

- $2B by 2002, $3B by 2007
- Grow EPS as fast as revenue
- Build a dominant brand
- Expand P/E multiple to 20+

POLARIS
RIDE THE BEST

Achieved by ...

Product Innovation — "The Foundation"

- **ATVs**
  - $700M business growing double digit
  - Strong #2 and growing share
- **Motorcycles**
  - $300–500MM opportunity
  - Superior product
- **Snowmobiles**
  - Maintain leadership
  - Generate cash
- **Personal Watercraft**
  - Minimum investment
  - Upside only

Growth Initiatives — "The Catalysts"

- **Financial Services**
  - Rapidly grow retail portfolio
- **Parts, Garments & Accessories**
  - Double in 3 years
- **International**
  - Grow from 6% to 15% of revenue
  - Motorcycle is game changer
- **Alliances**
  - Brand extensions/partnerships
  - Acquisitions/JVs
- **New Management**

*Reprinted from *Organizational Dynamics*, 29 (1), Carole K. Barnett and Noel M. Tichy, 'How new leaders learn to take charge', page 26. Copyright 2000, with permission from Elsevier.

Cadbury Schweppes Cadbury Schweppes reorganized its senior management structure in March 2000 to separate responsibility for operational performance from strategic development, with a remit covering mergers and acquisitions, e-commerce and knowledge management.[78] Its 'governing objective' is stated as 'growth in shareholder value'.[79] Without a quantified target, and considering the criteria for effective visions, missions and strategies, I would regard this governing objective really as a governing strategy: growth in shareholder value is a means to the end – the company's vision and mission (see Chapter 3). The company states its strategy ('to achieve this [governing] objective', or perhaps in support of its governing strategy) as to:

- Focus on its core businesses of beverages and confectionery
- Develop robust and sustainable positions in regional markets
- Grow organically and via acquisition

While the CEO, John Sunderland, says 'Cadbury Schweppes' success has been built on its clarity of purpose',[80] its purpose could perhaps be a greater source of employee motivation if redefined. The company, however, recognizes 'the power of strategic insight'.[81] Its annual report for 2001 states:

> Successful companies in the confectionery and beverage business are those that are able to develop appropriate strategic responses to the changing needs of their consumers. They have to acquire the kind of strategic flexibility which can only come from genuine insight into the behaviour of the people who buy their products...we focus on our consumers intensely so that we are able to find new and profitable ways of broadening our offering to meet the ever-widening spectrum of consumer demand.

Trinity Mirror Trinity Mirror, publisher of the *Daily Mirror* and *Sunday Mirror* and the largest publisher of regional newspapers in the UK, was described by Alan Ruddock (2004) as in a 'strategic quagmire' at the time a new CEO, Sylvia ('Sly') Bailey, took over in early 2003. Bailey's initial strategies were to cut costs, improve management and rationalize the portfolio – 'a rehashing of old solutions to old problems'. With a mission to increase shareholder value, she laid out a strategy in three phases:

- Stabilization – through cost reduction, involving centralization of finance, HR and IT, management delayering and accelerated regionalization, and immediate revenue enhancement
- Revitalization – through redesigning internal processes
- Growth – through exploring the 'options and routes that may lie open'[82]

Kingfisher In a year (2000) which saw 'strong sales growth and important strategic progress [but which] did not translate satisfactorily into growth in earnings', Kingfisher made a major strategic change – to demerge the British general merchandise companies (Woolworths, Superdrug and its entertainment businesses) from the internationally focused home improvement, electrical and furniture businesses, thus creating the 'new' Kingfisher.[83] The aim was to enable 'new' Kingfisher 'to concentrate on its international management skills and finances on accelerating its growth record' and British General Merchandise to 'focus on the development of its customer propositions through destination stores, and stores offering convenience "everyday" shopping, as it exploits its strong positions in a range of growth markets'.

BAT For British American Tobacco (BAT), its four strategies for pursuing its vision – 'leadership of the tobacco industry in order to create long term shareholder value'[84] – are:

- Growth – to increase volume and value share of the global tobacco market through organic growth and mergers and acquisitions
- Productivity – to effectively deploy global resources to increase profits and generate funds to reinvest in the business
- Responsibility – to continue to balance commercial objectives with the expectations of a broader range of stakeholders, thus ensuring a sustainable business
- 'Winning Organisation' – to ensure there are the right people and the right environment to deliver the Vision

BAT's 'Winning Organisation' strategy reflects four HR 'drivers': 'A great place to work:

- Leadership
  - Develop leaders at all levels who have a clear vision for the business, align, energies and enable those around them, foster innovation, and contribute to building our global enterprise.
  - Continuously build and strengthen our leadership pipeline.
- Culture
  - Foster an open, confident culture that encourages change & innovation, is shaped by the Guiding Principles (Enterprising Spirit, Open Minded, Freedom through Responsibility and Strength from Diversity) and inspires people to perform & enjoy.

Outstanding people:

- Talent
  - Attract, grow and retain the right people who have the ability and hunger to drive and deliver competitive advantage and superior performance.
  - Continuously upgrade the Group talent pool.
- Learning
  - Develop a learning culture by building the capabilities of our organisation and people, with a focus on coaching.'

Boots A FTSE100 company, Boots was experiencing flat sales and profits in April 2000, coupled with pricing pressures and losses from an overseas initiative. Steve Russell, then newly appointed Group Chief Executive, decided to tap into the 'prevailing wisdom' in the beauty and healthcare industry that people are prepared to spend more on 'things that make us feel good' by forging new strategic directions (Hall, 2001):

- Opening 65 upmarket health and beauty stores selling designer brands
- Restructuring shops, with 1,000 local stores selling standard Boots offerings, 275 complete health and beauty stores, and 140 megastores offering dentistry, body treatments and optician services

The new strategy in the opinion of key institutional investors, however, was not working by December 2002: increased competition from supermarkets had failed to be addressed, and the share price had fallen from 715p in May 2002 to 550p (Goodman, 2002; Lewis and Goodman, 2002). Both Russell and the chairman were forced to resign.

University of Strathclyde An example of strategies in the higher education sector is that of the University of Strathclyde. Captured in its mission statement, they are to:

- Contribute to the advancement of the knowledge society, social cohesion and the quality of life in Scotland and elsewhere
- Generate new ideas, knowledge and skills
- Provide a high-quality education to all its students
- Offer opportunities for all staff to develop their full potential[85]

Thailand's National Economic and Social Development Board In the public sector, an example of strategies linked to a vision for national transformation comes from Thailand. The country's head of the National Economic and Social Development Board, Chakramon Phasukavanich, calls these the 'seven dreams':

- 'An economic development platform giving growth as stable as Switzerland's, with small and medium-sized enterprises as strong as Taiwan's and Italy's, a tourism industry on the scale of Spain's, along with commensurate healthcare, education and infrastructure
- An active foreign policy of coordinating regional investment and production
- Becoming a leader in global or Asian niche products such as food, health services, fashion, tourism and automobiles
- Inculcating innovative learning in the individual
- Creating a society of entrepreneurs
- To create cultural pride and global awareness among Thais, with the open-mindedness of the British and the pride of the French, but without the notable excesses of the latter
- To make Thailand a country of decency and a sound living environment.'

(Changsorn and Janviroj, 2003)

Chakramon is quoted as saying that these 'dreams' assumed continuing global trends such as changing geopolitics, the digital revolution, global deflation, changes in global culture, environment and health, and the demographic shift towards an ageing world. They are the result of considering three questions: 'Where we are; where we want to be; and how to get there.'

The Leadership Trust Foundation In the voluntary or 'third' sector, The Leadership Trust Foundation's strategies for pursuing its mission – 'to inspire academic and aspirational leadership thinking, development and education' – and its vision – 'to be the premier centre for leadership, with a global reach' – are:

- Knowledge creation and idea generation
- Leadership development and education
- Creation of an aspirational environment

Manchester United In the sports arena, Manchester United, while not communicating any clear vision for the club, does set out clear and detailed strategies for pursuing its mission (see Chapter 4):

- Maintaining the team's playing success
- Developing the value of media rights
- Leveraging the global brand
- Converting more fans to customers[86]

The arts In the arts world strategies are perhaps more challenging and controversial than in conventional business because the arts do not generate profits like business and are largely dependent on external funding. For example, Sir Peter Hall says that, 'In theatre, in serious music and the other arts, there is a huge amount of creative talent that is failing to find outlets, for lack of adequate funding ... [which] ... wastes our cultural resources.'[87] And, Sir John Tusa says, 'too many arts organisations ... [are] ... weighed down by a surfeit of pseudo-strategy'.[88]

Developing the strategy

'Strategy development,' Colin Eden (1993: 118) says, 'is about discovering how to manage and control the future .... It is concerned with capturing the experience and wisdom of organizational members about how they believe an attractive vision of the future can be attained.'

This is exactly what the British Geological Survey (BGS) did. With a clear, new vision of what he wanted BGS to be, when he was appointed its head in January 1998, David Falvey immediately invited all non-managerial employees to apply to join a strategy team (Management Today, 2001). Within 21 months, seven 'pillars' of new or better ways of working were agreed in the team, and in April 2000 a project-based organizational structure was introduced. Commitment and ownership in respect of strategic vision and plans are critical to success, as is clear from a survey of successful middle-market manufacturing firms in the UK by The Manufacturing Foundation (2003).

'Strategic conversation' (Van der Heijden, 1996) needs to replace what James Champy (1997) calls 'mere consultation and the broadcasting of messages'. Peter Linkow (1999) makes the point that organizations that do not involve employees in the strategy process in strategic conversation will not survive. *Organization-wide* strategic thinking, he says, is a source of competitive advantage. This is an intrinsic element of strategic leadership capacity or institutional leadership (O'Shea, 2000; Pasternack et al., 2001). Linkow (1999) says that unrelenting environmental pressures require strategic agility in 'constantly monitoring the competition, scanning for changes in the external environment, and identifying emerging market opportunities'. As a result of delayering and downsizing, he says, more middle-level managers need to be part of the strategic conversation process and hence first to understand it. This has leadership implications for empowerment, which is discussed in Chapter 7.

Strategy can be viewed through different 'lenses'. One view is that strategy is about *alignment*. The argument is that successful change entails leaders bringing people along with them – achieving a common vision. Alignment entails not a grudging acceptance or tolerance of personal sacrifice but a deep emotional commitment to change. A Booz Allen & Hamilton and World Economic Forum study suggests that alignment to vision and strategy, contrary to common wisdom, does not necessarily entail lack of adaptability (Pasternack et al., 2001).

Strategy results from design, experience or ideas, according to Johnson and Scholes (2002: 37–89). Strategy most often results from design – analysis, evaluation and planning by top management. However, this process is influenced by the individual and collective experience of people in the organization and by the organizational culture, for example subconscious assumptions and procedural routines that are taken for granted. Johnson and Scholes point out that this may lead to future strategies that are merely adaptations of past strategies. Innovative strategies, they say, result not only from experience but also from diversity and variety of ideas. Organizations therefore respond to the often rapidly changing and uncertain business environment through a process of 'logical incrementalism' – learning by doing – which relies more on emergent strategy than on top-down direction and control.

Organizations sometimes face the imposition of strategy by external forces or agencies. For example, in the public sector – and indeed in the private sector in the case of the railways since their privatization in the UK – some industries are regulated.

Strategy development involves:

- Articulating strategic vision
- Identifying major strategic issues facing the organization, requiring both insight and foresight
- Generating options and building scenarios
- Identifying stakeholders and their possible response in relation to their own goals
- Developing goals
- Setting strategies within the goal context
- Establishing strategic programmes
- Creating a mission statement
- Developing strategic controls

(After Eden, 1993: 117)

In the business context, Hambrick and Fredrickson (2001) say a strategy provides answers to five questions:

1 Where will we be active?
  This question concerns product categories, market segments, geographical areas, core technologies and value-creation stages.

2 How will we get there?
Options are internal development, joint ventures, licensing or franchising, and mergers and acquisitions.

3 How will we win in the marketplace?
Differentiators are image, customization, price, styling, and product or service reliability.

4 What will be our speed and sequence of moves?
This question concerns speed of expansion and the sequence of initiatives.

5 How will we obtain our returns?
Economic logic focuses on achieving the lowest costs through advantages of scale, scope and replication, and premium prices as a result of unmatchable service and proprietary product features. Hambrick and Fredrickson cite IKEA, the highly successful global furniture retailer, as an example of a company with a coherent strategy (for the past 25 years) that contains all five elements that are consistent with – and reinforce – one another.

Understanding the strategy process has been aided by research in the field of managerial and organizational cognition (Johnson et al., 2001). The cognitive element of strategy development entails individual attention, encoding, storage and information retrieval as a basis for action and, within the strategy team, the cognitive processes of sharing meanings, constructing interpretative frameworks and socialization processes for choosing and coordinating action (Corner et al., 1994). CEOs have the additional task of collating and making sense of their top teams' views (Calori et al., 1994). The strategic leader, Karl Weick (1995) says, is a 'sense-maker'.

Christopher Bartlett (2000) further argues that CEOs and top-level executives must be 'sense-makers' rather than 'grand strategists'. He says that they 'rarely have the detailed business and technical knowledge to set anything but the general direction of a complex organization'. He describes how Intel was forced to move from making memory chips to making microprocessors not as a result of a strategic decision reflecting a clear corporate vision but as a result of the wisdom of front-line managers who, Intel's CEO Andy Grove said, 'really knew what was going on'. Bartlett also believes that top-level executives need to focus not on strategic fit and organizational alignment but on creating 'dynamic disequilibrium, challenging the organization's working assumptions, and creating the discomfort that prompts creative action'.

Managers in leadership roles have to make sense of their strategic environments – for example, using mental models – as a basis for making informed strategic choices. Kevin Daniels et al. (1995) found that an organization's managers may not share the same perceptions of the strategic environment. They say that effective behaviour in this case is to start from cognitive commonality and to work on reconciling diversity later. This later task requires encouraging dissent and expert opinion, empathy – appreciating others' perspectives – and coming to a consensus that reflects multiple perspectives and multiple-stakeholder acceptability.

Strategy formation is a group process based on discussion. But, Mirela Schwarz and Joe Nandhakumar (2002) say, there is insufficient understanding of how strategic ideas are generated. They suggest that leaders need to acknowledge and emphasize the importance of strategic debate. They need to create an atmosphere of openness in eliciting and discussing controversial views from people with diverse intellectual, social and cultural backgrounds. And they need to encourage strategic conversation based on a common understanding of strategic language.

An important cognitive skill in strategic thinking is the development of strategic ideas – a major source of sustained competitive advantage (Barney, 1986, 1991; Hart and Banburry, 1994). These ideas are expressed as new products or services that maintain or develop an organization's market position (Mintzberg, 1994).

Linkow (1999) analyses the cognitive competencies required for strategy formation:

- *Reframing.* Reframing is about challenging and restating the underlying beliefs, values and assumptions – mental models – that form the basis of organizational relationships and action, for example through brainstorming.
- *Scanning.* This is the constant search for information that relates to beliefs, values and assumptions. Demographic and cultural information (part of the social context) and industry and market information (part of economic analysis) might be included. Conclusions as a basis for decision making are made iteratively – through successive approximation.
- *Abstracting.* Abstracting is grasping the essential message in disparate information. An example would be capturing and describing the essence of Charles Rennie Mackintosh's architectural design based on studying the houses he designed. Many tools are available for abstracting, such as nominal group technique and cluster and factor analysis.
- *Multivariate thinking.* This is the balancing of many dynamic variables simultaneously to discern the relationship among them. In metaphorical terms, it is about seeing the forest *before* seeing the trees, but nevertheless also seeing the trees, the spaces around them and the surrounding flora and fauna, that is the 'helicopter view' (which we discussed in Chapter 3). Multivariate thinking enables seeing how actions or decisions affect one another. Useful tools are mathematical modelling and simulation.
- *Envisioning.* Envisioning, or simply visioning, was discussed in Chapter 4. It is about seeing future states as vivid mental images. Vision is the result of analysis, imagination and intuition. Useful tools for visioning are the Delphi method and scenario planning.
- *Inducting.* This is the ability to arrive at beliefs and generalizations from information. The converse process is deduction, which starts with a theory from which hypotheses are generated and tested and leads to confirmation or disconfirmation. An example of induction is the small-scale piloting of a programme in a low-risk situation before introducing it organization-wide.
- *Valuating.* Valuating is seeking to know and understand the underlying beliefs, values and assumptions of stakeholders. The rationale is that their interests are important and that successful strategic action requires incorporating a balance of interests. This process involves stakeholder analysis.

How individuals make sense of information and use knowledge (through mental models) in strategic thinking has been explored using 'cognitive mapping' methods (Gioia and Sims, 1986; Huff, 1990; Fiol and Huff, 1992; Huff, 1997). In Chapter 3 in the section on the cognitive skills of leadership, it was pointed out that such models and methods are associated with well-developed cognitive skills. Mental models, Phyllis Johnson et al. (2001) say, 'can hasten decision making but can also lead to misdiagnosis of strategic issues'. The importance of leader briefing and team interaction skills in developing mental models and communication processes for handling unfamiliar situations has been established by research (Marks et al., 2000). This has important implications for strategy formation in novel and adverse business environments.

The strategy development process is not only a cognitive process but also a social and emotional process, involving, for example, the desire to conform to group expectations and 'social loafing' (Williams et al., 1979) – not sharing the consensus but not being willing to make the effort to change it. Moreover, complicating this analysis, individuals may vary in their behaviour from situation to situation (Johnson et al., 2001) and they may vary from one another because of personality traits such as introversion/extraversion (Hampson, 1999). Emotions of anxiety and sadness – 'negative affectivity' – can be associated with industry complexity and poor organizational performance, in particular industry competitiveness and decline (Daniels, 1998, 1999). Anger and fatigue too can lead to adverse strategies (Daniels, 1999). Information processing may be adversely affected by 'emotional contagion', where one person's affective state induces that state in others through unconscious signals (Hatfield et al., 1992).

Board directors appear to be particularly prone to acting in ways that do not necessarily reflect their thinking. Reasons are fear of failure and unwillingness to seek help, risk of material loss associated with failure, and expectations of other board members for individuals to comply with the status quo (Garratt, 1996). This may result in top teams performing less well than other groups in the organization (Katzenbach, 1997). This in turn is likely to result in unfavourable perceptions of the organization's top-level leaders.

Methods of strategic analysis

Strategies derive from environmental scanning, PESTLE analysis, industry and competitor analysis, SWOT analysis, benchmarking and scenario planning. Let us briefly review each method.

Environmental scanning

The initial task for a leader in the strategy process is environmental scanning and strategic analysis (Calori et al., 1994) – on the face of it a cognitive process. The purpose of this is:

> **to determine positive and negative trends that could impact organizational performance...it's how managers determine the opportunities and threats which face their organization.(Coulter, 2002: 66)**

Environmental scanning and strategic analysis are fraught with difficulties and risk, such as misinterpretation of threats and opportunities. For example, Phyllis Johnson et al. (2001: 81–82) say:

> **[Individuals may] selectively attend to information that is consistent with their mental models when scanning and analyzing their strategic environment...[and they may be]... pressured by [lack of] time...[or] other cognitive demands or feel they are already familiar with the issues.**

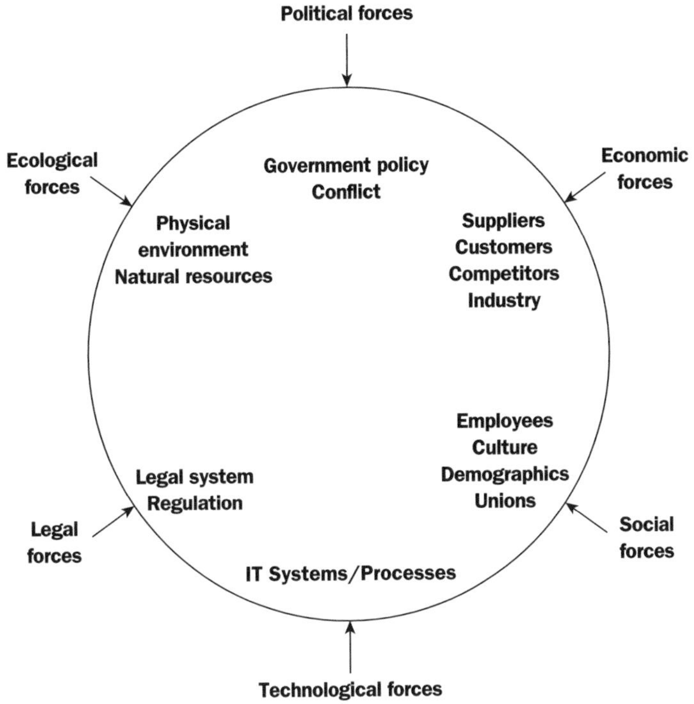

Figure 6.3 *Environmental analysis: the PESTLE model*

Environmental scanning is particularly important during uncertain times. Bruce Pasternack (2002) says, 'The leadership challenge is to read economic signals to understand if they presage either recovery or harder times ahead.' Uncertainty, however, is more than just economic: it is also political, social, technological, legal and ecological.

PESTLE analysis

'PESTLE' refers to the organization's political, economic, social (and demographic), technological, legal and ecological environment. Figure 6.3 shows the PESTLE model for environmental analysis.

Industry and competitor analysis

Industry analysis focuses on competitors, business ideas and distinctive competencies in the industry. Porter's 'five forces' model, which was discussed earlier in this chapter, is a popular framework for competitor analysis (Porter, 1980: 4). Competitive advantage essentially grows out of the value a firm is able to create for its buyers that exceeds the firm's cost in creating it.

Kim and Mauborgne (2002) suggest the use of a 'strategy canvas' in which the horizontal axis identifies the factors in which the industry competes and the vertical axis shows the extent to which firms in the industry offer these competitive factors. The strategy canvas provides a strategic profile of firms in the industry. An example they give is the hotel industry in France, which emerges from their analysis as comprising

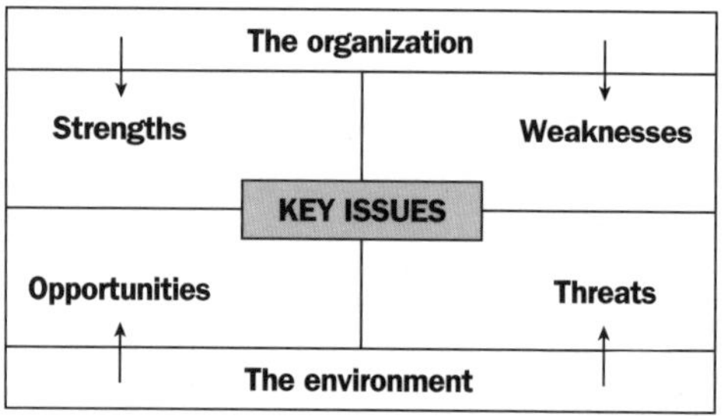

Figure 6.4 *SWOT analysis*

hotels that copy one another, fail to stand out in the eyes of customers, do not have a devoted following among them, and fail to generate significant economic returns. They describe how the successful Formule 1 hotel group has a clear, divergent and focused strategy, with a memorable 'tagline' – 'Two-star comfort, one-star price.'

The process for developing a strategy canvas involves four steps:

1 'Visual awakening' – creating a common perception of reality among the company's senior managers
2 'Visual exploration' – visits by the managers themselves to customers (not commissioned reports) to assess the latter's opinions on the company's products or services to identify what is valued by them; next to draw up strategic profiles depicting how the company could stand out in the market
3 'Strategy fair' – presentations by teams of managers of their strategy canvases, voting on them and drawing up a strategic profile for the future
4 'Communication' – communicating the new strategy on a single page, – so that it is readily understood by all employees, can remain constantly visible, and clearly states where the company currently stands and where they have to focus their efforts for the future

SWOT analysis

SWOT analysis – referring to the organization's strengths, weaknesses, opportunities and threats – is the basis for identifying key issues in matching the organization's internal resources and distinctive competencies (Selznick, 1957) with environmental threats and opportunities (see Figure 6.4). A strategy is chosen that will capitalize on the organization's strengths, control its weaknesses, neutralize threats and exploit its opportunities (Barney, 1997).

Benchmarking

Benchmarking is a commonly used technique for identifying 'best practice' and improving business performance. According to Morgen Witzel (2003), the process entails asking three questions:

1 What tasks are we not doing well?
2 Are others performing these tasks better than we are?
3 Can we adapt their methods to our own business to improve our performance?

Benchmarking is carried out most usually by companies in one sector, but it has also become popular between different sectors and between divisions within one company. Proponents of benchmarking, Witzel says, argue that benchmarking, through learning from others' successes and failures, diffuses best practice and innovation. On the other hand, companies may not wish to disclose information. And, more seriously, benchmarking may lead to convergence, whereby companies try to imitate one another rather than focusing on innovation, as was discussed earlier in this chapter. Competitive advantage results not from following current best practice but from creativity and innovation that go beyond it. Andrew Neil (2003), the publisher, writer and broadcaster on media affairs, goes even further: he advocates creating *new products and markets* rather than merely responding to customers' needs, wishes and expectations.

Scenario planning

What does the future hold for the organization? And how does that affect its strategies for pursuing its vision and mission? According to Hamel and Prahalad (1994), most managers on average devote less than 3% of their time thinking about the future. The urgent drives out the important. The future is left unexplored. The capacity to act, rather than think and imagine, becomes the measure of leadership. On the other hand, Pasternack (2002) says:

> **When I meet with CEOs these days, I usually hear the same questions: When will our business recover? What risks does our company face? How can we gain more control over our destiny?**

Uncertainty is an unavoidable feature of the current business environment. Pasternack and O'Toole (2002) call the kind of leadership required in these conditions 'yellow-light' leadership. We cannot forecast merely by extrapolating the past into the future. So-called experts may not be helpful here. Experts are better able to defend their point of view: they use their knowledge (experience) not to explore the future but to reflect the past.

Scenario planning focuses on assumptions, values and mental models in thinking 'outside the box' and on identifying possible future scenarios and planning for them. Thinking outside the box is about escaping from the patterns of experience that are stored in the brain and do most of our thinking. Merely using these patterns creates all manner of heuristics and biases in thinking which prevent us from *imagining* what might be. The antidote to such cognitive constriction in strategy formation is scenario planning.

Scenario planning makes a difference in strategy development: thinking 'outside the box', more creative strategies result, and these provide a route map if anticipated futures change. Van der Heijden (1996), former head of scenario planning at Shell, lists the benefits of scenario planning, among them:

- More robust decisions and projects
- Better thinking about the future by 'stretching mental models'
- Enhancing corporate perception, recognizing events as part of a pattern and understanding their implications

Invented by Herman Kahn of the Rand Corporation in the 1940s, scenario planning is a process that has gained currency after Shell in the early 1970s pioneered the approach in the business context. All possible futures for the company are identified, evaluated and planned for (Van der Heijden, 1996). This process enabled Shell to become one of the strongest oil companies in the world, foreseeing the energy crises of 1973 and 1979, the rise in the importance of energy conservation, the development of the global environment movement and the break-up of the Soviet Union (Dearlove, 1997b). Through scenario planning Shell was able to react quickly to the 1973 oil embargo by OPEC and emerge as the most profitable oil company. More recently (October 2001), Shell has updated its scenarios up to 2050. These are captured as 'dynamics as usual' and 'the spirit of the coming age', focusing on a gradual shift from carbon fuels to renewable energy and a technical revolution respectively (*The Economist*, 2001b). Van der Heijden (1996: 21) says:

> **Scenario thinking now underpins the established way of making decisions at Shell. It has become part of the culture, such that people throughout the company, dealing with significant decisions, normally will think in terms of multiple but equally plausible futures to provide a context for decision making... . The distinguishing feature of the scenario culture is that it has invested in assumptions, values and mental models.**

Scenarios are stories about the future. Scenario planning takes the views of managers and external experts to identify how political, economic, social, technological, legal and ecological forces might affect the organization in the long-term future and how it might respond through contingent strategies. Peter Schwartz, president of the Global Business Network, and architect of scenario planning in Shell, stresses the need for companies to add security issues in scenario planning, as a result of the September 11 attacks on the United States (*The Economist*, 2001b). In particular, he questioned the extent to which Islamic fundamentalism might hinder the spread of Western capitalism and democracy.

When the Hart–Rudman Commission on 'American security in the twenty-first century' considered recent futurist studies, it identified a weakness: they concentrated only on present concerns and rarely identified 'other possibilities that produce startling emergent behaviour' (*The Economist*, 2001b). Most futurist studies had failed to carry out a full and proper scenario planning exercise. Peter Schwartz (2003) argues that the future is not as uncertain as many think. He cites the lengthening of the human life span, changing patterns of migration, the dominance of US economic and military power, and the likelihood of disorderly nations that can unleash terror, disease and disruption on the rest of the world. Schwartz reveals that Global Business Network provided a US presidential commission in early 2001 with several possible scenarios about terrorism on US soil, including the flying of aircraft into the World Trade Center, but that this was ignored by the intelligence services.

A Scotch whisky distiller, aiming to increase output by 50%, discovered through scenario planning that it was making the wrong assumptions: it faced losing control of its business to distributors who were taking control of the product supply chain (Eglin, 2001c). And Iain Borthwick, marketing manager for UPM-Kymmene, a wood products and paper company, at the company's Caledonian Paper Mill in Scotland, says:

> **We would plan on the basis that the future was going to be rather like the past. [Scenario planning] helped us to see that maybe it was going to be dramatically different. (Maitland, 2001b)**

Borthwick also points out that the process was 'intellectually stressful and radically different from what most companies do' (Eglin, 2001c). One participant in a scenario planning exercise at UPM-Kymmene says, 'We're really good at what we do, but what we do is the wrong thing.' The company was failing to consider the communications revolution and how this would affect the role of paper.

According to Awi Federgruen and Garrett van Ryzin (2003), three intellectual challenges present themselves in scenario planning:

1 Constructing meaningful scenarios, requiring expert analysis of the factors that influence the outcomes
2 Determining the likelihood of each of the scenarios
3 Deciding on good criteria for selecting strategies, analysing the benefit/risk relationship

Scenario planning is increasing in popularity because of increasing turbulence in the business environment and in our lives as a whole, according to Federgruen and van Ryzin. Examples they quote are terrorism, political instability, threats of war, accounting scandals that invalidate what was previously taken for granted, and natural biological disasters such as SARS (Severe Acute Respiratory Syndrome), BSE and foot-and-mouth disease. A further reason they suggest is the advent of sophisticated computer software that allows efficient analysis of large-scale scenario planning.

George Burt says that scenario planning makes a positive long-term impact on a firm and increases its managers' self-confidence: 'We will never know everything about the future. But you can control and manage it rather than having the future running you around' (Eglin, 2001c). The test of a useful scenario is not whether it was right or wrong, but whether it led to better decision making.

CASE EXAMPLE

Marks & Spencer

Marks & Spencer's decline in the late 1990s from its pre-eminent position in the retail industry is an example of poor strategic management. When Luc Vandevelde took over as chairman and CEO in 2000, he identified the major problem as a lack of understanding of the company's fundamental strengths – what customers valued most about the business – and then using that information to develop its brand (Vandevelde, 2002). He said:

> **Once you lose your confidence, the tendency is to spread your risks and then you start becoming average in everything you do – and your customers know that.**

His strategy for recovery was two phased. The first phase, for 2001–2002, he says was 'simple, radical and all-encompassing':

- To focus on the heart of the business – the retail and financial services operations in the UK and to get back to the fundamental strengths that had made Marks & Spencer great in the past
- To stop all activities which were non-core or making a loss
- To achieve the right capital structure to make the balance sheet more efficient and to generate greater value for shareholders[89]

This strategy was carried out successfully. The second phase, from 2002, addressed future growth, looking at 'how we deliver value, both for our shareholders and for the communities in which we operate':

- Regain our leadership in clothing and speciality food by translating our scale and authority into superior quality, value and appeal
- Build on our unique customer relationships through new products and services, particularly in home and financial services
- Shape our store locations, formats and offer products to meet the changing needs of our customers
- Reassert our position as a leading socially responsible business

The annual review for 2002 declared: 'things are looking up'. By early 2004, however, improvements had reversed in certain areas, and Vandevelde was asked to leave the company. A new CEO, Stuart Rose, took over, and better prospects came into sight.

Decision making and emergent strategy

Deciding on a strategy entails reconciling a variety of individual interpretations and choices to achieve consensus (Johnson et al., 2001). Strategic decision making is usually described either as a sequence of steps or in terms of a set of characteristics or dimensions, such as comprehensiveness and rationality, politicization, centralization and formalization (Sharfman and Dean, 1998: 179–203). Strategic decisions essentially are unusual in that they have no precedents, entail the commitment of substantial resources, and influence or dictate decision making throughout the organization.

Although there is little evidence that top management teams influence the process of making strategic decisions (Rajagopalan et al., 1993), some research suggests that personality and demographic characteristics of CEOs and the top management team as a whole do play an important part (Nahavandi and Malekzadeh, 1993; Lewin and Stephens, 1994). High achievers tend to favour formal processes both for decision making and for communication, and risk-averse CEOs reduce uncertainty by exercising greater control and direct supervision (Lewin and Stephens, 1994). Longer-serving CEOs tend to minimize internal political debate by developing a top management team of their own choosing (Haleblian and Finkelstein, 1993), and by standardizing communication (Smith et al., 1994).

Cognitive skills undoubtedly aid more rational processes to decision making and more creative solutions to complex problems (Bantel and Jackson, 1989). In reviewing

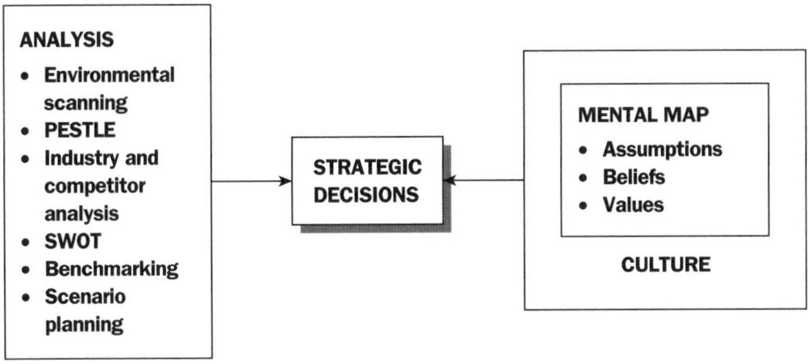

Figure 6.5 *Relationship between analysis, mental maps and strategic decisions*

this and related research, Papadakis and Barwise (2002) conclude that both the CEO and the top management team affect the process, but their influence is limited by internal and external contextual factors. In their study of industrial companies in Greece, they found that the characteristics of the top management team mattered more than those of the CEO, suggesting the importance of team-based leadership. They suggest that CEOs cannot rely on their position power to influence strategic decision making, but they need to concentrate on building an assertive top management team that is strongly committed to innovation and beating the competition. The implication for effective leadership is that CEOs need to ensure their top management teams are empowered, both individually and as a 'performing' team.

Gerry Johnson (1989) suggests that strategic decisions reflect political processes as much as analysis: managers' perception is influenced by mental maps as well as analysis, and these mental maps are the product of the organization's culture. This relationship is depicted at Figure 6.5. Indeed corporate culture interacts with all aspects of business strategy:

> **A positive business strategy and positive corporate culture go hand in hand. An effective strategy must grow out of the culture and the culture must be strategically shaped. (Deetz et al., 2000: 3)**

The political processes involved in strategic decision making include the use of power (which we discuss in the context of influence in Chapter 8), which may lead to repression of the least powerful members in the group (Walsh et al., 1988). For example, in their leadership role, non-executive directors need to draw on both their political will and their political skill to exercise influence (Pettigrew and McNulty, 1995).

Mintzberg (1987) uses the analogy of the potter's wheel to describe the strategy process as a craft. He says strategies do not need to be deliberate but can emerge through circumstances. Strategies can *form*; they need not necessarily be *formulated.* What often happens is that strategy emerges – not necessarily in line with strategic intent – as a result of 'patterns or consistencies realized despite, or in the absence of, intentions [and through] strategic learning' (Mintzberg and Waters, 1985). Strategies that are implemented may be the result of an emergent stream of actions recognized as a pattern *post hoc.* Strategic learning is key: effective strategies may be formed and discovered by experimentation rather than by formal analysis and decision making (Mintzberg et al., 1998). Emergent strategy is more viable in times of turbulent environments.

Influences on strategy development

Strategy development is not dependent solely on leadership. Following Mintzberg's distinction between strategy formulation and strategy formation (Mintzberg, 1978, 1987), it can be argued that:

> **The leader is just one important element in [a] model of strategy formation. History and context are the other two. [What is needed] is the examination of how leadership, context and history interact in the formation of an organisation's strategy and how this changes over time. (Leavy and Wilson, 1994: 2)**

Understanding this interaction is important in gaining a complete picture of leadership, for the same leader may succeed in one organizational context and fail in another (Leavy and Wilson, 1994: 3). Situational context is characterized by political, economic, social/cultural, technological and ecological features. Andrew Pettigrew (1985, 1990) agrees that the interaction between strategy content and process and organizational context requires study. We know more about the content of strategy – for example, the laws of the marketplace, the 'experience curve', the 'business portfolio matrix', 'generic' strategies and the 'value chain' – than about how strategy is formed (Leavy and Wilson, 1994: 9). These 'voluntaristic' theories assume the leader is the formulator of strategy, with the necessary will, intellect and administrative skill (1994: 9). The leadership role itself varies according to context and history in the form of institutionalized patterns of strategic behaviour (1994: 16). Farjoun (2002) says, 'History matters in the sense that prior events and developments condition current choices.' 'Deterministic' theories of organizations focus on structure, technology, the task environment, socio-technical systems, resource dependency and natural selection, and they demote leadership to a minimal or symbolic role (Leavy and Wilson, 1994: 11).

Strategy requires context, as Lord (John) Browne of BP Amoco (Garten, 2001: 149) says:

> **The most important thing a leader can do to communicate is to keep the bigger picture in focus, to set the context...to explain or reconcile the complexities that cloud the overall picture of what's important and why.**

Examples of strategy in context are writing off one failed multi-million-pound investment, an apparent disaster, in the context of a multi-billion-pound raft of investments that overall help a company fulfil its vision and mission, and how strategies deal with maintaining or strengthening a company's position in a market affected by volatile equity markets (Garten, 2001: 149–151).

This model can help to explain why expectations of leaders in Japan have been quite different from those of leaders in the West. Gary Stead, as head of mergers and acquisitions at Merrill Lynch in Tokyo, said, 'In Japan, nobody falls off the chair if the president doesn't know what the strategy is or doesn't have a strategy' (Nakamoto, 2001). The behaviour of Japanese leaders has been strongly conditioned by organizational history and national culture, but there is now an increasing force for change, driven by dissatisfaction with economic and political failures. In the UK only 41% of boards of directors in PLCs, according to research by Philip Stiles (2001), are exclusively responsible for developing corporate strategy, and some 15% leave it mostly or exclusively to management. Their primary role in the strategy process is review and discussion of strategy.

A study of four organizations representing the mixed economy of Ireland revealed the strong influences of context and history in strategy formation and in constraining or facilitating what leaders do (Leavy and Wilson, 1994: 170). The nature of leadership therefore has to do with more than just the leader's characteristics and behaviour. The situational context and history of an organization present challenges and opportunities to a leader, which need to be understood. Only with this understanding can a leader transform people's expectations and motivation through vision and inspiration (Leavy and Wilson, 1994: 185–187).

In reviewing the fortunes of well-known companies over the past half-century, including Collins and Porras's 18 'visionary' companies (Collins and Porras, 1994), Hamel and Välikangas (2003) conclude that 'success has never been so fragile'. Success, they say, 'rides on resilience – on the ability to dynamically reinvent business models and strategies as circumstances change'. And strategic resilience is displayed by continuously anticipating and adjusting to trends that may permanently damage the business. 'A turnaround', they say, 'is a transformation tragically delayed'.

Strategies eventually decay, according to Hamel and Välikangas, for four reasons:

- They are replicated by competitors and thus lose their distinctiveness, e.g. SUVs
- They become supplanted by better strategies through product or technological innovation, e.g. flat-pack furniture from IKEA
- They become 'exhausted' as markets become saturated, customers become bored or strategic programmes start to produce diminishing returns, e.g. mobile phones
- They become 'eviscerated' through the new-found power of consumers using the Internet, e.g. airline and hotel bookings in the travel business

Hamel and Välikangas point out that the human body responds to changes in the environment automatically, spontaneously and reflexively; organizations generally do not. Maintaining strategic resilience as an autonomic process requires developing a capacity for continuous renewal and reconstruction. 'Any company that can make sense of its environment, generate strategic options, and realign its resources faster than its rivals,' Hamel and Välikangas say, 'will enjoy a decisive advantage.'

Strategic leaders, according to Charles Farkas and Suzy Wetlaufer (1996), use various approaches to managing strategy and change:

- The 'strategy approach' – focusing on personal responsibility in searching for future opportunities and developing the strategy
- The 'human assets approach' – focusing on developing people who can take responsibility for strategy locally
- The 'expertise approach' – focusing on a particular area as a source of competitive advantage

- The 'control box approach' – focusing on the development and communication of a set of controls to ensure uniform behaviour and standards
- The 'strategic change approach' – focusing on continual reinvention of the organization

In dynamic or turbulent environments, leaders need to have insight – the cognitive flexibility to reconfigure their mental models to suit the circumstances (Daniels and Henry, 1998). The effective leader is likely to encourage dissenting views in the early stages of strategy formation so that consensus is based on reasoned discussion (Weick, 1979; Quinn, 1980; Eisenhardt, 1992; Larson et al., 1996).

Implementing strategy

Eden (1993) points out the importance of implementation:

> **The key issue with strategy for the chief executive is not its development, content or correctness but making it have an impact throughout the organization, gaining commitment to it, ownership of it and strategic control.**

Strategy implementation concerns a range of administrative activities that include designing the required structure and processes of the organization (Chandler, 1962). Implementing strategy is above all a process of communication. Communication underlies understanding of and commitment to strategy, which in turn are required for effective teamwork in implementing strategy. This means reaching not just managers throughout the organization, but all employees and in different cultures in which they live and work (Garten, 2001: 147–149).

Few strategic plans turn into action, according to Kim and Mauborgne (2002), because of 'paralysis by analysis'. This paralysis, they say, is caused by the muddle of a:

> **lengthy assembly of a mishmash of data and analysis into a hefty tome teeming with industry assessments, jargon-laden presentations on cost savings or market share expansion, topped off with a torrent of budgetary spreadsheets... . One company we worked with had so many strategic priorities it called a general meeting to prioritise the priorities.**

Robert Mittelstaedt (2003) relates how people time and time again complain that they do not understand their companies' strategies, yet CEOs typically say, 'They've been briefed a hundred times – they should understand it by now.' He says multiple strategies often reflect a lack of focus. And 'corporate wordsmiths massage [their] communication ... until [they become] all things to all people ... and meaning nothing to the person trying to do his or her job every day'. Mittelstaedt recommends using performance indicators and rewards aligned to strategy, easily remembered mnemonics (but not slogans) and corporate storytelling to bring strategy alive for every employee.

Strategic leadership and management

'Strategic leadership' is about providing a sense of purpose and a clear direction to guide the formulation of strategies. Donald Hambrick (1989) is more specific: strategic leadership involves aligning the organization with anticipated external forces such as technological developments, market trends, regulatory constraints and competitors' actions.

Leaders who focus on strategy in pursuing a presumed vision or long-term goals can be called strategic leaders. A key function of a leader, particularly the CEO, Calori et al. (1994) say, is to form and implement strategy – to provide strategic leadership. The CEO and top management team certainly play a significant role in strategic leadership (McNulty and Pettigrew, 1999). But Brian Leavy and David Wilson (1994: 16–17) suggest that top management's role in strategy formation may be one of the following:

- Directly formulating the content of strategy
- Shaping the strategy indirectly through managing the organizational context and the strategy process
- Overcoming the institutionalized forces for continuity in an organization – inertia – in pursuing new strategic departures

Strategic leadership is a universal process that is not culture bound, reflecting the adage: 'Think globally; act locally.' Rowe (2001) defines strategic leadership as:

> **the ability to influence others to voluntarily make day-to-day decisions that enhance the long-term viability of the organization, while at the same time maintaining its short-term financial stability.**

Strategic leadership tends to suffer from a diversity of interpretations and definitions. Richard Byrd (1987) regards it as anticipating, envisioning, maintaining flexibility and empowering others to create strategic change. Adair (1989) sees it as direction (vision, purpose and communication), teambuilding and creativity. Alan Hooper and John Potter (2001) see it as vision, purpose, communication and values. They see the ultimate test of strategic leadership as its impact at the front-line level. Duane Ireland and Michael Hitt (1999) see it as determining the firm's purpose or vision, exploiting and maintaining core competencies, developing human capital, sustaining an effective organizational culture, emphasizing ethical practices and establishing balanced organizational controls. Senge (1996) follows Elliott Jaques' concept of time span of discretion in suggesting that strategic leaders need to be providing insight and vision about how the world will be evolving over the next 10 to 20 years. This poses a challenge in most high-tech industries.

Strategic leadership entails strategic thinking: environmental scanning, strategic analysis, strategy formation and strategy implementation (Milliken and Volrath, 1991). However, all of these activities are informed by the vision, mission and shared values of the organization. Strategies are implemented usually through short-term business objectives in pursuit of the vision and mission of the organization.

Strategies that turn out to be highly effective often have challenged preconceived views of the world or the apparently rational or possible (Middleton and Gorzynski, 2002: 3). Such strategies reflect a state of mind rather than the expert use of strategy tools and techniques. Such strategies therefore are the consequence of leadership that breaks the mould, of leadership with an unconventional, pioneering or innovative vision. Middleton and Gorzynski suggest that the challenge of strategy lies in its inherent paradox: for example, 'a vision of the future' and 'a firm footing in reality', 'stretching the organization beyond what is currently possible' and 'core competencies', and 'seeing the big picture' and 'attention to detail'. Effective leadership goes beyond merely choosing between such opposites or even reconciling them, namely, Hamel and Prahalad (1994) say, 'to find the higher ground'.

Leaders are implementers of strategy, according to Anil Gupta (1988): this even applies to top-level leaders who assume strategies as a given. This is arguable: leaders certainly are accountable for the implementation of strategy, but implementation is usually delegated. Nevertheless, a far-reaching vision can fail when the top-level leader takes on too many roles and does not build a top management team to implement the necessary strategies, as in the case of Richard Huber at Aetna; when strategies are implemented too fast to get understanding and commitment, as in the case of Xerox; and when the vision is too grandiose and is dependent on business and political influences coming together, as in the case of the Azurix Corporation (Garten, 2001: 159–166). CEOs need to be not only visionaries and strategists, Garten (2001: 166) says, but also implementers.

There is some empirical evidence of the effect of emotion and mood ('affect') in strategic management (Daniels, 1998, 1999). Emotion and mood may influence the environmental information that is attended to or the recall processes in information processing (Walsh, 1995). Anxious individuals attend more to the threatening or negative aspects of a situation (Dalgleish and Watts, 1990; MacCleod, 1991; Mathew, 1993). Daniels found significant relationships between negative affectivity – the tendency to experience the negative emotions of anxiety and sadness – and poor organizational performance, industry decline and industry competitiveness (Daniels, 1998). This suggests that individuals with negative affectivity might tend to favour strategies that reflect pessimistic interpretations of the strategic environment (Johnson et al., 2001). Daniels suggests that anger may influence individuals to allocate more resources to existing strategies or to reposition them against the sources of such anger such as competitors (Daniels, 1999). He also suggests that positive affectivity may influence individuals to initiate radical strategic change and that fatigue makes individuals less likely to consider fully all strategic options. Emotional contagion (Hatfield et al., 1992) – where one person's affective state induces the same state in others through unconscious signals – may influence:

> a management team collectively to attend closely to a new, but small, entrant into the industry; to recall that in the past their own company was slow to respond to competitive moves of other new entrants; or to interpret the market positioning of the entrant as a direct competitive threat to their market position. (Johnson et al., 2001)

While the empirical evidence is scant so far, it is clear that emotion and mood can influence how leaders use information about their strategic environments (Johnson et al., 2001). This makes a case for leaders to have well-developed emotional intelligence. What we know about emotion and mood in strategic thinking and decision making suggests that leaders require self-awareness, awareness of others' emotions and behaviour, and the ability to respond skilfully in appropriate ways.

CASE STUDY

Business Strategy at CGU Asia

This case study illustrates an analytical approach to business strategy that underscores the importance of the intellectual dimension of leadership. Of importance to the effective implementation and sustainability of the strategy, however, was not only its validity and 'intellectual' acceptance throughout the organization. The fit between the strategy and the company's values, the empowerment of staff, their motivation and commitment to the strategy in carrying it out, and effective leadership development were perhaps even more important.

CGU Asia was the Far East wing of CGNU, which was formed in 2000 through a merger between CGU and Norwich Union, creating the UK's largest insurer and Europe's fifth largest.[90] The merger was a strategic move due to pressure on general insurance premiums because of excess capacity and extra pressure on British life insurance companies from government-approved 'stakeholder pensions', which limited annual charges to 1% a year (*The Economist*, 2000). This was in line with consolidation in the insurance industry throughout Europe. UK-based insurance companies had lost ground in Europe over the 20 years between 1978 and 1998, with six in the top 10 (57%) in 1978 and only one – Prudential – (7%) by 1998.

CGNU's first post-merger chief executive, Bob Scott, had a vision for the marriage for CGNU to be a 'British champion' (*The Economist*, 2000). CGNU's corporate strategic intent was to develop European business, in which it was relatively weak, in particular in Spain, Italy and Germany, and to shift the emphasis away from volatile general insurance into long-term savings. A new CEO, Richard Harvey, took over in April 2001 and on 1 July 2002 CGNU became known as Aviva, with Aviva Asia succeeding CGU Asia and comprising both financial services and general insurance businesses. The strategy of CGU Asia's general insurance arm during the period 2000–2001 is the subject of this case.

CGU Asia's 'governing objective' (mission) was to generate consistently superior returns for its shareholders – superior to its peers and superior to the market. It pursued its mission through several strategies including a 'heartland strategy'.

CGU Asia's overall strategy was to maximize EVA (Economic Value Added), which is a measure of economic profits on existing business less a charge for capital and including discounted future profits emerging from existing business. EVA is based on the assumptions that companies with the best track records in value creation have a competitive advantage in attracting and utilizing capital and human resources and are best at managing human resources and customer satisfaction, and that, wherever shareholders subsidize other stakeholders to any great extent, the financial health of the company is diminished, ultimately to the detriment of all stakeholders. Target EVAs were established for each country operation within CGU Asia. Key EVA drivers were changes in quality

Table 6.2 *CGU Asia's balanced performance scorecard*

Financial	Customer/market
• EVA increase • Profitability premium growth	• 'Heartland' • Brand
Internal processes: operational effectiveness	**Learning and growth**
• Operational effectiveness • Technological capacity • Reporting	• Organizational growth • Personal growth • Innovation and development

of business, volume of business, risk-rating adequacy in terms of prices, expected claims costs and expenses, and investment return. CGU Asia's balanced performance scorecard is given in Table 6.2.

EVA was endorsed by CGU Asia's senior executives and business unit heads, established in revised reporting systems and embedded in business planning guidelines and planning forms. Further steps in its strategic implementation were:

- Roll-out in each country, tailoring it to the needs of each
- Ensuring understanding of the company's value drivers
- Leadership by local EVA champions and reinforcement by training
- Support from the centre and financial management consultants
- Linking of rewards to EVA achievement

CGU Asia's heartland strategy, coordinated by a three-member heartland work-group, was to focus on those business sectors which would produce long-term profitability and in which CGU Asia could be a leader. 'Heartland' could be any of the following:

- A product or product line (e.g. healthcare)
- A defined customer or affinity group (e.g. motor franchise holder)
- A form of distribution (e.g. *Bancassurance*)
- A geographical region (e.g. rural Thailand)

Other supporting strategies focused on learning and growth, both organizational and individual, through training, innovation and development, and managing for value, through ensuring a clear understanding of the means for profitable growth, setting and meeting objectives, accountability and measuring performance.

CGU Asia defined its portfolio, with descriptors, thus:

- The heartland – core business that the company wished to strengthen and grow
- Edge of heartland – growth sectors with real prospects of becoming heartland ('heart warming')

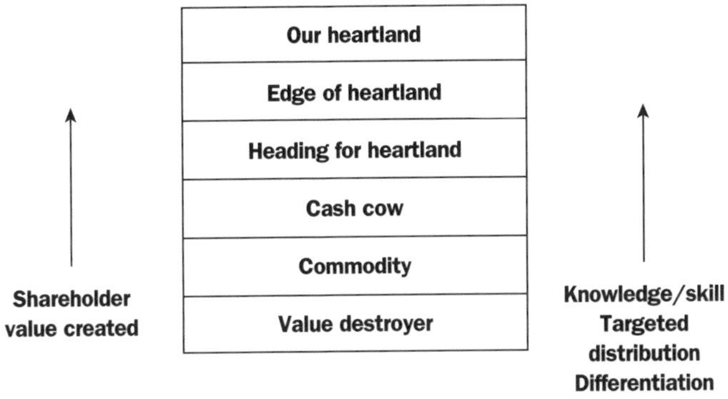

Figure 6.6 *Heartland portfolio management in CGU Asia*

- Heading for heartland – real development prospects, but not yet delivering strong results ('heart to heart')
- Cash cow – good profitability but uncertain prospects, and to be exploited ('heart burn')
- Commodity – opportunistic in character, and not always profitable ('heart break')
- Value destroyer – to be exited ('heart attack')

Heartland portfolio management was depicted in the terms shown in Figure 6.6.

Success with the heartland strategy was defined by the superior shareholder value created, riding the underwriting cycle, clearly identified competition, maturity of the business and strong differentiation, with a return on capital of at least 20% before tax over five years. A CVI (Customer Value Index) for each portfolio category was calculated by weighting business from –2 to +10, resulting in an overall business focus index.

Examples of heartland insurance lines in 1999 were house and contents packages and preferred intermediaries schemes (both 'personal lines'). Examples of value destroyers were motorcycle insurance and motor fleet insurance.

From 2001 CGU Asia aggressively pursued a strategy of service excellence over and above the focus on operational effectiveness and other strategies described above. And from 2002, on changing its name to Aviva Asia, the company pursued a new brand identity and a company values awareness campaign. In September 2004 Aviva Asia's general insurance arm was sold to Mitsui Sumitomo Insurance. The remaining financial services arm is now the sole business of Aviva Asia, which has replaced EVA with ROCE (Return On Capital Employed) and has dropped the concept of 'heartland' as inappropriate and made associated changes to its Balanced Scorecard.

Case study questions

1 What is your opinion of CGU Asia's 'governing objective' (mission): to generate consistently superior returns for its shareholders?
2 Comment on CGU Asia's balanced performance scorecard.

3 Is the concept of 'heartland strategy' a useful one?
4 If you had been the CEO of CGU Asia, what would you have changed in the company's strategies and how would you have exercised strategic leadership?

Focusing primarily on maximizing shareholder value, Medtronic's William W. George says, may lead to short-term improvements but not sustainable long-term growth (George, 2001). This is what happened to GEC in the UK according to former chairman Lord Weinstock after his retirement in 1996 (Aris, 2002). In line with the model of leadership described in this book, George (2001) advises:

> **Pursue a worthy mission with a passion that inspires your employees, stay true to your purpose, practice your values with an unyielding consistency, and employ an adaptable business strategy to match changing market conditions. The long-term increases in shareholder value will far surpass the highest expectations of those who would seek only to maximize shareholder value.**

These are suitable words with which to conclude our three chapters on vision and mission, shared values and culture, and strategy. Vision, mission and strategies require the ability and desire to pursue them. We therefore now turn our attention to how this is achieved through leadership: empowerment, influence, motivation and inspiration.

Further reading

Christopher A. Bartlett and Sumantra Ghoshal (1998), *The Individualized Corporation*. London: Heinemann.

Gary Hamel (2001), *Leading the Revolution*. New York: McGraw-Hill.

J. Hendry, G. Johnson and J. Newton (Editors) (1993), *Strategic Thinking: Leadership and the Management of Change*. Chichester: John Wiley & Sons.

Gerry Johnson, Kevan Scholes and Richard Whittington (2005), *Exploring Corporate Strategy, 7th Edition*. Harlow: Pearson Education.

Brian Leavy and David Wilson (1994), *Strategy and Leadership*. London: Routledge.

John Middleton and Bob Gorzynski (2002), *Strategy Express*. Oxford: Capstone Publishing.

Discussion questions

1 Why is strategic thinking a common management weakness?
2 Should strategy be geared solely or largely to maximizing shareholder value?
3 Should strategy be formulated or allowed to 'form'?
4 How can commitment to strategies be achieved throughout the whole organization?
5 Is 'strategic leadership' any different from 'effective leadership'?

7 Leadership and Empowerment

As for the best leaders, the people do not notice their existence.
The next best the people honour and praise.
The next, the people fear.
And the next, the people hate.
But when the best leaders' work is done, the people say,
'We did it ourselves'.

Lao Tzu (*c.* 500 BC), *The Way of Lao Tzu, Number 17*

Overview

- Empowerment is a topic that is much misunderstood and is interpreted in different ways. Unsurprisingly, therefore, it often arouses passion and heated debate whenever it is mentioned. One of the issues concerns some managers' belief that, in empowering other people, they have to 'give away' some of their power. The proposition of this chapter is that effective leaders empower people to be *able to do* what needs to be done.
- The various concepts of empowerment are reviewed in this chapter. I propose that empowering people is giving them the knowledge, skills, self-awareness, authority, resources, opportunity and freedom to manage themselves and be accountable for their behaviour and performance.
- Studies show that empowering people enhances both job satisfaction and organization performance measured in various ways.
- Barriers to empowerment include bureaucracy, risk aversion, the need for control over others, fear of loss of control, lack of trust, the skill and time required to do it, and resistance to being empowered among those receiving it due to their distrust of motives and anxiety over the consequences. Empowering others requires both ethical justification and emotional intelligence.
- We review cultural variations and considerations in empowerment, using Hofstede's model and examples of empowerment practices, including delegation, and the risks involved and reasons for resistance to it.
- If knowledge is power, then empowering people also means sharing knowledge with them. We review how empowerment is necessary to create a learning organization in which people are creative.

Why did the people say this? Because they were empowered. Effective leaders transfer credit for achievement from themselves to their followers or group members. Empowering leaders may frequently be anonymous or even invisible, but they are among the most effective leaders (Lenz, 1993: 160). Says Lenz (1993: 157), 'At the other extreme is the leader who takes on the mantle of "hero" or "messiah" ... who positions himself or herself as the central protagonist of organizational drama and origin of ideas and actions crucial to the future of an enterprise.'

Empowering people is a principle Nelson Mandela followed. For his wish, as president of a newly liberated South Africa, was not merely to lead his people but to empower them to lead themselves (Stengel, 1994). Expressing Lao Tzu in a contemporary way, Goyder (2001) says, 'Good leaders keep out of the way'; having found the best managers they create the conditions in which the managers can best manage. What are these conditions? And how do effective leaders create them?

The term 'empowerment' often arouses passion whenever it is mentioned. It is a term like 'total quality management' and 'business process re-engineering' that often provokes strong negative reactions among many senior executives – and indeed among the workforce at large. Why?

There are several reasons for this. The meaning of empowerment is 'anything but consistent' across different organizations or even people in one organization, say Deetz et al. (2000: 100). And its implementation has not been easy for many organizations, meeting with resistance at all levels. As Chris Argyris (1998) says, empowerment of employees is notably difficult to achieve. A strong organizational culture can either help or hinder a move towards greater empowerment. There are those who reject the idea as dangerously subversive to managerial authority and control. Some regard 'empowerment' as merely another word for delegation and therefore nothing new. And there are those who immediately reject the idea as yet another management fad – although apparently the idea has been around for at least 2,500 years.

But there are also those who see empowerment as liberating – as simply good leadership. Argyris (1998) reports one CEO as saying, 'No vision, no strategy, can be achieved without able and empowered employees.' And Dess and Picken (2000) say:

> **Inspiring the organization and its stakeholders with a clear vision and compelling sense of purpose is a *necessary* but not a *sufficient* condition for the development of an organization that can learn, adapt, and respond effectively to a rapidly changing environment. Empowerment, providing motivated employees with the responsibility and authority to implement the vision, is equally important.**

Empowerment can also help an organization move towards a stronger culture of initiative, creativity, innovation and accountability. The relationship between empowerment and education and its implications for leadership were recognized in the nineteenth century by the Scottish lawyer and Lord Chancellor, Lord Brougham: 'Education makes a people easy to lead, but difficult to drive; easy to govern, but impossible to enslave' (Jay, 1996: 58).

Recent research in the private and public sectors in the UK revealed that leadership is perceived as:

- Engaging others as partners in developing and achieving a shared vision and enabling staff to lead
- Creating a fertile, supportive environment for creative thinking and for challenging assumptions about how a service or business should be delivered
- Displaying sensitivity to the needs of a range of internal and external stakeholders

(Alimo-Metcalfe and Alban-Metcalfe, 2002a)

This research also suggested that vision and charisma are less important for British managers than for American managers, that collaboration with others is more important, and that the most important issue for British managers is concern for individuals' well-being and development. The research also provides a case for the importance of empowerment in leadership.

What is empowerment?

Empowering people, according to the *Oxford English Dictionary*, is giving people power: giving people the ability, or making them able, to do or act. 'Power' has connotations of vigour, energy, authority, influence. Effective leadership entails empowering people: enabling them to do what needs to be done to pursue a vision, mission, objective or strategy and to fulfil their potential. Robert Heller (1997) sees empowering people as 'setting them free to think for themselves'. As Olivier (2001: 37) says, 'Alignment happens when the right "thing" (outside) is linked to the right "feeling" (inside).' And Goethe in the eighteenth century said, 'Whatever you can do, or dream you can, begin it. Boldness has genius and power and magic in it' (Anster, 1888).

Empowerment was also understood by St Thomas Aquinas, the thirteenth-century philosopher and Dominican friar. He said it is immoral to abuse people and to underuse them (Flanagan, 2000). Developing this point, Fran Yammarino (1994: 45–46) says:

> **it is 'immoral' not to develop others or to not allow them to develop to their fullest potential because of the resulting tremendous waste of human talent.**

One of the first books about empowerment, written in the genre of a modern fable, is that by William C. Byham (1988). Byham defines empowerment as '[having] responsibility, a sense of ownership, satisfaction in accomplishments, power over what and how things are done, recognition for ... ideas, and the knowledge that [one is] important to the organization'. The term 'empowerment' has now become part of everyday management language (Collins, 1994; Cunningham et al., 1996; Hennestad, 1998).

It is only recently, however, that the idea of empowerment has been extended to encompass sharing power, energizing employees, enhancing self-efficacy by reducing powerlessness, and increasing opportunities for intrinsic motivation at work (Menon, 2001). Is the need for power that characterizes effective leaders incompatible with empowering followers? Empowerment must be distinguished from the need for control. Sharing power does not diminish power; in fact it multiplies power. According to Pedler et al. (2004), distributing power to others is necessary for empowerment but not sufficient:

> **Empowerment is a confidence trick unless it comes with real power attached. The idea of empowerment is faulty because power is rarely given away and has to be taken.**

Empowerment is not a clear-cut concept, according to Toby Wall et al. (2002). Sometimes it refers to employees' feelings of competence, meaningful work, autonomy and contribution, and sometimes to the managerial or leadership practices that determine such feelings. The roots of its modern empirical study are in the Hawthorne studies at Western Electric in the United States in the 1920s (Locke and Schweiger, 1979: 265–339). Though the term is relatively new, the practice of empowerment is not new; for example, delegation, job enrichment and giving decision-making authority to employees. The concept is well rooted in theory: McGregor's Theory Y (McGregor, 1960), Likert's 'new patterns of management' (Likert, 1961), Herzberg's job enrichment (Herzberg, 1966), Hackman and Oldham's Job Characteristics Model (Hackman and Oldham, 1976), and the Quality of Working Life movement of the 1970s (Davis and Cherns, 1975). Empowerment also captures the two dimensions of individualized consideration and intellectual stimulation in Bass's model of transformational leadership (Bass, 1985).

Patrick Waterson et al. (1999) say that empowerment is now 'a theme in contemporary strategic thinking as well as a prescription for good management practice'. But definitions of empowerment have been many and varied, leading to some confusion in management circles. Peter Mills and Gerardo Ungson (2003) say that scholars use the term when they mean other things, such as an empowered *feeling*, and that the term is used to mean the same as delegation and employee participation. For example, Jerald Greenberg and Robert Baron (2000) define empowerment as:

> **the passing of responsibility and authority from managers to employees [involving] power being shifted down the ladder to workers who are allowed to make decisions themselves.**

This is a very limited view of empowerment, focusing only on giving authority power and expecting responsibility in return. This is not true empowerment: it is delegation. Holly Rudolph and Joy Peluchette (1993) make the point that delegation (and participation) 'only create[s] the conditions necessary for empowerment to take place'. Monica Lee (1999) takes a somewhat cynical view of empowerment: 'From an "organizational" perspective, empowerment is about the ability to set and achieve goals that are valued by the "organization".'

The term 'structural empowerment' can be used to denote horizontal decentralization of authority whereby decisional power flows to employees from the formal structure' (Mintzberg, 1979; Mills and Ungson, 2003). Structural empowerment, they say, arises in conditions of uncertainty and 'information asymmetry' and where employees need to exchange information and other resources. In addition to individual variables, group and organizational characteristics – group effectiveness, worth of the group and status in the hierarchy – also influence feelings of empowerment, according to a study in the healthcare sector (Koberg et al., 1999).

Roy Herrenkohl et al. (1999) identify several different uses of the term 'empowerment':

- Sharing power with, or transferring power to, those who do the work
- Redistributing authority and control

- Sharing equal responsibility (between employees and managers) for results
- Maximizing employees contribution to an organization's success
- Full participation of workers and leaders in decision making
- Pursuit of a shared vision and purpose through team effort
- Self-motivation through a full understanding of responsibility and authority
- The capability to make a difference in the attainment of goals
- Synergistic interaction among individuals that emphasizes cooperation and leads to expansion of power for the group

Herrenkohl and colleagues define empowerment as shared vision, a supportive organizational structure and governance, responsibility for knowledge and learning, and institutional recognition, all of which together encourage employees using initiative to improve processes and take action. A shared vision provides meaning and value in work. Self-efficacy (the feeling of capability or competence to perform a task) and personal control (a belief that one can make a difference by influencing the environment and outcomes) are also important features of empowerment. Bradley Kirkman and Benson Rosen (1999) similarly define empowerment in terms of potency, meaningfulness, autonomy and impact.

Kirkman and Rosen (1999) make a distinction between self-managing teams and empowered teams. Both are autonomous, they argue, but empowered teams 'also share a sense of doing meaningful work that advances organizational objectives ... team empowerment is a much broader concept'. They found that team effectiveness is determined by team empowerment in addition to individual autonomy, and that highly empowered teams are more effective than less empowered teams.

Scott Seibert et al. (2004) investigated at the level of the work unit the 'empowerment climate' – a shared perception of the extent to which an organization uses structures, policies and practices that support employee empowerment. They found that empowerment climate is empirically distinct from psychological empowerment and positively related to work-unit performance. Psychological empowerment – empowerment at the individual level – was defined as an individual's experience of intrinsic motivation based on personal cognitions in relation to work role (meaning, competence, self-determination and impact). The relationship between empowerment climate and individual performance and job satisfaction, Seibert *et al.* found, is mediated by psychological empowerment.

A popular view of empowerment involves a leader in *doing something to employees* – sharing information, encouraging participation, teambuilding, providing training and development, and rewarding them for taking initiatives and risks. An alternative view is that true empowerment comes from self-determination and intrinsic motivation (Frohman, 1997). This is captured in Phil Lowe's definition of empowerment:

> **The process as a result of which individual employees have the autonomy, motivation and skills necessary to perform their jobs in a way which provides them with a genuine sense of ownership and fulfilment while achieving shared organizational goals. (Lowe, 1994)**

Ken Blanchard and colleagues (Blanchard et al., 1995; Randolph, 1995) suggest that empowerment requires, first, recognizing the importance of knowledge, experience and intrinsic motivation in improving performance and, second, releasing that power by sharing accurate information, creating autonomy within boundaries and replacing hierarchy with self-managing teams.

Empowering people literally *is* giving people power – making them *able to* … . Harvey-Jones says that 'the leader is an enabler as much as a driver' (Harvey-Jones, 1988: 87). Menon (2001) suggests that power has to do not only with control but also with competence and being energized to achieve valued goals. He says:

> **The psychologically empowered state is a cognitive state characterised by a sense of perceived control, competence, and goal internalisation.**

Goal internalization reflects belief in, and commitment to, the vision, mission, causes and goals of the organization. This, Menon says, is the 'energising aspect of empowerment'. He found in his study that goal internalization and perceived control are strongly related. He says:

> **Goal internalisation is...the ownership of the organisational goal, while perceived control is...ownership (or control) of the means (e.g. decision-making authority) to achieve that goal.**

Argyris (2000) argues that there is a great deal of confusion about empowerment. One problem, he says, is the conflict between 'internal commitment' and 'external commitment'. This is the inconsistency of asking employees to 'own' situations and problems and to behave like owners (internal commitment), yet expecting them to meet job requirements as specified by bosses (external commitment). The problem occurs when managers ask for internal commitment and the organizational system rewards external commitment. Asking people to act like owners when they have not set the objectives is a psychological paradox. Argyris says:

> **When someone else defines objectives, goals, and the steps to reach them, whatever commitment exists will be external. Employees may feel responsible for producing what is required of them, but they will not feel responsible for the way the situation is defined.**

An empirical study of empowerment by Menon (2001) explains empowerment as self-perceptions of competence (self-efficacy), perception of control over the work environment, and the internalization of organizational goals. Self-efficacy is an important ingredient in feeling empowered and can be explained by the expectancy–valency theory of motivation (see Chapter 8). Perception of control results from delegation and autonomy. Menon's work adds to our understanding of empowerment, however, by emphasizing the importance of goal internalization. Goals can be motivating if they are valued as a cause or worthy purpose. If personal needs and objectives are congruent with the organization's objectives, people will feel that they control their own lives and that their actions make a difference.

Effective leaders do not 'manage' people; they empower them (you may recall the United Technologies notice, 'Let's get rid of management', in Chapter 1). Empowering people means treating people as valued individuals, giving power to them, expecting responsibility in return, and enabling them to perform and achieve – in other words, giving people the skills, resources and freedom to manage themselves with accountability for their performance. As Margot Morrell and Stephanie Capparell (2001: 9) say:

> **[Employees today]...resent being managed and driven; they want to be inspired and led. They expect to have intelligent exchanges with their bosses and to help guide the direction of their companies.**

Rob Lebow says:

> **Unless you link accountability and responsibility...you'll never get accountable employees. It's the 'strings' that are placed on employees - policies, incentives and performance standards - that destroy accountability. (Creelman, 2003b)**

Empowerment implies the need for concomitant capability. Henry Coleman (1996) describes how Airtouch wanted, through cross-training, to empower its call-centre staff in dealing with customers. Unfortunately these lowly paid staff did not have the intellectual capacity to take on the additional responsibility. Argyris (1998) points out that there is also a limit to employees' emotional commitment to their work and employer and hence their desire for empowerment. Stress may increase as a result of greater responsibility (Wright, 1996), although stress may be due to fear of failure and its consequences.

People cannot perform unless they have the opportunity to do so. Providing opportunities to people and the freedom and resources to do what they can do – and to do what they have not done before – is part of good leadership. Giving people the knowledge and skills they need to perform, for example through training and coaching, is hardly a case that needs to be argued. In the words of the ancient Chinese saying: 'Give a man a fish and you feed him for a day. Teach him how to fish and you feed him for a lifetime.'

Underlying empowerment, however, is self-awareness and 'perceived competence' or self-efficacy – belief in one's own capabilities to do what needs to be done (Wood and Bandura, 1989). In Jay Conger and Rabindra Kanungo's model, empowerment is a process of psychological enabling, primarily through enhancing belief in self-efficacy (Conger and Kanungo, 1988). In a more recent extension of this model, Menon (2001) adds perception of control over the work environment and the internalization of organizational goals. He says:

> **If employees in modern organisations are to be...enjoined in the organisational cause, then they need to internalise the goals of the organisation.**

We see empowerment displayed where people are allowed to write their own job descriptions, work in self-managing teams, take part in decision making and are delegated meaningful and challenging tasks and responsibilities (Yammarino, 1994: 46).

My research suggests that transactional leaders – who emphasize management-by-exception and reward that is contingent on performance – are primarily directive in their leadership style, and strongly so, while the more effective transformational leaders (who display Bass's four 'I's) use all the leadership styles – directive, consultative, participative and delegative – to a significant extent (Gill, 1999a). They are likely to use such styles according to the situation, as situational leadership and contingency theories recommend. The conclusion is that transactional leaders are less empowering than transformational leaders.

Popper and Mayseless (2003) sum up the relationship between transformational leadership and empowerment as:

- Increasing followers' autonomy and encouraging them to think independently and critically
- Raising their level of self-efficacy, self-confidence, competence, self-worth and self-management
- Augmenting their creativity and risk taking

Transformational leadership through vision and inspiration transforms the beliefs and attitudes of citizens or employees in line with national or organizational mission and objectives: such leadership creates internalized goals.

Shackleton was an empowering leader. He spelt out exactly what was required of each man and provided the best possible equipment. He understood and accepted each man's quirks and weaknesses, identified his unique talents, matched what needed to be done with these abilities, and helped each one to reach his potential through challenging and meaningful work. Perhaps above all, he was a nurturing, caring leader, even serving tea in bed to the ship's 'cry-baby'.

What specific actions or behaviour – in leaders or followers – constitute empowerment? My review of the literature suggests the following:

- Self-awareness of one's strengths and limitations, interests, preferences and motivational drivers, and values, beliefs and attitudes
- Delegation of challenging tasks and the authority to make decisions and take action
- Stimulating people's intellects, imagination and intuition, questioning the status quo, and getting them to do likewise
- Providing the opportunity, resources and support for people to perform
- Sharing knowledge and rewarding *learning* as well as performance
- Coaching and training for skills acquisition or improvement
- Allowing or encouraging self-determination and autonomy – the freedom of people to manage themselves
- Acceptance of responsibility (sense of duty or obligation) and accountability (willingness to admit to being the source of actions or decisions that cause given outcomes)

In summary, empowerment is giving people the knowledge, skills, self-awareness, authority, freedom, resources and opportunity to manage themselves. This definition reflects key ideas and research findings in the practitioner and scholarly literature (Blau and Alba, 1982; Sashkin, 1984; Burke, 1986; Smits et al., 1993; Donovan, 1994; Hayes, 1994; Labianca et al., 1997). However, along with empowerment comes accountability for behaviour and performance. Just as rights entail responsibilities, power entails accountability. So my definition of empowerment includes accountability for one's behaviour and performance.

The impact of empowerment

David Myers (1993: 130) points out that 'study after study finds that when workers have more control – when they can help define their own goals and hours and when they participate in decision making – their job satisfaction rises'. He quotes the case of

Herman Miller, the American office furniture manufacturer and in 1989 one of *Fortune* magazine's top 10 most-admired companies, whose investment in employee empowerment was repaid with a 25-times increase in stock value between 1970, when it went public, and 1991 (1993: 131).

Using a participative leadership style is a feature of empowering people. A positive relationship has been established between participation, satisfaction, motivation, quality, productivity and performance (Hollander and Offerman, 1990; Bartol and Martin, 1991). And Peter Turney (1993) found that empowered employees have a sense of ownership and responsibility, satisfaction in their accomplishments, a sense of control over what and how things are done, and the knowledge that they are important to the organization. Gervase Bushe et al. (1996) in a study of empowerment report increased productivity and efficiency, measured by increased customer satisfaction and innovation. Continuous improvement, responsiveness to customers, quality and efficiency are achieved by empowered workers rather than bureaucrats (Greenhalgh, 2001a).

Empowerment as a management practice, Adrian Wilkinson (1998) says, is the very antithesis of the principles of scientific management according to Frederick W. Taylor, namely clear limits to authority, separation of planning from operations, the need for incentives for workers, task specialization and management-by-exception. One of Henry Ford's patriarchal aphorisms intoned: 'leadership is perfect when it so simplifies operations that orders are not necessary' (Nevins and Hill, 1954). Leadership may be 'perfect' when orders are not necessary, but not because operations are so simple. Bureaucracy is at odds with empowerment: it is associated with powerlessness, lack of initiative, non-fulfilment and emotional 'homelessness' (Blauner, 1964; Weber, 1964; Bennis, 1973).

The bureaucratic organization is the antithesis of the learning organization. More than 40 years ago Michel Crozier (1964) depicted the bureaucratic organization as unable to learn from past mistakes, therefore engaging in a retreat from reality. This results, in terms of transactional leadership, either from passive management-by-exception that reinforces the status quo or from active management-by-exception that may punish initiative (if it results in adverse outcomes) and the risk taking necessary in learning (Pitt et al., 1996). Long ago Tom Burns and George Stalker (1969) suggested that bureaucratic organization and leadership styles would disadvantage companies operating in fast-moving and unpredictable environments, including those occupying a particular technological niche.

The restructuring of traditional bureaucratic organizations to encourage 'intrapreneurship' and create a learning organization, Bala Chakravarty and Martin Gargiulo (1998) argue, requires employee empowerment during the process. They describe how, typically, such a transformation is characterized by first an authoritarian restructuring and then a more participative revitalization. This, they say, often fails. This is due to top management's inability to empower employees because of a loss of the necessary trust during restructuring.

Senior staff in the higher education sector in the UK complain of institutional bureaucracy that discourages teaching initiatives and innovative teaching and learning methods, according to Ian McNay (2004). Bureaucracy is an enemy of empowerment, for which it substitutes system controls. McNay suggests that one reason for this problem may be the lack of confidence and leadership skills of senior management:

> **This lack of confidence leads to control strategies where even minor decisions have to go further up the decision-making hierarchy than is efficient... . Subsidiarity is a good principle...[whereby]...leadership and management are distributed, and small, agile, adaptive units are created.**

Lack of empowerment can lead to no change, even when change is needed. For example, leaders often do not change because they are not challenged (Kotter, 1996). Being empowered means being willing and able to challenge the status quo:

> **Visions don't work unless the people who have to find their way to the vision are given sufficient empowerment to take the actions necessary to reach the vision without continually needing to refer back to their leader. (Hodgson and White, 2001)**

Empowerment, however, does not always enhance work performance (Wall et al., 2002). Empowerment is likely to be more effective when there is a high degree of operational uncertainty than when work processes are more predictable and understood.

Is the empowering leader at risk of becoming laissez-faire and losing control? Bass (1998) suggests that, if a person's goals are not aligned with the organization's, then, through being empowered, he or she may pursue self-interest at the expense of the organization. He also suggests that 'groupthink' and 'social loafing' may result in dysfunctional self-managing teams: members avoid being critical of one another and nobody takes responsibility. Alan Randolph (1995) suggests that, to avoid this, more rather than less structure is needed in empowered teams. In this respect *The Economist* (2002e) is somewhat cynical about empowerment:

> **The empowered, flattened organisational structure is fatally flawed. Empowerment has an unintended and paradoxical effect upon organisations whereby employees attempt to maximise the degree of individual freedom and responsibility during expansionist times, then abdicate leadership responsibility and actively undermine innovative strategic solutions when threatened by potential loss of power and income.**

Empowerment nevertheless can enhance organizational performance. Edward Lawler et al. (1992) report a greater return on sales when people are given more control and responsibility. In fact supervisors who are more empowered are perceived by their subordinates as more innovative, influential upwards and inspirational (Spreitzer et al., 1999).

When challenges engage our skills, we often become so absorbed in the flow of an activity that we lose awareness of self and time (Csikszentmihalyi and Csikszentmihalyi, 1988: 261). Painters and writers (like me), for example, know this only too well. Challenge is essential to satisfying work.

Myers (1993: 134) says, 'As people accumulate a history of productivity in high-challenge, high-skill situations they develop positive self-esteem.' Gretchen Spreitzer and Robert Quinn (1996) found that managers with low levels of self-esteem, negative feelings about their jobs and poor support from their colleagues and bosses were less likely to effect organizational change through transformational leadership. Self-esteem, for the nineteenth-century psychologist and philosopher William James (1890), is 'the ratio of a person's successes to his or her pretensions', where pretensions are viewed as goals, purposes or aims. Self-esteem is a powerful motivator. And self-esteem is perfectly acceptable morally, and indeed desirable. Self-esteem is what Sir Kenneth Wheare (1974) calls 'proper pride', as distinct from the 'sin of inordinate pride', which shows itself as 'self-love, self-satisfaction, self-admiration ... and self-glorification', as we see in Malvolio, Mr Toad and some celebrities.

An empirical study of operators of complex technology by Desmond Leach et al. (2003) showed that empowerment can result in employees' increased job knowledge and self-confidence, but not necessarily motivation or job satisfaction. However, Daniel Denison (1984) suggests that empowerment can also lead to improvements in employee absenteeism and turnover, which may reflect poor morale, as well as problem solving and decision making.

Empowerment and emotional intelligence

The concept of emotional intelligence (EQ) has helped us to understand empowering leadership. Emotional intelligence is about being aware of one's own abilities, needs and feelings, recognizing those of others, displaying trust and self-control, and responding to others in appropriate ways through well-developed interpersonal skills. Awareness of – and overcoming – one's own need for control, for example, is necessary if one is to empower people sincerely and effectively.

Lack of trust is the enemy of empowerment. So is fear of the consequences of taking risks. Such distrust and fear lead to a desire for control. The 'control freak' is an all-too-common phenomenon. However, control does not necessarily mean controlling other people: 'it means the organization is "in control" – the parts work together responsibly to create the desired results' (Covey, 1992: 213). Empowerment means letting go. Fear of losing control and lack of trust are emotional responses.

Trust in fact is a *sine qua non* for empowerment, as Warren Bennis affirms in conversation with Richard Hodgetts (1996):

Hodgetts: ...even if you have the best vision in the world, if you can't generate trust, it doesn't matter. And it's not just trust in an abstract sense. It's the ability to connect with people in their gut and in their heart and not just in their head.

Bennis: Absolutely, and that's particularly true in this era of re-engineering and downsizing, where trust continues to be a major concern for the employees. If leaders can't establish that trust, then participation and empowerment will be cynical relics of a distopian nightmare. The problem is squarely in the hands of management, and it's a challenge that will confront us well into the next century.

It is only when we learn to manage our emotions and have the courage to make changes that we can be truly empowering.

When intentions and decisions are challenged, a single-minded leader may ignore the challenge and lead an organization or nation into difficulty or disaster. Witness Adolf Hitler's refusal to heed his generals' advice that led to Germany's defeat (contrasted with Winston Churchill's acceptance of dissent over his strategies) and British prime minister Tony Blair's diminishing popularity after charges of ignoring ambivalent legal advice about joining the Iraq War in early 2003.

In a BBC2 television series on *Secrets of Leadership*, Andrew Roberts describes how Hitler at first deliberately empowered his commanders but then, as his trust in them waned, reversed his leadership strategy.[91] Initially he introduced 'Mission Control', whereby he empowered his army leaders in the field. High Command set the objectives and commanders in the field were enabled to act on their own initiative and respond to situations without waiting for orders. Lower ranks were trained in leadership on the rationale that every follower had the potential to be a leader. Hitler displayed trust in his commanders to use their initiative and expertise to fulfil the mission, and he adopted this approach in his leadership of the German government, devolving decision-making responsibility to ministers, while he happily stayed in his Bavarian retreat. However, his growing distrust of his army generals in the struggle to take over Russia led him to abandon his empowerment strategy and Mission Control and to 'micro-manage' activity at the fighting front. The outcome was disastrous: hundreds of thousands of German soldiers were killed, the fight against Russia was lost, and the Allies broke through in western Europe. Abandoning empowerment was the disastrous result of distrusting his subordinates. In fact it is not uncommon for managers to recall empowerment and take control when the chips are down.

Empowering people means taking the risk that mistakes will be made and, when they are made, treating them as opportunities to learn. During the Second World War, Churchill won the confidence of his service chiefs through empowerment:

> **He brought [to them] the sure knowledge that they might take calculated risks of even the most hair-raising kind without having to look over their shoulders. (Ferrier, 1965: 6)**

Effective leaders identify and develop the potential of other people, they question and they criticize. Criticism, Tom Kirby (1998) says, has wrongly become regarded as a bad thing. Gerry Randell (1998) agrees: criticism must be constructive and objective, and it entails the skilful use of questions, statements and body language to influence behaviour and handle emotions. Empowerment characterizes the learning organization. While the CEO of a telecommunications company intellectually stimulated his management team and gained their openness in expressing ideas and suggestions, he publicly humiliated them when they did so. That was the end of ideas and suggestions from his managers.

The extent of empowerment by the leader depends on the leader's need for control of others, self-awareness, self-control, self-confidence, trust in others, interpersonal skills and desire for empowerment or acceptance of it by subordinates or followers. Another enemy of empowerment is involvement in 'the minutiae of management' – expense claims, sick leave and the like (Street-Porter, 2000). Letting go and taking risks that mistakes will be made require courage – the courage to fail (Furnham, 2001a). 'In failure, it is important to acknowledge it and even more important to learn from it' (Flanagan, 2000). Risk aversion, lack of trust, and selfishness or self-centredness on the part of the manager clearly impede this. Organizational initiatives to empower people have failed often because of managers' inability to delegate effectively, their need for power, their own job insecurity, and role ambiguity (Fleming, 1991).

Effective leaders know their own strengths and they use and nurture them. Ensuring self-awareness is the starting point in effective leadership development programmes.

Effective leaders empower both themselves and their followers or subordinates by recognizing both their own strengths and weaknesses and those of others and capitalizing on strengths (Hooper and Potter, 2001: 9).

Empowerment and culture

It should be clear that empowerment both influences and reflects organizational culture. Empowerment varies according to culture and leadership style, which in turn are determined by situations and other contingencies:

> **We made a mess of our empowerment initiative at the outset. We did not think about the changes in corporate values that would be needed to make it work. We simply thought our people would be glad to have a job in this once-proud organisation and thus go along with our blueprint for change...we forgot to ask the basic question: 'Why would staff want to be empowered in a climate of exponential change?' But more than that, we forgot to ask, 'What's in it for the staff?' (Rajan, 2000b)**

Empowerment varies across cultures according to cultural values, requiring understanding of local values and flexible leadership behaviour. Ignoring cultural differences in empowering people may make the effort a failure. Despite its shortcomings, Hofstede's model of the dimensions of culture can provide a useful framework for understanding the implications of culture for empowerment (Hofstede, 1994). Alan Randolph and Marshall Sashkin (2002) suggest the following guidelines.

When power distance is high, people may not feel comfortable in making decisions and taking action that have been the prerogative of their managers previously. There may be a mutual reluctance to share information and replace hierarchy with self-managing teams. When power distance is low, managers and employees are more likely to welcome empowerment.

When uncertainty avoidance is high, employees prefer goals, policies, procedures and assignments to be precisely spelled out. Information sharing, provided it is understandable, and clarifying boundaries when creating autonomy are welcomed. However, self-managing teams may suffer from the need for management to clarify team goals and roles. When uncertainty avoidance is low, people tolerate unclear structure in relation to roles and procedures, though empowerment may lead to chaos. And a greater tolerance of ambiguity does not excuse accountability, so boundaries that set expectations are needed. Self-managing teams tend to be comfortable with setting their own goals, roles and procedures.

When individualism is strong, there may be difficulty in moving towards team empowerment. However, individualistic people prefer control over their own destinies, and they therefore seek information that gives them such control. Moreover, those with such information feel a stronger compulsion to act responsibly (Blanchard et al., 1995). Individualistic people respond positively to autonomy, but they may have difficulty in self-managing teams. When collectivism is strong, information sharing and team accountability are preferred.

The effects of 'masculinity/femininity' as a cultural dimension on empowerment are likely to be moderated by other cultural elements. In masculine cultures (where assertiveness and a focus on results are strong), information is likely to be shared where it relates to results, and clear and meaningful goals and responsibilities will be sought. In feminine cultures (where the emphasis is more on nurturing and caring), information is more likely to be sought on processes and relationships, which are emphasized over tasks and goals, and there is likely to be a focus on the team development process.

Implementing empowerment in a multicultural organization or environment is likely to be more difficult than in a single-culture one because of the complexities that have been described.

Empowerment in practice

Robert Quinn and Gretchen Spreitzer (1997) say that 'this promising concept [of empowerment] often proves elusive'. A basic problem, they say, is the lack of consensus on what empowerment is and how to implement it. For example, half of the 12 most senior executives in a *Fortune 50* manufacturing company believed that empowerment is about delegation and accountability. Their implicit strategy for empowerment, they say, was to:

- Start at the top
- Clarify the organization's vision, mission and values
- Clearly specify the roles, tasks and rewards for employees
- Delegate responsibility
- Hold people accountable for results

The other six senior executives, Quinn and Spreitzer say, viewed empowerment very differently, as about risk taking, growth and change. It meant:

> **trusting people and tolerating their imperfections...[asking] for forgiveness rather than permission...[acting] as entrepreneurs...with a sense of ownership in the business... engaging in creative conflict, constantly challenging each other.**

Their implicit strategy for empowerment was to:

- Start at the bottom by understanding the needs of employees
- Model empowered behaviour for employees
- Build teams to encourage cooperative behaviour
- Encourage intelligent risk taking
- Trust people to perform

A fear expressed by one senior executive (in the first group) was: 'We can't afford loose cannons around here', to which another, from the second group, retorted, 'When was the last time you saw a cannon of any kind around here?' Quinn and Spreitzer point out an important and incorrect assumption in mechanistic, top-down strategies for empowerment: that 'empowerment is something managers do to their people'. They argue that truly empowered people have a sense of:

- Self-determination: they are free to choose how to do their work – they are not 'micro-managed' (or, if we follow United Technology's advice, they are not 'managed' at all; they manage themselves)
- Meaning: they feel their work is important to them, and they care about it
- Competence: they are confident about their ability to do their work well
- Impact: they believe they can influence their work unit, that others will listen to their ideas

The three major barriers to empowerment, according to research by Quinn and Spreitzer, are a bureaucratic culture that emphasizes maintenance of the status quo and impedes change, conflict among organizational functions such as production and customer service, and personal time constraints due to workload. They describe how an empowerment programme such as The Ford Motor Company's can create the shared values and beliefs necessary for true empowerment. The organizational requirements are a clear vision, mission and challenge, openness and teamwork, individual goals aligned clearly to the vision, with clear boundaries for decision making and clear task responsibilities, and mutual support and a sense of security. The last-mentioned requirement is about reinforcing efforts to take the initiative and risk rather than punishing failure when people do this.

A survey by Development Dimensions International found that British companies, such as Shell UK Exploration & Production and telecommunications company Orange, empower their staff more than those in other countries through information sharing and 'high-involvement' strategies with employees.[92] Shell estimates it saved £19 million in production costs as a result of its high-involvement programme.

One useful approach to empowering people at work (Covey, 1992: 190–199) focuses on achieving several conditions:

1. Win–win agreements whereby followers satisfy their own needs, goals and aspirations by achieving what is expected of them at work. This is done by ensuring a clear mutual understanding and commitment regarding expectations in five areas:
   - Specifying desired results
   - Setting guidelines
   - Identifying and providing available resources
   - Defining and agreeing accountability and how results will be evaluated
   - Clarifying and delivering the consequences – in terms of rewards or benefits
2. Self-management – whereby people manage themselves according to that agreement. The leader provides help and support, together with the necessary organizational structures and systems. People appraise themselves according to the agreed results and criteria.
3. The character traits associated with a genuine desire for other people's accomplishment and success:
   - Integrity, whereby the leader's habits are congruent with corporate values, words are congruent with actions and expressions with feelings
   - Maturity, whereby courage is balanced with consideration, for example clear and assertive expression moderated by listening and empathy
   - 'Abundance mentality', whereby the leader is willing to share the rewards and benefits of success

4 Skills of communication, planning and organization, and synergistic problem solving to enable the foregoing conditions. Synergistic decision making entails getting several people at different levels in the organization to work together on a problem and make a recommendation.

Empowering people entails delegating challenging tasks to them. Delegation is the assignment of responsibility or authority to another person (Kuhnert, 1994: 10–25). Managers delegate to others for a variety of reasons – often to improve their own time management or to get more things done. These aims may reflect a preoccupation with self-interest on the part of the leader: a concern with his or her own personal needs, goals, interests or agenda without a genuine concern for the well-being of subordinates (1994: 13). This is not true empowerment. Delegation is often not deliberately done specifically to develop people – true empowerment. Effective leaders empower people through delegation by taking account of both the long-term goals and interests of the organization and those of the individual rather than the immediate or short-term ones (1994: 18–24).

Delegation carries two main benefits. First, it empowers and develops people: it enhances their knowledge and skills, it provides opportunities for growth and advancement, it increases people's motivation and job satisfaction, and it enhances their value to the organization. Second, it frees up time for other, more critical tasks that need to be carried out personally. Barriers to effective delegation centre on reluctance to delegate and managers' lack of delegation skills. How often do we hear, 'If you want something done right, do it yourself'? Reluctance arises from fear that the task will be done badly, a desire for personal control and achievement, perceived staff workload, and lack of time to do it – a 'chicken-and-egg' situation. Lack of delegation skills tends to concern inability to analyse staff workload, critical tasks, and staff abilities, interests and potential, and poor communication skills in explaining and gaining commitment to objectives, tasks and responsibilities.

Lowe (1994) describes the process of effective empowerment as follows:

- Coaching – whereby leaders help people to apply or improve knowledge and skills on the job
- Sponsorship – sponsoring projects by employees
- Facilitating – suggestion schemes, quality circles, self-directed work teams, training events and project teams
- Mentoring – providing counselling and guidance to less experienced or mature employees
- Providing learning and development opportunities – for example, job rotation schemes
- Accrediting – recognizing the acquisition of specific competencies
- Taking ownership of employee development

An example of empowerment comes from the British Army. 'Mission Command' recognizes that success on the battlefield is related to the speed with which commanders make decisions. It involves telling subordinate commanders what to achieve and why, but not what to do and how. They are allowed to take the initiative within defined limits. Ronit Kark et al. (2003) in a study found that transformational leadership is simultaneously associated with both empowerment and dependence on the leader.

Whether this is a paradox depends on what kind of dependence. In the British Army example, this is clear and consistent with true empowerment.

Eileen Shapiro (2000) suggests, however, that the best examples of employee empowerment are found not in organizations that educate and coach their managers to empower people but in 'fast-paced entrepreneurial companies typified by high-growth Internet start-ups'. These circumstances – extremely rapid speed and growth – require high-impact decisions by junior people without consultation with bosses, motivated by the prospect of huge rewards fairly quickly. This is, Shapiro says, empowerment 'by default' rather than 'by design'. Shapiro expressed this view in 2000, before the Internet 'bubble' burst. She says, 'Entrepreneurs often have an abnormally high need for control; that's partly why they dump ... employers and start their own enterprises.' But it is those entrepreneurs who are genuinely empowering of their employees, she says, who succeed most.

Empowerment, risk and resistance

A Nepalese Buddhist mantra says, 'Take into account that great love and great achievements involve great risk.' Empowerment carries risks. One is the risk of perceived abdication by a leader; others are fear of loss of control and fear of failure. For example, in one telecommunications company I worked with, some managers expressed discomfort with the risk of anarchy as the result of empowerment. They preferred limits to subordinates' authority. Empowerment requires a distinction to be made between *leading* an organization and *controlling* it.

When the Bank of Scotland failed to gain control of NatWest in 2000, the chief executive, Peter Burt, said, 'People have to learn to fail ... . If you don't try you may never lose, but you'll never win.'[93] The Bank of Scotland's arch-rival, the Royal Bank of Scotland, pipped it to the post – after two failed attempts at taking over Barclays Bank and Birmingham Midshires. People learn more from failure than from success. In fact failure is necessary for success. This requires us to understand *why* we have failed in a particular situation and to use this understanding in future risk taking. Another Nepalese Buddhist mantra says, 'When you lose, don't lose the lesson.' Empowering people, therefore, may carry a risk of failure, but this risk is necessary and worthwhile if we are to help them to succeed.

Peter Mills and Gerardo Ungson (2003) say:

> **The success or failure of employee empowerment depends on the ability of the organization to reconcile loss of control inherent in empowerment practices with the fundamental organizational need for goal congruence.**

They propose two ways of exercising control for the risks of empowerment: the organizational constitution and the building of organization-wide (routine) trust. The organization constitution is 'a set of agreements and understandings that define the limits and goals of the group ... as well as the responsibilities and rights of participants' (Zald, 1970). Mills and Ungson (2003) distinguish between 'routine trust' and 'basic trust'. The former is a limited form of trust built up over time and seen in everyday relationships, entailing the belief that a person has the ability to perform specific tasks under specific conditions (Bigley and Pearce, 1998). Basic trust arises in situations where people have little information about the object of their trust (Rotter, 1980), and it carries greater risk than routine trust (Granovetter, 1985). Basic trust, according to Blair Sheppard and Dana Sherman (1998):

> **[has] the potential for the individual to behave in ways contrary to the interests of the organization, primarily because the empowered employee's behavior is often outside the purview of the organization and therefore difficult to control.**

According to Graham Clark, the need for control determines the extent to which empowerment is possible (Eadie, 1999). Organizations with a strong need for control and low tolerance of risk – 'compliant organizations' – include mass-production firms, fast-food restaurants, retail financial services and airlines.

Empowerment has disadvantages, both perceived and real. Some employees may abuse the increased power they gain. Some may not have the desire or aptitude for the increased responsibility. Managers of empowered employees need to have new or better skills in facilitation and information sharing. Some fear loss of control (Capozzoli, 1995). The vertical chain of command, and the associated emphasis on control, is still common in organizations. The problem is that control seeks conformity to the plan, policies and procedures. The emotional reaction it engenders is captured in the saying 'Trust flees authority.' This problem has greatest adverse impact in the realms of middle-level management. Yet middle managers are expected, and ought, to be leaders themselves (R.E. Colvin, 2001). In fact most resistance to empowerment comes from middle-level managers (Keighley, 1993). J.P. Scully (1993) says that some employees may regard empowerment as abdication by managers that leads to organizational anarchy.

Many managers resist empowerment. For example, 'Some are like parents who want their children to make decisions for themselves but want them to make only the decisions that [they] ... would have made' (Deetz et al., 2000: 103). This approach creates mutual distrust and cynicism and leads to the excuse by managers that empowerment does not work. A Harbridge House survey revealed that some 62% of middle-level managers and one-third of senior and junior managers felt threatened by empowerment: the three most common barriers to empowerment are unwillingness to let go, fear of the new, and risk aversion (Lowe, 1994). Such resistance is illustrated by the admission of Robert Haas, former CEO of Levi Strauss: 'It has been difficult for me to accept the fact that I don't have to be the smartest guy on the block' (Howard, 1990).

Argyris (2000) describes such resistance to empowerment by managers as examples of what he calls 'Model 1' – unilateral control. This is characterized by:

- Needing to maximize winning and minimize losing
- Perceiving challenges to authority, policies and strategies as signs of weakness
- Going to great lengths to avoid such conflicts and covering up efforts to do so
- Achieving the desired outcomes while minimizing the stimulation or expression of negative feelings

On the other hand Argyris's Model 2 managers:

- Confront issues
- Debate assumptions

- Share information
- Express feelings
- Involve and empower people
- Focus on winning collectively as an enterprise rather than winning as an individual

Shapiro (2000), in a review of Argyris's models, questions the assertion that empowerment is the result of confronting issues, debating assumptions, sharing information and expressing feelings. Instead she posits the structural circumstances of the economy as an alternative explanation for empowerment described earlier in this chapter, quoting fast-paced entrepreneurial situations with empowerment 'by default' as an example.

More junior managers and non-managerial employees may resist empowerment because of several forms of anxiety. Their new freedom to take risks may lead to a fear of lack of support from their bosses when they fail. They may fear failure itself in what they perceive to be a 'blame' culture. And they may fear losing their job either because of failure or because of handing it away and becoming redundant. They may also fear that accepting greater responsibility and accountability may mean it is harder to blame others when things go wrong. Empowering people includes giving them the power to say 'no' to being empowered – if they do not want it.

Managers may also fear loss of power and control when they delegate authority to subordinates, with little benefit in return for themselves. In fact, empowering subordinates implies a redefinition of the manager's role – as leader, rather than manager, of people. As was quoted in Chapter 1, ' We manage *things*, but we *lead* people.'

Empowerment, knowledge management and creativity

If knowledge is power, then empowering people means sharing knowledge with them. Yet, according to research on strategies for the knowledge economy by Windle Priem and David Finegold, nine out of every ten people in global firms say they do not have access to lessons learned by their firms (Coles, 2000). In their report Priem and Finegold say:

> **Leaders should participate in development programmes, mentor high-potential managers, have executives share publicly their mistakes and what they learned, recognise those who took carefully calculated risks but didn't succeed, and promote people who actively share knowledge to help the whole organisation. (Coles, 2000)**

Priem and Finegold's report also makes the point that employees must feel that sharing knowledge is part of their job and that it is recognized and rewarded. Many leaders sadly miss the mark by failing to ensure this: they reward performance but not learning. Most people feel they do not share in the success of the organization, and half feel they do not have a stake in improving corporate performance.

Knowledge management is nothing new. And it is an example of leadership through empowerment. Knowledge management is about people, not IT: it is about learning, communication, using knowledge from various sources and developing a culture of knowledge sharing (Windle, 2001). Effective leaders share information and ideas across the organization and encourage and cultivate informal sources of information (Dess and Picken, 2000).

Creating a learning organization is about learning how to learn, facilitating the learning of all its members and continuous organizational change (Senge, 1990). A survey of 532 CEOs and senior managers in the top 100 companies in 15 countries by the PA Consulting Group in 1996 revealed a significant global consensus on the need to create learning organizations characterized by agility, continuous adaptation, creativity and innovation, facilitated by empowering leadership (PA Consulting Group, 1996).

A model organization in this respect, management consultant Chris Collison says, is BP (Coles, 2000). In 1996 Sir John (later Lord) Browne, the company's group CEO, initiated a successful knowledge management programme using an intranet that saved millions of dollars. This programme involved a task force to identify best practice, teams about to carry out a new project getting together with peers from other parts of the organization to identify the best way to do it, reviews of action taken compared with those intended and the lessons learned, and proof of learning about what the firm knows about running a similar project before getting approval and funding for a new project.

Nurturing the creativity of gifted people entails empowering them. Some create new things and ideas from scratch. Some rearrange existing things or ideas and put them into a new order or perspective. And creative people require leaders who themselves are creative. What do we mean by 'creativity'? Creativity is the ability to generate new and original ideas, associations, methods, approaches and solutions – a process known as 'ideation' – and to relate them to a given problem. Creativity – popularly associated with the right hemisphere of the brain – is characterized by artistic, intuitive, conceptual, emotional, holistic, 'divergent' and 'lateral' thinking and the associated behaviour. Analytical thinking – 'left brain' – in contrast is logical, rational, mathematical, technical, controlled, administrative, 'convergent' and 'vertical'.

Creativity must be contrasted with *innovation*. Innovation is not invention; that is creativity. Innovation is a process of implementation, Joe Prochaska (2002) says, 'identifying an existing resource and, through knowledge, elevating it to a new level of utility and value to the customer'. He believes:

> **The biggest roadblocks to innovation are a lack of understanding of when to take intelligent risks...and insufficient knowledge of the skills and principles needed to develop innovation into a managerial practice...innovation is largely knowledge driven.**

The intelligence shown by creative people is evident through their conceptual fluency and flexibility, originality and preference for complexity (Steiner, 1965). Conceptual fluency is the ability to generate many ideas rapidly. Conceptual flexibility ('dimensionality') is the ability to 'shift gears', to discard a frame of reference and one approach in favour of another. Originality is the ability to give unusual interpretations or responses to situations. And creative people display a preference for complexity as an enjoyable challenge. This preference has important implications for the effective leadership of creative people.

Creativity is impaired by a belief that there is always one right answer, by the discipline and requirements of bureaucracy, such as standard operating procedures, and by authoritarianism in managers. This, together with fear of evaluation – often premature – and fear of criticism, leads to conformity or convergent thinking. Another barrier is the lack of recognition and use of creativity in people. Prochaska (2002) believes that creativity is often misunderstood by top management in an organization:

> **The biggest roadblock to creativity is that it is not precisely defined or well understood as a managerial practice that can have an attractive return on investment when put to work in an organization. It is especially misunderstood among top management, from whom a high level of support is needed to sponsor any change in an organization.**

What does this mean for empowering leadership? John Hafile (1962) says that creative people need appropriate roles and goals, appropriate infrastructure and support, permission and freedom to experiment and make mistakes, and recognition and reward of their achievements and for these to be put into use. Using the results of creative work sometimes fails: 'The operation was a success though the patient died.'

There are some further implications for leadership. Creative people's bosses must welcome disagreement and contrary views, using empathy and suspending judgement. Creative people must be made accountable for the changes they suggest. Creative ideas must reach the decision makers. In addition, in their analysis of 'breakthrough thinking', Gerald Nadler and Shozo Hibino (1994) suggest that those who are expected to implement others' creative solutions must be involved in the creating thinking process at the group level, with flexibility in applying them. All of this is required to create or reinforce a culture of creativity.

There are many well-known techniques of creative thinking. What they have in common during the ideation process is the banning of criticism, evaluation and judgement – what Edward de Bono (1977) calls 'PO', or 'Give the idea a chance, don't kill it yet' – encouragement of unusual – even 'wild' – ideas, a delegative leadership style during individual creative activity, intellectual stimulation, and clarity of purpose of the creative process. Group creative activity, for example brainstorming, requires a participative leadership style. Problem solving requires not only creativity, however, but also evaluation – for the truth or correctness of facts, relevance to the goal or need, and feasibility of implementation.

Concluding comments

I defined empowering people as giving them the knowledge, skills, self-awareness, authority, freedom, resources and opportunity to manage themselves. Some concepts of empowerment explicitly include the feeling of intrinsic motivation. We now turn in the next chapter to the relationship between leadership and influence, motivation and inspiration.

Further reading

Chris Argyris (2000), *Flawed Advice and the Management Trap.* Oxford: Oxford University Press.

K. Blanchard, J.P. Carlos and A. Randolph (1995), *Empowerment Takes More Than a Minute.* San Francisco, CA: Berrett-Koehler.

William C. Byham (1988), *Zapp! The Lightning of Empowerment.* Pittsburgh, PA: Development Dimensions International Press.

Discussion questions

1 Why is empowerment much misunderstood? Why do some managers resist empowering their people?
2 How can the barriers to empowerment be overcome or reduced?
3 Is empowerment universally applicable and effective? What are the cross-cultural considerations?

8 Leadership and Influence, Motivation and Inspiration

Inspire others and you will feel inspired yourself.

Theodore Zeldin (2004)

Overview

- Leadership is most commonly associated with influencing, motivating and inspiring people. Transformational leadership is associated with people who are motivated to levels beyond what is normal and to contribute to the common good of their group, organization or nation. The proposition of this chapter is that effective leaders influence, motivate and inspire people to *want to do* what needs to be done.
- Inspirational leadership, however, is a major weakness among many of those in leadership positions, in what they stand for, how they communicate it and the example they set. It is this area of leadership that calls for the greatest attention and improvement.
- Inspiring leaders create or catalyse motivation by aligning organizational goals with individuals' goals. They treat threats, problems and failures as opportunities to learn and challenges to do better. They are 'traders in hope'. They may personally display a unique or exceptional competency, yet they share success, recognize others' accomplishments and enhance their self-esteem – a powerful motivator. They show courage and take personal risks and responsibility. They motivate and inspire people to action through the way they speak. They identify and appeal to a common purpose; they communicate with optimism, feeling and expression. They believe in what they are saying, demonstrate their personal conviction and set an example.
- This chapter considers the fifth and last element in our model of leadership, reviewing the major concepts and theories of motivation and how understanding and applying them can contribute to leadership effectiveness, the different forms of power and its use (and misuse) in the influencing process, the relationship between inspirational leadership and charisma, and the use of inspirational language and speech in leadership, in particular the framing of language and the use of rhetoric.

'Transformational leaders,' Bernard Bass and Bruce Avolio (1994: 3) say, motivate and inspire those around them by providing meaning and challenge to their followers' work.' Joe Pence (1998) adds that 'There can be no inspiration without passion, and without inspiration we cannot move forward in any meaningful way.'

Inspiration and passion are inextricably interlinked. For Randy Komisar (2002) passion is not about zeal for success, making money or even building a company. He says that passion instead is about:

> what...individuals care about, what difference they hope to make, what constructive change they propose to lead. Passion is an undeniable force generated from within... the best entrepreneurs are people driven by vision and ardor. They don't talk to me about money but about products, services, technologies, and customers...[about] how things will be better when they succeed. When I find passion aligned with vision, I know the venture is authentic...the real secret to reawakening passion in one's work is integrating what we do with who we are.

Motivation may be thought of as associated more with transactional leadership, inspiration more with transformational leadership. Burns (1978) relates transformational leadership to Maslow's theory of the hierarchy of needs (Maslow, 1987): followers of transformational leaders are motivated to achieve the highest possible level of need satisfaction – self-actualization. Bass's research for the Full-Range Leadership model suggests that transformational leaders:

> [provide] meaning and challenge to their followers' work. Team spirit is aroused. Enthusiasm and optimism are displayed. Leaders get followers involved in envisioning attractive future states; they create clearly communicated expectations that followers want to meet and also demonstrate commitment to goals and the shared vision. (Bass, 1998: 5)

Intellectual stimulation is often also inspiring (Bass, 1988). It contributes to subordinates' or followers' independence and autonomy by encouraging them to think for themselves, to look at problems in new ways, to think through action before taking it. However, Bass says that leader competency alone does not guarantee intellectual stimulation and inspiration of subordinates or followers. He quotes former US presidents Jimmy Carter and Herbert Hoover as technically competent but failures at inspiring people, and John F. Kennedy and Franklin D. Roosevelt as less intellectually astute but superior in intellectual stimulation and inspirational leadership. Bass says:

> A *sine qua non* of intellectual stimulation is arousing consciousness and awareness in followers of what is right, good and important, which new directions must be taken, and why.

Shackleton was an inspirational leader. He drew his own inspiration from his faith, other people and the literature of great thinkers. He set an example, made personal sacrifices, focused on the future, not the past, and inspired his men with his unflinching confidence of success, insisted on being treated no differently from others, and never asked anybody to do anything that he would not do himself. Shackleton made a lifelong impact on his men: some were still gathering to honour him 50 years after the Endurance mission of

1914–1916, some 42 years after his early death at 47 in 1922. He was the archetypal transformational leader: he transformed the expectations and motivation of his men beyond what they had ever thought possible. Centuries before (c. 1520), the explorer Ferdinand Magellan wrote of the courage that Shackleton's leadership would display:

> **The sea is dangerous and its storms terrible, but these obstacles have never been sufficient reason to remain ashore... . Unlike the mediocre, intrepid spirits seek victory over those things that seem impossible... . It is with an iron will that they embark on the most daring of all endeavours...to meet the shadowy future without fear and conquer the unknown.**

What does it take to engage people and arouse their commitment to the work of the organization, to pursue its objectives? The ability to influence, motivate and inspire followers or subordinates is one of the biggest challenges facing leaders today, particularly business leaders. In my use of Bass and Avolio's Multifactor Leadership Questionnaire, self-ratings on inspirational motivation consistently emerge as lower than those for individualized consideration, intellectual stimulation and idealized influence (Gill, 1999a,b). This finding is corroborated by a survey finding that only 5% of British managers aged under 45 years have confidence in their ability to motivate others and only 6% had confidence in their communication skills (Beckett, 1999). And the ability to motivate people and communication skills emerged in a 1997 KPMG survey as the two most lacking characteristics of British business leaders, identified by 40% and 35% of respondents respectively (KPMG, n.d.: 10). And while 55% of managers identified inspiration as one of the three most important leadership characteristics, only 11% said their leaders provide it, according to a 2001 survey by DEMOS, the think tank, conducted for the Institute of Management (Institute of Management, 2001; Hayhurst, 2002; Professional Manager, 2002).[94]

In the United States Kouzes and Posner (1991: 124–125) have found much the same inspiration deficit:

> **inspiring a shared vision is the least frequently applied of the...fundamental practices of exemplary leadership. People also report that inspiring a shared vision is the leadership practice with which they feel most uncomfortable. And when we ask people whether they consider themselves to be inspiring, only 10 percent say that they are.**

Mark Scott (2000) writes about the 'reinspired' corporation. He describes how companies 'seem to be operating at considerably less than their full potential' not necessarily because of a failure of business strategies, but 'simply a lack of vigour, of will to grow, of enthusiasm; an absence of joy about the process of being in business'. It is time, he says, 'to reinspire ourselves'. Scott defines a reinspired corporation as one in which people are committed to it with a passion: 'they understand its mission, they have bought into its ethos'. He suggests: 'The foundation of a reinspired corporation is a sense of community – a grouping of people ... [who] share common ideas and feelings on important issues.' They share identity and values. Many 'excellent' and even 'built to last' companies may falter, but Scott suggests that the best examples of reinspired organizations are the world's seven great religions: they share common characteristics in how they unify and inspire their members. Scott suggests they inspire adherence to them – as can business organizations – by:

- Providing a context of moral authority that binds the community of the company together behind a unified purpose
- Emphasizing looking beyond the individual to a good that is beyond limited self-interest
- Using deeply ingrained ritual and symbolism
- Being founded on well-understood tradition – where it has come from and what it stands for
- Being optimistic in their outlook – a clear vision of the future that is worth fighting for
- Encouraging the asking of 'big' questions – objectives, status quo, reinvention, sharing ideas
- Cloaking themselves in mystery – they are not easily understood

Inspiring leaders create or catalyse motivation by aligning organizational goals with individuals' goals. They treat threats, problems and failures as opportunities to learn and challenges to do better. They may personally display a unique or exceptional competency, yet they recognize others' accomplishments and enhance their self-esteem – a powerful motivator. They show courage and take personal risks and responsibility. And they motivate and inspire people to action through the way they speak. They identify and appeal to a common purpose; they communicate with feeling and expression, thereby bringing the vision to life so that people can see themselves as part of it; they believe in what they are saying and they demonstrate their personal conviction (Kouzes and Posner, 1991: 129).

Inspirational leaders tend to share a passion for their cause, commitment to its pursuit, energy and courage (Wallington, 2000). But inspiration has its dark side. Inspiring people through vision and passionately communicating it may have destructive effects. Inspiration, Tim Wise (1999) suggests, is contagious. It may create sheep-like followers who tread the road to perdition. Likewise, commitment displayed as will and determination may lead to inflexibility and resistance to change for the common good.

Useful lessons about how leaders create commitment and inspiration can be learned from the psychological phenomenon of hypnotism. Stephen Armstrong (2001) relates how the psychologist and hypnotist Paul McKenna demonstrates how hypnotized people can become excited about what they are going to do:

> **At first, McKenna...talked to me about visualising things and...got me to experience a huge rush of endorphins that filled my body with an excited pleasure merely by telling me what I was going to do.**

McKenna suggests that the way cults work is in effect through hypnotism. This is also an interesting aspect of effective leadership. He says cult leaders 'bombard [devotees] with messages, setting out a vision of the way things are' – and presumably the way things could (should?) be. This is what effective leaders do. They then 'shape [devotees'] behaviour, making them do things they would never otherwise have done', such as '[persuading] 19 people to crash airliners into buildings full of innocent people' (in the September 11 terrorist attacks on the United States). This is central to the idea of transformational leadership – getting people to want to do what they never imagined they could do, to go beyond their immediate self-interest. McKenna suggests that this helps to explain such otherwise 'utterly bewildering … so frighteningly inexplicable' behaviour. Cult leaders and religious fanatics – such as Osama bin Laden, Jim Jones, Adolf Hitler – who have achieved this have shown remarkable leadership. The issue, of course, is not how they did it but the validity of their vision and values. Values, and visions based on them, are interminably arguable. But effective leaders get commitment to visions and inspire people to pursue them, often against their immediate self-interest, in the interest of the group, organization or society.

Leaders are 'traders in hope', according to a Chinese saying. As a combination of expectation and desire, hope is motivating, even inspiring. As Paxman (2002: 290) says, 'if you can offer hope, you can inspire enchantment'. As a trader in hope Winston Churchill was:

> a statesman whose services to his country are unexampled in modern times, one to whose courage, clear-sightedness and gift for leadership the world owes many debts of gratitude. Yet if we must remember him for one thing above all, it is bound to be for the inspiration, the will to fight on, that he injected into [his] country and her allies in the dark days of 1940. (Ferrier, 1965: 5)

Churchill was modest about this. He said:

> I have never accepted what many people have kindly said – namely, that I inspired the nation… . It was the nation and the race dwelling all round the globe that had the lion's heart. I had the luck to be called upon to give the roar. I also hope that I sometimes suggested to the lion the right place to use his claws.[95]

According to British historian Andrew Roberts, Churchill had been a domineering leader before the Second World War – ruthless, egotistic and lacking pragmatism (Roberts, 2003). But for Ian McKenzie, chief executive of Blue Circle Cement, Churchill was a source of both learning and inspiration: '[His] writings and speeches conveyed to me the power of communication and inspiration. [He] gave me a can-do mentality' (Rajan, 2000a). Anthony Storr, the psychiatrist, says of Churchill:

> In that dark time what England needed was not a shrewd, equably balanced leader. She needed a prophet, a heroic visionary, a man who could dream dreams of victory when all seemed lost. Winston Churchill was such a man; and his inspirational quality owed its dynamic force to the romantic world of fantasy in which he had his true being. (Gardner, 1996: 262)

What is motivation?

The popular view of leadership is that effective leaders influence, motivate and inspire people. Understanding how this happens entails understanding *what* influences, motivates and inspires people, how it does so, what leaders do when they influence, motivate and inspire other people, and how they create the conditions in which motivation or inspiration can emerge.

The key understanding of this lies in a good working definition of motivation, for example: 'those psychological processes that cause the arousal, direction, and persistence of voluntary actions that are goal-directed' (Mitchell, 1982). George Miller (1962) says,

'The study of motivation is the study of all those pushes and prods – biological, social and psychological – that defeat our laziness and move us, either eagerly or reluctantly, to action.' Unless we are motivated, we will do nothing. Motivation concerns our needs and wants (Atkinson et al., 1990: 361).

The earliest recorded views of motivation are those of the ancient Greeks: that hedonism – the pursuit of pleasure and the avoidance of pain – is the principal driving force. It was not until the end of the nineteenth century that 'the issue of motivation began to migrate from the realm of philosophy to the newly emerging science of psychology' (Steers et al., 2004). Hedonism as the key principle was superseded by the instinct theories of William James, Sigmund Freud and William McDougal and subsequently by theories of drive and reinforcement of, for example, Thorndike (the law of effect) and Skinner (operant or instrumental conditioning). Social influences on behaviour now began to be understood through the work of Elton Mayo and Roethlisberger and Dickson, and multiple influences in motivation through Abraham Maslow's hierarchy of needs and David McClelland's model of affiliation, power, achievement and autonomy.

The term 'motivation' comes from the Latin *movere*, 'to move'. A motive thus is something that moves us into action – a push or a prod. Effective leaders, then, tap people's psychological processes that arouse, direct and maintain voluntary behaviour towards goals. Inspiring people means stimulating, instilling or arousing thoughts or feelings that strongly animate or energize them to act in a particular way.

We may regard inspiration as a high level of motivation. The word 'inspiration' comes from the Latin *inspirare*, which means 'to breathe in'. Vision, Olivier (2001: 33) says, 'is like a breath of fresh air, it gives energy'. In a religious context, 'inspiration' in the Koran (*wahy*) can be read as 'revelation' and 'the inspired' (*yuha*) as 'the revealed' (Dabash, 2000). This implies that being inspired is associated with revelation of a goal, purpose or meaning. When people understand these and identify with them, they are inspired. Inspiration therefore may be a consequence of spiritual leadership, which, as we saw in Chapter 3, creates meaning and value for people in what they do.

The psychology of motivation

Motivation arises from both extrinsic and intrinsic sources. Extrinsic motivation drives the performance of an activity to gain a specific externally offered or required outcome. The motivation that leaders or managers through their actions create in people is extrinsic: people are motivated to do something or not to do it as a result of a manager's or a leader's behaviour (deCharms, 1968). Motivation is not just a consequence of good leadership. People may be motivated to achieve the required results through bullying or fear in order to avoid unpleasant consequences. This is negative reinforcement. People may be motivated by the prospect of extrinsic rewards, such as money, recognition (e.g. praise) and other externally provided rewards and benefits. Extrinsic motivation entails a feeling of compulsion to do things for an external source to achieve an outcome that satisfies usually lower-order needs like money to survive. Extrinsic motivation entails seeking and securing a reward to work.

On the other hand people may be motivated by intrinsic needs – for example, the need for the satisfaction that accompanies performing meaningful, interesting, enjoyable or challenging work, a desire to belong to a social group, a sense of responsibility, achievement, self-esteem, creativity, or making a difference in some way. This is intrinsic motivation. People may be motivated in the absence of leaders, managers or anybody else: they perform an activity for the inherent satisfaction of the activity itself.

Mihaly Csikszentmihalyi studied why people such as artists, musicians, chess players, mountaineers and actors love to do what they do, despite the absence of material reward. He found that they all said, 'experiencing the activity was in itself the reward .... This is the feeling I labelled "flow"' (Creelman, 2003c). He reports that the British prime minister Tony Blair asked his Cabinet to use flow as a basis for social policy. He also reports that vehicle manufacturer Volvo uses it in restructuring work. The leadership challenge is to structure work according to individuals' needs and interests so that it is the reward in itself. Richard Ryan and Edward Deci (2000) argue that intrinsic motivation relates to three innate psychological needs: competence, autonomy and relatedness (interaction with other people and security in relationships). With intrinsic motivation, 'my work is my reward' (Fry, 2003).

The motivation of creative people poses a special leadership challenge. Extrinsic motivation, such as targets, deadlines and performance-related pay, appears to be detrimental to creativity. Intrinsic motivation, on the other hand, is conducive to it. The single best stimulus to creativity is freedom – the power to decide what to do and how to do it, and a sense of control over one's destiny (Amabile, 1996).

There can be no better way of being intrinsically motivated at work, to do what needs to be done, than when organizational goals are aligned with our individual goals. This enables us to create a 'win–win agreement' – a psychological contract between leader and followers that 'represents a clear mutual understanding and commitment regarding expectations in five areas: ... desired results, ... guidelines, ... resources, ... accountabilities, and ... consequences [rewards or benefits]' (Covey, 1992: 191–192).

Leadership in part, then, is about eliciting motivation in people by creating motivational environments. Motivation is an individualized phenomenon. Leaders therefore have to know their followers and provide the opportunities for individuals' idiosyncratic needs to be satisfied, as Bass's theory of transformational leadership suggests in relation to individualized consideration.

The problem is that the study of motivation is beset by inconsistency and confusion in its findings. This is a source of frustration to managers who want to understand motivation better and create motivational conditions at work. For example, Timothy Judge and Remus Ilies (2002) used meta-analysis to try to clarify the link between personality and motivation. They found that neuroticism was inversely correlated with motivation, and that conscientiousness was positively correlated, whereas correlations for extraversion, openness to experience and agreeableness were unclear. Nevertheless motivation theorists have tried to paint a clear picture of what motivates people: people are motivated to satisfy their needs. The picture of motivation, however, is much like that of leadership: a variety of disparate theories that each offer some clues and insights.

Maslow's hierarchy of needs

Needs exist at several successive levels, according to Abraham Maslow (1970): survival, safety and security, affiliation, challenge, achievement, recognition and self-esteem, and self-actualization (self-fulfilment). Clayton Alderfer (1972) suggests a condensed model: existence needs, relatedness needs and growth needs ('ERG'). William James, the 'father' of modern psychology, believed that 'the deepest principle of human nature is the craving to be appreciated' (James, 1920).

McGregor's Theory X and Theory Y

McGregor's ideas about motivation had a profound effect on management and leadership during the 1960s. He contrasted two sets of assumptions and attitudes in managers in respect of human nature: Theory X and Theory Y (McGregor, 1960).

Theory X postulates that the average human being inherently dislikes and tries to avoid work, has little ambition, wants security above all, and therefore must be coerced, controlled, directed and threatened to do what needs to be done. Theory Y on the other hand postulates that:

- Physical and mental work is as natural as play or rest
- Human beings will exercise self-direction and self-control in pursuing objectives to which they are committed
- Commitment results from rewards associated with achievement
- The average human being will not only accept responsibility but even seek it
- The capacity to exercise imagination, ingenuity and creativity is widely, not narrowly, distributed
- The potential of the average human being generally is only partially utilized

McGregor's ideas stimulated the development of motivation programmes such as participative management and management-by-objectives, job enrichment, employee involvement, job redesign, and suggestion schemes providing rewards to employees for suggesting method improvements.

Shiba's 'Theory W'

Shoji Shiba (1998) argues that McGregor's Theory X and Theory Y do not adequately explain human nature and motivation. He formulated 'Theory W', which 'embraces the duality of the nature of people':

> **People want both a stable, controlled environment and to create something new (and in many ways these two are in conflict). We want strong clear leadership that tells us what to do and makes us secure. However, we also want to contribute to something new that changes our present existence and makes us feel uncomfortable.**

My contention that our understanding of leadership draws on many disciplines, including non-traditional ones, is illustrated by Shiba. He arrived at Theory W, he says, by studying Paul Gauguin's painting *D'ou venons nous? Que sommes nous? D'ou allons nous?* (Where do we come from? What are we? Where are we going?). Shiba (1998) says:

> **This masterpiece symbolically represents the questions all leaders must answer to successfully lead their organizations to sustained ('eternal') existence.**

> **The painting is divided into three parts, and there is an arc of...narrative that flows from right to left. The right side of the painting illustrates a baby and its growing up – this represents the question *'Where do we come from?'* The middle of the painting illustrates adults in the fullness of life – this represents the question *'Where are we [now]?'* The left side of the painting illustrates the decline of old age – this represents the question *'Where are we going?'***
>
> **However, the top right and the top left corners of the painting are in a light color and have a shape that matches...a cycle from the top left back to the right side in a cylinder...[indicating the] possibility of 'eternal life' of the human species... .**
>
> **We are all faced with the duality indicated by Gauguin in his painting. We know we cannot sustain ourselves if we allow no change; but we like working on clear goals and we are uncomfortable with change... . Successfully answering [the three] questions can bring enlightenment and transformation, and move both a corporation and the people within it through a threshold to a place where all kinds of masterpieces can be created. Leaders who can demonstrate and catalyse this will not only achieve breakthroughs, but also enable people to understand and become 'Who they are'.**

Shiba (1998) relates Theory X to control, Theory Y to continuous improvement, and Theory W to breakthrough.

Herzberg's motivation–hygiene theory

Frederick Herzberg's motivation–hygiene theory offers another view of motivation and contrasts it with dissatisfaction (Herzberg et al., 1959; Herzberg, 1964). This theory proposes that there are some elements in the work situation that, when present, tend to lead to satisfaction ('motivators') and other elements that, when present, tend to lead to dissatisfaction ('hygiene factors').

Motivators include the nature of the work itself, achievement, recognition and opportunities for advancement. Hygiene factors – dissatisfiers – include poor technical supervision, pay and working conditions. The implications for leadership are clear. Effective leaders minimize dissatisfiers and maximize motivators.

Expectancy–valence theory

One of the best-known and most useful theories of motivation is expectancy–valence theory, first formulated in relation to the workplace by Victor Vroom (1964) and later expanded to include the role of individual differences in ability by Lyman Porter and Edwin Lawler (1968). This theory has added considerable value in our understanding of human motivation at work and has important practical implications for leadership.

This theory suggests that individuals act through self-interest and take action that they perceive as maximizing the likelihood of desirable outcomes for themselves, whether these are to avoid pain or enhance pleasure. Whether self-interest is a necessary assumption is a moot point: desirable outcomes may equally relate to collective interests. Scott (2000) argues that:

> **Community, shared beliefs, alignment with collective interest are the dominant psychological needs; more dominant than the drive for individual accomplishment... . We all long for a higher collective purpose; a reunification...[which] in fact leads to greater success.**

Expectancy–valence theory explains motivation in terms of value (worth) and probability:

- The likelihood (p) that we will gain a particular outcome (reward) if we do what is needed ($P \rightarrow O$) – known as 'instrumentality'
- The value of that outcome or reward to us (V) – known as 'valence'
- The likelihood (p) that we will be able to do what is needed if we try to do so ($E \rightarrow P$) – known as 'expectancy'

An individual's motivational state (M) can be represented by the following formula:

$$M = p(E \rightarrow P) \times p(P \rightarrow O) \times V$$

The attractiveness of outcomes varies among individuals (Sneade and Harrell, 1994). The theories of Maslow, Herzberg, McClelland and others help us to understand the various kinds of valences – satisfaction associated with various and differing rewards, in turn associated with the various and differing physical and psychological needs that people have. Expectancy–valence theory explains how people individually are motivated by the prospect of these various kinds of outcomes or rewards. The theory is supported by a wealth of empirical evidence (Harrell and Stahl, 1984; Hope and Pate, 1988; Klein, 1991; Sneade and Harrell, 1994; Fudge and Schlacter, 1999).

There has been little research, however, on the relationship between motivation and positive feelings (affect). One study suggests that positive feelings may be an important determinant of the value of outcomes or rewards (George and Brief, 1996). Another study investigated this further, and extended it to the relationship between positive feelings and instrumentality and expectancy. It found that positive feelings do enhance motivation and performance, influencing the cognitive processes underlying motivation (Erez and Isen, 2002). The implication for effective leadership behaviour is clear, though Chester Schriesheim and Steven Kerr (1977: 9–45) believe that using expectancy theory to explain leader influence is unrealistic because it fails to take account of emotional responses to decision dilemmas that interfere with rationality in decision making.

Let us now identify the implications of expectancy–valence theory for what we might do to influence other people and create the optimum conditions for motivation and inspiration.

Applying the concept of expectancy

- Provide challenging tasks that match a person's competencies.

  Unchallenging work leads to boredom, frustration and marginal performance, whereas challenge that is perceived as impossible to meet is rejected, and little or no performance ensues (Moussa, 1996).
- Assess the person's perception of his or her competencies (self-confidence).

  If a person lacks the confidence to perform the task, motivation to do so will be weak (Moussa, 1996). Individuals choose to perform tasks that are sufficiently likely to provide feedback that is congruent with their self-image (Leonard et al., 1999). Self-confidence can be boosted by reinforcement (showing recognition) of progress towards a goal, encouragement when there are setbacks, forgiveness over honest mistakes or failure, and coaching.

- Clarify and agree precisely what outcomes constitute acceptable performance and those that do not (Katzenbach, 1996).
- Clarify how the person's work contributes to pursuing the organization's vision.
  Expending effort in doing meaningful work increases motivation and job satisfaction (Brown and Peterson, 1994).

One might reasonably infer that empowerment is a necessary condition for motivation: a perception of unempowerment or disempowerment is likely to lead to a lack of motivation.

Applying the concept of instrumentality

- Consistently ensure that promises of outcomes and associated rewards for performance are fulfilled (Daly and Kleiner, 1995).
  Excuses for non-fulfilment weaken instrumentality (Karathanos et al., 1994) – and managers' credibility.
- Provide fair rewards in a predictable way.
  'Fair rewards' does not mean the same rewards for everybody: it means rewards according to people's needs that are perceived (by people and their peers) as fair. Predictability enhances instrumentality.
- Give accurate, timely and honest but tactful feedback.
  Positive feedback needs to be contiguous in time, negative feedback delivered in a positive (developmental or constructive) way.

One area where instrumentality frequently breaks down is in appraisal schemes where high ratings of performance have a tenuous or inadequate association with monetary rewards.

Applying the concept of valence

- Determine the value of each of the available rewards to the individual.
  Outcomes must be highly valued to induce heightened motivation. While most people need – or at least want – money, most also respond positively to rewards that come 'free of charge', for example appreciation and recognition (Beavers, 1996; Rigsbee, 1996). 'Cafeteria compensation' as part of pay and benefits policy is an example of an individualized approach (reflecting the dimension of 'individualized consideration' in Bass's model of transformational leadership). Rewards associated with outcomes continually change in their value to individuals throughout life as personal circumstances change: this requires investing time and effort to determine for each individual (Miller, 1999).
- Ensure alignment between the personal goals of individuals and the goals of the organization.
  This means knowing individuals' interests, goals and aspirations and 'creatively [framing] the organization's vision in such a way that [they perceive] congruency between personal and organizational [aims]' (Isaac et al., 2001). Alignment can be a source of inspired effort.

Equity theory

In evaluating the outcome of reward, one consideration is the fairness or equity of that reward in relation not only to effort expended but also to other people. This idea is the basis for equity theory, associated mainly with Adams (1965). The tension that results from a sense of inequity, usually adverse, creates motivation to resolve it through several kinds of action: reduction of inputs (e.g. effort, working time), efforts to increase outputs (e.g. negotiating more pay), 'cognitive distortion' of the facts, any of the foregoing in relation to others, changing the object of the comparison, and withdrawal from the work situation.

Goal theory

Goal theory is usually associated with Locke (1968). Effective leaders in their relationship with individuals need to understand the expectancy–valence process and accordingly provide the appropriate goals, resources (e.g. opportunities, infrastructure, time, information, authority, competencies), outcomes and rewards, and a link between achievement and rewards (need satisfaction). Robert Isaac et al. (2001) say:

> **[The] desire to maximize self-interest provides aspiring leaders with unique opportunities to assume leadership roles by simultaneously meeting both follower needs and organizational requirements.**

Organizational requirements are usually stated as goals. In fact the management process known as MBO (Management-By-Objectives) is virtually taken for granted today: a goal is a result or outcome that is intended to be achieved. A goal can also be defined as an internal representation of a desired state, where the state is an outcome, event or process (Austin and Vancouver, 1996). In addition to their cognitive role in providing information and direction, 'Goals serve to … energize, and sustain people's actions' (Locke and Latham, 1990).

McClelland's motivational needs theory

David McClelland (1988) proposed that the style and behaviour of human beings are characterized by the needs for affiliation ('n-affil'), authority or power ('n-pow') and achievement ('n-ach'). The mix of these needs characterizes a person's leadership style and behaviour. McClelland believed that a strong affiliation need undermines a manager's objectivity because of the need to be liked, and a strong power need may be associated with strong work ethic and commitment to the organization but not necessarily with flexibility and interpersonal skills. Strong achievement motivation is associated with effective leadership.

McClelland also suggested that achievement-motivated managers value achievement more than material or financial reward (a measure of success rather than an end in itself) or praise or recognition from other people. For them, security and status matter little, but feedback is essential for measurement of success and constant improvement. A strongly achievement-motivated manager focuses on the task (see Adair's model, described in Chapter 2), sometimes to the detriment of the individual and the team, and may demand too much of others, who may not be similarly motivated.

Other theories and concepts of motivation

It is well known that what we expect of other people strongly influences their behaviour (Livingstone, 1969). People tend to do what they believe is expected of them. This is known as the *Pygmalion effect* (after Pygmalion in Greek mythology).

This was first demonstrated in pupils' performance as a result of their school teachers' expectations (Rosenthal and Jacobson, 1968). Effective leaders harness the Pygmalion effect for increased performance among their followers or subordinates (Locke et al., 1981; Eden and Ravid, 1982; Eden and Shani, 1982; Eden, 1984). Their language expresses confidence in their people and arouses expectations of achievement among them. This creates the self-fulfilling prophecy: expectations of success increase the chances of success. Almost anything is possible if you share the glory: giving other people credit is a simple, effective way to get results (Goodwin, 1998). Self-esteem is a powerful motivator and source of inspiration.

'Optimists ... enjoy greater success. Rather than see setbacks as signs of their incompetence, they view them as flukes or as suggesting a new approach' (Myers, 1993: 117). 'They can because they think they can', according to Virgil's *Aeneid* (Humphries, 1951: 121). This, for Norman Vincent Peale (1952), is 'the power of positive thinking'. But, Myers (1993: 119) suggests, 'The recipe for well-being ... requires neither positive nor negative thinking alone, but a mix of ample *optimism* to provide hope, a dash of *pessimism* to prevent complacency, and enough *realism* to discriminate those things we can control from those we cannot.' This recipe reflects attribution theory, associated with Fritz Heider (1958), which suggests that behaviour can be explained by 'locus of control' – the extent to which individuals perceive outcomes as controlled by themselves (related to their ability or effort) vis-à-vis external factors (such as policies, rules, the weather, the boss).

Treating threats, problems and failures as opportunities to learn can be a source of great inspiration among one's subordinates or followers. It prevents, removes or reduces the emotional contagion of loss of self-esteem. Quite the contrary, it maintains or enhances self-esteem. It is part and parcel of creating a 'can-do mentality'. Recognizing and emphasizing accomplishments – contingent reward, a positive feature of transactional leadership – also enhances self-esteem.

A happy worker is not necessarily a motivated worker. This finding continues to be replicated in studies, for example a study by the Chartered Institute of Personnel and Development in the UK (McHenry, 1997). At work no one factor alone, for example pay, results in motivation. What matters is how employees perceive their work and how they behave as a result. Robert McHenry (1997) suggests, for example, that a greater amount of higher-quality work might result from greater commitment to work, which results from feeling that it is safe to get involved, in turn depending on having an opportunity to express oneself. The key to understanding motivation, he says, is the causal chain, which is unidirectional.

Work involvement for sales people appears to depend on 'psychological safety' – authority and support to make decisions, clarity of the role (performance expectations), and recognition of work that is done (and the meaningfulness of work), opportunity for self-expression, perceived contribution in making a difference, and challenge (Leigh and Brown, 1996). Targets or goals alone are not motivating (unless the deadline for submitting a report or making a sale is tomorrow!). Work involvement is displayed by people who work intensely and enjoy making the maximum effort.

McHenry's study suggests that, for HR professionals, the basis for motivation is work meaningfulness (McHenry, 1997). This leads successively to work involvement, committing considerable time to work and working intensely, perceptions of support and safety, and ultimately high-quality performance. He makes the point that different elements are likely to apply to different groups and there are likely to be individual differences within different groups. Open communication and empowerment thus appear to be more effective in motivation than 'carrot-and-stick' approaches such as performance-related pay.

Social cognition and self-efficacy also play a part in motivation. Albert Bandura (1977a,b; 1997) proposed a social cognition theory in which the motivation of an individual to act or be proactive depends on his or her self-confidence. Self-efficacy, moderated by task complexity and locus of control, is a significant determinant of performance at work (Stajkovic and Luthans, 1998; Stajkovic and Luthans, 2003: 126–140).

As a result of this work, a new movement in organizational studies and organizational development known as 'Positive Organizational Behavior [or Scholarship]' has emerged. Recent studies of 'positive deviance' in organizations have suggested that it is associated with a high level of employee motivation (Luthans, 2001; Cameron et al., 2003). Positive deviance, Kim Cameron says, is characterized by appreciation, collaboration, virtuousness, vitality, optimism and meaningfulness reflecting a culture of trust and trustworthiness, resilience, humility, authenticity, respect and mutual forgiveness among employees (Salopek, 2003). Welcoming feedback from others, a rare phenomenon, is an example. Cameron reports that focusing on the positive attributes of employees, rather than on their weaknesses and problem solving, leads to significantly better performance of their organizations (Salopek, 2003).

Given that in most work organizations, at least in developed nations, the needs for survival, safety and security are already well met, we can draw together the theories of Maslow, McGregor, Herzberg, McClelland and others in answering the question 'What motivates people at work?':

- A need to survive
- A need for money (as a means to survival and other ends)
- A need to belong to a group – affiliation
- A need for interesting, meaningful and challenging work
- A need for recognition, trust and self-esteem
- A need to influence others – power
- A need to achieve and contribute
- A need to fulfil themselves

Today there is a common belief that 'the highest level of human motivation is a sense of personal contribution' (Covey, 1992: 70) – a sense of fulfilling a 'transcending purpose or meaning' (1992: 284). One advantage that the world's seven great religions have over business organizations is their moral authority, which, Scott (2000) suggests, is:

the framework that provides some guarantee that the positive efforts we have put in will lead somewhere...[that] they will bring endorsement, recognition...[that] we should continue to strive.

Creating meaning, according to a more recent view (Dent and Brent, 2001), is the key to influence:

Creating meaning implies that you actively consider the other person's point of view, that you listen attentively to what the person has to say and respond accordingly.

While this view of creating meaning reminds us of emotional intelligence, creating meaning is, as was discussed in Chapter 3, the essence of spiritual leadership.

Motivation, influence and the use of power

Managers get things done through using authority, manipulation ('politicking') or influence. They motivate people by using various forms of power. Power is the ability to influence the thoughts and actions of another person or group of people. If leadership is the use of power to win the minds and hearts of people to strive towards a common purpose, where does the leader's power come from? While managers are appointed, leaders are not. Managers have authority or position power, which is associated with rank, status or position in an organization. This is the power that entitles them to give direction and material or financial rewards to subordinates or others. However, managers who rely on authority to get things done will usually foster only reluctance or compliance at best rather than commitment – a *desire* to do what needs to be done.

There are several forms of power described by John French and Bertram Raven (1986; Raven, 1993): legitimate power, coercive power, reward power, referent power, information power and expert power. These forms of power depend for their effectiveness on followers' perceptions of them in leaders. For example, influence due to one's perceived possession of information that others do not have is *information power*. In true leaders, their power resides not so much in the authority or right to make things happen as in their *personal power* regardless of their position, status or rank. Ultimately effective leadership depends on personal power – the ability to win the hearts and minds of other people. Table 8.1 shows how these forms of power might be classified.

Legitimate power

Legitimate power and coercive power are associated with authority and are forms of position power. Legitimate power is based on people's perception of the manager's or leader's right or authority to make them do something because of his or her role or position in the organization (and it has nothing to do with personality or personal relationships). Isaac et al. (2001) make this distinction: 'managers use legitimate power to push employees towards desired ends, whereas leaders use their influence to pull followers towards goals'.

Table 8.1 *Forms of position power and personal power*

Authority (position power)	Personal power
• Legitimate power	• Psychological reward power
• Coercive power	• Referent power
• Material/financial reward power	• Expert power

Coercive power

Coercive power, associated with position or authority, is based on the perceived ability of a leader or manager to bring about undesirable or unpleasant outcomes for those who do not comply with expectations, instructions or directives, for example withholding of pay rises or bonuses, promotion or privileges; allocation of undesirable or unpleasant tasks or responsibilities; reprimands or disciplinary action including dismissal; and even the threat or infliction of physical punishment including pain and death. Coercive power does not bring about voluntary action, only necessary action. Nor does it foster followership.

The least effective leaders use coercive power, which creates fear among people of the adverse consequences of not complying with the wishes of the leader. It is temporary in its impact and it creates negative feelings and attitudes. It is associated with an extreme form of the directive style of leadership – tyranny. An example is Saddam Hussein, who used authority, manipulation and coercive power with the Iraqi people. John Laughland (2000) says he 'inspire[d] terror in Iraq but loyalty too': he combined 'extraordinary brutality with occasional acts of exceptional kindness – the classic hallmarks of a psychopath ... the Anglo-American sanctions ... actually bolstered Saddam by offering him ... the means by which to entrench his own organised self-adulation, while impoverishing ... ordinary Iraqis'. George Orwell (1949, 3: 3) recognized how dictators use power. For them:

> **Power is not a means, it is an end. One does not establish a dictatorship in order to safeguard a revolution; one makes the revolution in order to establish the dictatorship.**

Reward power – material/financial

A common form of power is reward power or utility power, which offers a material or financial benefit in return for acquiescence, cooperation or followership, for example a pay increase, bonus, privileges or promotion. This is a common feature of transactional leadership (contingent reward), and such reward power is usually associated with position and authority to dispense a material or financial reward.

One problem with reward power when used in a one-to-one situation is that it tends to encourage individualism at the expense of teamwork (Covey, 1992: 103–104), but conversely team-based reward can alienate individuals who are high achievers that stand out in a team. And of course such power may be abused.

Personal power

Personal power comes from many sources. It is not necessarily based on charisma, though sometimes it is. *Referent power* is one form of personal power that is influence due to one's perceived attractiveness, charisma, personal characteristics, social skills or reputation. A study of US presidents suggested that those who were regarded as charismatic – Jefferson, Jackson, Lincoln, Theodore Roosevelt, Franklin Roosevelt and Kennedy – possessed stronger power needs than those regarded as low in charisma – Tyler, Pierce, Buchanan, Arthur, Harding and Coolidge (House et al., 1988). Our personal power comes primarily from:

- Our personality, values and personal standards of behaviour
- Our personal knowledge, competency or expertise in some field – expert power
- Our interpersonal skills of empathy, influence and persuasion
- The clarity and intellectual and emotional appeal of our vision of the future and our strategies for pursuing it

Power is exhilarating: it is ego boosting. Indeed it may be, as former US secretary of state Henry Kissinger famously said, 'the great aphrodisiac'.[96] Yet true leaders are willing to share power with those they lead – to empower them to be freer, more autonomous and hence more capable (Marshall, 1991: 71–73).

The issue of power needs raises the question of motivation to lead others. To perform well as a leader implies not only the cognitive and interpersonal abilities to do so, but also the desire to do so. Motivation to lead appears to be determined by leadership self-efficacy, past leadership experience, collectivist values and a sense of social duty and acceptance of social hierarchies (Chan and Drasgow, 2001). Leadership self-efficacy in turn is determined by several personality factors – extraversion, agreeableness, conscientiousness, emotional stability and openness to learning from experience.

Personal power is 'the ability to affect others' attitudes, beliefs and behaviours without using force or formal authority' (Dent and Brent, 2001). US president George W. Bush, for example, is said 'not [to] have Ronald Reagan's or Bill Clinton's skills at crowd-pleasing politics, but he is a master at the one-on-one politics of personal persuasion' (Steltzer, 2001: 3.4). In contrast, historian A.J.P. Taylor (1965) said of Lord Northcliffe, 'He aspired to power [authority] instead of influence, and as a result forfeited both.'

Psychological reward power

This form of power is personal rather than positional, for it requires no authority to use it. The form it takes is giving praise and recognition for achievement, and it requires perceptual and behavioural skills and a willingness to use them effectively. Like providing material or financial reward, however, it is a form of contingent reward. But it should be remembered, as was discussed in Chapter 2, that contingent reward is more closely associated with effective leadership overall than Bass's original Full-Range Leadership model postulated.

Referent power

Referent power is influence that leaders can exert as a result of their perceived attractiveness, personal characteristics or social skills (e.g. charm), reputation or charisma in the eyes of followers and the respect or esteem that followers have for them. This is power that leaders have as a result of followers' belief in them and what they are trying to do. It is associated with being trusted and respected, shared values and followers' desire to follow. Idealized influence in Bass's model of transformational leadership is related to referent power.

People identify with leaders when they display insight into their needs, values and aspirations and respond positively to them (with emotional intelligence) in a timely fashion. They display empathy in passionate and realistic ways with them (Goffee and Jones, 2000). Showing courage and taking personal risk and responsibility instil trust. The leader gains referent power. Leaders like Churchill and Eisenhower took the blame for their failures; Hitler did not. Effective leaders also display a sense of purpose, persistence and trust in others. An example of purposefulness and persistence and its inspirational effects based on her resulting referent power is Margaret Thatcher, former British prime minister:

> **What cannot be doubted is her belief in her basic principles and her unflinching courage in holding her corner when she has decided that a battle must be fought – qualities that brought so many people to her banner. (Butler, 2000)**

Thatcher saw having conviction and principle as incompatible with consensus politics (Kavanagh, 1990: 57) and, presumably, with the participative style of leadership.

Displaying the values they espouse in their behaviour has been shown to motivate others to behaviour similarly. For example, Jonathan Haidt's research, mentioned in Chapter 5, showed that morally 'beautiful' behaviour can lead to an emotion in others ('elevation'), felt physically in the chest, that creates this desire (Carpenter, 2001).

Confidence in oneself and in others counts: this means not only having self-confidence but extending this faith to others and sincerely believing in their talents (Goodwin, 1998). This leads to respect, trust and confidence in the leader, a willingness to exert extra effort, to 'go the extra mile', and the desire to achieve in order to show support for the leader. In this respect Thatcher was a paradox. According to Lord (Robin) Butler (2000), her principal private secretary and later cabinet secretary, her image of self-confidence and the reality were at odds:

> **In consequence, she never took any event lightly, however trivial... . When she talked too much it was often to cover her nervousness. Yet [again contrary to the popular view] she listens as she talks.**

An important source of referent power for leaders is credibility. People look for credibility – honesty, inspiration and competence – in their leaders (Kouzes and Posner, 1991). Effective leaders display the values they promote, exceptional personal competence and self-confidence. Jean Vanhoegaerden (1999) says, 'Credibility means doing what you say you will do.'

> **I worked for someone who proclaimed that he was really committed to empowerment. He bought the entire department a book on the topic so we could better understand his management philosophy. As the book suggested, the limits of autonomy were agreed. But, the first time I took a decision within that limit which he did not like, he resorted to bullying. His actions were completely alien to what he had preached.**

Credibility also comes from leading 'from the front'. In the Second World War:

> **Where the bombing was worst, there Churchill would be, and only the direct intervention of King George VI prevented him from arriving as an interested observer (or, who knows, even a participant in the struggle) on the D-Day beaches. (Ferrier, 1965: 6)**

Competence contributes to credibility. But no leader today is expected to be all things to all people, to be as competent in everything as followers or subordinates. Outstanding, charismatic leaders, however, are competent in extraordinary ways (Bass's idealized influence). And they are competent in understanding what other people do (Vanhoegaerden, 1999). But, at least in Anglo-Saxon culture (but not in southern European and Asian cultures), effective leaders also admit to not knowing when this is the case, and they often disclose a flaw: contrary to a common view, this does not reduce their credibility; indeed it may increase it (Vanhoegaerden, 1999). Goffee and Jones (2000) agree: the approachability and humanity of leaders are thus revealed.

Credibility is also built through previous reliability in providing correct information. Such 'source' credibility in a leader results in a greater ability to influence attitudes and behaviour and hence change (Lam and Schaubroeck, 2000). It comes from sharing knowledge. Informal leadership, or opinion leadership, depends for its effectiveness on source credibility and similarity of the leader's social status to that of the followers (Weiman, 1991).

Effective leaders share knowledge and encourage others to do so. Sharing knowledge, however, potentially may diminish one's value to an organization. But, in transactional terms, people are willing to do so if they expect useful knowledge in return, if they see their reputation enhanced as a result, or are altruistic about doing so, according to Tom Davenport and Larry Prusak (1998). Trust underlies willingness to share knowledge.

Shackleton is an example of credible and inspirational leadership through referent power gained by treating people with respect and encouragement when things went wrong (Morrell and Capparell, 2001). Interestingly, Shackleton had the intellectual skills to back up his inspirational leadership: he paid painstaking attention to detail and used what we now call scenario planning.

Another example is Scotland's former football manager, Craig Brown. He 'retain[ed] a knack for persuading players to do things they did not know they could, or did not imagine they wanted to do' (Northcroft, 2000) – fitting exactly Bass's concept of a true transformational leader. For example, in speaking to one of his players he said, 'You can do everything Beckham can do on the right and you can tackle.' And he makes requests to players that 'sound like a gentle errand. "Can you do me a favour … ?"'

Expert power

Knowledge is a source of power, sometimes referred to as 'information power'. Socrates placed great emphasis on the right of those who have knowledge to lead. 'Expert power', the more general term, is another form of personal power, based on others' perception of a leader's competency or special knowledge or expertise. People are willingly influenced by those who are perceived as knowledgeable or skilful.

However, there is a danger in expert power. St Paul said that knowledge 'puffs up',[97] to which Marshall (1991: 42) adds:

> [Knowledge] feeds our feelings of self importance to know things that other people don't know and to be able to make decisions on the basis of inside knowledge.

Misuse and abuse of power

Power may be misused. Many senior executives are highly competent at planning, organizing, directing and controlling. But some are 'command-and-control freaks'. And some are bullies. They get things done, but by using coercive power, through fear or threat of sanctions and consequential compliance by others. We briefly discussed the example of Saddam Hussein earlier in this chapter. Such power-mongers may succeed but they do so despite, not because of, their leadership style and behaviour. Such leaders possess unsocialized power motives and, as a result, fail to empower their subordinates and they even disempower them. Richard Sorensen says:

> You can have a very effective leader who has no ethics, such as Hitler or Stalin; but a leader who does not have ethics creates a disastrous situation. (Shinn, 2003)

Power is dangerous, as Lord Acton, the British statesman, indicated in his famous dictum 'Power tends to corrupt and absolute power corrupts absolutely.'[98] It is not power itself that is corrupt but its immoral use. Powerlessness is hardly to be argued for as morally more desirable.

Marshall (1991: 45–51) presents an insightful account of the corrupting consequences of the misuse of power. One problem with the use of power in leadership has to do with its potential consequence of pride: self-importance, superiority, vanity and conceit may lead to what the ancient Greeks called 'hubris' – impious pride. This is not the same as self-confidence – a necessary requirement for effective leadership. A Biblical reference makes the point:

> Everyone who is proud in heart is an abomination to the Lord. Pride goes before destruction and a haughty spirit before a fall.[99]

Power can also lead to arrogance. Arrogance shows itself in an unwillingness to be checked, questioned, advised or opposed. It is 'the wrongness of those who think they are always right' (Marshall, 1991: 47). Arrogance in turn can lead to self-deception, grandiose delusions, poor judgement and lack of critical examination. Marshall (1991: 48) says:

> The more successful we are as leaders, the more we need critics, even when they are wrong, because at the very least they help to save us from the dangers of arrogance.

Power can lead to self-aggrandisement too, as we see with the obscene indulgence of some leaders of impoverished nations and some captains of industry even when they have failed. Power can also lead to insensitivity to others' needs (a lack of emotional intelligence) and the consequential loss of commitment from followers, domination of others, the maintaining of one's position at any cost, and tyranny – the ultimate misuse of power.

Power and domination, then, are often associated with the opposite of humility – arrogance. Adair (1989: 39) calls this the 'deepest flaw in leadership'. Arrogance, he says, comes from 'an inflated pride that makes a person in a position of leadership act in an excessively determined, over-bearing, or domineering way'. This in turn is caused by an exaggerated self-perception of wealth, position, learning or achievement. This was understood as far back as the fourth century BC, by the Chinese philosopher Lao Tzu.

Closely related to power, particularly position power, and worthy of comment here, is status. We all are familiar with status symbols. Examples are the chief executive's large office in a prime location, reserved car parking spaces and special forms of address. Other manifestations of status are pay, special employment benefits, limited access to the 'leader', and leaders being singled out for praise for achievements as if they were solely responsible for them.

The effects of status are much the same as those of the misuse of power. Status creates deference, feeds pride and fosters vanity, conceit and aggrandisement. It also increases psychological distance between leaders and followers. Marshall (1991: 88–89) adduces from the story of Jesus washing the disciples' feet[100] that, while 'leadership is a special function ... it carries no status with it whatsoever'. What effective leaders do deserve, Marshall argues, is honour – recognition and respect for a job well done. He defines honour as the recognition of *value* that is mutual between leaders and followers.

Dysfunctional leaders sometimes exercise power without responsibility – in Rudyard Kipling's words, 'the prerogative of the harlot throughout the ages'.[101] Contrast this with the perceived impotence of the UK's House of Lords: 'an illusion to which I have never been able to subscribe – responsibility without power, the prerogative of the eunuch throughout the ages' (Stoppard, 1966: part 6).

Carl Jung, the psychologist, suggested that love and power have an inverse relationship: 'Where love rules, there is no will to power, and where power predominates, love is lacking' (Jung, 1917). In his farewell broadcast in 1961, US president Dwight D. Eisenhower said, 'The potential for the disastrous rise of misplaced power exists and will persist.'[102] We find examples at both ends of the political spectrum – communists and fascists – as well as in business. In national socialist movements:

> At the head...is the Leader in whose name everything is done, who is said to be 'responsible' for all, but whose acts can nowhere be called into question. (Sabine and Thorson, 1973: 824)

The charismatic leader may use propaganda to great effect. Hitler, for example, both characterized the leader this way and practised what he preached:

> No trick was overlooked: the advantage of oratory over written argument; the effects of lighting, atmosphere, symbols, and the crowd; the advantage of meetings held at night when the power to resist suggestion is low. Leadership works by a skilful use of suggestion, collective hypnosis, and every kind of subconscious motivation; the key to its success is 'clever psychology'... . The leader manipulates the people as an artist molds clay. (Sabine and Thorson, 1973: 825)

Manipulation occurs in more subtle ways too. Richard Olivier says there is a 'thin line' between inspiring and manipulating others (Bailey, 2000). He says:

> **Sometimes managers need to inspire those around them to do what they want them to do. This is justifiable when all parties know the purpose and agree that there is a potential benefit to individuals and the organisation. In this respect, inspiration is a part of the persuasion process.**

As Bass (1985: 65–66) points out:

> **Inspirational leadership has been most applauded by the masses and most derided by skeptical intellectuals who [equate] it with demagoguery, manipulation, exploitation, and mob psychology. Its emphasis on persuasive appeals to faith rather than reason, to the emotions rather than to the intellect, and to various mechanisms of social reinforcement rather than to logical discourse has made it seem fit only for the immature and the undereducated.**

The very best leaders, Collins (2002) says, have ambitions 'first and foremost for the organization, the cause [vision and mission], the work – not [themselves]'. This is why, he says, such leaders can get people to do what they might otherwise not do, and like doing it. Ultimately, the American journalist Walter Lippmann said, 'The final test of a leader is that he leaves behind him in other men the conviction and the will to carry on.'[103]

Inspiration and charisma

A crisis calls for inspirational leadership. Sir John Egan, as chairman of Inchcape and former head of the UK's Chartered Institute of Management, said, 'It is really inspirational leaders who stand out in a crisis. The Chinese characters for "crisis" are "opportunity" and "danger". That's what it should be seen as – an opportunity' (Simms, 2002).

Inspiring leaders are often regarded as charismatic – a double-edged sword, as was discussed in Chapter 1. They are perceived to have a special talent or power to attract followers and inspire them with devotion and enthusiasm. One view is that charismatic leaders are emotionally expressive, self-confident, self-determined and free from internal conflict (Bass, 1992). They also show empathy with followers, they use compelling, emotive language, they display personal competency, they display confidence in their followers, and they provide followers with opportunities to achieve (Behling and McFillen, 1996). However, whether, and to what extent, charisma is essential to effective leadership – or the result of it – is arguable (Drucker, 1992; Sayles, 1993):

> **Many of the organisations we know do not have charismatic leaders… . [Their leaders] are usually modest, sometimes even self-effacing, losing no opportunity to stress that real achievement has come from teamwork, not the inspiration of just one individual. (Binney and Williams, 1995)**

This raises the question of ego. Maccoby (2000) stimulated a debate about whether effective leaders are egotistical and narcissistic, arguing that because of their vision, charisma and energy, they help organizations, which they see as extensions of their egos, become great. But Collins (2001b) found in a research programme that the most effective leaders – who have successfully transformed their business organizations – suppress their egos: they are self-effacing, humble and shy, but resolute. Perhaps the real issue is *authenticity*: inspirational leaders inspire others because they communicate *themselves* – their virtues and their flaws (Goffee and Jones, 2000). An example is Mahatma Gandhi, who said, 'My life is its own message' (Lulla, 2002). While charisma is generally viewed as a social process between leader and follower, where the leader might well have some very special gifts, such as oratory, charisma is very much a 'manufactured' phenomenon today (Bryman, 1992: 30), especially among politicians.

Leadership is often thought of as a process of *influencing* others in getting them to want to do what needs to be done. One new view of influencing put forward by Eric Knowles concerns removing people's inhibitions, or lowering their resistance (*The Economist*, 2002c). Knowles defines 'alpha' and 'omega' strategies of persuasion. Alpha strategies are concerned with making an offer more attractive, whereas omega strategies focus on minimizing resistance to it. Resistance, of course, is not necessarily logical or rational.

Sir Richard Branson of the Virgin Group – the best business leader in KPMG surveys in 1997 and 1999 (Beckett, 1999) – is an example of a contemporary business leader who inspires loyalty among the Group's employees and is well liked by them and admired among other business leaders. The story is told of how he praised an engineer on board his first transatlantic flight when it ran into difficulties and he solved the problem and how every year the engineer received a handwritten birthday card thanking him for saving the reputation of Virgin Atlantic (Reynolds, 2000). Sidney Harman, chairman of the American top-of-the-line entertainment and hi-fi systems company Harman International, cut costs with 'un-American compassion': he placed surplus workers in spun-off companies, including one that made clocks from waste wood (*The Economist*, 2002d). Harman says workers 'should have a serious emotional connection to the company'. These examples of leadership behaviour illustrate responding positively to the emotional needs of people.

We find many examples of inspirational leadership in the world of sports. For example, a member of the winning yachting team in the 1996–1997 BT Global Challenge round-the-world race, Humphrey Walters, says the team had 'a feeling that they [had] done something they never thought they could do … [and] … stretched themselves and reached aspirations and achievement far beyond their thinking' (Walters, 2002).

Inspiration may also come from communicating a clear vision eloquently, confidently and with confidence in it, using appealing language and symbols.

Inspirational language and speech

'Nothing is so akin to our natural feelings as the rhythms and sounds of voices', wrote Cicero (Schama, 2002). The Chinese translation of the word 'speech' is two words that separately mean 'act' and 'talk'. So to make a speech is 'to perform a talking show' (Leung, 2000).

Inspirational speeches contain simple language, imagery and plays on words in a colourful way. They are delivered with sincerity and passion, with confidence and conviction, and often with expansive body language – in particular facial expressions, gestures of the hand, head movements and eye contact. Eye contact gives the audience impressions of spontaneity and being addressed directly (Atkinson, 1984). Inspiring leaders express emotions through their body language. For one CEO, John Robins of Guardian Insurance, 'leadership is about communicating emotions and excitement' (Rajan, 2000a).

On two inspirational speakers Bass (1989: 56) says:

> In the United States, Martin Luther King and Jesse Jackson stirred disadvantaged blacks into believing that by their own personal efforts combined with collective action they could reshape American society to advance their place in it, ultimately for the benefit of all Americans.

Whether you agree with his political ideas or not, 1988 US presidential candidate Jesse Jackson touches hearts in the way he speaks. P.J. O'Rourke (1992: 24), the American journalist, says of him:

> He is the only living American politician with a mastery of classical rhetoric. Assonance, alliteration, litotes, pleonasm, parallelism, exclamation, climax and epigram – to listen to Jesse Jackson is to hear everything mankind has learned about public speaking since Demosthenes.

O'Rourke (1992: 25) gives an example from his 'A Call to Common Ground' speech:

> So many guided missiles and so much misguided leadership, the stakes are very high. Our choice? Full participation in a democratic government or more abandonment and neglect. So this night, we choose not a false sense of independence... . Tonight we choose interdependency.

Peggy Noonan captures the essence of inspirational public speaking.

> A speech is a soliloquy, one man on a bare stage with a big spotlight. He will tell us who he is and what he wants and how he will get it and what it means that he wants it and what it will mean when he does or does not get it... . He looks up at us...and clears his throat. 'Ladies and gentlemen...' We lean forward, hungry to hear. Now it will be said, now we will hear the thing we long for. A speech is part theatre and part political declaration; it is personal communication between a leader and his people; it is an art, and all art is a paradox, being at once a thing of great power and great delicacy. A speech is poetry: cadence, rhythm, imagery, sweep! A speech reminds us that words...have the power to make dance the dullest beanbag of a heart. (MacArthur, 1999: xxiv)

Language is one's most powerful tool: without communication skills a leader will fail to have an impact (Goodwin, 1998). Yet most senior executives 'don't make the strong audience connection – visceral, personal, emotional – needed to inspire trust and action', according to Nick Morgan (2001), a communications consultant.

Brian MacArthur (1999: xvii), like Simon Schama, laments the lack of oratory in leaders today: 'Where are the visions and where are the words that inspire men and women to greater things and make them vote with enthusiasm, even passion?' Modern egalitarianism may have tended to discourage flights of high rhetoric. Disraeli said of his legendary adversary William Gladstone, 'A sophisticated rhetorician, inebriated with the exuberance of his own verbosity.'[104] Using an esoteric, even if right, quote or allusion may seem pretentious, but politicians today sometimes forget that the common people are actually educated. According to Peggy Noonan, they 'go in for the lowest common denominator – like a newscaster' (MacArthur, 1999: xvi–xvii) – or perhaps a tabloid newspaper. But Morgan (2001) suggests that people in business increasingly expect speakers to connect with them 'viscerally, personally and emotionally'.

Jeremy Paxman, the broadcaster, writer and political commentator, describes how 'the Leader' at party conferences has 'largely discarded the rousing vision, the cloudy imagery and the rhetorical resonance of even twenty years ago' (Paxman, 2002: 151–152). The reason, he says, is that such oratory does not suit television, which is 'a medium of impressions and more intimate tone'. Political conference speeches therefore have become 'an awkward hybrid, part talk, part declamation'. And, he says, it is all 'a sham', for such speeches, and the punctuating and final euphoric hand-clapping and subsequent theatrical departure, are engineered, timed and planned, and the speeches are even not written by the speaker but by teams of speechwriters.

Outstanding leaders do influence and persuade people through inspirational language. This is perhaps the most obvious behavioural characteristic of an outstanding leader. But this poses a problem, even a paradox. If humility is a characteristic of effective leadership, as we find in the teachings of Jesus and Lao Tzu and in the opinion of many successful business leaders, how does this square with the power of oratory, exalted by the Greeks and Romans? 'Silence is of the gods,' says a Chinese proverb; yet 'Silence is the virtue of fools,' said Francis Bacon (1561–1626) (Watts, tr. 1640). Adair (1989: 44) suggests the answer is *listening*: humility lies in listening rather than speaking or waiting to speak.

Great leaders, however, have often been elevated to iconic status through their use of language. How do they do it? They inspire people through what they say and how they say it.

> **The speeches of Moses, Jesus of Nazareth and Muhammad to their followers are still inspiring men and women to lead lives based on a moral code and still, today, changing the course of history...the greatest speeches...move hearts or inspire great deeds [and] uplift spirits. (MacArthur, 1996: xv)**

The prophet Muhammad 'was noted for superb eloquence and fluency … [as] an accurate, unpretending straightforward speaker … [with] the strength and eloquence of bedouin language and the decorated splendid speech of town' (al-Mubarakpuri, 1995: 496–497). Inspirational speeches by leaders 'articulate dreams, offer hope, stir hearts and minds, and offer their audiences visions of a better world' (MacArthur, 1999: xxiv).

Inspiring leaders communicate a clear vision eloquently and confidently, using appealing language and symbols. They use a 'charismatic tone … [they] speak with a captivating voice, make direct eye contact, show animated facial expressions, and have a dynamic interaction style' (Kirkpatrick and Locke, 1996).

The ability to communicate a clear, simple vision is a key characteristic: 'The power of language … [gives] life to vision' (Kouzes and Posner, 1991). David E. Berlew says, 'Leaders must communicate a vision in a way that attracts and excites members of the organization' (Kouzes and Posner, 1991: 121). In the words of William Hazlitt (1807):

> **The business of the orator is not to convince, but persuade; not to inform, but to rouse the mind; to build upon the habitual prejudices of mankind (for reason of itself will do nothing) and to add feeling to prejudice, and action to feeling.**

Table 8.2 *Inspirational speeches*

Martin Luther King, Jr
'I have a dream…'

Abraham Lincoln
'…government of the people, by the people, for the people, shall not perish from the earth.'

Winston Churchill
'Never in the field of human conflict was so much owed by so many to so few.'

'We shall fight on the beaches…we shall fight in the fields and in the streets, we shall fight in the hills, we shall *never* surrender.'

John F. Kennedy
'Ask not what your country can do for you; ask what *you* can do for your country.'

'Let every nation know, whether it wishes us well or ill, that we shall pay any price, bear any burden, meet any hardship, support any friend, oppose any foe, in order to ensure the survival and the success of liberty.'

Tony Blair
'Now make the good that is in the heart of each of us serve the good of all of us. Give to our country the gift of our energy, our ideas, our hopes, our talents. Use them to build a country each of whose people will say that "I care about Britain because I know that Britain cares about me." Britain, head and heart, will be unbeatable. That is the Britain I offer you. That is the Britain that together can be ours.'

Table 8.2 shows the famous parts of well-known inspirational speeches by Martin Luther King Jr, Abraham Lincoln, Winston Churchill, John F. Kennedy and Tony Blair.

Martin Luther King Jr delivered his speech before a crowd of 250,000 in Washington, DC. His speech, Kouzes and Posner (1991: 125) say, was rooted in fundamental values, cultural traditions and personal conviction, and stirred hearts and passions. It is a masterpiece of connecting with an audience and crafting rhetoric. Abraham Lincoln, who 'demonstrated … passionate conviction allied to simple but eloquent words, quietly spoken' (MacArthur, 1996: xv) in 270 words spoken in three minutes, gave possibly 'the greatest and noblest speech of modern times' – his famous Gettysburg address. Winston S. Churchill's Battle of Britain speech[105] and his Dunkirk speech[106] inspired the nation. President Kennedy's inaugural presidential address on 20 January 1961 did likewise, rallying the youth of his country in one part of it and displaying its far-reaching influence, on George W. Bush after 9/11, in another part.[107] And Tony Blair's speech to his first Labour Party conference as newly elected prime minister[108] was both triumphal and indicative of radical change in the ideology of Labour:

> [emphasizing] duty over rights, the importance of family life, zero tolerance on crime and a more positive approach to European unity as he appealed for Britain to become a beacon to the world. Even right-wing commentators hailed the speech as a historic statement of intent. (MacArthur, 1999: 511–512)

Following the attacks on the World Trade Center in New York and the Pentagon in Washington, DC, on 11 September 2001, President George W. Bush addressed Congress on 20 September 2001. Extracts appear as a case example below.

CASE EXAMPLE

Extracts from President George W. Bush's Address to a Joint Session of the United States Congress on Thursday night, September 20, 2001[109]

Mr. Speaker, Mr. President Pro Tempore, members of Congress, and fellow Americans, in the normal course of events, presidents come to this chamber to report on the state of the union. Tonight, no such report is needed; it has already been delivered by the American people.

We have seen it in the courage of passengers who rushed terrorists to save others on the ground. Passengers like an exceptional man named Todd Beamer. And would you please help me welcome his wife Lisa Beamer here tonight?

We have seen the state of our union in the endurance of rescuers working past exhaustion.

We've seen the unfurling of flags, the lighting of candles, the giving of blood, the saying of prayers in English, Hebrew and Arabic.

We have seen the decency of a loving and giving people who have made the grief of strangers their own.

My fellow citizens, for the last nine days, the entire world has seen for itself the state of union, and it is strong.

Tonight, we are a country awakened to danger and called to defend freedom. Our grief has turned to anger and anger to resolution. Whether we bring our enemies to justice or bring justice to our enemies, justice will be done.

All of America was touched on the evening of the tragedy to see Republicans and Democrats joined together on the steps of this Capitol singing "God Bless America."

And you did more than sing. You acted, by delivering $40 billion to rebuild our communities and meet the needs of our military. Speaker Hastert, Minority Leader Gephardt, Majority Leader Daschle and Senator Lott, I thank you for your friendship, for your leadership and for your service to our country.

And on behalf of the American people, I thank the world for its outpouring of support.

America will never forget the sounds of our national anthem playing at Buckingham Palace, on the streets of Paris and at Berlin's Brandenburg Gate.

We will not forget South Korean children gathering to pray outside our embassy in Seoul, or the prayers of sympathy offered at a mosque in Cairo.

This is not, however, just America's fight. And what is at stake is not just America's freedom. This is the world's fight. This is civilization's fight. This is the fight of all who believe in progress and pluralism, tolerance and freedom.

> We ask every nation to join us...
>
> Our nation, this generation, will lift the dark threat of violence from our people and our future. We will rally the world to this cause by our efforts, by our courage. We will not tire, we will not falter and we will not fail.
>
> Some will remember an image of a fire or story or rescue. Some will carry memories of a face and a voice gone forever.
>
> And I will carry this. It is the police shield of a man named George Howard who died at the World Trade Center trying to save others.
>
> It was given to me by his mom, Arlene, as a proud memorial to her son. It is my reminder of lives that ended and a task that does not end.
>
> I will not forget the wound to our country and those who inflicted it. I will not yield, I will not rest, I will not relent in waging this struggle for freedom and security for the American people. The course of this conflict is not known, yet its outcome is certain. Freedom and fear, justice and cruelty, have always been at war, and we know that God is not neutral between them.
>
> Fellow citizens, we'll meet violence with patient justice, assured of the rightness of our cause and confident of the victories to come.
>
> In all that lies before us, may God grant us wisdom and may he watch over the United States of America. Thank you.

Dom Anthony Sutch says, 'He came across as "one of us" – he found the mood … . He said what the world wanted to hear' (Sutch, 2001). Bush's speech displays the characteristics of inspirational language that are reminiscent of wartime Churchill:

- Vivid imagery of the terrorist enemy, their goal of 'remaking the world', and of life in Afghanistan
- Personalization, by welcoming Lisa Beamer, widow of a passenger on United Airlines flight 93 who died storming the hijackers, and colleagues of the police, firefighters and military who died in the World Trade Center inferno
- His invocation of God
- The symbolism in his display of the police shield of George Howard, who died at the World Trade Center trying to save others
- His stirring language: 'I will not yield, I will not rest, I will not relent in waging this struggle for freedom and security for the American people'; and 'We will not tire, we will not falter, and we will not fail'

While his speech is said to have been written by a speechwriter, and a key feature of inspirational language is authenticity, the speechwriter nevertheless on this occasion seems to have captured his master's voice: simple, direct, natural.

Political leaders may express core values and beliefs in inspirational speech, with potentially productive or dangerous consequences. Examples of those more likely to lead to negative outcomes are a sense of superiority, perceived injustice to oneself or one's group, a sense of vulnerability, distrust and a sense of helplessness (Eidelson and Eidelson, 2003). Effective leaders through their rhetoric may inspire their followers to change the status quo, even violently (Homer-Dixon, 1999), especially when they also communicate innocence and victimization (Stern, 1995). Examples of mutual perceptions of vulnerability and consequential threat are the Israelis and Palestinians in the Middle East and the Protestants and Catholics in Northern Ireland.

We cannot leave this discussion of inspirational speech without a comment on Adolf Hitler. 'Hitler, undoubtedly the greatest speaker of the century ... changed a nation by his oratory,' says MacArthur (1999: xvii). He was able to arouse a mass audience and work it up to a frenzy, with a mixture of appeals to idealism, power, hatred and action, the use of symbols, the assertion of a grandiose identity – 'Deutschland über Alles' – and the projection of all evil outside. His moving speeches captured the minds and hearts of a vast number of the German people: he virtually hypnotized his audiences. The inspirational effect of a brilliant speech is illustrated by Hitler's address in 1932 to the Düsseldorf Industry Club. On his arrival:

> his reception...was cool and reserved. Yet he spoke for two and a half hours without pause and made one of the best speeches of his life, setting out all his stock ideas brilliantly dressed up for his audience of businessmen. At the end they rose and cheered him wildly. Contributions from German industry started flowing into the Nazi treasury. (MacArthur, 1999: xix–xx)

Norman Lebrecht (2000) concurs: 'Hitler was nothing if not a spellbinder ... Mixed with revulsion at the deeds he inspired, one cannot avoid a sneaking admiration for a lone individual who overturned an entire civilization.'

Central to inspirational language are two skills: framing and rhetorical crafting (Georgiades and Macdonnell, 1998). Inspirational language is not the exclusive domain of the speaker's podium or rostrum. The skills of framing and rhetorical crafting apply just as much in any one-to-one conversation between leader and follower, manager and subordinate, or indeed between any two people – where the purpose is to influence, motivate or inspire.

Framing language and speech

Framing is connecting your message with the needs and interests of those whose commitment you need (Conger, 1999). This means first knowing your audience. Framing is the management of meaning, which requires careful thought and forethought (Fairhurst and Sarr, 1996). Meaning is found in the image of the organization, its place in the environment, and its collective purpose, according to Bass (1990a: 208). Jay Conger (1999) says that:

> The most effective leaders study the issues that matter to their colleagues...in...conversations...they collect essential information... . They are good at listening. They test their ideas with trusted confidants, and they ask questions of the people they will later be persuading. These explorations help them think through the arguments, the evidence, and the perspectives they will present.

Framing is about developing a shared sense of destiny through dialogue (Kouzes and Posner, 1991), something both Martin Luther King Jr and Nelson Mandela did so well. Leadership is about building connections with people: effective leaders *make people feel they have a stake in common problems* (Goodwin, 1998). Giving people an identity as stakeholders creates shared ownership and thereby wholehearted commitment to solving problems and building futures together. Framing involves several specific behaviours:

Catching attention. First, catching people's attention at the start with something surprising or attention grabbing. Morgan recommends avoiding a joke or rhetorical question and instead telling a carefully crafted 'personal parable' or anecdote that captures your overall theme that the audience can identify with (Morgan, 2001).

Timing. Timing is (almost) everything: knowing when to introduce an initiative and when to hold off is a crucial skill (Goodwin, 1998). Hunt (1998) calls this 'exercising theatre'.

Appealing to common interests. Your message must be linked to the benefits for everybody involved. This extends to incorporating the values and beliefs of those you are communicating to, appealing to common bonds – noting that 'what is white in one culture may be black in another' (Leung, 2000).

Avoiding statistics. Using statistics usually should be avoided. Statistical summaries are regarded by most people as mostly uninformative and unmemorable: 'information is absorbed by listeners in proportion to its vividness' (Conger, 1999). However, as Nick Georgiades and Richard Macdonnell (1998: 111) say, telling a group that a project has an 80% chance of success rather than a 20% chance of failure is more likely to win over the group.

Use of vocabulary. Framing also entails using vocabulary that matches the listeners' and generally not using a two- or three-syllable word where a one-syllable word will do. Charles Goldie and Richard Pinch (1991) also advocate 'economic representation' in communication: using one word rather than several words to express oneself.

Showing feelings. A key element in framing is showing that you are feeling what you are saying, speaking with passion and emotion, and reinforcing the verbal message by using appropriate body language. In the words of Shakespeare's Hamlet's advice to the travelling players – 'Suit the action to the word, the word to the action.' This refers to tone of voice, posture and gestures – what Morgan (2001) calls the 'kinesthetic connection' with the audience.

Authenticity. This, of course, requires authenticity in communication. Framing language may be more difficult, however, for a speaker who has strong emotion about a subject, whose authenticity is all too obvious (Rogers and Greenberg, 1952). Inspiring others requires finding out what inspires you and speaking 'from the heart', according to Richard Olivier: 'If the speaker is inspired and moved, it generally follows that the audience will empathise' (Bailey, 2000). MacArthur (1999: xxi–xxii) says:

> **However brilliant the words, it is also the manner of delivery, the sincerity of the speaker, that makes a speech great… . Speeches succeed, according to Lloyd George, by a combination of word, voice and gesture in moving their audiences to the action the orator desires.**

Lack of authenticity has become an issue for leaders, particularly those in politics and government. The professional speechwriter has been used for a long time.

Public orators in ancient Greece employed *rhetores* to produce speeches. Simon Schama (2002) notes that former US president Andrew Jackson's best speeches were written by Chief Justice Roger Taney and that Samuel Rosenmann wrote for Franklin D. Roosevelt.

But the rise of the adviser – the 'spin doctor' – has created scepticism among audiences about whether leaders are speaking their own words sincerely or those invented by experts in image management. In fact leaders themselves have been 'invented'. Gardner (1996: 60) says, 'even the claim for authenticity can be manufactured ... good actors know how to feign sincerity'. Image management, or impression management, taken to extremes, however, can backfire and have a 'boomerang' effect (Bass, 1988). Authenticity, however, like so many other usually positive leadership characteristics, may have adverse consequences. Saying what you mean may demonize sections of a community, as, for example, it has done in Northern Ireland (de Bono, 1998: 55).

Inclusivity. In framing your speech, you move from 'I' to 'we' – using words like 'we' and 'our' rather than 'them' and 'they'. This characterizes inclusive language that unifies rather than divides followers (Fiol et al., 1999). This extends to comparing your group and situation with other groups and situations, for example with competitors ('We can do better than ... '), with ideals ('We can achieve our best performance yet), with goals ('We can achieve whatever we set our mind to'), with the past ('We can do better than we've ever done before') with traits ('This is what we could look like if ... ') and with stakeholders ('We can make our employees our strongest advocates) (Bass, 1990a: 208; Conger, 1999).

Presenting a solution and a challenge. Finally, framing includes presenting a solution, challenging the audience to implement it (Morgan, 2001), and then 'reading' the audience's reaction – their non-verbal signals – of receptivity, engagement with you, agreement and commitment to your message and adjusting to it accordingly and – better still – involving the audience in some form of physical activity related to your message (Morgan, 2001).

Television has made a difference in public speaking, whether for education, entertainment or to win hearts and minds to a cause. Morgan (2001) says that the 'grand gesture ... sweeping phrases, the grand conceits' and voice projection were *de rigueur* for centuries and, of course, still are so in theatre. But television (and video) has enabled the illusion of people talking to you from a few feet away, more personally, more intimately and therefore more trustworthily. Trust in the speaker – and winning hearts and minds – depends on the connection between the verbal message and the kinesthetic message, in other words, authenticity in communication. Tongue in cheek, Schama (2002) gives a contemporary interpretation of Cicero's five characteristics of oratory:

- *Intentio* – 'the main idea dreamt up and carefully monitored by staff'
- *Dispositio* – 'the arrangement, tailor-made for television and punctuated by gestures to "real life" heroes inserted into the gallery'
- *Memoria* – 'supplied by the invisible teleprompter'
- *Actio* – 'the oxymoronic homely gravitas studded with reassuring simplicities'
- *Elocutio* – 'a delivery finely tuned to reassure that the incumbent can complete sentences but equally finely judged to make them short'

Rhetorical crafting of language and speech

Inspiring leaders not only frame their language; they also craft their rhetoric. Speaking in West Berlin in 1987, then US President Ronald Reagan said:

> General Secretary Gorbachev, if you seek peace, if you seek prosperity for the Soviet Union and eastern Europe, if you seek liberalization: come here to this gate. Mr Gorbachev, open this gate. Mr Gorbachev, tear down this wall. (Allen-Mills, 2004)

Reagan is widely regarded as having been a great communicator, skilled in both framing his message and in crafting his rhetoric.

Rhetoric is the art of verbal expression. According to Beard (2000), rhetoric was taught in British schools long before English language and literature as we know it came into being. Bass (1988) describes how inspirational leaders substitute simple words, metaphors and slogans for complex ideas, such as glasnost and perestroika representing complex social, economic and political change in the former Soviet Union, and 'Never again!' to convey a response to the Holocaust. Inspiring leaders give examples, tell anecdotes, give quotations and recite slogans. They tell stories.

Storytelling Screenwriting coach and award-winning writer and director Robert McKee (2003) believes that 'most executives struggle to communicate, let alone inspire'. He argues for engaging people's emotions not through 'dry' memos, missives, PowerPoint slides or conventional rhetoric, but through storytelling. He says that the former methods are an intellectual exercise whereby one tries to convince or influence people on the basis of facts and logic but that 'people are not inspired to act by reason alone'. A much more powerful way is to unite an idea with feeling – by telling a story. Talula Cartwright (2002) says:

> People naturally gravitate to stories. Nearly everyone can remember stories from childhood that captured the imagination, touched the heart, and helped determine ideals, heroes, religious beliefs.

McKee (2003) suggests that people identify more with a story about struggle against adversity than with rosy pictures because they see it as more truthful. Once again, as has been discussed earlier, self-knowledge is a *sine qua non*. McKee (2003) says:

> A storyteller...[asks] the question, 'If I were this character in these circumstances, what would I do?' The more you understand your own humanity, the more you can appreciate the humanity of others.

Use of rhythm, metaphor and symbols Inspiring leaders vary their speaking rhythm. They use familiar images, metaphors and analogies to make the message vivid – as did Nelson Mandela with the image of the new South Africa as the 'Rainbow Nation'. They use symbols which capture the imagination – for example, the eagle symbolizes strength, the olive branch peace, the lion courage (Kouzes and Posner, 1991: 145). The cross symbolizes suffering, sacrifice and redemption; 'the hammer and sickle signifies the worker and peasant whose proletarian dictatorship would bring forth a communist utopia' (Bass, 1988). Hitler used to great effect symbols such as the swastika, the goose step, the 'Heil Hitler' salute and the 'Horst Wessel' song (Gardner, 1995: 261).

Tihamér von Ghyczy (2003) says, 'Metaphors … [involve] the transfer of images or ideas from one domain of reality to another.' The rhetorical metaphor is well known and heavily used in the business world. It is part of inspirational language, for example 'winning the match', 'star performers', and so on. But linguistics scholars say such metaphors have a 'shelf life', eventually becoming 'dead metaphors'. The 'cognitive metaphor', von Ghyczy points out, serves a different function. He quotes Aristotle's view that good metaphors surprise and puzzle us: while they have familiar elements, their relevance and meaning are not immediately clear. It is in this 'delicately unsettled [state] of mind that we are most open to creative ways of looking at things': 'something relatively unfamiliar (for example, evolutionary biology) [is used] to spark creative thinking about something familiar (business strategy)'.

Expression of hope Inspiring leaders express hope and possibilities. They wax lyrical, as did Martin Luther King Jr, with phrases like 'the jangling discords of our nation' and 'a beautiful symphony of brotherhood'. But, as Adair (1988) says, such leadership is about having the courage to take people forward in a positive way, not about demoralizing them through language filled with threats and fears.

Repetition Inspiring leaders also use repetition. This promotes easier recall (Ormrod, 1995). As Churchill said:

> **If you have an important point to make, don't try to be subtle or clever. Use a pile-driver. Hit the point once. Then come back and hit it a second time – a tremendous whack! (Fitton, 1997)**

Inspiration through language comes not only from magical manipulation and set-piece speeches. The idea of crafting rhetoric underlies the use of poetry by management consultant and poet David Whyte in his leadership development programmes – described in the next chapter – to inspire participants to inspire their people (Hoare, 2001). The idea is that poetry – using words that far better capture the essence of issues that leaders have to deal with – can help them to define a powerful vision and the courage to challenge preconceptions.

Speeches have always had memorable phrases or what today we call 'sound bites' – the invention of their impression managers, the spin doctors, rather than (political) leaders themselves. Examples are: 'With malice towards none … With charity towards all' (Lincoln); 'He has not a single redeeming defect' (Disraeli on Gladstone); 'The only thing we have to fear is fear itself' (Churchill); and 'Ask not what your country can do for you' (Kennedy) (MacArthur, 1999: xvii).

Michael Ignatieff (1985) said, 'We need words to keep us human.' And in the words of Raja Zarith Sofiah Sultan Idris Shah, Crown Princess of Johor (Malaysia), in a speech at the Malaysian Association of Modern Languages:

> **To be touched by...words...is not a sign of gullibility but of being human. We are not ashamed that we are moved to tears by what someone has written or said... . We should be really proud that we possess such human-ness within us. (Ahmad, 2002)**

Aristotle in *The Art of Rhetoric*[110] also recognized the importance in leadership of rhetoric; Socrates, on the other hand, regarded rhetoric as 'sleight of hand' and a 'poor handmaiden to logic' (Wardy, 1996; Grint, 2000). Yet Confucius said, 'He who does not understand the force of words can never know his fellow-men' (Giles, 1976: 94). And I say: he who does not know his fellow men cannot inspire them. Outstanding leaders know their followers. They use inspiring language.

Today's world has seen the creation of the World Wide Web and global conglomerates whose influence now exceeds that of any national government. Already we have witnessed the adverse consequences of such creations as well as their benefits. Tomorrow's world consists of many possible futures – scenarios. The scenarios that bring about the greatest good for the greatest number of people depend for their realization on leaders who have the right vision, values and strategies. But leaders will not – and cannot – do this without followers who share the vision, values and strategies and are both empowered and inspired to display them in their everyday behaviour, particularly when times are difficult.

Olivier's analysis of Shakespeare's Henry V as a leader – presented in the following case study – illustrates how he did this, with salutary lessons for our leaders of today and tomorrow (Olivier, 2001). Olivier suggests that inspirational leaders think in terms of the big picture: they go beyond immediate goals, such as making a profit, and they focus on what would serve the community at large. They have, he says, access to 'a muse of fire' (Olivier, 2001: 4).[111] The historian Theodore Zeldin (2004) has provided just such access: he established a foundation called 'The Oxford Muse':

> **to bring together people who want inspiration to think more imaginatively, to cultivate their emotions through practice of the arts, to understand the past better and to have a clearer vision of the future.**

'Inspire others,' Zeldin says, 'and you will feel inspired yourself.'

CASE STUDY

Shakespeare's Henry V and Inspirational Leadership[112]

The fictional Henry V is Shakespeare's greatest leader – inspired and inspiring, visionary but pragmatic, powerful yet responsible. Richard Olivier, son of Sir Laurence, who introduced him to *Henry V* at an early age, follows the progress of the play and, based on his use of the text in mythodrama seminars and workshops,[113] describes how Henry develops as a paragon of inspirational leadership. In particular, we see how Henry defines, communicates and gathers support for his vision, faces his critics, changes direction without losing support, leads by example and inspires his followers.

Act I in *Henry V* starts with an assessment of the past and depicts visions of the future and Henry building consent around his mission to reclaim the territory of France. He believes this is his right and he visibly commits to it. The Chorus asks for a 'muse of fire' that will exceed the 'brightest heaven of invention'. It is a call to the imagination. Henry's big idea – his mission – is to reunite England

and France. He now meets with his nobles to gather support. He starts by ensuring there is proof of his right to do so. And he wants to pick not only the right fight but also the one he knows he has a right to pick.

Henry next marshals and allocates his resources, and he identifies and deals with those who would oppose his mission. Effective leaders identify the forces ranged both for and against them. But they also need to understand their own habits and behaviours that might get in the way of achieving success. Henry disguises his awareness of treachery until an appropriate moment, when he reveals his feeling of betrayal. The culprits are sentenced to death. Dealing with naysayers, critics (both overt and covert) and traitors is important. And objective rather than subjective judgements, even apparently harsh ones at the time, may preserve the trust of others around the leader and save much trouble later.

In Act III, Henry takes the first steps into France, meets the first barriers to success, overcomes them, stages a strategic withdrawal, and ends up being surrounded by a vastly superior force to whom he is asked to surrender – or die. He starts with a plan – to arrive in August with 10,000 troops, take the first foothold in a week, and march on Paris by Christmas. He lands at the coastal town of Harfleur as planned. But three months later is still there, having lost 2,000 men and with another 3,000 ill. He makes his famous rousing speech to his exhausted troops:

> **Once more unto the breach, dear friends, once more,**
> **Or close the wall up with our English dead...**
> **Then imitate the action of the tiger.**
> **Stiffen the sinews, conjure up the blood,**
> **Disguise fair nature with a hard-favoured rage...**
> **Now set the teeth and stretch the nostril wide,**
> **Hold hard the breath, and bend up every spirit**
> **To his full height. On, on, you noblest English,**
> **Whose blood is fet from fathers of war-proof...**
> **Follow your spirit, and upon this charge**
> **Cry, 'God for Harry! England and Saint George!'**

Olivier comments: however grand the vision or mission, there must be a practical place to start. When things get stuck – especially when it is not the followers' fault – an effective leader will have to speak passionately and imaginatively to motivate them through the blocks. Says Olivier, 'At [this] point the "troops" [would be] about as keen to fight as they would be to jump off a cliff.' Henry's troops have been living in a marsh for three months, watching their mates die, and they *know* what went wrong. What they need is something that will change their energy and create a different result. To do this Henry includes himself in the conversation – 'dear friends'. Olivier comments: 'When was the last time you were three months behind delivery on an important project and your boss called you a dear friend?' What the demotivated troops need is a sense that 'we're in this together'.

The key to re-motivating his troops is Henry's use of imagery. He does not tell them what to do – they already know that – but how they can be successful when they get there. This approach reflects 'active imagination' used in psychology: 'see' the desired result first; next think what energy you need to achieve it; then imagine yourself doing it; finally do it. Framing and rhetoric are key skills in inspirational language, as we have discussed earlier in the chapter. Sparing use of such language and authenticity and careful timing are crucial. Otherwise such language becomes a cliché and leads to cynicism.

Henry appeals to the troops' natural desire to make their parents and ancestors proud of them. And he confirms his hope that they are motivated to move forward, displaying the hallmark of transformational leadership that we discussed in Chapter 2: 'You're doing this not just for your parents, or for me, but for our country, and for the great spirit that guides it.' Henry has motivated his troops to go beyond immediate self-interest and serve a greater good. He has transformed their motivation to go beyond what they had previously expected of themselves.

The night before battle, Henry faces up to his fears and duties. He has to inspire his troops to achieve an evidently miraculous victory against all the odds. The Chorus tells us that the English are waiting, like ghosts, to die. At 3 a.m. Henry walks around, visiting all his troops, 'thawing cold fear'. Olivier comments: Henry does what is required of him, not what is easy or comfortable. He displays visible leadership. He is seen by others, and he sees them; he displays confidence. By acting confidently, Henry bolsters his troops' confidence. As we have seen in Chapters 3 and 7, self-confidence is a hallmark of successful leaders.

Henry tells his brother, 'We are in great danger.' He is asked to meet with his nobles but refuses to do so: 'I and my bosom must debate awhile and then I would no other company.' He takes off his crown, puts on a cloak and walks around unrecognized. He talks to some ordinary soldiers who believe they will die and that if they do not die well 'it will be a black matter for the King that led us to it'.

Leaders need to put on a brave face for their followers. But they also need to face their inner reality, their 'private truth', and reflect on the situation they are in. Henry has the courage to listen (anonymously) to his troops – they, like people in a crisis the world over, are blaming the boss. But by practising what we now call MBWA ('Management By Walking Around') and listening carefully to what they are saying he may be able to inspire them later. He feels the weight of responsibility of what people project onto their leaders, the cause of many sleepless nights for leaders. He needs to unload this: failing to do so may lead to decisions based on what others want rather than what he thinks is right. This is what Olivier calls 'appropriate selfishness'. Finally, in praying he faces his own 'inner demons'. The activities of the 'dark night' have stripped away layers to reveal Henry's core values: why he is doing this. And it is from these core values that he speaks to inspire others. Now he is ready to enter the fray.

Henry returns to his nobles and speaks to them from the heart. He tells them why he believes they are doing the right thing. He says their resources are enough to win honourably or die trying:

> **No, my fair cousin.**
> **If we are marked to die, we are enough**
> **To do our country loss; and if to live,**
> **The fewer men, the greater share of honour.**

He says that those who do not wish to fight may leave, but that any who choose to fight and who survive will remember this day for the rest of their lives. A foolhardy offer, perhaps, but Henry has sown the seeds of inspiration well. He does not talk about the battle to come and what he expects of his troops, but about their retirement! He offers the gift of a future, but without false promises. Now they have something to fight for. He makes an extraordinary offer of equality and turns the outrageous odds against winning into an inspiring challenge:

> **We few, we happy few, we band of brothers.**
> **For he today that sheds his blood with me**
> **Shall be my brother; be he ne'er so vile,**
> **This day shall gentle his condition.**

This speech impressed Winston Churchill so much during the Second World War that he asked Richard's father, Sir Laurence Olivier, to make his film of *Henry V* to enhance morale for the Normandy landings. Churchill himself drew from Henry's image of 'the happy few' in his Battle of Britain speech to the House of Commons on 20 August 1940: 'Never in the field of human conflict was so much owed by so many to so few.'

The battle goes well for the English. The French surrender, Henry thanks God, and he forbids anyone to boast of the victory: he says, 'Boast of this, or take that praise from God, which is His only.' Olivier comments: Henry did not claim credit for the victory: it happened because it was right. Outstanding leaders do not seek credit or applause. Olivier says:

> **An insecure leader will feel the need to claim the credit for the victory, to be seen as the superhero who 'made' it happen. The more secure we are, and the less driven by ego, the more we will surrender credit to others.**

Further reading

Kim S. Cameron, Jane E. Dutton and Robert E. Quinn (Editors) (2003), *Positive Organizational Scholarship: Foundations of a New Discipline*. San Francisco, CA: Berrett-Koehler.

Gail Fairhurst and Robert Sarr (1996), *The Art of Framing*. San Francisco, CA: Jossey-Bass.

Nick Georgiades and Richard Macdonnell (1998), *Leadership for Competitive Advantage*. Chichester: John Wiley & Sons.

L.W. Porter, G.A. Bigley and R.M. Steers (Editors) (2003), *Motivation and Work Behavior, 7th Edition*. Burr Ridge, IL: Irwin/McGraw-Hill.

Mark C. Scott (2000), *Reinspiring the Corporation: The Seven Seminal Paths to Corporate Greatness*. Chichester: John Wiley & Sons.

Discussion questions

1 List and prioritize what motivates or inspires you in the context of work, study or home.
2 Consider the forms of power and influence that you exert over work colleagues, friends and relatives and apply the descriptions outlined in this chapter under the headings of authority (position power) and personal power.
3 Review George W. Bush's speech to the US Congress provided as a case example and identify what makes it appealing or inspirational in terms of the way it was framed and his use of rhetoric.
4 Analyse the leadership behaviour of Shakespeare's *Henry V* using the leadership model, with particular reference to his ability to inspire his followers.

9 Leadership Development

It is not a matter of whether leaders are born or made. They are born and made.

Jay Conger (2004)

Overview

- Are leaders 'born' or 'made'? This question has dominated debate about leadership development ever since the ancient Greeks. However, there is now a common view that, while there may be genetic effects, leadership can be developed and that this process starts early in life.
- Leadership development programmes are plentiful and costly. They can be effective when they are focused on specific leadership behaviour, they are based on feedback, practice and application, and there is a desire to exercise and develop effective leadership behaviour.
- There are several barriers to both leadership and leadership development. Most barriers are internal to the individual but some are due to organizational culture or politics or a lack of time to undertake leadership development activities. Internal barriers include low self-esteem, lack of self-confidence, fear of failure, shame or social disapproval, cognitive constriction (thinking 'inside the box'), and the adverse consequences of stress. These barriers can be removed or reduced by the use of psychological principles and experiential learning methods that are discussed in the chapter.
- Self-awareness as a leader is the necessary basis for effective leadership development: leadership development begins with learning to know and control oneself first to enable self-confidence to grow. There are several other principles to be followed as well as other considerations in designing leadership development programmes (e.g. the nature of the environmental and organizational contexts) that are discussed.
- Essential to the leadership development process are feedback and follow-up in application of learning. The 360-degree assessment and feedback process in particular is potentially useful and has become popular.
- Leadership development programmes tend to focus only on one specific or limited aspect of leadership and often employ one particular model or theory of leadership

and sometimes one particular learning method, thereby limiting their effectiveness. There are, however, a variety of learning and development methods that serve different purposes. Examples that are discussed are case studies, skill practice through role play, e-learning, mentoring, projects and assignments, and use of the arts, for example theatre, and the use of outstanding leaders themselves as teachers. There are also several 'triggers' or catalysts, both planned and opportunistic, in the development of leadership. We discuss principles that guide the effective design of leadership programmes, and examples are provided.

- There are many examples and studies of leadership development programmes with positive validated or documented results. Some examples are given. The chapter concludes with an answer to the question 'Can leadership be "taught"?'

Are leaders 'born' or 'made'?

'Leaders are born, not made. Discuss.' This is one my favourite assignment topics for my MBA leadership classes. The issue has dominated debate about leadership development ever since Plato raised the question, the Greek historian and general Xenophon argued that leadership can be developed, and Aristotle contrarily asserted that men are destined from the moment of birth either to rule or to be ruled.

William Shakespeare was well aware of the nature–nurture issue: 'Some are born great, some achieve greatness, and some have greatness thrust upon them.'[114] The Romantic movement of the eighteenth century, in particular the writings of Jean-Jacques Rousseau (*The New Heloise* in 1761 and *Emile* in 1762) ushered in a period of emphasis on environmental and social influences on human behaviour. Then the publication of Darwin's *On the Origin of Species* in 1859 suggested the part that heredity and chance play in determining the human condition, and the popular view reverted to 'leaders are born, not made'.

Some people – including both successful chief executives and young people – argue passionately that leadership is innate. Interestingly, most of the candidates in the 2001 Leaders of Tomorrow competition believed that people are 'born rather than made' leaders. One 17-year-old shortlisted finalist, Kieran Ferguson, says, 'I don't think for a second that leadership can be taught, but it can be discovered and developed' (Hilpern, 2001).

What is meant by 'innate' is ambiguous. Is it that there is a 'leadership' gene? Or is leadership something that is acquired early in life that cannot be changed – or developed – by the time one starts work on the bottom rung of the corporate ladder? Others argue that leadership can be developed, learned or even taught. A somewhat ambivalent view is expressed by Harold Geneen (1984), former CEO of the ITT Corporation:

> **Leadership is learned, although I cannot explain entirely how it is learned. The ability to lead and inspire others is far more instinctual than premeditated and it is acquired through the experiences of one's everyday life, and the ultimate nature and quality of that leadership comes out of the innate character and personality of the leader himself.**

David Norburn provocatively takes a more 'born rather than made' stance:

> **[Leadership] is basically genetic - but it can be encouraged.The teacher (the bellows) can accelerate the embryonic leader (the spark) to burst forth (the crackling fire). The result? (Hopefully): paradigm busters, full of spirit and empathy.Those with no sign of spark - lower-quartile MBAs, perhaps - join investment banks and become androids.[115]**

Nigel Nicholson (2001) is less equivocal:

> **The big lie sold to us by much of the management literature is the myth that any man or woman can be turned into a leader, given the right developmental intervention... . The new science of behavior genetics is steadily accumulating evidence about how much of individual character, style, and competence is inborn. As every parent with more than one child knows, each is born different and stays different.**

Nicholson admits to some 'reworking' of our traits during childhood and by radical change in adulthood, but believes that by the twenties these are largely fixed, and that one of these traits is motivation to lead. On the other hand, Nelson Mandela (1995: 1) says:

> **Apart from life, a strong constitution and an abiding connection to the Thembu royal house, the only thing my father bestowed upon me was a name, *Rolihlahla*.**

Even accepting that there are genetic influences on personality – DRD4 on chromosome 11 (Okuyama et al., 2000) – and, by implication, on leadership, there is still enormous scope for changing our leadership behaviour. Susan Greenfield (2003) says that genes 'make things possible' but much may happen between them and behaviour and feelings – nurture may 'trump' nature. In other words, genes are necessary but not sufficient. And Winston (2003) says that we are not merely the product of our genes: environment has a huge impact, but in a mysterious way.

Leadership potential has its roots partly in genetics, partly in childhood development – the Jesuits have a saying, 'Give me the boy until he is seven and I will give you back a man' – and partly in adult experience. We might therefore say, 'Give me the manager until ... and I will give you back a leader.' Kets de Vries and Florent-Treacy (1999) describe how early childhood and family influences shape character in general and leadership potential in particular. The early years of a person's development are well established as a formative period. It is therefore not surprising that research carried out for the global HR consultancy DDI reinforces the link between early leadership experience and business leadership in adulthood (Eglin, 2005). Seventy per cent of over 100 business leaders interviewed had been school prefects, 50% had been sports team captains, 30% head or deputy head boy or girl, and nearly 90% had held at least two leadership positions at school, with 40% holding three.

However, scepticism, and even cynicism, dogs such findings. For example, they are sometimes regarded as self-evident and so hardly worth the cost of the research, evidently not true – school prefects are 'creeps' with 'a special badge' rather than leaders-in-waiting – or self-serving as 'a blatant attempt to crack the code of dinner party chat' about one's own gifted children who are 'going straight to the top' (Appleyard, 2005). Nevertheless, the role of childhood experience in developing emotional literacy, for example, is starting to be recognized, with programmes in British primary schools (*The Economist*, 2001c).

Developing leadership potential is a combination of the accidental, the incidental and the planned. All of us have the potential to improve our leadership effectiveness, some no doubt more than others. As Rajan (2000a) says:

> **Some may not possess enough skills or emotional strength. Some may do so, but lack the necessary motivation. Some may have the ability and will, but lack the necessary opportunities.**

The key question about leadership development is not of whether leadership can be developed, but *how* and *how much*. For example, can leadership be *taught*? All of us have learned most of what we know and can do through experience. And this experience has very largely come from 'real life' rather than the classroom. Indeed Oscar Wilde (1891, 1894) said that 'nothing that is worth knowing can be taught'. Opinions about whether leadership can be 'taught' vary, with a tendency towards agreeing that, while little if anything can be taught, it can be learned. For example, Hilarie Owen says:

> **Leadership cannot be taught as a list of skills. Nor can it be bolted on to management development, as leadership is totally different to management and requires different thinking. Leadership potential is already in the individual and therefore requires recognition, development, growth and practice. A week's training course will not achieve this – it requires much more.[116]**

The METO project on *Management and Leadership in the Changing Economy* found a high degree of agreement that leadership capabilities can be learned, developed or released (METO, 2000). And according to *The Economist* (2001d):

> **The truth is that there are many people within every corporation who are capable of leading if they are given the right experience and encouraged to develop certain talents.**

Even Nicholson (2001) admits to this: leadership behaviour can be 'moderated' – 'but not transformed' – by training people who are not naturally gifted leaders in key behaviours and habits that are associated with effective leadership.

Approaches to leadership development

Leadership development programmes are plentiful – they have superseded 'management development' programmes in many organizations (Cacioppe, 1998a) – and they are expensive. In the United States they may cost as much as $100,000 to $250,000 to develop and $50,000 to $150,000 per session to deliver, according to Robert Fulmer (1997).

The remark by successful CEOs, 'I didn't get where I am by attending leadership courses', is familiar. However, training practitioners know that training can speed up the learning process and provide a cognitive, emotional and skills framework and sense of meaning and value that eases and enables the learning process. There is no reason why this argument should not apply to leadership development. Leadership development involves *knowing what, knowing how to, wanting to apply it,* and then *actually applying it,* just as much as learning any other set of skills.

At the core of effective leadership, according to Randell (1998), are the 'micro-skills' of asking questions, active listening, making statements and 'body language'. His colleagues Peter Wright and David Taylor (2000) describe in detail the interpersonal skills of leadership, which comprise verbal and non-verbal questions and responses, the way interactions with subordinates are structured, and managing emotion at work. Randell, describing the Bradford approach to leadership development, argues that leadership can be developed, but:

- Only if desired: a person must be motivated to be a leader and to develop the necessary leadership skills
- Only if focused on specific leadership behaviour
- Only by practising leadership skills and getting feedback in either real-life or training situations

It has been claimed that 'conventional leadership training strategies are not enough to transform individuals into leaders' and that 'character' should be reinstated in leadership development (Chakraborty, 1995). And Warren Bennis has observed, 'Leadership courses can only teach skills. They can't teach character or vision and indeed they don't even try' (Chakraborty, 1995: 155). How can personal integrity, trust and credibility be 'taught'? This issue has been the basis of criticism of business schools for 'training technicians' (Lenz, 1993: 173) and for turning out 'highly skilled barbarians'.[117]

One study investigated the circumstances in which a transformational leadership development programme actually produced the intended changes in participants' leadership behaviour (Avolio and Bass, 1998). Whether it did so appears to depend on whether the participants were aware of the need to change and had a plan to do so. A further consideration was how constrained participants were in changing their behaviour by the culture of their organization, their own boss and colleagues and the particular tasks they were performing. Time pressures inhibited implementation of leadership development plans for some 25% of participants.

In addition, however, Lenz (1993: 173) points out that there are 'personal experiences central to [leaders'] capacity to lead that are beyond the purview of formal education'. Furthermore, leadership also depends on self-development, whereby people deliberately put themselves into situations from which they expand their repertoire of leadership behaviours (Bennis, 1989). This is the focus of many leadership development approaches, such as that at The Leadership Trust.

Such approaches use techniques borrowed from outdoor training. In addition to The Leadership Trust, well-known examples in the UK include Outward Bound, Brathay and programmes run at the Royal Military Academy at Sandhurst. The theory is that leadership techniques under conditions of physical stress can be successfully applied to the high-pressure office, according to Rick Chattell, project manager for leadership development courses at RMA Sandhurst:

> **It is all about inspiration: inspiring yourself and others to succeed, if necessary against the odds. In business, as in other areas, there are usually obstacles to overcome such as lack of resources or time. Inspiration can be the secret to winning through. (White, 2000a)**

The impact of leadership development programmes depends to a significant extent on the emergence of self-awareness. For example, self-discipline is often tested and revealed in leadership development programmes, and one of the critical success factors in leadership development is self-discipline in implementing leadership development plans. Self-awareness gives rise to reflective thinking about better leadership strategies. This is the foundation for leadership development. And The Leadership Trust is constantly told of the way its experiential-learning 'Leadership in Management' course has dramatically changed participants' lives.

Leadership development must also focus on environmental and organizational contexts. A conceptual framework that relates the use of power and influence to contextual conditions is necessary to understand the connections between action and context in terms of the range of discretion and the feasibility of action options (Lenz, 1993: 173–177). Porter's work on the economic and competitive characteristics of firms and nations (Porter, 1980, 1990) is also helpful, as is an understanding of decision making in organizations (Lenz, 1993: 174).

Whether leadership research is useful to leadership development, Chester Schriesheim (2001) argues, is dubious. He says that the 'misfit between the complexity of research and the limited ability of managers to use complex information on a daily basis' is a fundamental problem and that leadership development should focus on methods of skill-based training, building confidence, and replacing habitual behaviours with a broader repertoire of responses. Lenz (1993: 172) says:

> **Leadership is assumed to be largely comprised of learned behaviors – some proportion of these involve higher-order cognitive abilities, while others involve interpersonal and other related types of skills (e.g. verbal and written communication).**

However, Lenz (1993: 175) also says 'An overarching conception of leadership may provide a conceptual framework for relating [leadership skills] subject matter taught rather than independently in a variety of courses and training experiences.'

The Council for Excellence in Management and Leadership (CEML), set up by the British government, made recommendations, based on its research published in 2001, for leadership development across British society:

- For small and medium sized organizations, to establish a more coherent approach to counteract the 'confusing plethora' of initiatives from various sources
- For larger organizations, to improve the spread of best practice by promoting both IIP (Investors in People) and the use of a Leadership Development Best Practice Guide and to adopt a voluntary scheme of corporate reporting of leadership capacity
- For the professions, to introduce leadership development into their pre-qualification and Continuing Professional Development (CPD) programmes
- For government, to develop a framework of measures for leadership capacity as the basis for a management and leadership development index.

(CEML, 2001)

The CEML (2001: 8) found that some 50% of newly recruited or promoted managers stay with their employer for six or more years. This low churn rate implies a significant benefit from taking leadership development seriously in organizations. The report says:

We still find that a high proportion of managers...are lacking in skills which are considered to be important. These are the softer 'leadership' skills – to do with strategic thinking, communication, leading teams and developing and promoting cultural and ethical standards for the organisation.

The Leadership Development: Best Practice Guide for Organisations promotes three strategic principles for leadership development:

1 Leadership development must be driven from the top: if the CEO is not intimately involved and committed to it, it is not worth starting
2 Leadership development supports and drives the business: if it is not core to an organization's strategy, it will not happen
3 A leadership model must be culturally attuned: it must reflect the culture of the organization

(James and Burgoyne, 2001)

Feedback and follow-up in leadership development

Essential to any performance improvement and development process are feedback and follow-up. Drucker (1999a) says, 'a person can perform only from strength. One cannot build performance on weaknesses' and that discovering one's strengths requires feedback analysis. Drucker used to keep a record of his decisions and actions and what he expected would happen, and after some nine to twelve months compared results against his expectations. This approach can be very revealing. It is nothing new, having been used by John Calvin and Ignatius Loyola, who founded the dominant Calvinist Church and the Jesuit order respectively. This approach, Drucker says, enables one to concentrate on using strengths and on improving them as well as discovering one's intellectual arrogance.

Feedback analysis also gives information on how one performs. For example, people are either readers or listeners. Not knowing which one is can greatly reduce effectiveness, as it did, Drucker (1999a) says, for former US presidents Dwight D. Eisenhower and Lyndon B. Johnson. Another example is learning style. He quotes Churchill as doing badly at school because there was only one way of learning, which did not suit him: by listening and reading, rather than by writing – his preferred way. Drucker quotes a chief executive who learns by talking to his senior group for two or three hours. How we learn – learning style – has been captured in the well-known theories of David Kolb (1985) and Peter Honey and Michael Mumford (1992). Other aspects of how one performs best concern oneself in relation to other people – some people learn best alone, others in groups, some as subordinates, some as advisers rather than decision makers, some under stress.

Henry Wadsworth Longfellow (1807–1882), the American poet, said, 'We judge ourselves by what we feel capable of doing, while others judge us by what we have done already.'[118] The author George Eliot (1819–1880), alias Mary Ann Evans, thought likewise: 'We judge others according to results; how else? – not knowing the process by which results are arrived at.'[119] The importance of self-awareness as part of emotional intelligence in leadership was discussed in Chapter 3. A major contribution to enhancing self-awareness as a basis for personal development as an effective leader has come from 360-degree feedback (Ward, 1997).

In 360-degree feedback, a profile of the manager's leadership behaviour in terms of strengths and development needs is synthesized from feedback from the manager's boss, peers and subordinates as well as from him- or herself. The rationale for this approach is that managers' bosses, who traditionally are the sole source of information about managers' leadership development needs, mostly see only 'upward' leadership behaviour by them, whereas leadership behaviour is exercised with peers and subordinates and even clients or customers too. As Beverly Alimo-Metcalfe (1996) says:

> **Aspects of a manager's behaviour that are deemed to be important by a boss are very different from those regarded as important by subordinates. Bosses tend to focus on technical managerial skills, such as decision making and problem solving. Subordinates are more concerned with interpersonal skills, sensitivity, empowerment and visionary leadership.**

It can be argued that no complete picture of leadership development needs or a personal development action plan can be gained without comprehensive feedback. However, a study of organizational leaders participating in a transformational leadership development programme and their subordinates found that training and feedback each had a positive effect on the participants' transformational leadership behaviour, though incorporating both did not enhance it (Holloway et al., 2000). This suggests that training and feedback may be interchangeable approaches to leadership development. On the other hand, there is good evidence that effective leaders have a more realistic self-image than less effective leaders (Gill, 1998). Upward feedback can result in a sustained change over a long time (Reilly et al., 1996). However, upward feedback may be limited to the extent to which a manager or leader meets subordinates' needs and therefore may fail to account for actual performance or achievement as a whole (Mukhopadhyay, 1996).

While there is strong evidence for the value of 360-degree feedback in leadership development, factors other than the process and its content also make a difference. Todd Maurer et al. (2002) suggest, for example, the organization's culture: its development orientation and the involvement of the leader's own team in the feedback process.

The use of 360-degree feedback in leadership development has produced positive results, for example, in the Royal Bank of Canada, where it helped managers to become less focused on 'oppositional' power behaviour and instead to use more effective humanistic, coaching and achievement-oriented leadership styles (Crossley and Taylor, 1995). The leadership development programme for Britax International, run by The Leadership Trust and employing 360-degree feedback, 'revolutionised' the culture of the organization in breaking down communication barriers, according to Morice Mendoza (2000).

But not all authorities are believers in 360-degree feedback. For example, Edgar Schein says it is 'inappropriate' (Schein and Coutu, 2002): managers may be 'too fragile' to accept negative feedback from their subordinates, and in this case managers may benefit more from 'real-time' objections during meetings and discussions based on their subordinates' 'reading' of them.

The failures in applying what has been learned – in what psychologists call transfer of learning – characterize all 'training', including leadership development. The requirements for effective transfer of learning are well known. Follow-up of training is necessary – on what has been learned, what has been applied, the difficulties in applying what has been learned, the lack of inclination to apply it, and the further help that is needed.

Follow-up can take many forms: checks on whether participants are working on their application objectives, feedback instruments to measure behavioural change and measures of the impact on the group and the organization (Martineau and Steed, 2001). These methods can motivate participants to focus on application of learning, enhance the development process through the additional feedback, validate the process by identifying the specific impacts of the process, and gain the support of participants' managers, a key influence in transfer of learning.

Failure to apply what has been learned can also be due to the intrinsic nature of the leadership 'training' that most organizations carry out and to the organization's structure, culture and rigid processes which do not allow people to be 'leaders', according to Hilarie Owen (2001). Owen's central thesis is that organizations in their present state do not encourage people to find their leadership potential or use it. She explains how organizations can transform themselves to become places where the potential of existing leaders and would-be leaders can be expressed – where leadership can be 'unleashed'.

Overcoming the barriers to leadership and leadership development

A survey of some 300 leaders in manufacturing industry in the UK by the Manufacturing Foundation and The Leadership Trust Foundation found that just over half of them experienced barriers to leadership development during their careers, mostly due to themselves but also due to organizational culture or politics and lack of time to undertake leadership development activities (Bentley and Turnbull, 2005: 5).

One of the barriers to transfer of learning is emotional, yet the traditional cognitive approach has ignored this (Fineman, 1997). Benjamin Franklin, undoubtedly a leader himself, said, 'How few there are who have the courage enough to own their own faults, or resolution enough to mend them' (McCormick, 2000).

A useful starting point in leadership development, therefore, is to understand what stops people – managers – from becoming effective leaders. Once we know the psychological barriers to effective leadership and effective leadership development, we can use psychological techniques to overcome them and develop the cognitive, emotional and behavioural skills needed. Leadership development begins with learning to know and control oneself first – an essential element of emotional intelligence. Then, and only then, by building self-confidence and developing emotional intelligence, can we lead and enable others. For example, would you expect people to trust you if you did not trust yourself?

Norman Dixon describes the psychological barriers to effective leadership and leadership development (Dixon, 1985a,b,c):

- Low self-esteem – which leads to depression and lack of motivation. Self-esteem is a powerful motivator, as I have said constantly throughout this book.
- Lack of self-confidence – as a result of not coming to terms with oneself, which in turn leads to lack of confidence in other people. Howard Hass (1992) points out, based on analysis of 150 business leaders, that most people lack the self-confidence to practise and develop leadership. And a KPMG Management Consulting survey reported in 1999 revealed the insecurity and lack of self-confidence of British managers, particularly in their communication skills and ability to motivate people (M. Beckett, 1999).
- Fear of failure, shame or social disapproval – adults fear failure, whereas, Struan Robertson (2002) says, 'children keep trying to walk until they can'.
- Cognitive constriction – thinking 'inside the box' and over-rationalization, leading to 'paralysis by analysis'.
- Adverse consequences of stress – cognitive, managerial and physical.

These psychological barriers mean that many natural talents are impaired rather than improved by training. They can be removed in leadership development programmes through experiential learning in teams.

The process at The Leadership Trust involves generating or surfacing anxiety by imposing challenging tasks in work-related leadership projects such as a business simulation and physical activities which include rock climbing, scuba diving or caving and field projects. Anxiety is extinguished by enabling participants to discover their personal strengths. The focus is on handling aggression, resolving conflict, reviewing individual and team performance, and establishing effective working relationships. The tasks and activities comprise defining and solving problems, establishing objectives, planning, organizing team and physical resources, and implementing team action. Competition among teams is fostered but without risk of ego damage, and group dynamics among participants are facilitated. An underlying rationale for programme activities is presented for cognitive and emotional buy-in to the process.

Dixon (1985a,b,c) describes the psychological techniques and processes used in this process:

- *Desensitization*. The gradual overcoming of fear and anxiety by equally gradual increases in difficulty of the tasks and activities, with the surmounting of each hazard being reinforced by approval and an increment in personal satisfaction.
- *Reinforcement theory*. Emphasis on reward and recognition for effort and progress, not results, rather than punishment and blame, to bring about desired changes in behaviour, feelings and attitudes. Activity and task reviews are conducted in a positive, friendly, non-recriminatory and democratic way to build self-esteem.
- *Psychoanalytical re-enactment*. Review of what was done and what (if anything) went wrong in projects and physical activities, with facilitation but minimal interference from the tutor, who primarily asks open questions of the team (e.g. 'How did you feel about that?'). This is a process of self-discovery.

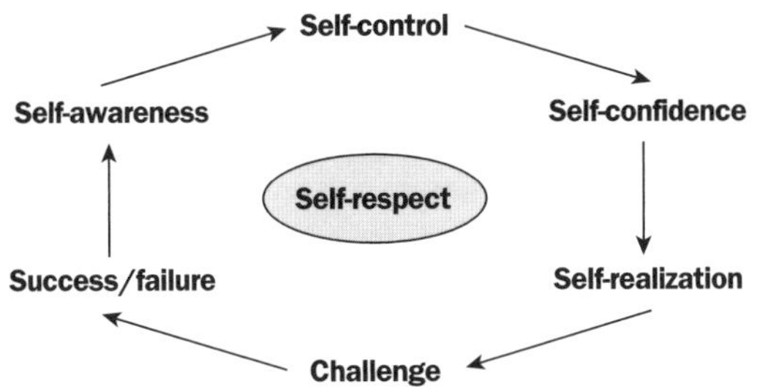

Figure 9.1 *The Leadership Trust's leadership self-development model*

- *Acquisition of social skills.* Focuses mainly on trust and honesty and uses a tool called *Spectrum* that assesses the degree of social control versus nurturing. The rationale is that self-esteem leads to honesty, and honesty leads to trust. In addition, humour is used liberally. Humour is a way of managing our emotions (Funes, 2000). Furnham (2001b) says:

  > [Humour] can generate a sense of group solidarity and belongingness...and help individuals cope with threatening experiences...[it is] an excellent defence mechanism and a means of coping with difficulties...it makes things funny and therefore tolerable. For many, it can be a coping strategy.

  Humour thus discharges hostility to negative feedback in building self-awareness and consequently self-esteem.

- *Group dynamics theory.* Teams are formed of up to nine members, each with its own identity, facilities and resources. They work and eat together, and they compete with one another. Team members develop cohesiveness through mutual helping, protection, support and friendships.

The outcome is increased self-awareness, followed in turn by increased self-control, self-confidence and self-realization as a leader (Edwards et al., 2002: 29-34). The Leadership Trust's leadership self-development model that underpins this process is shown in Figure 9.1.

Self-awareness develops through examining how one reacts to situations and why one does so in those ways. Self-control is thereby enabled. Self-confidence results from knowing that one has the mechanisms for coping with situations. Self-realization occurs when one maximizes one's strengths, controls for one's weaknesses and stands up for one's values. The ultimate consequence is self-respect (self-esteem).

The results that The Leadership Trust has achieved through this process are remarkable, according to feedback received (Berry, 2001). Dixon (1985a,b,c) in an evaluation of this approach reports that:

> Unless I've been duped by an astonishing illusion...[the programme is]...one of the best applications of sound psychological principles I [have] ever witnessed. Where else could one find sleek businessmen, past their prime, emerging all the better from a course of treatment that threatens, but never quite succeeds in, the breakage of every bone in one's body, the permanent wrecking of one's reproductive capabilities

> and the destroying of every illusion one might have about being a tough, virile, macho jungle fighter with a tank-like ego? If there are such places, I know them not.

Outdoor leadership development sometimes goes even further in presenting daunting challenges, not least physical. For example, the Wharton School in the United States offers its MBA students and participants in executive education programmes several leadership development ventures: a three-week journey to the Mount Everest area, reaching over 18,000 feet above sea level, and visits to Ecuador, the Marine Corps base in Quantico, Virginia, and the site of the disastrous 1949 fire in Montana. Michael Useem believes such escapades help to understand what it takes to be a leader (*The Economist Global Executive*, 2002). Such an approach in leadership development is underscored in management consultant Hugh Aldous's view:

> Leadership development is fundamentally about experience that tests individuals in hostile or difficult situations. It is about creating an environment in which ordinary people can have unusual experiences. (Rajan, 2000c)

Such 'unusual' experiences provide the vehicle for truly knowing oneself: we all have vast, hidden and unused potential which most of us underestimate in ourselves, acting in effect as leaders without formal subordinates (S. Smith, 2000).

Leadership development programmes

I have addressed the psychological barriers to effective leadership and leadership development and how they can be overcome by enhancing emotional intelligence. However, leadership development must also address other aspects of effective leadership. Ed Kur and Richard Bunning (1996) say that:

> Most leadership development programmes focus only on a part of leadership. For example, executive programmes often deal with strategic and/or visionary aspects of leadership, what we call 'macroleadership', without addressing the skills associated with leading individuals or small groups. Other programmes ... focus on leading teams but fail to address leadership of individuals or of total organizations. Still others, especially those for first-line supervisors and technical leaders, emphasize one-to-one or microleadership.

Rajan (2000a) reports a survey of CEOs on the leadership development methods they favour. In rank order of importance, these are:

1 Coaching by the CEO
2 Learning from peers
3 Experience
4 Skills training

The more recent survey by the Manufacturing Foundation and The Leadership Trust Foundation revealed 10 key 'triggers' or catalysts of leadership development in the British manufacturing sector listed in Table 9.1.

Triggers of leadership development appear to be both planned, for example experiential leadership development courses, and opportunistic, such as encounters with

Table 9.1 *Key triggers of leadership development**

1	Significant leadership challenge at an early age
2	Positive role models
3	Being 'thrown in at the deep end'
4	Mentoring, coaching and consultant relationships
5	Experiential leadership development courses
6	Negative role models
7	MBA and professional qualifications
8	International or multicultural exposure
9	Voluntary and community work
10	Team sports

Source: Bentley and Turnbull (2005), *Stimulating Readers: Developing Manufacturing Leadership Skills*. Birmingham: The Manufacturing Foundation. Reproduced with permission.

*In order of frequency of occurrence.

other leaders (Bentley and Turnbull, 2005: 15). And a mix of learning methods appears to be crucial to leadership development in manufacturing:

> **For most, the learning was derived from a powerful mix of learning from doing (work-based learning); learning from books or courses (ideas and concepts) and learning from people (social interaction). (Bentley and Turnbull, 2005: 5)**

In an online survey on global leadership development issues and practices, international assignments were the most used practices to develop global leaders, followed by experience in managing global functional or process teams (Lanto and Mobley, 1998). This survey also found that participating in global task forces to address specific organization problems or opportunities was the predominant best practice for developing global leaders with the capabilities that their organization needed. Peter Lorange (2003) argues that business schools need to refine their approaches to developing global leaders: creating a 'global meeting place', face-to-face or virtual; providing opportunities for experimentation; encouraging learning from failure; juxtaposing new business models with cherished traditional ones; and avoiding 'silo' cultures and encouraging single global 'families'. Lorange quotes Roger Schmenner: global leadership has 'no dominant culture'.

The United Nations University has an International Leadership Academy,[120] which employs various methods of leadership development on the premise that leadership cannot be taught but the skills associated with leadership can be learned. These mainly comprise direct instruction from and interaction with distinguished leading politicians, civil servants and academics and seminars, workshops and experiential learning.[121]

An early approach to developing interpersonal and intergroup relations through 'learning for leadership' in an experiential manner in the Tavistock tradition is that of Kenneth Rice (1965). The Bradford approach to leadership development is similar and focuses on the 'micro skills' of leadership – for example, perception, questioning, active listening, judgement and responding verbally and non-verbally through body language (Wright and Taylor, 1994; Randell, 1998).

The learning methods that are employed are many and varied. These include action learning (Revans, 1998), 'e-learning' (Ulrich and Hinkson, 2001), theatre at Cranfield School of Management (Olivier, 2001), cinema, for example in Roffey Park Management College's programme on 'Images of Leadership' (Lucas, 2001), and even the use of the martial arts (Clawson and Doner, 1996) and transcendental meditation (Harung et al., 1995), as well as more conventional methods such as case studies, skill practice in role-play exercises, leadership simulations and leadership projects.

Case studies

Case studies are detailed investigations of an individual, group or organization that contain background, contextual and historical information and detail on one or more aspects of leadership. Case studies require participants to make sense of complex problems or situations using appropriate theories to do so, identify the implications, and make recommendations for action or answer specific questions about leadership in the case.

Films or movies are often used as case studies. For example, Francis Beckett (1999) describes how London Business School has used the 1957 Henry Fonda film *Twelve Angry Men*, about a jury in a murder case, to discuss how to use influence rather than authority and create a 'boardroom presence'. And the University of Bradford School of Management used the 1949 Gregory Peck film *Twelve O'Clock High*, in which a US bomber leader is replaced for being too accommodating to his men and his successor soon has the men carrying out dangerous missions and also finds out how much he cares about his men.

Case studies, according to Henry Mintzberg and Joseph Lampel, are often seen as artificial ways of learning management, especially leadership (Eadie, 2001b). They can only teach *about* leadership, and 'taught' courses, especially on leadership, also tend to receive a critical press. For example, John Rink says:

> I've just been on a six-week leadership course at Harvard. It raised my awareness about things that I had not thought of. But the problem is it didn't give me [as managing partner] the soft skills that are crucial in managing this place [Allen & Overy]. (Rajan, 2000a)

Skill practice through role play

Role play in leadership development also meets with mixed responses. In the absence of other feedback, it allows a manager to display their leadership skills and to learn how to improve them. However, Hunt (2002) says:

> Unfortunately, the fact that these role-plays [occur] in front of other participants in a ferociously well lit CCTV studio [can] be inhibiting. For that minority of senior executives who are extraverts, this challenge to their thespian leanings can produce Oscar-winning performances. As luck has it, most senior executives are introverts. Role-playing [terrifies] them... . As for stimulating post-course development, it often [has] the opposite effect.

However, Hunt believes that 360-degree feedback, which we discussed earlier in this chapter, has reduced much of this anxiety, especially where role play requires participants to play themselves, not to act. And combined with 360-degree feedback, he says, role plays can produce dramatic improvements.

E-learning

E-learning, or the use of web-based learning, can make a contribution in leadership development:

> as long as the technology builds on the established principles of adult learning: learn by doing; learn from others; learn ideas that are relevant and practical; learn from experimentation and reflection; and learn over time, not in one event. (Ulrich and Hinkson, 2001)

Mentoring

Coaching and mentoring are examples of leadership one-to-one. 'Mentor' comes from Greek mythology and refers to one who inspires and helps a person in resolving difficulties and in personal development. The usefulness of mentoring – and a dismissal of role playing as a leadership development practice – is evident in the following remark by a company chairman:

> Having the opportunity to have a risk-free conversation with a trusted third party has been enormously helpful. You can bring our your doubts and anxieties without seeming to look weak or silly...the mentors I had helped me to be 'me'. That has helped because I am my own worst critic and I am also terrible at role playing, which still passes for leadership development in many organisations. In this age of sound-bite leadership, it is important to harbour self-doubts and discuss them...leaders must never take themselves too seriously. (Rajan, 2000d)

Leadership projects and assignments

Leadership projects are gaining popularity as part of leadership development. Participants carry out a project focused on applying leadership theory and practice, individually or in teams, which is expected to deliver measurable business results for the organization. For example, Vodafone's 'Global Leadership Model',[122] aimed at leadership development for its most senior positions, comprises several elements, including a succession of assignments and projects:

- One-year experiences in a 'senior assignment position' in the 'home' function in the home country, in the home function in another country, in another function in the home country, and in general management
- Business improvement projects
- Participation in an MBA programme
- Individual tailored experiences
- Sponsorship and mentoring by a board member and country and functional mentors
- Employee communication through presentations, team briefings, e-mail, intranet sites, focus groups, conferences and an International Employee Communications Forum

The use of the arts in leadership development

In addition to film (which we discussed in the section on case studies), the arts – music, poetry, literature and theatre in particular – have been used increasingly in leadership development in recent years. Why, and how?

Music plays a part in Henley Management College's courses and in LBS courses, where Ben Zander, conductor of the Boston Symphony Orchestra, talks about the contribution of the conductor to the orchestra (we discussed leadership as a 'performing art' in Chapter 1). Poetry is also used in leadership development. The poet David Whyte, who also works as a management consultant, uses poetry in his 'creative leadership' development programmes to inspire participants to inspire their people (Hoare, 2001). He used parts of the Anglo-Saxon epic *Beowulf* as a powerful metaphor to initiate the change process at Boeing. He also uses the poem *Tramps* by Robert Frost to stimulate reflection among the consultants he advises on the leader as communicator and motivator.

At the new Globe theatre in Southwark, London, Sir Laurence Olivier's son, Richard Olivier, has led the trend in applying theatre in leadership development by using the learning process he calls *mythodrama* in partnership with Cranfield School of Management. Mythodrama combines theatre techniques with mythology, psychology and the techniques of organizational development (Olivier, 2001: xxii–xxiii). For example, in leadership development programmes for business leaders, he asks participants to bring a short poem, play or speech that they have found to be inspirational (Bailey, 2000). The common theme that emerges in whether the audience is inspired is the use of imagery and how much speakers themselves are inspired. Mythodrama entails imagining and invoking characters that participants want to play – behaviours they want to display – and 'acting them in', a form of role playing. Olivier says that using these images opens up previously unimagined possibilities. It is 'literally "rehearsing" new ways of being'. Rehearsal – involving experimentation – is essential, he says, just as footballers and actors warm up before a performance.

Another technique Olivier uses is to examine the leadership behaviour of Shakespeare's King Henry V in inspiring an undisciplined mob to follow him into battle against the French (Nurden, 1999; Olivier, 2001), which we analysed in Chapter 8. Key learning points are Henry's mission – to gain the territory he covets – and how he overcomes his setbacks through his inspirational language. Role playing is used, as in conventional management and leadership development programmes (which we discussed earlier), but using Shakespeare brings imagination and creativity to the learning process – it adds the essential emotional aspect to the process and helps develop emotional intelligence. Olivier compares Henry V's journey from his misspent youth to the battlefield of Agincourt and beyond with the challenges faced by all leaders. He uses Jungian psychology to explore the 'roles and characters we can inhabit as leaders at work' and how Henry exemplifies how effective leaders adapt their behaviour to changing situations.

Olivier also uses *Julius Caesar* to illustrate emotional and political intelligence in leadership, showing how Caesar lacked insight into people's motives. And *The Winter's Tale* enables participants to explore change and regeneration in organizational life. Robert Nurden describes how this helped a director with NatWest 'move from seeing business solutions in terms of black and white to one with shades of grey'. Shakespeare undoubtedly was an insightful writer about leadership.

Opinion about using theatre in leadership development, however, is mixed. Francis Beckett (1999) quotes David Norburn of Imperial College Management School in London, for example, as strongly against it on the ground that business schools need to provide rigorous and relevant training. However, Beckett also quotes Robert Owen of AMBA[123] as supporting the use of theatre but only for teaching presentation skills, and Patricia Hodgins of the LBS as saying that 'the heart of creativity is about intuition .... Using arts, music and theatre helps us to find that.' Olivier (2001: 5) believes that arts-based leadership development, a rapid growth area in the late 1990s, helps people to be more creative, flexible and adaptable – perhaps the greatest challenge of the twenty-first century.

The effectiveness of leadership development programmes

There are many examples of leadership development programmes with positive validated or documented results. Bass and Avolio's Full-Range Leadership Programme focuses on developing transformational leadership, for which positive results drawn from many applications are reported (Bass, 1998: 85–86, 99, 102–116, 171). A small-scale study by Julian Barling et al. (1996) in a Canadian bank showed that training in transformational leadership had a positive impact on subordinates' perceptions of leaders' leadership behaviour, particularly individualized consideration, intellectual stimulation and charisma, subordinates' own organizational commitment, and the financial performance of branches. Kur and Bunning's three-track leadership development process in Pilkington Glass, British Aerospace, Greenall Whitley, SmithKline Beecham (now GlaxoSmithKline) and Motorola, among other outcomes, has yielded cost savings and revenue improvements, successful project implementation and enhanced credibility of participants due to enhanced project leadership competence (Kur and Bunning, 1996). And a report on the DfEE Leadership Development Programme for Serving Headteachers produced significant improvements in both organizational climate and pupils' performance (Topple, 2000).

The Institute of Management survey on leadership in the UK published in December 2001 indicated a correlation between effective leadership development in organizations and perceptions of the quality of leadership. Fifty-seven per cent rated the quality of leadership highly in organizations that develop leadership potential effectively, consistently and fairly compared to 21% in other organizations (Institute of Management, 2001; *Professional Manager*, 2002). Favoured leadership development methods comprise *in situ* activities focused on working relationships, formal mentoring, action learning and 360-degree feedback. Traditional classroom-based programmes have little sustained impact on leadership development, according to a 1999 study (PIU, 2001: 6.8).[124]

Research by DDI found a strong relationship between the perceived quality of leadership development programmes and the financial measures of revenue growth, profitability and market share as well as non-financial measures such as customer satisfaction, retention and employee engagement (Wellins and Weaver, 2003). Other research by DDI found that leadership development delivered positive changes valued at $500,000 to $1 million.

The classic study supporting the effectiveness of management training and leadership development programmes is that of Michael Burke and Russell Day (1986) in which they carried out a meta-analysis of 70 studies between 1951 and 1982. Doris Collins and Elwood Holton (2004) carried out another meta-analysis of 83 studies of the effectiveness of leadership development programmes between 1982 and 2001. They found clear evidence of the effectiveness of such programmes in terms of leadership knowledge and skill provided that prior analysis was conducted to ensure that the appropriate development was offered to the appropriate persons. Collins and Holton recommend nevertheless that organizations should evaluate the return on their investment in leadership development.

The survey by the Manufacturing Foundation and The Leadership Trust Foundation found that leadership development was believed to impact strongly in both 'hard' respects – productivity, quality, delivery performance and reduced overhead costs – and 'soft' respects, for example staff motivation and morale (Bentley and Turnbull, 2005: 5). There are many qualitative and anecdotal accounts of the impact of leadership development. For example, says David Wills of the Motherwell Bridge Group:

> **I sense a maturity about some people that wasn't obvious beforehand, increased awareness of self-impact, better leadership, improved communication in the group and positive behavioural changes... . In time, I see this leading to a more efficient business, as more of our managers and directors join this club... . It is only when the people change that the company will, and the [leadership development experience at The Leadership Trust] facilitates the long, hard look in the mirror that we all need from time to time. (Abrahams, 2001)**

Research studies show beyond doubt that *managers can learn to lead* through training (Conger, 1992). But, like leadership itself, leadership development is a process, not an event. It takes place in a variety of situations, including job assignments, relationships, experiencing hardship and other activities unrelated to work (McCauley et al., 1998). Leadership development, however, depends for its success on the readiness for development of both the individual *and* the organization. Without such readiness, the effectiveness of leadership development is seriously at risk. Such readiness therefore has to be diagnosed prior to designing or launching any leadership development programme. Of course, the lack of such readiness may itself be the focus of leadership development.

Designing leadership development programmes

John Burgoyne expresses scepticism about proof of the effectiveness of management development in general (Pickard, 2001). Leadership development in particular frequently suffers from several methodological and practical problems. Terry Gillen (2003), a training consultant, suggests that the key problems are the following:

1 The criteria for effective leadership that form the basis for leadership development programmes may not be valid. Such criteria reflect only self-reports or analyses of so-called role models such as Ernest Shackleton, Jack Welch and Sven-Goran Eriksson rather than what followers seek in their leaders.

2 Managers often feel compelled to demote leadership in favour of meeting short-term demands for high performance, particularly by 'doing more themselves and managing processes rather than leading people'.
3 What is 'taught' in such programmes contradicts what apparently successful managers ('the more senior ones') do, evidenced by the frequent comment that 'it's my manager who ought to be here'; yet human beings tend to imitate those perceived as 'successful'.
4 The clash between the espoused values and the actual behaviour of managers, for example customer satisfaction versus tight cost control, discourages implementation of learning.
5 Programme methodologies, such as outdoor activities and using 'videos of Kenneth Branagh as Henry V' reciting 'Once more unto the breach', may be inappropriate for their purpose: practical relevance – transferability of learning – may be questionable.

Formal leadership development programmes vary in their form and structure. Some run on intensive, one-off bases over, for example, five days (e.g. Motorola), others on a modular basis (e.g. Halifax), with intranet support, projects and coaching (Reynolds, 2000). Apart from the classroom, leadership development takes place, of course, mostly on the job. In fact most of what we know and can do is learned through experience in real life rather than in the classroom.

Formal training programmes in general, and leadership development programmes in particular, aim to speed up the learning process and make it more efficient through exploration, instruction or coaching, practice, feedback and reflection. Real-life experience provides a lot more opportunity for leadership development for most people. Examples are job rotation, taking on the leadership of special projects or assignments, deputizing for the boss and leading cross-functional teams. As *The Economist* (2001d) says:

> **The value of real experience is well demonstrated by the way in which some of the top consulting firms have become a rich source of CEOs. It is almost as if the experience that consultants gain from hand-holding clients through hard times constitutes the ideal leadership programme.**

Fiat's leadership development programme aims to integrate leadership styles with company goals and diffuses Bass's transformational leadership model throughout the company (Testa, 2000). This programme provides assisted self-development, individual counselling, and project-based action learning and development. The underlying philosophy is 'to promote learning by starting from the individual's own leadership situation and to support development through real experiences of exercising leadership'.

Ford Motor Company, through its Leadership Development Center, focuses on creating a 'transformational mindset', using action learning projects and e-tools and integrating work and life in what it calls 'total leadership' (Friedman, 2001). Ford runs several leadership development programmes, focusing variously on the new business leader, leadership for the New Economy, experienced leaders, leadership in senior positions and strategic change initiatives. Programme alumni serve as 'leader–teachers', started by CEO Jacques Nasser. Projects are evaluated for their impact on the organization, with impressive cost savings resulting. Stewart Friedman, director of the Center, says not only do 'our leadership programs pay for themselves many times over' but 'We're accelerating the process of creating leaders at every level' and 'the return on this ... is exponential', creating a leadership 'brand' that is unparalleled.

Two examples of leadership development in the public education sector come from the Department of Education in Victoria, Australia, and the Department for Education and Employment (DfEE)[125] Leadership Programme for Serving Headteachers in the UK (PIU, 2001: 6.5). The Australian programme was based on a research model linking competencies, leadership styles and organizational climate, focusing on:

- Behavioural characteristics causally related to success in leadership positions
- Raising participants' awareness of the factors – both conscious and unconscious – that drive behaviour in themselves and others
- Understanding their own motives and behavioural drivers and their impact on others
- Understanding the links between behaviour, leadership styles and organizational performance
- Clarifying the steps needed to develop defined skills

The DfEE programme was based on a similar research model and includes 360-degree diagnostic feedback and a follow-up event 9–12 months later. An interim study of some 2,500 participants suggested a direct and conclusive relationship between organizational climate and performance.

The Leadership Trust Foundation in the UK has pioneered leadership development within the context of accredited business and management education by introducing an MBA programme with a specialism in Leadership Studies in collaboration with the University of Strathclyde's Graduate School of Business. The aim was to respond to the needs of senior managers and directors of the future, a unique attempt to create an integrated leadership development programme. This programme combines the standard core curriculum of the Strathclyde MBA with a 'taught' course in leadership (focused on learning *about* leadership), experiential learning courses at The Leadership Trust (focused on developing emotional intelligence and leadership skills) and a leadership project (focused on application of leadership theory and practice). The aim is to produce graduates who are not only knowledgeable and skilled in business and management but also effective leaders. This initiative counters the increasingly frequent and strident criticisms of MBA programmes that they fail to help develop leadership in their students.

Effective leadership development is more than just focusing on current real-life leadership issues and problems, experiential learning, and even using varied methodologies, according to Stephen Kaagan (1998). Dealing with unfamiliar issues poses a real leadership challenge. Anticipating problems that leaders will face in the future while pursuing corporate strategies and solidifying corporate values is part of Fiat's aim. Experiential learning requires well-facilitated discussion of the experience to capture the learning and connect it with the workplace. And methodology must follow from learning objectives and not just be sophisticated (and expensive) or 'varied' for its own sake.

A useful model and approach for designing leadership development programmes proposes seven stages:

1 Articulate strategic issues, objectives and competencies
2 Set objectives for development
3 Identify appropriate methods
4 Select providers and design the specific learning programme
5 Evaluate programme delivery and effectiveness
6 Integrate the leadership development programme with management and human resource systems
7 Assess the overall value of the programme, broad objectives and programme philosophy.

(Cacciope, 1998a)

The content and learning methods that deliver 'moments of truth' – a term coined by the SAS's Jan Carlzon (1987) to describe a moment during a human interaction when a critical judgement about service attitude is made – need to:

- Improve self-knowledge and self-worth
- Reshape perspectives and mindsets
- Allow the testing of behaviours and ideas through action learning
- Improve skills and relationships
- Provide leadership behaviour models
- Provide opportunities for participating in changing the direction and culture of the organization
- Provide a global focus
- Link up with other people relevant to participants' jobs

(Cacciope, 1998a)

Roya Ayman (2001) says that a comprehensive leadership development programme has the following characteristics:

- Ongoing (long-term) involvement
- Cognitive training – the facts about what works
- Insight through diverse experiences – reading case studies
- Opportunity for self-reflection and self-awareness through personal feedback
- Leadership experiences through the opportunity to lead

These characteristics, he suggests, reflect the Kolb learning cycle: concrete experience, reflective observation, abstract conceptualization and active experimentation (Kolb, 1985).

Leaders as teachers

Many organizations fail to appreciate their intrinsic leadership development resources: their own leaders. Many great leaders are great teachers, for example Jesus Christ, Mahatma Gandhi and Martin Luther King Jr, who transformed their followers into leaders themselves (Cacciope, 1998b). Management consultant Stephen Yearout concurs: 'Today's leaders need to be adept at making decision makers, not making decisions' (O'Shea, 2000). An example of such empowerment through teaching is the approach of Kevin Newman, who set up the very successful First Direct, the telephone banking company, ranked in *The Sunday Times* 2002 survey of the 100 best companies in the UK to work for.[126] When asked about how he takes important decisions, Newman said:

> **I avoid taking decisions as much as possible. As chief executive, my job is to teach other people how to make the decisions. (Reynolds, 2000)**

The idea of the leader as teacher has gained much popularity. Barnett and Tichy (2000) believe that top leaders need to take personal responsibility for developing other leaders in the organization and to energize them to be teachers. In fact this is one of the most important tasks facing a leader (Cohen and Tichy, 1997). CEOs identify having a manager as a role model early in their career as a major contribution to their development as a leader (Margerison and Kakabadse, 1984). And the most successful organizations – for example General Electric, Hewlett-Packard, the US Navy Seals, and Intel – use leaders to develop leaders by sharing their experience in creative and 'teachable' ways (Cohen and Tichy, 1997). This extends to the participation in leadership development programmes of CEOs themselves in companies like GE, PepsiCo and Shell (Cacciope, 1998b) and in the United Nations at its International Leadership Academy mentioned earlier.

The key prerequisites are 'leader–teachers' who themselves are credible and respected and who can articulate their own views well and facilitate group discussion, a learning environment that fits the leader–teacher's own style and personality, and clarity and organization of what is to be imparted (Russell, 1997). The University of Chicago's Graduate School of Business has a programme for leaders that recognizes the importance of the leader–teacher in building collaborative enterprises where information is co-created and shared.[127] Using senior and chief executives as leader–teachers has several benefits to themselves, their organizations and those participating in leadership development programmes: it reinforces new ideas and directions, the thinking behind them and the behaviours required; it enables them to test the reality of their ideas; and it provides frameworks for decisions by managers (Tichy, 1997). The leadership development programme run by The Leadership Trust for the board and senior managers of Britax International (mentioned earlier), in which the CEO and directors participated as 'teachers', is an example of a programme in which precisely these outcomes were achieved.

Concluding comments

In answer to our earlier question – can leadership be 'taught'? – the conclusion is 'yes', but only at the intellectual or cognitive level. *Knowing* what to do and how to do it is necessary but it is not sufficient. *Wanting to do it* entails 'it' making sense both cognitively and spiritually, and there are considerable emotional factors involved too. And *doing* it – using the cognitive and interpersonal skills of leadership – can be learned only by actually doing it, feedback, application and practice. We can *learn* leadership and we can develop it.

Further reading

Gareth Edwards, Paul K. Winter and Jan Bailey (2002), *Leadership in Management.* Ross-on-Wye: The Leadership Trust Foundation.

K. James and J. Burgoyne (2001), *Leadership Development: Best Practice Guide for Organisations.* London: Council for Excellence in Management and Leadership.

C. McCauley, R. Moxley and E. Van Velsor (1998), *The Center for Creative Leadership's Handbook of Leadership Development.* San Francisco, CA: Jossey-Bass.

Hilarie Owen (2001), *Unleashing Leaders: Developing Organizations for Leaders.* Chichester: John Wiley & Sons.

P. Ward (1997), *360-degree Feedback.* London: Institute of Personnel and Development (CIPD).

Peter L. Wright and David S. Taylor (1994), *Improving Leadership Performance: Interpersonal Skills for Effective Leadership.* London: Prentice Hall.

Discussion questions

1. Are leaders 'born' or 'made'?
2. How can the barriers to leadership development be removed or reduced?
3. Why is self-awareness the necessary basis for leadership development?
4. What events or processes have triggered or catalysed your own leadership development?

10 Rethinking the Leadership Challenge

With a strong wind, even turkeys can fly. But on winds of change, only eagles will soar.[128]

Overview

- In this chapter we consider some of the pressing issues of our time and analyse them in the light of the leadership model – vision and purpose, shared values, intelligent strategies, empowerment and influence, motivation and inspiration.
- First we consider trends and challenges concerning leadership and the public sector; leadership and quality and the quest for excellence; and leadership and organization, in particular the decline of bureaucracy, outsourcing, strategic alliances and the virtual organization.
- We next consider some of the major leadership challenges ahead – the 'big issues': globalization, terrorism, gender and cultural diversity, and technology and the knowledge economy.
- Mergers and acquisitions (M&As) pose a particular leadership challenge, especially in light of the high failure rate. We consider reasons for failure, the importance of leadership and culture in the success of M&As, and how assessment and audit methods and leadership development can help.
- Finally we discuss the only constant in today's world and what in fact is the focus of leadership (as distinct from 'management'): change. I emphasize that, while organizational change must be well managed, even more important is how well led it is, and we use the leadership model to discuss this.

The challenges ahead are at once demanding, scary, exciting and in significant measure as yet unknown. They concern the many political, economic, social, demographic, technological, legal and ecological pressures for change that are becoming evident. Commentators speak and write about today's turbulent times, in which uncertainty and chaos are now the norm. On the prolific prescriptions for the kind of leadership that is needed, Garten (2001: 112–113) says:

> **Leaders should be coaches, they should be nannies, they should be servants, leadership should flow from the bottom to the top. Most CEOs do not pay much attention to these sound-bite philosophies. In fact, most are much more pre-occupied with a few basics, which themselves are hard enough to maintain these days.**

Henry Mintzberg is not optimistic about the ability of top-level organizational leaders to rise to the challenge:

> **During the boom years, many chief executives became separated from the feeling and culture of their organisations, as evidenced by their extraordinarily high rates of pay compared with the rest of their staff. (Skapinker, 2001)**

And Skapinker (2001) says that the high rate of turnover among chief executives itself creates leadership problems: the average tenure of a British or American CEO is little more than four years – not enough time to understand the organization and its strengths and opportunities. Lord Taylor of Warwick, a British barrister and former MP for Cheltenham, portrays the pressures at the top in a Jamaican proverb: 'The higher up the mountain, the more the wind blows' (Taylor, 2000).

How might we know the likely challenges ahead? One way to identify trends, the futurist John Naisbitt suggests, is to count the column-inches on topics in the newspapers (Creelman, 2003b). Daniel Muzyka (2000) suggests that today's turbulence is being fuelled by several particular trends: accelerating human discovery, in particular advances in scientific knowledge; changing expectations of a growing population; globalization; and human mobility. In business organizations, according to another commentator, five powerful forces are changing the nature of effective leadership: the digital or knowledge economy, globalization, corporate restructuring, employee empowerment and the pace of change (Millar, 1996). To these trends must now be added terrorism. Cycles of economic recession, which the world as a whole last faced in 2001 and was exacerbated by the effects of the September 11 terrorist atrocities that year in the United States, also create new leadership challenges.

Among the 'big issues' confronting global leaders that Nixon (2002) identifies are:

- The ecological crisis and sustainability
- The increasing gap between rich and poor people and nations
- How to make diversity a source of delight, wisdom, creativity and wealth
- Providing all human beings – 80% of whom live in developing countries – with the opportunity for a healthy and fulfilling life
- Creating successful and sustainable workplaces
- The need for companies to be good corporate citizens as well as profitable
- Harnessing the power of transnational corporations for the common good
- The gap between strategy makers and those not involved
- Products, lifestyles and events that damage quality of life
- A yearning for meaning and balance in life, uniting body, mind, heart and spirit

The global balance of wealth and power is perhaps the key leadership challenge ahead for global leaders, for political and business leaders, and particularly for the wealthy nations. In the 26th Richard Dimbleby Lecture in December 2001, in the aftermath of 9/11, former US president Bill Clinton said:

> **I am absolutely confident that we have the knowledge and the means to make the twenty-first century the most peaceful, prosperous, interesting time in all human history. The question is whether we have the wisdom and the will. (Clinton, 2001)**

The wisdom and the will cannot but be reflected in the vision, sense of purpose, shared values and intelligent strategies, and the desire and ability to empower and inspire the peoples of this world – in other words, in a new kind of leadership.

On the business front organizational capability is receiving increasing attention today. Business opportunities arise and vanish more quickly than ever before (Muzyka, 2000). Prahalad (1999) predicts that business organizations will have to understand global forces, react quickly and innovate in their business models. Organizations are addressing several key areas of capability: building confidence (Fombrun, 1996), becoming flatter (Cannon, 2000) and boundary-less (Ohmae, 1990; Ashkenas et al., 1995), achieving capacity for change and flexibility that allows innovation (Kanter et al., 1992; Goldman et al., 1994; Drucker, 1995), and building learning organizations that are knowledge driven (Argyris and Schon, 1978; Senge, 1990; Wick, 1993). More flexible organization is necessary to exploit key opportunities for innovation while outsourcing and subcontracting more routine activities. The alternative is obsolescence.

One of the big issues is the diminishing loyalty and commitment of employees to employers. Reasons posited include increasing employee mobility, downsizing by organizations, and outsourcing of human resources:

> **There is a greater sense of self-determination, an expectation of rewards and recognition for efforts expended, and a growing appetite for a better life. These forces are interacting in complex ways to move and change markets, businesses and the economic fortunes of regions. (Muzyka, 2000)**

Employee compliance will no longer be enough – or even possible. Leaders will need to seek and gain employees' commitment. It is becoming harder to recruit and retain young, technologically competent workers who are attracted to vibrant workplaces (Greenhalgh, 2001a). Former chairman of ICI, Sir John Harvey-Jones, recognized this as long ago as 1988, when, quite radically at the time, he said:

> **In the future the organization will have to adapt to the needs of the individual, rather than expecting the individual to adapt to the needs of the organization. (Harvey-Jones, 1988: 254)**

Let us first consider the government and public sector. The public and private sectors need to be treated separately, says Jane Steele of the Public Management Foundation, because their predominant values and motives are different (PIU, 2001: 5.6). Public sector leaders (including those in the voluntary sector) focus largely on societal improvement through providing benefits to service users in international, national or local communities, whereas private sector leaders focus primarily on financial targets, company prosperity and shareholder value through meeting customer and market needs.

Leadership issues in the public sector

The British government report *Strengthening Leadership in the Public Sector* (PIU, 2001) recognizes the challenges of leadership in the public sector:

Britain's public services face unprecedented challenges at the start of the 21st century. The public sector must ensure that its leaders can meet these challenges.

These challenges are:

- Demands to modernize public services and orient them more closely to the needs and wishes of customers
- Higher expectations of the general public, who expect public services to keep up with the private sector
- Increased opportunities, and requirements, for partnerships, both across the public sector and with private and voluntary organizations
- Pressures to harness new technology and deliver government services electronically

The report recommends, among other things, a better balance between the freedom to lead and holding public service leaders accountable for their performance and more intensive leadership development. The report says, 'Above all, there is a need for leaders who are able to see the whole picture, and create a common vision with other agencies' (PIU, 2001: 2.11).

The May 2003 Scottish parliamentary elections provide an example of the leadership challenge for politicians. My review of the leaflets sent out by nine political parties reveals interesting findings. Only three parties (33%) communicated any clear vision of the future under them. Five (56%) communicated a mission for the party in Scotland. None communicated clearly any set of values, other than those implicit in their vision or missions. A wider range of strategies (25 different ones) was evident. Seven parties promoted similar strategies in each of the areas of education, health and crime. Three parties did likewise in the areas of the economy and rural communities. Some 20 strategies were unique to individual parties. Some conclusions and lessons may be drawn from this. Regional and local political party leadership needs to pay more attention particularly to identifying and communicating its vision and values and, in some cases, to providing a clear mission statement. And while most parties identified three key strategic areas, they also need to identify distinctive strategies for these areas. A party leadership that does not address the community's needs and wishes is not likely to be elected or effective if elected.

The UK's Cabinet Office sees the way forward for the public services as follows:

> **A vision for effective leadership...needs to recognise personal characteristics that are not based solely around magnetism or charisma but also around the ability to motivate and bring the best out of others; organisational skills that recognise the complexity of modern organisations and focus on defining and communicating mission and strategy rather than issuing commands; working well with other organisations to define and achieve common goals. (PIU, 2001: 3)**

The need for 'joined-up' government has become a pressing matter. The government report says:

> **Partnership working with other agencies requires skills which have not been demanded of the public sector before. It requires collaborative work with other services, including the voluntary and private sectors, in relationships which are built on mutual respect, not**

> **formal authority, and in groups where they do not share a common 'language', cultural references or history. Goals may need to be achieved in ways which are perceived to 'disadvantage' one organisation. (PIU, 2001: 3.21)**

In their study of collaboration and leadership in the public sector, Chris Huxham and Siv Vangen (2000) conceptualize leadership in collaborations as stemming from three leadership media – structures, processes and the participants. None of these is wholly within the control of the parties to collaboration:

> **structures and processes are often imposed upon or emerge from the activities of the collaboration, and many of the participants who influence and enact the collaborative agenda are not members of the collaborating organizations.**

It has been argued that many political processes, and peace processes in particular, are essentially driven by elites (Darby and MacGinty, 2000). A relatively small number of people take responsibility for making the final decisions and implementing policies. In other words, they use the directive or consultative styles. The question arises as to the commitment to those decisions and policies by their constituency members.

Do the private and public sectors require different kinds of leadership? This question is particularly topical in the UK in the light of the current debates about public sector reform and public–private partnership. Michael Fogden (2001) points out that the major change in the public sector concerns the growing awareness of the primacy of the customer. Public sector issues concern cost pressures, quality demands, delivery of services and relationship with the private sector, all of which place new demands on public sector managers. Such demands are further increased by drivers of change in the labour market and the workforce – technology, demography and education. For example, current British government policy is for one in every two of the eligible population to be in higher education by 2010. A better educated workforce means higher performance and greater challenge to management policies, decisions and actions. Having more women in the workforce has an impact on the workplace and work/life balance. Technology is changing both patterns of work and the physical location of work. And a more diverse and complex workforce leads to issues of mobility and insecurity, commitment and 'contractorization'. All of this produces more opportunities as well as more threats.

Public sector culture, according to Fogden, has been characterized by bureaucratic structures in which top-level managers are paid to 'manage', complicated internal procedures, and a paucity of performance information that in any case has gone only to top-level managers. The public sector has been centralized, inwardly focused, slow in decision making and risk averse.

The traditional management model in the public sector has been front-line managers as operational deliverers, middle managers as administrative supervisors and top-level managers as resource allocators. But this model in practice stifles initiative, fragments resources and capabilities, and discourages reform. Both 'management' and 'leadership' are needed to meet developing needs and to deliver the required results. Management is concerned with planning and budgeting, control, problem solving, and organizing and staffing. Management creates stability and order and delivers short-term results. Leadership, however, establishes direction, aligns people to it, and motivates and inspires them towards it. Leadership creates change and commitment and new approaches and improved services as a result.

Where does the public sector need to be going in the twenty-first century? Fogden identifies three development areas: structure, systems and culture. There need to be fewer rules and greater delegation, fewer managerial levels, and top-level managers who are paid not to manage but to lead. Procedures need to be designed to serve customer needs. Performance data are needed for critical success factors and should be more widely distributed. Public sector culture needs to be outward looking, empowering, open and frank, and supportive of fast decision making and risk taking.

A new focus on leadership in management, Fogden says, is needed: top-level managers as coaches, not 'kings'; middle managers in support roles rather than suppressors; and front-line managers as developers and sharers – as opportunity creators and opportunist innovators rather than merely operational deliverers – who are performance driven and capability builders. Middle managers have to become organizational strategists, business developers and people 'exploiters' in the most positive sense. Top-level managers need to become shapers of purpose, architects of processes and moulders of people – above all, inspiring leaders. They need to be credible, approachable and visible. The new management doctrine must be liberating rather than constraining. The organization is not just an economic entity; it is also a social institution. It is not an aggregation of activities and tasks; it is a set of roles and relationships. People are not 'replaceable parts'; they are key corporate assets.

One of the problems between the public and private sectors is the lack of empathy as a result of different management procedures and the different nature of the stakeholders. The public sector is characterized by a more complex stakeholder community than the private sector's, with implications for the kind of leadership required. And the 'dependency culture' in the public sector is shifting to an interdependency culture. 'Joined-up' thinking in government and public–private partnership are challenges yet to be met. Such partnership needs to extend to tapping the ideas and wisdom of *all* staff in the organization and indeed those of players in the private and third sectors too to create a greater synergy, for example local strategic partnerships involving local authorities. A greater emphasis needs to be placed on encouraging and recognizing emergent leaders in the organization. The organization needs to become a *learning organization.*

The challenges ahead for the European Union call for visionary leadership. Hamish McRae (2001) argues that, following the introduction of the euro currency, Europe needs a new 'Big Idea' to 'invoke pride … animate it … [and avoid] descending into petty squabbling' – a 'new sense of mission'. Examples might be, he suggests, taking the lead on the environment, creating a new welfare system, or helping Africa.

The increasing attention to leadership in local government has been reflected in new research studies to develop ways of assessing it. Alimo-Metcalfe and Alban-Metcalfe (2003a) developed their *Transformational Leadership Questionnaire* initially for this purpose and found significant strengths in local government in the areas of decisiveness, problem solving and empowerment. But they also found weaknesses in, among other areas, encouraging change, values concerning people such as individualized consideration and honesty, and the ability to inspire people. They also report the Audit Commission's finding that lack of effective leadership is a major obstacle to reform. Jean Hartley and Anna Morgan-Thomas (2003) report the development of a *Political Leadership Questionnaire* specifically to assess the development needs of elected councillors and to deepen understanding of the changing contexts, challenges and capabilities they have to confront.

Leadership and quality: the quest for excellence

The increasing emphasis on the management of change has spawned a variety of techniques: economic value added (EVA), business process re-engineering (BPR), the Balanced Scorecard, TQM, etc. But where they have not yielded the intended results, O'Toole (1995: xii) says, the missing element is *leadership*. According to Mohamed Zairi (1994), 'Leadership in the context of TQM is not about power, authority and control ... it is more about empowerment, recognition, coaching and developing others'. This is true, except for 'power': leadership is about *personal* power rather than position power.

Empowering others means creating a climate of freedom in the organization. Customers and clients now expect the quality standards of the products and services they buy formerly associated only with luxury goods (Greenhalgh, 2001a). 'Total quality' requires quality built in at every point, in the work carried out by every employee, in the supply chain. Part of total quality is the customer transaction. Effective customer transactions, Rob Lebow says, require a freedom-based workplace rather than a control-based one, in which shared values is the 'glue' (Creelman, 2003b). Lebow quotes Jack Welch as saying: 'If you're facing me, then your rear-end is facing our customer.' 'In a control-based environment,' Lebow says, 'the front-line worker tells the customer, "I'd love to do that for you, but our policies don't allow it".' Effective leadership entails empowering people in a freedom-based work environment in which key values are shared.

Management is about achieving efficiency and stability; leadership is about increasing effectiveness through change and transformation. Christopher Hart and Leonard Schlesinger (1991) on TQM say:

> **Successful TQM implementation calls for a cultural shift in the organization with a change in values...the way people work together, and the way people feel about participation and involvement.**

TQM is not the preserve of only commercial business organizations. Geoff Berry (1997) describes how it is a viable paradigm for developing a quality culture in schools too, where leadership is the critical factor in handling cultural, political and organizational issues. J. Paine et al. (1992: 40) rename TQM as 'TQE' (Total Quality Education). The application of TQM in educational settings raises the question of what we mean by 'quality'. Berry concludes from his analysis that quality in education can be defined as commonly accepted standards or as fitness for purpose (as judged by users).

A study by Benjamin Schneider and David Bowen (1985) demonstrated unequivocally that how bank employees in the United States felt about the way they were managed was related to how customers felt about the way they were treated. John Seddon (1991) reports a British study of customer satisfaction and staff attitudes in a service organization. The study found that customers were more satisfied when staff said they understood the company's mission, they felt empowered, they felt they had good inter-unit relations, and their manager was open to suggestions for change. Similar findings in 1998 resulted from a study in the US retail store Sears Corporation (Rucci et al., 1998), and a study of restaurants in the UK (Georgiades and Macdonnell, 1998).

Using a participative leadership style is a feature of empowering people. A positive relationship has been established between participation, satisfaction, motivation, quality, productivity and performance (Hollander and Offerman, 1990; Bartol and Martin, 1991). Organizational climate is associated with quality management practices (Kuei et al., 1997). Work-unit climate is defined by Burke and Litwin as 'the collective current impressions, expectations and feelings that members of local work units have that in turn affect their relations with their boss, with one another, and with other units' (Burke and Litwin, 1989). Cannon (2004) discovered in the European division of a global financial services firm that leadership has a significant impact on work-unit climate, twice as great as that on corporate culture.

The need for leadership and vision in quality management has been argued by both W. Edwards Deming (1986) and J.M. Juran (1988, 1994). Despite the widespread acceptance that leadership is the driving force for the successful implementation of TQM, Wen-Hsien Chen (1997) found a lack of awareness among top executives in local firms of how to exercise leadership in TQM when he investigated American, Japanese and local firms in Taiwan. In a study of public sector construction projects, Robin Holt and David Rowe (2000) argue the need for 'critical leadership' in achieving total quality. Critical leadership entails self-assessment of both technique and attitude to promote continuous learning. 'Attitude' includes responding to client or customer input. Holt and Rowe say, 'For critical leaders, authority is a by-product of activity, not its legitimization.'

The importance of leadership is recognized in the well-known Excellence Model promoted by the European Foundation for Quality Management (EFQM) and the British Quality Foundation (BQF) (EFQM, 2000).

Leadership is also important in other quality concepts such as those of Deming (1986) and others (Dale, 1994; Oakland, 1999) and in quality programmes such as the Malcolm Baldridge National Quality Award. Zairi reports the analysis by George Easton (1993) of the applications for the Malcolm Baldridge National Quality Award (MBNQA) in 1993 and winners of that award, the European Quality Award and the Australian Quality Award (Zairi, 1994). In the area of leadership, Easton found that senior management had developed a vision and a set of values to create a quality culture in their organization, reflected by an obsession with the customer – both external and internal – and continuous improvement.

One reason for the failure of so many dotcom companies, Internet guru Patricia Seybold says, is their lack of vision in how they can competitively deliver market needs (Maruca, 2000). Deetz et al. (2000: 53) say that 'A strong long-term vision gives cohesion to the work of an organization.' Without it, initiatives like TQM, BPR, quality circles, benchmarking, etc., become ineffectual fads. Co-founder of Sony, Akio Morita, envisioned high quality as connoted by the Sony brand name. Marks & Spencer's vision is: 'The standard against which all others are measured.'[129]

By the mid 1990s there was a marked shift in strategic thinking away from a preoccupation with the attractiveness of products and services towards the competencies and capabilities that underpin them, for example visionary transformational leadership, according to Sonny Nwanko and Bill Richardson (1996). They say:

> Many UK-based visionary leaders have used the concept of quality to improve their market-place performances. Visionaries have [grown] their organizations' competitive strengths through using quality as an underpinner of...product-market developments.

Zairi (1994) concludes that the leadership aspects of quality are:

- Setting the vision and strategy
- Communicating the vision and gaining corporate commitment to it
- Developing a process-based culture (focusing on processes and teamwork rather than the individual)
- Recognizing people as assets through empowerment, participation in decision making, encouraging creativity and innovation, and motivation through reward and recognition

Quality improvement requires organization-wide change. Change requires good management, but above all it requires effective leadership (Gill, 2003). This is the key challenge in the quest for quality.

Leadership and organization

Innovation and change require structural flexibility, but with the stability to deliver products and services on time. Tom Peters (1992) calls this 'permanent flexibility'. It is well established in the management literature that structure must serve strategy, not the converse.

An example of how structures have changed is short-term, project-focused teams superseding permanent functional, departmental or cross-departmental teams. They come together for a specific purpose and, on achieving it, disband. The consequences are work roles that frequently change and leadership roles that are also temporary and varied. Networks of power and influence and 'horizontal' relationships are replacing the formal hierarchies we find in bureaucratic organizations (Gill et al., 1998). New organizational cultures are supplanting bureaucratic cultures that are characterized by hierarchy, boundaries, internal orientation, control and the need to avoid mistakes (Hastings, 1993). And organizations are becoming increasingly culturally diverse and dispersed geographically: they are increasingly becoming 'virtual'.

The (partial) demise of bureaucracy and the rise of 'adhocracy'

Violina Rindova and William Starbuck (1997) point out that bureaucracy, contrary to the views of Max Weber (Gerth and Mills, 1946) and Warren Bennis (1966: 3), was not an invention of the Industrial Revolution but a system already operating as long ago as *c.*1100 BC – in government in ancient China and prescribed in a book, *The Officials of Chou* (Biot, 1851; Gingell, 1852). The system provided rules to define departments, allocate responsibilities, specify coordination, define standard operating procedures and exceptions to them, and audit officials' performance.

Robert Sanders (1997) defines bureaucracy as 'administration over a contiguous area or organization, using written regulations and centralized procedures'. Bureaucratic organizations are notoriously slow to respond to environmental change and unable to learn from mistakes. Leadership is almost irrelevant in bureaucracies:

standard operating procedures make the decisions. Bureaucracies, Max Weber said, speaking at a meeting of an academic political club (Verein für Sozialpolitik) in 1909, are frightening for their capacity to dehumanize people – constituting a 'parcelling-out of the soul' (Kariel, 1964: 152). They trap individuals in an 'iron cage' of rule-based, rational control. They stifle individual initiative and cause individual powerlessness and alienation. An example of a response to such bureaucracy was the uprising and near-strike by school teachers over excessive 'red tape' in the education system in the UK in 1998. Goffee and Jones (2000) comment:

> **The tragic novels of Franz Kafka bear stark testimony to the debilitating effects of bureaucracy. Even more chilling was the testimony of Hitler's lieutenant Adolf Eichmann that 'I was just a good bureaucrat'.**

Weber's antidote to bureaucracy, charismatic leadership, they say, has had its notable failures, for example Hitler, Stalin and Mao Zedung. This raises the question of whether there is any relationship between charismatic leadership and bureaucratic followership. Weber was concerned about the potential tyranny of bureaucracy less in business organizations than in the state – for example, the 'psychopathic national socialism of Nazi Germany, communism of Stalinist Soviet rule and fascism of Imperial Japan' (*The Economist*, 2004).

The development of our thinking about leadership has paralleled the development of organizational theory. The old paradigm of the bureaucratic organization can be explained by the model of laissez-faire and transactional leadership, and the new post-bureaucratic organizational paradigm reflects the currently popular model of transformational leadership (Gill et al., 1998). The 'new leadership' now means:

> **scenario thinking, providing a compelling vision of the possible future, showing the way through rational strategies, truly empowering people through individualized consideration and intellectual stimulation, developing their competencies, providing appropriate resources and opportunity, and inspiring people to want to do the things that enable the organization attain its vision.**

Handy (1995) says, 'It is no longer the manager and the managed … . [It is now] a different relationship, one built more on trust and mutual respect than on control.' Peter Senge (1993: 340) says:

> **In a learning organization, leaders are designers, stewards and teachers. They are responsible for building organizations where people continually expand their capabilities to understand complexity, clarify vision, and improve shared mental models.**

'The post-heroic leader,' in the words of James Eicher (2000), 'operates in … an influencing relationship where there is little direct control.' The leader's role is to empower followers by encouraging participation and facilitating continuous learning and development. This idea has been taken further in Robert Greenleaf's concept of 'servant leadership' (see Chapter 2), in which the leader's sole purpose is to serve the needs of others and to help them develop emotionally and spiritually.

The traditional organization structure is becoming inverted, with customers at the top and 'top' management at the bottom, playing a supportive role (e.g. John Timpson's 'Upside-Down Management' model applied in his key-cutting and shoe-repair firm

(Timpson, 2002)). Organizations are moving away from bureaucracy to 'adhocracy', with flatter and project-based structures. 'Bureaucracy is no more appropriate to the information age than serfdom was to the industrial era,' say Gifford Pinchot and Elizabeth Pinchot (1994). The need for organization, however, remains. In fact the need for organization will become even greater, according to Drucker (1997):

> **Precisely because there will be so much ambiguity, so much flexibility, so many variations, far more clarity will be needed in respect to mission, values and strategy, in balancing long-range and short-range goals, in defining results. Above all, absolute clarity will be needed as to who ultimately makes the decisions and who is in command in a crisis.**

Flattening organizations through 'delayering' entails the need for greater empowerment owing to a wider span of control. However, flatter organizations may make individualized consideration more difficult. Ways of maintaining or strengthening this – greater empowerment combined with sufficient individualized consideration – need to be addressed.

The old management paradigm is giving way to a new leadership paradigm. In the words of Kreitner and Kinicki (1997):

> **Traditional organizations and the associated organizational behaviors they created have outlived their usefulness. Management must seriously question and challenge the ways of thinking that worked in the past...**
>
> **For example, the old management paradigm of planning, organizing and control might be replaced with one of vision, values and empowerment.**

The 'new organization' that is emerging is characterized by several features. We are seeing more internal and external networking, particularly through IT, as well as partnerships between the public and private sectors and between customers and suppliers. There is an increasing emphasis on 'knowledge workers', in whom 'headwork' will count for more than 'handwork'. We are witnessing the liberalization and empowerment of people at work. Self-managed project teams in 'permanently flexible' organizations that take an organic or matrix form are increasingly evident. And it will be the 'learning organization' that survives by collectively learning and adapting to new demands. Not least interesting is the development of the 'virtual organization'.

The ability to use language persuasively, says Conger (1999), is ever more important today as the spread of electronic communication and the increase in decision-making power of middle-level managers result from greater pressures to serve customers, solve problems and respond to opportunities. Electronic communication means that managers and subordinates have access to the same information and therefore subordinates can assess their managers' ideas and decisions more critically. Managers therefore need to be more persuasive in explaining and justifying them.

However, technological innovation, with its promise of 'liberating' people and enhancing customer service, has led, according to some commentators such as Darcus Howe, to the 'new enslavement', as in 'barn-like' call centres, with their highly routinized and controlled working practices reminiscent of the worst examples of Frederick

W. Taylor's 'scientific management' philosophy.[130] Howe's assessment of the Internet bank Egg, for example, is that the Egg culture is 'hollow and shallow', with individuality overridden by 'Egg [corporate] personality'. Leadership there, he says, in effect merely comprises providing incentives and rewards, creating opportunities for having fun, propaganda and giving 'pep talks'.

We have not seen the end of bureaucracy, as is evident in the dotcom companies that have emerged in recent years. According to one advertising agency, they have been adopting traditional business practices, including bureaucracy. In the words of Andy Law of St Luke's:

> **[Dotcoms] are still set up along the model established by Henry Ford. Dot coms are terribly traditional...look at the mind-numbing casualness with which dot coms treat their human resources. They're owned and managed conventionally. People don't count. (Law and Coutu, 2000)**

Outsourcing

Greater outsourcing is one of the trends identified in a study by the CIPD-sponsored Tomorrow Project on the future workplace (Moynagh and Worsley, 2001a, b). The implications for leadership are more remote supervision, more indirect control (targets, performance measurement and financial incentives replacing rules, observation and command), and greater self-management of work and careers. Likewise for the trend towards virtual organizations, particularly those on a global scale. But Peter Nolan (2001) says:

> **The new economy may yet succeed in transforming the future world of work, but all the signs today are pointing to the emergence of an hourglass economy.**

In addition to more outsourced, specialized and autonomous workers, Nolan says, will be a growth in 'low-paid, routine and unglamorous jobs', resulting in an adverse impact on national productivity, work life balance, the quality of business strategies and relationships at work.

The need for rapid response and innovation has created a culture of 'intrapreneurship' in many companies. Innovation has become the province of *all* employees, not just those in the product development department. Encouraging intrapreneurship is an example of empowerment. Cannon (2000) adds further examples of capability building: networking, IT development, increased customer and stakeholder orientation, emphasizing value added and quality, emphasizing shared values, and becoming more trust based.

Bennis (1999a) suggests that a shrinking world with increasing technological and political complexity offers fewer and fewer arenas for effective top-down leadership: the key to real change is empowered teams. Larry Hirschhorn (1997) suggests that, in post-industrial society:

> **upward identification [with the leader] is no longer sufficient. Because of the wider technological and economic changes enterprises now face and manage, bosses can no longer project the certainty, confidence and power that once facilitated employees' identification with them.**

Strategic alliances and collaboration

Organizations increasingly do not compete alone with others. They are forming either networks based on value-chain partnerships that compete with others (Greenhalgh, 2001a) or more formal strategic alliances – the contractual pooling of resources to achieve a long-term strategic purpose that is not possible for a single organization (Zuckerman and Kaluzny, 1991). The high rate of failure with strategic alliances – more than half (Ellis, 1996; Segill, 1998) – has led to examination of the associated leadership issues. It is a question of power and authority, in particular the compatibility of CEOs (Bucklin and Sengupta, 1993) and the other senior executives (Zajac and D'Aunno, 1994). According to Leonard Greenhalgh (2001b), the issues concern power, organizational politics and networking. One example of the difficulties in cross-cultural strategic alliances is the difference across national cultures in negotiation styles: 'Chinese managers value relationships in business, while American managers do not' (Sanches, 2001).

William Judge and Joel Ryman (2001) argue that the key consideration for successful strategic alliances is the mutual ability to collaborate from a distance, focus on creating customer value above all else, and experiment with and implement innovative ways of competing in the industry with a partner. Collaborating from a distance is particularly difficult. It requires focusing on *mutual* benefits rather than either partner's, shared decision making, agreement on what constitutes 'success', and mutual trust – 'the glue that binds people together in relationships' (Peters, 1997: 142). In other words, successful strategic alliances are founded on shared vision, values and strategies.

The virtual organization

Technological advances in computing and telecommunications have enabled people to work together at geographically distant locations and across time zones. The physical workplace has been giving way in many industries to a 'virtual' one, removing physical and geographical boundaries. Many people are members of what are now called *virtual teams,* whose existence is partly a consequence of globalization, the rise of e-commerce and the increase in mergers and acquisitions (Lipnack and Stamps, 1997; Boudreau et al., 1998; Hughes et al., 1999). And this development has been fuelled by information communication technologies or computer-mediated communication technologies such as the World Wide Web, e-mail and video conferencing. Interacting in a virtual organization and interacting in physical proximity differ in important ways (Joinson, 1998). Research on the relationship between virtual teams or virtual organizations and leadership is still in its infancy.

John Sosik and colleagues, for example, report that transformational leadership in virtual groups using group decision support systems is positively associated with creativity, effort, performance and satisfaction (Sosik, 1997; Sosik et al., 1997) and with group (collective) self-efficacy (Sosik et al., 1998). However, Crystal Hoyt and Jim Blascovich (2003), in a study of leadership in proximal face-to-face and in virtual settings, found that group members were more satisfied with their leader when interacting face to face than when using 'immersive' virtual environment technology or intercom, though there were no differences between face-to-face and virtual settings in group performance or group cohesiveness.

'Tele-leadership' (Shamir and Ben-Arie,1999) – the leadership of virtual teams – is a new challenge. Many new questions arise concerning the leadership of virtual teams and the creation and maintenance of trust and performance at a geographical distance and with time separation using only or mostly telecommunication (Avolio et al., 2001). Avolio et al. (2001) suggest that virtual teams with transformational leaders (rather than transactional or laissez-faire leaders) are more likely to identify a common purpose and shared mental models of the challenges and opportunities facing them. Penny Horner-Long and Richard Shoenberg (2002) found that leaders in e-businesses tend to be more entrepreneurial and risk taking and less conservative than traditional leaders, who are more collaborative.

The key issues for leadership in the virtual organization appear to be concerned with:

- Human relationships as a result of the lack of face-to-face interaction, for example building and maintaining trust (Avolio and Kahai, 2000; Yukl, 2002; Jarvenpaa and Tanriverdi, 2003; Pauleen, 2003; Zaccaro and Bader, 2003; Zigurs, 2003)
- Knowing how to work together in the virtual setting (Zigurs, 2003; Avolio and Kahai, 2003)
- A need for greater flexibility and empowerment (Cascio and Shurygailo, 2003)

Confronting the big issues

Globalization

Globalization is the integration of economic activity across national or regional boundaries (Middleton and Gorzynski, 2002: 30). Purely domestic business of any importance is now rare: businesses have become global, 'drawing on supply chains that transcend national boundaries and serve customers worldwide' (Greenhalgh, 2001a). We are living in a 'global village' in which there are instant global communication, rapid international travel, and freer economic and social barriers to business and financial markets. Individuals too are more mobile internationally. Globalization is a convergence among nations and companies towards a common way of doing things. In the economic arena, globalization has provided huge increases in the power, control and profits of multinational companies.

Baroness Helena Kennedy has said, 'Globalisation has the power and the desire to embrace us all, but it ... will never fulfil the deeper needs of people' (Willan, 2002).[131] A globalized, homogenized culture, she says, cannot provide the necessary sense of identity: cultural pluralism within nations and cultural dialogue across nations are more urgent than ever before. This is the basis of the global compact launched in 2000 by Kofi Annan, secretary-general of the United Nations.

Multinational and global firms cross national boundaries and seek competitive advantage without necessarily considering the economic welfare of countries they touch. In some cases they exceed the economic strength of those nations. Such firms move in and out of nations in pursuit of their own long-term survival and prosperity. Martyn Hobrough (2001) suggests that competition for inward investment leads to the shaping of economic and industrial policies by governments as part of their foreign policies to attract inward investment:

Thus we see the power of international firms to shape and influence international relations. And we can understand the fear with which many, especially developing and transitioning economies, view this power.

According to a survey of 1,161 chief executives across the globe by Pricewaterhouse Coopers in 2001, the vast majority believe that globalization will bring about positive economic change and is a catalyst for social change.[132] However, about one-third believe it will widen the gap between developed and developing countries. Yet nearly half of the CEOs polled believe that the anti-globalization movement does not 'pose a genuine threat' to global business.

The World Economic Forum (WEF) poll of 25,000 people in 25 nations conducted at the same time (last quarter of 2001) yielded a mix of opinions on this, according to Daniel Sternoff.[133] According to the poll, most people believe globalization will raise personal living standards but will also increase world poverty and damage the environment. The most optimistic views were expressed by people in North America, northern Europe (in particular the Dutch), and the developing nations in Asia. Turkey was the most pessimistic. The conclusion from the poll was that more effective global integration can be achieved by tackling poverty, access to world markets and growth in jobs.

Jeremy Warner (2002) says, 'Third World poverty has risen beyond being the concern only of bleeding heart liberals to the top of everyone's political agenda ... 80% of the world's wealth is owned by 20% of its population'. He says, 'a real determination to do something about ... [this] morally indefensible divide may be one of the lasting legacies of those terrible events [on 11 September 2001]'. Understanding of the wealth divide is one reason, and the second is less altruistic: 'the growing maturity of Western economies and the need to create new markets onto which global capitalism can expand' by creating a prosperous middle class throughout the world.

While countering the World Economic Forum, the World Social Forum is trying to shed its image of being 'anti' the WEF and globalization and replace it with its vision of 'global democracy, equality, diversity, justice and quality of life'.[134] Its criticism is levelled particularly strongly against the World Trade Organization, which is, it says, 'a protectionist vehicle' against free trade and 'for the rich countries'.

Whether the threat from the anti-globalization movement is real remains to be seen. But clearly dismissing such a threat is a high-risk strategy, which proper scenario planning needs to counter. Effective leadership is characterized not only by responsiveness to threats and opportunities but also by proactivity – anticipating and acting on them.

Globalization makes obvious sense intellectually, according to Micklethwait and Wooldridge (2000). It creates more efficient use of resources. But, they say, its advocates have failed to recognize social and cultural issues – in particular, the adverse outcome for those who lose out on the one hand, and the advantage it brings of freedom and opportunity on the other. Globalization is not just an economic or business phenomenon; it is political, social and cultural. Adair Turner says:

Free markets are not in themselves sufficient to achieve prosperity, nor is the achievement of prosperity sufficient in itself to resolve all social or environmental challenges.[135] (Willan, 2002)

Hanan Ashrawi, the Palestinian politician and human rights campaigner, comments that, while political power carries responsibility and a moral imperative, economic power, which is still seeking ethical legitimacy, can sometimes be at odds with social justice (Willan, 2002).[136]

Globalization creates new leadership challenges for a company: ethics, cultural differences, and communicating with a geographically dispersed workforce (Lansdell, 2002: 30). Issues include the treatment of workers in low-wage economies and the use of tropical hardwoods from non-sustainable forests. Companies' visions and values therefore have had to address the issue of social responsibility. The importance of shared values was discussed in Chapter 5. Even in award-winning firms, corporate social responsibility audits have revealed discrepancies between corporate and employee values (Waddock and Smith, 2000). Globalization brings increasing diversity in the workforce and in our communities, and leadership will face the challenge of reconciling different traditions and habits, often in the context of prejudice, discomfort and fear.

The leadership challenge facing Western democracies and trading blocs is summarized by Helena Kennedy:

> **As the world shrinks and homogenises and as authentic cultures consequently see their identities threatened, the deep and long-evolving currents which travel subsurface and that create the diversity of the world's peoples need to be more profoundly understood... . It is understanding of difference that roots the surface sway of political and economic relationship in cultural meaning and respect.[137] (Willan, 2002)**

Global leadership is leadership across borders and cultures. Institutionalized attempts at providing global leadership started with the League of Nations at the end of the First World War. It failed, the UN's Adel Safty (1999) says, because it 'became a congress of European powers determined to defend colonialism at all costs against the rising tide of self-determination and the challenge of communism [and] turned a blind eye to the danger of fascism'. The League of Nations' successor was the United Nations at the end of the Second World War. In line with our model of leadership, its mission was global leadership based on universally shared values – peace, democracy and development. Despite constraints on resources, the UN's global leadership achievements have been considerable.

Safty believes that globalization, however, whatever its merits, has overlooked universally shared values and that economic and social benefits to society at large have been incidental rather than a primary purpose of business. He says that, while globalization has not caused the poverty gap between rich and poor nations, 'it has created the environment in which a market-driven survival-of-the-fittest attitude had undercut political leadership'. Global leadership will require not only vision, empowerment and the ability to inspire commitment, but also a clear sense of shared values, perhaps the most difficult of all to achieve. As Safty says:

> **When we talk about the globalization of business, we will also talk about the globalization of human concerns...management that is driven by economic interests must grow into leadership that is driven by human interests.**

Kets de Vries and Florent-Treacy (1999) suggest that leaders in global organizations need to have well-developed skills and attitudes in several areas. On the cognitive dimension, they say, they need to have 'a strategic awareness of, and a deep interest in, the socio-economic and political scene of the countries in which they operate'. They also need to be 'masters of disorganization', displaying intellectual curiosity, creativity and innovation. On the emotional dimension, they need to have resilience – a positive outlook and persistence – and emotional intelligence, as well as tolerance of diversity, cross-cultural empathy and tolerance of frustration and uncertainty. On the behavioural dimension, they need to have relational skills – verbal and non-verbal communication skills, teambuilding skills and an 'authoritative' rather than authoritarian style of leadership, which entails 'distributed' leadership.

Effective leaders in global organizations, Kets de Vries and Florent-Treacy (1999) say, create 'authentizotic' organizations (from the Greek words *authenteekos* – authentic – and *zoteekos* – 'vital to life'). These are organizations that are rational and therefore worthy of trust and reliance and in which their vision, mission, culture and structure have a 'compelling connective quality' for their employees. Their leaders have communicated the *how* and the *why*. They are also organizations in which people are 'invigorated' by their work. Kets de Vries and Florent-Treacy (1999) quote Franklin Delano Roosevelt:

> **We have learned that we cannot live alone, at peace; that our well-being is dependent on the well-being of other nations, far away. We have learned that we must live as men, not as ostriches, nor as dogs in the manger. We have learned to be citizens of the world, members of the human community.**

This could be, they say, the 'epithet for today's successful global organizations and their employees'. The challenges are immense, but using the model of leadership in this book can provide a concept and a practical framework for action.

Terrorism

The infamous events of 11 September 2001 in the United States (known as '9/11') brought a new leadership challenge. Terrorists from the Al-Qaeda movement headed by Osama bin Laden attacked what it saw as the very heart of Western capitalism, civilization and democracy and punished the United States for its support of Israel in its conflict with the Palestinians, its presence and interests in Saudi Arabia and the Middle East, and its alleged exploitation of the developing world and 'imperialist' global agenda.

Terrorism has emerged as a major challenge to world order. There is no single, universally accepted definition of terrorism. According to the FBI, it is 'the unlawful use of force or violence against persons or property to intimidate or coerce a government, the civilian population, or any segment thereof, in furtherance of political or social objectives'.[138] The US Department of Defense adds religious and ideological objectives. Intimidation includes the generation of a climate of fear among innocent people.

One explanation for the rise of terrorism is a global lack of effective leadership. Rohan Gunaratna (2003) of the Centre for the Study of Terrorism and Political Violence at St Andrews University in the UK believes, based on his interviews with terrorist groups around the world, that 'it is not poverty or lack of literacy that drives people to join terrorist groups, but ideology'. He reports:

> **Most of those I met had tried for years to gain their rights through democratic means but had failed miserably... . Very few leaders [in governments and international organizations] took any notice of these non-violent groups and dismissed protesters as a nuisance. But they did take note of [terrorists].**

Terrorism results from dissatisfaction with a political or social system or policy and an inability to change it through mainstream or non-violent means. It is less the consequence of poverty or illiteracy than of the failure of democracy and a failure of leadership: it is, Gunaratna says, the consequence of being ignored.

The solution, therefore, may lie therein, at least in part.

What kind of global leadership is needed to remove terrorism and the causes of terrorism? This is one of the most difficult questions of our time. The issue of Western values vis-à-vis Islam appears to be insoluble without mutual understanding and tolerance. The only glimmer of light may lie in finding common ground in values – highly desirable though seemingly a remote possibility. The issue of Western – in particular American – domination or exploitation of Islamic nations appears more open to resolution. The path in this case may lie in the West and Muslim nations determining a shared vision and implementing agreed strategies for the latter's economic development where they are alleged to have been disadvantaged or exploited by the West. The key to resolving the terrorism issue must lie in achieving a shared global vision for the world, common values and agreed strategies for dealing with its causes rather than its consequences.

Gender and cultural diversity

Much has been written of the leadership traits associated with gender, even of the twenty-first century as the 'age of the female leader'. Indeed Alimo-Metcalfe and Alban-Metcalfe (2003b) found that female leaders are rated significantly higher than male bosses on 10 out of 14 leadership dimensions.

Yet women at present are under-represented demographically in senior management and leadership positions in organizations. Alimo-Metcalfe (1998) suggests that male bias, both in assessment, selection and promotion and in research studies, has reinforced stereotypes about women. Common conceptions of why women fail to reach through the 'glass ceiling' are lack of management experience (a 'vicious circle'), lack of career opportunities, gender differences in linguistic style and socialization, gender-based stereotypes, the 'old boy' network at the top of organizational hierarchies, and tokenism. But Judith Oakley (2000) suggests other explanations, such as a mismatch between leadership styles demonstrated and those required and the possibility that the most talented women in business prefer entrepreneurial careers rather than corporate life.

It has often been claimed that women can bring certain 'female' qualities to the leadership role, namely those that characterize relationship building (Grant, 1992). It is more often than not assumed that men and women differ in their leadership styles and behaviour. In particular, female leaders are perceived as more empowering, nurturing and participative than male leaders, who are seen as more controlling, assertive and directive. The reason for this, Judy Rosener (1990) suggests, is that women have been socialized to manage relationships in the home and different career paths. Indeed a former president of the American Psychological Association, Norine Johnson (2001), says:

'Two of the traditional characteristics of women's leadership are consensus building and inclusiveness.' For example, female leaders have been found to use the participative style of leadership and individualized consideration, to be more caring and nurturing, than male leaders (Alimo-Metcalfe, 1998). And brain researchers Raquel Gur and Ruben Gur found that women may be more sensitive than men to emotional cues and verbal nuances (Schrage, 1999).

In general, however, gender studies of leadership tend to show mixed and sometimes contradictory results. Jan Grant (1988) concluded from a literature review that there are no significant differences between male and female leaders, probably because women identify with 'male' characteristics as they take on leadership roles. In Singapore, Van Kit Meng (2002) found that female leaders display stereotypically 'male' characteristics even more than male leaders do. Robert Hooijberg and Nancy DiTomaso (1996) found that male and female leaders behave very similarly in their leadership roles. And Marloes Van Engen et al. (2001) found no gender differences in leadership behaviour in Dutch department stores.

Bass (1990a: 11–18), however, found that women are less likely to practise management-by-exception (transactional leadership) than men. And Cary Cooper suggests that men tend to use punishment (a threat perceived in excessive management-by-exception) and women tend to use reward or reinforcement (Morris, 1992: 271). On the other hand, B.R. Envik (1998) found that female entrepreneurial leaders tend to more controlling behaviour than their male counterparts.

Oshagbemi and Gill (2003) found that female leaders delegate less than male leaders and display less inspirational motivation than males, but that male and female leaders did not differ significantly in other leadership styles (directive, consultative and participative), other dimensions of transformational leadership, or in laissez-faire or transactional leadership. Yet a study by Sarah Burke and Karen Collins (2001) found that female accountants are more likely than their male counterparts to see themselves as transformational in their leadership behaviour. And Alice Eagly and Mary Johannesen-Schmidt (2001) found that female leaders are more likely to be more transformational and to use contingent reward more than male leaders. Several studies have suggested that male and female leaders tend to behave differently but are equally effective.

Gender may be a consideration in designing leadership development programmes. According to Liz Cook and Brian Rothwell (2000), men may be more action oriented than women and bond through tasks, whereas women are more relationship oriented and bond through conversation. Kay Payne et al. (1997) found in their review of the literature that men and women generally do differ in leadership style along stereotypical lines when untrained but do not differ when they have been trained. And another study found that women report less positive affective reactions after leadership development programmes than men (Klein et al., 1992). Edward Klein et al. (1996) suggest that leadership development programmes for women may need to have a 'gender-balanced' learning environment and include not only traditionally 'male' activities but instead a range of activities.

Some of the largest and most successful firms around the world – General Motors, Exxon, General Electric and IBM in the United States, Bayer in Germany, and ICI, Shell, GEC and Glaxo in the UK – at one time favoured 'organization man' in preference to individualistic and entrepreneurial leaders (METO, 2000: 23). Speakers at the

2001 National Conference of the UK's Chartered Institute of Personnel and Development, however, agreed that only an end to 'executive cloning', which suppresses diversity and fails to recognize the talents of women, can provide the leaders with the 'kindness, courage and energy' that the UK needs.

Members of minority ethnic groups, like women, are demographically underrepresented in senior management. Yet formerly homogeneous workforces and customers have become heterogeneous (Greenhalgh, 2001a). In responding to this issue, 'political correctness' may cause more problems than it prevents. For example, the Center for Creative Leadership (2001) in the United States reports how its single-audience programme – for black African Americans – avoids the positively distorted feedback that formerly came from Caucasian participants because of the latter's fear of appearing racist if they were honest.

The leadership model described in this book takes no account of gender, race, ethnic origin, religion, sexual preference or any other aspect of 'diversity'. The practical issue is how to overcome diversity barriers and create the opportunities for more people who are competent and want to take on a leadership role, regardless of gender or other irrelevant characteristics that are the cause of unfair, unethical or illegal discrimination. This itself is a leadership challenge.

Leadership, technology and the knowledge economy

Today's leaders cannot know everything: they often have to lead people who know more than they do (Cockburn, 2000). 'Human capital' has become a competitive battleground with the rising importance of employees as producers and users of information and knowledge that enables organizations to compete (Drucker, 1995). David Potter (1999) says that:

> **We are in the relatively early phases of a major economic revolution. This revolution is based around the concept of a post-industrial era where making things is increasingly automated and routine, creating things is difficult and value therefore derives from creation and from the intellectual capital or knowledge base of the firm or nation.**

What is the 'knowledge' in the knowledge economy and the knowledge worker? Peter Drucker points out that knowledge is not data – objective facts presented without context or judgement. Nor, he says, is it information – 'data endowed with relevance and purpose', what Laura Empson (1999) calls raw data put into a context to aid analysis and understanding. A knowledge worker is not somebody who merely handles or processes data or information. Knowledge is information that is used to make comparisons, assess consequences, establish relationships and engage in a dialogue. Knowledge is 'information that comes laden with experience, judgement, intuition and values' (Empson, 1999).

The economy, at least in parts of the Western world, is more and more dependent on services rather than production, and it is people rather than machines who are the key assets. Knowledge-based companies increasingly are the key to economic success (Cleveland, 1985). This point is emphasized in the following comment by an executive quoted by Muzyka (2000):

> **I wouldn't value a company strongly on what it sells today or even the growth potential in these products, but what future options its current competencies and customers create for future opportunities.**

Senge (1993) was one of the first to highlight the different needs and expectations of knowledge workers and how their leaders have to gain their commitment and tap their capacity to learn.

The rise of the knowledge worker means a different kind of 'followership': collaborative rather than passive, with new opportunities for leadership (Heller and Van Til, 1982). Knowledge workers do not think of themselves as 'subordinates': they expect to be given goals and to be free to achieve them without 'micro-management' and to be helped rather than directed and controlled by their bosses (Greenhalgh, 2001a). Mintzberg (1998) puts it more strongly:

> **Such professionals hardly need in-house procedures or time-study analysts to tell them how to do their jobs. That fundamental reality challenges many preconceptions that we have about management and leadership.**

The traditional definition of management as 'getting things done through other people' has been superseded by leadership, as 'creating frameworks for participation that draw in and coordinate the efforts of disparate actors' (Moore, 1998). This view is endorsed by Jack Welch, former CEO and chairman of General Electric:

> **People within the company are going to have so much data in their hands that they will be able to challenge [a CEO's] decisions all the time. The pace of events is going to be so fast that people aren't going to wait for the next level of approvals. There's going to have to be far more delegation. There's going to have to be far more participation. The leader must become an ever more engaging coach, an ever more engaging person. (Garten, 2001: 111)**

Where knowledge is the key competitive advantage, power has shifted from organizational 'leader' to organizational members. The leader of the future will create a 'learning organization', which 'facilitates the learning of all its members and continuously transforms itself' (Pedler et al., 1991) and in which:

> **people continually expand their capacity to create the results they truly desire, where new and expansive patterns of thinking are nurtured, where collective aspiration is set free and where people are continually learning how to learn together. (Senge, 1990)**

Leadership, mergers and acquisitions

It is frequently said in the acquisitions world that 'integration would be easy without people involved' (Ashkenas and Francis, 2000). Effective integration is not an engineering exercise, however, but one that affects people's livelihoods, requiring emotional and spiritual intelligence and cross-cultural competency.

A survey of 447 HR professionals, primarily in North America but also including Europe, Latin America and Asia–Pacific, revealed that 43% of M&As had been successful, 33% partially so and 24% unsuccessful.[139] Two-thirds of respondents had been involved in three or more M&As or joint ventures in the previous five years. The key finding was that M&As depend for their success on the effective management of people issues at all stages of the M&A process.

A survey in 2002 by KPMG revealed that over one-third of recent international takeovers and mergers were being reversed, with the perceived benefits of the original deals proving hard to realize.[140] The survey also found that 32% of the CEOs or financial directors who proposed the deals were being replaced. Two-thirds of the companies bought between 1996 and 1998 were still not integrated fully with the purchasing company. 'The 1990s "urge to merge" ... created a huge hangover of unfinished business,' said John Kelly, head of M&A integration at KPMG Consulting.

Mergers of 'equals' in terms of size may be a better bet than acquisitions. JP Morgan, in a study of 22 such mergers among European companies, found that two-thirds created shareholder value (*The Economist*, 1998). However, there is little academic support for this claim. Mergers between equals are especially difficult: 'they disrupt two strong corporate cultures, and they often throw up intractable problems of leadership' (*The Economist*, 1999). Leadership style impacts significantly on the satisfaction of employees with a merger (Covin et al., 1997). But the leadership styles associated with merger satisfaction are different for the acquiring and acquired firms. In the acquiring firm, reward power is the strongest predictor of merger satisfaction, followed by coercive power, legitimate power and referent power.[141] In the acquired firm, transformational leadership is the strongest predictor, followed by reward power and coercive power. It should be noted that effective leaders rely more on expert and referent power; using legitimate, coercive and reward use tends to lead to a loss of trust among employees (Schriesheim et al., 1991; Frost and Mossavi, 1992). Leadership development focusing on using expert and referent power can therefore play a useful part in enhancing merger satisfaction (Rahim, 1989; Palich and Hom, 1992).

A rare example of a successful acquisition is Cisco System's $7 billion investment in Cerent and Monterey Network – both companies produce devices for Internet development (Clutterbuck and Cage, 2001). Another example is the merger of Lloyds Bank and the TSB in 1995. One reason for their success was their complementary qualities. For example, Lloyds was strong in tackling challenges in project mode, displaying thoroughness in planning and prioritizing and a clear sense of direction; TSB was strong in proactivity, innovation and speed (Deboo, 2000).

One of the problems of change during M&As is that change is exciting when we do it and threatening when it is done to us. The solution is to get people to participate in it. When ScottishPower acquired Manweb and Southern Water, it created 'transition teams' with managers from the acquired company to create shared values and HR policies and practices. Similarly Commercial Union Assurance and General Accident, when they merged to form CGU, set up a carefully thought-out process of management and employee involvement in the change process and cultural integration. Participation in change creates ownership of it, and ownership of it brings commitment to it. But some five to seven years are typically needed for employees to feel truly assimilated into a merged entity (Stybel, 1986).

Management buy-outs (MBOs) and management buy-ins are different forms of acquisition. MBOs are the purchase of a business from its existing owners by a group of its managers in conjunction with one or more financial institutions. The latter tend to play a more aggressive role in the United States than in the UK.[142] In MBOs, some executives share in the value of the business as well as realizing their entrepreneurial ambitions. MBOs go against the trend to divorce control from ownership, which clearly influences organizational objectives and culture. An important requirement for success with MBOs is agreement among the owner–managers on the vision and objectives for the company. Commitment to existing products, services and practices may hinder change. Some owner–managers – especially those nearing retirement – may be more concerned with security and risk minimization, while others may be more risk and growth oriented. Change in corporate culture clearly may be required. The expectations of all parties therefore must be compatible.

Management buy-ins (MBIs) take place when a group of managers is brought in to run a company which is sold to them and their financial backers rather than to existing managers. There are pros and cons for MBIs: on the one hand the introduction of fresh ideas, but on the other hand loss of continuity and lack of insight and experience.[143] Investors are usually willing to accept higher risks than those associated with MBOs, and the failure rate is likely to be higher. Even greater faith and trust are therefore required by investors in the MBI management team.

With an MBI, issues concerning culture and change are also even more important than with MBOs. A new professional management team may have ideas which are very different from those of a fairly stable, complacent, family-owned company, for example new systems, efficiency improvements and cuts in overheads. MBIs, especially small companies bought from private ownership, show a higher failure rate than MBOs because of the greater difficulty in matching keen and suitable managers with appropriate acquisitions. Such managers – from large companies – may be unfamiliar with the culture and problems of small companies.

Well-known examples of MBOs and MBIs are as diverse as Hornby Hobbies (toys), Parker Pen, Dolland and Aitchison (opticians), Charles Letts (diaries), Standard Fireworks, Shepperton Film Studios and Premier Brands (the foods and confectionery arms of Cadbury Schweppes). Examples of management buy-backs of publicly quoted companies are the MFI buy-back from ASDA, Richard Branson's Virgin and Andrew Lloyd-Webber's Really Useful Group.

Reasons for failure

The reasons for failure and disappointment with M&As increasingly are human ones (Mirvis, 1985; Buono and Bowditch, 1989). One of the main reasons why mergers fail is because the fears, uncertainties and culture clashes among the people they affect are ignored (Devine et al., 1998; Holbeche, 1998). Sir John Harvey-Jones, former chairman of ICI, says that takeovers are presented as tough, shareholder-focused activities when in reality they are about the softer side of management (Finn, 1998).

'Merger syndrome' sets in after the announcement, with stress reactions, imagining the worst, crisis management (Marks and Mirvis, 1997; Marks, 1998). M&As increase uncertainty among employees, which leads to decreases in satisfaction, commitment, intention to remain with the organization, and perceptions of management's trustworthiness, honesty and caring (Schweiger and DeNisi, 1991). And these attitudes can spread and become endemic (Fulmer and Gilkey, 1988).

Julia Galosy (1990) says that 'the watchword when looking at a merger or acquisition from the employee's perspective is loss'. Loss is felt in many ways:

- Loss of position
- Hierarchical status – the acquirer becomes 'boss'
- Knowledge of the firm – procedures and people change
- Trusted subordinates – people are moved around
- Network – new connections are formed
- Control – acquirers usually make the decisions
- Future – no one knows what will happen
- Job definition – a state of flux prevails for some time
- Physical location – moving is typical in mergers
- Friends and peers – people often leave, are fired or are transferred

Such losses create a state of acute anxiety, which can lead to a variety of dysfunctional behaviours, such as psychological withdrawal or even sabotage.

The Towers Perrin/SHRM Foundation survey[144] revealed that four among the top seven obstacles to M&A success were:

- Incompatible cultures
- Clash of management (including leadership) styles or egos
- Inability to manage or implement change
- Lack of understanding of objectives and synergies.

A survey of *Forbes 500* chief financial officers showed that the top 10 pitfalls in achieving synergies in M&As are mostly due to people or people-related organizational and cultural issues, highlighted in bold in Table 10.1.[145] In a study of 24 acquisitions, in 11 out of the 12 cases with poor performance, there was inadequate target evaluation (Hitt et al., 1998). Success or failure depends on 'degree of fit' not only in terms of goals or resources of the parties to a merger but also in terms of culture (Garnsey, 1999).

A key element in corporate culture and successful organizational change is leadership style. Richard Schoenberg found in a study of M&As that some 35% of 129 major

Table 10.1 *Pitfalls ranked by negative impact on M&As*

Rank	Pitfall
1	**Incompatible cultures**
2	**Inability to manage targets**
3	**Inability to implement change**
4	Non-existent or overestimated synergies
5	**Lack of anticipation of foreseeable events**
6	**A clash of management styles**
7	Overly high acquisition premium
8	Unhealthy acquisition target
9	Need to spin off or liquidate too much
10	Incompatible marketing systems

companies' acquisitions had different leadership styles and that the larger the difference in leadership style, the less likely the takeover was to succeed (van de Vliet, 1997; Finn, 1998). Half of the managers in those companies judged the merger or acquisition to be a failure.

The importance of leadership and culture

'Leadership is probably the single most powerful and misunderstood variable in the success of a merger or acquisition,' says Mary Cianni (2002). She says that the key role of the senior leadership role during an M&A is to engage, inform and motivate workers. The new company's leaders have to get to know one another, establish norms, clarify roles, assign accountabilities, determine how decisions will be made, and, most important, decide how exactly they will guide the development of the new organization. The commitment of people in leadership roles is vital to the success of M&As. This depends in part on their satisfaction with their new roles and rewards, as well as the acquirer's actions and culture.

Effective leadership in M&As, Jeffrey Schmidt (2002) says, means creating a new vision for the new company and communicating it in an inspiring way, setting out clear corporate values, formulating goals for the transition, monitoring and responding to employee attitudes and feelings, teambuilding, and communication. Building trust is fundamental, and perhaps the most difficult.

M&As entail organizational change. Resistance to change essentially has to do with self-interest. People need to understand the potential consequences of mergers or acquisitions and to believe in their benefit for themselves. While M&As – indeed any organizational change – have to be managed well, even more important is leadership: not so much getting people to accept change but getting them to *want* it.

Leaders cannot assume they can 'paint the culture on' after companies have merged, research at Roffey Park Management Institute revealed (Devine et al., 1998). And this research suggested that the merger experience itself shapes the culture of the new company. Leaders must harness the synergies among people in terms of values, behaviours and working styles.

Applying the new leadership model

Let us now consider each of the five elements of the new leadership model in turn in relation to M&As, MBOs and MBIs.

Corporate vision and mission

A vision and mission that are perceived by employees as both intellectually rational and emotionally appealing must be communicated and committed to. Venture capital firms (VCFs) themselves need to have a clear vision and mission for their business. These may be, for example, high returns on their investments, success rates, and contribution of additional jobs to the economy or additional revenue to the public purse. Lack of agreement or understanding of vision, mission and objectives is a key obstacle to success in M&As, MBOs and MBIs. VCFs need to be assured of the clarity and validity of vision and mission of their targets' management and the latter's commitment to these.

For a merger or acquisition to be successful, a shared vision of the industry's future is essential. This was the case for SmithKline and Beecham, but differences caused a broken engagement subsequently between SmithKline Beecham and Glaxo Wellcome: Jan Leschly of SmithKline Beecham believed in integrated healthcare but Sir Richard Sykes of Glaxo Wellcome envisioned innovative R&D to sell drugs. Moreover, according to Widget Finn (1998), egos intervened: they could not agree who should be boss.

Change requires direction, and the leaders at the top must have a clear and credible vision of where the change will take the company and its people – and to communicate this in an inspiring way. The new leadership agenda for M&As entails making sure that the new vision for the company serves all stakeholders' interests, is perceived as such, and touches the hearts of those who will make or break it – the employees.

Corporate culture and values

Corporate culture shows itself in the symbols an organization holds dear, its heroes and the rituals people perform – 'the way we do things here'. In turn these symbols and rituals become embodied in the organization's structure, information flows, decision making, distribution of authority, and HR management policies and practices. Culture clash between two organizations inevitably leads to all sorts of dysfunctional outcomes if not outright disaster (Cartwright and Cooper, 1993; Marren, 1993).

Many companies underestimate the importance of integration, and it requires a huge amount of effort and resources (Ashton, 2000). One consulting firm reports several examples of incompatible cultures:

- Open, sharing v. adversarial
- Solution based v. product based
- Commercial v. process
- Performance v. employee
- Continuous improvement v. cost control

(Ashton, 2000)

Table 10.2 shows the significant gaps between successful and unsuccessful firms in cultural integration revealed in the Towers Perrin/SHRM Foundation survey (Schmidt,

Table 10.2 *Gaps between successful and unsuccessful firms in cultural integration*

Cultural factor	Successful firms	Unsuccessful firms
HR involved in addressing cultural integration issues	64	33
Behaviours supporting culture rewarded	48	20
Desired cultural behaviours considered during management selection	41	20
Culture aligned with vision	41	23
Attributes of the desired culture agreed to	37	20

Note: Figures indicate the percentages of respondents who strongly agreed with each statement.

2002).[146] These gaps are important because cultural factors influence the design of HR policies and practices, including leadership development. Successful companies also make more accurate assessments of potential synergies from M&As influenced by cultural factors and are better able to realize them. One respondent observed, however, that unfortunately 'culture is simply not on the map with senior management'.

Culture issues that typically arise, according to David Clutterbuck and Stephanie Cage (2001), include:

- Clash between a bureaucratic acquiring company and an entrepreneurial acquired company – for example, WH Smith's 'brief encounters' with Our Price and Waterstones failed partly because staff in the latter were uncomfortable with the 'near-military' discipline of WH Smith (which used to recruit many staff from the armed services)
- Clashing reward systems and management styles – for example, when Wells Fargo and First Interstate merged, Wells Fargo staff felt their job titles were devalued when First Interstate handed out prestigious titles as rewards; and Wells Fargo's style was very decisive and action oriented, while First Interstate operated through committees and discussion
- Power struggles
- Disparate national cultures

M&As across national boundaries are particularly sensitive to cultural differences. Hofstede (1994: 227) says:

> **Foreign takeovers are to greenfield starts as the bringing up of a foster child, adopted in puberty, is to the bringing up of one's own child.**

Transatlantic M&As have included BP and Amoco, Deutsche Bank and Bankers Trust, GlaxoWellcome and SmithKline Beecham, and Unilever and Ben & Jerry's. Cross-cultural differences are well known. For example, Americans favour contractual arrangements, Europeans favour rationality and detailed planning, and Far Eastern firms emphasize the long-term development of trust and respect (Gill, 1999c). And within Europe, the French are systematic in conducting meetings, which they use to rubber-stamp the boss's decision, whereas the British debate cases on their merits.

Perceptions of cultural compatibility influence preferences. For example, in one study, managers in British, Dutch and Swedish companies appear to prefer partnerships with American companies and managers in American companies prefer British partners, in both cases because of a mutual perception of professionalism (Davenport, 2002).

Jan Leschly, formerly of SmithKline Beecham, however, believes that mergers between American and European companies are difficult, owing to different management styles and philosophies, though his view may be affected by his own unhappy experience in the merger with GlaxoWellcome. But Bill Avery of Crown Cork & Seal, a global leader in consumer-goods packaging, points to such differences in attitudes towards cost cutting during budget shortfalls (Carey, 2000).

The study also showed that managers in British, French, German and American companies least favoured a merger with a Japanese company because of language barriers and lack of cultural understanding. M&As by Western companies in Japan are particularly difficult for cultural reasons, according to Jan Leschly (Carey, 2000). M&As in Japan are unusual for cultural reasons (Guild, 2000). Corporate boards generally have many long-service members, and business arrangements and investments often reflect family ties, long-standing relationships with suppliers and distributors, and loyalty to employees rather than economic or strategic goals. Decision making is complex, with no single decision maker, even the CEO.

Emotional intelligence in cross-cultural situations – particularly the ability to perceive and respond appropriately to differences in values and beliefs – is a prerequisite for success. Blending corporate cultures is like blending families, Gloria Allen (1999) says. Considerations are values, traditions, and dominant and recessive roles. Ignoring these differences can lead to prolonged chaos, lowered employee morale and reduced productivity. The skills required are the abilities to resolve conflict (despite prevention strategies), achieve consensus on solutions, resist premature resolutions to problems, and gather data and carry out research.

Leadership and strategy

M&As require a strategic approach to be successful (Gill, 1999d). Jeffrey Schmidt (2002) says, 'Strategic people management is as crucial to a successful merger as a sound strategy and fair valuation.' This entails careful merger planning and management and effective leadership.

Andrew Griffin (2002) suggests several questions that need to be asked about the target company's strategic expectations:

- Are the target company's *de facto* strategies consistent with its vision and stated direction?
- Do senior managers involved in the deal (from both companies in the case of M&As) have consistent views of these strategies?
- In the case of M&As, are the two companies' strategies historically similar, or are they in conflict?
- Do managers understand and accept the business rationale for the deal?
- In the case of M&As, do managers share the same vision, values and strategic objectives (e.g. profit, growth and community responsibility) for the new company?
- In the case of M&As, do managers appreciate the scope and implications of integration of businesses, organizations and management teams?

Leadership and empowerment

Corporate culture and empowerment are inextricably linked, for example through the distribution of power and power relationships among management. The cultural differences between Chrysler and Daimler-Benz illustrate this. Managerial talent is a key determinant of creating value in leveraged buy-outs, and MBOs rely on the ability of former divisional or business unit managers to become effective directors or owner–managers. Moreover, during M&As, MBOs and MBIs, some senior executives and managers lose out and some gain. The sources and distribution of power, opportunities, resources, and training and development needs all change. And in MBIs in particular, management teams brought in with fresh ideas need to empower those who will implement them.

Inability to manage or implement change is a key obstacle in M&As. Participation by managers and employees in change processes requires consideration of empowerment strategies. In M&As, MBOs and MBIs, special attention needs to be given to risk taking, ownership of opportunities and challenges, accountability, willingness to trust intuition, and decision making. Empowerment enables people to perform and achieve.

Leadership and influence, motivation and inspiration

Leadership style and behaviour and the use of power and influence greatly impact on motivation and inspiration. And change, actual or impending, can be motivating, even inspiring, or quite the contrary. Participation in the change process is a form of ownership of change, which in turn generates commitment and motivation to change. We all know that people treat what they own with greater care and commitment than they treat what they rent, borrow or merely contract to provide. However, loss or the fear of loss can bring demoralization and motivate widespread dysfunctional behaviour, even sabotage. Handling such situations during times of merger or acquisition is a test of leadership.

In the case of MBOs, the values and commitment of owner–managers to the vision and strategies of their company affect the motivation of all those involved in implementing them effectively.

Assessment and audit methods

The process of determining, through assessment and audits, whether the acquirer is paying the right price for the right target company is known as 'due diligence'. Its purposes are to:

- Verify strategic expectations
- Validate the price
- Discover significant liabilities and exposures
- Confirm legal ability to combine
- Verify expected organizational capabilities
- Analyze people issues such as retention, cost and cultural fit
- Evaluate IT position
- Understand variations among company units and jurisdictions
- Confirm leadership commitment

(Griffin, 2002)

Due diligence thus encompasses the 'human' side of M&As. Griffin (2002) quotes an acquisition of a consumer services company by a competitor with the intention of leveraging its distribution capability. The due diligence process failed to discover the fact that the company's sales representatives were so dissatisfied with working conditions that many were planning to leave *en masse*. After the deal they did so, and the value of the distribution synergy was drastically reduced.

In-depth investigation and analysis are also needed to reveal any concerns about management competence and honesty, such as:

- Are the managers in command of operational details?
- How well do they work as a team?

- How do they react when challenged – for example, flustered or hostile?
- To what extent are they enthused by the transaction or concerned about their personal futures?

'Due diligence' from an HR perspective, Ruth Bramson (2000) says, entails a comparative assessment of:

- Culture
- Employee demographics and competencies
- Key talent
- Pay and benefits
- Legal issues regarding outstanding employee litigation, workers' compensation and industrial relations

Due diligence is the most time-consuming and least creative part of the acquisition process. According to the Towers Perrin and the SHRM Foundation survey, it took 60% of respondents three months or less and 90% six months or less.[147] The process is often delegated by senior executives to business development staff, accountants, lawyers and bankers (Aiello and Watkins, 2000). Robert Aiello and Michael Watkins say that 'a deal that dies at the due diligence stage almost always dies for the right reasons' (Aiello and Watkins, 2000).

Taking the time and effort to assess culture fit and take the appropriate action reduces culture clash. But only 28% of companies in a survey by the US Bureau of Business Research felt they had done a satisfactory job of assessing the culture of their merging organizations prior to the merger, and only 15% said they had successfully communicated the vision and goals after the merger (Bramson, 2000). Mitchell Lee Marks and Philip Mirvis (2001) speak of preparation for a merger as being as critical as preparation for an organ transplant. Leo F. Brajkovich (2001) in the same vein says that cultural analysis is 'analogous to typing and cross matching the blood in a surgical operation'. Yet, Griffin (2002) says, 'Cultural due diligence, while crucial, is often overlooked [partly] because HR professionals ... lack the required assessment competencies.'

Corporate culture can be assessed from an analysis of information about internal and external communications obtained from both the organization and employees including managers and directors (Table 10.3).

Such an audit might cover the following features of the organization and its people:

- Vision for the future, how it is communicated and the extent to which it is shared
- Corporate mission (statement of purpose), how it is communicated and the extent to which it is shared
- Corporate values that inform and support the vision, mission and strategies
- Strategies for pursuing the vision and mission, how they are communicated and the extent to which they are shared; strategies in commercial organizations are likely to fall into the following categories: product/service development and implementation, marketing, distribution, HR (the extent to which employees act in concert with the strategies) and financial

Table 10.3 *Sources of information for profiting an organization's culture**

Organization	Employees
• Memos	• Interviews
• Newsletters	• Focus groups
• Employee handbooks	• Culture and climate surveys
• Policies and procedures	• 360-degree assessments
• Performance review process	• Turnout data
• Succession planning	• Promotion practices
• Annual report	• Retention actions
• Press releases	• Complaints and grievances
• Marketing materials	• Legal and regulatory compliance
• Financial information	• Union avoidance or relationships
• Speeches and presentations by senior executives	• Health and safety record
	• Training and development
	• Reward policy and practices
	• Work flexibility
	• Work/life balance

*Based on Don Howard, *HIGH Performance Strategies*, SPHR, quoted by Brent L. Rice (2002).

- How strategies are developed or formed and implemented
- Corporate culture and leadership, for example risk orientation, extent of shared values, empowerment, motivational climate (i.e. performance-related pay, self-fulfilment, job satisfaction, recognition, enthusiasm, commitment), emotional intelligence
- Teamwork and teambuilding efforts, including top-team teamwork and politics
- Communication – especially preferred communication methods (e.g. 'e-mail culture' versus 'face-to-face culture' and the use of inspirational language)
- Change orientation – attitudes to change, communication of change, employee participation in change, commitment and resistance to change, change processes

Finally we turn to the role of management and leadership in the change process in organizations.

Leadership and change

> *All things change, nothing is extinguished. There is nothing in the whole world which is permanent. Everything flows onward; all things are brought into being with a changing nature; the ages themselves glide by in constant movement.*

So wrote the Roman poet, Ovid, in *Metamorphoses.*[148] And in the contemporary context, James Champy (1997) writes likewise that organizational change is 'a journey that never ends'. In the graphic words of an African proverb, it is a journey that must take place every day:

> **Each morning a gazelle wakes up knowing that it must outrun the fastest lion or be eaten. And every morning the lion wakes up knowing that it must outrun the slowest gazelle or starve. Gazelle or lion, every morning you must run. That's what change is all about.**[149]

Today change that is continuous or discontinuous, not stability, is the order of the day. Like Ovid, Alvin Toffler (1971: 439–440), in his disturbing and challenging book *Future Shock*, says, 'Change is essential to man … . Change is life itself' and that 'a strategy for capturing control of change' is essential to avoiding future trauma and to the future well-being of the human race. In the words of Bennis (2000: xvi), 'Change is the only constant' in our society.

The challenges ahead, more than ever before, require organizations, industries and societies to change and to keep changing. Change may be planned, proactive and about creating the future. Or it may be unplanned, reactive and about adaptation. In Bennis's view, 'Leaders have to … create an environment that embraces change, not as a threat but as an opportunity' (Bennis, 1999b). The change imperative itself has changed. Charles Darwin is supposed to have said, 'It is not the strongest species that survive, nor the most intelligent, but the ones most responsive to change.'[150] But the imperative used to be to respond positively to the need for change. Now it is the need actively to *create* change. This was expressed forcefully by the former chairman of British Leyland, Sir Michael Edwardes:

> **And they [the new breed of top executives] have a particular drive, a desire to bring order out of chaos, or if something is too cosy, to create chaos in order to bring change. (Goldsmith and Ritchie, 1987)**

Change requires effective management: clear objectives; planning; organizing roles, responsibilities and resources, and compatible and supportive corporate policies, practices and systems; monitoring and control. The challenges are to find new and better ways of motivating people, especially to make effective change happen, satisfy people's needs and expectations, and win their hearts and minds.[151] Raymond Caldwell (2003), using a Delphi process with change agents, found that managing and leading change are two distinct but complementary processes.

A recent model of leadership proposes seven competencies: setting direction, making decisions, effective communication, creating alignment, setting an example, bringing the best out of people, and acting as a change agent (Hooper and Potter, 1997: 2; Hooper and Potter, 2001: 10). The key to successful change, according to a 1994 American Management Association survey of 259 senior executives in *Fortune 500* companies in the United States, is leadership (Table 10.4).

Change requires effective leadership to be successfully introduced and sustained. The early 1980s saw a marked growth in interest in the leadership of change. Rosabeth Moss Kanter's concept of the 'change master' focused on entrepreneurship and innovation in organizations (Kanter, 1983). New models of transformational leadership that we have discussed describe how leaders change how people feel about themselves and can be inspired to achieve beyond their previous expectations. Kanter (1991) notes how there has been a shift of emphasis from managing change to leading change. The new model of leadership described in this book shows how change may be managed and led effectively (Gill, 2003).

Table 10.4 *Keys to successful change*

	% mentioning this as important
Leadership	92
Corporate values	84
Communication	75
Teambuilding	69
Education and training	64

Source: AMA (1994)

For the chief executive and top management team change leadership means 'developing a vision of the future, crafting strategies to bring that vision into reality [and ensuring] that everybody in the organisation is mobilising their energies towards the same goals ... the process we call "emotional alignment"' (Hooper and Potter, 2001: 5). It can be argued that the most difficult challenges facing leaders today are making sure that people in the organization can adapt to change and that leaders can envisage where the organization is currently placed in the market and where it should be in the future (Heifetz and Laurie, 1997). Change is now driven by a global orientation and customer needs and demands. It requires an 'authoritative (or respect-based) leadership rather than authoritarian (position-based) leadership' (Kets de Vries, 2001: 61). Change that is participative generates ownership of it, commitment to it and creativity in the process.

The most negative reaction that people display at work concerns change, not money. People resist change for many reasons. Milan Kubr (1996) identified the following:

- Lack of conviction that change is needed
- Dislike of *imposed* change
- Dislike of surprises
- Fear of the unknown
- Reluctance to deal with unpopular issues
- Fear of inadequacy and failure: lack of know-how
- Disturbed practices, habits and relationships: 'We've always done it this way'; moving people from their 'comfort zone' means moving from the familiar, secure and controllable to the unfamiliar, insecure and uncontrollable
- Lack of respect and trust in the person(s) promoting change

O'Toole (1995: 11) says that:

> **To be effective, leaders must [set] aside that 'natural' instinct to lead by push, particularly when times are tough. Leaders must instead adopt the unnatural behavior of *always* leading by the pull of inspiring values.**

He says that reverting to paternalistic behaviour at any time will break trust with followers: the ultimate lack of respect for others is 'to impose one's will on them without regard for what they want or need and without consulting them' (1995: 12). In fact, O'Toole in his analysis concludes: 'the major source of resistance to change is ... having the will of others imposed on us' (1995: 15).

In addition, self-interest and shifts in power and influence hinder change efforts. Loss or change of role is an example. That change in this respect is difficult has been long recognized, for example by Machiavelli (1469–1527):

> **There is no more delicate matter to take in hand, nor more dangerous to conduct, nor more doubtful in its success, than to set up as a leader in the introduction of changes. For he who innovates will have for his enemies all those who are well off under the existing order of things, and only lukewarm supporters in those who might be better off under the new. (Machiavelli, 1532: 55)**

There are many reasons why change efforts fail:

- Lack of communication or inconsistent messages
- Lack of commitment to change due to lack of compelling evidence for the benefits of change – based on unrealistic expectations of the change effort; lack of commitment shows itself in objections, unwillingness to consider options or look at process issues and the use of 'hidden agendas' or delaying tactics
- Lack of commitment by top-level management
- Lack of dedicated effort
- Lack of expertise
- Poor planning and coordination
- Lack of necessary resources, including training
- Inconsistent HR policies or systems, such as performance criteria used in performance appraisal and the way people are rewarded for their performance
- Conflict between functional areas
- Imposition of 'intellectual' solutions on emotional problems: lack of emotional intelligence

Traumatic change brings a well-known reaction: first, denial that it has happened; then anger about its having happened, bargaining over what to do, depression, and finally acceptance (Kübler-Ross, 1969). Mulligan and Barber speak of the *yin* and *yang* of change: the social and emotional considerations and the technical aspects respectively (Sadler, 1998: 66–81). The model of response to change used at The Leadership Trust is first immobilization (non-response or 'freezing'), then minimization – 'This doesn't concern or affect us', self-doubt and depression, the low point, at which either change fails or its reality is accepted, in which case change is tested in a search for its meaning and benefits, followed by internalization. Perhaps the simplest model of change is that of Kurt Lewin (1948):

- Unfreezing – creating anxiety or dissatisfaction in relation to the status quo or a problem and a desire for change
- Changing – new behaviour and activity which people identify with and internalize
- Refreezing – positively reinforcing the initial change successes

Kotter (1995b: 21) provides a model for creating effective change:

1 Create a sense of urgency and importance to change.
   Examine the market in which the organization operates and the competitive realities.
2 Create the guiding coalition.
   Put together a group with enough power to lead the change and get it to work together as an effective team.
3 Develop a vision and strategy.
   Create a vision for a desired future state as a basis for directing the change effort. Develop strategies for achieving the vision.
4 Communicate the change
   Use every method possible to communicate constantly and explain the new vision and strategy and ensure the guiding coalition models the behaviour expected of employees.
5 Empower people for action.
   Get rid of obstacles to change, change systems or structures that undermine the vision, and encourage risk taking, new ideas and innovative activities.
6 Generate short-term wins.
   Plan and create visible improvements in performance, or 'wins'. Visibly recognize and reward people who made the wins possible.
7 Consolidate gains and continue the change effort.
   Use increased credibility to change all systems, structures and policies that do not fit together and do not fit the vision. Recruit, promote and develop people who can implement the change vision. Reinvigorate the change process with new projects, themes and change agents.
8 Embed the new approaches in the culture.
   Create better performance through customer-oriented and productivity-oriented behaviour and more effective management and leadership.

Kotter's model of change is criticized by Argyris (2000). He says that it reflects Model 1 behaviour (command and control) that is aimed at getting compliance from people rather than Model 2 behaviour that is genuinely people centred. Moreover, he questions whether creating a new sense of urgency would lead to desired outcomes and whether people in these circumstances would fully understand what they have to do and produce new ideas for overcoming obstacles.

Philip Sadler (1998) distinguishes between incremental and transformational change: incremental change concerns activities within a given culture and transformational change concerns changing the culture. Malcolm Higgs and Deborah Rowland (2003) report a study in seven organizations that found emergent change was more successful than directed change. The most effective change–leadership behaviour was framing change rather than shaping behaviour or creating capacity. In fact leader-centric shaping of behaviour impaired the implementation of change. During strategic change, consensus appears to develop, but less through gaining strength and more through increasing scope, according to Livia Markoczy (2001). Consensus during the early stages of successful strategic change tends to appear mainly not in the top management team but in the key interest groups, for example product development or marketing.

Meeting the challenges ahead

If leadership is the key to successful change, then the changing shape of organizations in response to the new challenges they are facing implies a new emphasis in leadership development. Tomorrow's leaders will need to be transformational rather than merely transactional. They will make change happen, rather than merely respond to it. They will encourage and develop teamwork. They will use power and influence rather than authority. They will understand and be able to respond effectively to different values and expectations in different cultures. And they will create a culture in which achieving the organization's goals will also lead to the satisfaction of individuals' personal goals.

Tomorrow's leaders will need to transform the expectations that people have of themselves, especially women and members of historically disadvantaged groups. They will need to create and communicate an appealing vision of the possible and desired future. They will need to understand and treat people as valued individuals. They will need to create team spirit based on mutual trust, respect and support, a particular challenge in virtual teams. And they will need to empower and inspire people to make the vision a reality.

Some writers foresee a shift in the 'distribution' of leadership in organizations, reflecting the shift to innovation and knowledge management. More capable leadership at the top is not necessarily what is needed. In fact, as has been pointed out, the stresses of life at the top have today approached the limits of human endurance. What is needed is for leaders to '"loosen up" the organization, encouraging innovation, creativity and responsiveness, and [to] learn to manage continuous adaptation to change – without losing strategic focus or spinning out of control' (Dess and Picken, 2000). Dess and Picken (2000) see visioning and empowerment as key to success in the new competitive environment.

Owen (2001) believes that organizations in their present state do not encourage people to find their leadership potential or use it. She explains how organizations need to transform themselves to become places where the potential of existing leaders and would-be leaders can be expressed – where leadership can be 'unleashed'. For her, the starting point is dialogue. Not just conversation and discussion, but an exploration throughout the organization of 'deeply held assumptions, beliefs, culture, meaning and identity' (Owen, 2001: 136). From this come its purpose or mission and a shared vision of the future.

Effective emotional and behavioural leadership without visioning and intelligent strategic thinking is dangerous. The converse is impotent. Outstanding leaders display both. Great achievers – who make the positive difference in our lives at work – are not mere masters of business administration; they are masters of leadership. Popper and Mayselass (2001) suggest that several particular characteristics are required to become a 'master of leadership':

- A disposition towards social dominance
- A belief in one's ability to influence others
- Optimistic orientation towards oneself, others and the future
- A motivation and a capacity to treat others in a positive and encouraging way while serving as a role model
- Intellectual openness, curiosity and flexibility

This analysis takes us back to where we started: trait theory. But the roots of these characteristics, it can be argued, lie in childhood and early-career experiences as well as genes.

Today will be looked back on by historians who describe:

> **shifting political, economic and social forces and the strenuous efforts of individual business leaders who confronted powerful trends and even tried to shape them... captains of ships in a turbulent sea – unable to chart a steady course and to maintain control of their own fate. (Garten, 2001: 277)**

For Jeffrey Garten, technology, globalization, rapid change, communicating and implementing a vision – one that depicts not just the future of a company but the contribution of business to society at large – and balancing the interests of all stakeholders in the company pose a challenge that few leaders can match. Leadership has changed contexts, from the industrial age to the information age, and now to the knowledge age (the age of understanding has yet to come). The CEOs and leaders of the future will need to address more than profits and shareholder value. Today's leaders of the future are reflecting changes in values that concern the environment, poverty and health or, as Susan Beresford, president of the Ford Foundation, says, 'how the world should be for their own lives and for their children' (Garten, 2001: 285). We still await the age of wisdom.

A century ago (in 1908), M. Louise Haskins wrote in *The Desert*:

> **And I said to the man who stood at the gate of the century: 'Give me light that I may tread safely into the unknown'.[152] (Haskins, 1940)**

We have now passed through the gate of the twenty-first century. I have attempted to illuminate a path ahead into the uncertain new world that leaders face. Leadership is a challenging and rewarding journey of discovery, and effective leaders show – and share – the way.

Further reading

Warren Bennis (2000), *Managing the Dream: Reflections on Leadership and Change.* New York: Perseus Publishing.

Jeffrey E. Garten (2001), *The Mind of the CEO.* New York: Basic Books.

Charles Handy (1995), *The Empty Raincoat.* London: Arrow Books.

Frances Hesselbein, Marshall Goldsmith and Richard Beckhard (Editors) (1997), *The Organization of the Future.* San Francisco, CA: Jossey-Bass.

Larry Hirschhorn (1997), *Reworking Authority: Leading and Following in the Post-Modern Organization.* Cambridge, MA: MIT Press.

Mitchell Lee Marks and Philip H. Mirvis (1997), *Joining Forces: Making One Plus One Equal Three in Mergers, Acquisitions, and Alliances.* San Francisco, CA: Jossey-Bass.

J. Oakland (1999), *Total Organizational Excellence: Achieving World Class Performance.* Oxford: Butterworth–Heinemann.

Jeffrey A. Schmidt (Editor) (2002), *Making Mergers Work: The Strategic Importance of People.* Alexandria, VA: SHRM Foundation and Towers, Perrin, Foster, & Crosby, Inc.

Discussion questions

1 Is leadership in the public sector different from that in the private sector?
2 Does bureaucracy mitigate the need for leadership?
3 How does the nature of leadership that is needed vary across permanent office-based workers, home workers, outsourced workers, and those in virtual teams dispersed around the world?
4 What sort of leadership on the world stage do (a) increasing globalization and (b) the rise of terrorism call for?
5 Some commentators have labelled the twenty-first century as the age of the female leader. Do you agree?
6 Do 'knowledge' workers require a special kind of leadership?
7 What leadership challenges do mergers and acquisitions pose?

Notes

Chapter 1

1 Edinburgh International Festival 2003, *Festival 2003*, brochure.
2 Paul Keating, prime minister of Australia 1991–1996, quoted in *Time* magazine, January 9, 1995.
3 Tony Blair, leader of the British Labour Party, quoted in the *Mail on Sunday*, 2 October 1994.
4 Isaiah 42: 16.
5 Sun Tzu, *The Art of War*, *c.* 100 BC.
6 Also reported in *Professional Manager*, July 2003, 6.
7 US Army (1999), *U.S. Army Vision Statement*, 7. Available at www.army.mil/vision/Documents/The%20-Army%20Vision.pdf.
8 Profile of Tony Hall, based on an interview with Sue Mann, *Professional Manager*, May 2005, 16–19.
9 From the brochure for the Hart Leadership Program, *Leadership in the Arts*, in which Duke University undergraduate students spend a semester in New York City.
10 Also reported in 'Leadership – from the followers' perspective', *Professional Manager*, 11 (1): 2, January 2002; and 'UK leaders fail to win hearts and minds (but they do if they try)', http://www.instmgt.org.uk/press/hearts.htm, Institute of Management, 4 December 2001.
11 *The Sunday Times 100 Best Companies to Work for*, 24 March 2002.
12 *The Sunday Times 100 Best Companies to Work for*, 24 March 2002, 19.
13 *The Sunday Times 100 Best Companies to Work for 2004*, 7 March 2004, 14.
14 *The Sunday Times 100 Best Companies to Work for 2005*, 6 March 2005, 4–5, 16.
15 *The Sunday Times 100 Best Companies to Work for*, 24 March 2002, 46.
16 The Industrial Society, www.indsoc.co.uk/cforl, 15 January 2001.
17 Paul Staman, reported from an interview with writer Joe Tye. See www.joetye.com.

Chapter 2

18 1 Corinthians 9: 19.
19 Quoted in *Annual Report 1998*, Center for Effective Organizations, Marshall School of Business, University of Southern California, Los Angeles, 13.
20 Attributed.
21 Paul 'Bear' Bryant, quoted in http://coachlikeapro.tripod.com.
22 The Industrial Society, www.indsoc.co.uk/cforl, 15 January 2001.

23 Bruce J. Avolio, in a speech at the Bernard M. Bass Festschrift, State University of New York at Binghamton, New York, May 31–June 1, 2001.
24 James MacGregor Burns, in a teleconference at the Bernard M. Bass Festschrift, State University of New York at Binghamton, New York, May 31–June 1, 2001.

Chapter 3

25 Michel de Montaigne (1533–1592), *Essais*, III, xii. Ed. Maurice Rat (1958).
26 *The Concise Oxford English Dictionary, 11th Edition.* Oxford: Oxford University Press, 2004.
27 William Wordsworth (1770–1850), *Daffodils.*
28 Measured in the Emotional Competency Inventory published by HayMcBer.
29 Measured in the Emotional Intelligence Questionnaire published by ASE, Windsor.
30 Robert Burns (1759–1796), *To a Louse.* On Seeing One on a Lady's Bonnet, At Church (1786).
31 Philip Massinger (1624), *The Bondman*, I, iii.
32 With an average turnover of £87 million, average turnover per employee of £138,000, and a 13% return on capital employed.
33 *SFI [Sugar for Industry] Core Values and Leadership Competency Framework*, August 2000. Peterborough: British Sugar. Reproduced by permission.
34 This analysis is based on my meetings and correspondence with senior executives of BAT and material provided to me on the company's Global Agenda Context and Update, August 2005. By permission.

Chapter 4

35 Also reported in *Professional Manager*, July 2003, 6.
36 *The Concise Oxford English Dictionary, 11th Edition.* Oxford: Oxford University Press, 2004.
37 Quoted in The University of Strathclyde – *The* place of useful learning. *Prism*, 186, January/February 2002, 7.
38 McDonald's Corporate Webpage (2000), November. Website: http://www.mcdonalds.com/corporate/investor/about/vision/index.html.
39 *Annual Report & Accounts 2000*, Domino's Pizza UK & IRL plc.
40 *Wall Street Journal* (1993), October 4.
41 Reproduced from *Sheer Inspiration: The UK's 100 Most Visionary Companies*, London: Management Today, 2001, 20–22. By permission.
42 *The Concise Oxford English Dictionary, 11th Edition.* Oxford: Oxford University Press, 2004.
43 Transforming Travel, *Annual Review 2002*, FirstGroup plc.
44 *Annual Report/Form 10-K*, Perot Systems Corporation, 2001.
45 *Annual Review and Summary Financial Statement 2001*, Tesco PLC.
46 *Annual Review and Summary Financial Statement 2003*, Marks & Spencer Group p.l.c.
47 *Annual Review 2000*, Lloyds TSB Group.
48 *Annual Review and Summary Financial Statement 2002*, Barclays PLC.

Chapter 5

49 Reported from Reuters in 'US corporate culture at fault, says Schroeder', *The Straits Times*, Singapore, July 11, 2002, A14.
50 *The Sunday Times 50 Best Companies to Work for*, 4 February 2001.
51 *The Sunday Times 100 Best Companies to Work for*, 24 March 2002.
52 *Best Workplaces 2003*, Special Report, *Financial Times*, 28 March 2003.
53 *Best Workplaces 2004*, Special Report, *Financial Times*, 28 April 2004.
54 For example, the *Code of Professional Management Practice* published by the Chartered Management Institute, Corby, July 2002.
55 *Principles for Business.* Caux Round Table, The Hague, 1996.

56 *An Interfaith Declaration: A Code of Ethics on International Business for Christians, Muslims and Jews.* London, 1994 (reproduced in *Business Ethics – A European Review*, 5 (1): 55–57, 1996).
57 Hartley William Shawcross, quoted by *The Economist*, Obituary, 19th July 2003, 76.
58 William Clay Ford, Jr (2000), *Corporate Citizenship Report*, Ford Motor Company.
59 *Annual Report & Accounts 2000*, Domino's Pizza UK & IRL plc.
60 Sun Tzu (*The Art of War*) and Confucius (*Analects*).
61 W.B. Yeats (1895), The Countess Cathleen, act 3. *Poems.*
62 *The Sunday Times 100 Best Companies to Work for*, 24 March 2002, 41.
63 Michael West, *Trust in Business.* BBC Radio 4, 14 February 2002.
64 For example, *Horkulak* v. *Cantor Fitzgerald*, (unreported, 2003/1918QB/HQ01X02541); *Ogilvie* v. *Neyfor-Weir Ltd* (unreported, EAT/0055/02).
65 Walker Information and the Hudson Institute, *National Employee Relationship Report*, Boston: Bain & Company, May 5, 2000.
66 William Shakespeare (1564–1616), *Hamlet*, Act I, Scene 3.
67 *Annual Review and Summary Financial Statement 2001*, Tesco PLC.
68 Sir Chris Gent, former chief executive of Vodafone Group Plc, *Annual Review & Summary Financial Statement 2001.*
69 *Vodafone future*, Corporate Social Responsibility Report 2000–2001, Vodafone Group plc.
70 *Annual Report/Form 10-K*, Perot Systems Corporation, 2001.
71 Mahathir Mohamad (1997), *New Straits Times*, 4 September.
72 T.C. Dougherty (1999), The challenge continues. *Lockheed Martin Today*, http://www.lmco.com/files3/lmtoday/9904/challenge.html.
73 *The Corporation*, Big Picture Media Corporation, 2003.
74 Ian Russell, chief executive of ScottishPower plc, *Annual Review 2000/2001.*
75 *Getting Things Done: Annual Review 2001/2002*, ScottishPower plc.
76 Ian MacLaurin, chairman of Vodafone Group Plc, *Annual Review & Summary Financial Statement 2001.*
77 *Annual Report and Form 20-F 2001*, Cadbury Schweppes plc, 2002, 18–19.

Chapter 6

78 *Annual Report 2000*, Cadbury Schweppes plc, 13.
79 *Annual Report and Form 20-F 2001*, Cadbury Schweppes plc, 2002, 4.
80 *Annual Report and Form 20-F 2001*, Cadbury Schweppes plc, 2002, 18.
81 *Annual Report and Form 20-F 2001*, Cadbury Schweppes plc, 2002, 20.
82 Trinity Mirror plc, *Interim Report 2003*, 2–4.
83 Chairman's Statement, *Annual Report and Accounts 2001*, Kingfisher plc.
84 Based on the BAT Group Strategy Review, July 2004. By permission.
85 Quoted in The University of Strathclyde – *The* place of useful learning. *Prism*, 186, January/February 2002, 7.
86 *Annual Report 2003*, Manchester United PLC.
87 Sir Peter Hall, chairman of the Shadow Arts Council, launching its *Election Manifesto for the Arts*, 14 May 2001.
88 Sir John Tusa, quoted in the Shadow Arts Council's news release on its *Election Manifesto for the Arts*, 14 May 2001.
89 Chairman's message, *Annual Review and Summary Financial Statement 2002*, Marks & Spencer plc.
90 CGU itself was the result of a previous merger between Commercial Union Assurance and General Accident.

Chapter 7

91 Andrew Roberts, *Hitler – Military Command.* 'Secrets of Leadership' series. London: BBC2, 2003.
92 Quoted in British firms lead the way in empowerment, *Management Skills & Development*, March 1998, 4–5.
93 *Financial Times*, 18 February 2000.

Chapter 8

94 UK leaders fail to win hearts and minds (but they do if they try), http://www.inst-mgt.org.uk/press/hearts.htm, Institute of Management, 4 December 2001.
95 Winston Churchill (1954), speech at Westminster Hall, 30 November. Reported in *The Times*, 1 December.
96 Henry Kissinger, quoted in the *New York Times*, January 19, 1971, 12.
97 1 Corinthians 8: 1.
98 Lord Acton (1834–1902), Letter to Bishop Mandell Creighton, 3 April 1887 (*Life and Letters of Mandell Creighton*, 1904, i.372).
99 Proverbs 16: 5, 18.
100 John 13: 12–15.
101 A phrase used by Rudyard Kipling of Max Aitken after Aitken's acquisition of the *Daily Express*, reported by Earl Baldwin in a speech to the Kipling Society, 5 October 1971, and published in the *Kipling Journal*, December 1971.
102 Dwight D. Eisenhower (1961), Farewell broadcast, January 17, reported in the *New York Times*, January 18.
103 Walter Lippmann (1945), *New York Herald Tribune*, April 14.
104 Benjamin Disraeli (1878), Speech at a banquet at the Riding School, Knightsbridge, London, 17 July.
105 Winston Churchill (1940), *Hansard*, 20 August, col. 1166.
106 Winston Churchill (1940), *Hansard*, 4 June, col. 796.
107 John F. Kennedy (1961), Inaugural presidential address, 20 January. Published in *Vital Speeches*, February 1, 1961, 226–227.
108 Brighton, 30 September 1997.
109 Available from CNN at http://archives.cnn.com/2001/US/09/20/gen.bush.transcript.
110 Aristotle (384–322 BC), *The Art of Rhetoric*, Harmondsworth: Penguin, 1997.
111 A muse is a spirit of inspiration and a source of genius for those involved in the creative process, says Richard Olivier.
112 Based on Richard Olivier's *Inspirational Leadership: Henry V and the Muse of Fire*, published by Spiro Press (formerly The Industrial Society press), London, 2001, with kind permission of the author and the publisher. Richard Olivier is Director of Olivier Mythodrama Associates and Artistic Director of 'Mythodrama – Creative Management Development' at London's Globe theatre in association with Cranfield School of Management (www.oliviermythodrama.com).
113 The use of mythodrama in leadership development is described in Chapter 9.

Chapter 9

114 William Shakespeare (1564–1616), *Twelfth Night*. Malvolio, Act II, Scene 5.
115 David Norburn (2001), quoted by *Ambassador* magazine, AMBA (Association of MBAs), March, 6.
116 Hilarie Owen (2001), quoted by *Ambassador* magazine, AMBA (Association of MBAs), March, 6.
117 The cover story in an issue of *Newsweek* in the early 1980s.
118 Henry Wadsworth Longfellow (1807–1882), *Kavanagh*, chapter 1.
119 George Eliot (1819–1880), *The Mill on the Floss*, book VII, chapter II.
120 See the UNU/ILA's website at www.unu.edu/ila/index.htm.
121 See the UNU/ILA's programme at its website at www.unu.edu/ila/ila-pg-frmwrk.html.
122 *Vodafone future*, Corporate Social Responsibility Report 2000–2001, Vodafone Group plc.
123 The Association of MBAs, the UK's MBA accreditation agency.
124 *Best Practices in Leadership Development*, by Warren Bennis and Linkage, Inc.
125 Later renamed the Department for Education and Skills (DES).
126 *The Sunday Times 100 Best Companies to Work for*, 24 March 2002.
127 *Enhancing Leadership Performance: The Leader as Teacher*, The University of Chicago Graduate School of Business.

Chapter 10

128 With acknowledgement to Charnchai Charuvastr, sometime president and CEO of Samart, Thailand, and Ian C. Buchanan, formerly chairman, Asia Pacific, Booz Allen & Hamilton, management consultants, Sydney, Australia.

129 *Annual Review and Summary Financial Statement 2003,* Marks & Spencer Group p.l.c.

130 Darcus Howe, in *Slave Nation: Work.* Channel 4 Television, 15 August 2001.

131 Baroness Helena Kennedy, *Cultural Conundrums in the Brave New World.* Lecture to the Royal Society of Arts, 28 November 2001.

132 PricewaterhouseCoopers (2002), *Fifth Annual Global CEO Survey,* reported from Reuters by *The Jakarta Post,* February 2, 2002, 14.

133 In a Reuters report of the World Economic Forum poll conducted by Environics International Ltd (Canada) in association with polling firms worldwide, published in *The Jakarta Post,* February 4, 2002, 14.

134 Second Annual World Social Forum, Porto Alegre, February 1, reported by Agence France-Presse and published in *The Jakarta Post,* February 4, 2002, 14.

135 Adair Turner, *Towards a Just Society: Capitalism in the 21st Century.* Lecture to the Royal Society of Arts.

136 Hanan Ashrawi, *Global Ethics and Values: West Is Best?* Royal Society of Arts/BBC World Service Lecture.

137 Baroness Helena Kennedy, *Cultural Conundrums in the Brave New World.* Lecture to the Royal Society of Arts, 28 November 2001.

138 Quoted in the website of the Terrorism Research Center, based in Virginia, USA, www.terrorism.com.

139 Towers Perrin and the SHRM Foundation (2001), *The Strategic Importance of People in Mergers and Acquisitions: A Survey of HR Executives.* The SHRM Foundation is the non-profit affiliate of the Society for Human Resource Management.

140 Reported in the Institute of Management Consultancy *UPDAT-E Newsletter,* 4 March 2002, www.imc.co.uk.

141 These forms of power base are part of the well-established typology of J.R. French and B. Raven (1986).

142 www.itpe.com/busmgt/strategy/thompson4/knowmore/iv buyout.htm.

143 www.itpe.com/busmgt/strategy/thompson4/knowmore/iv buyout.htm.

144 Towers Perrin and the SHRM Foundation (2001), *The Strategic Importance of People in Mergers and Acquisitions: A Survey of HR Executives.*

145 Survey by the Bureau of Business Research, American International College, Springfield, MA, reported in *CFO Magazine,* April 1996.

146 Also see Towers Perrin and the SHRM Foundation (2001), *The Strategic Importance of People in Mergers and Acquisitions: A Survey of HR Executives.*

147 Towers Perrin and the SHRM Foundation (2001), *The Strategic Importance of People in Mergers and Acquisitions: A Survey of HR Executives.*

148 Ovid (43 BC–AD 17), Pythagoras's teachings: the eternal flux, Book XV: 176–198, *Metamorphoses.*

149 Courtesy of Ian C. Buchanan, Booz Allen & Hamilton, Sydney.

150 Charles Darwin (1809–1882), source unknown.

151 Conclusions from the Inaugural Annual Conference, 'Leadership Development: The Challenges Ahead', The Leadership Trust Foundation, Ross-on-Wye, 2–3 February 1998.

152 Minnie Louise Haskins (1875–1957), Introduction, *The Desert,* 1908 (private printing). Quoted by King George VI in a Christmas Day broadcast, 1939. Published in M. Louise Haskins (1940), *The Gate of the Year.* London: Hodder and Stoughton.

References

Abdalla, I.A. and Al-Homoud, M.A. (2001), Exploring the implicit leadership theory in the Arabian Gulf states. *Applied Psychology: An International Review,* 50 (4), 506–531.

Abrahams, G. (2001), Leading lights. *Herald,* Appointments section, Glasgow, 20 March, 26.

Ackerman, L.D. (2000), *Identity is Destiny: Leadership and the Roots of Value Creation.* San Francisco, CA: Berrett-Koehler.

Ackroyd, S. and Crowdy, P. (1990), Can culture be managed? *Personnel Review,* 19 (5), 3–13.

Adair, J. (1973), *Action-Centred Leadership.* New York: McGraw-Hill.

Adair, J. (1983), *Effective Leadership.* Aldershot: Gower.

Adair, J. (1984), *The Skills of Leadership.* Aldershot: Gower.

Adair, J. (1988), *The Action Centred Leader.* London: The Industrial Society.

Adair, J. (1989), *Great Leaders.* Guildford: The Talbot Adair Press.

Adams, J.S. (1965), Injustice in social exchange. In L. Berkowitz (Editor), *Advances in Experimental Social Psychology.* London: Academic Press.

Adams, S. (1997), *The Dilbert Principle.* London: Boxtree.

Ahmad, A. (2002), The power of language. *New Straits Times,* Malaysia, April 17, 10.

Aiello, R.J. and Watkins, M.D. (2000), The Fine Art of Friendly Acquisition. *Harvard Business Review,* November–December.

Albert, S. and Whetten, D. (1985), Organizational identity. In L.L. Cummings and B.M. Staw (Editors), *Research in Organizational Behavior, Vol. 7,* 263–295. Greenwich, CT: JAI Press.

Alderfer, C.P. (1972), *Existence, Relatedness and Growth.* London: Collier Macmillan.

Alimo-Metcalfe, B. (1996), The feedback revolution. *Health Service Journal,* 13 June, 26–28.

Alimo-Metcalfe, B. (1998), Leadership development: the gender agenda. Paper presented at the Inaugural Annual Conference, 'Leadership Development: The Challenges Ahead', The Leadership Trust Foundation, Ross-on-Wye, 2–3 February.

Alimo-Metcalfe, B. and Alban-Metcalfe, J. (2001), The development of a new Transformational Leadership Questionnaire. *Journal of Occupational and Organizational Psychology,* 74, 1–27.

Alimo-Metcalfe, B. and Alban-Metcalfe, J. (2002a), The great and the good. *People Management,* 10 January, 32–34.

Alimo-Metcalfe, B. and Alban-Metcalfe, J. (2002b), *Leadership: Time to Debunk the Myths.* Cabinet Office report. Leeds: Leadership Research and Development.

Alimo-Metcalfe, B. and Alban-Metcalfe, J. (2003a), Under the influence. *People Management,* 6 March, 32–35.

Alimo-Metcalfe, B. and Alban-Metcalfe, J. (2003b), Leadership: a masculine past, but a feminine future? Paper presented at the Annual Occupational Psychology Conference, British Psychological Society, Bournemouth, 8–10 January.

Allen, G. (1999), Blending merging corporate cultures. *Performance in Practice*, Spring.

Allen, R. (1995), On a clear day you can have a vision. *Leadership & Organizational Development Journal*, 16, 39–45.

Allen-Mills, T. (2004), Deceptive face of the man they always underestimated. *The Sunday Times*, 6 June, 1.26.

Allinson, C.W., Armstrong, S.J. and Hayes, J. (2001), The effects of cognitive style on leader-member exchange: a study of manager-subordinate dyads. *Journal of Occupational and Organizational Psychology*, 74, 201–220.

Allport, G.W. (1983), Preface. In Viktor E. Frankl, *Man's Search for Meaning*. New York: Washington Square Press.

al-Mubarakpuri, Safi-ur-Rahman (1995), *Ar-Raheeq Al-Makhtum (The Sealed Nectar): Biography of the Noble Prophet*. Riyadh, Saudi Arabia: Maktaba Dar-us-Salam.

Alvesson, M. (2002), *Understanding Organizational Culture*. Thousand Oaks, CA: Sage Publications.

AMA (1994), *Survey on Change Management*. New York: American Management Association.

Amabile, T.M. (1996), *Creativity in Context*. Boulder, CO: Westview Press.

Ansoff, I. (1962), *Corporate Strategy, an Analytic Approach to Business Policy for Growth and Expansion*. New York: McGraw-Hill.

Anster, J. (1888). Translation from the German of 'Prelude at the Theatre', *Faust*, 214–230, by Johann Wolfgang von Goethe (1749–1832). London: White and Allen.

Antonakis, J. (2001), Construct validation of the Full-Range Leadership Model using independent data sets. Paper presented at the Festschrift for Bernard M. Bass, State University of New York at Binghamton, May 31–June 1.

Appleyard, B. (2004), Are you sinning comfortably? *The Sunday Times Magazine*, 11 April, 18–28.

Appleyard, B. (2005), The maverick art of leadership. *The Sunday Times*, 9 January, 4.3.

Ardrey, R. (1970), *The Social Contract*. London: Collins.

Argyris, C. (1998), Empowerment: the emperor's new clothes. *Harvard Business Review*, May–June, 98–105.

Argyris, C. (2000), *Flawed Advice and the Management Trap: How Managers Can Know When They're Getting Good Advice and When They're Not*. Oxford: Oxford University Press.

Argyris, C. and Schon, D.A. (1978), *Organizational Learning: A Theory of Action Perspective*. Reading, MA: Addison-Wesley.

Aris, S. (2002), Weinstock: I wanted to string up Simpson. *The Sunday Times*, 28 July, 3.8.

Arkin, A. (2004), Serve the servants. *People Management*, 23 December, 30–33.

Armstrong, S. (2001), Look into my eyes. Culture, *The Sunday Times*, 18 November, 28.

Ashkanasy, N.M. and Daus, C. (2002), Emotion in the workplace: the new challenge for managers. *Academy of Management Executive*, 16 (1), 76–86.

Ashkanasy, N.M., Wilderom, C. and Peterson, M.F. (Editors) (2000), *Handbook of Organizational Culture and Climate*. Thousand Oaks, CA: Sage Publications.

Ashkenas, R.N. and Francis, S.C. (2000), Integration managers. *Harvard Business Review*, November–December.

Ashkenas, R.N., Ulrich, D., Todd, J. and Kerr, S. (1995), *The Boundaryless Organization*. San Francisco, CA: Jossey-Bass.

Ashton, G. (2000), Merger integration – the new organisational capability. *Topics: The Journal of Business Management*, 3, 2–6.

Atkinson, J.M. (1984), *Our Masters' Voices: The Language and Body Language of Politics*. London: Methuen.

Atkinson, R.L., Atkinson, R.C. and Hilgard, E.R. (1990), *Introduction to Psychology, 10th Edition*. San Diego, CA: Harcourt Brace Jovanovich.

Atwater, L.E., Penn, R. and Rucker, L. (1991), Personal qualities of charismatic leaders. *Leadership & Organization Development Journal*, 12, 7–10.

Austin, J. and Vancouver, J. (1996), Goal constructs in society: structure, process, and content. *Psychological Bulletin*, 120, 338–375.

Avery, G. (2004), *Understanding Leadership*. London: Sage Publications.

Avolio, B.J. and Bass, B.M. (1990), *Basic Workshop in Full Range Leadership Development*. Binghamton, NY: Bass, Avolio and Associates.

Avolio, B.J. and Bass, B.M. (1994), Conclusion and Implications. In B.M. Bass and B.J. Avolio (Editors), *Improving Organizational Effectiveness through Transformational Leadership.* Thousand Oaks, CA: Sage Publications.

Avolio, B.J. and Bass, B.M. (1995), Individual consideration viewed at multiple levels of analysis: a multi-level framework for examining the diffusion of transformational leadership. *Leadership Quarterly,* 6, 199–218.

Avolio, B.J. and Bass, B.M. (1998), You can drag a horse to water but you can't make it drink unless it is thirsty. *Journal of Leadership Studies,* 5 (1), 4–17.

Avolio, B.J., Bass, B.M. and Jung, D.I. (1999), Re-examining the components of transformational and transactional leadership using the Multifactor Leadership Questionnaire. *Journal of Occupational and Organizational Psychology,* 72, 441–462.

Avolio, B.J. and Kahai, S.S. (2000), E-leadership: implications for theory, research, and practice. *Leadership Quarterly,* 11 (4), 615–668.

Avolio, B.J. and Kahai, S.S. (2003), Adding the 'E' to E-leadership: how it may impact your leadership. *Organizational Dynamics,* 31 (4), 325–338.

Avolio, B.J., Kahai, S., Dumdum, R. and Sivasubramaniam, N. (2001), Virtual teams: implications for e-leadership and team development. In M. London (Editor), *How People Evaluate Others in Organizations,* 181–202. Mahwah, NJ: Erlbaum.

Awamleh, R. and Gardner, W. (1999), Perceptions of leader charisma and effectiveness: the effects of vision content, delivery, and organizational performance. *Leadership Quarterly,* 10 (3), 345–373.

Ayman, R. (2001), Leadership development in higher education: present and future. Paper presented at the 11th Annual Kravis-deRoulet Conference, 'The Future of Leadership Development', Claremont McKenna College, Claremont, CA, March 23–24.

Badaracco, J.L.E. and Ellsworth, R.R. (1989), *Leadership and the Quest for Integrity.* Boston, MA: Harvard Business School Press.

Bailey, R. (2000), Great expectations. *Management Skills & Development,* 3 (1), 58–59.

Bakan, J. (2004), *The Corporation: The Pathological Pursuit of Profit and Power.* New York: Free Press.

Baldoni, J. (2004), Highlighting others: sharing the leadership spotlight. *Wharton Leadership Digest,* 8 (10): http://leadership.wharton.upenn.edu/digest/index.shtml.

Bales, R. (1950), *Interaction Process Analysis: A Method for the Study of Small groups.* Cambridge, MA: Addison-Wesley.

Bandura, A. (1977a), Self-efficacy: toward a unifying theory of behavioural change. *Psychological Review,* 84, 191–215.

Bandura, A. (1977b), *Social Learning Theory.* Englewood Cliffs, NJ: Prentice Hall.

Bandura, A. (1997), *Self-efficacy: The Exercise of Control.* New York: Freeman.

Bantel, J.A. and Jackson, S.E. (1989), Top management and innovation in banking: does the composition of the top team make a difference? *Strategic Management Journal,* 10, 107–124.

Barling, J., Weber, T. and Kelloway, E.K. (1996), Effects of transformational leadership training on attitudinal and financial outcomes: a field experiment. *Journal of Applied Psychology,* 81 (6), 827–832.

Barlow, W. (2002), The harm done by regulators. *Ingenia,* Royal Academy of Engineering, 11, February, 4–5.

Barnard, C.I. (1938), *The Functions of the Executive.* Cambridge, MA: Harvard University Press.

Barnett, C.K. and Tichy, N.M. (2000), How new leaders learn to take charge. *Organizational Dynamics,* 29 (1), 16–32.

Barney, J.B. (1986), Organizational culture: can it be a source of sustained competitive advantage? *Academy of Management Review,* 11, 656–665.

Barney, J.B. (1991), Firm resources and sustained competitive advantage. *Journal of Management,* 17 (1), 99–120.

Barney, J.B. (1997), *Gaining and Sustaining Competitive Advantage.* Reading, MA: Addison-Wesley.

Barrick, M.R. and Mount, M.K. (1991), The big five personality dimensions and job performance: a meta-analysis. *Personnel Psychology,* 44, 1–26.

Bart, C.K. and Tabone, J.C. (1998), Mission statement rationales and organizational alignment in the not-for-profit heath care sector. *Health Care Management Review,* 23 (4), 54–70.

Bartels, R. (Editor) (1963), *Ethics in Business.* Columbus, OH: Bureau of Business Research, College of Commerce and Administration, Ohio State University.

Bartlett, C.A. (2000), Closing the strategic generation gap. *Leader to Leader,* 15, Winter, 27–32.

Bartlett, C.A. and Ghoshal, S. (1989), *Managing across Borders: The Transnational Solution.* London: Century Business.

Bartlett, C.A. and Ghoshal, S. (1994), Changing the role of top management beyond strategy to purpose. *Harvard Business Review*, November–December.

Bartlett, C.A. and Ghoshal, S. (1995a), Changing the role of top management beyond structure to processes. *Harvard Business Review*, January–February.

Bartlett, C.A. and Ghoshal, S. (1995b), Changing the role of top management beyond systems to people. *Harvard Business Review*, May–June.

Bartlett, C.A. and Ghoshal, S. (1998), *The Individualized Corporation*. London: Heinemann.

Bartol, K.M. and Martin, D.C. (1991), *Management*. New York: McGraw-Hill.

Bass, B.M. (1976), A systems survey research feedback for management and organizational development. *Journal of Applied Behavioral Science*, 12 (2), 215–229.

Bass, B.M. (1985), *Leadership and Performance Beyond Expectations*. New York: Free Press.

Bass, B.M. (1988), The inspirational processes of leadership. *Journal of Management Development*, 7 (5), 21–31.

Bass, B.M. (1989), Evolving perspectives on charismatic leadership. In J.A. Conger and R.N. Kanungo (Editors), *Charismatic Leadership: The Elusive Factor in Organizational Effectiveness*. San Francisco, CA: Jossey-Bass.

Bass, B.M. (1990a), *Bass and Stogdill's Handbook of Leadership: Theory, Research and Managerial Applications, 3rd Edition*. New York: Free Press.

Bass, B.M. (1990b), From transactional to transformational leadership: learning to share the vision, *Organizational Dynamics*, 18, 19–31.

Bass, B.M. (1992), Assessing the charismatic leader. In M. Syrett and C. Hogg (Editors), *Frontiers of Leadership*. Oxford: Blackwell.

Bass, B.M. (1996), *A New Paradigm of Leadership: An Inquiry into Transformational Leadership*. Alexandria, VA: US Army Research Institute for the Behavioral and Social Sciences.

Bass, B.M. (1997a), *The Ethics of Transformational Leadership*. Kellogg Leadership Studies Program: Transformational Leadership, Working Papers. College Park, MD: Academy of Leadership Press.

Bass, B.M. (1997b), Does the transactional-transformational leadership paradigm transcend organizational and national boundaries? *American Psychologist*, 52, 130–139.

Bass, B.M. (1998), *Transformational Leadership: Industrial, Military, and Educational Impact*. Mahwah, NJ: Erlbaum.

Bass, B.M. and Avolio, B.J. (1993), Transformational leadership: a response to critiques. In M.M. Chemers and R. Ayman (Editors), *Leadership Theory and Research*. Orlando, FL: Academic Press.

Bass, B.M. and Avolio, B.J. (1994), Introduction. In B.M. Bass and B.J. Avolio (Editors), *Improving Organizational Effectiveness through Transformational Leadership*. Thousand Oaks, CA: Sage Publications.

Bass, B.M. and Avolio, B.J. (1997), *Revised Manual for the Multifactor Leadership Questionnaire*. Palo Alto, CA: Mind Garden.

Bass, B.M. and Valenzi, E.R. (1974), Contingent aspects of effective management styles. In J.G. Hunt and L.L. Larson (Editors), *Contingency Approaches to Leadership*. Carbondale, IL: Southern Illinois University Press.

Bass, B.M., Valenzi, E.R., Farrow, D.L. and Solomon, R.J. (1975), Management styles associated with organizational, task, personal, and interpersonal contingencies. *Journal of Applied Psychology*, 60 (6), 720–729.

Bass, B.M. and Yammarino, F.J. (1991), Congruence of self and others: leadership ratings of naval officers for understanding successful performance. *Applied Psychology: An International Review*, 40, 437–454.

Bateman, T.S., O'Neill, H. and Kenworthy-U'Ren, A. (2002), A hierarchical taxonomy of top managers' goals. *Journal of Applied Psychology*, 87 (6), 1134–1148.

Baum, J.R., Locke, E.A. and Kirkpatrick, S.A. (1998), A longitudinal study of the relation of vision and vision communication to venture growth in entrepreneurial firms. *Journal of Applied Psychology*, 83 (1), 43–54.

Baumeister, R.F. (1991), *The Meanings of Life*. New York: Guildford.

Baumhart, R. (1961), How ethical are businessmen? *Harvard Business Review*, July–August.

Beard, A. (2000), *The Language of Politics*. London: Routledge.

Beatty, K. and Quinn, L. (2002), Strategic command: taking the long view for organizational success. *Leadership in Action*, 22, 2, May/June, 3–7.

Beavers, K. (1996), Supermotivation: a blueprint for engineering your own organization from top to bottom. *Business Credit*, 98 (2), 23–24.

Beckett, F. (1999), Creative way to better management. *Financial Times*, 8 November, 16.

Beckett, M. (1999), Tomorrow's leaders filled with self-doubt. *Daily Telegraph*, 26 August, 26.

Behling, O. and McFillen, J.M. (1996), A syncretical model of charismatic/transformational leadership. *Group & Organization Management*, 21 (2), 163–185.

Bennis, W. (1966), *Changing Organizations: Essays on the Development and Evolution of Human Organizations.* New York: McGraw-Hill.

Bennis, W. (1973), *Beyond Bureaucracy.* New York: McGraw-Hill.

Bennis, W. (1989), *On Becoming a Leader.* Reading, MA: Addison-Wesley.

Bennis, W. (1994), *On Becoming a Leader, 2nd Edition.* Reading, MA: Addison-Wesley.

Bennis, W. (1998), The leadership challenge: generating intellectual capital. The Brathay Conference: 'The Leadership Odyssey', Windermere, 14–15 May.

Bennis, W. (1999a), The end of leadership: exemplary leadership is impossible without full inclusion, initiatives, and cooperation of followers. *Organizational Dynamics*, 27, July, 71.

Bennis, W. (1999b), Recreating the company. *Executive Excellence*, September, 5–6.

Bennis, W. (2000), *Managing the Dream: Reflections on Leadership and Change.* New York: Perseus Publishing.

Bennis, W. and Goldsmith, J. (1997), *Learning to Lead.* London: Nicholas Brealey.

Bennis, W. and Nanus, B. (1985), *On Leaders: Strategies for Taking Charge.* New York: Harper and Row.

Bennis, W. and O'Toole, J. (2000), Don't hire the wrong CEO. *Harvard Business Review*, May–June, 171–176.

Bennis, W. and Thomas, R. (2002), *Geeks & Geezers: How Era, Values, and Defining Moments Shape Leaders.* Boston, MA: Harvard Business School Press.

Bentley, J. and Turnbull, S. (2005), *Stimulating Leaders: Developing Manufacturing Leadership Skills.* Birmingham: The Manufacturing Foundation.

Bernard, L.L. (1926), *An Introduction to Social Psychology.* New York: Holt.

Berry, A. (2001), The tide of change. *Business South West*, February.

Berry, G. (1997), Leadership and the development of quality culture in schools. *International Journal of Educational Management*, 11 (2), 52–64.

Beyer, J.M. and Nino, D. (2001), Culture as a source, expression, and reinforcer of emotions in organizations. In R. Payne and C.L. Cooper (Editors), *Emotions at Work*, 173–197. New York: Wiley.

Bigley, G.A. and Pearce, J.L. (1998), Straining for shared meaning in organizational science: problems of trust and distrust. *Academy of Management Review*, 23, 405–421.

Binney, G. and Williams, C. (1995), *Leading into the Future*. London: Nicholas Brealey.

Biot, E. (1851), *Le Tcheou-Li.* Paris: L'Imprimerie Nationale.

Blake, R.R. and Mouton, J.S. (1964), *The Managerial Grid.* Houston, TX: Gulf.

Blake, R.R. and Mouton, J.S. (1978), *The New Managerial Grid.* Houston, TX: Gulf.

Blakemore, S. (1999), *The Meme Machine.* New York: Oxford University Press.

Blanchard, K., Carlos, J.P. and Randolph, A. (1995), *Empowerment Takes More Than a Minute.* San Francisco, CA: Berrett-Koehler.

Blatner, A. (2000), Personal meaning and emotional intelligence. Paper presented at the International Conference on Searching for Meaning in the New Millennium, International Network on Personal Meaning: http://www.meaning.ca.

Blau, J.R. and Alba, R.D. (1982), Empowering nets of participation. *Administrative Science Quarterly*, 27, 363–379.

Blauner, R. (1964), *Alienation and Freedom.* Chicago: University of Chicago Press.

Boal, K.B. and Bryson, J.M. (1988), Charismatic leadership: a phenomenological and structural approach. In J.G. Hunt, B.R. Baliga, H.P. Dachler and C.A. Schriesheim (Editors), *Emerging Leadership Vistas.* Lexington, MA: Heath.

Boal, K.B. and Hooijberg, R. (2000), Strategic leadership research: moving on. *Leadership Quarterly*, 11 (4), 515–549.

Bolden, R. (2004), *What is Leadership?* Research Report, Leadership South West, Centre for Leadership Studies, University of Exeter.

Bono, J.E. and Judge, T.A. (2004), Personality and transformational and transactional leadership: a meta-analysis. *Journal of Applied Psychology*, 89 (5), 901–910.

Bottger, P.C. (2000), Leaders as implementers of strategy. Unpublished paper, IMD, Lausanne.

Boudreau, M., Loch, K.D., Robey, D. and Straud, D. (1998), Going global: using information technology to advance the competitiveness of the virtual transnational organization. *Academy of Management Executive*, 12, 120–129.

Bourgeois, L.J. (1984), Strategic management and determinism. *Academy of Management Review*, 9 (4), 586–596.

Bourgeois, L.J. (1985), Strategic goals, perceived uncertainty, and economic performance in volatile environments. *Academy of Management Journal*, 28, 548–573.

Bowie, N. (1998), A Kantian theory of meaningful work. *Journal of Business Ethics*, 17 (9–10), July, 1083–1092.

Boyett, J.H. and Boyett, J.T. (1996), *Beyond Workplace 2000*. New York: Plume.

Bradshaw, D. (2002), The hero model falls into disrepute. *Financial Times*, 9 September, 3.

Bradshaw, D. (2003), Dean presents a case study in evangelism. *Financial Times*, 28 April, 14.

Brajkovich, L.F. (2001), Executive commentary on Mitchell Lee Marks and Philip H. Mirvis, Making mergers and acquisitions work: strategic and psychological preparation. *Academy of Management Executive*, 15 (2), 92–94.

Bramson, R.N. (2000), HR's role in mergers and acquisitions. *Training & Development*, October, 59–66.

Bray, D.W. (1982), The assessment center and the study of lives. *American Psychologist*, 37, 180–189.

Bray, D.W., Campbell, R.J. and Grant, D.L. (1974), *Formative Years in Business: A Long-Term AT&T Study of Managerial Lives*. New York: John Wiley & Sons.

Brief, A.P., Dietz, J., Cohen, R.R., Pugh, S.D. and Vaslow, J.B. (2000), Just doing business: modern racism and obedience to authority as explanations for employment discrimination. *Organization Behavior and Human Decision Processes*, 81, 72–97.

Britten, F. (2005), Office OM. *Style* magazine, *The Sunday Times*, 17 April, 15.

Brodbeck, F.C., Frese, M., Akerblom, S., Andia G. and Bakacsi, G. (2000), Cultural variation of leadership prototypes across 22 European countries. *Journal of Occupational and Organizational Psychology*, 73, 1–29.

Brodbeck, F.C., Frese, M. and Javidan, M. (2002), Leadership made in Germany: low on compassion, high on performance. *Academy of Management Executive*, 16 (1), 16–29.

Brookes, N.J. and Leseure, M. (2003), The influence of top managers on their organizations: a cognitive perspective. Paper presented at the Annual Conference of the British Academy of Management, Harrogate, 15–17 September.

Brosnahan, J. (1999), Public sector reform requires leadership. Paper presented at the Symposium on Government of the Future: Getting from Here to There. Organisation for Economic Cooperation and Development, Paris, 14–15 September.

Brown, A. (1995), *Organisational Culture*. London: Pitman.

Brown, D.J. and Lord, R.G. (2001), Leadership and perceiver cognition: moving beyond first order constructs. In M. London (Editor), *How People Evaluate Others in Organizations*, 181–202. Mahwah, NJ: Erlbaum.

Brown, M.E. and Goia, D.A. (2002), Making things click: distributive leadership in an online division of an offline organization. *Leadership Quarterly*, 13 (4), 392–419.

Brown, S.P. and Peterson, R.A. (1994), The effect of effort on sales performance and job satisfaction. *Journal of Marketing*, 58 (2), 23–24.

Bryman, A. (1992), *Charisma and Leadership in Organizations*. London: Sage Publications.

Bryman, A. (1996), Leadership in organizations. In S.R. Clegg, C. Hardy and W.R. Nord (Editors), *Handbook of Organizational Studies*. London: Sage Publications.

Buchanan, D. and Huczynski, A. (1997), *Organizational Behaviour: An Introductory Text, 3rd Edition*. London: Prentice Hall.

Buckingham, M. (2005), What great managers do. *Harvard Business Review*, March, 70–79.

Bucklin, L. and Sengupta, S. (1993), Organizing successful co-marketing alliances. *Journal of Marketing*, 57, 32–46.

Bullis, R.C. (1992), *The Impact of Leader Behavioral Complexity on Organizational Performance*. Unpublished doctoral dissertation, Texas Tech University, Lubbock, TX.

Buono, A.F. and Bowditch, J.L. (1989), *The Human Side of Mergers and Acquisition*. San Francisco, CA: Jossey-Bass.

Burke, M.J. and Day, R.R. (1986), A cumulative study of the effectiveness of management training. *Journal of Applied Psychology*, 71, 232–245.

Burke, R.J. (1986), The present and future status of stress research. *Journal of Organizational Behaviour Management*, 8, 249–267.

Burke, S. and Collins, K.M. (2001), Gender differences in leadership styles and management skills. *Women in Management Review*, 16 (5), 244–257.

Burke, W.W. (1986), Leadership as empowering others. In S. Srivasta and Associates (Editors), *Executive Power: How Executives Influence People and Organizations*. San Francisco, CA: Jossey-Bass.

Burke, W.W. and Litwin, G.H. (1989), A causal model of organizational performance. In J.W. Pfeiffer (Editor), *The 1989 Annual: Developing Human Resources*. San Diego, CA: University Associates.

Burke, W.W. and Litwin, G.H. (1992), A causal model of organizational performance. *Journal of Management*, 18 (3).

Burns, J.M. (1978), *Leadership*. New York: Harper and Row.

Burns, J.M. (2005), Leadership. *Leadership*, 1 (1), February, 11–12.

Burns, T. and Stalker, G.M. (1969), *The Management of Innovation*. London: Tavistock.

Bushe, G.R., Havlovic, S.J. and Coetzer, G. (1996), Exploring empowerment from the inside out. *Journal for Quality and Participation*, 19 (2), 36–45.

Butcher, D. and Meldrum, M. (2001), Defy gravity. *People Management*, 28, June, 40–44.

Butler, R. (2000), The road from fruit and veg to purest iron. Review of John Campbell, *Margaret Thatcher Volume One: The Grocer's Daughter*, London: Jonathan Cape. *The Times Higher Education Supplement*, 20 October, 29.

Bycio, P., Hackett, R. and Allen, J.S. (1995), Further assessment of Bass's (1985) conceptualization of transactional and transformational leadership. *Journal of Applied Psychology*, 80, 468–478.

Byham, W.C. (1988), *Zapp! The Lightning of Empowerment*. Pittsburgh, PA: Development Dimensions International Press.

Byrd, R.E. (1987), Corporate leadership skills: a new synthesis. *Organizational Dynamics*, 16, 34–43.

Byrne, J.A. (1998), How Jack Welch runs GE. *Business Week*, June 8.

Cacioppe, R. (1998a), An integrated model and approach for the design of effective leadership development programs. *Leadership & Organization Development Journal*, 19 (1), 44–53.

Cacioppe, R. (1998b), Leaders developing leaders: an effective way to enhance leadership development programs. *Leadership & Organization Development Journal*, 19 (4), 194–198.

Cacioppe, R. (2000), Creating spirit at work: re-visioning organization development and leadership – part 1. *Leadership & Organization Development Journal*, 21, 48–54.

Caldwell, R. (2003), Change leaders and change managers: different or complementary? *Leadership & Organization Development Journal*, 24 (5), 285–293.

Calori, R., Johnson, G. and Sarnin, P. (1994), CEOs' cognitive maps and the scope of the organization. *Strategic Management Journal*, 15 (6), 437–457.

Cameron, K.S., Dutton, J.E. and Quinn, R.E. (Editors) (2003), *Positive Organizational Scholarship: Foundations of a New Discipline*. San Francisco, CA: Berrett-Koehler.

Cannon, F.W. (2004), *Leadership and Culture as Determinants of Organisational Climate: An Exploration of Perceptions in a European Division of a Global Financial Services Firm*. Unpublished DBA thesis, Henley Management College and Brunel University.

Cannon, T. (2000), Leadership in the new economy. Paper presented at The National Leadership Conference, MCI-METO, The Royal Military Academy, Sandhurst, 24 May.

Capozzoli, T.K. (1995), Managers and leaders: a matter of cognitive difference. *Journal of Leadership Studies*, 2 (3), 20–29.

Cappelli, P. (1995), Can this relationship be saved? *Wharton Alumni Magazine*, Spring, 36–41.

Carden, S.D. and Darragh, O. (2004), A halo for investors. *McKinsey Quarterly*, 1.

Carey, D. (2000), A CEO roundtable on making mergers succeed. *Harvard Business Review*, May–June, 145–154.

Carless, S.A. (1998), Assessing the discriminant validity of transformational leader behaviour as measured by the MLQ. *Journal of Occupational and Organizational Psychology*, 71, 353–358.

Carlzon, J. (1987), *Moments of Truth*. Cambridge, MA: Ballinger.

Carpenter, S. (2001), They're positively inspiring. *Monitor on Psychology*, 32 (7), July/August, 74–76.

Cartwright, D. and Zander, A. (1968), Leadership and performance of group functions: introduction. In D. Cartwright and A. Zander (Editors), *Group Dynamics: Research and Theory, 3rd Edition*. New York: Harper and Row.

Cartwright, S. and Cooper, C.L. (1993), If cultures don't fit, mergers may fail. *New York Times*, August 29, 93.

Cartwright, T. (2002), A question of leadership. *Leadership in Action*, 22 (2), May/June, 12.

Cascio, W.F. and Shurygailo, S. (2003), E-leadership and virtual teams. *Organizational Dynamics*, 31 (4), 363–376.

Cassell, C. and Daniels, K. (1998), A missed opportunity? The contribution of occupational psychology to strategic management research. *The Occupational Psychologist*, August, 35, 17–21.

CEML (2001), *Excellent Managers and Leaders: Meeting the Need.* London: Council for Excellence in Management and Leadership.
CEML (2002), *Managers and Leaders: Raising Our Game.* London: Council for Excellence in Management and Leadership.
Center for Creative Leadership (2001), The African-American leadership program – a unique experience. *Update,* Winter, 1–2.
Chakraborty, S.K. (1995), *Ethics in Management: Vedic Perspective.* Delhi: Oxford University Press.
Chakravarty, B. and Gargiulo, M. (1998), Maintaining leadership legitimacy in the transition to new organizational forms. *Journal of Management Studies,* 35 (4), 437–456.
Chaleff, I. (1995), *The Courageous Follower.* San Francisco, CA: Berrett-Koehler.
Chalofsky, N. (2003), Meaningful work. *Training & Development,* December, 52–58.
Champy, J.A. (1997), Preparing for organizational change. In F. Hesselbein, M. Goldsmith and R. Beckhard (Editors), *The Organization of the Future.* San Francisco, CA: Jossey-Bass.
Champy, J.A. and Nohria, N. (2000), *The Arc of Ambition.* Chichester: John Wiley & Sons.
Chan, K.-Y. and Drasgow, F. (2001), Toward a theory of individual differences and leadership: understanding the motivation to lead. *Journal of Applied Psychology,* 86 (3), 481–498.
Chandler, A.D. (1962), *Strategy and Structure: Chapters in the History of the Industrial Enterprise.* Cambridge, MA: MIT Press.
Changsorn, P. and Janviroj, P. (2003), 10 years to a new Thailand. *Nation,* Bangkok, February 24, 1.
Charan, R. and Colvin, G. (1999), Why CEOs fail. *Fortune,* 21, 68–75.
Charan, R. and Useem, J. (2002), Why companies fail. *Fortune,* May 27, 36–44.
Charlesworth, K., Cook, P. and Coozier, G. (2003), *Leading Change in the Public Sector: Making the Difference.* London: Chartered Management Institute.
Chatman, J.A. (1991), Matching people and organizations: selection and socialization in public accounting firms. *Administrative Science Quarterly,* 36, 459–484.
Chatman, J.A. and Eunyoung Cha, S. (2003), Leading by leveraging culture. *California Management Review,* 45 (4), Summer, 20–34.
Chen, C.Y. (2002), The world's most admired companies 2002. *Fortune,* March 4, 26–32.
Chen, W.-H. (1997), The human side of total quality management in Taiwan: leadership and human resource management. *International Journal of Quality & Reliability Management,* 14 (1), 24–45.
Church, A.H. (1997), Managerial self-awareness in high-performing individuals in organizations. *Journal of Applied Psychology,* 82 (2), 281–292.
Church, A.H. and Waclawski, J. (1999), The impact of leadership style on global management practices. *Journal of Applied Social Psychology,* 29 (7), 1416–1443.
Cianni, M. (2002), Implementation stage. In J.A. Schmidt (Editor), *Making Mergers Work: The Strategic Importance of People,* 127–151. Alexandria, VA: SHRM Foundation and Towers, Perrin, Foster, & Crosby, Inc.
Ciulla, J. B. (1999), The importance of leadership in shaping business values. *Long Range Planning,* 32 (2), 166–172.
Clawson, J.G. and Doner, J. (1996), Teaching leadership through aikido. *Journal of Management Education,* 20 (2), 182–205.
Cleaver, A. (2001), *Foreword. Excellent Managers and Leaders: Meeting the Need.* London: Council for Excellence in Management and Leadership.
Clemens, J. (1986), A lesson from 431 B.C. *Fortune,* October 13, 161, 164.
Cleveland, H. (1985), *The Knowledge Executive: Leadership in a Knowledge Economy.* New York: Dutton.
Clinton, R.J. (1988), *The Making of a Leader: Recognizing the Lessons and Stages of Leadership Development.* Colorado Springs, CO: NavPress.
Clinton, W.J. (2001), *The Struggle for the Soul of the 21st Century.* The 26th Richard Dimbleby Lecture, BBC1, 16 December.
Cloud, S. (1996), *Nixon.* New York: Harper and Row.
Clutterbuck, D. and Cage, S. (2001), Communications in mergers and acquisitions: keeping the ship on course. *Training Journal,* May, 16–20.
CMI (2003), *Leading Change in the Public Sector: Making the Difference.* London: Chartered Management Institute.
Cockburn, B. (2000), Leadership during change. Paper presented at The National Leadership Conference, 'Leaders and Managers: Fit for the Future', The Royal Military Academy, Sandhurst, 24 May.

Cohen, D.V. (1995), Creating ethical work climates: a socioeconomic perspective. *Journal of Socio-Economics,* 24, 317–343.
Cohen, E. and Tichy, N. (1997), How leaders develop leaders. *Training & Development,* 51 (5), May, 58–63, 65–67, 69–73.
Coleman, H.J. (1996), Why employee empowerment is not just a fad. *Leadership & Organization Development Journal,* 17 (4), 28–35.
Coles, M. (1998), Vision is key to good leadership. *The Sunday Times,* 18 October, 7.20.
Coles, M. (1999), Life at the top is brutal and short. *The Sunday Times,* 13 June, 7.26.
Coles, M. (2000), Sharing knowledge boosts efficiency. *The Sunday Times,* 30 April, 7.16.
Collins, A. (2004), Where they lead we will follow. *The Sunday Times 100 Best Companies to Work for 2004,* 7 March, 8.
Collins, D. (1994), The disempowering logic of empowerment. *Empowerment in Organizations,* 2 (2), 14–21.
Collins, D. and Holton, E.F. (2004), The effectiveness of managerial leadership development programs: a meta-analysis of studies from 1982 to 2001. *Human Resource Development Quarterly,* 15 (2), Summer, 217–248.
Collins, J.C. (1996), Aligning action and values. *Leader to Leader,* 1, Summer, 19–24.
Collins, J.C. (2001a), *Good to Great: Why Some Companies Make the Leap – and Others Don't.* New York: HarperBusiness.
Collins, J.C. (2001b), Level 5 leadership: the triumph of humility and fierce resolve. *Harvard Business Review,* January–February.
Collins, J.C. (2002), Foreword. In F. Hesselbein, *Hesselbein on Leadership.* San Francisco, CA: Jossey-Bass.
Collins, J.C. and Porras, J.I. (1991), Organizational vision and visionary organizations. *California Management Review,* 34 (1), 30–52.
Collins, J.C. and Porras, J.I. (1994), *Built To Last: Successful Habits of Visionary Companies.* New York: HarperCollins.
Collins, J.C. and Porras, J.I. (1995), The ultimate vision. *Across the Board,* January.
Collins, J.C. and Porras, J.I. (1996a), *Built to Last: Successful Habits of Visionary Companies.* London: HarperBusiness.
Collins, J.C. and Porras, J.I. (1996b), Building your company's vision. *Harvard Business Review,* September–October.
Collins, J.C. and Porras, J.I. (1997), *Built To Last: Successful Habits of Visionary Companies, 2nd Edition.* London: Century/Random House Business Books.
Collinson, D. and Grint, K. (2005), Editorial: The Leadership Agenda. *Leadership,* 1 (1), February, 5–9.
Colvin, G. (2001), Should companies care? *Fortune,* June 11, 26.
Colvin, R.E. (2001), Leading from the middle: a challenge for middle managers. Paper presented at the Bernard M. Bass Festschrift, State University of New York at Binghamton, May 31–June 1.
Conference Board (2002), *Developing Business Leaders for 2010.* New York: The Conference Board.
Conger, J.A. (1989), *The Charismatic Leader: Behind the Mystique of Exceptional Leadership.* San Francisco, CA: Jossey-Bass.
Conger, J.A. (1992), *Learning to Lead.* San Francisco, CA: Jossey-Bass.
Conger, J.A. (1999), The new age of persuasion. *Leader to Leader,* Spring, 37–44.
Conger, J.A. (2004), Developing leadership capability: what's inside the black box? *Academy of Management Executive,* 18 (3), 136–139.
Conger, J.A. and Kanungo, R.N. (1987), Toward a behavioral theory of charismatic leadership in organizational settings. *Academy of Management Review,* 12, 637–647.
Conger, J.A. and Kanungo, R.N. (1988), The empowerment process: integrating theory and practice. *Academy of Management Review,* 13, 471–482.
Cook, L. and Rothwell, B. (2000), *The X and Y of Leadership.* London: The Industrial Society.
Cook, P. (2000), Jazz and leadership. *Strategy,* January, 9–10.
Cooley, C. (1902), *Human Nature and the Social Order.* New York: Scribners.
Cooper, J. and Hartley, J. (1991), Reconsidering the case for organisational commitment. *Human Resource Management Journal,* 3, Spring, 18–32.
Cooper, R. (1997), Applying emotional intelligence in the workplace, *Training & Development,* December, 31–38.
Cooper, R. (1998), Sentimental value. *People Management,* 2 April, 48–50.

Cooper, R. and Sawaf, A. (1997), *Executive EQ*. London: Orion Business.
Corner, P., Kinicki, A.J. and Keats, B.W. (1994), Integrating organizational and individual processing perspectives on choice. *Organization Science*, 5 (3), 294–308.
Coulter, M. (2002), *Strategic Management in Action, 2nd Edition*. Upper Saddle River, NJ: Prentice Hall.
Covey, S.R. (1989a), Universal mission statement. *Executive Excellence*, March, 7–9.
Covey, S.R. (1989b), *The Seven Habits of Highly Effective People*. New York: Fireside.
Covey, S.R. (1992), *Principle-centered Leadership*. London: Simon and Schuster.
Covin, T.J., Kolenko, T.A., Sightler, K.W. and Tudor, R.K. (1997), Leadership style and post-merger satisfaction. *Journal of Management Development*, 16 (1), 22–33.
Cowe, R. (2002), Embracing companies' social role. *Financial Times*, 12 July, 10.
Crainer, S. (1996), Bridging the gap between noble aspirations and reality. *Professional Manager*, July, 7.
Crainer, S. (1999), Group leaders. *Management Skills & Development*, 2 (18), June/July, 38–40.
Craven, R. (1998), Let's take it from the top. *Independent on Sunday*, Smart Moves, 15 February, 2.
Creelman, D. (2003a), Thinking out loud with Barry Gibbons: www.HR.com.
Creelman, D. (2003b), *Interview: Rob Lebow on Accountability, Freedom and Responsibility:* www.HR.com, 14 November.
Creelman, D. (2003c), *Interview: Dr Csikszentmihalyi on Flow and Leadership:* www.HR.com, 31 October.
Creelman, J. (1996), Why money's only part of the score. *Financial Director*, April.
Cross, T. (1998), *Christian Leadership*. Speech at Welbeck College, London, 5 July.
Crossley, T. and Taylor, I. (1995), Developing competitive advantage through 360–degree feedback. *American Journal of Management Development*, 1 (1), 11–15.
Crozier, M. (1964), *The Bureaucratic Phenomenon*. Chicago: Tavistock.
Csikszentmihalyi, M. (1999), If we are so rich, why aren't we happy? *American Psychologist*, 54, 821–827.
Csikszentmihalyi, M. and Csikszentmihalyi, I.S. (1988), *Optimal Experience: Psychological Studies of Flow in Consciousness*. Cambridge: Cambridge University Press.
Csoka, L.S. (1998), *Bridging the Leadership Gap*. New York: Conference Board.
Cummings, S. and Davies, J. (1994), Mission, vision, fusion. *Long Range Planning*, 27 (6), 147–150.
Cunningham, B.J. (2002), Brand leadership. Paper presented at a conference on The Successful Leader, Institute of Directors, London, 3 May.
Cunningham, F. (2001), Interview with Henry Mintzberg. *Business Voice*, June, 49–52.
Cunningham, I., Hyman, J. and Baldry, C. (1996), Empowerment: the power to do what? *Industrial Relations Journal*, 27 (2), 143–151.
Dabash, H. (2000), In the absence of the face. *Social Research*, 67 (1), 127.
Dahl, A.B. (1998), *Command Dysfunction: Minding the Cognitive War*. Maxwell Air Force Base, AL: Air University Press.
Dalai Lama XIV (1999), *Ethics for the New Millennium*. New York: Putnam.
Dale, B.G. (Editor) (1994), *Managing Quality*. New York: Prentice Hall.
Dalgleish, T. and Watts, F.N. (1990), Biases of attention and memory in disorders of anxiety and depression. *Clinical Psychology Review*, 10, 589–604.
Daly, D. and Kleiner, B.H. (1995), How to motivate problem employees. *Work Study*, 44 (2), 5–7.
Daniels, K. (1998), Toward integrating emotions into strategic management research: trait affect and the perception of the strategic environment. *British Journal of Management*, 9, 163–168.
Daniels, K. (1999), Affect and strategic decision making. *The Psychologist*, 12 (1), 24–29.
Daniels, K., De Chernatony, L. and Johnson, G. (1995), Validating a method for mapping managers' mental models of competitive industry structures. *Human Relations*, 47, 975–991.
Daniels, K. and Henry, J. (1998), Strategy: a cognitive perspective. In S. Segal-Horn (Editor), *The Strategy Reader*. Oxford: Blackwell Business.
Dansereau, F., Graen, G. and Haga, W.J. (1975), A vertical dyad linkage approach to leadership within formal organizations: a longitudinal investigation of the role making process. *Organizational Behavior and Human Performance*, 14, 46–78.
Darby, J. and MacGinty, R. (Editors) (2000), *The Management of Peace Processes*. New York: St Martin's Press.
Dastmalcian, A., Javidan, M. and Alam, K. (2001), Effective leadership and culture in Iran: an empirical study. *Applied Psychology: An International Review*, 50 (4), 532–558.

Davenport, T.A. (2002), M&A in the new millennium. In J.A. Schmidt (Editor), *Making Mergers Work: The Strategic Importance of People*, 218–234. Alexandria, VA: SHRM Foundation and Towers, Perrin, Foster, & Crosby, Inc.

Davenport, T. and Prusak, L. (1998), *Working Knowledge: How Organizations Manage What They Know.* Boston, MA: Harvard Business School Press.

David, F.R. (1989), How companies define their mission. *Long Range Planning*, 22 (1), 90–97.

Davidson, J.E., Deuser, R. and Sternberg, R.J. (1994), The role of metacognition in problem solving. In J. Metcalf and A.P. Shimamura (Editors), *Metacognition: Knowing about Knowing.* Cambridge, MA: MIT Press.

Davis, I. (2003), Learning to grow again. *The World in 2004.* London: The Economist.

Davis, J.H., Shoorman, F.D., Mayer, R.C. and Hwee, H.T. (2000), The trusted general manager and business unit performance: empirical evidence of a competitive advantage. *Strategic Management Journal*, 21, 563–576.

Davis, L.E. and Cherns, A.B. (1975), *The Quality of Working Life, Vol. 1.* London: Free Press.

Dawkins, R. (1998), *Unweaving the Rainbow.* New York: Penguin.

Day, D.V. (2001), Assessment of leadership outcomes. In S.J. Zaccaro and R.J. Klimoski (Editors), *The Nature of Organizational Leadership: Understanding the Performance Imperatives Confronting Today's Leaders.* San Francisco, CA: Jossey-Bass.

Day, D.V. and Lord, R.G. (1988), Executive leadership and organizational performance: suggestions for a new theory and methodology. *Journal of Management*, 14, 453–464.

Deacon, T. (1997), *The Symbolic Species.* London: Penguin.

Deal, T. and Kennedy, A. (1982), *Corporate Cultures: The Rites and Rituals of Corporate Life.* Reading, MA: Addison-Wesley.

DeAngelis, T. (2003), Why we overestimate our competence. *Monitor on Psychology*, February, 60–62.

Dearlove, D. (1997a), No substitute for bright ideas. Management Plus, *The Times*, 3 July, 5.

Dearlove, D. (1997b), Just imagine. *Human Resources*, July/August.

de Bono, E. (1977), *Lateral Thinking: A Textbook of Creativity.* Harmondsworth: Penguin.

de Bono, E. (1998), *Simplicity.* Harmondsworth: Penguin.

Deboo, A. (2000), Lloyds TSB – a story of a successful merger. *Topics: The Journal of Business Management*, 3, 19–21.

deCharms, R. (1968), *Personal Causation: The Internal Affective Determinants of Behavior.* New York: Academic Press.

de Mirecourt, E. (1857), *Histoire Contemporaine*, no. 79, Ledru-Rollin.

Deetz, S.A., Tracy, S.J. and Simpson, J.L. (2000), *Leading Organizations through Transition.* Thousand Oaks, CA: Sage Publications.

Deming, W.E. (1986), *Out of Crisis: Quality, Productivity and Competitive Position.* Cambridge: Cambridge University Press.

Den Hartog, D.N., House, R.J., Hanges, P.J., Ruiz-Quintanilla, S.A., Dorfman, P.W. et al. (1999), Culture specific and cross-culturally generalizable implicit leadership theories: are attributes of charismatic/transformational leadership universally endorsed? *Leadership Quarterly*, 10 (2), 219–256.

Den Hartog, D.N., Van Muijen, J.J. and Koopman, P.L. (1997), Transactional versus transformational leadership: an observational field study. *Journal of Occupational and Organizational Psychology*, 70, 19–34.

Den Hartog, D.N. and Verburg, R.M. (1997), Charisma and rhetoric: communicative techniques of international business leaders. *Leadership Quarterly*, 8, 355–391.

Denison, D. (1984), Bringing corporate culture to the bottom line. *Organizational Dynamics*, 13 (2), 4–22.

Dent, F. and Brent, M. (2001), Influencing: a new model. *Training Journal*, July, 14–17.

Denton, D.K. (2001), Mission statements miss the point. *Leadership & Organization Development Journal*, 22 (7), 309–314.

Dess, G.G. and Picken, J.C. (2000), Changing roles: leadership in the 21st century. *Organizational Dynamics*, 28 (3), 18–34.

Devine, M., Hirsh, W., Garrow, V. and Holbeche, L. (1998), *Mergers and Acquisitions: Getting the People Bit Right.* Horsham: Roffey Park Management Institute.

Diamond, M. (2002), Academic leadership: turning vision into reality. *Forum*, European Foundation for Management Education, April, 14–18.

Dickson, M.W., Smith, D.B., Grojean, M.W. and Ehrhart, M. (2001), An organizational climate regarding ethics: the outcome of leader values and the practices that reflect them. *Leadership Quarterly*, 12 (2), 197–217.

Digman, J.M. (1990), Personality structure: emergence of the five-factor model. *Annual Review of Psychology,* 41, 417–440.
Dingfelder, S.F. (2004), A presidential personality. *Monitor on Psychology,* American Psychological Association, November, 26–28.
Dirks, K.T. (2000), Trust in leadership and team performance: evidence from NCAA basketball. *Journal of Applied Psychology,* 85 (6), 1004–1011.
Divyanathan, D. (2002), SIA is 'best employer' among Singapore firms. *Straits Times,* Singapore, July 11, A18.
Dixon, N. (1976), *On the Psychology of Military Incompetence.* London: Jonathan Cape.
Dixon, N. (1985a), Why lefties make the best leaders. *Personnel Management,* November, 36–39.
Dixon, N. (1985b), The Leadership Trust: an examination of their concepts and methods. Unpublished paper. Ross-on-Wye: The Leadership Trust.
Dixon, N. (1985c), The training of leader. Unpublished paper. Ross-on-Wye: The Leadership Trust.
Donovan, M. (1994), The empowerment plan. *Journal for Quality and Participation,* July/August, 12–14.
Döös, M. and Wilhelmson, L. (2003), Work processes of shared leadership. Paper presented at the Annual Conference of the British Academy of Management, Harrogate, 15–17 September.
Dorcas, A. (2000), Qigong: an invitation to take a break from intellection and discover intuition. College seminar, 1995–96. *The Millennium Journal 2000,* Robert Black College, University of Hong Kong, 65.
Downton, J.V. (1973), *Rebel Leadership: Commitment and Charisma in the Revolutionary Process.* New York: Free Press.
Doyle, P. (1996), The loss from profits. *Financial Times,* 25 October.
Drath, W.H. (2001a), The third way: a new source of leadership, *Leadership in Action,* 21 (2), May/June, 7–11.
Drath, W.H. (2001b), *The Deep Blue Sea: Rethinking the Source of Leadership.* San Francisco, CA: Jossey-Bass.
Drucker, P.F. (1966), *The Effective Executive.* New York: HarperBusiness (revised edition, 2002).
Drucker, P.F. (1992), *Managing for the Future.* Oxford: Butterworth–Heinemann.
Drucker, P.F. (1995), *Managing in a Time of Great Change.* New York: Penguin.
Drucker, P.F. (1997), Introduction: toward the new organization. In F. Hesselbein, M. Goldsmith and R. Beckhard (Editors), *The Organization of the Future.* San Francisco, CA: Jossey-Bass.
Drucker, P.F. (1999a), Managing oneself. *Harvard Business Review,* March–April, 65–74.
Drucker, P.F. (1999b), *Management Challenges for the 21st Century.* New York: HarperCollins.
Dubrin, A.J. (2001), *Leadership: Research Findings, Practice and Skills, 3rd Edition.* Boston, MA: Houghton Mifflin.
Dulewicz, V. and Higgs, M. (2000), Emotional intelligence: a review and evaluation study. *Journal of Managerial Psychology,* 15 (4), 341–372.
Dulewicz, V. and Higgs, M. (2002), *Emotional Intelligence, Motivation and Personality: A Study of Leaders and Teams in a Round-the-World Yacht Race.* Henley Working Paper 0203, Henley Management College.
Dulewicz, V., Higgs, M. and Cranwell-Ward, J. (2002), Ocean's twelve. *People Management,* 30 May, 32–35.
Dutton, J.E., Fahey, L. and Narayanan, V.K. (1983), Understanding strategic issue diagnosis. *Strategic Management Journal,* 14, 307–323.
Dutton, J.E. and Jackson, S. (1987), Categorizing strategic issues: links to organizational action. *Academy of Management Review,* 12 (1), 76–90.
Dutton, J.E. and Penner, W.J. (1993), The importance of organizational identity for strategic agenda building. In J. Hendry, G. Johnson and J. Newton (Editors), *Strategic Thinking: Leadership and the Management of Change.* Chichester: John Wiley & Sons.
Dutton, J.E., Walton, E.J. and Abrahamson, E.C. (1989), Important dimensions of strategic issues: separating the wheat from the chaff. *Journal of Management Studies,* 26, 379–396.
Eadie, A. (1999), When empowerment may be bad for you. *Daily Telegraph,* 29 July, A14.
Eadie, A. (2001a), Leadership looking for a 21st century direction. *Sunday Telegraph,* 10 June.
Eadie, A. (2001b), Class acts with MBAs are no guarantee of success as a chief executive. *Daily Telegraph,* 22 February.
Eagly, A.H. and Johannesen-Schmidt, M.C. (2001), The leadership styles of men and women. *Journal of Social Issues,* 57 (4), 781–797.
Easton, G.S. (1993), The 1993 state of US Total Quality Management: A Baldridge Examiners' Perspective. *California Management Review,* Spring, 32–54.
Eden, C. (1993), Strategy development and implementation: cognitive mapping for Group Support. In J. Hendry, G. Johnson and J. Newton (Editors), *Strategic Thinking: Leadership and the Management of Change.* Chichester: John Wiley & Sons.

Eden, D. (1984), Self-fulfilling prophecy as a management tool: harnessing Pygmalion. *Academy of Management Review*, 9 (1), 64–73.
Eden, D. (1990), *Pygmalion in Management: Productivity as a Self-fulfilling Prophecy.* San Francisco, CA: New Lexington Press.
Eden, D. and Ravid, G. (1982), Pygmalion vs. self-expectancy: effects of instructor- and self-expectancy on trainee performance. *Organizational Behavior and Human Performance*, 30, 351–364.
Eden, D. and Shani, A.B. (1982), Pygmalion goes to boot camp: expectancy, leadership, and trainee performance. *Journal of Applied Psychology*, 67, 194–199.
Edwards, C. (2004), Five-star strategy. *People Management*, 8 April, 34–35.
Edwards, G. (2000), *In Search of the 'Holy Grail': Leadership in Management.* Working Paper no. LT-GE-00–15. Ross-on-Wye: The Leadership Trust Foundation.
Edwards, G., Bailey, J. and Winter, P.K. (2002), *Leadership in Management.* Ross-on-Wye: The Leadership Trust Foundation.
Edwards, G. and Gill, R. (2003a), Hierarchical level as a moderator of leadership behaviour: a 360-degree investigation. Paper presented at the Annual Occupational Psychology Conference, British Psychological Society, Bournemouth, 8–10 January.
Edwards, G. and Gill, R. (2003b), An investigation of the 'Full Range Leadership' model at different hierarchical levels of an organisation using multiple ratings. Paper presented at the Annual Conference of the British Academy of Management, Harrogate, 15–17 September.
EFQM (2000), *Assessing for Excellence: A Practical Guide for Self Assessment.* Brussels: European Foundation for Quality Management.
Eglin, R. (2001a), No more Mr Nice Guy as times get tough. *Sunday Times*, 4 March.
Eglin, R. (2001b), Preaching fails to convert workforce. *Sunday Times*, 11 March.
Eglin, R. (2001c), Think ahead to avoid nasty surprises. *Sunday Times*, 29 April, 7.16.
Eglin, R. (2002a), Wanted: real leaders who can be trusted. *Sunday Times*, 28 July, 7.4.
Eglin, R. (2002b), High flying bosses know their history. *Sunday Times*, 17 March, 7.7.
Eglin, R. (2003), Why business is no place for yes men. *Sunday Times*, 8 September, 7.6.
Eglin, R. (2004), A third of Britons are bored at work. *Sunday Times*, 7 March, 7.6.
Eglin, R. (2005), Leadership begins in the playground. *Sunday Times*, 9 January, 7.9.
Ehrhart, M.G. and Klein, K.J. (2001), Predicting followers' preferences for charismatic leadership: the influence of follower values and personality. *Leadership Quarterly*, 12 (2), 153–179.
Eicher, J. (2000), *Post-Heroic Leadership: Managing the Virtual Organization.* Performance Improvement Global Network:
www.pignc-ispi.com.
Eidelson, R.J. and Eidelson, J.I. (2003), Dangerous ideas: five beliefs that propel groups towards conflict. *American Psychologist*, 58 (3), 182–192.
Eisenhardt, K.M. (1992), Speed and strategic choice: accelerating decision making. *Planning Review*, 20, 30–34.
Elgie, R. (1995), *Political Leadership in Liberal Democracies.* Basingstoke: Macmillan.
Elliott, J. (2003), Think happy, *Sunday Times*, 23 November, 1.23.
Ellis, C. (1996), Making strategic alliances succeed. *Harvard Business Review*, 74 (4), 8–9.
Ellsworth, R.R. (2002), *Leading with Purpose: The New Corporate Realities.* Stanford, CA: Stanford Business Books.
Empson, L. (1999), The challenge of managing knowledge. Mastering Strategy: Part Two. *Financial Times*, 4 October, 8–10.
Envik, B.R. (1998), Behaviours of entrepreneurs: a gender comparison. *Journal of Business and Entrepreneurship*, March, 106–115.
Erez, A. and Isen, A.M. (2002), The influence of positive affect on the components of expectancy motivation. *Journal of Applied Psychology*, 87 (6), 1055–1067.
Etzioni, A. (1961), *A Comparative Analysis of Complex Organizations.* New York: Free Press.
Evans, M.G. (1970), The effects of supervisory behavior on the path-goal relationship. *Organizational Behavior and Human Performance*, 5, 277–298.
Evans, R. (1997), Follow the leader. *Report on Business*, November, 56–63.
Evered, R. (1980), *So What Is Strategy?* Working Paper. Monterey, CA: Naval Postgraduate School.
Fairholm, G.W. (1996), Spiritual leadership: fulfilling whole-self needs at work. *Leadership & Organization Development Journal*, 17 (5), 11–17.
Fairhurst, G. and Sarr, R. (1996), *The Art of Framing.* San Francisco, CA: Jossey-Bass.

Farjoun, M. (2002), Towards an organic perspective on strategy. *Strategic Management Journal*, 23, 561–594.
Farkas, C.M. and Wetlaufer, S. (1996), The ways chief executives lead. *Harvard Business Review*, May–June, 110–123.
Faruk, A. (2002a), Corporate responsibility: beyond niceness. *Ashridge Journal*, Summer, 28–31.
Faruk, A. (2002b), *Ashridge Corporate Responsibility Survey*. Berkhamsted: Ashridge Management College.
Federgruen, A. and van Ryzin, G. (2003), New risks put scenario planning in favour. *Financial Times*, 19 August, 11.
Ferrier, N. (Editor) (1965), *Churchill: The Man of the Century*. London: Purnell.
Ferris, G.R., Hochwarter, W.A., Douglas, C., Blass, R., Kolodinsky, R.W. and Treadway, D.C. (2002), Social influence processes in human resources systems. In G.R. Ferris and J.J. Martocchio (Editors), *Research in Personnel and Human Resources Management, Vol. 21*, 65–127. Oxford: JAI Press/Elsevier Science.
Festinger, L. (1957), *A Theory of Cognitive Dissonance*. Evanston, IL: Row, Peterson.
Fiedler, F.E. (1969), Leadership – a new model. In C.A. Gibb (Editor), *Leadership*. Harmondsworth: Penguin.
Fiedler, F.E. (1986), The contribution of cognitive resources and leader behaviour to organizational performance. *Journal of Applied Social Psychology*, 16, 532–548.
Fiedler, F.E. (2002), The curious role of cognitive resources in leadership. In R.E. Riggio, S.E. Murphy and F.J. Pirozzolo (Editors), *Multiple Intelligences and Leadership*. Mahwah, NJ: Erlbaum.
Fiedler, F.E. and Garcia, J.E. (1987), *New Approaches to Effective Leadership: Cognitive Resources and Organizational Performance*. New York: JohnWiley & Sons.
Fineman, S. (1996), Emotion and organizing. In S.R. Clegg, C. Hardy and W.R. Nord (Editors), *Handbook of Organization Studies*. London: Sage Publications.
Fineman, S. (1997), Emotion and management learning. *Management Learning*, 28 (1), 13–25.
Fineman, S. (2001), Emotions and organizational control. In R. Payne and C. L. Cooper (Editors), *Emotions at Work*, 214–239. New York: JohnWiley & Sons.
Fineman, S. (2003), *Understanding Emotion at Work*. London: Sage Publications.
Finkelstein, S. (2003a), How do you spot the signs of disaster? *Financial Times*, 6 August, 11
Finkelstein, S. (2003b), *Why Smart Executives Fail and What You Can Learn from Their Mistakes*. New York: Portfolio.
Finn, W. (1998), Personal aspect important in marriage. *Sunday Telegraph*, 5 April, A5.
Finnie, B. and Norris, M. (1997), On leading change: a conversation with John P. Kotter. *Strategy and Leadership*, 25 (1), 18.
Fiol, C.M., Harris, D. and House, R.J. (1999), Charismatic leadership: strategies for effecting social change. *Leadership Quarterly*, 10, 440–482.
Fiol, C.M. and Huff, A.S. (1992), Maps for managers: where are we? Where do we go from here? *Journal of Management Studies*, 29 (3), 267–285.
Fiol, C.M. and O'Connor, E.J. (2002), Future Planning + Present Mindfulness = Strategic Foresight. Paper presented at the International Conference on 'Probing the Future: Developing Organizational Foresight in the Knowledge Economy', University of Strathclyde Graduate School of Business, Glasgow, 11–13 July.
Fiske, S.T. and Taylor, S.E. (1991), *Social Cognition*. New York: McGraw-Hill.
Fitton, R.A. (1997), *Leadership: Quotations from the World's Greatest Motivators*. Oxford: Westview Press.
Flanagan, R. (2000), Leadership during cultural and institutional change. Paper presented at the National Leadership Conference, MCI-METO, The Royal Military Academy, Sandhurst, 24 May.
Fletcher, C. (1976), Editor's Foreword. In Ralph Rolls, *Image and Imagination*. Nutfield: Denholm House Press.
Fleishman, E.A. (1953), The description of supervisory behaviour. *Journal of Applied Psychology*, 37 (1), 1–6.
Fleishman, E.A. and Harris, E.F. (1962), Patterns of leadership behavior related to employee grievances and turnover, *Personnel Psychology*, 15 (1), 43–56.
Fleishman, E.A., Mumford, M.D., Zaccaro, S.J., Levin, K.Y., Korotkin, A.L. and Hein, M.B. (1991), Taxonomic efforts in the description of leader behavior: a synthesis and functional interpretation. *Leadership Quarterly*, 2, 245–287.
Fleming, P.C. (1991), Empowerment strengthens the rock. *Management Review*, 80 (12), 34–37.
Flynn, F.J. and Staw, B.M. (2004), Lend me your wallets: the effect of charismatic leadership on external support for an organization. *Strategic Management Journal*, 25, 309–330.
Fogden, M. (2001), Do the private and public sectors require different leadership? A public sector perspective. Paper presented at the Leadership Forum, The Leadership Trust Foundation, Ross-on-Wye, 11 October.

Follett, K. (2000), *Code to Zero.* London: Macmillan.
Fombrun, C. (1996), *Reputation: Realizing Value from the Corporate Image.* Boston, MA: Harvard Business School Press.
Ford, R.C. (2002), Darden Restaurants CEO Joe Lee on the importance of core values: integrity and fairness. *Academy of Management Executive,* 16 (1), 31–36.
Foti, R.J. and Miner, J.B. (2003), Theoretical letters. Individual differences and organizational forms in the leadership process. *Leadership Quarterly,* 14, 83–112.
Frankl, V.E. (1984), *Man's Search for Meaning, 3rd Edition.* New York: Simon and Schuster.
Fray, P. (2001), Rewards of running a happy workplace. *Liverpool Daily Post,* 15 February, 20–21.
French, J.P. and Raven, B.H. (1986), The bases of social power. In D. Cartwright and A.F. Zander (Editors), *Group Dynamics: Research and Theory,* 3rd *Edition.* New York: Harper and Row.
Frese, M., Beimel, S. and Schoenborn, S. (2003), Action training for charismatic leadership: two evaluations of studies of a commercial training module on inspirational communication of a vision. *Personnel Psychology,* 56, 671–697.
Friedman, M. (1962), *Capitalism and Freedom.* Chicago: Chicago University Press.
Friedman, S.D. (2001), Leadership DNA: The Ford Motor story. *Training & Development,* March, 23–29.
Frohman, A. (1997), Igniting organizational change from below: the power of personal initiative. *Organizational Dynamics,* Winter, 39–53.
Frost, P.J. (2003), *Toxic Emotions at Work: How Compassionate Managers Handle Pain and Conflict.* Boston, MA Harvard Business School Press.
Frost, T. and Mossavi, F. (1992), The relationship between leader power base and influence: the moderating role of trust. *Journal of Applied Psychology,* 78 (4), 9–14.
Fry, L.W. (2003), Toward a theory of spiritual leadership. *Leadership Quarterly,* 14, 693–727.
Fudge, R.S. and Schlacter, J.L. (1999), Motivating employees to act ethically: an expectancy theory approach. *Journal of Business Ethics,* 18 (3), 195–304.
Fukuyama, F. (1995), *Trust: The Social Values and the Creation of Prosperity,* London: Hamish Hamilton.
Fuller, R.W. (2001), A new look at hierarchy. *Leader to Leader,* Summer, 6–12.
Fulmer, R.M. (1997), The evolving paradigm of leadership development, *Organizational Dynamics,* 25 (4), 59–72.
Fulmer, R.M. and Gilkey, R. (1988), Blending corporate families: management and organization development in a post-merger environment. *Academy of Management Executive,* 2 (4), 275–283.
Funes, M. (2000), *Laughing Matters: Live Creatively with Laughter.* Dublin: Newleaf.
Furnham, A. (2001a), Industry needs more captains courageous. *Financial Times,* 5 September, 13.
Furnham, A. (2001b), Cut the comedy? You must be joking. *Daily Telegraph,* 22 February.
Gabris, G.T., Maclin, S.A. and Ihrke, D.M. (1998), The leadership enigma: toward a model of organizational optimism. *Journal of Management History,* 4 (4), 334–349.
Galosy, J. (1990), The human factor in mergers and acquisitions. *Training & Development Journal,* April, 90–95.
Gardner, H. (1985), *The Mind's New Science: A History of the Cognitive Revolution.* New York: Basic Books.
Gardner, H. (1993), *Frames of Mind: The Theory of Multiple Intelligences.* New York: Basic Books.
Gardner, H. (1995), *Leading Minds: An Anatomy of Leadership.* New York: Basic Books.
Gardner, J.W. (1990), *On Leadership.* New York: Free Press.
Gardner, L. and Stough, C. (2002), Examining the relationship between leadership and emotional intelligence in senior level managers. *Leadership & Organization Development Journal,* 23 (2), 68–78.
Garnsey, E. (1999), *Acquisition for Innovation: A Report into the Organisation and Human Dynamics of Acquiring Innovative Companies.* Cambridge: ER Consultants.
Garratt, B. (1996), *The Fish Rots from the Head: The Crisis in Our Boardrooms.* London: HarperCollins.
Garten, J.E. (2001), *The Mind of the CEO.* New York: Basic Books.
Gary, L. (2001), Strategy as process. *Burning Questions 2001, Harvard Management Update,* July, 8.
Geneen, H. (1984), *Managing.* New York: Avon.
George, J.M. and Brief, A.P. (1996), Motivational agendas in the work-place: the effects of feelings on focus of attention and work motivation. *Research in Organizational Behavior,* 18, 75–109.
George, W.W. (2001), *Keynote Address.* Academy of Management Annual Conference, Washington, DC, August. In *Academy of Management Executive,* 15 (4), 39–47.
Georgiades, N. and Macdonnell, R. (1998), *Leadership for Competitive Advantage.* Chichester: John Wiley & Sons.

Gerth, H.H. and Mills, C.W. (1946), *From Max Weber: Essays in Sociology.* New York: Oxford University Press.

Giddens, A. (2000), *Runaway World: How Globalization Is Reshaping Our Lives.* New York: Routledge.

Gilbert-Smith, D. (2003), *Winning Hearts and Minds.* London: Pen Press.

Giles, L. (1976), *The Analects of Confucius, XII.7.* Translated from the Chinese. Norwalk, CT: The Easton Press.

Gill, R. (1980), Intelligence and trainability in managerial prioritizing and decision-making: an empirical investigation. Paper presented at the British Psychological Society Annual London Conference, London, December.

Gill, R. (1982), A trainability concept for management potential and an empirical study of its relationship with intelligence for two managerial skills, *Journal of Occupational Psychology,* 55 (2), 139–147.

Gill, R. (1998), The Impact of 360-degree feedback on leadership behaviour. Paper presented at a Symposium on 'What Can Be Learned from the Analysis of 360-degree/Multirater Feedback Data and Its Applications in Organizations?' at the 24th International Congress of Applied Psychology, San Francisco, CA, August 9–14.

Gill, R. (1999a), *The Leadership Styles of Transactional and Transformational Leaders.* Working Paper (LT-RG-97–1 revised). Ross-on-Wye: The Leadership Trust Foundation.

Gill, R. (1999b), *Cross-cultural Similarities and Differences in Leadership Styles and Behaviour: A Comparison between UK and Southeast Asian Managers.* Working Paper (LT-RG-97–6 revised). Ross-on-Wye: The Leadership Trust Foundation.

Gill, R. (1999c), Making transition a working reality. *Guardian,* 28 August.

Gill, R. (1999d), Mergers and acquisitions: the route to failure? *Training Journal,* November, 20–23.

Gill, R. (2001a), Does executive education really improve business performance? *Independent on Sunday,* 16 December.

Gill, R. (2001b), Leadership sans frontiéres. *City to City,* 12, September/October, 32–33.

Gill, R. (2003), Change management – or change leadership? *Journal of Change Management,* 3 (4), 307–318.

Gill, R., Levine, N. and Pitt, D.C. (1998), Leadership and organizations for the new millennium. *Journal of Leadership Studies,* 5 (4), 46–59.

Gillen, T. (2003), Leadership training: how to give it practical impact. *Training Journal,* December, 16–21.

Gingell, W.R. (1852), *The Ceremonial Uses of the Chinese, B.C.1121, as Prescribed in the 'Institutes of the Chow Dynasty Strung as Pearls.' Or Chow le Kwan Choo.* London: Elder.

Gioia, D.A. and Sims, H.P. (1986), *The Thinking Organization: Dynamics of Organizational Social Cognition.* San Francisco, CA: Jossey-Bass.

Goffee, R. and Jones, G. (2000), Why should anyone be led by you? *Harvard Business Review,* September–October, 62–70.

Gold, J. and Harris, A. (2003), Leading in schools: studying distribution. Paper presented at the Second Annual International Conference on Leadership Research, 'Studying Leadership', Lancaster University Management School, Lancaster, 15–16 December.

Goldie, C.M. and Pinch, R.G.E. (1991), *Communication Theory.* New York: Press Syndicate of the University of Cambridge.

Goldman, R.N., Nagel, R. and Preiss, K. (1994), *Agile Competitors and Virtual Organizations: Strategies for Enriching the Customer.* New York: Van Nostrand Reinhold.

Goldsmith, W. and Ritchie, B. (1987), *The New Elite.* London: Weidenfeld & Nicolson.

Goldstein, M. (1992), Management succession – plan now or pay later. *CPA Journal,* 62 (8), 14.

Goleman, D. (1995), *Emotional Intelligence.* New York: Bantam Books.

Goleman, D. (1997), Beyond IQ: developing the leadership competencies of emotional intelligence. Paper presented at the Second International Competency Conference, London, October.

Goleman, D. (1998a), The emotional intelligence of leaders. *Leader to Leader,* Fall, 20–26.

Goleman, D. (1998b), *Working with Emotional Intelligence.* London: Bloomsbury.

Goleman, D., Boyatzis, R. and McKee, A. (2001), Primal leadership: the hidden driver of great performance. Breakthrough Leadership, *Harvard Business Review,* December, 43–51.

Gonen, J.Y. (2000), *The Roots of Nazi Psychology: Hitler's Utopian Barbarism.* Lexington, KY: University of Kentucky Press.

Goodman, M. (2002), Getting the boot. *The Sunday Times,* 15 December, 3.5.

Goodpaster, K.E. (1983), *The Beliefs of Borg-Warner.* Case 9–383–091, Boston, MA: Harvard Business School.

Goodwin, D.K. (1998), Lessons of presidential leadership, *Leader to Leader*, 9, 23–30.

Gordon, G.G. and DiTomaso, N. (1992), Predicting corporate performance from organizational culture. *Journal of Management Studies*, 29, 783–798.

Goyder, M. (1999), Value and values: lessons for tomorrow's company. *Long Range Planning*, 32 (2), 217–224.

Goyder, M. (2001), Learn to lead, not manage. *The Sunday Times*, 18 November, 7.9.

Graen, G. (1976), Role-making processes within complex organizations. In M.D. Dunnette (Editor), *Handbook of Industrial and Organizational Psychology*. Chicago: Rand McNally.

Graen, G., Cashman, J., Ginsburgh, S. and Schiesmann, W. (1977), Effects of linking-pin quality upon the quality of working life of lower participants: a longitudinal investigation of the managerial understructure. *Administrative Science Quarterly*, 22, 491–504.

Graham, J.W. (1991), Servant-leadership in organizations: inspirational and moral. *Leadership Quarterly*, 2 (2), 105–19.

Granovetter, M. (1985), Economic action and social structure: the problem of embeddedness. *American Journal of Sociology*, 91, 481–510.

Grant, J. (1988), Women as managers: what they can offer to organizations. *Organizational Dynamics*, 16 (3), 56–63.

Grant, J. (1992), Women as managers. What they can offer organizations. In M. Syrett and C. Hogg (Editors), *Frontiers of Leadership*. Oxford: Blackwell.

Gratton, L. (1997), Tomorrow people. *People Management*, 24 July, 22–27.

Gratton, L. (2003), La dolce vita. *People Management*, 11 September, 20.

Gray, J.R., Braver, T.S. and Raichle, M.E. (2002), *Monitor on Psychology*, American Psychological Association, 33 (6), 18.

Grayling, A.C. (2004), What is the good life? Richer not happier: a 21st century search for the good life. Debate on 11 February 2004 at the Royal Society of Arts, London. *RSA Journal*, July, 36–39.

Grayson, D. and Hodges, A. (2004), *Corporate Social Opportunity!* Sheffield: Greenleaf.

Greenberg, J. and Baron, R.A. (2000), *Behavior in Organizations*. Harlow: Prentice Hall.

Greene, C.N. (1975), The reciprocal nature of influence between leader and subordinate, *Journal of Applied Psychology*, 60, 187–193.

Greenfield, S. (2003), The intuitive brain – what is its future? Paper presented at the Sixth Annual Leadership Conference, 'Intuition, Leadership, Instinct', The Leadership Trust Foundation, Ross-on-Wye, 23–24 September.

Greenhalgh, L. (2001a), Managers face up to the new era. Mastering Management, *Financial Times*, 22 January.

Greenhalgh, L. (2001b), *Managing Strategic Relationships*. New York: Free Press.

Greenleaf, R.K. (1977), *Servant Leadership*. New York: Paulist Press.

Greenleaf, R.K. (1991), *The Servant as Leader*. Indianapolis, IL: The Robert K. Greenleaf Center.

Grensing-Pophal, L. (2000), Follow me. *HR Magazine*, 45 (2), February, 36–41.

Griffin, A.F. (2002), The due diligence stage. In J.A. Schmidt (Editor), *Making Mergers Work: The Strategic Importance of People*, 75–97. Alexandria, VA: SHRM Foundation and Towers, Perrin, Foster, & Crosby, Inc.

Griffiths, G. (1999), The cross-cultural chessboard at BT. Paper presented at the Second Annual Conference of The Leadership Trust Foundation on 'Leadership sans Frontières', Ross-on-Wye, February 1–2.

Grint, K. (1997a), Introduction. In K. Grint (Editor), *Leadership: Classical, Contemporary and Critical Approaches*. Oxford: Oxford University Press.

Grint, K. (1997b), TQM, BPR, JIT, BSCs and TLAs: managerial waves or drownings? *Management Decision*, 35 (10), 731–738.

Grint, K. (2000), *The Arts of Leadership*. Oxford: Oxford University Press.

Gronn, P. (1995a), Greatness revisited: the current obsession with transformational leadership, *Leading and Managing*, 1 (1), 14–27.

Gronn, P. (1995b), A realistic view of leadership. Paper presented at the ELO-AusAsia online conference on Educational Leadership for the New Millennium:
http://elo.eddirect.com.

Gronn, P. (1999), Substituting for leadership: the neglected role of the leadership couple. *Leadership Quarterly*, 10 (1), 41–62.

Gronn, P. (2002), Distributed leadership as a unit of analysis, *Leadership Quarterly*, 13 (4), 423–451.

Gronn, P. (2003), Leadership: who needs it? *School Leadership and Management*, 23 (3), 267–290.

Guardian (2000), Briefcase: Watch out for: Rentokil Initial. *Guardian*, 17 May.

Guba, E.G. and Lincoln, Y.S. (1982), Epistemological and methodological bases of naturalistic enquiry, *Educational Communication and Technology Journal*, 30, 233–252.

Guild, T. (2000), Making M&A work in Japan. *McKinsey Quarterly*, 4, 87–93.

Gunaratna, R. (2003), Cooking for terrorists. *The Times Higher*, 14 February, 20–21.

Gupta, A.K. (1988), Contingency perspectives in strategic leadership: current knowledge and future research directions. In D.C. Hambrick (Editor), *The Executive Effect: Concepts and Methods for Studying Top Managers*. Greenwich, CT: JAI Press.

Hackman, J.R. and Oldham, G.R. (1976), Motivation through the design of work: test of a theory. *Organizational Behavior and Human Performance*, 15, 250–279.

Hackman, R. (2001), Foreword. In H. Seifter and P. Economy, *Leadership Ensemble: Lessons in Collaborative Management from the World's Only Conductorless Orchestra*. New York: Henry Holt.

Hafile, J.W. (1962), *Creativity and Innovation*. New York: Reinhold.

Hagen, A., Haile, S. and Yousef, M. (2003), CEOs' perceptions of strategic flexibility and its impact on organizational performance: empirical investigation. *Research Journal of the Olu Olu Institute Academy International Congress*, 1 (1).

Haire, M., Ghiselli, E. and Porter, L. (1966), *Managerial Thinking: An International Study*. New York: John Wiley & Sons.

Haleblian, J. and Finkelstein, S. (1993), Top management team size, CEO dominance, and firm performance: the moderating roles of environmental turbulence and discretion. *Academy of Management Journal*, 36 (4), 844–863.

Hall, A. (2000), What on earth is Stelios Haji-Ioannou up to now? *Real Business*, March, 12–14.

Hall, A. (2001), Russell's prescription for Boots. *Sunday Telegraph*, 3 June.

Hambrick, D.C. (1989), Guest editor's introduction: putting top managers back in the strategy process. *Journal of Strategic Management*, Summer, 5–15.

Hambrick, D.C. and Fredrickson, J.W. (2001), Are you sure you have a strategy? *Academy of Management Executive*, 15 (4), 48–59.

Hambrick, D.C. and Mason, P. (1984), Upper echelons: the organization as a reflection of its top managers. *Academy of Management Review*, 9, 193–206.

Hamel, G. (2001), *Leading the Revolution*. New York: McGraw-Hill.

Hamel, G. (2002), *Leading the Revolution*. Boston, MA: Harvard Business School Press.

Hamel, G. and Prahalad, C.K. (1994), *Competing for the Future: Breakthrough Strategies for Seizing Control of Your Industry and Creating the Markets of Tomorrow*. Boston, MA: Harvard Business School Press.

Hamel, G. and Välikangas, L. (2003), The quest for resilience. *Harvard Business Review*, September, 52–63.

Hamlin, R.G. (2004), In support of universalistic models of managerial and leadership effectiveness: implications for HRD research and practice. *Human Resource Development Quarterly*, 15 (2), 189–215.

Hampson, S. (1999), State of the art: personality. *The Psychologist*, 12 (6), 284–288.

Handy, C. (1992a), The language of leadership. In M. Syrett and C. Hogg (Editors), *Frontiers of Leadership*. Oxford: Blackwell.

Handy, C. (1992b), *Waiting for the Mountain to Move*. London: Arrow Books.

Handy, C. (1995), *The Empty Raincoat*. London: Arrow Books.

Handy, C. (1997), *The Hungry Spirit: Beyond Capitalism – A Quest for Purpose in the Modern World*. London: Hutchinson.

Haplin, A.W. and Winer, B.J. (1957), A factorial study of leader behavior descriptions. In R.M. Stogdill and A.E. Coons (Editors), *Leader Behavior: Its Description and Measurement*. Columbus, OH: Bureau of Business Research, Ohio State University.

Harrell, A.M. and Stahl, M.J. (1984), Modeling managers' effort-level decisions for a within-persons examination of expectancy theory in a budget setting. *Decision Sciences*, 15, 52–73.

Hart, C. and Schlesinger, L. (1991), Total quality management and the human resource professional: applying the Baldridge framework to human resources. *Human Resource Management*, Winter, 30 (4), 433–454.

Hart, S.L. and Banburry, C. (1994), How strategy-making processes can make a difference. *Strategic Management Journal*, 15, 251–269.

Hart, S.L. and Quinn, R.E. (1993), Roles executives play: CEOs, behavioral complexity, and firm performance. *Human Relations*, 46 (5), 543–574.

Härtel, C.E.J. and Fujimoto, Y. (2000), Diversity is not the problem: openness to perceived dissimilarity is. *Journal of the Australian and New Zealand Academy of Management*, 5, 14–27.

Hartley, J. and Morgan-Thomas, A. (2003), The development of the Political Leadership Questionnaire: conceptual framework and measurement properties. Paper presented at the Second Annual International Conference on Leadership Research, 'Studying Leadership', Lancaster University Management School, Lancaster, 15–16 December.

Harung, H.S., Heaton, D.P. and Alexander, C.N. (1995), A unified theory of leadership: experiences of higher states of consciousness in world-class leaders. *Leadership & Organization Development Journal*, 16 (7), 44–59.

Harvey-Jones, J. (1988), *Making It Happen*. London: HarperCollins.

Haskins, M.L. (1940), *The Gate of the Year*. London: Hodder and Stoughton.

Hass, H. (1992), *The Leaders Within: An Empowering Path of Self-discovery*. New York: Harper Business.

Hastings, C. (1993), *The New Organization*. London: IBM/McGraw-Hill.

Hater, J.J. and Bass, B.M. (1988), Supervisors' evaluations and subordinates' perceptions of transformational leadership. *Journal of Applied Psychology*, 73, 695–702.

Hatfield, E., Cacioppo, J.T. and Rapson, R.L. (1992), Primitive emotional contagion. In M.S. Clark (Editor), *Review of Personality and Social Psychology, Vol. 14: Emotion and Social Behaviour*. Newbury Park, CA: Sage Publications.

Hayashi, A.M. (2001), When to trust your gut. *Harvard Business Review*, February, 59–65.

Hayes, B.E. (1994), How to measure empowerment. *Quality Progress*, February, 41–46.

HayGroup (2001), *Top Teams: Why some work and some do not*. Working Paper. Boston, MA: HayGroup, Inc.

Hayhurst, C. (2002), The power to inspire. *Peak Performance*, Spring, 7–11.

Hazell, R. (1997), *Heroes: Great Men through the Ages*. New York: Abbeville Press.

Hazlitt, W. (1807), *The Eloquence of the British Senate*. In Geoffrey Keynes (Editor) (1946), *Selected Essays of William Hazlitt: 1778–1830*. London: Nonesuch Press.

Heenan, D. and Bennis, W. (1999), *Co-leaders: The Power of Great Partnership*. New York: John Wiley & Sons.

Heider, F. (1958), *The Psychology of Interpersonal Relations*. New York: John Wiley & Sons.

Heifetz, R.A. and Laurie, D.L. (1997), The work of leadership. *Harvard Business Review*, January-February, 124–134.

Heller, R. (1997), *In Search of European Excellence*. London: HarperCollins Business.

Heller, T. and Van Til, J. (1982), Leadership and followership: some summary propositions. *Journal of Applied Behavioral Science*, 18 (3), 405–414.

Hennestad, B. (1998), Empowering by de-powering: towards an HR strategy for realizing the power of empowerment. *International Journal of Human Resource Management*, 9 (5), 934–953.

Herrenkohl, R.C., Judson, G.T. and Heffner, J.A. (1999), Defining and measuring employee empowerment. *Journal of Applied Behavioral Science*, 35 (3), September, 373–389.

Hersey, P. and Blanchard, K.H. (1969), The life cycle theory of leadership. *Training and Development Journal*, 23 (5), 26–34.

Hersey, P. and Blanchard, K.H. (1993), *Management of Organizational Behavior: Utilizing Human Resources, 6th Edition*. Englewood Cliffs, NJ: Prentice Hall.

Herzberg, F. (1964), The motivation-hygiene concept and problems of manpower. *Personnel Administrator*, 27, 3–7.

Herzberg, F. (1966), *Work and the Nature of Man*. Cleveland, OH: World Publishing.

Herzberg, F., Mausner, B. and Snyderman, B.B. (1959), *The Motivation to Work, 2nd Edition*. New York: John Wiley & Sons.

Hesselbein, F. (2002), *Hesselbein on Leadership*. San Francisco, CA: Jossey-Bass.

Hicks, D.A. (2002), Spiritual and religious diversity in the workplace: implications for leadership. *Leadership Quarterly*, 13, 370–396.

Higgs, M. and Dulewicz, V. (1999), *Making Sense of Emotional Intelligence*. Windsor: NFER-Nelson.

Higgs, M. and Dulewicz, V. (2002), *Making Sense of Emotional Intelligence, 2nd Edition*. London: ASE.

Higgs, M. and Rowland, D. (2003), Is change changing? An examination of approaches to change and its leadership. Paper presented at the Second Annual International Conference on Leadership Research, 'Studying Leadership', Lancaster University Management School, Lancaster, 15–16 December.

Hilpern, K. (2001), Driven by a need to help others. Leadership supplement. *Independent* in association with PricewaterhouseCoopers, 10 April.

Hinkin, T.R. and Tracey, J.B. (1999), The relevance of charisma for transformational leadership in stable organizations. *Journal of Organizational Change Management*, 12 (2), 105–119.

Hirschhorn, L. (1997), *Reworking Authority: Leading and Following in the Post-Modern Organization*. Cambridge, MA: MIT Press.

Hirshberg, G. (2002), Profits with a conscience. *Leader to Leader*, Winter, 24–28.

Hitt, M.A., Harrison, J., Ireland, R.D. and Best, A. (1998), Attributes of successful and unsuccessful acquisitions of US firms. *British Journal of Management*, 9, 91–114.

Hitt, M.A., Ireland, R.D. and Hoskisson, R.E. (1995), *Strategic Management: Competitiveness and Globalization*. Minneapolis/St Paul, MN: West.

Hitt, M.A. and Tyler, B.B. (1991), Strategic decision models: integrating different perspectives. *Strategic Management Journal*, 12, 327–351.

Hjelt, P. (2003), The world's most admired companies 2003. *Fortune*, March 3, 24–33.

Hoad, T.F. (Editor) (1988), *The Concise Oxford Dictionary of English Etymology*. Oxford: Oxford University Press.

Hoar, R. (2004), Work with meaning. *Management Today*, May, 44–53.

Hoare, S. (2001), Rhymes with leadership. Sunday Business, *Sunday Telegraph*, 4 March, 4.

Hobrough, M. (2001), Globalisation – it's a foreign affair. *The Analyst*, 1, 1–3.

Hodgetts, R. (1996), A conversation with Warren Bennis on leadership in the midst of downsizing. *Organizational Dynamics*, 25 (1), 79.

Hodgson, P. and White, R. (2001), Leadership – the ne(x)t generation. *Directions: The Ashridge Journal*, Summer, 18–22.

Hofstede, G. (1984), *Culture's Consequences*. Thousand Oaks, CA: Sage Publications.

Hofstede, G. (1991), *Cultures and Organizations*. London: McGraw-Hill.

Hofstede, G. (1994), *Cultures and Organizations: Software of the Mind, Paperback Edition*. London: HarperCollins.

Hofstede, G. (1998), Identifying organizational subcultures: an empirical investigation. *Journal of Management Studies*, 35 (1), 1–12.

Hogg, M.A. (2001), A social identity theory of leadership. *Personality and Social Psychology Review*, 5, 184–200.

Holbeche, L. (1998), Scary splice, *People Management*, October 15, 44–46.

Holden, P. (2000), Ethics for leaders. Paper presented at a seminar, The Leadership Trust Foundation, Ross-on-Wye, 16 March.

Holladay, S.J. and Coombs, W.T. (1994), Speaking of visions and visions being spoken: an exploration of the effects of content and delivery on perceptions of leader charisma. *Management Communication Quarterly*, 8, 165–189.

Hollander, E.P. and Offerman, L.R. (1990), Power and leadership in organizations. *American Psychologist*, February, 179–188.

Holloway, E.K., Baring, J. and Helleur, J. (2000), Enhancing transformational leadership: the roles of training and feedback. *Leadership & Organization Development Journal*, 21 (3), 145–149.

Holt, R. and Rowe, D. (2000), Total quality, public management and critical leadership in civil construction projects. *International Journal of Quality & Reliability Management*, 17 (4, 5), 541–553.

Homer-Dixon, T.F. (1999), *Environment, Scarcity, and Violence*. Princeton, NJ: Princeton University Press.

Honey, P. and Mumford, A. (1992), *The Manual of Learning Styles, 3rd Edition*. Maidenhead: Peter Honey.

Hooijberg, R. (1996), A multidirectional approach toward leadership: an extension of the concept of behavioral complexity. *Human Relations*, 49 (7), 917–946.

Hooijberg, R. and DiTomaso, N. (1996), Leadership in and of demographically diverse organizations. *Leadership Quarterly*, 7 (1), 1–19.

Hooijberg, R., Hunt, J.G. and Dodge, G.E. (1997), Leadership complexity and development of the leaderplex model. *Journal of Management*, 23, 375–408.

Hooker, R. (Editor) (1993), *Manoeuvre Warfare: An Anthology*. Novato: Presidio Press.

Hooper, A. and Potter, J. (1997), *The Business of Leadership: Adding Lasting Value to Your Organization*. Aldershot: Ashgate.

Hooper, A. and Potter, J. (2001), *Intelligent Leadership: Creating a Passion for Change*. London: Random House Business Books.

Hoopes, D.G., Madsen, T.L. and Walker, G. (2003), Guest editors' introduction to the special issue: why is there a resource-based view? Toward a theory of competitive heterogeneity. *Strategic Management Journal*, 24, 889–902.

Hope, J.W. and Pate, L.E. (1988), A cognitive expectancy analysis of compliance decisions. *Human Relations*, 41, 739–751.

Horn, C. (2001), Leading by example. *Personnel Today*, 12 June.
Horner-Long, P. and Shoenberg, R. (2002), Does e-business require different leadership characteristics? An empirical investigation. *European Management Journal*, 20 (6), 611–619.
Hosmer, L.T. (1982), The importance of strategic leadership. *Journal of Business Strategy*, 3 (2), Fall, 47–57.
Hough, J.R. and Ogilvie, dt (2005), An empirical test of cognitive style and strategic decision outcomes. *Journal of Management Studies*, 42 (2), 417–448.
House, R.J. (1973), A path-goal theory of leadership effectiveness. In E.A. Fleishman and J.G. Hunt (Editors), *Current Developments in the Study of Leadership*. Carbondale, IL: Southern Illinois University Press.
House, R.J. (1977), A 1976 theory of charismatic leadership. In J.G. Hunt and L.L. Larson (Editors), *Leadership: The Cutting Edge*. Carbondale, IL: Southern Illinois University Press.
House, R.J. (1995), Leadership in the twenty-first century: a spectacular inquiry. In A. Howard (Editor), *The Changing Nature of Work*, 411–450. San Francisco, CA: Jossey-Bass.
House, R.J. and Aditya, R.N. (1997), The social scientific study of leadership: quo vadis? *Journal of Management*, 23 (3), 409–465.
House, R.J., Hanges, P.J., Ruiz-Quintanilla, S.A., Dorfman, P.W., Javidan, M., Dickson, M., Gupta, V. and GLOBE (1999), Cultural influences on leadership and organizations. *Advances in Global Leadership*, 1, 171–233, Stamford, CT: JAI Press.
House, R.J. and Howell, J.M. (1992), Personality and charismatic leadership. *Leadership Quarterly*, 3, 81–108.
House, R.J., Javidan, M. and Dorfman, P. (2001), Project GLOBE: an introduction, *Applied Psychology: An International Review*, 50 (4), 489–505.
House, R.J. and Mitchell, R.R. (1974), Path-goal theory of leadership. *Journal of Contemporary Business*, 3 (4), 81–98.
House, R.J. and Shamir, B. (1993), Towards and integration of transformational, charismatic, and visionary theories. In M.M. Chemers and R. Ayman (Editors), *Leadership Theory and Research: Perspectives and Directions*. Orlando, FL: Academic Press.
House, R.J., Woycke, J. and Foder, E.M. (1988), Charismatic and non-charismatic leaders: differences in behavior and effectiveness. In J.A. Conger and R.N. Kanungo (Editors), *Charismatic Leadership: The Elusive Factor in Organizational Effectiveness*. San Francisco, CA: Jossey-Bass.
Howard, A. and Bray, D.W. (1988), *Managerial Lives in Transition: Advancing Age and Changing Times*. New York: Guilford Press.
Howard, M. and Paret, P. (Editors and Translators) (1984), Karl von Clausewitz (1780–1831), *On War*. Princeton, NJ: Princeton University Press.
Howard, R. (1990), Values make the company: an interview with Robert Haas. *Harvard Business Review*, September–October.
Howell, J.M. and Avolio, B.J. (1993), Transformational leadership, transactional leadership, locus of control, and support for innovation: key predictors of business unit performance. *Journal of Applied Psychology*, 78, 891–902.
Howell, J.M. and Frost, P.J. (1989), A laboratory study of charismatic leadership. *Organizational Behavior and Human Decision Processes*, 43, 243–269.
Howell, J.M. and House, R.J. (1993), *Socialized and Personalized Charisma*. London, Ontario: University of Western Ontario, Western Business School.
Hoyle, S. (2004), Leadership in the arts and creative industries. Paper presented at 'The Art of Leadership' conference on the challenge of leadership in the arts, Birmingham, 24 February.
Hoyt, C.L. and Blascovich, J. (2003), Transformational and transactional leadership in virtual and physical environments. *Small Group Research*, 34 (6), 678–715.
Huff, A.S. (1990), *Mapping Strategic Thought*. Chichester: John Wiley & Sons.
Huff, A.S. (1997), A current and future agenda for cognitive research in organisations. *Journal of Management Studies*, 34 (6), 947–952.
Hughes, O. (2003), Making vision a reality. *Charity Times*, 10 (1), January, 43.
Hughes, R.L., Ginnett, R.C. and Curphy, G.J. (1999), *Leadership: Enhancing the Lessons of Experience*. Boston, MA: Irwin McGraw-Hill.
Humphries, R. (Translator) (1951), *The Aeneid of Virgil*. New York: Charles Scribner's Sons.
Hunt, J.G. (1999), Transformation/charismatic leadership's transformation of the field: an historical essay. *Leadership Quarterly*, 10 (2), 129–144.
Hunt, J.W. (1998), A differential equation. *Financial Times*, 25 March, 25.
Hunt, J.W. (2002), Fertile feedback. *Financial Times*, 21 June.

Huxham, C. and Vangen, S. (2000), Leadership in the shaping and implementation of collaboration agendas: how things happen in a (not quite) joined-up world. *Academy of Management Journal*, 43 (6), 1159–1175.
Ignatieff, M. (1985), *The Needs of Strangers*. New York: Viking.
Ilmihal (1999), *Divantas Publications*. Istanbul: Medya Ofset.
Institute of Management (2001), *Leadership: The Challenge for All?* Report by DEMOS in association with the Council for Excellence in Management and Leadership. London: Chartered Management Institute.
Ireland, R.D. and Hitt, M.A. (1992), Mission statements: importance, challenge, and recommendations for development. *Business Horizons*, May–June, 34–42.
Ireland, R.D. and Hitt, M.A. (1999), Achieving and maintaining strategic competitiveness in the 21st century: the role of strategic leadership. *Academy of Management Executive*, 13 (1), February.
Isaac, R.G., Zerbe, W.J. and Pitt, D.C. (2001), Leadership and motivation: the effective application of expectancy theory. *Journal of Managerial Issues*, 13 (2), 211–226.
Itami, H. and Roehl, T.W. (1987), *Mobilizing Invisible Assets*. Cambridge, MA: Harvard University Press.
Jackson, T. (1999), Reflections of a knowledge worker. *Financial Times*, 27 April, 14.
Jacobs, T.O. and Jaques, E. (1987), Leadership in complex systems. In J. Zeidner (Editor), *Human Productivity Enhancement, Vol. 2*. New York: Praeger.
Jacobs, T.O. and Jaques, E. (1990), Military executive leadership. In K.E. Clark and M.B. Clark (Editors), *Measures of Leadership*. Greensboro, NC: Center for Creative Leadership.
Jacobs, T.O. and Jaques, E. (1991), Executive leadership. In R. Gal and A.D. Manglesdorf (Editors), *Handbook of Military Psychology*. New York: John Wiley & Sons.
Jacobs, T.O. and McGee, M.L. (2001), Competitive advantage: conceptual imperatives for executives. In S.J. Zaccaro and R.J. Klimoski (Editors), *The Nature of Organizational Leadership: Understanding the Performance Imperatives Confronting Today's Leaders*. San Francisco, CA: Jossey-Bass.
James, H. (Editor) (1920), Familiar Letters of William James, II. *Atlantic Monthly*, August.
James, K. and Burgoyne, J. (2001), *Leadership Development: Best Practice Guide for Organisations*. London: Council for Excellence in Management and Leadership.
James, W. (1890), *The Principles of Psychology*. New York: Holt.
Janis, I. (1982), *Victims of Groupthink: A Psychological Study of Foreign Policy Decisions and Fiasco, 2nd Edition*. Boston, MA: Houghton Mifflin.
Jarvenpaa, S.L. and Tanriverdi, H. (2003), Leading virtual knowledge networks. *Organizational Dynamics*, 31 (4), 403–412.
Javidan, M. and Dastmalchian, A. (2003), Culture and leadership in Iran: the land of individual achievers, strong family ties, and powerful elite. *Academy of Management Executive*, 17 (4), November, 127–142.
Jaworski, J. (1996), *Synchronicity: The Inner Path of Leadership*. San Francisco, CA: Berrett-Koehler.
Jay, A. (Editor) (1996), *The Oxford Dictionary of Political Quotations*. Oxford: Oxford University Press.
Jehn, K.A., Chadwick, C. and Thatcher, S.M.B. (1997), To agree or not to agree: the effects of value congruence, individual demographic dissimilarity, and conflict on workgroup outcomes. *International Journal of Conflict*, 8, 287–305.
Johnson, G. (1987), *Strategic Change and the Management Process*. Oxford: Basil Blackwell.
Johnson, G. (1989), Rethinking incrementalism. In D. Asch and C. Bowman (Editors), *Readings in Strategic Management*. London: Macmillan.
Johnson, G. and Scholes, K. (2002), *Exploring Corporate Strategy, 6th Edition*. Harlow: Pearson Education.
Johnson, G., Scholes, K. and Whittington, R. (2005), *Exploring Corporate Strategy, 7th Edition*. Harlow: Pearson Education.
Johnson, N.G. (2001), Women leadership: in health and in war. *Monitor on Psychology*, December, 5.
Johnson, P. (1998), *A Study of Cognition and Behaviour in Top Management Team Interaction*. Unpublished PhD thesis, Cranfield University.
Johnson, P., Daniels, K. and Huff, A. (2001), Sensemaking, leadership and mental models. In S.J. Zaccaro and R.J. Klimoski (Editors), *The Nature of Organizational Leadership: Understanding the Performance Imperatives Confronting Today's Leaders*. San Francisco, CA: Jossey-Bass.
Joinson, A. (1998), Causes and implications of disinhibited behaviour on the internet. In S. Kiesler (Editor), *Culture of the Internet*, 43–59. Mahwah, NJ: Erlbaum.
Jones, P. and Kahaner, L. (1995), *Say It and Live It: 50 Corporate Mission Statements that Hit the Mark*. New York: Currency/Doubleday.
Joni, S.A. (2004), The geography of trust. *Harvard Business Review*, March, 82–88.
Joseph, A.M. (1972), *Put It In Writing*. Cleveland, OH: Industrial Writing Institute.

Joseph, A.M. (1986), *Put It In Writing, 3rd Edition*. Cleveland, OH: International Writing Institute.

Joyce, P. (2003), Leading change in the public sector. *Strategy Magazine*, 1, 11–13.

Joyce, P. and Woods, A. (2001), *Strategic Management: A Fresh Approach to Developing Skills, Knowledge and Creativity*. London: Kogan Page.

Judge, T.A., Bono, J.E., Ilies, R. and Gerhardt, M.W. (2002), Personality and leadership: a qualitative and quantitative review. *Journal of Applied Psychology*, 87, 765–780.

Judge, T.A., Colbert, A.E. and Ilies, R. (2004), Intelligence and leadership: a quantitative review and test of theoretical propositions. *Journal of Applied Psychology*, 89 (3), 542–552.

Judge, T.A. and Ilies, R. (2002), Relationship of personality to performance motivation: a meta-analytic review. *Journal of Applied Psychology*, 87 (4), 797–807.

Judge, T.A. and Piccolo, R.F. (2004), Transformational and transactional leadership: a meta- analytic test of their relative validity. *Journal of Applied Psychology*, 89 (5), 755–768.

Judge, T.A., Piccolo, R.F. and Ilies, R. (2004), The forgotten ones? The validity of consideration and initiating structure in leadership research. *Journal of Applied Psychology*, 89 (1), 36–51.

Judge, W.Q. and Ryman, J.A. (2001), The shared leadership challenge in strategic alliances: lessons from the US healthcare industry. *Academy of Management Executive*, 15 (2), 71–79.

Jung, C.G. (1917), Über die Psychologie des Unbewussten (On the psychology of the unconscious). In C.G. Jung (1958), *Gesammelte Werke, Vol. 7*, 58. Zürich/Stuttgart: Rascher.

Jung, D.I. and Avolio, B.J. (2000), Opening the black box: an empirical investigation of the mediating effects of trust and value congruence on transformational and transactional leadership. *Journal of Organizational Behaviour*, 21, 949–964.

Juran, J. (1988), *Juran on Planning for Quality*. New York: Free Press.

Juran, J. (1994), The quality trilogy: a universal approach for managing quality. In H. Costin (Editor), *Total Quality Management*. New York: Dryden.

Kaagan, S.S. (1998), Leadership development: the heart of the matter. *International Journal of Educational Management*, 12 (2), 74–81.

Kabasakal, H. and Bodur, M. (1998), *Leadership, Values and Institutions: the Case of Turkey*. Research Paper. Istanbul: Bogaziçi University.

Kabasakal, H. and Dastmalchian, A. (2001), Introduction to the special issue on leadership and culture in the Middle East. *Applied Psychology: An International Review*, 50 (4), 479–488.

Kakabadse, A. (2001), What is vision? *Sheer Inspiration: The UK's 100 Most Visionary Companies*, 4–5. London: Management Today.

Kakabadse, A. and Kakabadse, N. (1996), *Essence of Leadership*. London: International Thomson Business Press.

Kanaga, K. and Prestridge, S. (2002), The right start: a team's first meeting is key. *Leadership in Action*, 22 (2), May/June, 14–17.

Kanter, R.M. (1983), *The Change Masters*. London: Allen and Unwin.

Kanter, R.M. (1991), *World Leadership Survey: The Boundaries of Business*. Boston, MA: Harvard Business School Press.

Kanter, R.M. (2003a), Leadership and the psychology of turnarounds. *Harvard Business Review*, June.

Kanter, R.M. (2003b), Inspire people to turn round your business. *Financial Times*, 25 August, 11.

Kanter, R.M., Stein, B.A. and Jick, T.D. (1992), *The Challenge of Organizational Change*. New York: Free Press.

Kanungo, R.N. and Conger, J.A. (1992), Charisma: exploring new dimensions of leadership behavior. *Psychology and Developing Societies*, 4, 21–38.

Kanungo, R.N. and Mendonca, M. (1996), *Ethical Dimensions in Leadership*. Beverly Hills, CA: Sage Publications.

Kaplan, R.S. and Norton, D.P. (1992), The balanced scorecard: measures that drive performance. *Harvard Business Review*, January–February, 70–79.

Kaplan, R.S. and Norton, D.P. (2000), Having trouble with your strategy? Then map it. *Harvard Business Review*, September–October, 167–176.

Kaplan, R.S. and Norton, D.P. (2001a), *The Strategy-Focused Organization: How Balanced Scorecard Companies Thrive in the New Business Environment*. Boston, MA: Harvard Business School Press.

Kaplan, R.S. and Norton, D.P. (2001b), Using the Balanced Scorecard to create strategy-focused organizations. *Ivey Business Journal*, May/June, 12–19.

Karathanos, P., Pettypool, M.D. and Troutt, M.D. (1994), Sudden lost meaning: a catastrophe? *Management Decision*, 32 (1), 15–19.

Kariel, H. (1964), *In Search of Authority: Twentieth-Century Political Thought.* New York: Free Press.

Kark, R., Shamir, B. and Chen, G. (2003), The two faces of transformational leadership: empowerment and dependency. *Journal of Applied Psychology,* 88 (2), 246–255.

Karlgren, B. (1950), *The Book of Documents.* Stockholm: Museum of Far Eastern Antiquities.

Karlgren, B. (1970), *Glosses on the Book of Documents.* Stockholm: Museum of Far Eastern Antiquities.

Katz, D. and Kahn, R.L. (1978), *The Social Psychology of Organizations.* New York: John Wiley & Sons.

Katz, D., Maccoby, N., Gurin, G. and Floor, L. (1951), *Productivity, Supervision and Morale Among Railroad Workers.* Ann Arbor, MI: University of Michigan Institute for Social Research.

Katz, D., Maccoby, N. and Morse, N.C. (1950), *Productivity, Supervision and Morale in an Office Situation.* Ann Arbor, MI: University of Michigan Institute for Social Research.

Katz, R. (1977), The influence of group conflict on leadership effectiveness. *Organizational Behavior and Human Performance,* 20, 265–286.

Katzenbach, J. (1996), Real change leaders. *McKinsey Quarterly,* 1, 148–163.

Katzenbach, J. (1997), The myth of the top management team. *Harvard Business Review,* November, 83–91.

Katzko, M.W. (2002), The rhetoric of psychological research and the problem of unification in psychology. *American Psychologist,* 57, 262–270.

Kavanagh, D. (1990), *British Politics: Continuities and Change, 2nd Edition.* Oxford: Oxford University Press.

Kay, J. (1996), Happy combination. *Financial Times,* 25 October, 18.

Kaye, B. and Jacobson, B. (1999), True tales and tall tales: the power of organizational storytelling. *Training & Development,* March, 45–50.

Keighley, T. (1993), Creating an empowered organization. *Training and Development in Australia,* December, 6–11.

Kellaway, L. (2003), Only an idiot asks leaders why they are so brilliant. *Financial Times,* 25 August, 10.

Keller, R.T. (1986), Predictors of the performance of project groups in R&D organizations. *Academy of Management Journal,* 29, 715–726.

Kellerman, B. (2004a), Leadership: warts and all. *Harvard Business Review,* January, 40–45.

Kellerman, B. (2004b), *Bad Leadership: What It Is, How It Happens, Why It Matters.* Boston, MA: Harvard Business School Press.

Kelley, R.E. (1992), *The Power of Followership.* New York: Doubleday.

Kelloway, E. and Barling, J. (2000), What have we learned about developing transformational leaders? *Leadership & Organizational Development Journal,* 22 (5), 221–229.

Kelly, J. (1993), *Facts against Fictions of Executive Behavior: A Critical Analysis of What Managers Do.* Westport, CT: Quorum Books.

Kennett, M. (2004), First-class coach. *Management Today,* January, 72.

Kerr, S., Schriesheim, C.A., Murphy, C.J. and Stogdill, R.M. (1974), Towards a contingency theory of leadership based upon the consideration and initiating structure literature. *Organizational Behavior and Human Performance,* 12, 62–82.

Kets de Vries, M. (2000), Beyond Sloan: trust is at the core of corporate values. Mastering Management, *Financial Times,* 2 October.

Kets de Vries, M. (2001), *The Leadership Mystique.* London: Pearson Education.

Kets de Vries, M. and Florent-Treacy, E. (1999), *AuthentiZiotic Organizations: Global Leadership from A to Z.* Working Paper no. 99/62/ENT, INSEAD, Fontainebleau, France.

Kibby, L. and Härtel, C. (2003), Noetic leadership: leadership skills that manage the existential dilemma. Paper presented at the Annual Conference of the British Academy of Management, Harrogate, 15–17 September.

Kim, W.C. and Mauborgne, R. (2002), Pursuing the holy grail of clear vision. *Financial Times,* 6 August, 11.

Kim, W.C. and Mauborgne, R. (2003), Think for yourself – stop copying a rival. *Financial Times,* 11 August, 9.

Kirby, T. (1998), The games workshop experience: our concept of leadership and experience with leadership development. Paper presented at The Leadership Trust Foundation Inaugural Conference on 'Leadership Development: The Challenges Ahead'. The Leadership Trust Foundation, Ross-on-Wye, 2–3 February.

Kirkman, B. and Rosen, B. (1999), Beyond self-management: antecedents and consequences of team empowerment. *Academy of Management Journal,* 42 (1), 58–74.

Kirkpatrick, S.A. and Locke, E.A. (1991), Leadership: do traits matter? *The Executive,* 5, 48–60.

Kirkpatrick, S.A. and Locke, E.A. (1996), Direct and indirect effects of three core charismatic leadership components on performance and attitudes. *Journal of Applied Psychology,* 81, 36–51.

Klein, E.B., Astrachan, J.H. and Kossek, E.E. (1996), Leadership education: the impact of managerial level and gender on learning. *Journal of Managerial Psychology*, 11 (2), 31–40.

Klein, E.B., Kossek, E.E. and Astrachan, J.H. (1992), Affective reactions to leadership education: an exploration of the same-gender effect. *Journal of Applied Behavioral Science*, 28, 102–117.

Klein, H.J. (1991), Further evidence on the relationship between goal setting and expectancy theories. *Organizational Behavior and Human Decision Processes*, 49, 230–257.

Koberg, C.R., Senjem, J.C. and Goodman, E.A. (1999), Antecedents and outcomes of empowerment. *Group & Organization Management*, 24 (1), 71–91.

Koene, B.A.S., Vogelaar, L.W. and Soeters, J.L. (2002), Leadership effects on organizational climate and financial performance: local leadership effect in chain organizations. *Leadership Quarterly*, 13, 193–215.

Kolb, D.A. (1985), *Experiential Learning: Experience as the Source of Learning and Development*. Harlow: Prentice Hall.

Komisar, R. (2002), Letter to the Editor. *Harvard Business Review*, July, 119–120.

Korman, A.K. (1966), Consideration, initiating structure, and organizational criteria – a review. *Personnel Psychology*, 19, 349–361.

Korn/Ferry (1989), *Reinventing the CEO*. New York: Korn/Ferry International and Columbia Business School.

Kotter, J.P. (1988), *The Leadership Factor*. New York: Free Press.

Kotter, J.P. (1990a), What leaders really do. *Harvard Business Review*, May–June, 156–167.

Kotter, J.P. (1990b), *A Force for Change: How Leadership Differs from Management*. New York: Free Press.

Kotter, J.P. (1995a), Leading change: why transformation efforts fail. *Harvard Business Review*, March–April.

Kotter, J.P. (1995b), *The New Rules: How to Succeed in Today's Post-Corporate World*. New York: Free Press.

Kotter, J.P. (1996b), *Leading Change*. Boston, MA: Harvard Business School Press.

Kotter, J.P. (1997a), *Matsushita Leadership: Lessons from the 20th Century's Most Remarkable Entrepreneur*. New York: Free Press.

Kotter, J.P. (1997b), Leading by vision and strategy. *Executive Excellence*, October, 15–16.

Kotter, J.P. and Heskett, J.L. (1992), *Corporate Culture and Performance*. New York: Free Press.

Kouzes, J.M. and Posner, B.Z. (1987), *The Leadership Challenge*. San Francisco, CA: Jossey-Bass.

Kouzes, J.M. and Posner, B.Z. (1991), *The Leadership Challenge*. San Francisco, CA: Jossey-Bass.

Kouzes, J.M. and Posner, B.Z. (1993), *Credibility: How Leaders Gain and Lose It, Why People Demand It*. San Francisco, CA: Jossey-Bass.

Kouzes, J.M. and Posner, B.Z. (1995), *The Leadership Challenge*. San Francisco, CA: Jossey-Bass.

Kouzes, J.M. and Posner, B.Z. (2002), *The Leadership Challenge, 3rd Edition*. San Francisco, CA: Jossey-Bass.

KPMG Management Consulting (n.d.), *British Business Leadership Survey*. London: KPMG Management Consulting.

Krause, D.G. (1997), *The Way of the Leader*. London: Nicholas Brealey.

Kreitner, R. and Kinicki, A. (1997), *Organizational Behavior*. Homewood, IL: Richard D. Irwin.

Kreitner, R. and Kinicki, A. (1998), *Organizational Behavior, 4th Edition*. Boston, MA: Irwin/McGraw-Hill.

Kübler-Ross, E. (1969), *On Death and Dying*. New York: Macmillan.

Kubr, M. (1996), *Management Consulting: A Guide to the Profession, 3rd (Revised) Edition*. Geneva: International Labour Office.

Kuei, C., Manu, C.N., Lin, C. and Lu, M.H. (1997), An empirical investigation of the association between quality management practices and organisational climate. *International Journal of Quality Science*, 2, 121–137.

Kuhnert, K.W. (1994), Transforming Leadership: Developing People through Delegation. In B.M. Bass and B.J. Avolio (Editors), *Improving Organizational Effectiveness through Transformational Leadership*, 10–25. Thousand Oaks, CA: Sage Publications.

Kunda, G. and Barley, S. (1988), Designing devotion: corporate cultures and ideologies of workplace control. Paper presented at the 83rd Annual Meeting of the American Sociological Association, San Francisco, August.

Kur, E. and Bunning, R. (1996), A three-track process for executive leadership development. *Leadership & Organization Development Journal*, 17 (4), 4–12.

Labianca, G., Gray, B. and Brass, D.J. (1997), A grounded model of organizational schema change during empowerment. Paper presented at the National Academy of Management meeting, August 8–12, Boston, MA.

Lam, S.S.K. and Schaubroeck, J. (2000), A field experiment testing frontline opinion leaders as change agents. *Journal of Applied Psychology*, 85 (6), 987–995.

Lane, H.W., DiStefano, J.J. and Maznevski, M.L. (2000), *International Management Behavior, 4th Edition.* Cambridge, MA: Blackwell.

Lansdell, S. (2002), *The Vision Thing.* Oxford: Capstone.

Lanto, A. and Mobley, W. (1998), Summary of participant interactive voting on global leadership development issues and practices. Paper presented at The Global Leadership Development Conference, London, 19–20 November.

Larson, J.R., Christensen, C., Abbott, A.S. and Franz, T.M. (1996), Diagnosing groups: charting the flow of information in medical decision-making teams. *Journal of Personality and Social Psychology,* 71, 315–330.

Larson, L.L., Hunt, J.G. and Osborn, R.N. (1976), The great hi-hi leader behavior myth: a lesson from Occam's razor. *Academy of Management Journal,* 19, 628–641.

Laughland, J. (2000), The great dictator. *The Spectator,* 28 October, 16.

Law, A. and Coutu, D.L. (2000), Creating the most frightening company on earth: an interview with Andy Law of St Luke's. *Harvard Business Review,* September.

Law, S. (2002), Getting the measure of leadership. *Professional Manager,* July, 26–28.

Lawler, E.E., Mohrman, S.A. and Ledford, G.E. (1992), *Employee Involvement and Total Quality Management.* San Francisco, CA: Jossey-Bass.

Lawrence, P. and Lorsch, J. (1967), *Organization and Environment.* Boston, MA: Harvard Business School Division of Research.

Lawrence, S.V. (2002), Daring to raise a taboo topic. *Far Eastern Economic Review,* September 12, 37.

Leach, D.J., Wall, T.D. and Jackson, P.R. (2003), The effect of empowerment on job knowledge: an empirical test involving operators of complex technology. *Journal of Occupational and Organizational Psychology,* 76 (1), 27–53.

Leavy, B. and Wilson, D. (1994), *Strategy and Leadership.* London: Routledge.

Lebrecht, N. (2000), The humanising of Hitler. *The Spectator,* 28 October, 60–61.

Lee, M. (1999), The lie of power: empowerment as impotence. *Human Relations,* 52 (2), 225–262.

Leigh, A. and Maynard, M. (2000), Making sense of culture. *Training Journal,* December, 26–29.

Leigh, T. and Brown, S. (1996), A new look at psychological climate and its relationship to job involvement, effort, and performance. *Journal of Applied Psychology,* 81 (4), 358–368.

Lencioni, P.M. (2002), Make your values mean something. *Harvard Business Review,* July, 113–117.

Lennick, D. and Kiel, F. (2005), *Moral Intelligence: Enhancing Business Performance and Leadership Success.* Upper Saddle River, NJ: Wharton School Publishing.

Lenz, R.T. (1993), Strategic management and organizational learning: a meta-theory of executive leadership. In J. Hendry, G. Johnson and J. Newton (Editors), *Strategic Thinking: Leadership and the Management of Change.* Chichester: John Wiley & Sons.

Leonard, N.H., Beauvais, L.L. and Scholl, R.W. (1999), Work motivation: the incorporation of self-concept-based processes. *Human Relations,* 52 (2), 969–998.

Lester, T. (2004), When a bullseye can be a miss. Special Report on Public Sector Recruitment. *Financial Times,* 7 June, 5.

Leung, V. (2000), The making of an impressive speech. End-of-millennium Lecture. *The Millennium Journal 2000,* Robert Black College, University of Hong Kong.

Levering, R. and Moskowitz, M. (1993), *The 100 Best Companies to Work for in America.* New York: Currency/Doubleday.

Levicki, C. (1998), *The Leadership Gene: The Genetic Code for a Life-long Leadership Career.* London: Financial Times Management.

Levin, I.M. (2000), Vision revisited: telling the story of the future. *Journal of Applied Behavioral Science,* 36 (1), 91–107.

Levin, L. (2000), Transforming our business through people. Paper presented at the Third Annual Leadership Conference, 'The Head and Heart of Leadership', The Leadership Trust Foundation, Ross-on-Wye, 6–7 September.

Lewin, A.Y. and Stephens, C.U. (1994), CEO attributes as determinants of organizational design: an integrated model. *Organization Studies,* 15 (2), 183–212.

Lewin, K. (1948), Group decision and social change: readings in psychology. In G.W. Lewin (Editor), *Resolving Social Conflicts, Selected Papers on Group Dynamics (1935–1946).* New York: Harper.

Lewis, P. and Jacobs, T.O. (1992), Individual differences in strategic leadership capacity: a constructive/development view. In R.L. Phillips and J.G. Hunt (Editors), *Strategic Leadership: A Multiorganizational Perspective.* Westport, CT: Quorum Books.

Lewis, W. and Goodman, M. (2002), Boots chairman and chief executive to check out. *The Sunday Times*, 15 December, 3.1.

Liden, R.C. and Graen, G. (1980), Generalizability of the vertical dyad linkage model of leadership. *Academy of Management Journal*, 23, 451–465.

Likert, R. (1961), *New Patterns of Management.* New York: McGraw-Hill.

Linkow, P. (1999), What gifted strategic thinkers do. *Training & Development*, 53 (7), July, 34–37.

Lipman-Blumen, J. (2005), *The Allure of Toxic Leaders.* New York: Oxford University Press.

Lipnack, J. and Stamps, J. (1997), *Virtual Teams: Reaching Across Space, Time, and Organizations with Technology.* New York: JohnWiley & Sons.

Lipton, M. (1996), Demystifying the development of an organizational vision. *Sloan Management Review*, 37, June, 83–92.

Lissack, M. and Roos, J. (2000), *The Next Common Sense.* London: Nicholas Brealey.

Livingstone, S. (1969), Pygmalion in management. *Harvard Business Review*, 47, 81–89.

Llinas, R. and Ribary, U. (1993), Coherent 40–Hz oscillation characterizes dream state in humans. *Proceedings of the National Academy of Science, USA*, 90, March, 2078–2081.

Locke, E.A. (1968), Towards a theory of task motivation and incentives. *Organizational Behavior and Human Performance*, 3, 157–189.

Locke, E.A. (1997), The motivation to work: what we know. In M. Maehr and P. Pintrich (Editors), *Advances in Motivation and Achievement, Vol. 10*, 375–412. Greenwich, CT: JAI Press.

Locke, E.A. and Latham, G. (1990), *A Theory of Goal Setting and Task Performance.* Englewood Cliffs, NJ: Prentice Hall.

Locke, E.A., Saari, L.M., Shaw, K.N. and Latham, G.P. (1981), Goal setting and task performance: 1969–1980. *Psychological Bulletin*, 90, 125–152.

Locke, E.A. and Schweiger, D.M. (1979), Participation in decision making: one more look. In B.M. Staw (Editor), *Research in Organizational Behavior, Vol. 1*, 265–339. Greenwich, CT: JAI Press.

Lodges, W.E. and Kidder, R.M. (1997), *Global Values, Moral Boundaries*. London: Institute for Global Ethics.

London, S. (2002), The geezer with lessons for geeks. *Financial Times*, 17 September, 8.

Lorange, P. (2003), Developing global leaders. *BizEd*, AACSB, September/October, 24–27.

Lord, R.G., Foti, R.J. and De Vader, C.L. (1984), A test of leadership categorization theory: internal structure, information processing, and leadership perceptions. *Organizational Behavior and Human Performance*, 34, 343–378.

Lord, R.G. and Maher, K.J. (1991), *Leadership and Information Processing.* London: Routledge.

Lowe, K.B., Kroeck, K.G. and Sivasubramaniam, N. (1996), Effectiveness correlates of transformational and transactional leadership: a meta-analytic review of the MLQ literature. *Leadership Quarterly*, 7, 385–425.

Lowe, P. (1994), Empowerment: management dilemma, leadership challenge. *Executive Development*, 7 (6), 23–24.

Lubitsh, G. and Higgins, J. (2001), Thinking from the heart. *Directions: The Ashridge Journal*, Summer, 32–35.

Lucas, E. (2001), And the winner is … everyone. *Professional Manager*, January, 10–12.

Lulla, S. (2002), Leadership = character × competence. *Indian Management*, Journal of the All-India Management Association, June.

Luthans, F. (2001), The case for positive organizational behaviour. *Current Issues in Management*, 1 (1), 10–21.

MacArthur, B. (Editor) (1996), *The Penguin Book of Historic Speeches.* London: Penguin.

MacArthur, B. (Editor) (1999), *The Penguin Book of Twentieth-Century Speeches, 2nd Revised Edition.* London: Penguin.

MacCleod, C. (1991), Clinical anxiety and the selective encoding of threatening information. *International Review of Psychiatry*, 3, 272–292.

Maccoby, M. (2000), Narcissistic leaders: the incredible pros and the inevitable cons. *Harvard Business Review*, January–February.

Maccoby, M. (2004), The power of transference. *Harvard Business Review*, September, 77–85.

MacDonald, S. (1999), A crisis in leadership. *The Times*, First Executive, 12 November, 2.

Machiavelli, N. (1532), *The Prince.* Translated from the Italian by H. Thompson (1980). Norwalk, CT: Easton Press.

Maitland, A. (2001a), Solitary geniuses need not apply. *Financial Times*, 14 November, 17.

Maitland, A. (2001b), Time to think the unthinkable. *Financial Times*, 21 March, 19.
Maitland, A. (2002), The hearts are won but not the minds. *Financial Times*, 18 June, 16.
Management Today (2001), *Sheer Inspiration: The UK's 100 Most Visionary Companies*. London: Management Today.
Mandela, N. (1995), *A Long Walk to Freedom*. London: Abacus.
Mangan, K. (2002), Leading the way in leadership: the unending quest of the discipline's founding father, James MacGregor Burns. *Chronicle of Higher Education*, 31 May, 1.
Mangham, I. (2004), Leadership and integrity. In J. Storey (Editor), *Leadership in Organizations: Current Issues and Key Trends*. London: Routledge.
Margerison, C.J. and Kakabadse, A.P. (1984), *How American Chief Executives Succeed*. AMA Survey Report. New York: American Management Association.
Marino, S.F. (1999), Where there is no visionary, companies falter. *Industry Week*, March 15.
Markoczy, L. (2001), Consensus formation during strategic change. *Strategic Management Journal*, 22, 1013–1031.
Marks, M.A., Zaccaro, S.J. and Mathiue, J.E. (2000), Performance implications of leader briefings and team-interaction training for team adaptation to novel environments. *Journal of Applied Psychology*, 85 (6), 971–986.
Marks, M.L. (1998), Learning from the failed mergers and acquisitions of the 20th century to better manage organizational combinations in the new millennium. Paper presented to the 24th International Congress of Applied Psychology, San Francisco, CA, August.
Marks, M.L. and Mirvis, P.H. (1997), *Joining Forces: Making One Plus One Equal Three in Mergers, Acquisitions, and Alliances*. San Francisco, CA: Jossey-Bass.
Marks, M.L. and Mirvis, P.H. (2001), Making mergers and acquisitions work: strategic and psychological preparation. *Academy of Management Executive*, 15 (2), 80–92.
Marren, J. (1993), *Mergers and Acquisitions: A Valuation Handbook*. Homewood, IL: Business One Irwin.
Marshall, T. (1991), *Understanding Leadership*. Tonbridge: Sovereign World.
Martin, M.W. (2000), *Meaningful Work: Rethinking Professional Ethics*. New York: Oxford University Press.
Martin, R. (2002), The virtue matrix: calculating the return on corporate responsibility. *Harvard Business Review*, March, 69–75.
Martin, S. and Fahy, S. (2003), Mind your language. *People Management*, 11 September, 17.
Martineau, J.W. and Steed, J.L. (2001), Follow-up: a valuable tool in leadership development. *Leadership in Action*, Center for Creative Leadership, 21 (1), 1–6.
Maruca, R.F. (2000), State of the new economy. *Fast Company*, September, 105.
Maslow, A. (1970), *Motivation and Personality*. New York: Harper and Row.
Maslow, A. (1987), *Motivation and Personality, 3rd Edition*. New York: Harper and Row.
Mathew, A. (1993), Biases in processing emotional information. *The Psychologist*, 6, 493–499.
Matsushita, K. (1978), *My Management Philosophy*. Kyoto: PHP.
Maurer, T.J., Mitchell, R.D. and Berbeiti, F.G. (2002), Predictors of attitudes towards a 360-degree feedback system and involvement in post-feedback management development activity. *Journal of Occupational and Organizational Psychology*, 75 (1), March, 87–107.
Mavrinac, S. and Siesfeld, T. (1998), *Measures that Matter: An Exploratory Investigation of Investors' Information Needs and Value Priorities*. Ernst & Young Center for Business Innovation and the Organization for Economic Cooperation and Development (OECD).
Mayer, J.D., Caruso, D.R. and Salovey, P. (1999), Emotional intelligence meets traditional standards for an intelligence. *Intelligence*, 27, 267–298.
Mayer, R.C., Davis, J.H. and Schoorman, F.D. (1995), An integrative model of organizational trust. *Academy of Management Review*, 20, 709–734.
McCaffrey, M. and Reynolds, L. (2003), Small group, big impact: how to facilitate a vision workshop. *Training Journal*, March, 18–21.
McCall, A. (2004), Inspired all the way to the top. *The Sunday Times 100 Best Companies to Work for 2004*, 7 March, 4–5.
McCall, M.W. and Lombardo, M.M. (1978), Leadership. In M.W. McCall and M.M. Lombardo (Editors), *Leadership: Where Else Can We Go?* Durham, NC: Center for Creative Leadership.
McCauley, C., Moxley, R. and Van Velsor, E. (1998), *The Center for Creative Leadership's Handbook of Leadership Development*. San Francisco, CA: Jossey-Bass.

McClelland, D.C. (1988), *Human Motivation.* Cambridge: Cambridge University Press.
McCormick, B. (2000), *Ben Franklin's 12 Rules of Management.* Irvine, CA: Entrepreneur Press.
McCrae, R.R. and Costa, P.T. (1987), Adding *Liebe* and *Arbeit*: the full five-factor model and well-being. *Personality and Social Psychology Bulletin*, 17, 227–232.
McGregor, D. (1960), *The Human Side of Enterprise.* London: McGraw-Hill.
McHenry, R. (1997), Spurring stuff. *People Management*, 24 July, 28–31.
McKean, J. and Baxter, C. (2000), *Charles Rennie Mackintosh: Architect, Artist, Icon.* Edinburgh: Lomond Books.
McKee, R. (2003), Storytelling that moves people. *Harvard Business Review*, June, 51–55.
McNay, I. (2004), More than a branch of UKHE plc. *The Times Higher*, 2 January, 12.
McNulty, T. and Pettigrew, A. (1999), Strategists on the board. *Organization Studies*, 20 (1), 47–74.
McRae, H. (2001), Europe needs a new Big Idea. *Fortune*, August 13, 15.
Meglino, B.M. and Ravlin, E.C. (1998), Individual values in organizations: concepts, controversies, and research. *Journal of Management*, 24, 351–389.
Mendoza, M. (2000), Eye of the storm. *Human Resources*, August.
Menon, S.T. (2001), Employee empowerment: an integrative psychological approach. *Applied Psychology: An International Review*, 50 (1), 153–180.
Messick, S. (1976), Personality consistencies in cognition and creativity. In S. Messick (Editor), *Individuality in Learning*, 4–22. San Francisco, CA: Jossey-Bass.
METO (2000), *Management and Leadership in the Changing Economy.* Project Report. London: Management and Enterprise National Training Organisation.
Micklethwait, J. and Wooldridge, A. (2000), *A Future Perfect: The Challenge and Promise of Globalization.* New York: Crown Business.
Middleton, J. and Gorzynski, B. (2002), *Strategy Express.* Oxford: Capstone.
Milgram, S. (1963), Behavioral study of obedience. *Journal of Abnormal and Social Psychology*, 67, 371–378.
Millar, W. (1996), Leadership at the crossroads. *Industry Week*, 19 August, 42.
Miller, A. and Dess, G.G. (1996), *Strategic Management, 2nd Edition.* New York: McGraw-Hill.
Miller, C. (1999), The Renaissance manager: embracing the three dimensions of dynamic leadership. *Supervision*, 60 (2), 6–8.
Miller, C.C. and Ireland, R.D. (2005), Intuition in strategic decision making: friend or foe in the fast-paced 21st century? *Academy of Management Executive*, 19 (1), 19–30.
Miller, D. and O'Whitney, J. (1999), Beyond strategy: configuration as a pillar of competitive advantage. *Business Horizons*, 42 (3), May–June, 5–17.
Miller, G.A. (1962), *Psychology, the Science of Mental Life.* New York: Harper and Row.
Milliken, F.J. and Volrath, D.A. (1991), Strategic decision-making tasks and group effectiveness: insights from theory and research on small group performance. *Human Relations*, 44 (2), 1229–1253.
Mills, P.K. and Ungson, G.R. (2003), Reassessing the limits of structural empowerment: organizational constitution and trust as controls. *Academy of Management Review*, 28 (1), 143–153.
Minchin, J. (1986), *No Man Is an Island: A Study of Singapore's Lee Kuan Yew.* Sydney: Allen and Unwin.
Mintzberg, H. (1978), Patterns in strategy formation. *Management Science*, 24 (9), 934–948.
Mintzberg, H. (1979), *The Structuring of Organizations.* Englewood Cliffs, NJ: Prentice Hall.
Mintzberg, H. (1982), If you're not serving Bill and Barbara, then you're not serving leadership. In J.G. Hunt, U. Sakaran and C.N. Schriesheim (Editors), *Leadership: Beyond Establishment Views.* Carbondale, IL: Southern Illinois University Press.
Mintzberg, H. (1983), *Power in and around Organizations.* Englewood Cliffs, NJ: Prentice Hall.
Mintzberg, H. (1985), The organization as a political arena. *Journal of Management Studies*, 22, 133–154.
Mintzberg, H. (1987), Crafting strategy. *Harvard Business Review*, July–August, 65–75.
Mintzberg, H. (1994), *The Rise and Fall of Strategic Planning.* New York: Free Press.
Mintzberg, H. (1998), Covert leadership: notes on managing professionals. *Harvard Business Review*, November–December, 140–147.
Mintzberg, H., Ahlstrand, B. and Lampel, J. (1998), *The Strategy Safari: A Guided Tour through the Wilds of Strategic Management.* New York: Free Press.
Mintzberg, H. and Quinn, J.B. (1996), *The Strategy Process: Concepts, Contexts, Cases, 3rd Edition.* Upper Saddle River, NJ: Prentice Hall.
Mintzberg, H. and Waters, J.A. (1985), Of strategies, deliberate and emergent. *Strategic Management Journal*, 6 (3), 257–272.

Mirvis, P.H. (1985), Negotiations after the sale: the roots and ramifications of conflict in a acquisition. *Journal of Occupational Behavior,* 6, 65–84.
Mitchell, T.R. (1982), Motivation: new directions for theory, research, and practice. *Academy of Management Review,* 7 (1), 80–88.
Mitroff, I.I. and Denton, E.A. (1999a), *A Spiritual Audit of Corporate America: A Hard Look at Spirituality, Religion, and Values in the Workplace.* San Francisco, CA: Jossey-Bass.
Mitroff, I.I. and Denton, E.A. (1999b), A study of spirituality in the workplace. *Sloan Management Review,* 40, 83–92.
Mittelstaedt, R. (2003), Why don't they understand our strategy? *Financial Times,* 20 August, 11.
Mobbs, B. (2004), Linking the Balanced Scorecard to the [EFQM] Excellence Model. Paper presented at the 'Quest for Excellence' Conference, Quality Award Secretariat and Department of Economic Development, Dubai, UAE, and the British Quality Foundation, Dubai, UAE, March 15.
Moncrieff, J. (1998), Making a difference. *Directions,* Ashridge Management College, November.
Monks, J. (2000), Engaging the work force during change. Paper presented at the National Leadership Conference. MCI-METO, Sandhurst, 24 May.
Montefiore, H. (1976), The theology of accountability. Paper presented at the Spring Conference on Power and Accountability in Business, The Christian Association of Business Executives.
Moore, B.V. (1927), The May Conference on leadership. *Personnel Journal,* 6, 124.
Moore, J.F. (1998), *The Death of Competition.* New York: HarperCollins.
Morden, T. (1997), Leadership as vision. *Management Decision,* 35, 664.
Morgan, N. (2001), The kinesthetic speaker: putting action into words. *Harvard Business Review,* April, 113–120.
Morrell, M. and Capparell, S. (2001), *Shackleton's Way.* London: Nicholas Brealey.
Morris, R. (1992), Management: why women are leading the way. In M. Syrett and C. Hogg (Editors), *Frontiers of Leadership.* Oxford: Blackwell.
Moskowitz, M. and Levering, R. (2003), Where are the best workplaces? *Best Workplaces 2003,* Special Report. *Financial Times,* 28 March, 3.
Moussa, F.M. (1996), Determinants and process of the choice of goal difficulty. *Group & Organization Management,* 21 (4), 414–438.
Moxley, R.S. (2000), *Leadership and Spirit.* San Francisco, CA: Jossey-Bass.
Moynagh, M. and Worsley, R. (2001a), Prophet sharing. *People Management,* 27 December, 24–29.
Moynagh, M. and Worsley, R. (2001b), *Tomorrow's Workplace: Fulfilment or Stress?* London: Tomorrow Project/Chartered Institute of Personnel and Development (CIPD).
Mukhopadhyay, N. (1996), *Performance Appraisal: A Critical Analysis.* Unpublished MSc dissertation, University of Strathclyde.
Mumford, M.D., Baughman, W.A., Threlfall, K.V., Constanza, D.P. and Uhlman, C.E. (1993a), Personality, adaptability, and performance: performance on well-defined and ill-defined problem-solving tasks. *Human Performance,* 6, 245–285.
Mumford, M.D., Constanza, D.P., Threlfall, K.V., Baughman, W.A. and Reiter-Palmon, R. (1993b), Personality variables and problem construction activities: an exploratory investigation. *Creativity Research Journal,* 6, 365–389.
Mumford, M.D. and Strange, J.M. (2002), Vision and mental models: the case of charismatic and ideological leadership. In B.J. Avolio and F.J. Yammarino (Editors), *Charismatic and Transformational Leadership: The Road Ahead.* New York: JAI Elsevier.
Mumford, M.D. and Van Dorn, J.R. (2001), The leadership of pragmatism: reconsidering Franklin in the age of charisma. *Leadership Quarterly,* 12, 279–309.
Murphy, E.C. (1996), *Leadership IQ.* New York: John Wiley & Sons.
Murphy, P.E. (1998), *80 Exemplary Ethics Statements.* Notre Dame, IN: University of Notre Dame Press.
Muzyka, D. (2000), Thriving on the chaos of the future. Mastering Management, *Financial Times,* 2 October.
Myers, D.G. (1993), *The Pursuit of Happiness.* London: Aquarian Press.
Nadin, S.J., Cassell, C.M. and Older, M.T. (1998), *The Change Management Needs of South Yorkshire SMEs: A Needs Analysis.* Sheffield: IWP.
Nadler, G. and Hibino, S. (1994), *Breakthrough Thinking: The Seven Principles of Creative Problem Solving.* Rocklin, CA: Prima.
Nahavandi, A. and Malekzadeh, A.R. (1993), Leader style in strategy and organizational performance: an integrative framework. *Journal of Management Studies,* 30 (3), 405–425.

Nakamoto, M. (2001), Sparing the pheasants that cry out. Japanese Management, Part 1. *Financial Times*, 14 March.

Nanus, B. (1992), *Visionary Leadership: Creating a Compelling Sense of Direction for Your Organization*. San Francisco, CA: Jossey-Bass.

Nash, L. and Stevenson, H. (2004), Success that lasts. *Harvard Business Review*, February, 102–109.

Neil, A. (2003), *Intuition, Leadership and the Media*. Speech at the Sixth Annual Leadership Conference, The Leadership Trust Foundation, Ross-on-Wye, 23–24 September.

Nevins, A. and Hill, F.E. (1954), *Ford: the Times, the Man, the Company*. New York: Charles Scribner.

Nice, D.C. (1998), The warrior model of leadership: classic perspectives and contemporary relevance. *Leadership Quarterly*, 9 (3), 321–332.

Nicholls, J. (1994), The 'heart, head and hands' of transforming leadership. *Leadership & Organization Development Journal*, 15 (6), 8–15.

Nicholson, N. (2001), Gene politics and the natural selection of leaders. *Leader to Leader*, 20, 46–52.

Nicotera, A. and Cushman, D. (1992), Organizational ethics: a within-organization view. *Journal of Applied Communication Research*, 20, 437–463.

Nixon, B. (2002), Responding positively to the big issues. *Professional Consultancy*, 4, April, 24–26.

Nolan, P. (2001), Shaping things to come. *People Management*, 27 December, 30–31.

Nordstrom, K. (2000), *Funky Business*. Edinburgh: Pearson Education.

Northcroft, J. (2000), Head man Elliott. *The Sunday Times*, 8 October.

Northouse, P.G. (1997), *Leadership: Theory and Practice*. Thousand Oaks, CA: Sage Publications.

Novak, M. (1982), *The Spirit of Democratic Capitalism*. New York: Simon and Schuster.

Nurden, R. (1999), Henry's lesson in leadership. *Independent on Sunday*, 23 May.

Nussbaum, M.C. (2001), *Upheavals of Thought: The Intelligence of Emotions*. Cambridge: Cambridge University Press.

Nutt, P.C. and Backoff, R.W. (1997), Crafting vision. *Journal of Management Inquiry*, 6, 308–328.

Nwanko, S. and Richardson, B. (1996), Quality management through visionary leadership. *Managing Service Quality*, 6 (4), 44–47.

Nystrom, P.C. (1978), Managers and the hi-hi leader myth, *Academy of Management Journal*, 21, 324–331.

Oakland, J. (1999), *Total Organizational Excellence: Achieving World Class Performance*. Oxford: Butterworth–Heinemann.

Oakley, J.G. (2000), Gender-based barriers to senior management positions: understanding the scarcity of female chief executive officers. *Journal of Business Ethics*, 27 (4), 321–324.

O'Brien, F. and Meadows, M. (2000), Corporate visioning: a survey of UK practice. *Journal of the Operational Research Society*, 51.

O'Brien, T. (2001), A storyteller for our time. SiliconValley.com, February 4.

O'Connor, J.A., Mumford, M.D., Clifton, T.C., Gessner, T.E. and Connelly, M.S. (1995), Charismatic leaders and destructiveness: a historiometric study. *Leadership Quarterly*, 6, 529–555.

Offermann, L.R., Hanges, P.J. and Day, D.V. (2001), Leaders, followers, and values: progress and prospects for theory and research. *Leadership Quarterly*, 12 (2), 129–131.

Ogbonna, E. and Harris, L.C. (1998), Organizational culture: it's not what you think … . *Journal of General Management*, 23 (3), 35–48.

Ogbonna, E. and Harris, L.C. (2000), Leadership style, organizational culture and performance: empirical evidence from UK companies. *International Journal of Human Resource Management*, 11 (4), 766–788.

Ogbonna, E. and Harris, L.C. (2001), The founder's legacy: hangover or inheritance? *British Journal of Management*, 12, 13–31.

Ohmae, K. (1990), *The Borderless World: Managing Lessons in the New Logic of the Global Marketplace*. New York: Harper.

Okuyama, Y., Ishiguro, H., Nankai, M., Shibuya, H., Watanabe, H.A. and Arinami, T. (2000), Identification of a polymorphism in the promoter region of DRD4 associated with the human novelty seeking personality trait. *Molecular Psychiatry*, January, 5 (1), 64–69.

Oliva, L. (2004), Ethics edges on to courses. *Financial Times*, 16 February, 11.

Olivier, R. (2001), *Inspirational Leadership: Henry V and the Muse of Fire*. London: The Industrial Society (The Spiro Press).

O'Neill, O. (2002), *A Question of Trust: The BBC Reith Lectures 2002*. Cambridge: Cambridge University Press.

Ormrod, J.E. (1995), *Human Learning, 2nd Edition*. Columbus, OH: Merrill.

O'Rourke, P.J. (1992), *Parliament of Whores.* London: Picador.
Orwell, G. (1949), *Nineteen Eighty-Four, a Novel.* London: Secker & Warburg.
Oshagbemi, T. and Gill, R. (2003), Gender differences and similarities in the leadership styles and behaviour of UK managers. *Women in Management Review,* 18 (6), 288–298.
Oshagbemi, T. and Gill, R. (2004), Differences in leadership styles and behaviour across hierarchical levels in UK organisations. *Leadership & Organization Development Journal,* 25 (1), 93–106.
O'Shea, S. (2000), The changing composition of leadership. *Financial Executive,* 16 (4), 35.
Ostell, A. (1996), Managing dysfunctional emotions in organisations. *Journal of Management Studies,* 33, 525–557.
Ostell, A., Baverstock, S. and Wright, P. (1999), Interpersonal skills of managing emotion at work. *The Psychologist,* 12 (1), 30–34.
O'Toole, J. (1995), *Leading Change: Overcoming the Ideology of Comfort and the Tyranny of Custom.* San Francisco, CA: Jossey-Bass.
O'Toole, J. (2001), When leadership is an organizational trait. In W. Bennis, G.M. Spreitzer and T.G. Cummings (Editors), *The Future of Leadership.* San Francisco: Jossey-Bass.
O'Toole, J., Galbraith, J. and Lawler, E.E. (2002), When two (or more) heads are better than one: the promise and pitfalls of shared leadership. *California Management Review,* Summer, 44 (4), 65–83.
Ouchi, W. (1981), *Theory Z.* Reading, MA: Addison-Wesley.
Overell, S. (2002), The search for corporate meaning. *Financial Times,* 13 September, 12.
Owen, H. (2001), *Unleashing Leaders: Developing Organizations for Leaders.* Chichester: John Wiley & Sons.
Owen, J. (2002), Alexander the reasonable? *Daily Telegraph,* 7 July.
PA Consulting Group (1996), *Leading into the Millennium.* London: PA Consulting Group.
Paine, J., Turner, P. and Pryke, R. (1992), *Total Quality in Education.* Sydney, NSW: Ashton Scholastic.
Palich, L.E. and Hom, P.W. (1992), The impact of leader power and behavior on leadership perceptions. *Group & Organization Management,* 17, 279–296.
Palmer, B., Walls, M., Burgess, Z. and Stough, C. (2001), Emotional intelligence and effective leadership. *Leadership & Organization Development Journal,* 22 (1), 5–10.
Palus, C.J. (1999), The art and science of leadership. *Leadership in Action,* 19 (1), 12–13.
Papadakis, V.M. and Barwise, P. (2002), How much do CEOs and top managers matter in strategic decision making? *British Journal of Management,* 13, 83–95.
Parker, A. (2003), Study criticises companies for poor reports. *Financial Times,* 6 February, 27.
Parkinson, B. (1995), *Ideas and Realities of Emotion.* London: Routledge.
Parry, K.W. (1998), Grounded theory and social process: a new direction for leadership research. *Leadership Quarterly,* 9 (1), 85–105.
Parry, K.W. and Proctor-Thompson, S.B. (2001), Validation of the Social Process of Leadership scale (SPL). Paper presented at the *Festschrift* for Dr Bernard M. Bass, State University of New York at Binghamton, New York, June.
Parry, K.W. and Proctor-Thomson, S.B. (2002), Do our chief executives have their finger on the pulse? *University of Auckland Business Review,* 4 (1), 1–11.
Pasa, S.F., Kabasakal, H. and Bodur, M. (2001), Society, organisations, and leadership in Turkey. *Applied Psychology: An International Review,* 50 (4), 559–589.
Pasternack, B.A. and O'Toole, J. (2002), Yellow-light Leadership: *How the World's Best Companies Manage Uncertainty.* McLean, VA: Booz Allen & Hamilton.
Pasternack, B. Williams, T.D. and Anderson, P.F. (2001), Beyond the cult of the CEO: building institutional leadership. *Strategy and Business,* 1st quarter, 1–12.
Pauleen, D. (2003), Leadership in a global virtual team: an action learning approach. *Leadership & Organizational Development Journal,* 24 (3), 153–162.
Paxman, J. (2002), *The Political Animal: An Anatomy.* London: Penguin/Michael Joseph.
Payne, K.E., Fuqua, H.E. and Canegami, J.P. (1997), Women as leaders. *Journal of Leadership Studies,* 4 (4), 44–63.
Peale, N.V. (1952), *The Power of Positive Thinking.* New York: Prentice Hall.
Pearce, J.A. (1981), An executive-level perspective on the strategic management process. *California Management Review,* 24, 39–48.
Pearce, J.A. (1982), The company mission as a strategic tool. *Sloan Management Review,* Spring, 15–24.
Pedler, M. Burgoyne, J. and Boydell, T. (1991), *The Learning Company: A Strategy for Sustainable Development.* Maidenhead: McGraw-Hill.

Pedler, M., Burgoyne, J. and Boydell, T. (2004), *A Manager's Guide to Leadership.* Maidenhead: McGraw-Hill.

Pence, J. (1998), The Ps, not Qs, that count (qualities of effective government managers). *Public Management,* 80 (11), 22.

Perot, R. (2000), *Annual Report 2000.* Plano, TX: Perot Systems Corporation.

Perrewé, P.L., Zellars, K.L., Ferris, G.R., Rossi, A.M. and Ralston, D.A. (2004), Neutralizing job stressors: political skill as an antidote to the dysfunctional consequences of role conflict stressors. *Academy of Management Journal,* 47, 141–152.

Persaud, J. (2003), In good company. *People Management,* 10 July, 36–37.

Persinger, M.A. (1996), Feelings of past lives as expected perturbations within the neurocognitive processes that generate the sense of self: contributions from limbic lability and vectorial hemisphericity. *Perceptual and Motor Skills,* 83, December, 1107–1121.

Peters, T.J. (1987), *Thriving on Chaos.* New York: HarperCollins.

Peters, T.J. (1992), *Liberation Management: Necessary Disorganization for the Nanosecond Nineties.* New York: Alfred A. Knopf.

Peters, T.J. (1997), *The Circle of Innovation.* London: Hodder and Stoughton.

Peters, T.J. and Austin, N. (1985), *A Passion for Excellence.* New York: Random House.

Peters, T.J. and Waterman, R.H. (1982), *In Search of Excellence: Lessons from America's Best-Run Companies.* New York: Harper and Row.

Peterson, R.S., Smith, D.B., Martorana, P.V. and Owens, P.D. (2003), The impact of chief executive officer personality on top management team dynamics: one mechanism by which leadership affects organizational performance. *Journal of Applied Psychology,* 88 (5), 795–808.

Pettigrew, A.M. (1985), *The Awakening Giant,* Oxford: Blackwell.

Pettigrew, A.M. (1987), Context and action in the transformation of the firm. *Journal of Management Studies,* 24, 649–670.

Pettigrew, A.M. (1990), Longitudinal field research on change: theory and practice. *Organisational Science,* 1, 267–292.

Pettigrew, A.M. and McNulty, T. (1995), Power and influence in and around the board room. *Human Relations,* 48 (8), 845–873.

Pettigrew, A.M. and Whipp, R. (1993), *Managing Change for Competitive Success.* Oxford: Blackwell.

Pfeffer, J. (1981), Management as a symbolic action. In L.L. Cummings and B.M. Staw (Editors), *Research in Organizational Behavior, Vol. 3,* 1–52. Greenwich, CT: JAI Press.

Pfeffer, J. and Salancik, G.R. (1978), *The External Control of Organizations.* New York: Harper and Row.

Pickard, J. (2001), Tester of faith. *People Management,* 22 February, 32–34.

Pickles, H. (2000), I feel, therefore I am. *Business Life,* July/August, 37–41.

Pillai, R., Williams, E.A., Lowe, K.B. and Jung, D.I. (2003), Personality, transformational leadership, trust, and the 2000 U.S. presidential vote. *Leadership Quarterly,* 14, 161–192.

Pinchot, G. and Pinchot, E. (1994), *The End of Bureaucracy and the Rise of the Intelligent Organization.* San Francisco, CA: Berrett-Koehler.

Pitt, D.C., Yan, X. and Levine, N. (1996), Touching stones to cross the river: evolving telecommunication policy priorities in contemporary China. *Journal of Contemporary China,* 5, 347–365.

PIU (2001), *Strengthening Leadership in the Public Sector.* Research study by the Performance Improvement Unit, Cabinet Office, UK Government: www.cabinet-office.gov.uk/innovation/leadershipreport.

Podsakoff, P.M., MacKenzie, S.B., Moorman, R.H. and Fetter, R. (1990), Transformational leader behaviors and their effects on followers' trust in leader, satisfaction, and organizational citizenship behaviour. *Leadership Quarterly,* 1, 107–142.

Pollard, C.W. (2000), Mission as an organizing principle. *Leader to Leader,* 16, Spring, 17–21.

Popper, M. and Mayseless, O. (2001), The internal world of transformational leaders. Paper presented at the Bernard M. Bass Festschrift, Binghamton University, Binghamton, New York, May 31–June 1.

Popper, M. and Mayseless, O. (2003), Back to basics: applying a parenting perspective to transformational leadership. *Leadership Quarterly,* 14, 41–65.

Porter, L.W. and Lawler, E.E. (1968), *Managerial Attitudes and Performance.* Homewood, IL: Irwin.

Porter, M.E. (1980), *Competitive Strategy: Techniques for Analyzing Industries and Competitors.* New York: Free Press.

Porter, M.E. (1985), *Competitive Advantage: Creating and Sustaining Superior Performance.* New York: Free Press.

Porter, M.E. (1990), *The Competitive Advantage of Nations*. New York: Free Press.

Porter, M.E. (1991), Towards a dynamic theory of strategy. *Strategic Management Journal*, Winter Special Issue, 12, 95–117.

Porter, M.E. (1997), Creating tomorrow's advantages. In R. Gibson (Editor), *Rethinking the Future*. London: Nicholas Brealey.

Potter, D. (1999), *Wealth Creation in the Knowledge Economy of the Next Millennium*. Third Millennium Lecture, Downing Street, 27 May. Available at: www.number-10.gov.uk/textsite/news/features_display.asp?id=665.

Prahalad, C.K. (1999), Changes in the competitive battlefield. Mastering Strategy: Part Two. *Financial Times*, 4 October, 2–4.

Price, T.L. (2003), The ethics of authentic transformational leadership. *Leadership Quarterly*, 14, 67–81.

Prochaska, J. (2002), A new view of creativity and innovation. Letter to the Editor. *Leadership in Action*, 22 (2), May/June, 24.

Professional Manager (2002), Leadership – from the followers' perspective, *Professional Manager*, 11 (1), January, 2.

Quinn, J.B. (1980), *Strategies for Change: Logical Incrementalism*. Homewood, IL: Richard D. Irwin.

Quinn, R.E. (1984), Applying the competing values approach to leadership: toward an integrative framework. In J.G. Hunt, D.M. Hosking, C.A. Schriesheim and R. Stewart (Editors), *Leaders and Managers: International Perspectives on Managerial Behavior and Leadership*. New York: Pergamon.

Quinn, R.E. and Spreitzer, G.M. (1997), The road to empowerment: seven questions every leader should consider. *Organizational Dynamics*, 26 (2), 37–49.

Quirke, B. (2002), Managers must convey the big picture. *Professional Management*, May, 24–25.

Rafferty, A.E. and Griffin, M.A. (2004), Dimensions of transformational leadership: conceptual and empirical extensions. *Leadership Quarterly*, 15, 329–354.

Rahim, M.A. (1989), Relationship of leader power to compliance and satisfaction with supervision: evidence from a national sample of managers. *Journal of Management*, 15, 545–556.

Rajagopalan, N., Rasheed, A.M.A. and Datta, D.K. (1993), Strategic decision processes: critical review and future directions. *Journal of Management*, 19 (2), 349–384.

Rajan, A. (2000a), *Does Management Development Fail to Produce Leaders?* Tonbridge, Kent: Centre for Research in Employment & Technology in Europe.

Rajan, A. (2000b), *How Can Leaders Achieve Successful Culture Change?* Tonbridge, Kent: Centre for Research in Employment & Technology in Europe.

Rajan, A. (2000c), *How Can Companies Identify Leadership Potential?* Tonbridge, Kent: Centre for Research in Employment & Technology in Europe.

Rajan, A. (2000d), *What Are Mentoring and Coaching and Why Are They Central to Leadership Development?* Tonbridge, Kent: Centre for Research in Employment & Technology in Europe.

Ramachandran, V.S. and Blakeslee, S. (1998), *Phantoms in the Brain*. London: Fourth Estate.

Randell, G.A. (1998), *The Micro-skills Approach to Leadership Development*. Paper presented to the Inaugural Conference of The Leadership Trust Foundation: 'Leadership Development: The Challenges Ahead', Ross-on-Wye, February 2–3.

Randolph, W.A. (1995), Navigating the journey to empowerment, *Organizational Dynamics*, 23 (4), 19–32.

Randolph, W.A. and Sashkin, M. (2002), Can organizational empowerment work in multinational settings? *Academy of Management Executive*, 16 (1), 102–115.

Rangan, V.K. (2004), Lofty missions, down-to-earth plans. *Harvard Business Review*, March, 112–119.

Rao, H.R., Jacob, V.S., Lin, F., Robey, D. and Huber, G.P. (1992), Hemispheric specialisation, cognitive differences, and their implications for the design of decision support systems. *MIS Quarterly*, 16, 145–151.

Raven, B.H. (1993), The bases of power: origins and recent developments. *Journal of Social Issues*, 49 (4), 227–251.

Raynor, H. (2004), Leadership is all very well … . *Arts Professional*, 23 February, 8.

Raynor, M. (1998), That vision thing: do we need it? *Long Range Planning*, 31 (3), 368–376.

Reddin, W.J. (1970a), The tri-dimensional grid. *Canadian Personnel and Industrial Relations Journal*, January, 13–20.

Reddin, W.J. (1970b), *Managerial Effectiveness*. New York: McGraw-Hill.

Reddin, W.J. (1987), *How To Make Your Management Style More Effective*. Maidenhead: McGraw-Hill.

Reichheld, F.F. (2001), Lead for loyalty. *Harvard Business Review*, July–August, 76–84.

Reilly, R.R., Smither, J.W. and Vasilopoulos, N.L. (1996), A longitudinal study of upward feedback. *Personnel Psychology*, 49, 599–612.

Rennie, D.L. (2000), Grounded theory methodology: the pressing need for a coherent logic of justification, *Theory and Psychology*, 10, 481–502.

Revans, R.W. (1998), *ABC of Action Learning, 3rd Edition*. London: Lemos and Crane.

Reynolds, L. (2000), What is leadership? *Training Journal*, November, 26–27.

Rice, A.K. (1965), *Learning for Leadership: Interpersonal and Intergroup Relations*. London: Tavistock.

Rice, B.L. (2002), Integration planning stage. In J.A. Schmidt (Editor), *Making Mergers Work: The Strategic Importance of People*, 100–125. Alexandria, VA: SHRM Foundation and Towers, Perrin, Foster, & Crosby, Inc.

Riddell, P. (2001), Blair as prime minister. In A.Seldon (Editor), *The Blair Effect*. London: Little, Brown.

Rigby, D.K. (2001), Management Tools 2001. *Forum*, European Foundation for Management Development, December, 24–26.

Rigby, R. (1998), Mission statements. *Management Today*, March.

Rigsbee, E.R. (1996), Employee motivation. *Executive Excellence*, 13 (6), 19.

Rindova, V. and Starbuck, W. (1997), Ancient Chinese theories of control. *Journal of Management Inquiry*, 6, 144–159.

Robbins, S.R. and Duncan, R.B. (1988), The role of the CEO and top management in the creation and implementation of strategic vision. In D.C. Hambrick (Editor), *The Executive Effect: Concepts and Methods for Studying Top Managers*. Greenwich, CT: JAI Press.

Roberts, A. (2003), *Hitler and Churchill: Secrets of Leadership*. London: Weidenfeld and Nicolson.

Robertson, S. (2002), Transformational leadership. Paper presented at a conference on 'The Successful Leader', Institute of Directors, London, 3 May.

Robinson, D.N. (2000), Paradigms and the 'myth of framework': how science progresses, *Theory and Psychology*, 10, 39–47.

Roddick, A. (2000), *Beautiful business*. Lecture delivered to the Royal Society of Arts, London, 29 March, and published in synopsis form in *RSA Journal*, 4 April.

Roe, R. and Ester, P. (1999), Values and work: empirical findings and theoretical perspectives. *Applied Psychology: An International Review*, 48, 1–21.

Rogers, C.R. and Greenberg, H.M. (1952), Barriers and gateways to communication. *Harvard Business Review*, republished November 1, 1991.

Rolls, R. (1976), *Image and Imagination*. Nutfield: Denholm House Press.

Rosener, J. (1990), Ways women lead. *Harvard Business Review*, 68 (6), 119–125.

Rosenthal, R. and Jacobson, L. (1968), *Pygmalion in the Classroom: Teacher Expectations and Pupils' Intellectual Development*. New York: Holt, Rinehart and Winston.

Rosnow, R.L., Skleder, A.A., Jaeger, M.E. and Rind, B. (1994), Intelligence and the epistemics of interpersonal acumen: testing some implications of Gardner's Theory. *Intelligence*, 19, 92–116.

Rost, J.C. (1991), *Leadership for the Twenty-First Century*. New York: Praeger.

Rost, J.C. (1993), Leadership development in the new millennium. *Journal of Leadership Studies*, November, 91–110.

Roth, G. and Wittich, C. (Editors) (1968), *Economy and Society, 3 Vols (Wirtschaft und Gesellschaft)*, by Max Weber, 1925. New York: Bedminster.

Rotter, J. (1980), Generalized expectancies for interpersonal trust. *Journal of Personality*, 35, 651–665.

Rowe, W.G. (2001), Creating wealth in organizations: the role of strategic leadership. *Academy of Management Executive*, 15 (1), 81–94.

RSA (1995), *Tomorrow's Company Inquiry*. London: Gower.

Rubenzer, S.J. and Faschingbauer, T.R. (2004), *Personality, Character & Leadership in the White House: Psychologists Assess the Presidents*. Washington, DC: Brassey's.

Rucci, J., Kirn, S.P. and Quinn, R.T. (1998), The employee-customer-profit chain at Sears. *Harvard Business Review*, January–February.

Ruddock, A. (2004), Paper tigress. *Management Today*, February, 59–61.

Rudolph, H.R. and Peluchette, J.V. (1993), The power gap: is sharing or accumulating power the answer? *Journal of Applied Business Research*, 9 (3), 12–20.

Rush, S. and Wilcox, M. (2001), Visionary leadership: a talk with Jay Conger. *Leadership in Action*, 21 (2), 19–22.

Rushe, D. and Durman, P. (2002), The enforcers: crackdown on crony capitalism. *The Sunday Times*, 28 July, 3.5.

Russell, P. (1997), *The PepsiCo Leadership Center: How PepsiCo's Leaders Develop Leaders. Conference Proceedings*, 97–138. The Second Annual Leadership Development Conference, Linkage, Inc., San Francisco, California.

Ryan, R.M. and Deci, E.L. (2000), Self-determination theory and the facilitation of intrinsic motivation, social development, and well-being. *American Psychologist,* 55 (1), 68–78.
Sabine, G.H. and Thorson, T.L. (1973), *A History of Political Theory, 4th Edition,* 824. Fort Worth, CO: Holt, Rinehart and Winston.
Sadler, P. (1997), *Leadership.* London: Kogan Page.
Sadler, P. (1998), *Management Consultancy: A Handbook of Best Practice.* London: Kogan Page.
Safty, A. (1999), A view on global leadership. *Leadership in Action,* 19 (1), 1–5.
Sagie, A., Zaidman, N., Amichal-Hamburger, Y., Te'eni, D. and Schwartz, D.G. (2002), An empirical assessment of the loose-tight leadership model: quantitative and qualitative analyses. *Journal of Organizational Behaviour,* 23, 303–320.
Salmon, P. (2003), How do we recognise good research? *The Psychologist,* 16 (1), 24–27.
Salopek, J.J. (2003), Accentuate the positive. *Training & Development,* September, 19–21.
Salovey, P. and Mayer, J.D. (1990), Emotional intelligence. *Imagination, Cognition and Personality,* 3 (3), 185–211.
Salz, P.A. (2003), Redefining corporate value. *Fortune,* Europe Edition, 148 (2), S2–S4.
Sanches, C.M. (2001), Review of L. Greenhalgh, *Managing Strategic Relationships,* New York: The Free Press. *Academy of Management Executive,* 15 (2), 136–138.
Sanders, R.L. (1997), The future of bureaucracy. *ARMA Records Management Quarterly,* 31 (1), 44–52.
Sands, S. (2003), Does Howard mean business or is he acting? *Daily Telegraph,* 6 November, 24.
Sarros, J.C. and Santora, J.C. (2001), Leaders and values: a cross-cultural study. *Leadership and Organization Development Journal,* 22 (5), 243–248.
Sashkin, M. (1984), Participative management is an ethical imperative. *Organizational Dynamics,* 12, 4–22.
Sashkin, M. (1986), The visionary leader. *Training and Development Journal,* 40 (5), 58–61.
Sashkin, M. (1988), The visionary leader. In J.A. Conger and R.N. Kanungo (Editors), *Charismatic Leadership: The Elusive Factor in Organizational Effectiveness.* San Francisco, CA: Jossey-Bass.
Sashkin, M. (1992), Strategic leadership competencies: what are they? How do they operate? What can be done to develop them? In R.L. Phillips and J.G. Hunt (Editors), *Leadership: A Multiorganizational-level Perspective.* New York: Quorum Books.
Sashkin, M. and Fulmer, R.M. (1988), Toward an organizational leadership theory. In J.G. Hunt, B.R. Baliga, H.P. Dachler and C.A. Schriesheim (Editors), *Emerging Leadership Vistas.* San Francisco, CA: New Lexington Press.
Sashkin, M. and Rosenbach, W.E. (1998), A new vision of leadership. In W.E. Rosenbach and R.L. Taylor (Editors), *Contemporary Issues in Leadership, 4th Edition.* Boulder, CO: Westview Press.
Sashkin, M. and Sashkin, M.G. (2003), *Leadership That Matters: The Critical Factors for Making a Difference in People's Lives and Organizations' Success.* San Francisco, CA: Berrett-Koehler.
Sayles, L.R. (1993), *The Working Leader.* New York: Free Press.
Scarnati, J.T. (1997), Beyond technical competence: honesty and integrity. *Career Development International,* 2 (1), 24–27.
Scase, R. (2004), Are mission statements a waste of space? *Business Voice,* February, 22.
Schama, S. (2002), Friends, Romans, Eminem, lend me your ears. *The Sunday Times,* 21 July, 4.7.
Schein, E.H. (1990), Organizational culture. *American Psychologist,* 45 (2), 109–119.
Schein, E.H. (1991), The role of the founder in the creation of organizational culture. In P.J. Frost, L.F. Moore, M.R. Louis, C. Lundberg and J. Martin (Editors), *Organizational Culture.* London: Sage Publications.
Schein, E.H. (1992), *Organizational Culture and Leadership, 2nd Edition.* San Francisco, CA: Jossey-Bass.
Schein, E.H. and Coutu, D.L. (2002), The anxiety of learning: an interview with Edgar H, Schein. *Harvard Business Review,* March, 100–106.
Schleicher, D.J., Watt, J.D. and Greguras, G.J. (2004), Reexamining the job satisfaction-performance relationship: the complexity of attitudes. *Journal of Applied Psychology,* 89 (1), 165–177.
Schmidt, F. (1992), What do data really mean? Research findings, meta-analysis, and cumulative knowledge in psychology. *American Psychologist,* 47, 1171–1181.
Schmidt, F., Hunter, J. and Outerbridge, A. (1986), The impact of job experience and ability on job knowledge, work sample performance, and supervisory ratings of job performance. *Journal of Applied Psychology,* 71, 432–439.
Schmidt, J.A. (2002), The strategic importance of people. In J.A. Schmidt (Editor), *Making Mergers Work: The Strategic Importance of People,* 3–21. Alexandria, VA: SHRM Foundation and Towers, Perrin, Foster, & Crosby, Inc.

Schminke, M., Wells, D., Peyrefitte, J. and Sebora, T.C. (2002), Leadership and ethics in work groups. *Group & Organization Management*, 27 (2), 272–293.
Schneider, B. and Bowen, D.E. (1985), Employee and customer perceptions of service in banks. *Journal of Applied Psychology*, 60, 318–328.
Schneider, S.C. and Rentsch, J. (1988), Managing climates and cultures: a futures perspective. In J. Hage (Editor), *Futures of Organizations: Innovating to Adapt Strategy and Human Resources to Rapid Technological Change*. Lexington, MA: Lexington Books.
Schrage, M. (1999), Why can't a woman be more like a man? *Fortune*, August 16, 184.
Schriesheim, C.A. (2001), Why leadership research is irrelevant for leadership development. Paper presented at the 11th Annual Kravis-deRoulet Conference, 'The Future of Leadership Development', Claremont McKenna College, Claremont, CA, March 23–24.
Schriesheim, C.A., Hinkin, T. and Podsakoff, T. (1991), Can ipsative and single-item measures produce erroneous results in field studies of French and Raven's five bases of power? An empirical examination. *Journal of Applied Psychology*, 76, 106–114.
Schriesheim, C.A. and Kerr, S. (1977), Theories and methods of leadership: a critical appraisal of current and future directions. In J.G. Hunt and L.L. Larsen (Editors), *Leadership: The Cutting Edge*. Carbondale, IL: Southern Illinois University Press.
Schriesheim, C.A. and Murphy, C.J. (1976), Relationships between leader behavior and subordinate satisfaction and performance: a test of some situational moderators. *Journal of Applied Psychology*, 61, 634–641.
Schriesheim, J.F. (1980), The social context of leader-subordinate relations: an investigation of the effects of group cohesiveness. *Journal of Applied Psychology*, 65, 183–194.
Schwarz, M. and Nandhakumar, J. (2002), Conceptualizing the development of strategic ideas: a grounded theory analysis. *British Journal of Management*, 13, 67–82.
Schwartz, P. (2003), *Inevitable Surprises*. New York: Free Press.
Schwartz, S.H. (1992), Universals in the content and structure of values: theoretical advances and empirical tests in 20 countries. In M.P. Zanna (Editor), *Advances in Experimental Social Psychology, Volume 25*, 2. San Diego, CA: Academic Press.
Schweiger, D. and DeNisi, A. (1991), Communication with employees following a merger: a longitudinal field experiment. *Academy of Management Journal*, 34 (1), 110–135.
Scott, M.C. (2000), *Reinspiring the Corporation: The Seven Seminal Paths to Corporate Greatness*. Chichester: John Wiley & Sons.
Scully, J.P. (1993), A point of view: actions speak louder than buzzwords. *National Productivity Review*, Autumn, 453–456.
Seddon, J. (1991), Attitudes and behaviour. *Management Service Quality*, May, 193–196.
Segil, L. (1998), Strategic alliances for the 21st century. *Strategy and Leadership*, September/ October, 4–16.
Seibert, S.E., Silver, S.R. and Randolph, W.A. (2004), Taking empowerment to the next level: a multiple-level model of empowerment, performance, and satisfaction. *Academy of Management Journal*, 47 (3), 332–349.
Seldon, A. with Baston, L. (1997), *Major: A Political Life*. London: Weidenfeld and Nicolson.
Seligman, M. (2002), *Authentic Happiness*. New York: Free Press.
Selznick, P. (1957), *Leadership in Administration; A Sociological Interpretation*. Evanston, IL: Row Peterson.
Senge, P.M. (1990), *The Fifth Discipline: The Art and Practice of the Learning Organization*. New York: Doubleday.
Senge, P.M. (1993), *The Fifth Discipline*. London: Century Business.
Senge, P.M. (1996), The ecology of leadership. *Leader to Leader*, 2.
Senge, P.M., Roberts, C., Ross, R.B., Smith, B.J. and Kleiner, A. (1994), *The Fifth Discipline Fieldbook: Strategies and Tools for Building a Learning Organization*. London: Nicholas Brealey.
Shamir, B. (1995), Social distance and charisma: theoretical notes and an exploratory study. *Leadership Quarterly*, 6, 19–47.
Shamir, B., Arthur, M. and House, R.J. (1994), The rhetoric of charismatic leadership: a theoretical extension, a case study, and implications for research. *Leadership Quarterly*, 5, 25–42.
Shamir, B. and Ben-Arie, E. (1999), Leadership in an open army? Civilian connections, interorganizational frameworks, and changes in military leadership. In J.G. Hunt, G.E. Dodge and L. Wong (Editors), *Out-of-the-box Leadership: Transforming the Twenty-first Century Army and Other Top-performing Organizations*, 15–42. Stamford, CT: JAI Press.

Shamir, B., House, R.J. and Arthur, M.B. (1993), The motivational effects of charismatic leadership: a self-concept based theory, *Organization Science*, 4, 577–594.
Shapiro, E. (1996), *Fad Surfing in the Boardroom: Managing in the Age of Instant Answers*. Reading, MA: Addison-Wesley.
Shapiro, E.C. (2000), Managing in the cappuccino economy. Review of Chris Argyris (2000), *Flawed Advice and the Management Trap*, Oxford: Oxford University Press. *Harvard Business Review*, March–April, 177–184.
Sharfman, M.P. and Dean, J.W. (1998), The effects of context on strategic decision making processes and outcomes. In V. Papadakis and P. Barwise (Editors), *Strategic Decisions*, 179–203. Boston, MA: Kluwer Academic.
Sharplin, A. (1985), *Strategic Management*. New York: McGraw-Hill.
Sheppard, B.H. and Sherman, D.M. (1998), The grammars of trust: a model and general implications. *Academy of Management Review*, 23 (3), 422–437.
Shiba, S. (1998), Leadership and breakthrough. *Center for Quality of Management Journal*, 7 (2), 10–22.
Shinn, S. (2003), The leader within us. *BizEd* magazine, American Association for the Advancement of Collegiate Schools of Business, November/December, 30–35.
Simms, J. (2002), Is Britain being led astray? *Director*, January, 48–51.
Simon, H.A. (1957), *Administrative Behavior: A Study of Decision-Making Processes in Administrative Organization, 2nd Edition*. New York: Macmillan.
Simons, T.L. (1999), Behavioral integrity as a critical ingredient for transformational leadership. *Journal of Organizational Change Management*, 12 (2), 89–104.
Singer, W. (1999), Striving for coherence. *Nature*, 397, February, 391–393.
Singer, W. and Gray, C.M. (1995), Visual feature integration and the temporal correlation hypothesis. *Annual Review of Neuroscience*, 18, 555–586.
Skapinker, M. (2001), Search for a new pattern in face of a downturn. *Financial Times*, 25 October.
Skapinker, M. (2002), Straight from the stick. *Financial Times*, 2 May, 13.
Skapinker, M. (2003), Building trust and profits by telling staff the truth. *Best Workplaces 2003*, Special Report, *Financial Times*, March 28, 2.
Skapinker, M. (2004), Trust and respect make you happy. *Best Workplaces 2004*, Special Report. *Financial Times*, 28 April, 3.
Smircich, L. and Calás, M. (1987), Organizational culture: a critical assessment. In F. Jablin, L. Putnam, K. Roberts and L. Porter (Editors), *Handbook of Organizational Communication*. Newbury Park, CA: Sage Publications.
Smith, G. (2000), A Battle of Britain hero we forgot, *The Sunday Times*, 10 September.
Smith, K.G., Smith, K.A., Olian, J.D., Sims, H.P., O'Bannon, D.P. and Scully, J.A. (1994), Top management team demography and process: the role of social integration and communication. *Administrative Science Quarterly*, 39, 413–438.
Smith, P.B. (1999), Similarities and differences in leadership across cultures: a 43–nation study. Paper presented at the Second Annual Conference of The Leadership Trust Foundation on 'Leadership sans Frontières', Ross-on-Wye, 1–2, February.
Smith, S. (2000), *Inner Leadership: REALise Your Self-Leading Potential*. London: Nicholas Brealey.
Smits, S.J., McLean, E.R. and Tanner, J.R. (1993), Managing high-achieving information systems professionals. *Journal of Management Information Systems*, 9 (4), 103–120.
Sneade, K.C. and Harrell, A.M. (1994), An application of expectancy theory to explain a manager's intention to use a decision support system. *Decision Sciences*, 25 (4), 499–513.
Snook, S.A. (2003), Review of Richard R. Ellsworth (2002), *Leading with Purpose: The New Corporate Realities*. Stanford, CA: Stanford Business Books. *Academy of Management Review*, October, 675–677.
Snow, C.P. (1959), *The Two Cultures and the Scientific Revolution*. The 1959 Rede Lecture. Cambridge: Cambridge University Press.
Sooklal, L. (1991), The leader as a broker of dreams. *Human Relations*, 44 (8), 833–856.
Sorensen, J.B. (2002), The strength of corporate culture and the reliability of firm performance. *Administrative Science Quarterly*, 47 (1), 70–91.
Sosik, J.J. (1997), Effects of transformational leadership and anonymity on idea generation in computer-mediated groups. *Group & Organization Management*, 22, 460–487.
Sosik, J.J., Avolio, B.J. and Kahai, S.S. (1997), Effects of leadership style and anonymity on group potency and effectiveness in a group decision support system environment. *Journal of Applied Psychology*, 82, 89–103.

Sosik, J.J., Avolio, B.J., Kahai, S.S. and Jung, D.I. (1998), Computer-supported work group potency and effectiveness: the role of transformational leadership, anonymity, and task interdependence. *Computers in Human Behavior,* 14, 491–511.

Sosik, J.J., Kahai, S.S. and Avolio, B.J. (1999), Leadership style, anonymity, and creativity in group decision support systems: the mediating role of optimal flow. *Journal of Creative Behavior,* 33, 227–256.

Sosik, J.J. and Magerian, L.E. (1999), Understanding leader emotional intelligence and performance. *Group & Organization Management,* 24 (3), 367–391.

Sperry, R.W. (1973), Lateral specialization of cerebral functions in the surgically separated hemispheres. In F.J. McGuigan and R.A. Shoonover (Editors), *The Psychophysiology of Thinking,* 209–229. New York: Academic Press.

Spreier, S. and Sherman, D. (2003), Staying ahead of the curve. *Fortune,* March 3, 35–37.

Spreitzer, G.M., De Janasz, S.C. and Quinn, R.E. (1999), Empowered to lead: the role of psychological empowerment in leadership. *Journal of Organizational Behaviour,* 20, 511–526.

Spreitzer, G.M. and Quinn, R.E. (1996), Empowering middle managers to be transformational leaders. *Journal of Applied Behavioral Science,* 32 (3), 237–261.

Stajkovic, A.D. and Luthans, F. (1998), Self-efficacy and work-related performance, a meta-analysis. *Psychological Bulletin,* 124, 240–261.

Stajkovic, A.D. and Luthans, F. (2003), Social cognitive theory and self-efficacy: implications for motivation theory and practice. In L.W. Porter, G.A. Bigley and R.M. Steers (Editors), *Motivation and Work Behavior, 7th Edition,* 126–140. Burr Ridge, IL: Irwin/McGraw-Hill.

Starobin, P. (2002), What is Moscow's Role? Special Report: A Fragile World. *Business Week,* 11 February, 31.

Stech, E.L. (2004), Psychodynamic approach. In P.G. Northouse, Editor, *Leadership: Theory and Practice, 3rd Edition.* London: Sage Publications.

Steers, R.M., Mowday, R.T. and Shapiro, D.L. (2004), The future of work motivation theory. *Academy of Management Review,* 29 (3), 379–387.

Steiner, G.A. (1965), Introduction. In G.A. Steiner (Editor), *The Creative Organization.* Chicago: University of Chicago Press.

Steiner, G.A. (1975), *Business and Society, 2nd Edition.* New York: Random House.

Stelzer, I. (2001), Bush gets higher grades from the university of life. *The Sunday Times,* 12 August, 3.4.

Stengel, R. (1994), The making of a leader. *Time,* 143 (19), 6–12.

Stern, P.C. (1995), Why do people sacrifice for their nations? *Political Psychology,* 16, 217–235.

Stern, S. (2003), If you think you're hard enough. *Management Today,* March, 46–51.

Stern, S. (2004), The perils of CSR. *RSA Journal,* January, 32–35.

Sternberg, R.J. (1985), *Beyond IQ.* Cambridge, MA: Cambridge University Press.

Sternberg, R.J. (1996), *Successful Intelligence.* New York: Simon and Schuster.

Sternberg, R.J. and Vroom, V. (2002), Theoretical letters: the person versus the situation in leadership. *Leadership Quarterly,* 13, 301–323.

Sternberg, R.J., Wagner, R.K., Williams, W. and Horvath, J. (1995), Testing common sense. *American Psychologist,* 50 (11), 912–927.

Stevenson (Lord) of Coddenham (2004), *Keynote Address.* Leadership in Culture Conference, The Clore Leadership Programme, Royal Society for Arts, London, 8 June.

Stewart, S. and Donleavy, G. (1995), *Whose Business Values?* Hong Kong: Hong Kong University Press.

Stiles, P. (2001), The impact of the board on strategy: an empirical investigation. *Journal of Management Studies,* 38 (5), 627–650.

Stoppard, T. (1966), *Lord Malquist and Mr Moon,* part 6. London: Faber and Faber.

Strange, J.M. and Mumford, M.D. (2002), The origins of vision: charismatic versus ideological leadership. *Leadership Quarterly,* 13, 343–377.

Street-Porter, J. (2000), Radical approaches to leadership. Paper presented at The National Leadership Conference, MCI-METO, The Royal Military Academy, Sandhurst, 24 May.

Streufert, S. and Swezey, R.W. (1986), *Complexity, Managers, and Organizations.* Orlando, FL: Academic Press.

Stybel, L. (1986), After the merger. *New England Business,* 2 June, 67–68.

Sutch, A. (2001), Case study: leadership the St Benedictine way. Paper presented at the Fourth Annual Conference, 'Leading with Personal Power', The Leadership Trust Foundation, Ross-on-Wye, 25–26 September.

Symonds, M. (2003), When trust is going, the going gets tough. *The World in 2004.* London: The Economist.
Tait, R. (1996), The attributes of leadership. *Leadership & Organization Development Journal,* 17 (1), 27–31.
Tannenbaum, M.A. (2003), Organizational values and leadership. *Public Manager,* 32 (2), 19–20.
Tannenbaum, R. and Schmidt, W.H. (1968), How to choose a leadership pattern. *Harvard Business Review,* 36, 95–101.
Taylor, A.J.P. (1965), *English History, 1914–1945,* chapter 1. New York: Oxford University Press.
Taylor (Lord) of Warwick (2000), Diversity and ethics. Paper presented at The National Leadership Conference, 'Leaders and Managers: Fit for the Future', MCI-METO, The Royal Military Academy, Sandhurst, 24 May.
Testa, G. (2000), How to develop leadership: the Isvor Fiat training proposal. *EFMD Forum,* European Foundation for Management Development, December, 27–31.
Thatcher, M. (2002), *Statecraft: Strategies for a Changing World.* London: HarperCollins.
The Economist (1997), Making strategy. 1 March, 81.
The Economist (1998), Sharing the limelight. 18 April, 81.
The Economist (1999), How to make mergers work. 9 January, 15–16.
The Economist (2000), Gnu surprise. 26 February, 128.
The Economist (2001a), The voters give Koizumi a chance. Will the LDP? 4 August, 21–23.
The Economist (2001b), The next big surprise, 13–19 October, 76.
The Economist (2001c), The feelgood factor. 15 February, p. 37.
The Economist (2001d), Chief executives: churning at the top. 17 March, 101.
The Economist (2002a), Churning heads. 22 June, 80–83.
The Economist (2002b), Fallen idols. 4 May, 11.
The Economist (2002c), Persuasion. 4 May, 95–96.
The Economist (2002d), Dr Feelgood. 16 March, 84.
The Economist (2002e), Like herding cats. 20 April, 78.
The Economist (2003), Tough at the top. Survey: corporate leadership: www.economist. com, 27 October.
The Economist (2004), The lunatic you work for: www.economist.com, 6 May.
The Economist Global Executive (2002), High climbers. 28 January.
The Leadership Trust (2002), *Senior Management Attitude Survey.* Ross-on-Wye: The Leadership Trust.
The Manufacturing Foundation (2003), *Innovation Essentials.* Birmingham, August.
Theakston, K. (2003), Political skills and context in prime ministerial leadership in Britain. In E.C. Hargrove and J.E. Owens (Editors), *Leadership in Context.* Lanham, MD: Rowman & Littlefield.
Thomas, A.B. (1988), Does leadership make a difference to organizational performance? *Administrative Science Quarterly,* 33, 388–400.
Thomas, A.B. (2003), *Controversies in Management: Issues, Debates, Answers, 2nd Edition.* London: Routledge.
Thompson, J.D. (1967), *Organizations in Action.* New York: McGraw-Hill.
Thompson, J.W. (1992), Corporate leadership in the 21st Century. In J. Renesch (Editor), *New Traditions in Business.* San Francisco, CA: Berrett-Koehler.
Thorndike, E.L. (1920), A constant error in psychological ratings. *Journal of Applied Psychology,* 4, 25–29.
Thornhill, J., Jaggi, R. and McNulty, S. (2001), Imagination and vision to carve out future. *Financial Times,* 11 April.
Tichy, N.M. (1997), *The Leadership Engine: How Winning Companies Create Leaders at all Levels. Conference Proceedings,* 57–81. The Second Annual Leadership Development Conference, Linkage, Inc., San Franciso, California.
Tichy, N.M. and Cohen, E. (1997), *The Leadership Engine: How Winning Companies Build Leaders at Every Level.* New York: HarperCollins.
Tichy, N.M. and Devanna, M.A. (1986a), The transformational leader. *Training and Development Journal,* 40, 27–32.
Tichy, N.M. and Devanna, M.A. (1986b), *Transformational Leadership.* New York: John Wiley & Sons.
Tichy, N.M. and Devanna, M.A. (1990), *The Transformational Leader: The Key to Global Competitiveness, 2nd Edition.* New York: John Wiley & Sons.
Tichy, N.M. and Sherman, S. (1994), *Control Your Own Destiny or Someone Else Will.* New York: Harper Business.

Timpson, J. (2002), Upside-down management. Paper presented at the Conference on the Successful Leader, Institute of Directors, London, 3 May.
Tischler, L., Biberman, J. and McKeage, R. (2002), Linking emotional intelligence, spirituality and workplace performance: definitions, models and ideas for research. *Journal of Managerial Psychology,* 17 (3), 203–218.
Toffler, A. (1971), *Future Shock.* London: Pan Books.
Topple, S. (2000), Leadership programmes – a sketch. Paper presented at a Seminar on Leadership for the 21st Century, Cambridge University Local Industry Links, Wolfson College, Cambridge, 20 September.
Tourish, D. and Pinnington, A. (2002), Transformational leadership, corporate cultism and the spirituality paradigm: an unholy trinity in the workplace. *Human Relations,* 55, 147–172.
Treadway, D.C., Hochwarter, W.A., Ferris, G.R., Kacmar, C.J., Douglas, C., Ammeter, A.P. and Buckley, M.R. (2004), Leader political skill and employee reactions. *Leadership Quarterly,* 15, 493–513.
Triandis, H.C. (1996), The psychological measurement of cultural syndromes. *American Psychologist,* 51, 407–415.
Troiano, P. (1999), Sharing the throne. *Management Review,* 88 (2), 39–43.
Trompenaars, F. (2000), Cultural diversity within the head and heart of leadership. Paper presented at the Third Annual Conference, 'The Head and Heart of Leadership', The Leadership Trust Foundation, Ross-on-Wye, 6–7 September.
Turnbull, S. (2001), Corporate ideology – meanings and contradictions for middle managers. *British Journal of Management,* 12, 231–242.
Turnbull, S. (2003), The emotions of re-constructing leader identities after a leadership development programme. Paper presented at the Second Annual International Conference on Leadership Research, 'Studying Leadership', Lancaster University Management School, Lancaster, 15–16 December.
Turner, N., Barling, J., Epitropaki, O., Butcher, V. and Milner, C. (2002), Transformational leadership and moral reasoning. *Journal of Applied Psychology,* 87 (2), 304–311.
Turney, P.B.B. (1993), Beyond TQM with workforce activity-based management. *Management Accounting,* September, 28–31.
Ulrich, D. and Hinkson, P. (2001), Net heads. *People Management,* 7 (2), 25 January, 32–36.
Ulrich, D. and Smallwood, N. (2000), Leadership brand in fundamental change. *Training Journal,* September, 16–18.
Ulrich, D., Smallwood, N. and Zenger, J. (2000), Building your leadership brand. *Leader to Leader,* 15, Winter, 40–46.
US Army (1990), *Field Manual 22–100, Army Leadership.* Washington, DC: US Government Printing Office.
Useem, M. (1998), *The Leadership Moment.* New York: Times Business Books.
Uttal, B. (1983), The corporate culture vultures. *Fortune,* 108 (8), October 17, 66–72.
Van, K.M. (2002), *The Perception of Gender Differences in Leadership and Organisational Effectiveness: A Singapore Perspective.* Unpublished MBA dissertation, University of Strathclyde Graduate School of Business.
van Beek, M. (2000), *People Oriented Makes a Difference: A Comparative Study of Dutch, British, American, Swedish, Italian and French Organizational Leaders.* Unpublished Master's thesis, Leiden University.
Van der Heijden, K. (1993), Strategic Vision at Work: Discussing Strategic Vision in Management Teams. In J. Hendry, G. Johnson and J. Newton (Editors), *Strategic Thinking: Leadership and the Management of Change.* Chichester: John Wiley & Sons.
Van der Heijden, K. (1996), *Scenarios: The Art of Strategic Conversation.* Chichester: John Wiley & Sons.
Van Engen, M.L., Van der Leeden, R. and Willemsen, T.M. (2001), Gender, context and leadership styles: a field study. *Journal of Occupational and Organizational Psychology,* 74, 581–598.
Vandevelde, L. (2002), Speech at the Second Annual CBI Business Summit, 12 June, London. Reported in The CBI View: Strength through adversity. *Business Voice,* July/August 2002, 16.
van de Vliet, A. (1997), When mergers misfire. *Management Today,* June, 40–50.
Vanhoegaerden, J. (1999), Letting go. *Directions,* Ashridge Management College, April.
Vansina, L.S. (1988), The general manager and organisational leadership. In M. Lambrechts (Editor), *Corporate Revival: Managing into the Nineties.* Leuven: University Press.
Vansina, L.S. (1999), Leadership in strategic business unit management. *European Journal of Work and Organizational Psychology,* 8 (1), 87–108.
Van Sters, D.A. and Field, R.H.G. (1990), The evolution of leadership theory. *Journal of Organizational Change Management,* 3 (3), 29–45.

Vogt, J. (1994), Demystifying the mission statement. *Nonprofit World*, 12, 29–32.
von Ghyczy, T. (2003), The fruitful flaws of strategy metaphors. *Harvard Business Review*, September, 86–94.
Vroom, V. (1964), *Work and Motivation*. New York: John Wiley & Sons.
Waclawski, J. (2001), The real world: Abraham, Martin, and John: where have all the great leaders gone? *The Industrial-Organizational Psychologist*, 38 (1), January, 70–73.
Waddock, S. and Smith, N. (2000), Corporate responsibility audits: doing well by doing good. *Sloan Management Review*, Winter.
Waldman, D.A. and Javidan, M. (2001), Charismatic leadership at the strategic level: taking a new look at upper echelons theory. Paper presented at the Festschrift for state, Bernard M. Bass University of New York at Binghamton, May 31–June 1.
Waldman, D.A., Ramírez, G.G., House, R.J. and Puranam, P. (2001), Does leadership matter? CEO leadership attributes and profitability under conditions of perceived environmental uncertainty. *Academy of Management Journal*, 44 (1), 134–143.
Wall, T., Cordery, J.L. and Clegg, C.W. (2002), Empowerment, performance and operational uncertainty. *Applied Psychology: An International Review*, 51 (1), 146–169.
Wallington, P. (2000), Inspiring minds – total leadership. *CIO Magazine*, June 1.
Walsh, J.P. (1995), Managerial and organizational cognition: notes from a trip down memory lane. *Organization Science*, 6, 280–321.
Walsh, J.P., Henderson, C.M. and Deighton, J. (1988), Negotiated belief structures and decision performance: an empirical investigation. *Organizational Behavior and Decision Processes*, 42, 194–216.
Walters, H. (2002), Leadership and teambuilding in a hostile environment. Paper presented at a conference on 'The Successful Leader', Institute of Directors, London, 3 May.
Ward, P. (1997), *360-degree Feedback*. London: Institute of Personnel and Development.
Wardy, R. (1996), *The Birth of Rhetoric: Georgias, Plato and Their Successors*. London: Routledge.
Warner, J. (2002), Even corporations are getting a social conscience. *Independent*, 9 February, 19.
Warnock, M. (2002a), Being intelligent about love's uses. Review of Martha C. Nussbaum, *Upheavals of Thought: The Intelligence of Emotions*, Cambridge: Cambridge University Press. *The Times Higher*, 2 August, 22.
Warnock, M. (2002b), New cynics will never flourish. Review of Onora O'Neill, *A Question of Trust: The BBC Reith Lectures 2002*, Cambridge: Cambridge University Press. *The Times Higher*, 30 August, 21.
Wasti, S.A. (2003), The influence of cultural values on antecedents of organisational commitment: an individual-level analysis. *Applied Psychology: An International Review*, 52 (4), 533–554.
Waterson, P.E., Clegg, C.W., Bolden, R., Pepper, K., Warr, P.B. and Wall, T.D. (1999), The use and effectiveness of modern manufacturing practices. *International Journal of Production Research*, 37, 2271–2292.
Watkins, J. (2003), Spiritual guidance. *People Management*, 20 February, 16–17.
Watts, G. (Translator) (1640), *De Dignitate et Augmentis Scientarium* (Of the Advancement and Proficience of Learning, or, The Partitions of Sciences, IX Books), 1, vi, 31, Antiheta, 6, 1, by Francis Bacon. Oxford: Robert Young and Edward Forrest, publishers.
Waugh, P. and Morris, N. (2002), Ministers warn Blair that Labour lacks core values. *Independent*, 9 March.
Weber, M. (1964), *The Theory of Social and Economic Organization*. New York: Free Press.
Webley, S. (1992), *Business Ethics and Company Codes*. London: Institute of Business Ethics.
Webley, S. (1999), Sources of corporate values. *Long Range Planning*, 32 (2), 173–178.
Weick, K.E. (1979), Cognitive processes in organizations. In B. Staw (Editor), *Research in Organizational Behavior, Vol. 1*, 41–64. Greenwich, CT: JAI Press.
Weick, K.E. (1995), *Sensemaking in Organizations*. Newbury Park, CA: Sage Publications.
Weiman, G. (1991), The influentials: back to the concept of opinions? *Public Opinion Quarterly*, 55, 267–279.
Weiss, H.M. and Cropanzano, R. (1996), Affective events theory: a theoretical discussion of the structure, causes and consequences of affective experiences at work. *Research in Organizational Behavior*, 18, 1–74.
Wellins, R.S. and Weaver, P.S. (2003), From C-level to see-level leadership. *Training & Development*, September, 58–65.
Wheare, K. (1974), *On the Sin of Pride*. Quinquagesima Sermon, University of Oxford, 24 November. Reprinted in *Oxford*, the journal of the Oxford Society, LII, 2, November 2000, 26–28.
Whipp, R. and Pettigrew, A. (1993), Leading change and the management of competition. In J. Hendry, G. Johnson and J. Newton (Editors), *Strategic Thinking: Leadership and the Management of Change*. Chichester: John Wiley & Sons.
White, D. (2000a), Sandhurst style builds teamwork. *Sunday Telegraph*, 8 October.

White, D. (2000b), Use your head – check your EQ. *Sunday Telegraph*, Business File, 16 April.
White, R.P., Hodgson, P. and Crainer, S. (1996), *The Future of Leadership*. Lanham, MD: Pitman.
Whittington, R. (1993), Social structures and strategic leadership. In J. Hendry, G. Johnson and J. Newton (Editors), *Strategic Thinking: Leadership and the Management of Change*. Chichester: John Wiley & Sons.
Whyte, D. (1997), *The House of Belonging*. Langley, WA: Many Rivers Press.
Whyte, W.H. (1943), *Street Corner Society*. Chicago: University of Chicago Press.
Wick, C. (1993), *The Learning Edge: How Smart Managers and Smart Companies Stay Ahead*. New York: McGraw-Hill.
Wickens, P. (1999a), *Energise Your Enterprise*. Basingstoke: Macmillan.
Wickens, P. (1999b), Values added. *People Management*, 5 (10), 20 May, 33–38.
Wilde, O. (1891), The critic as artist. *Intentions*. London: James R. Osgood, McIvaine.
Wilde, O. (1894), *Intentions*. New York: Dodd, Mead.
Wilkinson, A. (1998), Empowerment theory and practice. *Personnel Review*, 27, 40–56.
Willan, B. (2002), Globalisation and Human Rights. *RSA Journal*, 1/6, 18–21.
Williams, J.M.G., Watts, F.N., MacCleod, C. and Mathews, A. (1996), *Cognitive Psychology and Emotional Disorders, 2nd Edition*. Chichester: John Wiley & Sons.
Williams, K., Harkins, S.G. and Latane, B. (1979), Many hands make light the work: the causes and consequences of social loafing. *Journal of Personality and Social Psychology*, 37, 822–832.
Williams, P. (1982), Changing styles of leadership. In Dennis Kavanagh (Editor), *The Politics of the Labour Party*. London: George Allen and Unwin.
Willmott, B. (2003), Documenting HR strategies is essential to people and profits. *Personnel Today*, 7 January.
Wilson, A. (2001), Civilising the corporation. *Directions: The Ashridge Journal*, Summer, 36–37.
Wilson, C. (1963), *The Outsider*. London: Pan Books.
Windle, I. (2001), Efficiency through knowledge. *Financial Times*, 21 February.
Winston, R. (2003), Human instinct. Paper presented at the Sixth Annual Leadership Conference, 'Intuition, Leadership, Instinct', The Leadership Trust Foundation, Ross-on-Wye, 23–24 September.
Wise, T. (1999), The threat of a good example (political activism). *Social Justice*, 26 (2), 182.
Witzel, M. (2003), The search for shortcomings. *Financial Times*, 6 August, 11.
Wong, L., Bliese, P. and McGurk, D. (2003), Military leadership: a context specific review. *Leadership Quarterly*, 14, 657–692.
Wood, R.E. and Bandura, A. (1989), Impact of conceptions of ability on self-regulatory mechanisms and complex decision making. *Journal of Personality and Social Psychology*, 56, 407–415.
Work Systems Associates (1996), *The Courage to Change*. Lexington, MA: Work Systems Associates/Linkage Incorporated.
Wortman, M.S. (1982), Strategic management and changing leader-follower roles. *Journal of Applied Behavioral Science*, 18, 371–282.
Wright, P.L. (1996), *Managerial Leadership*. London: Routledge.
Wright, P.L. and Taylor, D.S. (1994), *Improving Leadership Performance: Interpersonal Skills for Effective Leadership*. London: Prentice Hall.
Wright, P.L. and Taylor, D.S. (2000), *The Interpersonal Skills of Leadership: Behavioural Aspects*. Bradford: University of Bradford School of Management.
Yammarino, F.J. (1994), Indirect leadership: transformational leadership at a distance. In B.M. Bass and B.J. Avolio (Editors), *Improving Organizational Effectiveness through Transformational Leadership*. Thousand Oaks, CA: Sage Publications.
Yammarino, F.J., Spangler, W.D. and Bass, B.M. (1993), Transformational leadership and performance. *Leadership Quarterly*, 4, 81–102.
Yearout, S., Miles, G. and Koonce, R.H. (2001), Multi-level visioning. *Training & Development*, March, 31–39.
Yeung, A.K. and Ready, D.A. (1995), Developing leadership capabilities of global corporations. *Human Resource Management*, 34 (4).
Yukl, G. (1989), Managerial leadership: a review of theory and research. *Journal of Management*, 15 (2), 251–289.
Yukl, G. (1994), *Leadership in Organizations, 3rd Edition*. Englewood Cliffs, NJ: Prentice Hall.
Yukl, G. (1998), *Leadership in Organizations, 4th Edition*. Upper Saddle River, NJ: Prentice Hall.
Yukl, G. (1999), An evaluation of the conceptual weaknesses in transformational and charismatic leadership theories. *Leadership Quarterly*, 10 (2), 285–305.

Yukl, G. (2002), *Leadership in Organizations, 5th Edition*. Upper Saddle River, NJ: Prentice Hall.

Yukl, G. (2005), *Leadership in Organizations, 6th Edition*. Upper Saddle River, NJ: Prentice Hall.

Yukl, G. and Falbe, C.M. (1990), Influence tactics in upward, downward, and lateral influence attempts. *Journal of Applied Psychology*, 75, 132–140.

Yukl, G. and Tracey, B. (1992), Consequences of influence tactics used with subordinates, peers, and the boss. *Journal of Applied Psychology*, 77, 525–535.

Zaccaro, S.J. (1996), *Models and Theories of Executive Leadership: A Conceptual/Empirical Review and Integration*. Alexandria, VA: US Army Research Institute for the Behavioral and Social Sciences.

Zaccaro, S.J. (1999), Social complexity and the competencies required for effective military leadership. In J.G. Hunt, G.E. Dodge and L. Wong (Editors), *Out-of-the-box Leadership: Transforming the Twenty-first Century Army and Other Top-performing Organizations*. Greenwich, CT: JAI Press.

Zaccaro, S.J. and Bader, P. (2003), E-leadership and the challenges of leading e-teams; minimizing the bad and maximizing the good. *Organizational Dynamics*, 31 (4), 377–387.

Zaccaro, S.J. and Banks, D.J. (2001), Leadership, vision, and organizational effectiveness. In S.J. Zaccaro and R.J. Klimoski (Editors), *The Nature of Organizational Leadership: Understanding the Performance Imperatives Confronting Today's Leaders*. San Francisco, CA: Jossey-Bass.

Zaccaro, S.J., Gilbert, J.A., Thor, K.K. and Mumford, M.D. (1991), Leadership and social intelligence: linking social perceptiveness and behavioral flexibility to leader effectiveness. *Leadership Quarterly*, 2, 317–331.

Zaccaro, S.J. and Klimoski, R.J. (2001), The nature of organizational leadership: an introduction. In S.J. Zaccaro and R.J. Klimoski (Editors), *The Nature of Organizational Leadership: Understanding the Performance Imperatives Confronting Today's Leaders*. San Francisco, CA: Jossey-Bass.

Zaccaro, S.J., Ritman, A.L. and Marks, M.A. (2001), Team leadership. *Leadership Quarterly*, 12, 451–483.

Zadek, S. (2001), *The Civil Corporation*. London: Earthscan.

Zairi, M. (1994), Leadership in TQM implementation: some case examples. *TQM Manager*, 6 (6), 9–16.

Zajac, E. and D'Aunno, T. (1994), Managing strategic alliances. In S. Shortell and A. Kaluzny (Editors), *Healthcare Management: Organization Design and Behavior, 3rd Edition*. New York: Delmar.

Zald, M. (1970), Political economy: a framework for comparative analysis. In M. Zald (Editor), *Power in Organizations*. Nashville, TN: Vanderbilt University Press.

Zaleznik, A. (1990), The leadership gap. *Academy of Management Executive*, 4 (1), 7–22.

Zeldin, T. (2004), What is the good life? Richer not happier: a 21st century search for the good life. Debate on 11 February 2004 at the Royal Society of Arts, London. *RSA Journal*, July, 36–39.

Zigurs, I. (2003), Leadership in virtual teams: oxymoron or opportunity? *Organizational Dynamics*, 31 (4), 339–351.

Zohar, D. and Drake, J. (2000), On the whole. *People Management*, 6 (8), 13 April, 55.

Zohar, D. and Marshall, I. (2001), *Spiritual Intelligence: The Ultimate Intelligence*. London: Bloomsbury.

Zohar, D. and Marshall, I. (2004), *Spiritual Capital: Wealth We Can Live By*. San Francisco, CA: Berrett-Koehler.

Zuckerman, A. (2002), Strong corporate cultures and firm performance: are there tradeoffs? *Academy of Management Executive*, November, 158–160.

Zuckerman, H. and Kaluzny, A. (1991), The management of strategic alliances in health services. *Frontiers of Health Service Management*, 7 (5), 2–23.

Index

Please note that page references to non-textual information such as tables will be in *italic* print.